The Politics of Urban America

A Reader

THIRD EDITION

EDITED BY

Dennis R. Judd
University of Illinois at Chicago

Paul Kantor
Fordham University

Longman

New York   San Francisco   Boston
London   Toronto   Sydney   Tokyo   Singapore   Madrid
Mexico City   Munich   Paris   Cape Town   Hong Kong   Montreal

Publisher: Priscilla McGeehon
Senior Acquisitions Editor: Eric Stano
Marketing Manager: Megan Galvin-Fak
Production Manager: Mark Naccarelli
Project Coordination, Text Design, and Electronic Page Makeup: Nesbitt Graphics, Inc.
Cover Design Manager: John Callahan
Cover Designer: Kay Petronio
Cover Photo: Center B/W Photo: Hulton/Archive from Gettyone
Manufacturing Buyer: Al Dorsey
Printer and Binder: The Maple-Vail Book Manufacturing Group
Cover Printer: The Lehigh Press

Library of Congress Cataloging-in-Publication Data

The politics of urban America : a reader / [edited by] Dennis R. Judd,
Paul Kantor.—3rd ed.
  p. cm.
  Includes bibliographical references.
  ISBN 0-321-08728-3 (alk. paper)
1. Urban policy—United States. 2. Municipal government—United States. 3. Metropoli-
tan government—United States. 4. Urban renewal—United States. 5. City planning—
United States. I. Judd, Dennis R. II. Kantor, Paul, 1942- .
HT123 .P6 2001
320.8'5'0973—dc21   2001033170

Please visit our website at http://www.ablongman.com

ISBN 0-321-08728-3

  4 5 6 7 8 9 10—MA—04

The Politics of Urban America

A Reader

To my grandchildren, Dylan, Miranda, and—born just before this book was sent to the publisher—Jennifer.

Dennis R. Judd

To the most important women in my life: Anna, Elizabeth, and Pauline Kantor, and Mary Desmond.

Paul Kantor

Contents

Preface

The scholarship in urban politics is a moving target—so much so that over the years we have rarely, if ever, assigned exactly the same readings two semesters in a row. To keep up with this fast-changing literature, we have frequently found it necessary to assign selections from books or materials that may be difficult for students to find. Making the readings available has often proved to be frustrating for students, for us, and sometimes for the reserve librarians on our campuses. Like its predecessor, this edition of *The Politics of Urban America* is intended as a solution to this perennial problem. We have brought together a selection of readings that represents some of the most important trends and topics in urban scholarship today. This volume is a suitable companion for any good urban politics text, but its organization and themes fit particularly well with Dennis R. Judd and Todd Swanstrom's *City Politics*, a textbook also published by Longman Publishers.

The readings fit within a political economy framework so that, considered as a whole, they illustrate how public power and private resources interact in the governance of cities. The readings are grouped into chapters covering the essential topics in urban political economy, and each chapter is introduced by an editors' essay that places the selected readings into the context of current literature. Urban politics in the United States has always entailed a tension between the state and the market, or to put it differently, between a democratic politics involving electoral processes and a give-and-take among groups and the private institutions that supply capital and jobs in the pursuit of profit. The tensions arising in urban politics express themselves in a variety of ways. The conflicts arising from the struggle between political and market forces provide a recurring theme but so do social and cultural conflicts. Especially in the last few years, an "identity" politics involving racial, ethnic, and gender differences has come to the fore in international, national, and local political arenas. Within metropolitan areas, there has also been an emerging concern about regional issues—a consequence of the fact that some problems (social and racial segregation and inequality, urban sprawl) seem impossible to solve without a regional approach. The readings in this volume reflect these concerns; thus, we have added a new chapter made up of readings dealing with the new regionalism.

This book is intended to add depth and scope to the main text and other sources used in urban politics and related courses. By reading original sources, students are able to delve deeper into the subjects that they have read about elsewhere. Original sources also stimulate class discussion because students can discuss the various perspectives and interpretations provided by the readings. Because all citations and references have been retained in the original sources, the readings give students the opportunity to pursue further research on their own.

The scholarship on urban politics is so voluminous that a few readings can only scratch the surface. We have had to make many judgment calls; for many of the selections one or more alternatives might have worked just about as well. In addition, to keep the book of manageable length, we were forced to neglect some important topics. We have included no readings, for example, that deal with the history of federal programs or with urban fiscal problems. Except for these notable omissions, however, the readings cover the major topics of the field.

We wish to thank our reviewers: Aubrey Jewett at University of Central Florida and Timothy D. Mead at University of North Carolina—Charlotte.

Dennis R. Judd
Paul Kantor

The Politics of
Urban America

A Reader

Introductory Essay

❖❖❖

THE EVOLUTION OF URBAN POLITICS IN AMERICA

As the four readings making up Chapter 1 of this volume illustrate, over a span of about two decades, the literature on urban politics passed through an intellectual revolution, and it is now undergoing a second. The first scholarly revolution was characterized by the emergence of a "political economy" literature that focused on the interactions between the marketplace and the public sphere. This scholarly interest paralleled developments in national and local politics: all through the 1980s and into the early 1990s, the nation and its cities seemed preoccupied with issues of economic growth. The deep cuts in urban programs that were initiated in the 1980s came at a time when many cities were already experiencing job losses and fiscal retrenchment. In reaction, mayors began to focus on policies designed to stimulate private investment. Predictably, scholarly attention turned to an analysis of the effectiveness and consequences of these policies.

Scholars who began writing from a political economy perspective recognized that governments possess very significant resources, but in the United States they rarely, if ever, have the capacity to implement significant policies on their own. To do anything at all, governments require the cooperation and active participation of institutions and individuals who are not themselves part of the governmental apparatus. There is an economic and a political logic in urban politics (Swanstrom, 1989; see selection 3). The logic of the marketplace treats cities solely as locations for private economic activity—commerce, industry, finance, investment in land, jobs. The economic behavior of business and entrepreneurs is rarely, if ever, influenced significantly by a concern for the public at large because the discipline of the market does not reward—and it may actually penalize—business for doing so. In contrast, the political logic of democratic institutions motivates public officials to maintain and expand political support for what they do; otherwise, they do not remain in office for long. Political logic requires elected officials to pay attention not only to issues of prosperity but also to *governance*. City politics must be understood as complex conflict and accommodations among business, local governmental officials, interest groups, and urban voters.

In the 1990s, economic issues began to share space on the public agenda with racial, ethnic, and other social concerns. At the end of the Cold War, it seemed that age-old racial and ethnic hatreds erupted all over the world, from Bosnia, Israel, Russia, Sri Lanka, and many other places. In the United States,

1

these divisions took a milder form, but they became important nevertheless. Since the mid-1960s, the United States has experienced its heaviest period of immigration in almost 100 years. In cities undergoing rapid population change, racial and ethnic issues connected to policing, schooling, affirmative action hiring, and neighborhood change became lightening rods for political conflict. As before, the preoccupations of scholars who study cities are intimately connected to the real world. Accordingly, in the past few years the scholarship on race, ethnicity, gender, and other social issues has developed rapidly.

The readings that make up the chapters of Part One serve as useful reminders that these themes are timeless. The governance of American cities has always required urban leaders to nurture and promote local prosperity and at the same time to manage the conflicts that inevitably arise from racial, ethnic, and social diversity. The three readings that compose Chapter 2 comment on the period from the nation's founding to approximately the 1870s, when patricians and commercial elites formed governing coalitions devoted mainly to the task of boosterism and growth. The coalitions that governed cities regarded them as instruments to promote private opportunity, and little else. In the nineteenth century, the fate of individual cities—and the prospects of the individuals within them—depended on their ability to tie into a national and international system of trade and commerce. As a consequence, urban elites engaged in an intense inter-urban competition; in addition to extolling their alleged economic and cultural advantages, they invested heavily in canals, railroads, and an infrastructure to support local commerce. Today, the equivalent activities include such projects as sports stadiums, waterfront developments, entertainment districts, and convention centers.

After the Civil War, industrialization led to explosive urban growth. Lured by the jobs in the factories, foreign immigrants poured into the cities by the millions. Universal suffrage for white males meant that the immigrants possessed a significant resource that could be used to transform politics. As the readings in Chapter 3 illustrate, political entrepreneurs soon seized the opportunity to translate votes into political power. A new generation of politicians mobilized the Irish and other ethnic voters by distributing petty favors to needy constituents and by manipulating the symbols of ethnic solidarity. City hall typically became the forum for making deals, large and small. By the end of the nineteenth century, business and upper-class elements led a reaction to the free-wheeling, often notoriously corrupt practices of the immigrant politicians. The reformers pressed for new election laws and succeeded at instituting such reforms as voting registration, secret balloting, and nonpartisan elections. Wherever they could, they reorganized city government; although their banner was "efficiency," many of their proposals were explicitly designed to reduce the influence of immigrant voters. The readings of Chapter 4 provide insights into the often anti-democratic motives of the reformers.

Part Two is composed of readings that comment on the social and political consequences of one of the most significant developments of the twentieth century, the political separation of the suburbs from the central cities. Although suburbs were springing up in all metropolitan areas as early as the late nineteenth century and the movement picked up steam in the 1920s, the massive suburban migrations of the post-World War II era opened a chasm dividing suburbs from cities. This split became such a ubiquitous feature of American culture that people became accustomed to thinking in dualist metaphors: Suburbs connoted tree-lined subdivisons, affluent white neighborhoods, and safety; the cities called forth images of slums and ghettos, minorities, and poverty and crime (Beauregard, 1993). The readings composing Chapter 5 deal with the politics of the suburbs, especially emphasizing their tendency toward socioeconomic segregation. Chapter 6 provides commentary on the politics of the central cities, where race, ethnicity, and political representation are perennial issues.

In Part III we present selections that examine the policy issues of the 1990s. The readings in Chapter 7 deal with the ascendant issue facing cities, now as in the past: the imperative of economic growth. The issues discussed in these readings are vital for understanding the shape of urban politics in contemporary cities. Are cities becoming captive of top-down, corporate-led development strategies? What are the prospects for bottom-up, neighborhood-led development? Do cities still have some autonomy in dealing with business?

The selections making up Chapter 8 survey the inequalities that continue to characterize America's urban areas. To a considerable degree, urban residents live in segregated environments. In the 1960s, the concern with segregation was heightened by the riots and civil disorder that swept the cities for several years. More recently, the fracturing of the urban community is expressed not only by a segregation between suburbs and cities and between neighborhoods within cities, but also by a segmentation of urban space into defended enclaves. As William Julius Wilson points out (in reading 26), however, building multi-racial coalitions is difficult but not impossible, even in a deeply divided society.

We conclude the book with two chapters of readings that deal with policy responses. In Chapter 9, the selections deal with the question of how to divide policy responsibility between the cities and the national government. Both authors conclude that cities are not in a strong position to address problems caused by large-scale social and economic forces. The selections in Chapter 10 constitute part of a literature dealing with a new regional politics. Recently, many scholars and policymakers have noted that issues such as concentrated poverty, economic development, urban sprawl, and urban infrastructure can best be addressed not by individual local governments, but through regional cooperation.

In the remainder of this essay, we sketch in somewhat more detail the broad themes that inform the selection of readings for the three parts of the book. Detailed comments on the individual selections are contained within the brief essays that introduce the selections making up each chapter.

Part One: The Evolution of American Urban Politics

The Mercantile Cities

America's cities have always been pivotal in shaping national economic and cultural development. Before the industrial revolution, the nation's cities prospered by presiding over an economic system that relied on the exchange of agriculture and extractive products for goods shipped from abroad or produced by craft shops located mostly in cities. In the merchant cities, the streets "led past the warehouse to the piers," and later also to the rail lines (Glaab and Brown, 1967: 27). These trading centers were run by merchant elites and by aristocrats descended from the colonial families. Their domination over local affairs was ensured by the small size of the urban electorate; until the 1820s, and in many cases much later, less than 5% of white males met the property qualifications normally imposed on voters.

Even when the Jacksonian reforms of the 1830s ushered in universal male suffrage and mass involvement in political parties, the chief effect in most cities was to replace the colonial-era patricians, who asserted their authority by their education and social standing, with merchant and professional elites, who defined cities mostly by their economic activities (Taylor, 1951: 11). As cities grew in size and complexity, the local economic community became more specialized and fragmented. By the middle of the 19th century, larger investors, such as railway promoters, land speculators, and small industrialists, also emerged as important movers and shakers on the political scene. These political elites were indefatigable promoters of local growth because they instinctively understood that some cities—but not all—would prosper. The major obstacles to local economic growth were physical barriers that impeded the exchange of goods between a rural hinterland and the city, and between the city and other commercial centers. Those cities that succeeded in breaking down barriers to commerce gained a competitive advantage that contributed to local prosperity. Consequently, during several decades of the 19th century, an intense inter-urban competition became the singular dynamic that drove city politics.

The cities of the frontier fought their battles with one another on several fronts. They tried to attract investors and residents by extolling their alleged virtues and advantages. And they did much more. The building of the Erie Canal was a landmark event that precipitated several decades of interurban rivalry. In 1817, prodded by entrepreneurs in New York City, the state of New York authorized construction of the 364-mile waterway to connect the Hudson River with Lake Erie. After completion of the canal in 1825, New York City gained access to the vast agricultural hinterland of the old Northwest (now the upper midwest). The dramatic payoff from the construction of the Erie Canal encouraged other cities and states to begin their own somewhat more modest projects. Similarly, in the latter half of the 19th century, railroad building transformed the economic competition among cities into a truly national phenomenon. Cities everywhere, big and small, new or old, could use railroad lines to penetrate their hinterland in the expectation that they could gather up the trade of the back country and channel it through to their own commercial streets. Individual cities, as public corporations, provided massive assistance to railroad companies that agreed to build the necessary connections. By 1870, cities supplied an estimated one fifth of the construction costs for the railroad lines then in existence (Taylor, 1951: 92). Such a profligate use of municipal resources could only have occurred behind a strong, united leadership that shared a similar vision.

The politics of the merchant cities was characterized, for the most part, by remarkable political consensus. The economic interests of the governing elites were tied so closely to the growth of their cities that it drove them to close ranks and unite behind even the most ambitious and risky schemes to promote local development. Local political leadership became defined as the task of convincing all the factions in the community that it was in everyone's interest to support or contribute to some specific public works project, canal project, or railway venture. Most voters followed the lead of the governing class; they generally shared the belief that a growing economy would, indeed, benefit everyone. Such claims will sound familiar to anyone who remembers the supply-side economics of the 1980s. During that decade, the national political mood filtered down into local communities. Cities entered into an inter-urban competition that rivaled the railroad era. It is a competition that continues unabated.

Machine Politics

The industrial revolution and the development of mass democratic institutions transformed the politics of cities. The stability of the aristocrat/merchant coalitions can be explained by the persuasive power of an ideology of growth and by the near-absence of political competition. Eventually, however, a rapidly expanding urban electorate was bound to change the complexion of local politics. After the Civil War, city populations exploded when waves of immigrants from abroad and migrants from rural areas came in search of jobs in the factories. Wide-open political struggles began to replace oligarchic control by business and professional elites. A new generation of politicians learned how to mobilize the urban electorate. This new generation of politicians was often motivated by little more than a desire to use the political system for personal advancement. Public officials and those seeking favorable governmental action became accustomed to buying loyalty and favors with cash, jobs, contracts, and other material inducements.

In many cities, this style of politics became structured and regularized. By the turn of the century, several cities were governed by party machines that gathered the reins of power into the hands of a boss or a few ward politicians. The survival of this system was closely tied to two constituencies: voters and business. Machine politicians distributed jobs and favors to gain the loyalty of ethnic voters, and they also traded on the symbols of ethnic identity and solidarity. At the same time they made themselves useful—at a price—to business entrepreneurs who benefitted from stable, reliable relationships with politicians who could manipulate the powers of city government. Government officials routinely made important decisions granting franchises and setting utility rates; they approved contracts for the installation of street lights, gas, telephones, and trolley lines. Exclusive contracts for these services made fortunes; the politicians might receive bribes, but business entrepreneurs could make millions. The machines enabled business to operate freely in its own sphere; in exchange, the politicians expected that they would be allowed to operate freely within theirs. For this reason, urban businessmen were sometimes the main supporters and beneficiaries of machine governments.

Reform Politics

Machine politicians provoked their own opposition because they were often remarkably exclusionary. They represented some immigrant groups, but not others, and they were useful to only that fraction of the local business community that was willing or able to engage in deal-making and privilege-buying. Machine politicians often affronted middle- and upper-class sensibilities. The fledgling reform efforts that arose during the last years of the 19th century were mostly met with failure because they did not succeed at articulating a vision of the city that could unite enough groups behind a compelling cause. During the Progressive Era, however, a national movement coalesced behind the cause of municipal reform.

The system of boss politics found its most potent challenge in a municipal reform movement that became increasingly well-coordinated at the national level after the turn of the century. When national business corporations and organizations lined up behind the banner of municipal reform, the movement gained real strength. In principle, the reformers could have challenged the machines by destroying the machine's social base of support through appeals and programs designed to attract immigrants away from the machines—for instance, relief and housing programs could have competed with the bosses' unreliable dispensing of favors; taxes could have been imposed on business and the wealthy to pay for such programs. In reality, however, those who dominated municipal reform sought to limit the influence not only of bosses but also of immigrants, and they certainly did not imagine that the role of city government was to redistribute political power downward.

In fact, they took quite the opposite view. Most reformers wanted to gain control of municipal authority to use local government for their own purposes. They artfully obfuscated this agenda behind a rhetoric of "good government" that proposed that the public interest could be objectively defined and that this interest dictated only one objective: the delivery of basic city services at the lowest possible cost. This theory was directly related to local democratic politics in the reformers' assertion that elections and representation should be strictly separated from the day-to-day administration of services. To protect municipal government from "politics," the reformers said that experts with training, experience, and ability should run the public's business. In sum, the reformers asserted that urban politics was not about governance—that is, the task of brokering among various political interests—instead, city government was merely a matter of supplying services as efficiently as possible. "There is no Republican or Democratic way to pave the streets!" went the reform campaign slogan. Consistent with such a belief, the reformers fought to replace mayors with city managers, partisan elections with the nonpartisan ballot, and wards with at-large election systems. Despite all of their attempts to return power to the "better classes," however, the reformers could not return to the halcyon days when patricians and merchants ran city affairs. The industrial city was simply too big and complex for amateur, part-time government. It required a high level of municipal services and the construction of a public infrastructure. With the proliferation of administrative agencies, governments became more complex—and arguably less democratic. Ironically, this expansion of municipal authority often benefitted machines by vastly expanding the volume of city contracts and patronage. Outside of the older industrial cities, however, where the vast reservoir of ethnic votes made it impossible to replace machine organizations, reformers built their own edifices of power. Cities in the West and the Southwest met the challenge of modern governance by creating a multitude of special authorities to provide water and urban infrastructure. As one would expect (in light of the reformers' goals), these were put well beyond the reach of the urban electorate.

Part Two: The Politics of the Contemporary City

The Suburbs

It is impossible to understand the issues and controversies that define urban politics in America without reference to the great suburban–central city divide. The political separation of the suburbs and the cities is one of the most important stories of this century. People had begun to spill beyond the boundaries of the cities even in the 19th century, and by the decade of the 1920s, the streetcar and the first auto suburbs began proliferating. The suburban movement was stalled, for a time, by the Great Depression and World War II. But when prosperity returned in the postwar years, the floodgates were flung open. The suburbs grew by 35 million people in just the two decades from 1950 to 1960. Where people went, business followed—by the 1960s shopping centers began to spring up in the suburbs, and soon other businesses followed suit. Since World War II, older industrial cities have been faced with a steady erosion of populations and jobs.

Reflecting the stark differences between them, the politics of the suburbs and the central cities diverged sharply. Relatively affluent, white suburban governments rapidly proliferated as suburbanites formed new towns and cities beyond the boundaries of older core cities. By 1987, there were 83,237 local governments in the United States. In most major metropolitan areas, there are often hundreds of towns, villages, special districts, and other governmental units that govern the suburban fringes. Political separation allowed upper income and middle class whites to segregate themselves from the people and problems of the central cities and to maintain low taxes, high property values, and amenities not available elsewhere. By the 1960s, this trend made the older central cities home to large numbers of racial minorities, a pattern that has persisted. Even though African-Americans and other minority groups have been moving to the suburbs in substantial numbers, integrated neighborhoods are rare. Suburban black families are often segregated into small numbers of suburbs rather than being widely dispersed throughout suburban areas (Kantor, 1993: 235). And immigrants continue to pour into older neighborhoods of the central cities.

The social divisions described by the suburb-city divide are far more subtle and complex than the focus on race might suggest, however. The suburbs have long nurtured segmentation along many dimensions—and indeed, a more fine-tuned segregation may be a defining hallmark of suburbs today. There can be little doubt that the suburban housing tracts of the postwar era catered almost exclusively to standard-issue, middle-class families. The heterogeneity of urban life characterized city, and not suburban, neighborhoods. However, even within suburbia, an overlooked segregation took place; men commuted to work, wives stayed home. As the suburbs became more complex after the 1970s, suburbs became differentiated from one another, and they became more separated from the central cities. The old commuting patterns that pulled workers into the cities by day but pushed them back to the suburbs by night have been replaced by cross-commuting. Now Edge Cities—with their clusters of housing, office towers, campuses, and retailing complexes—compete with the central cities.

The Central Cities

Issues of race and ethnicity have always been central to the politics of American cities, and they remain important issues today. Since early in the 20th century, African-American populations in older cities have been increasing. In the 20 largest cities of the industrial belt, the white population fell sharply after 1950 while the black population grew rapidly. In some of these cities, and also in cities of the Sunbelt, the Latino population also increased dramatically, especially after 1960 (Kantor, 1993: 235). By the 1960s, conflicts over race and ethnicity affected virtually all the social and political institutions located in cities—from schools to neighborhoods to city halls.

Issues of race and ethnicity became contentious, even explosive, issues in the 1960s, and they have remained crucially important ever since. In the 1960s and 1970s, mayors looked to Washington in the hope that social and urban programs could help them cope with the racial tensions and social problems that confronted them. Since the withdrawal of the federal government from the cities, their task has been challenging, to say the least. On the one hand, mayors have been forced into strategies to rebuild downtown economies. On the other hand, they must also try to maintain some minimal degree of social cohesion, a task made even more difficult in those cities that have received waves of new immigrants coming from countries in Asia, Latin America, and the Caribbean. The 1980s was the second largest decade of legal immigration in American history, exceeding even the floodtide of 1900 to 1910. Most of the new immigrants have settled in the central cities. As a result, urban politics in the early millennium is likely to continue to revolve around interracial and inter-ethnic rivalries.

As their presence and political activism grew after the mid-1960s, African-Americans and Latinos began to capture roles as major power brokers in the big cities. By 1990, there were 7,935 black elected officials in the United States. Significantly, most of the increase in black representation occurred in central cities (Kantor, 1995: 83). The number of Latino officials has also grown, particularly in the cities. The ability of urban officials to leverage their access to government into tangible gains for inner-city populations is, however, constrained by the fact that the cities they govern lack the fiscal resources to tackle social problems in any serious way. For this reason, minority mayors who talk a language of social reform have been elected in large numbers, but they typically have ended up pursuing policies designed to promote investment and growth (Reed, 1987; Judd, 1986).

Part Three: Problems and Policy Issues

Entrepreneurial Cities

In trying to strike a balance between governance and growth, mayors seem to fall most often on the side of growth. For a few years, federal programs helped the cities stave off the consequences of economic decline. When Republicans won the White House in 1980, the cities' biggest source of new revenue since the early 1960s—federal dollars—dried up quickly. Because suburban and Sunbelt voters constituted the base of the national Republican party, advocates for the cities found that their pleas for a continuation of urban aid fell on deaf ears. Recognizing that their ability to lobby Washington had melted away, mayors began casting about for ways to stave off fiscal disaster. A new generation of mayors assumed office with the promise of fiscal austerity and economic revitalization. At the same time that they slashed budgets and trimmed services, cities offered tax abatements and subsidies for land and loans. They invested heavily in convention centers and sports stadiums; they renovated harbors and riverfronts. With all these efforts, mayors sought to make their cities hospitable environments for corporations, white-collar office workers, and tourists.

Urban leaders have little choice; they must compete vigorously for private investment. What began as the movement of manufacturing, wholesaling, and retailing firms from older cities in the 1970s has matured into an economic reality in which firms freely move from one city or region to another, or even outside the United States entirely. In recent decades, business has become increasingly mobile, forcing cities (and even nations) to compete with one another for investment. In the environment of a globalized economy, most cities are now fighting for a new niche in a new urban hierarchy of the twenty-first century. All of the older industrial cities have joined a fierce competition for corporate jobs, professional services, entertainment, and tourism. There is much debate about how much these entrepreneurial cities can control their own destinies. Mayors, however, must act as if they can.

The New Inequalities

The growing inequalities that characterize America in the new century are magnified in its urban areas. In the 1960s, the civil rights movement forced issues of racial justice onto the national agenda. A series of urban riots brought the message home with a vengeance. Short of a new round of violence—which, in any case, always provokes as much reaction as reform—is there any mechanism that might bring forth a new round of policies aimed at poverty and its associated ills? In the cities, the homeless still walk downtown areas, and although crime rates have declined, the signs of poverty and its ills are easily apparent. In downtown areas, fortress buildings, enclosed malls, and guarded condominiums keep out the poor. In the suburbs, gated communities are reminders of the walled cities of the medieval Europe. Building walls may sometimes appear to be a plausible response to intractable social divisions, but—apart from its moral implications—it is far from a foolproof remedy even for those who lived inside them. More and more suburbanites, for example, are finding that it is not so easy to escape the social ills of American society, however securely they think they are hidden behind their walls. The quality of life that suburbanites had hoped to achieve by physical separation from others is proving increasingly difficult to protect. Problems such as crime, social disorder, poverty, drugs, and environmental degradation often know no boundaries. Crime and drug problems have increased in suburban communities as well as in the cities. The fiscal cost of building more prisons, as well as for programs to assist the economically marginalized, is paid for by state and federal taxes, and not just by local governments (Downs, 1995).

National Policy and Local Governments

The urban politics of the 1990s has become transparently perverse. Homeless people sleep in cardboard boxes and on subway grates as busy business executives and public officials walk past into municipally subsidized office towers and downtown malls. Mayors discover that the resources and political cooperation they need to attend to the problems that face them are far from their grasp. Close by, wealthy suburbs may provide lavish services, and they can do so with a low tax base if property values and business investment are high enough. Early in the new millennium, exactly how these new dilemmas will be played out in national politics and in the cities is an intriguing question. On one hand, today's urban political order seems to have little capacity to bridge social inequalities or to build more inclusive political communities. Instead, metropolitan areas seem to be organized specifically to maintain and reinforce separation and segregation. On the other, the national government, with its huge revenue base and broad regulatory powers, clearly possesses the capacity to fund urban policy.

The New Regional Politics

It has often been observed that the costs of metropolitan fragmentation does not fall only on the poor and people at the margins of society. Metropolitan regions constitute economic systems, with the suburbs and the central cities sharing a mutual interdependence. In many urban areas, efforts are being made to organize political coalitions dedicated to the task of making key regional decisions. In Minneapolis, for example, the city has forged an alliance with the suburbs, which have not benefitted from a winner-take-all struggle for investment, jobs, and wealthy residents (Orfield, selection 30). Widespread popular frustration with urban sprawl may also bring about some attempts at regional cooperation. But it must be recognized that such reforms are likely to be partial. In the United States, the attachment to local government and suspicions about regional government run deep. Cooperation among local governments is more likely to emerge than true regional governance.

Bibliography

Beauregard, Robert A. 1993. *Voices of Decline: The Postwar Fate of U.S. Cities.* New York: Blackwell.

Downs, Anthony. 1994. *New Visions for Metropolitan America.* Washington, D.C.: The Brookings Institution.

Edsall, Thomas Byrne, and Mary D. Edsall. 1991. *Chain Reaction: The Impact of Race, Rights, and Taxes on American Politics.* New York: W.W. Norton & Co.

Garreau, Joel. 1991. *Edge City: Life on the New Frontier.* New York: Doubleday.

Glaab, Charles N., and A. Theodore Brown. 1967. *A History of Urban America.* New York: Macmillan.

Goodrich, Carter. 1960. *Government Promotion of American Canals and Railroads, 1800–1890.* New York: Columbia University Press.

Goodrich, Carter, ed. 1961. *Canals and American Economic Development.* New York: Columbia University Press.

Judd, Dennis R. 1986. "Electoral Coalitions, Minority Mayors, and the Contradictions in the Municipal Policy Agenda," pp. 145–170. in M. Gottdiener (ed.), *Cities in Stress: A New Look at the Urban Crisis.* Thousand Oaks, CA: Sage Publications.

Kantor, Paul. 1995. *The Dependent City Revisited. The Political Economy of Urban Development and Social Policy.* Boulder, CO: Westview Press.

Kantor, Paul. 1993. "The Dual City as Political Choice." *Journal of Urban Affairs,* 15 (3), 231–244.

Pomper, Gerald. 1985. "The Presidential Election." In Gerald Pomper (ed.), *The Election of 1984: Reports and Interpretations.* Chatham, NJ: Chatham House.

Reed, Adolph, Jr. 1987. "A Critique of Neo-Progressivism in Theorizing about Local Development Policy: A Case of Atlanta," pp. 199–215. In Clarence N. Stone and Heywood T. Sanders (eds.), *The Politics of Urban Development.* Lawrence, KS: University of Kansas Press.

Sassen, Saskia. 1991. *The Global City.* Princeton: Princeton University Press.

Shefter, Martin. 1985. *Political Crisis, Fiscal Crisis.* New York: Basic Books.

Stone, Clarence N. 1989. *Regime Politics: Governing Atlanta.* Lawrence, KS: University of Kansas Press.

Swanstrom, Todd. 1989. "Semisovereign Cities: The Politics of Urban Development," *Polity* 21, no. 1 (Fall): 83–110.

Taylor, George Rogers. 1951. *The Transportation Revolution: 1815–1860.* New York: Rinehart and Co.

***

THE NATURE OF URBAN REGIMES

The Nature of Urban Governance

Urban scholars often refer to cities as they would people, capable of independent thought and action. Such a construction is more than a mere rhetorical flourish; as public corporations, cities are invested with significant public powers that can be used for a variety of purposes. As Paul E. Peterson points out in Essay 1, there are constant debates about the "public interest" that cities ought to pursue. Some people might demand that cities spend their public resources on "redistributive" policies designed to help those most in need. Others might champion the view that city governments should do little more than provide the services necessary to make the city a healthy and functional environment. Peterson's view is that cities have no choice but to support policies that will stimulate economic growth. Such policies, he says, respond to a "unitary interest" that all urban residents hold in local economic vitality: "It is in the city's interest . . . to help sustain a high-quality local infrastructure generally attractive to all commerce and industry." Even the social health of a city, he says, depends on its economic prosperity: "When a city is able to export its products, service industries prosper, labor is in greater demand . . . tax revenues increase, city services can be improved, donations to charitable organizations become more generous, and the social and cultural life of the city is enhanced."

In Peterson's analysis, the leaders of cities cannot leave economic growth to chance because cities compete with one another. City governments are unable to control the movement of capital and labor across borders. In contrast to the national government, they lack the authority to regulate immigration, currency, prices, and wages, or the import or export of goods and services. City governments, therefore, are constrained to compete for capital investment or suffer decline in the economic well-being of the community. Although cities occupy a particular space, if the local business environment is not pleasing to them, investors and businesses can go elsewhere. This logic drives cities to minimize taxes, avoid expensive regulations, and offer a variety of subsidies to business. Put simply, politicians are advised to resist the clamor of other political interests when these might compromise the preferences of business in any way.

The book from which the Peterson selection is taken ignited a controversy among urban scholars. Many of them took Peterson to task for his apparent assertion that growth benefits everyone. Others accused him of ignoring the complexities of city politics, which can result in substantially different growth strategies and policies from city to city. At the very least, politicians must not only try to protect and enhance the economic base of a city, they must also mobilize sufficient political support to remain in office and implement their policies. In recent years, a literature on "urban regimes" has provided a way of understanding the specific mechanisms by which the tensions between the marketplace and local democracy are managed. Local regimes comprise of both political and economic actors who constantly negotiate settlements among political factions and interests. As described by Clarence N. Stone in Essay 2, the two most powerful components of urban regimes include city hall—the officials who are most motivated by electoral concerns—and the city's business elite. Governmental officials lack the resources to do much on their own. Likewise, the business community requires government to accomplish desirable goals. Thus, in Stone's account of politics in Atlanta, he notes that, "What makes governance in Atlanta effective is not the formal machinery of government, but rather the informal partnership between city hall and the downtown business elite. This informal partnership and the way it operates constitute the city's regime; it is the same means through which major policy decisions are made." Partnership suggests cooperation rather than control. If regime participants learn to work together to accomplish mutual goals, all are empowered, in the sense that they can accomplish things that none of them working alone can do.

The selection by Todd Swanstrom argues that the regime concept has been overly "economist" in its assumptions. Swanstrom believes that it is a mistake to think that most decisions over local development policies are driven by economic logic; the economic pressures on cities are almost always "slack," leaving room for internal political factors to shape behavior. He asserts that most public policies for development reflect a political logic; that is, they really function to serve the political needs of public officials and various interest groups. Often they do little more than provide symbolic reassurance that the government is trying to do something about the local economy. Thus, Swanstrom concludes that many of the policies designed to promote investment do not actually bring growth; it is enough for them to call attention to the actions of politicians. As such, they are often political successes even when they are economic failures.

With few exceptions, urban scholars have embraced Stone's premise that urban regimes require cooperation between governmental and nongovernmental actors. His claim, however, that a city hall–business coalition always constitutes the core of urban governance has been questioned, as has an assumption that economic issues are paramount. Issues connected to race and ethnicity have always been crucial features of urban politics. And as the selection by Elaine B. Sharp shows, just as the "culture wars" have become increasingly important in national politics, they have also penetrated into local communities. Accordingly, urban governments are forced to wrestle with contentious issues such as gay rights, pornography, the operation of abortion clinics, hate-group activity, and judicial decisions regarding sexual assault. Local governments are sometimes preoccupied with the task of maintaining the social order—all the more when volatile social conflicts emerge. But local governments do not only try to maintain order; as Sharp points out, sometimes local officials instigate controversy to press their own agendas. Just as urban governments take an entrepreneurial role in promoting economic growth, they also are active participants in the most volatile social issues of our time.

1

Paul E. Peterson

THE INTERESTS OF THE LIMITED CITY

Like all social structures, cities have interests. Just as we can speak of union interests, judicial interests, and the interests of politicians, so we can speak of the interests of that structured system of social interactions we call a city. Citizens, politicians, and academics are all quite correct in speaking freely of the interests of cities.[1]

Defining the City Interest

By a city's interest, I do not mean the sum total of the interests of those individuals living in the city. For one thing, these are seldom, if ever, known. The wants, needs, and preferences of residents continually change, and few surveys of public opinion in particular cities have ever been taken. Moreover, the residents of a city often have discordant interests. Some want more parkland and better schools; others want better police protection and lower taxes. Some want an elaborated highway system; others wish to keep cars out of their neighborhood. Some want more inexpensive, publicly subsidized housing; others wish to remove the public housing that exists. Some citizens want improved welfare assistance for the unemployed and dependent; others wish to cut drastically all such programs of public aid. Some citizens want rough-tongued ethnic politicians in public office; others wish that municipal administration were a gentleman's calling. Especially in large cities, the cacophony of competing claims by diverse class, race, ethnic, and occupational groups makes impossible the determination of any overall city interest—any public interest, if you like—by compiling all the demands and desires of individual city residents.

Some political scientists have attempted to discover the overall urban public interest by summing up the wide variety of individual interests. The earlier work of Edward Banfield, still worth examination, is perhaps the most persuasive effort of this kind.[2] He argued that urban political processes—or at least those in Chicago—allowed for the expression of nearly all the particular interests within the city. Every significant interest was represented by some economic firm or voluntary association, which had a stake in trying to influence those public policies that touched its vested interests. After these various groups and firms had debated and contended, the political leader searched for a compromise that took into account the vital interests of each, and worked out a solution all could accept with some satisfaction. The leader's own interest in sustaining his political power dictated such a strategy.

Banfield's argument is intriguing, but few people would identify public policies as being in the interest of the city simply because they have been formulated according to certain procedures. The political leader might err in his judgment; the interests of important but politically impotent groups might never get expressed; or the consequences of a policy might in the long run be disastrous for the city. Moreover, most urban policies are not hammered out after great controversy, but are the quiet product of routine decision making. How does one evaluate which of these are in the public interest? Above all, this mechanism for determining the city's interest provides no standpoint for evaluating the substantive worth of urban policies. Within Banfield's framework, whatever urban governments do is said to be in the interest of their communities. But the concept of city interest is used most persuasively when there are calls for reform or innovation. It is a term used to evaluate existing programs and to discriminate between promising and undesirable new ones. To equate the interests of cities with what cities are doing is to so impoverish the term as to make it quite worthless.

The economist Charles Tiebout employs a second approach to the identification of city interests.[3] Unlike Banfield, he does not see the city's interests as a mere summation of individual interests but as something which can be ascribed to the entity, taken as a whole. As an economist, Tiebout is hardly embarrassed by such an enterprise, because in ascribing interests to cities his work parallels both those orthodox economists who state that firms have an interest in maximizing profits and those welfare economists who claim that politicians have an interest in maximizing votes. Of course, they state only that their model will assume that firms and politicians behave in such a way, but insofar as they believe their model has empirical validity, they in fact assert that those constrained by the businessman's or politician's role must pursue certain interests. And so does Tiebout when he says that communities seek to attain the optimum size for the efficient delivery of the bundle of services the local government produces. In his words, "Communities below the optimum size seek to attract new residents to lower average costs. Those above optimum size do just the opposite. Those at an optimum try to keep their populations constant."[4]

Tiebout's approach is in many ways very attractive. By asserting a strategic objective that the city is trying to maximize—optimum size—Tiebout identifies an overriding interest which can account for specific policies the city adopts. He provides a simple analytical tool that will account for the choices cities make, without requiring complex investigations into citizen preferences and political mechanisms for identifying and amalgamating the same. Moreover, he provides a criterion for determining whether a specific policy is in the interest of the city—does it help achieve optimum size? Will it help the too small city grow? Will it help the too big city contract? Will it keep the optimally sized city in equilibrium? Even though the exact determination of the optimum size cannot presently be scientifically determined in all cases, the criterion does provides a useful guide for prudential decision making.

The difficulty with Tiebout's assumption is that he does not give very good reasons for its having any plausibility. When most economists posit a certain form of maximizing behavior, there is usually a good commonsense reason for believing the person in that role will have an interest in pursuing this strategic objective. When orthodox economists say that businessmen maximize profits, it squares with our understanding in everyday life that people engage in commercial enterprises for monetary gain. The more they make, the better they like it. The same can be said of those welfare economists who say politicians maximize votes. The assumption, though cynical, is in accord with popular belief—and therefore once again has a certain plausibility.

By contrast, Tiebout's optimum size thesis diverges from what most people think cities are trying to do. Of course, smaller communities are often seeking to expand—boosterism may be the quintessential characteristic of small-town America. Yet Tiebout takes optimum size, not growth or maximum size, as the strategic objective. And when Tiebout discusses the big city that wishes to shrink to optimum size, his cryptic language is quite unconvincing. "The case of the city that is too large and tries to get rid of residents is more difficult to imagine," he confesses. Even more, he concedes that "no alderman in his right political mind would ever admit that the city is too big." "Nevertheless," he continues, "economic forces are at work to push people out of it. Every resident who moves to the suburbs to find better schools, more parks, and so forth, is reacting, in part, against the pattern the city has to offer."[5] In this crucial passage Tiebout speaks neither of local officials nor of local public policies. Instead, he refers to "economic forces" that may be beyond the control of the city and of "every resident," each of whom may be pursuing his own interests, not that of the community at large.

The one reason Tiebout gives for expecting cities to pursue optimum size is to lower the average cost of public goods. If public goods can be delivered most efficiently at some optimum size, then migration of residents will occur until that size has been reached. In one respect Tiebout is quite correct: local governments must concern themselves with operating local services as efficiently as possible in order to protect the city's economic interests. But there is little evidence that there is an optimum size at which services can be delivered with greatest efficiency. And even if such an optimum did exist, it could be realized only if migration occurred among residents who paid equal amounts in local taxes. In the more likely situation, residents pay variable prices for public services (for example, the amount paid in local property taxes varies by the value of the property). Under these circumstances, increasing size to the optimum does not reduce costs to residents unless newcomers pay at least as much in taxes as the marginal increase in costs their arrival imposes on city government.[6] Conversely, if a city needs to lose population to reach the optimum, costs to residents will not decline unless the exiting population paid less in taxes than was the marginal cost of providing them government services. In most big cities losing population, exactly the opposite is occurring. Those who pay more in taxes than they receive in services are the emigrants. Tiebout's identification of city interests with optimum size, while suggestive, fails to take into account the quality as well as the quantity of the local population.

The interests of cities are neither a summation of individual interests nor the pursuit of optimum size. Instead, policies and programs can be said to be in the interest of cities whenever the policies maintain or enhance the economic position, social prestige, or political power of the city, taken as a whole.[7]

Cities have these interests because cities consist of a set of social interactions structured by their location in a particular territorial space. Any time that social interactions come to be structured into recurring patterns, the structure thus formed develops an interest in its own maintenance and enhancement. It is in that sense that we speak of the interests of an organization, the interests of the system, and the like. To be sure, within cities, as within any other structure, one can find diverse social roles, each with its own set of interests. But these varying role interests, as divergent and competing as they may be, do not distract us from speaking of the overall interests of the larger structural entity.[8]

The point can be made less abstractly. A school system is a structured form of social action, and therefore it has an interest in maintaining and improving its material resources, its prestige, and its political power. Those policies or events which have such positive effects are said to be in the interest of the school system. An increase in state financial aid or the winning of the basketball tournament are events that, respectively, enhance the material well-being and the prestige of a school system and are therefore in its interest. In ordinary speech this is taken for granted, even when we also recognize that teachers, pupils, principals, and board members may have contrasting interests as members of differing role-groups within the school.

Although social roles performed within cities are numerous and conflicting, all are structured by the fact that they take place in a specific spatial location that falls within the jurisdiction of some local government. All members of the city thus come to share an interest in policies that affect the well-being of that territory. Policies which enhance the desirability or attractiveness of the territory are in the city's interest, because they benefit all residents—in their role as residents of the community. Of course, in any of their other social roles, residents of the city may be adversely affected by the policy. The Los Angeles dope peddler—in his role as peddler—hardly benefits from a successful drive to remove hard drugs from the city. On the other hand, as a resident of the city, he benefits from a policy that enhances the attractiveness of the city as a locale in which to live and work. In determining whether a policy is in the interest of a city, therefore, one does not consider whether it has a positive or negative effect on the total range of social interactions of each and every individual. That is an impossible task. To know whether a policy is in a city's interest, one has to consider only the impact on social relationships insofar as they are structured by their taking place within the city's boundaries.

An illustration from recent policy debates over the future of our cities reveals that it is exactly with this meaning that the notion of a city's interest is typically used. The tax deduction that homeowners take on their mortgage interest payments should be eliminated, some urbanists have argued. The deduction has not served the interests of central cities, because it has provided a public subsidy for families who purchase suburban homes. Quite clearly, elimination of this tax deduction is not in the interest of those central city residents who wish to purchase a home in the suburbs. It is not in the interest of those central city homeowners (which in some cities may even form a majority of the voting population), who would then be called upon to pay higher federal taxes. But the policy might very well improve the rental market in the central city, thereby stimulating its economy—and it is for this reason that the proposal has been defended as being in the interest of central cities.

To say that people understand what, generally, is in the interest of cities does not eliminate debate over policy alternatives in specific instances. The notion of city interest can be extremely useful, even though its precise application in specific contexts may be quite problematic. In any policy context one cannot easily assert that one "knows" what is in the interest of cities, whether or not the residents of the city agree. But city residents do know the kind of evidence that must be advanced and the kinds of reasons that must be adduced in order to build a persuasive case that a policy is in the interest of cities. And so do community leaders, mayors, and administrative elites.

Economic Interests

Cities, like all structured social systems, seek to improve their position in all three of the systems of stratification—economic, social, and political—characteristic of industrial societies. In most cases, improved standing in any one of these systems helps enhance a city's position in the other two. In the short run, to be sure, cities may have to choose among economic gains, social prestige, and political weight. And because different cities may choose alternative objectives, one cannot state any one overarching objective—such as improved property values—that is always the paramount interest of the city. But inasmuch as improved economic or market standing seems to be an objective of great importance to most cities, I shall concentrate on this interest and only discuss in passing the significance of social status and political power.

Cities constantly seek to upgrade their economic standing. Following Weber, I mean by this that cities seek to improve their market position, their attractiveness as a locale for economic activity. In the market economy that characterizes Western society, an advantageous economic position means a competitive edge in the production and distribution of desired commodities relative to other localities. When this is present, cities can export goods and/or services to those outside the boundaries of the community.

Some regional economists have gone so far as to suggest that the welfare of a city is identical to the welfare of its export industry.[9] As exporters expand, the city grows. As they contract, the city declines and decays. The economic reasoning supporting such a conclusion is quite straightforward. When cities produce a good that can be sold in an external market, labor and capital flow into the city to help increase the production of that good. They continue to do so until the external market is saturated—that is, until the marginal cost of production within the city exceeds the marginal value of the good external to the city. Those engaged in the production of the exported good will themselves consume a variety of other goods and services, which other businesses will provide. In addition, subsidiary industries locate in the city either because they help supply the exporting industry, because they can utilize some of its by-products, or because they benefit by some economies of scale provided by its presence. Already, the familiar multiplier is at work. With every increase in the sale of exported commodities, there may be as much as a four- or fivefold increase in local economic activity.

The impact of Boeing Aircraft's market prospects on the economy of the Seattle metropolitan area illustrates the importance of export to regional economies. In the late sixties defense and commercial aircraft contracts declined. Boeing laid off thousands of workmen, the economy of the Pacific Northwest slumped, the unemployed moved elsewhere, and Seattle land values dropped sharply. More recently, Boeing has more than recovered its former position. With rapidly expanding production at Boeing, the metropolitan area is enjoying low unemployment, rapid growth, and dramatically increasing land values.

The same multiplier effect is not at work in the case of goods and services produced for domestic consumption within the territory. What is gained by a producer within the community is expended by other community residents. Residents, in effect, are simply taking in one another's laundry. Unless productivity increases, there is no capacity for expansion.

If this economic analysis is correct, it is only a modest oversimplification to equate the interests of cities with the interests of their export industries. Whatever helps them prosper redounds to the benefit of the community as a whole—perhaps four and five times over. And it is just such an economic analysis that has influenced many local government policies. Especially the smaller towns and cities may provide free land, tax concessions, and favorable utility rates to incoming industries.

The smaller the territory and the more primitive its level of economic development, the more persuasive is this simple export thesis. But other economists have elaborated an alternative growth thesis that is in many ways more persuasive, especially as it relates to larger urban areas. In their view a sophisticated local network of public and private services is the key to long-range economic growth. Since the world economy is constantly changing, the economic viability of any particular export industry is highly variable. As a result, a community dependent on any particular set of export industries will have only an episodic economic future. But with a well-developed infrastructure of services, the city becomes an attractive locale for a wide variety of export industries. As older exporters fade, new exporters take their place and the community continues to prosper. It is in the city's interest, therefore, to help sustain a high-quality local infrastructure generally attractive to all commerce and industry.

I have no way of evaluating the merits of these contrasting economic arguments. What is important in this context is that both see exports as being of great importance to the well-being of a city. One view suggests a need for direct support of the export industry; the other suggests a need only for maintaining a service infrastructure, allowing the market to determine which particular export industry locates in the community. Either one could be the more correct diagnosis for a particular community, at least in the short run. Yet both recognize that the future of the city depends upon exporting local products. When a city is able to export its products, service industries prosper, labor is in greater demand, wages increase, promotional opportunities widen, land values rise, tax revenues increase, city services can be improved, donations to charitable organizations become more generous, and the social and cultural life of the city is enhanced.

To export successfully, cities must make efficient use of the three main factors of production: land, labor, and capital.[10]

Land

Land is the factor of production that cities control. Yet land is the factor to which cities are bound. It is the fact that cities are spatially defined units whose boundaries seldom change that gives permanence to their interests. City residents come and go, are born and die, and change their tastes and preferences. But the city remains wedded to the land area with which it is blessed (or cursed). And unless it can alter that land area, through annexation or consolidation, it is the long-range value of that land which the city must secure—and which gives a good approximation of how well it is achieving its interests.

Land is an economic resource. Production cannot occur except within some spatial location. And because land varies in its economic potential, so do the economic futures of cities. Historically, the most important variable affecting urban growth has been an area's relationship to land and water routes.

On the eastern coast of the United States, all the great cities had natural harbors that facilitated commercial relations with Europe and other coastal communities. Inland, the great industrial cities all were located on either the Great Lakes or the Ohio River–Mississippi River system. The cities of the West, as Elazar has shown, prospered according to their proximity to East-West trade flows.[11] Denver became the predominant city of the mountain states because it sat at the crossroads of land routes through the Rocky Mountains. Duluth, Minnesota, had only limited potential, even with its Great Lakes location, because it lay north of all major routes to the West.

Access to waterways and other trade routes is not the only way a city's life is structured by its location. Its climate determines the cost and desirability of habitation; its soil affects food production in the surrounding area; its terrain affects drainage, rates of air pollution, and scenic beauty. Of course, the qualities of landscape do not permanently fix a city's fate—it is the intersection of that land and location with the larger national and world economy that is critical. For example, cities controlling access to waterways by straddling natural harbors at one time monopolized the most valuable land in the region, and from that position they dominated their hinterland. But since land and air transport have begun to supplant, not just supplement, water transport, the dominance of these once favored cities has rapidly diminished.

Although the economic future of a city is very much influenced by external forces affecting the value of its land, the fact that a city has control over the use of its land gives it some capacity for influencing that future. Although there are constitutional limits to its authority, the discretion available to a local government in determining land use remains the greatest arena for the exercise of local autonomy. Cities can plan the use of local space; cities have the power of eminent domain; through zoning laws cities can restrict all sorts of land uses; and cities can regulate the size, content, and purpose of buildings constructed within their boundaries. Moreover, cities can provide public services in such a way as to encourage certain kinds of land use. Sewers, gas lines, roads, bridges, tunnels, playgrounds, schools, and parks all impinge on the use of land in the surrounding area. Urban politics is above all the politics of land use, and it is easy to see why. Land is the factor of production over which cities exercise the greatest control.

Labor

To its land area the city must attract not only capital but productive labor. Yet local governments in the United States are very limited in their capacities to control the flow of these factors. Lacking the more direct controls of nation-states, they are all the more constrained to pursue their economic interests in those areas where they do exercise authority.

Labor is an obvious case in point. Since nation-states control migration across their boundaries, the industrially more advanced have formally legislated that only limited numbers of outsiders—for example, relatives of citizens or those with skills needed by the host country—can enter. In a world where it is economically feasible for great masses of the population to migrate long distances, this kind of restrictive legislation seems essential for keeping the nation's social and economic integrity intact. Certainly, the wage levels and welfare assistance programs characteristic of advanced industrial societies could not be sustained were transnational migration unencumbered.

Unlike nation-states, cities cannot control movement across their boundaries. They no longer have walls, guarded and defended by their inhabitants. And as Weber correctly noted, without walls cities no longer have the independence to make significant choices in the way medieval cities once did.[12] It is true that local governments often try to keep vagrants, bums, paupers, and racial minorities out of their territory. They are harassed, arrested, thrown out of town, and generally discriminated against. But in most of these cases local governments act unconstitutionally, and even this illegal use of the police power does not control migration very efficiently.

Although limited in its powers, the city seeks to obtain an appropriately skilled labor force at wages lower than its competitors so that it can profitably export commodities. In larger cities a diverse work force is desirable. The service industry, which provides the infrastructure for exporters, recruits large numbers of unskilled workers, and many manufacturing industries need only semiskilled workers. When shortages in these skill levels appear, cities may assist industry in advertising the work and living opportunities of the region. In the nineteenth century when unskilled labor was in short supply, frontier cities made extravagant claims to gain a competitive edge in the supply of ordinary labor.

Certain sparsely populated areas, such as Alaska, occasionally advertise for unskilled labor even today. However, competition among most cities is now for highly skilled workers and especially for professional and managerial talent. In a less than full-employment economy, most communities have a surplus of semiskilled and unskilled labor. Increases in the supply of unskilled workers increase the cost of the community's social services. Since national wage laws preclude a decline in wages below a certain minimum, the increases in the cost of social services are seldom offset by lower wages for unskilled labor in those areas where the unemployed concentrate. But even with high levels of unemployment, there remains a shortage of highly skilled technicians and various types of white collar workers. Where shortages develop, the prices these workers can command in the labor market may climb to a level where local exports are no longer competitive with goods produced elsewhere. The economic health of a community is therefore importantly affected by the availability of professional and managerial talent and of highly skilled technicians.

When successfully pursuing their economic interests, cities develop a set of policies that will attract the more skilled and white collar workers without at the same time attracting unemployables. Of course, there are limits on the number of things cities can do. In contrast to nation-states, they cannot simply forbid entry to all but the highly talented whose skills they desire. But through zoning laws, they can ensure that adequate land is available for middle-class residences. They can provide parks, recreation areas, and good-quality schools in areas where the economically most productive live. They can keep the cost of social services, little utilized by the middle class, to a minimum, thereby keeping local taxes relatively low. In general, they can try to ensure that the benefits of public service outweigh their costs to those highly skilled workers, managers, and professionals who are vital for sustaining the community's economic growth.

Capital

Capital is the second factor of production that must be attracted to an economically productive territory. Accordingly, nation-states place powerful controls on the flow of capital across their boundaries. Many nations strictly regulate the amount of national currency that can be taken out of the country. They place quotas and tariffs on imported goods. They regulate the rate at which national currency can be exchanged with foreign currency. They regulate the money supply, increasing interest rates when growth is too rapid, lowering interest rates when growth slows down. Debt financing also allows a nation-state to undertake capital expenditures and to encourage growth in the private market. At present the powers of nation-states to control capital flow are being used more sparingly and new supranational institutions are developing in their place. Market forces now seem more powerful than official policies in establishing rates of currency exchange among major industrial societies. Tariffs and other restrictions on trade are subject to retaliation by other countries, and so they must be used sparingly. The economies of industrialized nations are becoming so interdependent that significant changes in the international political economy seem imminent, signaled by numerous international conferences to determine worldwide growth rates, rates of inflation, and levels of unemployment. If these trends continue, nation-states may come to look increasingly like local governments.

But these developments at the national level have only begun to emerge. At the local level in the United States, cities are much less able to control capital flows. In the first place, the Constitution has been interpreted to mean that states cannot hinder the free flow of goods and monies across their boundaries. And what is true of states is true of their subsidiary jurisdictions as well. In the second place, states and localities cannot regulate the money supply. If unemployment is low, they cannot stimulate the economy by increasing the monetary flow. If inflationary pressures adversely affect their competitive edge in the export market, localities can neither restrict the money supply nor directly control prices and wages. All of these powers are reserved for national governments. In the third place, local governments cannot spend more than they receive in tax revenues without damaging their credit or even running the risk of bankruptcy. Pump priming, sometimes a national disease, is certainly a national prerogative.

Local governments are left with a number of devices for enticing capital into the area. They can minimize their tax on capital and on profits from capital investment. They can reduce the costs of capital investment by providing low-cost public utilities, such as roads, sewers, lights, and police and fire protection. They can even offer public land free of charge or at greatly reduced prices to those investors they are particularly anxious to attract. They can provide a context for business operations free of undue harassment or regulation. For example, they can ignore various external costs of production, such as air pollution, water pollution, and the despoliation of trees, grass, and other features of the landscape. Finally, they can discourage labor from unionizing so as to keep industrial labor costs competitive.

This does not mean it behooves cities to allow any and all profit-maximizing action on the part of an industrial plant. Insofar as the city desires diversified economic growth, no single company can be allowed to pursue policies that seriously detract from the area's overall attractiveness to capital or productive labor. Taxes cannot be so low that government fails to supply residents with as attractive a package of services as can be found in competitive jurisdictions. Regulation of any particular industry cannot fall so far below nationwide standards that other industries must bear external costs not encountered in other places. The city's interest in attracting capital does not mean utter subservience to any particular corporation, but a sensitivity to the need for establishing an overall favorable climate.

In sum, cities, like private firms, compete with one another so as to maximize their economic position. To achieve this objective, the city must use the resources its land area provides by attracting as much capital and as high a quality labor force as is possible. Like a private firm, the city must entice labor and capital resources by offering appropriate inducements. Unlike the nation-state, the American city does not have regulatory powers to control labor and capital flows. The lack thereof sharply limits what cities can do to control their economic development, but at the same time the attempt by cities to maximize their interests within these limits shapes policy choice.

Local Government and the Interests of Cities

Local government leaders are likely to be sensitive to the economic interests of their communities. First, economic prosperity is necessary for protecting the fiscal base of a local government. In the United States, taxes on local sources and charges for local services remain important components of local government revenues. Although transfers of revenue to local units from the federal and state governments increased throughout the postwar period, as late as 1975–76 local governments still were raising almost 59 percent of their own revenue.[13] Raising revenue from one's own economic resources requires continuing local economic prosperity. Second, good government is good politics. By pursuing policies which contribute to the economic prosperity of the local community, the local politician selects policies that redound to his own political advantage. Local politicians, eager for relief from the cross-pressures of local politics, assiduously promote goals that have widespread benefits. And few policies are more popular than economic growth and prosperity. Third, and most important, local officials usually have a sense of community responsibility. They know that, unless the economic well-being of the community can be maintained, local business will suffer, workers will lose employment opportunities, cultural life will decline, and city land values will fall. To avoid such a dismal future, public officials try to develop policies that assist the prosperity of their community—or, at the very least, that do not seriously detract from it. Quite apart from any effects of economic prosperity on government revenues or local voting behavior, it is quite reasonable to posit that local governments are primarily interested in maintaining the economic vitality of the area for which they are responsible.

Accordingly, governments can be expected to attempt to maximize this particular goal—within the numerous environmental constraints with which they must contend. As policy alternatives are proposed, each is evaluated according to how well it will help to achieve this objective. Although information is imperfect and local governments cannot be expected to select the one best alternative on every occasion, policy choices over time will be limited to those few which can plausibly be shown to be conducive to the community's economic prosperity. Internal disputes and disagreements may affect policy on the margins, but the major contours of local revenue policy will be determined by this strategic objective.

Notes

1. Flathman, R. E. 1966. *The public interest* (New York: John Wiley).
2. Banfield, E. C. 1961. *Political influence* (Glencoe, Illinois: Free Press). Ch. 12.
3. Tiebout, C. M. 1956. A pure theory of local expenditures. *Journal of Political Economy* 64: 416–424.
4. Ibid., p. 419.
5. Ibid., p. 420.
6. Bruce Hamilton, "Property Taxes and the Tiebout Hypothesis: Some Empirical Evidence," and Michelle J. White, "Fiscal Zoning in Fragmented Metropolitan Areas," in Mills, E. S., and Oates, W. E. 1975. *Fiscal zoning and land use controls* (Lexington, Massachusetts: Lexington Books). Chs. 2 and 3.
7. See Weber, "Class, Status, and Power," in Gerth, H. H., and Mills, C. W., trans. 1946. *From Max Weber* (New York: Oxford University Press).
8. For a more complete discussion of roles, structures, and interests, see Greenstone, J. D., and Peterson, P. E. 1976. *Race and authority in urban politics.* Phoenix edition (Chicago: University of Chicago Press). Ch. 2.
9. Cf. Thompson, W. R. 1965. *A preface to urban economics* (Baltimore, Maryland: Johns Hopkins University Press).
10. I treat entrepreneurial skill as simply another form of labor, even though it is a form in short supply.
11. Elazar, D. J. 1976. *Cities of the prairie* (New York: Basic Books).
12. Weber, M. 1921. *The city* (New York: Collier Books).
13. United States Department of Commerce, Bureau of the Census. 1977. *Local government finances in selected metropolitan areas and large counties: 1975–76.* Government finances: GF 76, no. 6.

2

Clarence N. Stone

URBAN REGIMES: A RESEARCH PERSPECTIVE

What makes governance in Atlanta effective is not the formal machinery of government, but rather the informal partnership between city hall and the downtown business elite. This informal partnership and the way it operates constitute the city's regime; it is the means through which major policy decisions are made.

The word "regime" connotes different things to different people, but in this [selection] regime is specifically about the *informal arrangements* that surround and complement the formal workings of governmental authority. All governmental authority in the United States is greatly limited—limited by the Constitution, limited perhaps even more by the nation's political tradition, and limited structurally by the autonomy of privately owned business enterprise. The exercise of public authority is thus never a simple matter; it is almost always enhanced by extraformal considerations. Because local governmental authority is by law and tradition even more limited than authority at the state and national level, informal arrangements assume special importance in urban politics. But we should begin our understanding of regimes by realizing that informal arrangements are by no means peculiar to cities or, for that matter, to government.

Even narrowly bounded organizations, those with highly specific functional responsibilities, develop informal governing coalitions.[1] As Chester Barnard argued many years ago, formal goals and formal lines of authority are insufficient by themselves to bring about coordinated action with sufficient energy to accomplish organizational purposes;[2] commitment and cooperation do not just spring up from the lines of an organization chart. Because every formal organization gives rise to an informal one, Barnard concluded, successful executives must master the skill of shaping and using informal organization for their purposes.

Attention to informal arrangements takes various forms. In the analysis of business firms, the school of thought labeled "transaction cost economics" has given systematic attention to how things actually get done in a world full of social friction—basically the same question that Chester Barnard considered. A leading proponent of this approach, Oliver Williamson,[3] finds that what he terms "private orderings" (as opposed to formal and legal agreements) are enormously important in the running of business affairs. For many transactions, mutual and tacit understanding is a more efficient way of conducting relations than are legal agreements and formal contracts. Williamson quotes a

---

business executive as saying, "You can settle any dispute if you keep the lawyers and accountants out of it. They just do not understand the give-and-take needed in business."[4] Because informal understandings and arrangements provide needed flexibility to cope with nonroutine matters, they facilitate co-operation to a degree that formally defined relationships do not. People who know one another, who have worked together in the past, who have shared in the achievement of a task, and who perhaps have experienced the same crisis are especially likely to develop tacit understandings. If they interact on a continuing basis, they can learn to trust one another and to expect dependability from one another. It can be argued, then, that transactions flow more smoothly and business is conducted more efficiently when a core of insiders form and develop an ongoing relationship.

A regime thus involves not just any informal group that comes together to make a decision but an informal yet relatively stable group *with access to institutional resources* that enable it to have a sustained role in making governing decisions. What makes the group informal is not a lack of institutional connections, but the fact that the group, *as a group,* brings together institutional connections by an informal mode of cooperation. There is no all-encompassing structure of command that guides and synchronizes everyone's behavior. There is a purposive coordination of efforts, but it comes about informally, in ways that often depend heavily on tacit understandings.

If there is no overarching command structure, what gives a regime coherence? What makes it more than an "ecology of games"?[5] The answer is that the regime is purposive, created and maintained as a way of facilitating action. In a very important sense, *a regime is empowering.* Its supporters see it as a means for achieving coordinated efforts that might not otherwise be realized. A regime, however, is not created or redirected at will. Organizational analysis teaches us that cognition is limited, existing arrangements have staying power, and implementation is profoundly shaped by procedures in place.[6] Shrewd and determined leaders can effect purposive change, but only by being attentive to the ways in which existing forms of coordination can be altered or amplified.[7]

We can think of cities as organizations that lack a conjoining structure of command. There are institutional sectors within which the power of command may be much in evidence, but the sectors are independent of one another.[8] Because localities have only weak formal means through which coordination can be achieved, informal arrangements to promote cooperation are especially useful. *These informal modes of coordinating efforts across institutional boundaries are what I call "civic cooperation."* In a system of weak formal authority, it holds special importance. Integrated with the formal structure of authority into a suprainstitutional capacity to take action, any informal basis of cooperation is empowering. It enables community actors to achieve cooperation beyond what could be formally commanded.

Consider the case of local political machines. When ward politicians learned to coordinate informally what otherwise was mired in institutional fragmentation and personal opportunism, the urban political machine was created and proved to have enormous staying power.[9] "Loyalty" is the shorthand that machine politicians used to describe the code that bound them into a cohesive group.[10] The political machine is in many ways the exemplar of governance in which informal arrangements are vital complements to the formal organization of government. The classic urban machines brought together various elements of the community in an informal scheme of exchange and cooperation that was the real governing system of the community.

The urban machine, of course, represents only one form of regime. In considering Atlanta, I am examining the governing coalition in a nonmachine city. The term "governing coalition" is a way of making the notion of regime concrete. It makes us face the fact that informal arrangements are held together by a core group—typically a body of insiders—who come together repeatedly in making important decisions. Thus, when I refer to the governing coalition in Atlanta, I mean the core group at the center of the workings of the regime.

To talk about a core group is not to suggest that they are of one mind or that they all represent identical interests—far from it. "Coalition" is the word I use to emphasize that a regime involves bringing together various elements of the community and the different institutional capacities they control. "Governing," as used in "governing coalition," I must stress, does not mean rule in command-and-control fashion. Governance through informal arrangements is about how some forms of coordination of effort prevail over others. It is about mobilizing efforts to cope and to adapt; it is not about absolute control. Informal arrangements are a way of bolstering (and guiding) the formal capacity to act, but even this enhanced capacity remains quite limited.

Having argued that informal arrangements are important in a range of circumstances, not just in cities, let me return to the specifics of the city setting. After all, the important point is not simply that there are informal arrangements; it is the particular features of urban regimes that provide the lenses through which we see the Atlanta experience. For cities, two questions face us: (1) Who makes up the governing coalition—who has to come together to make governance possible? (2) How is the coming together accomplished? These two questions imply a third: What are the consequences of the *who* and *how*? Urban regimes are not neutral mechanisms through which policy is made; they shape policy. To be sure, they do not do so on terms solely of the governing coalition's own choosing. But regimes are the mediating agents between the ill-defined pressures of an urban environment and the making of community policy. The *who* and *how* of urban regimes matter, thus giving rise to the further question of *with what consequences*. These three questions will guide my analysis of Atlanta.

Urban Regimes

As indicated above, an urban regime refers to the set of arrangements by which a community is actually governed. Even though the institutions of local government bear most of the formal responsibility for governing, they lack the resources and the scope of authority to govern without the active support and cooperation of significant private interests. An urban regime may thus be defined as the *informal arrangements by which public bodies and private interests function together in order to be able to make and carry out governing decisions.* These governing decisions, I want to emphasize, are not a matter of running or controlling everything. They have to do with *managing conflict* and *making adaptive responses* to social change. The informal arrangements through which governing decisions are made differ from community to community, but everywhere they are driven by two needs: (1) institutional scope (that is, the need to encompass a wide enough scope of institutions to mobilize the resources required to make and implement governing decisions) and (2) cooperation (that is, the need to promote enough cooperation and coordination for the diverse participants to reach decisions and sustain action in support of those decisions).

The mix of participants varies by community, but that mix is itself constrained by the accommodation of two basic institutional principles of the American political economy: (1) popular control of the formal machinery of government and (2) private ownership of business enterprise.[11] Neither of these principles is pristine. Popular control is modified and compromised in various ways, but nevertheless remains as the basic principle of government. Private ownership is less than universal, as governments do own and operate various auxiliary enterprises from mass transit to convention centers. Even so, governmental conduct is constrained by the need to promote investment activity in an economic arena dominated by private ownership. This political-economy insight is the foundation for a theory of urban regimes.[12]

In defining an urban regime as the informal arrangements through which public bodies and private interests function together to make and carry out governing decisions, bear in mind that I did not specify that the private interests are business interests. Indeed, in practice, private interests are not confined to business figures. Labor-union officials, party functionaries, officers in nonprofit organizations or foundations, and church leaders may also be involved.[13]

Why, then, pay particular attention to business interests? One reason is the now well-understood need to encourage business investment in order to have an economically thriving community. A second reason is the sometimes overlooked factor that businesses control politically important resources and are rarely absent totally from the scene. They may work through intermediaries, or some businesses may even be passive because others represent their interests as property holders, but a business presence is always part of the urban political scene. Although the nature of business involvement extends from the direct and extensive to the indirect and limited, the economic role of businesses *and the resources they control* are too important for these enterprises to be left out completely.

With revived interest in political economy, the regime's need for an adequate institutional scope (including typically some degree of business involvement) has received significant attention. However, less has been said about the regime's need for cooperation—and the various ways to meet it.[14] Perhaps some take for granted that, when cooperation is called for, it will be forthcoming. But careful reflection reminds us that cooperation does not occur simply because it is useful.

Robert Wiebe analyzed machine politics in a way that illustrates an important point: "The ward politician . . . required wider connections in order to manage many of his clients' problems . . . . Therefore clusters of these men allied to increase their bargaining power in city affairs. But if logic led to an integrated city-wide organization, the instinct of self-preservation did not. The more elaborate the structure, the more independence the ward bosses and area chieftains lost."[15] Cooperation can thus never be taken as a given; it must be achieved and at significant costs. Some of the costs are visible resources expended in promoting cooperation—favors and benefits distributed to curry reciprocity, the effort required to establish and maintain channels of communication, and responsibilities borne to knit activities together are a few examples. But, as Wiebe's observation reminds us, there are less visible costs. Achieving cooperation entails commitment to a set of relationships, and these relationships limit independence of action. If relationships are to be ongoing, they cannot be neglected; they may even call for sacrifices to prevent alienating allies. Forming wider connections is thus not a cost-free step, and it is not a step that community actors are always eager to take.

Because centrifugal tendencies are always strong, achieving cooperation is a major accomplishment and requires constant effort. Cooperation can be brought about in various ways. It can be induced if there is an actor powerful enough to coerce others into it, but that is a rare occurrence, because power is not usually so concentrated. More often, cooperation is achieved by some degree of reciprocity.

The literature on collective action focuses on the problem of cooperation in the absence of a system of command. For example, the "prisoner's dilemma" game instructs us that noncooperation may be invited by a number of situations.[16] In the same vein, Mancur Olson's classic analysis highlights the free-rider problem and the importance of selective incentives in inducing cooperation.[17] Alternatively, repeated interactions permit people to see the shortcomings of mutual noncooperation and to learn norms of cooperation.[18] Moreover, although Robert Axelrod's experiments with TIT FOR TAT computer programs indicate that cooperation can be instrumentally rational under some conditions, the process is not purely mechanical.[19] Students of culture point to the importance of common identity and language in facilitating interaction and promoting trust.[20] Size of group is also a consideration, affecting the ease of communication and bargaining among members; Michael Taylor, for example, emphasizes the increased difficulty of conditional cooperation in larger groups.[21]

What we can surmise about the urban community is thus twofold: (1) cooperation across institutional lines is valuable but far from automatic; and (2) cooperation is more likely to grow under some circumstances than others. This conclusion has wide implications for the study of urban politics. For example, much of the literature on community power has centered on the question of control, its possibilities and limitations: to what extent is domination by a command center possible and how is the cost of social control worked out. The long-standing elitist-pluralist debate centers on such questions. However, my line of argument here points to another way of viewing urban communities; it points to the need to think about cooperation, its possibilities and limitations—not just any cooperation, but cooperation of the kind that can bring together people based in different sectors of a community's institutional life and that enables a coalition of actors to make and support a set of governing decisions.

If the conventional model of urban politics is one of social control (with both elitist and pluralist variants), then the one proposed here might be called "the social-production model." It is based on the question of how, in a world of limited and dispersed authority, actors work together across institutional lines to produce a capacity to govern and to bring about publicly significant results.

To be sure, the development of a system of cooperation for governing is something that arises, not from an unformed mass, but rather within a structured set of relationships. Following Stephen Elkin, I described above the basic configuration in political-economy terms: popular control of governmental authority and private ownership of business activity. However, both of these elements are subject to variation. Populations vary in characteristics and in type of political organization; hence, popular control comes in many forms. The economic sector itself varies by the types of businesses that compose it and by the way in which it is organized formally and informally. Hence there is no one formula for bringing institutional sectors into an arrangement for cooperation, and the whole process is imbued with uncertainty. Cooperation is always somewhat tenuous, and it is made more so as conditions change and new actors enter the scene.

The study of urban regimes is thus a study of who cooperates and how their cooperation is achieved across institutional sectors of community life. Further, it is an examination of how that cooperation is maintained when confronted with an ongoing process of social change, a continuing influx of new actors, and potential break-downs through conflict or indifference.

Regimes are dynamic, not static, and regime dynamics concern the ways in which forces for change and forces for continuity play against one another. For example, Atlanta's governing coalition has displayed remarkable continuity in the post–World War II period, and it has done so despite deep-seated forces of social change. Understanding Atlanta's urban regime involves understanding how cooperation can be maintained and continuity can prevail in the face of so many possibilities for conflict.

Structure, Action, and Structuring

Because of the interplay of change and continuity, urban regimes are perhaps best studied over time. Let us, then, take a closer look at historical analysis. Scholars make sense out of the particulars of political and social life by thinking mainly in terms of abstract structures such as democracy and capitalism.

Although these are useful as shorthand, the danger in abstractions is that they never capture the full complexity and contingency of the world. Furthermore, "structure" suggests something solid and unchanging, yet political and social life is riddled with contradictions and uncertainties that give rise to an ongoing process of change and adjustment. Much of the change that occurs is at the margins of basic and enduring relationships, making it easy to think in terms of order and stability. Incrementalists remind us that the present is the best predictor of the near future. But students of history, especially those accustomed to looking at longer periods of time, offer a different perspective. They see a world undergoing change, in which various actors struggle over what the terms of that change will be. It is a world shaped and reshaped by human efforts, a world that never quite forms a unified whole.

In historical light, social structures are less solid and less fixed than social scientists have sometimes assumed. Charles Tilly has argued that there is no single social structure. Instead, he urges us to think in terms of multiple structures, which "consist of shifting, constructed social relations among limited numbers of actors."[22] Philip Abrams also sees structures as relationships, relationships that are socially fabricated and subject to purposive modification.[23]

Structures are real but not fixed. Action does not simply occur within the bounds set by structures but is sometimes aimed at the structures themselves, so that a process of reshaping is taking place at all times. Abrams thus argues that events have a two-sided character, involving both structure and action in such a way that action shapes structures and structures shape actions. Abrams calls for the study of a process he labels as "structuring," by which he means that events occur in a structured context and that events help reshape structure.[24]

Abrams therefore offers a perspective on the interplay of change and continuity. This continuity is not so much a matter of resisting change as coping with it. Because the potential for change is ever present, regime continuity is a remarkable outcome. Any event contains regime-altering potential—perhaps not in sudden realignment, but in opening up a new path along which subsequent events can cumulatively bring about fundamental change.[25] The absence of regime alteration is thus an outcome to be explained, and it must be explained in terms of a capacity to adapt and reinforce existing structures. Events are the arena in which the struggle between change and continuity is played out, but they are neither self-defining nor free-formed phenomena. They become events in our minds because they have some bearing on structures that help shape future occurrences. It is the interplay of event and structure that is especially worthy of study. To identify events, one therefore needs to have some conception of structure. In this way, the researcher can focus attention, relieved of the impossible task of studying everything.

There is no escaping the necessity of the scholar's imposing some form of analysis on research. The past becomes known through the concepts we apply. Abrams sees this as the heart of historical sociology: "The reality of the past is just not 'there' waiting to be observed by the resurrectionist historian. It is to be known if at all through strenuous theoretical alienation."[26] He also reminds us that many aspects of an event cannot be observed in a direct sense; too much is implicit at any given moment.[27] That is why the process, or the flow of events over time, is so important to examine. That is also why events are not necessarily most significant for their immediate impact; they may be more significant for their bearing on subsequent events, thus giving rise to modifications in structure.

Prologue to the Atlanta Narrative

Structuring in Atlanta is a story in which race is central. If regimes are about who cooperates, how, and with what consequences, one of the remarkable features of Atlanta's urban regime is its biracial character. How has cooperation been achieved across racial lines, particularly since race is often a chasm rather than a bridge? Atlanta has been governed by a biracial coalition for so long that it is tempting to believe that nothing else was possible. Yet other cities followed a different pattern. At a time when Atlanta prided itself on being "the city too busy to hate," Little Rock, Birmingham, and New Orleans pursued die-hard segregation and were caught up in racial violence and turmoil. The experience of these cities reminds us that Atlanta's regime is not simply an informal arrangement through which popular elections and private ownership are reconciled, but is deeply intertwined with race relations, with some actors on the Atlanta scene able to overcome the divisive character of race sufficiently to achieve cooperation.

Atlanta's earlier history is itself a mixed experience, offering no clear indication that biracial cooperation would emerge and prevail in the years after World War II. In 1906, the city was the site of a violent race riot apparently precipitated by inflammatory antiblack newspaper rhetoric.[28] The incident hastened the city's move toward the economic exclusion and residential segregation of blacks, their disenfranchisement, and enforcement of social subordination; and the years after 1906 saw the Jim Crow system fastened into place. Still, the riot was followed by modest efforts to promote biracial understanding, culminating in the formation in 1919 of the Commission on Interracial Cooperation.

Atlanta, however, also became the headquarters city for a revived Ku Klux Klan. During the 1920s, the Klan enjoyed wide support and was a significant influence in city elections. At this time, it gained a strong foothold in city government and a lasting one in the police department.[29] In 1930, faced with rising unemployment, some white Atlantans also founded the Order of Black Shirts for the express purpose of driving blacks out of even menial jobs and replacing them with whites. Black Shirt protests had an impact, and opportunities for blacks once again were constricted. At the end of World War II, with Atlanta's black population expanding beyond a number that could be contained in the city's traditionally defined black neighborhoods, another klanlike organization, the Columbians, sought to use terror tactics to prevent black expansion into previously all-white areas. All of this occurred against a background of state and regional politics devoted to the subordination of blacks to whites—a setting that did not change much until the 1960s.

Nevertheless, other patterns surfaced briefly from time to time. In 1932, Angelo Herndon, a black Communist organizer, led a mass demonstration of white and black unemployed protesting a cutoff of work relief. Herndon was arrested, and the biracial following he led proved short-lived. Still, the event had occurred, and Atlanta's city council did in fact accede to the demand for continued relief.[30] In the immediate postwar period, a progressive biracial coalition formed around the successful candidacy of Helen Douglas Mankin for a congressional seat representing Georgia's fifth district. That, too, was short-lived, as ultra-conservative Talmadge forces maneuvered to reinstitute Georgia's county-unit system for the fifth district and defeat Mankin with a minority of the popular vote.[31]

It is tempting to see the flow of history as flux, and one could easily dwell on the mutable character of political alignments. The Atlanta experience suggests that coalitions often give expression to instability. Centrifugal forces are strong, and in some ways disorder is a natural state. What conflict does not tear asunder, indifference is fully capable of wearing away.

The political incorporation of blacks into Atlanta's urban regime in tight coalition with the city's white business elite is thus not a story of how popular control and private capital came inevitably to live together in peace and harmony. It is an account of struggle and conflict—bringing together a biracial governing coalition at the outset, and then allowing each of the coalition partners to secure for itself an advantageous position within the coalition. In the first instance, struggle involved efforts to see that the coalition between white business interests and the black middle class prevailed over other possible alignments. In the second instance, there was struggle over the terms of coalition between the partners; thus political conflict is not confined to "ins" versus "outs." Those on the inside engage in significant struggle with one another over the terms on which cooperation will be maintained, which is one reason governing arrangements should never be taken for granted.

Atlanta's urban regime therefore appears to be the creature of purposive struggle, and both its establishment and its maintenance call for a political explanation. The shape of the regime was far from inevitable, but rather came about through the actions of human agents making political choices. Without extraeconomic efforts by the city's business leadership, Atlanta would have been governed in a much different manner, and Atlanta's urban regime and the policies furthered by that regime might well have diverged from the path taken. History, perhaps, is as much about alternatives not pursued as about those that were . . . .

The Political Ramifications of Unequal Resources

From Aristotle to Tocqueville to the present, keen political observers have understood that politics evolves from and reflects the associational life of a community. How people are grouped is important—so much so that, as the authors of the *Federalist* essays understood, the formation and reformation of coalitions [are] at the heart of political activity. Democracy should be viewed within that context; i.e., realizing that people do not act together simply because they share preferences on some particular issue.

Overlooking that long-standing lesson, many public-choice economists regard democracy with suspicion. They fear that popular majorities will insist on an egalitarian redistribution of benefits and thereby interfere with economic productivity. As worded by one economist, "The majority (the poor) will always vote for taxing the minority (the rich), at least until the opportunities for benefiting from redistribution run out."[32] In other words, majority rule will overturn an unequal distribution of goods and resources. This reasoning, however, involves the simple-minded premise that formal governmental authority confers a capacity to redistribute at the will of those who hold office by virtue of popular election. The social-production model of politics employed here offers a contrasting view. Starting from an assumption about the costliness of civic cooperation, the social production model suggests that an unequal distribution of goods and resources substantially modifies majority rule.

In operation, democracy is a great deal more complicated than counting votes and sorting through the wants of rational egoists. In response to those who regard democracy as a process of aggregating preferences within a system characterized by formal equality, a good antidote is Stein Rokkan's aphorism, "Votes count but resources decide."[33] Voting power is certainly not insignificant, but policies are decided mainly by those who control important concentrations of resources. Hence, governing is never simply a matter of aggregating numbers, whether for redistribution or other purposes. . . .

Of course, the election of key public officials provides a channel of popular expression. Since democracy rests on the principle of equal voting power, it would seem that all groups do share in the capacity to become part of the governing regime. Certainly the vote played a major role in the turnaround of the position of blacks in Atlanta. Popular control, however, is not a simple and straightforward process. Much depends on how the populace is organized to participate in a community's civic life. Machine politics, for example, promotes a search for personal favors. With electoral mobilization dependent upon an organizational network oriented toward patronage and related considerations, other kinds of popular concerns may have difficulty gaining expression.[34] The political machine thus enjoys a type of preemptive power, though the party organization is only one aspect of the overall governing regime.

On the surface, Atlanta represents a situation quite different from machine politics. Nonpartisan elections and an absence of mass patronage have characterized the city throughout the post–World War II era. Yet it would hardly be accurate to describe civic life in Atlanta as open and fluid. Nonpartisanship has heightened the role of organizations connected to business, and the newspapers have held an important position in policy debate. At the same time, working-class organizations and nonprofit groups unsupported by business are not major players in city politics.

Within Atlanta's civic sector, activities serve to piece together concerns across the institutional lines of the community, connecting government with business and each with a variety of nonprofit entities. The downtown elite has been especially adept at building alliances in that sector and, in doing so, has extended its resource advantage well beyond the control of strictly economic functions. Responding to its own weakness in numbers, the business elite has crafted a network through which cooperation can be advanced and potential cleavages between haves and have-nots redirected.

Consider what Atlanta's postwar regime represents. In 1946, the central element in the governing coalition was a downtown business elite organized for and committed to an active program of redevelopment that would transform the character of the business district and, in the process, displace a largely black population to the south and east of the district. At the same time, with the end of the white primary that same year, a middle-class black population, long excluded from power, mobilized its electoral strength to begin an assault on a firmly entrenched Jim Crow system. Knowing only those facts, one might well have predicted in 1946 that these two groups would be political antagonists. They were not. Both committed to an agenda of change, they worked out an accommodation and became the city's governing coalition. The alliance has had its tensions and even temporary ruptures, but it has held and demonstrated remarkable strength in making and carrying out policy decisions.

To understand the process, the Atlanta experience indicates that one must appreciate institutional capacities and the resources that various groups control. That is why simple preference aggregation is no guide to how coalitions are built. The downtown elite and the black middle class had complementary needs that could be met by forming an alliance, and the business elite in particular had the kind and amount of resources to knit the alliance together.

Politics in Atlanta, then, is not organized around an overriding division between haves and have-nots. Instead, unequally distributed resources serve to destabilize opposition and encourage alliances around small opportunities. Without command of a capacity to govern, elected leaders have difficulty building support around popular discontent. That is why Rokkan's phrase, "Votes count but resources decide," is so apt.

Unequal Resources and Urban Regimes

Regimes, I have suggested, are to be understood in terms of (1) who makes up the governing coalition and (2) how the coalition achieves cooperation. Both points illustrate how the unequal distribution of resources affects politics and what differences the formation of a regime makes. That the downtown elite is a central partner in the Atlanta regime shapes the priorities set and the trade-offs made. Hence, investor prerogative is protected practice in Atlanta, under the substantial influence of the business elite *within* the governing coalition. At the same time, the fact that the downtown elite is part of a governing coalition prevents business isolation from community affairs. Yet, although "corporate responsibility" promotes business involvement, it does so in a way that enhances business as patron and promoter of small opportunities.

Similarly, the incorporation of the black middle class into the mainstream civic and economic life of Atlanta is testimony to its ability to use electoral leverage to help set community priorities. The importance of the mode of cooperation is also evident. Although much of what the regime has done has generated popular resistance, the black middle class has been persuaded to go along by a combination of selective incentives and small opportunities. Alliance with the business elite enabled the black middle class to achieve particular objectives not readily available by other means. This kind of enabling capacity is what gives concentrated resources its gravitational force.

The pattern thus represents something more than individual cooptation. The black middle class as a group benefited from new housing areas in the early postwar years and from employment and business opportunities in recent years. Some of the beneficiaries have been institutional—colleges in the Atlanta University system and a financially troubled bank, for example. Because the term "selective incentives" implies individual benefits (and these have been important), the more inclusive term "small opportunities" provides a useful complement. In both cases, the business elite is a primary source; they can make things happen, provide needed assistance, and open up opportunities. At the same time, since the downtown elite needs the cooperation of local government and various community groups, the elite itself is drawn toward a broad community-leadership role. Although its bottom-line economic interests are narrow, its community role can involve it in wider concerns. Selective incentives, however, enable the elite to muffle some of the pressure that might otherwise come from the larger community.

Once we focus on the regime and the importance of informally achieved cooperation, we can appreciate better the complex way in which local politics actually functions. Public-choice economists, fearful that democracy will lead to redistribution, misunderstand the process and treat politics as a causal force operating in isolation from resources other than the vote. That clearly is unwarranted. Atlanta's business elite possesses substantial slack resources that can be and are devoted to policy. Some devotion of resources to political purposes is direct, in the form of campaign funds, but much is indirect; it takes on the character of facilitating civic cooperation of those efforts deemed worthy.

The business elite is small and homogeneous enough to use the norms of class unity and corporate responsibility to maintain its cohesion internally. In interacting with allies, the prevailing mode of operation is reciprocity, reinforced in many cases by years of trust built from past exchanges. The biracial insiders have also been at their tasks long enough to experience a sense of pride in the community role they play. Even so, the coalition is centered around a combination of explicit and tacit deals. Reciprocity is thus the hallmark of Atlanta's regime, and reciprocity hinges on what one actor can do for another. Instead of promoting redistribution toward equality, such a system perpetuates inequality.

Reciprocity, of course, occurs in a context, and in Atlanta, it is interwoven with a complex set of conditions. The slack resources controlled by business corporations give them an extraordinary opportunity to promote civic cooperation. Where there is a compelling mutual interest, as within Atlanta's downtown elite, businesses have the means to solve their own collective-action problem and unite behind a program of action. Their resources also enable them to create a network of cooperation that extends across lines of institutional division, which makes them attractive to public officials and other results-oriented community groups. In becoming an integral part of a system of civic cooperation, Atlanta's business elite has used its resource advantage to shape community policy and protect a privileged position. Because the elite is useful to others, it attracts and holds a variety of allies in its web of reciprocity. The concentration of resources it has gathered thus enables the elite to counter demands for greater equality.

Social Learning versus Privilege

Instead of understanding democratic politics as an instance of the equality (redistribution)/efficiency (productivity) trade-off, I suggest an alternative. Policy actions (and inactions) have extensive repercussions and involve significant issues that do not fit neatly into an equality-versus-efficiency mold. There is a need, then, for members of the governing coalition to be widely informed about a community's problems, and not to be indifferent about the information. That is what representative democracy is about.

For their part, in order to be productive, business enterprises need a degree of autonomy and a supply of slack resources. It is also appropriate that they participate in politics. However, there are dangers involved in the ability of high-resource groups, like Atlanta's business elite, to secure for themselves a place in the governing coalition and then use that inside position along with their own ample resources to shape the regime on their terms. Elsewhere I have called this "preemptive power,"[35] and have suggested that it enables a group to protect a privileged position. The ability to parcel out selective incentives and other small opportunities permits Atlanta's business elite to enforce discipline on behalf of civic cooperation by vesting others with lesser privileges—privileges perhaps contingently held in return for "going along."

The flip side of discipline through selective incentives is a set of contingent privileges that restrict the questions asked and curtail social learning. Thus, one of the trade-offs in local politics can be phrased as social learning versus privilege. Some degree of privilege for business may be necessary to encourage investment, but the greater the privilege being protected, the less the incentive to understand and act on behalf of the community in its entirety.

The political challenge illustrated by the Atlanta case is how to reconstitute the regime so that both social learning and civic cooperation occur. The risk in the present situation is that those who govern have only a limited comprehension of the consequences of their actions. Steps taken to correct one problem may create or aggravate another while leaving still others unaddressed. Those who govern can discover that only, it seems, through wide representation of the affected groups. Otherwise, choices are limited by an inability to understand the city's full situation.

No governing coalition has an inclination to expand the difficulties of making and carrying out decisions. Still, coalitions can be induced to attempt the difficult. For example, Atlanta's regime has been centrally involved in race relations, perhaps the community's most difficult and volatile issue. Relationships within the governing coalition have been fraught with tension; friction was unavoidable. Yet the coalition achieved a cooperative working relationship between the black middle class and the white business elite. In a rare but telling incident, black leaders insisted successfully that a 1971 pledge to build a MARTA spur to a black public-housing area not be repudiated. The newspaper opined that trust within the coalition was too important to be sacrificed on the altar of economizing. Thus the task of the governing regime was expanded beyond the narrow issue of serving downtown in the least expensive manner possible; concerns *can* be broadened.

Although no regime is likely to be totally inclusive, most regimes can be made more inclusive. Just as Atlanta's regime was drawn into dealing with race relations, others can become sensitive to the situations of a larger set of groups. Greater inclusiveness will not come automatically nor from the vote alone. Pressures to narrow the governing coalition are strong and recurring. Yet, if civic cooperation is the key to the terms on which economic and electoral power are accommodated, then more inclusive urban regimes can be encouraged through an associational life at the community level that reflects a broad range of perspectives. The problem is not an absence of associational life at that level but how to lessen its dependence on business sponsorship, how to free participation in civic activity from an overriding concern with protecting insider privileges, and how to enrich associational life so that nonprofit and other groups can function together as they express encompassing community concerns.

This step is one in which federal policy could make a fundamental difference. In the past, starting with the urban-redevelopment provision in the 1949 housing act and continuing through the Carter administration's UDAG program, cities have been strongly encouraged to devise partnerships with private, for-profit developers, thus intensifying already strong leanings in that direction. Since these were matters of legislative choice, it seems fully possible for the federal government to move in another direction and encourage nonprofit organizations. The federal government could, for example, establish a program of large-scale assistance to community development corporations and other nonprofit groups. Some foundations now support such programs, but their modest efforts could be augmented. Programs of community service required by high schools and colleges or spawned by a national-level service requirement could increase voluntary participation and alter the character of civic life in local communities. It is noteworthy that neighborhood mobilization in Atlanta was partly initiated by VISTA (Volunteers in

Service to America) workers in the 1960s and continued by those who stayed in the city after completing service with VISTA. This, however, is not the place to prescribe a full set of remedies; my aim is only to indicate that change is possible but will probably require a stimulus external to the local community.

Summing Up

If the slack resources of business help to set the terms on which urban governance occurs, then we need to be aware of what this imbalance means. The Atlanta case suggests that the more uneven the distribution of resources, the greater the tendency of the regime to become concerned with protecting privilege. Concurrently, there is a narrowing of the regime's willingness to engage in "information seeking" (or social learning). Imbalances in the civic sector thus lead to biases in policy, biases that electoral politics alone is unable to correct.

A genuinely effective regime is not only adept at promoting cooperation in the execution of complex and nonroutine projects, but is also able to comprehend the consequences of its actions and inactions for a diverse citizenry. The promotion of this broad comprehension is, after all, a major aim of democracy. Even if democratic politics were removed from the complexities of coordination for social production, it still could not be reduced to a set of decision rules. Arrow's theorem shows that majority choices cannot be neutrally aggregated when preference structures are complex,[36] as indeed they are bound to be in modern societies.

Democracy, then, is not simply a decision rule for registering choices; it has to operate with a commitment to inclusiveness. Permanent or excluded minorities are inconsistent with the basic idea of equality that underpins democracy. That is why some notion of social learning is an essential part of the democratic process; all are entitled to have their situations understood. Thus, to the extent that urban regimes safeguard special privileges at the expense of social learning, democracy is weakened.

Those fearful that too much community participation will lead to unproductive policies should widen their own understanding and consider other dangers on the political landscape. Particularly under conditions of an imbalance in civically useful resources, the political challenge is one of preventing government from being harnessed to the protection of special privilege. The social-production model reminds us that only a segment of society's institutions are under the sway of majority rule; hence, actual governance is never simply a matter of registering the preferences of citizens as individuals.

The character of local politics depends greatly on the nature of a community's associational life, which in turn depends greatly on the distribution of resources other than the vote. Of course, the vote is significant, but equality in the right to vote is an inadequate guarantee against the diversion of politics into the protection of privilege. If broad social learning is to occur, then other considerations must enter the picture. "One person, one vote" is not enough.

Notes

1. James G. March, "The Business Firm as a Political Coalition," *Journal of Politics* 24 (November 1962): 662–678.
2. Chester I. Barnard, *The Functions of the Executive* (Cambridge, Mass.: Harvard University Press, 1968).
3. Oliver E. Williamson, *The Economic Institutions of Capitalism* (New York: Free Press, 1985).
4. Ibid., 10.
5. See Norton E. Long, "The Local Community as an Ecology of Games," *American Journal of Sociology* 64 (November 1958): 251–261.
6. Cf. Graham T. Allison, *Essence of Decision* (Boston: Little, Brown, 1971).
7. See Philip Selznick, *Leadership in Administration* (New York: Harper & Row, 1957).
8. Cf. Bryan D. Jones and Lynn W. Bachelor, *The Sustaining Hand* (Lawrence: University of Kansas Press, 1986).
9. See especially Martin Shefter, "The Emergence of the Political Machine: An Alternative View," in *Theoretical Perspectives on Urban Politics,* by Willis D. Hawley and others (Englewood Cliffs, N.J.: Prentice-Hall, 1976).
10. Clarence N. Stone, Robert K. Whelan, and William J. Murin, *Urban Policy and Politics in a Bureaucratic Age,* 2d ed. (Englewood Cliffs, N.J.: Prentice-Hall, 1986, 104).
11. Stephen L. Elkin, *City and Regime in the American Republic* (Chicago: University of Chicago Press, 1987).
12. See ibid.
13. Cf. Jones and Bachelor, *The Sustaining Hand,* 214–215.
14. But see Elkin, *City and Regime;* Martin Shefter, *Political Crisis/Fiscal Crisis: The Collapse and Revival of New York City* (New York: Basic Books, 1985); and Todd Swanstrom, *The Crisis of Growth Politics* (Philadelphia: Temple University Press, 1985).
15. Robert H. Wiebe, *The Search for Order, 1877–1920* (New York: Hill and Wang, 1967), 10.
16. Russell Hardin, *Collective Action* (Baltimore: Johns Hopkins University Press, 1982); and Michael Taylor, *The Possibility of Cooperation* (Cambridge, Mass.: Cambridge University Press, 1987).
17. Mancur Olson, Jr., *The Logic of Collective Action* (Cambridge, Mass.: Harvard University Press, 1965).
18. Hardin, *Collective Action.*
19. Robert Axelrod, *The Evolution of Cooperation* (New York: Basic Books, 1984).
20. Hardin, *Collective Action;* and David D. Laitin, *Hegemony and Culture* (Chicago: University of Chicago Press, 1986).
21. Taylor, *Possibility of Cooperation.*
22. Charles Tilly, *Big Structures, Large Processes, Huge Comparisons* (New York: Russell Sage Foundation, 1984), 27.
23. Philip Abrams, *Historical Sociology* (Ithaca, N.Y.: Cornell University Press, 1982). For a similar understanding applied to urban politics, see John R. Logan and Harvey L. Molotch, *Urban Fortunes* (Berkeley and Los Angeles: University of California Press, 1987).
24. Cf. Anthony Giddens, *Central Problems in Social Theory* (Berkeley and Los Angeles: University of California Press, 1979).
25. Cf. James G. March and Johan P. Olsen, "The New Institutionalism," *American Political Science Review* 78 (September 1984): 734–749.
26. Abrams, *Historical Sociology,* 331.
27. Ibid.
28. Michael L. Porter, "Black Atlanta: An Interdisciplinary Study of Blacks on the East Side of Atlanta, 1890–1930" (Ph.D. diss., Emory University, 1974); Walter White, *A Man Called*

White (New York: Arno Press and the New York Times, 1969); and Dana F. White, "The Black Sides of Atlanta," *Atlanta Historical Journal* 26 (Summer/Fall 1982): 199–225.

29. Kenneth T. Jackson, *The Ku Klux Klan in the City 1915–1930* (New York: Oxford University Press, 1967); and Herbert T. Jenkins, *Forty Years on the Force: 1932–1972* (Atlanta: Center for Research in Social Change, Emory University, 1973).

30. Charles H. Martin, *The Angelo Herndon Case and Southern Justice* (Baton Rouge: Louisiana State University Press, 1976); Kenneth Coleman, ed., *A History of Georgia* (Athens: University of Georgia Press, 1977), 294; and Writer's Program of the Works Progress Administration, *Atlanta: A City of the Modern South* (St. Clairshores, Mich.: Somerset Publishers, 1973), 69.

31. Lorraine N. Spritzer, *The Belle of Ashby Street: Helen Douglas Mankin and Georgia Politics* (Athens: University of Georgia Press, 1982).

32. John Bonner, *Introduction to the Theory of Social Choice* (Baltimore: Johns Hopkins University Press, 1986), 34.

33. Stein Rokkan, "Norway: Numerical Democracy and Corporate Pluralism," in *Political Oppositions in Western Democracies,* ed. Robert A. Dahl (New Haven, Conn.: Yale University Press, 1966), 105; see also [Steven Erie, *Rainbow's End: Irish-Americans and the Dilemmas of Urban Machine Politics, 1840–1985* (Berkeley: University of California Press, 1988)].

34. Matthew A. Crenson, *The Un-Politics of Air Pollution* (Baltimore: Johns Hopkins University Press, 1971); see also Edwin H. Rhyne, "Political Parties and Decision Making in Three Southern Counties," *American Political Science Review* 52 (December 1958): 1091–1107.

35. Clarence N. Stone, "Preemptive Power: Floyd Hunter's 'Community Power Structure' Reconsidered," *American Journal of Political Science* 32 (February 1988): 82–104.

36. Norman Frohlich and Joe A. Oppenheimer, *Modern Political Economy* (Englewood Cliffs, N.J.: Prentice-Hall, 1978), 19–31.

8

Todd Swanstrom

SEMISOVEREIGN CITIES: THE POLITICS OF URBAN DEVELOPMENT

Economic theory has invaded political science with a vengeance. A case in point is Paul Peterson's *City Limits*, which applies neoclassical market theory to urban politics.[1] Winner of the 1981 Woodrow Wilson Foundation Award for the best book published in the United States on government, politics, or international affairs, *City Limits* argues that economic forces largely determine urban policy making. Cities must compete for mobile wealth in the intergovernmental marketplace, Peterson says, or face perpetual fiscal crises. The permeability

"Semisovereign Cities: The Politics of Urban Development," by Todd Swanstrom, *Polity*, Fall 1988. Reprinted by permission of the Northeastern Political Science Association.

of urban economies places "limits" on redistributive polices for the poor, for such policies "only make the city a more costly locale for the more productive community members."[2] Instead, Peterson argues, cities must pursue "developmental policies"—policies that provide incentives for investors and higher income residents to locate in the jurisdiction. While developmental policies may harm particular interests in a city, such as homeowners who are displaced by a highway project, all city residents benefit from publicly induced development insofar as it enhances the tax base and increases economic opportunity. Economic growth is a "unitary interest" that all citizens share.

Peterson's account replaces the pluralist image of the decision making process, which is rooted in conflict and bargaining, with a corporate image based on consensus and technical expertise. Peterson leaves room for pluralist politics in what he calls "allocational" policies, policies which do not affect the economy one way or the other. But since most policies do affect the economy, pluralist politics is restricted to a narrow sphere. Developmental policies, which dominate the agenda of urban politics, are decided, for the most part, by an economic elite, dominated by businessmen who possess the technical knowledge needed to design effective developmental policies. In predicting how cities will behave, however, we do not need to know the social background, values, or interests of the decision makers, since they are forced to make decisions by objective economic pressures. At a minimum, political sovereignty means the ability of decision makers to choose from alternative courses of action. In this sense, according to Peterson, cities lack internal sovereignty; unlike nation-states, cities have limited politics.

Peterson's economic approach to urban politics is not an isolated phenomenon. In many ways, *City Limits* simply sums up, albeit in a brilliant fashion, the trend toward economic approaches to urban politics, both theoretical and practical, in the present period. Public choice theory, for example, has applied economic concepts to urban reform and policy issues with increasing sophistication in recent years.[3] Since the economic troubles and fiscal crises of the 1970s, scholars have become increasingly aware of the market pressures on cities. Some, generally those on the right of the political spectrum, view the increased attention to economic factors as salutary;[4] others, generally on the left, deride the effects.[5] All agree, however, on the importance of economic factors. . . .

Critiques of Peterson's market approach to urban politics have proliferated in recent years. Many challenge the notion that there is a unitary interest in urban economic development. Bryan Jones, for example, asserts that cities must also be concerned with "social order and just government."[6] Susan and Norman Fainstein argue that there is little agreement on goals because the city is "a site for class and racial conflict."[7] Along similar lines, others attack Peterson's assumption that economic development benefits the entire city. Clarence Stone points out that taxes and housing costs go up in high growth cities, the fiscal dividend is often blocked by tax subsidies, and transportation policies frequently serve suburbanites better than city dwellers.[8] Finally, many have criticized Peterson's apolitical image of the decision-making process.[9] John Thomas argues that Peterson's notion of "groupless politics" is wrong; cities have sufficient free floating resources to sustain a rich political life at the neighborhood level.[10] Even in a declining industrial city like Detroit, Bryan Jones and Lynn Bachelor argue, politicians have resources to deal with multinational corporations. Political leadership does make a difference . . . .[11]

. . . The central problem with urban theory today is excessive abstractness. Peterson's theoretical approach is highly deductive: he starts with a set of assumptions derived from neoclassical economics; he then relaxes some of these assumptions to make the theory more "realistic"; finally, he deduces hypotheses from the model and tests them against the real world. While the deductive approach results in parsimonious and elegant theory, strong points of *City Limits*, it cannot do justice to the tremendous variety in urban politics. The abstractions of economic theory must be leavened with the concrete findings of political science.

Politics Between Cities: Slack in the Intergovernmental Marketplace

Pluralism is essentially a market model of the political process. The market thinking behind pluralism can be clearly seen in the pluralist classic, *Who Governs?*, where [Robert] Dahl develops a model of the political system based on an exchange relation between producers and consumers. Basically, professional politicians, or political entrepreneurs, offer policies in exchange for voter support at the polls. While most voters are passive consumers, competitive elections guarantee consumer sovereignty in the long run. At the same time, Dahl acknowledges the existence of what he calls "slack" in the political marketplace. Most people are subject to political inertia; they have unused political resources and, on most issues, do not carefully monitor the actions of elected officials. Dahl shows, however, how slack can be functional in the political system. Unused resources can be brought massively to bear if the central interests of voters are threatened, and the existence of slack gives leaders greater flexibility to be creative. Slack leaves room for political leadership.[12]

Like pluralism, Peterson's theory is based on a market model. Only in Peterson's case, instead of voters withdrawing their support at election time, the threat is that investors and residents will "vote with their feet." Peterson portrays the intergovernmental marketplace as taut. While allowing for some slack, Peterson restricts policy discretion to a narrow range of allocational issues which do not influence investment. Empirical research shows, however, that there is more slack than market theory acknowledges; indeed, considerable slack exists even in the area of economic development policy.

The question here is deceptively simple: what causal effect do local public policies have on the location of investment? Even in an experimental science, where all the relevant factors can be controlled, causal inference is extremely difficult. Public policy is not an experimental science. In the real world of public policy, many factors are varying at the same time that the independent variable, public policy, varies. To evaluate the causal effect of public incentive programs on investment, therefore, policy analysts have developed three surrogate methods. One is simply to ask the ultimate decision maker, the investor, what factors entered into the locational decision and see whether the public incentives were an important factor. The second method is to correlate various public policies with investment, controlling, as much as possible, for confounding variables. The third method is to examine the effects of public policies on investor profitability and compare these effects with other factors that vary between cities to see if the public policies could reasonably be expected to make a difference.

In what follows, I review the empirical evidence on the effects of local government policy using these three methods. Local governments can influence investment in three basic ways: through the power to subsidize or tax, the power to regulate, and the power to exhort or inform.[13] I will confine this review to the effect of local taxes and tax incentives. Local tax incentives, it should be noted, are "the most commonly offered municipal development incentive in the country."[14] No matter which method is used, the evidence points overwhelmingly to the conclusion that local taxes and incentives have very little effect on location decisions. Only a small portion of the evidence can be cited here, but I invite the reader to consult various surveys of the literature to confirm this generalization.[15]

Surveys

One of the problems with asking executives about taxes is that they have a conflict of interest: if they think their answers will affect policy, they will have a tendency to say that taxes are important in the hopes of stimulating more tax breaks. Nobody likes to pay taxes. However, numerous surveys have been conducted which effectively eliminate any motivation for self-interested replies. Local taxes are uniformly ranked low. Most surveys rank the accessibility to markets, availability of raw materials, and labor costs near the top. Taxes are ranked near the bottom. A 1958 *Business Week* study found that of 747 references to location decisions, only 5 percent referred to taxation.[16] More recently, Roger Schmenner conducted in-depth interviews with eight corporate executives and came to the conclusion that "taxes themselves are merely a minor consideration."[17]

Correlational Studies

Studies which correlate local taxes and incentives with investment have come to a similar negative conclusion. A 1967 study, for example, found "no clearcut relationship between the level of business taxes and manufacturing employment growth rates for states within the same region."[18] Other correlational studies have come to similar conclusions.[19] Some studies have even found a positive relationship between taxes and economic growth.[20] This may not mean that higher taxes cause economic growth, but it certainly does not mean the opposite. At one time, there was a great deal of concern that the cause of the booming economy in the Sunbelt and economic decline in the Northeast was the lower state and local taxes in the former compared to the latter. Actually, taxes had little to do with the matter. Today, the Northeastern economy is out-performing the Sunbelt for reasons that have little to do with taxes. In fact, some of the highest tax jurisdictions, Boston and New York, are experiencing rapid job growth and real estate booms while low tax cities, like Houston, are [in] the doldrums (primarily due to the sharp decline in the price of oil).

Effect of Taxes on Profits

Analyzing the effect of taxes on business profits explains why the correlation between taxes and growth is so low. Local taxes have little effect on business profits, and any effect different tax levels might have on investment is over-whelmed by other, more important, differences between cities. In Wisconsin, for example, local property taxes were estimated to be .68% of the value of all shipments for all manufacturing industries combined.[21] Barry Bluestone and Bennett Harrison estimate that total corporate income taxes plus property taxes on business were only 1.69 percent of total business sales for all states in the nation in 1975.[22] Moreover, state and local taxes can be deducted from income for federal taxes and therefore their burden to business is greatly reduced; the federal government subsidizes the payment of state and local taxes. By contrast, the U.S. Department of Labor estimated that labor was the single most important input into the production of a firm in 1977, "accounting for approximately sixty percent of all input payments on a national basis."[23] Not surprisingly, local taxes have only a minor impact on business location decisions, while wage rates have a major impact.

While the evidence for the limited impact of local taxes on investment is overwhelming, most of the evidence cited so far concerns competition *among* regions. What about competition among cities *within* regions? Some argue that within a single metropolitan area local taxes are important in location decisions. Since cities within a region are quite alike on most factors, differences in local taxation can make a difference in intra-regional location decisions. The evidence here is mixed. Some conclude that there is little effect. A study of the Cleveland metropolitan area, for example, found that "tax rates were insignificant in the intra-urban location decision."[24] Some studies, however, point in the other direction. T. E. McMillan argues that if you confine surveys to the question of site location within a single metropolitan area, taxes will be mentioned much more frequently.[25] A correlational analysis of the Cleveland metropolitan area showed that if cities that zone out industry are excluded, there is a significant positive correlation between low taxes and spending on business services and industrial investment.[26] Michael Wasylenko replicated the Cleveland study for the Milwaukee region and concluded that taxes and fiscal variables are significantly related to investment in manufacturing and wholesale but not to investment in construction, retail trade, finance, insurance and real estate, and services.[27]

In short, the evidence on the intrametropolitan effect of local taxing and spending decisions is mixed. There may be some effect with regard to highly footloose industries like routine manufacturing, but the M.I.T. research led by David Birch raises questions about the value of "smoke-stack chasing" as a strategy for economic development. First, very little employment change is due to the migration of firms; almost all the growth in jobs in cities is due to start-ups of new companies.[28] Now, local taxes may affect business start-ups, but almost all the studies have focused on business relocations. Moreover, the Birch study found that two-thirds of the net new jobs came from firms with twenty or fewer employees.[29] On the other hand, local tax incentives almost always go to the largest corporations.[30] In addition, the M.I.T. study found that manufacturing created only 5 percent of the net new jobs in the 1970s; 89 percent were created in services. Finally, other studies have shown that the multiplier effect of corporate industrial growth is less than generally believed.[31] The costs of additional services often outweigh the added tax base.[32] Clearly, smokestack chasing is not a viable long-term strategy for most cities.

Many central cities, realizing that growth in industrial employment is limited, have vigorously pursued white collar employment through various tax-cutting strategies. It is well known, however, that there are strong centripetal forces, independent of local public policy, centralizing high level white collar employment in the downtowns of central cities.[33] In fact, one author estimates, "almost half of the nation's post–1950 gain in office employment and construction was captured by the downtowns of our large cities."[34] The jobs that centralize tend to be high-level professional jobs, or what are sometimes called "advanced corporate services."[35] These advanced corporate services jobs are associated with high-level decision making in our information based economy. They tend to involve highly skilled functions that need downtown locations for the face-to-face contacts available there to aid in high-level decision making.

Although the growth of downtown white collar employment is a positive trend for depressed central cities, numerous studies have concluded that local tax incentives have little effect on boosting white collar employment.[36] In fact, since the service sector is more labor-intensive than is manufacturing, one would expect that local property taxes would play a less significant role in location decisions. A guidebook for local economic development, prepared by the U.S. Department of Housing and Urban Development (H.U.D.), analyzes the effect of a 75 percent tax abatement in a typical office development and concludes that it would only reduce office rents about one dollar per square foot per year (from $12.38 to $11.35).[37] Since office rent is only a small part of the cost of doing business, it is clear that the incentive will have little effect. Moreover, downtowns do not compete directly with suburbs for many types of white collar employment; many firms must locate downtown because of the prestige, business contacts, and specialized business services found there. In a study of the nation's largest tax abatement program, Andrew Parker showed that, even if it is effective in attracting new investment, the costs of office development often outweigh the benefits.[38] Even without tax incentives, there is considerable doubt whether downtown office development is a net fiscal benefit to cities.[39] In short, there is as much reason to suspect the efficacy of the "paper chase" as there is to suspect the effectiveness of smokestack chasing.

The impression created by Peterson and others, that the economic context of cities is a prison that determines most moves that cities make, is exaggerated. The point is not that the economic context is unimportant but that researchers must examine the particular city and type of mobile wealth before coming to any conclusions about the effect of the economic environment on policy making. Investors do not move from one city to another with the same ease that consumers switch from one brand of toothpaste to another. There is considerable friction in the movement of investment capital. "Transaction costs," to put it in the jargon of the economists, vary from one industry to another, from one locale to another. Some wealth is extremely mobile, as for example, routine manufacturing with low transportation costs, while other investment is not, as for example advanced corporate services that rely on sophisticated business services.

Slack in the intergovernmental marketplace creates room for political discretion. Recognizing the unique pulling power of their downtown areas, cities with strong white collar economies have enacted "linkage" policies that attempt to exploit their locational advantage. The opposite of tax abatement, linkage extracts an extra fee from developers, as a condition for development, in order to compensate for the external costs of growth, such as housing inflation for low income inner city residents. Boston, for example, expects to raise $52 million over a ten-year-period from its linkage fees to fund housing and employment programs. Linkage demonstrates that cities do sometimes possess what political analysts have long attributed to sovereign governments: the power, based on a territorial monopoly, to set policy according to internal political choices and values.[40]

Even where economic imperatives are tightest, however, development policy is never simply a rational response to the facts. No amount of objective and technical analysis can succeed in pinpointing the one best policy for the city as a whole. As we have seen, it is impossible to determine without error the effect of policies on investment. Moreover, information on the effect of policies is uneven.[41] Even if information were perfect, the goals of public sector decision makers are not predetermined; there is no agreed-upon public interest. Should decision makers, for example, seek to maximize jobs and investment next year or five years from now? Who should pay for the incentives to mobilize wealth? All development projects impose costs on part of the public, as in the case of displaced families. Who should pay these costs? Thus, even if policy makers had infinite resources to devote to planning and information gathering, it is unlikely they could agree on the one best policy to enhance the local economy. There is an almost infinite number of trade-offs that need to be evaluated across time, space, classes, and interest groups. Making these trade-offs is the job of politicians.

Politics Within Cities: The Political Logic of Urban Development

We know the basic structure of economic logic, and Peterson tells us how cities would behave if they followed economic logic. We have learned, however, that the economic pressures on cities are slack and that this leaves room for internal political factors to shape behavior. Urban politics, therefore, is a constant tension between economic and political logic. But what is the structure of political logic?

We could do worse than to begin with Dahl's market conception of pluralist democracy: professional politicians, or political entrepreneurs, compete for the votes of citizens who are for the most part passive consumers of politics. In order to get out the vote, politicians assemble subleaders who mobilize and organize voters in exchange for the prizes and perquisites of office, e.g., patronage and contracts. While the pluralist critique of the possibility of rational comprehensive decision making was correct as far as it went,[42] it would be a mistake to simply return to the internal political marketplace of pluralism, "in which all the active and legitimate groups in the population can make themselves heard at some crucial stage in the process of decision."[43]

While the currency of the political marketplace is votes, not money, it is not a free and fair competition. Slack in the political marketplace gives politicians room to maneuver and be influenced by other pressures, including economic ones. Generally, pluralists overlooked the way the economic context gave business a privileged position and ignored the biasing effect of political-economic structures, or what Clarence Stone calls "systemic power."[44] To simply return to pluralism, at this point, would be to throw out the baby, i.e., the legitimate insights of political economy, with the bathwater, i.e., economic determinism. The truth lies in the interaction between a slack internal political marketplace and a slack external economic marketplace.

While political institutions cannot be understood apart from their economic context, it is still possible to uncover a basic logic of what could be called representative democracy. It is based on the idea that professional politicians must compete for the votes of a basically self-interested, or apathetic, electorate. Political scientists have gradually accumulated knowledge about patterns of behavior in representative democracies, patterns which follow a political logic. Three kinds of political logic can be identified which contrast with economic logic and for which examples can be given of their application to urban development policy. Each of these will be discussed in turn:

The Economics of Growth versus the Politics of Distribution

Economic analysis of developmental policies is concerned first with the effect of the policies on the overall growth of the city, and only secondarily with the distributive effects. Sometimes the goal seems to be Pareto optimality: at least one person is made better off by the policy and no one is made worse off. Pareto optimality, however, is unrealistic. Seldom is no one hurt by a development project. If a highway is going to be built, some families are going to be displaced; if a city concentrates on attracting one kind of investment (industry), other kinds of investment (tourism) will be hurt. The logic behind the economic model then is the compensation principle, or the so-called Kaldor-Hicks principle: a policy is Kaldor-Hicks efficient if the resulting increase in aggregate wealth is sufficient to compensate the losers fully and still have something left over.[45] Economic logic, therefore, aims at maximizing the fiscal health of city government, even if that means favoring high income residents and corporations over small businesses and the poor.

Political logic, on the other hand, focuses first on the distributive effects of policies, who wins and who loses. Politicians are concerned, of course, with the size of the pie, but they are concerned first and foremost with slicing up the pie in order to feed their political coalition. The question politicians routinely ask themselves is: will supporting this policy increase or decrease my chances of getting reelected? Politically, it does not matter if a new highway will increase the tax base beyond the cost to the public. If the highway will displace residents who are at the heart of a politician's coalition, he or she, following political logic, will oppose the project.

Peterson acknowledges this difference between economic and political logic, but argues that the two logics will be kept separate: economic logic will be applied to developmental policies and political logic will be applied to allocational policies: Peterson develops what Clarence Stone and Heywood Sanders call a "policy determines politics" framework.[46] Developmental policy, because it benefits the whole city, is moved out of the political framework of interest group bargaining and is decided by a business elite using pure economic logic. A central contradiction of Peterson's theory, however, is that, while he bases it on rational decision making, he can give no account of why anyone would rationally participate in formulating urban development policy.

The problem stems from Peterson's identification of urban development policy as a public good. But if the benefits of development are a public good, the question then is how do you avoid the free rider problem?[47] Why should businessmen participate in developmental policy making, if the benefits, an enhanced local economy, are something they would enjoy even if they did not participate?[48] Peterson argues that businessmen participate in developmental policy in order to gain the civic respect that comes from the "halo effect" of benefiting the community as a whole. This solution, however, relies not on an economic theory of motivation but on social psychological assumptions— assumptions that hardly seem adequate to the problem at hand. After all, if public goods could be provided because people felt good about the respect they received for providing them, then there would be no need for the whole coercive apparatus of government.

Aside from coercion, which is not legally applicable to the problem of how to get people to participate in democratic politics, the solution to the free rider problem, preferred by Mancur Olson and others, is "selective incentives." People must be provided with benefits that they will receive only if they participate in the political organization. Professional politicians exercise political discretion over the jobs, contracts, and policies that they control to reward subleaders, who maintain an organization capable of winning elections. The internal political dynamics of how to put together a minimum winning coalition are just as important as the external imperatives of economic growth.

Matthew Crenson once observed that collective goods are not valuable to politicians, because they cannot be used to build a political organization. By definition, public goods can be enjoyed by all; they cannot be restricted to the party faithful. What politicians need are fluid assets, i.e., assets over which they can exercise political discretion to reward their friends and punish their ene-mies.[49] Development is indeed an excellent source of fluid assets. By its very nature, developmental policy is political. Development is not a public good that benefits everyone equally. Because development is a locational good, it naturally benefits, and harms, some more than others. In the words of David Harvey: "All localized public goods are 'impure' and the externality exists as a 'spatial field' of effects."[50] The spatial effects of developmental policy can be manipulated by professional politicians to enhance their political organization and power.

Two examples from the career of master planner Robert Moses illustrate the political uses of development. In 1925 Hempstead Township refused to cede a portion of its waterfront, thereby effectively killing Moses' dream of creating Jones Beach. According to Robert Caro, Moses met with leaders of the Hempstead Republican machine and gave them advance knowledge of where the causeway and other public improvements, would be built. The political leaders subsequently purchased land near the public improve-ments which they later sold at a great profit. The next year Hempstead Township ceded Moses the land he needed for Jones Beach. In another case, Moses placed the Manhattan terminus of the Triborough Bridge at 125th Street, not at 100th Street, the most rational location, according to Caro. While this action forces thousands of motorists each day to travel an extra $2\frac{1}{2}$ miles every time they cross the bridge, the 125th Street location had the political advantage of benefiting William Randolph Hearst, who sold his de-teriorating real estate at 125th Street to Moses for $782,000.[51]

Urban politics is decisively the politics of land use.[52] Real estate interests are key actors in urban political coalitions. The reason is that land values de-pend crucially on the uses of surrounding land. The most important powers of city government are powers over land use, especially powers over zoning and public improvements. To demonstrate how important city government is for land values, consider how much a parcel of urban land could fetch if it were not for the access provided by city streets. John Logan and Harvey Molotch have coined the term "place entrepreneurs" to refer to people who speculate on the value of land. Many place entrepreneurs are what Logan and Molotch call "structural speculators," real estate interests who shape future locational trends in order to enhance their land values. City government policy is a prime vehicle of structural speculation.[53]

Not only do real estate developers need politicians but politicians need real estate developers. Many of the traditional ways of steering selective benefits to political coalitions have been dried up by civil service laws and other reforms. The great advantage of manipulating the externalities of development projects is that it is a way of paying off political supporters without violating laws against bribery and corruption. George Washington Plunkitt once made the distinction between "honest graft" and "dishonest graft."[54] The externalities of city development policy are a form of honest graft. After all, a politician may reason, if one of our political allies does not make money on rising real estate values, somebody else will. This type of political patronage need not cost the public a single dollar. Moreover, the payments to political supporters are well laundered, so to speak, and hidden from public view.

The Economic Logic of Targeting versus the Political Logic of Dispersion

An economic approach to urban development policy naturally lends itself to a targeting strategy. The goal in economic policy making is to take advantage of external trends in the most efficient way possible to attract mobile wealth. Efforts should be concentrated in those areas where trends are positive and opportunities are the greatest. The logic is similar to efforts by corporate strategic planners to pick expanding markets and concentrate resources on those where the corporation has a comparative advantage. Success relies on anticipating trends and aggressively targeting resources to take advantage of those trends. Given the limited ability of city governments to affect investment trends, discussed earlier, the need to target in city development policy is even more apparent. Only by targeting subsidies can city governments have a reasonable chance of influencing new private investment.

The political logic of representative democracy, on the other hand, follows what Anthony Downs has called the Law of Political Dispersion.[55] In a democratic system, politicians must spread the fruits of policy around in order to construct a governing coalition. Targeting incentives to a few areas or industries might make economic sense, but it may not attract enough votes to sustain a minimum winning coalition.

The tendency to target or disperse resources is rooted in the different orientations economic and political actors have toward time. Economic analysis is oriented toward future payoffs, disregarding "sunk costs" if they do not make future sense. Politicians, on the other hand, take prior commitments into account and are reluctant to discard them. In economic logic, this is called throwing good money after bad; in political logic, it is known as honoring commitments. Political logic is oriented to the past as well as the future. Economic logic is only future oriented, theoretically willing to make brutal decisions, as in closing down whole factories if they are not profitably aligned with future trends. Presumably, corporations will be eliminated by the marketplace if they do not keep pace with a rapidly changing environment. There is no analogous flushing mechanism in the intergovernmental marketplace. Governments cannot go bankrupt; they have obligations, built up over the years, that cannot be jettisoned overnight. Political logic is conservative, in the strict meaning of the word.

Examples of dispersive political logic abound. James Schlesinger speaks of what he calls the "foot in door techniques" of politicians. "One wishes to attract the support of many groups, but there are limits to the size of the budget. Consequently, resources are applied thinly over a wide array of programs."[56]

One example of the Law of Political Dispersion is experience with the Community Development Block Grants (CDBG). Under the Carter Administration, regulations were written that strongly encouraged cities to target their funding to Neighborhood Strategy Areas (NSAs).[57] The idea was to concentrate block grant spending in order to increase the chances to turn around a neighborhood and attract new investment and residents. If CDBG spending were spread around the entire city, according to economic analysis, it would have little rejuvenating effect. In practice, however, there was a strong tendency to spread the funds to benefit many different areas, and political interests, in the city.[58] In Cleveland, the NSAs started out as relatively defined areas, but as time went on political pressures, including a call from the Council President to the White House, led to expansion of the target areas until they included almost all low and moderate income neighborhoods in Cleveland.[59] Under instrumental rationality, means are valued only as instruments for accomplishing given ends. Economic logic, then, values public policies as instruments for achieving agreed-upon goals. Policies are valued not for themselves but for their effects, which can be measured by cost-benefit analysis . . . .

Political logic is noninstrumental.[60] Policies, of course, are valued for their effects, but they are also valued for what they represent. Policies send messages. In getting policies passed through the political system, it matters as much what they symbolize to voters and politicians as what their effects will be on the world. . . .

Urban development policy is ripe for symbolic politics. Many cities are being buffeted about by economic forces over which they have little control. New production technologies, foreign competition, and the swift transition from a goods-producing to a service-based economy have left many cities with devastating pockets of unemployment and decline. Economic problems abound, yet cities have relatively little leverage, as we have seen, over mobile wealth or economic change. Moreover, knowledge in this area is weak; it is impossible to prove that any particular development policy did not have the desired effect. The temptation to engage in symbolic politics is great. The city is like a ship being so tossed about by the storms and currents that the captain has limited control over its progress. The crew desperately wants to believe that someone is in charge and can steer the ship out of troubled waters. It is not surprising that the captain, concerned about a mutiny, turns to symbolic acts to boost the morale of the crew.

Much local development policy is essentially a form of symbolic reassurance. Local tax abatement programs, for example, have been interpreted as forms of symbolic politics.[61] Even the most depressed industrial cities are enjoying growth in white collar office functions in downtown areas. Local tax abatement programs are an opportunity for politicians to claim credit for the one positive investment trend. As we have seen, the research shows that local taxes are such a small part of the cost of doing business that tax abatements are not effective instruments for influencing business location decisions. The appeal of tax abatement programs, however, lies not in their economic effect but in their political appearance. By giving tax breaks to new investments in the city, politicians can claim that the new jobs and investment would not have occurred without the incentive. It is the political version of the fallacy: *post hoc ergo propter hoc.*

Several characteristics of local property tax abatement programs lend support to this view of them as largely symbolic. As Michael Wolkoff pointed out, one of the odd characteristics of abatement programs is their invariant nature:

everyone who applies for an award within the eligible area gets the same award. No effort is made to determine how much incentive is needed to influence the investment location decision, and no assessment of the public benefits from the project, like jobs for city residents, is made.[62] In economic logic, this makes no sense. If tax abatement programs are understood not as instruments for achieving a certain result but as symbols for claiming credit, then the lack of rational planning makes perfect sense. Careful analysis of the costs and benefits of abatements would show that they do not produce new jobs and investment but only create windfall profits for developers. The public benefits do not justify the public costs.[63] Analysis would also show that if cities want to influence investment, they will target their incentives on a few projects. But this will expose the program to charges of political favoritism and will reduce the vaunted leverage ratio of incentives to investment. By drawing a line around an area and giving the same award to every developer, politicians can claim that they are encouraging huge amounts of investment without facing the political problems that would stem from making tough planning decisions.

Tax abatement programs are especially difficult to justify, since all of the subsidy comes out of local revenues. The temptation to engage in programs of symbolic reassurance is even greater, however, when federal grants are conditional upon granting subsidies to mobile wealth. Federal grants lessen the damage of such programs to the local tax base but they do not necessarily overcome the problem of spurious leveraging. Martin Anderson estimates that half of the urban renewal projects would have been built anyway, though perhaps in other areas of the city, without the subsidies.[64] After correlating urban renewal acreage with aggregate investment in housing and industry, Roger Friedland came to the following conclusion: "Urban renewal had no net additive effects on the level of new investment."[65]

More recent programs are not immune to this problem. John Gist points to the possibility that Urban Development Action Grant (UDAG) funds do not cause new investment at all, observing that sometimes the funds are applied for "*after* the private firms have committed themselves."[66] In the case of urban renewal, the federal government picked up two-thirds of the cost, but for UDAG the federal government pays the entire cost. Not only that, but when a developer repays a subsidized loan, the funds usually go to the local government to use as it sees fit within CDBG regulations. Moreover, projects that show a high leverage ratio between subsidy and investment are looked upon more favorably by federal evaluators who determine the grants, even though a high ratio increases the chances of spurious leveraging.[67] Obviously, local officials have little motivation to scrutinize projects to make sure the subsidy is necessary for the investment. In any case, they can use UDAGs to claim credit for new jobs and investment in their city . . . .

The view here is that political logic has its own value. The tendency of democratic politicians to focus on the distribution of growth and to spread the benefits around to put together a minimum winning coalition may be economically inefficient, but it does introduce the value of equality into developmental policy. The bias of economic logic to concentrate resources to maximize growth leads, in urban development, to the tendency to pull out of losing ventures and concentrate on winners. But politicians cannot close down an unprofitable neighborhood the way corporations can close down an unprofitable subsidiary. And a good thing it is. It was neighborhoods organizing through the political system, not the recommendations of economic planners, that eventually stopped the destruction of cities that resulted from urban renewal and high-way building.

The symbolic dimension of political logic also has its own value. As John Forrester observes, "Government policy not only produces regulations, incentives, or statements of intention, but it also recommends to its public a praise-worthy attitude to be adopted more generally."[68] Tax abatement programs for downtown office development not only give a false impression that something serious is being done about the problem of jobs and investment, but they signal that the way to do something about those problems is to "bribe" businessmen, who are expected to have only selfish motives, in order to persuade them to invest in the city. Linkage programs, on the other hand, which require downtown developers to contribute to a fund for neighborhood housing, daycare, employment training, or mass transit, send the signal that those who draw on the commonwealth of the city to reap large profits have obligations to contribute to the solution of the problems they helped cause. The lesson is simple yet profound: privileges are linked to obligations, downtown to neighborhoods, office development to housing. Cities are held together by mutual obligations, respect, and commitments—values that are not only overlooked by the economic paradigm but which are drowned "in the icy water of egotistical calculation."[69]

Notes

1. Paul Peterson, *City Limits* (Chicago: University of Chicago Press, 1981).
2. Ibid., p. 44.
3. See Robert L. Bish and Vincent Ostrom, *Understanding Urban Government: Metropolitan Reform Reconsidered* (Washington, DC: American Enterprise Institute for Public Policy Research, 1979); and Gary J. Miller, *Cities by Contract: The Politics of Municipal Incorporation* (Cambridge, MA: M.I.T. Press, 1981).
4. Irving Kristol, "Sense and Nonsense in Urban Policy," *Wall Street Journal*, 21 December 1977; Gurney Breckenfeld, "Refilling the Metropolitan Doughnut," in *The Rise of the Sunbelt Cities*, ed. David C. Perry and Alfred J. Watkins (Beverly Hills, CA: Sage Publications,, 1977); William E. Simon, *A Time for Truth* (New York: Berkley, 1978), ch. V; Donald A. Hicks, "Urban and Economic Adjustment to the Post-Industrial Era," *Hearings Before the Joint Economic Committee, Congress of the United States, Ninety-Seventh Congress, Part 2* (Washington, DC: U.S. Government Printing Office, 1982).
5. Harvey Molotch, "The City as a Growth Machine: Toward a Political Economy of Place," *American Journal of Sociology* 82 (1976): 309–332; Robert Goodman, *The Last Entrepreneurs: America's Regional Wars for Jobs and Dollars* (New York: Simon and Schuster, 1979); Barry Bluestone and Bennett Harrison, *The Deindustrialization of America* (New York: Basic Books, 1982); Roger Friedland, *Power and Crisis in the City: Corporations, Unions, and Urban Policy* (New York: Schocken, 1983); Michael D. Kennedy, "The Fiscal

Crisis of the City," in *Cities in Transformation: Class, Capital, and the State,* ed. Michael P. Smith (Beverly Hills, CA: Sage Publications, 1984).

6. Bryan Jones, "Contracting Limits: An End to City Government?" *Urban Affairs Quarterly* 17, no. 3 (1982): 383.

7. Susan S. Fainstein and Norman I. Fainstein, "Economic Change, National Policy, and the System of Cities," in *Restructuring the City,* ed. Susan Fainstein et al. (New York: Longman, 1983), pp. 2–3.

8. Clarence Stone, "City Politics and Economic Development: Political Economy Perspectives," *Journal of Politics* 46 (1984): 289. See also Douglas Muzzio and Robert W. Balley, "Economic Development, Housing, and Zoning: A Tale of Two Cities," *Journal of Urban Affairs* 8, no. 1 (Winter 1986): 1–18.

9. See Heywood T. Sanders and Clarence Stone, "Developmental Politics Reconsidered," *Urban Affairs Quarterly* 22, no. 4 (June 1987): 521–539.

10. John Clayton Thomas, *Between Citizen and City: Neighborhood Organizations and Urban Politics in Cincinnati* (Lawrence, KS: University of Kansas Press, 1986).

11. Bryan Jones and Lynn Bachelor, *The Sustaining Hand: Community Leadership and Corporate Power* (Lawrence, KS: University of Kansas Press, 1986).

12. Robert Dahl, *Who Governs? Democracy and Power in an American City* (New Haven, CT: Yale University Press, 1961). For a discussion of the value of slack in both economic and political systems, see Albert O. Hirschman, *Exit, Voice, and Loyalty.*

13. Ernest Sternberg, "A Practitioner's Classification of Economic Development Policy Instruments, with Some Inspirations from Political Economy," *Economic Development Quarterly* 1, no. 2 (1987): 149–161.

14. U.S. Department of Housing and Urban Development, *Local Economic Development Tools and Techniques* (Washington, DC: U.S. Government Printing Office, 1979).

15. John F. Due, "Studies of State-Local Tax Influences on the Location of Industry," *National Tax Journal* 14 (1961):163–173; David Mulkey and B. L. Dillman, "Location Effects of State and Local Industrial Development Subsidies," *Growth and Change* (April 1976): 37–42; Bennett Harrison and Sandra Kanter, "The Political Economy of State 'Job-Creation' Business Incentives," in *Revitalizing the Northeast,* ed. George Sternlieb and James W. Hughes (New Brunswick, NJ: Center for Urban Policy Research, Rutgers University, 1978); Jerry Jacobs, *Bidding for Business* (Washington, DC: Public Interest Research Group, 1979); Michael J. Wasylenko, "The Location of Firms: The Role of Taxes and Fiscal Incentives," in *Urban Government Finance,* ed. Roy Bahl (Beverly Hills, CA: Sage Publications, 1981); Michael Kieschnick, *Taxes and Growth: Business Incentives and Local Development* (Washington, DC: Council of State Planning Agencies, 1981); Advisory Commission on Intergovernmental Relations, *Regional Growth: Interstate Tax Competition* (Washington, DC: U.S. Government Printing Office, 1981); Roger W. Schmenner, *Making Business Location Decisions* (Englewood Cliffs, NJ: Prentice Hall, 1982).

16. *Business Week,* "Plant Site Preferences of Industry and Factors of Selection," *Business Week Research Report* (1958). See also Survey Research Center, *Industrial Mobility in Michigan* (Ann Arbor: University of Michigan Press, 1950); E. Mueller and J. Morgan, "Location Decisions of Manufacturers," Papers and Proceedings of the 74th Annual Meeting of the American Economics Association (1962); L. Lund, "Factors in Corporate Locational Decisions," Conference Board Information Bulletin Number 66; U.S. Department of Commerce, *Industrial Locations Determinants* (Washington, DC: U.S. Government Printing Office, 1975).

17. Schmenner, *Business Location Decisions,* p. 46.

18. Advisory Commission on Intergovernmental Relations, *State-Local Taxation and Industrial Location* (Washington, DC: U.S. Government Printing Office, 1967).

19. Raymond Struyk, "An Analysis of Tax Structure, Public Service Levels, and Regional Economic Growth," *Journal of Regional Science* (Winter 1967); D. Carlton, "Why Firms Locate Where They Do: An Econometric Model," in *Interregional Movements and Regional Growth*, ed. W. Wheaton (Washington, DC: The Urban Institute, 1979); and Kieschnick, *Taxes and Growth.*

20. C. C. Bloom, *State and Local Tax Differentials* (Iowa City: Bureau of Business Research, State University of Iowa); Thomas R. Plaut and Joseph E. Pluta, "Business Climate, Taxes and Expenditures, and State Industrial Growth in the United States," *Southern Economic Journal* 50 (July 1983): 99–119.

21. Benjamin Bridges, "State and Local Inducements for Industry: Part 2," in *Locational Analysis for Manufacturing* (Cambridge, MA: M.I.T. Press).

22. Bluestone and Harrison, *The Deindustrialization of America,* p. 186. For a review of the studies that examine the low impact of local taxes on business profits, see Due, "Studies of State-Local Tax Influences on the Location of Industry," pp. 165–168; Harrison and Kanter, "The Political Economy of State 'Job-Creation' Business Incentives," p. 63; and Susan Olson, *An Evaluation of Tax Incentives as a Means to Encourage Redevelopment* (Cleveland: Cleveland City Planning Commission, 1978), pp. 15–16.

23. Goodman, *The Last Entrepreneurs,* pp. 43–44.

24. C. J. Simon, "Analysis of Manufacturing Location and Relocation in the Cleveland Metropolitan Area: 1966–1971," *American Economist* 24 (1980): 35–42.

25. T. E. McMillan, Jr., "Why Manufacturers Choose Plant Locations vs. Determinants of Plant Locations," *Land Economics* (1965): 239–246.

26. William F. Fox, "Fiscal Differentials and Industrial Location: Some Empirical Evidence," *Urban Studies* 18 (1981): 105–11.

27. Michael Wasylenko, "Evidence of Fiscal Differentials and Intrametropolitan Firm Location," *Land Economics* 56 (1980): 339–349.

28. David L. Birch, "Who Creates Jobs?" *Public Interest* (Fall 1981): 3–14.

29. Ibid., p. 7.

30. Jacobs, *Bidding for Business.*

31. Bluestone and Harrison, *The Deindustrialization of America.*

32. Gene F. Summers and Kristi Branch, "Economic Development and Community Social Change," *Annual Review of Sociology* 10 (1984): 141–166. For a review of studies on the fiscal effects of growth, see John R. Logan and Harvey Molotch, *Urban Fortunes: The Political Economy of Place* (Berkeley, CA: University of California Press, 1987).

33. Thomas M. Stanback et al., *Services: The New Economy* (Totowa, NJ: Allanheld, Osmun, 1981); Jean Gottman, *The Coming of the Transactional City* (College Park, MD: Institute for Urban Studies, 1983).

34. Alexander Ganz, "Where Has the Urban Crisis Gone?" *Urban Affairs Quarterly* 20, no. 4 (1985): 456.

35. Robert Cohen, *The Corporation and the City* (New York: Conservation of Human Services Project, 1979).

36. New York Office of the Comptroller, Bureau of Performances Analysis, *Performance Audit of the Industrial and Commercial Incentive Board* (New York: Office of the Comptroller, 1979); Todd Swanstrom, "Tax Abatement in Cleveland," *Social Policy* (Winter 1982): 24–30; Andrew Parker, "Local Tax Subsidies as a Stimulus for Development: Are They Cost-Effective? Are They Equitable?" *City Almanac* 17, no. 1 (1983): 8–15. One of the few exceptions is a study of tax abatement in St. Louis: Daniel R. Mandleker, Gary Feder, and Margaret P. Collins, *Reviving Cities with Tax Abatement* (New Brunswick, NJ: Center for Urban Policy Research, 1980). The authors argue that tax abatement produced a huge fiscal surplus for St. Louis, but they never present any convincing evidence that the projects in question would not have been built without the tax incentives.

37. U.S. Department of Housing and Urban Development, *Local Economic Development Tools and Techniques,* p. 51.
38. Parker, "Local Tax Subsidies as a Stimulus for Development."
39. For a review of numerous studies done in San Francisco with mixed results, see Chester Hartman, *The Transformation of San Francisco* (Totowa, NJ: Rowman and Allenheld, 1984), pp. 26–266; and Douglas Muzzio, "Downtown Development: Boon or Bane?" prepared for delivery at the Annual Meeting of the Urban Affairs Association, Akron, Ohio, April 23–25, 1987.
40. The best overviews of linkage policies are Douglas Porter, ed., *Downtown Linkages* (Washington, DC: Urban Land Institute, 1985); and Dennis Keating, "Linking Downtown Development to Broader Community Goals: An Analysis of Linkage Policy in Three Cities," *Journal of the American Planning Association* (Spring 1986): 133–141.
41. John P. Blair, Rudy H. Fichtenbaum, and James A. Swaney, "The Market for Jobs: Locational Decisions and the Competition for Economic Development," *Urban Affairs Quarterly* 20, no. 1 (September 1984): 71; Jones and Bachelor, *The Sustaining Hand,* p. 203.
42. Charles Lindblom, "The Science of 'Muddling Through,'" *Public Administration Review* (Spring 1959): 79–88.
43. Robert A. Dahl, *A Preface to Democratic Theory* (Chicago: University of Chicago Press, 1956), p. 137.
44. Charles Lindblom, *Politics and Markets* (New York: Basic Books, 1977); John Forrester, "Rationality and the Politics of Muddling Through," *Public Administration Review* (Jan./Feb. 1984): 23–31; Clarence Stone, *Economic Growth and Neighborhood Discontent* (Chapel Hill: University of North Carolina Press, 1976).
45. N. Kaldor, "Welfare Propositions and Interpersonal Comparisons of Utility," *Economic Journal* 49 (1939): 549–552. For a critical discussion of the Kaldor-Hicks principle, see Gordon Clark, *Interregional Migration, National Policy, and Social Justice* (Totowa, NJ: Rowman and Allanheld, 1983).
46. Clarence Stone and Heywood T. Sanders, "Development Politics Reconsidered," unpublished manuscript, n.d.
47. Mancur Olson, *The Logic of Collective Action: Public Goods and the Theory of Groups* (New York: Schocken, 1965).
48. Indeed, the paradox of how to get rational individuals to provide collective goods is at the center of contract theory and economic theories of politics generally. In contract theory, the problem is how to move from the state of nature to civil society; economic theories of democracy have long struggled with the problem of how rationally to explain voting participation.
49. Matthew Crenson, *The Unpolitics of Air Pollution: A Study of Nondecisionmaking in the Cities* (Baltimore: Johns Hopkins University Press, 1971), p. 138.
50. David Harvey, *Social Justice and the City* (Baltimore: Johns Hopkins University Press, 1973), p. 60.
51. Robert Caro, *The Power Broker: Robert Moses and the Fall of New York* (New York: Vintage, 1975), pp. 209–210 and 390–391.
52. Stephen L. Elkin, *City and Regime in the American Republic* (Chicago: University of Chicago Press, 1987).
53. Logan and Molotch, *Urban Fortunes.*
54. William L. Riordon, *Plunkitt of Tammany Hall* (New York: E. P. Dutton, 1963).
55. Anthony Downs, "Using the Lessons of Experience to Allocate Resources in the Community Development Program," in *Housing Urban America,* ed. Jon Pynoos, Robert Schafer, and Chester W. Hartman (New York: Aldine, 1980), p. 530.
56. James R. Schlesinger, "Systems Analysis and the Political Process," *Journal of Law and Economics* XI (1968): 286.

57. *Code of Federal Regulations* (1978), 570.301.
58. For evidence on the CDBG dispersion effect, see Jack Fyock, "The Housing and Community Development Act of 1974: A Study of Policy Formulation, Administration, and Impact," paper delivered at the 1978 Meeting of the American Political Science Association, New York; Donald F. Kettl, *Managing Community Development in the New Federalism* (New York: Praeger, 1980).
59. Todd Swanstrom, *The Crisis of Growth Politics: Cleveland, Kucinich, and the Challenge of Urban Populism* (Philadelphia: Temple University Press, 1985), p. 200.
60. For an insightful discussion of the contrast between economic and political rationality, including the noninstrumental, or "constitutive," nature of the latter, see Stephen Elkin, "Economic and Political Rationality," *Polity* 18, no. 2 (1985): 253–271.
61. Swanstrom, "Tax Abatement in Cleveland"; and *The Crisis of Growth Politics,* ch. 6; Richard C. Feiock and James Clingermayer, "Municipal Representation, Executive Power, and Economic Development Policy," paper presented at the 1985 Southern Political Science Association Meeting; Irene S. Rubin and Herbert J. Rubin, "Economic Incentives: The Poor (Cities) Pay More," *Urban Affairs Quarterly* 2, no. 1 (September 1987): 37–62.
62. Michael J. Wolkoff, "The Nature of Property Tax Abatement Awards," *American Planning Association Journal* (Winter 1983): 77–84.
63. Parker, "Local Tax Subsidies as a Stimulus for Development."
64. Martin Anderson, *The Federal Bulldozer* (New York: McGraw-Hill, 1964), p. 167.
65. Roger O. Friedland, *Class, Power, and the Central City: The Contradictions of Urban Growth* (Ph.D. Dissertation, University of Wisconsin–Milwaukee, 1977).
66. John R. Gist, "Urban Development Action Grants: Design and Implementation," in *Urban Revitalization,* ed. Donald B. Rosenthal (Beverly Hills, CA: Sage Publications, 1980), p. 243.
67. David Cordish, "Overview of UDAG," in *The Urban Development Action Grant Program,* ed. Richard P. Nathan and Jerry Webman (Princeton, NJ: Princeton Urban and Regional Research Center, 1980).
68. John Forrester, "Public Policy and Respect," *Democracy* (Fall 1982): 94.
69. Karl Marx and Friedrich Engels, *The Communist Manifesto* (New York: Appleton-Century-Crofts, 1955), p. 12.

4

Elaine B. Sharp

CULTURE WARS AND CITY POLITICS
Local Government's Role in Social Conflict

In communities across the United States, strident social conflicts are posing thorny problems for local governance. In some communities, these stem from controversy over abortion and the efforts of the pro-life movement to disrupt the functioning of abortion clinics. In other communities, controversy surrounds

"Culture Wars and City Politics," by Elaine B. Sharp, in *Urban Affairs Review*, Vol. 31, No. 6, July 1996, pp. 738–758.

gay rights initiatives as struggles emerge over ordinances to provide civil rights protections for gays or efforts to ban such protections. In still other communities, episodes over book banning and antipornography crusades, sometimes spearheaded by public officials, have sparked controversy over free speech, women's civil rights, and the community's efforts to enforce moral standards. And, in a number of communities, the efforts of authorities to deal with the emergence of neo-Nazi groups or with particular hate crimes directed at religious minorities have been embedded in controversy. In contemporary America, such controversies reflect a new era of conflict, and they have, on many occasions, placed city governments in the eye of a firestorm.

These various conflicts and controversies exemplify what Hunter (1991) called *culture wars* or what others have variously referred to as the politics of *social regulatory policy* (Tatalovich and Daynes 1988). They involve strident social conflict over issues of morality. Treatments of this category of issues emphasize the intensity and persistence of the controversies that they evoke (Tatalovich and Daynes 1988, 3) and their potential for violence (Hunter 1994).

Several social theorists offer insights into the reasons for the spate of contemporary culture wars. Bellah et al. (1985), for example, treated culture wars as manifestations of an ongoing tension between four discrete themes or strands in our cultural heritage: the biblical strand, with its emphasis upon the shared building of a "community in which a genuinely ethical and spiritual life could be lived" (p. 29); the republican strand, with its emphasis upon participation in a politically egalitarian community; the strand of utilitarian individualism, with its emphases on individual self-improvement and material advancement through pragmatism and industry; and the strand of expressive individualism, with its emphasis upon the freedom to realize goals that transcend materialism—goals of self-actualization and personal fulfillment through emotional expression. Bellah and colleagues argued that the biblical and republican strands have been partly supplanted by utilitarian and then expressive individualism as a result of industrialization followed by the rise of postwar technological affluence. By the same token, they suggested that there are remaining currents of all four themes in American life and that challenges to the newest cultural themes "have arisen from a variety of quarters, from those left out of that prosperity, as well as from those who, while its beneficiaries, criticize it for moral defects" (p. 50).

Hunter (1991) portrayed culture wars as the manifestations of tensions between orthodox, denominationally grounded religion and progressive, ecumenical religious forces. In this characterization, competing moral visions give rise to strident disagreement across an array of policy issues because orthodox forces, or cultural conservatives, "tend to define freedom economically (as individual economic initiative) and justice socially (as righteous living)," and "progressives tend to define freedom socially (as individual rights) and justice economically (as equity)" (p. 115).

In his analysis, Inglehart (1990) posited an intergenerational culture shift, premised upon the fact that those who have come of age after World War II have been socialized in an era of relative economic security. Unlike older generations, whose materialist values are rooted in scarcity and the priorities of ensuring physical sustenance and safety, the post-World War II generation takes economic security more for granted and places a "heavier emphasis on belonging, self-expression, and the quality of life" (p. 66). Furthermore, Inglehart suggested that postmaterialists are also less likely to adhere to traditional sexual norms or to be strongly religious than those with materialist values, because "it is precisely those who experience the least economic security in their lives who have the greatest need for the guidance and reassurance that familiar cultural norms and absolute religious beliefs provide" (p. 185).

These various analyses offer differing interpretations of the roots of contemporary culture wars, but there are important commonalities as well. Hunter's (1991) orthodox religious forces, like the materialists in Inglehart's (1990) analysis, are characterized by an emphasis upon what Bellah et al. (1985) referred to as the biblical strand in American culture. And the importance of participation and self-expression for Inglehart's postmaterialists makes that category quite consistent with the expressive individualist category of Bellah and colleagues. For the purposes of this article, however, neither a synthesis of these approaches nor an extended critical comparison is necessary. The important point is that each of these interpretations highlights cultural fault lines that inevitably lead to strident political conflicts, conflicts that are not a simple function of economic cleavages.

This is not to say that economic conditions are irrelevant. As these theorists have acknowledged, they are part of the context for the emergence of cultural tensions. Hunter (1991, 62), for example, noted that the struggle between orthodox and traditional forces rises to the surface at times of societal transition, such as the economic transformation to a postindustrial society in recent decades. He also acknowledged that the progressive side of the religious divide is more likely to be populated by the better-educated and professionalized upper-middle classes and that orthodox forces are composed more heavily of lower-middle and working-class individuals (p. 63). Inglehart (1990) was even more explicitly concerned with economic conditions because of the contextual importance in his theory of economic security versus economic scarcity. But Bellah et al. (1985), Inglehart, and Hunter are distinctively theorists of *cultural* conflict. They emphasized the ways in which traditional left-right distinctions are not adequate to understand the new social movements (Inglehart 1990) and the ways in which contemporary culture wars simply are not reducible to class or economic conflicts (Hunter 1991, 118).

Urban Scholarship and Culture Wars

Scholars of urban politics have largely overlooked this category of conflict. There are exceptions, of course. There are some relevant case studies, several of which will be referred to often in this article. However, relatively few of these case studies are written by urban scholars or approached with a focus on local government's role in the controversy. There is also a substantial body of work on racial and ethnic conflict and protest activity in U.S. cities. However, the culture wars that are the focus of this analysis are arguably distinct from racial and ethnic conflict, even if there are some important commonalities between the two.[1] And, if anything, contemporary treatments of protest over racial issues are moving toward rational self-interest explanations rather than explanations that emphasize the cultural bases and nonmaterial stakes that underlie the controversies of interest in this article (Green and Cowden 1992).

There are several likely reasons for urban scholars' lack of attention to the sorts of social conflict at issue here. For one thing, police, prosecutors, and the local judiciary are likely to play a relatively central role in these controversies because decisions are made about parade permits, arrest tactics for protesters, enforcement of hate-crimes statutes, changes in human rights ordinances; yet changes to and prosecutions stemming from pornography laws, and the like, yet these institutions are among the least well integrated into mainstream theories of urban politics and are less often incorporated in urban research.

Lack of attention may also stem from the ideological complexity of the issues in contemporary culture wars. In the 1960s, activism was associated with the Left, and studies of social protest and civil rights agitation attracted the research interest of sympathetic intellectuals (Hunter 1991, 161). However, the *status quo challengers*[2] in contemporary culture-war controversies include activists such as abortion clinic protesters and pornography crusaders (representing Hunter's category of orthodox forces) as well as gay rights activists and feminists (better fitting Hunter's category of progressive forces).

The character of this issue domain is an obstacle to scholarly attention in another way as well. The elevation of *interests* over *values* as the focus of inquiry in political science leaves the matter of morals-based social conflict on the periphery of the intellectual enterprise. For example, there has long been an assumption that groups based on expressive and solidary values are unstable and less likely to be of relevance to policy formation than are materially based interest groups (Salisbury 1969, 18–19), and the groups at issue in these culture wars are expressive and solidary groups par excellence. Furthermore, the very intensity that makes these conflicts attractive to the media marginalizes them as a topic for urban scholarship:

> The events themselves tend to be presented as flashes of political insanity—spasmodic symptoms of civic maladjustment—against the routine conduct of public affairs. Such events are rarely related to one another, but appear to be merely "disparate" outbursts by disparate (and sometimes "desperate") individuals and groups. Commentators make little effort to explain and interpret these stories and the issues that underlie them, to place them in a broader frame of reference. (Hunter 1991, 33).

To the extent that the social conflicts emerging from contemporary culture wars are viewed as irrational flashes of political insanity on the fringes of the normal life of the community, they are also distanced from the mainstream of urban political theory in particular. To a large extent, theories of urban politics are theories in the political-economy tradition: They emphasize the material stakes that various organizations and interests have in the life of the city. This is most clearly true of Peterson's (1981) theoretical formulation, with its emphasis on the unitary interests of cities in fostering a competitive economy, the implications that this has for the *unpolitics* of redistribution, and the materially based distributional conflicts that are the heart of the politics of allocation. Although Stone's (1989) work on regime theory differs markedly from Peterson's approach in many respects, like Peterson's, it is essentially based in political economy. Regime theory focuses on the building of coalitions for urban governance—that is, a social production model that emphasizes the assembling of resources for problem solving. Although this theory reasserts the value of the political side of political economy, it emphasizes divisible benefits and assemble-able resources. But the symbolic politics and morality issues that are at the heart of local culture wars are not readily treated as divisible benefits, and the compromise and coalition building that are central to regime theory are less relevant for understanding the uncompromising social conflicts of interest here. The gap between theories of urban politics and the character of social conflicts of the culture-war variety stands as yet another reason why these conflicts tend to be overlooked by urban scholars.

Some may be inclined to argue that culture-war conflicts have also been marginalized in the study of urban politics because they are not properly viewed as issues for urban government. Important as they are, some might claim that the conflicts that constitute the contemporary culture wars occur essentially at the national level. From such a perspective, community controversies over cultural issues are local manifestations of broader social tensions. Local government is not as relevant for the development of these controversies as are the federal courts, politicians at the federal level, and nationally based interest groups, nor does understanding the unfolding of these controversies in local communities have the potential to contribute to fundamental knowledge about urban governance.

Culture-war conflicts are critical aspects of urban governance, however, for several reasons. Although Congress, the federal courts, and state governments are significant institutions in the ongoing development of policy regarding abortion, pornography, hate crimes, and the like, city governments are critical to the policy process as well, in initiating policy change and in implementing federal and state policy. With respect to policy initiation, for example, a number of cities have enacted local ordinances that offer civil rights protections for homosexuals, and others are grappling with the issue. City governments have also been on the front line in attempting to deal with the potential, and in some cases the reality, of violence around abortion clinics. The concept of a buffer zone around abortion clinics clearly emerged from the difficulties that local police experienced in handling this potential for violence—experience that led to congressional passage of the Freedom of Access to Clinic Entrances Act (1993).

It is important to note that social conflict and the implementation of policies addressing it involve local government in a web of intergovernmental relations that are at least as important, and as complex, as are intergovernmental relations surrounding policies with material stakes. The rights-based federal laws that are at issue in the social regulatory realm affect large numbers of individuals, often receive minimal federal enforcement attention, and often are implemented by state and local authorities "who are permitted much discretion" (Tatalovich and Daynes 1988, 224–25). In the case of pornography, the primary regulatory is "state and local government with the principal emphasis at the municipal level" because of the Supreme Court's ruling that "community values" must shape the regulation of pornography (Hawkins and Zimring 1991, 210–11).

Culture-war controversies are also important phenomena from the local government perspective because of the substantial consequences that such controversies can have for local officials and the communities they serve. The dollar costs of maintaining social order in the face of strident social conflicts can be quite high, and the outcomes of local elections can turn on the dynamics of these culture-war issues. Furthermore, because the emergence of these explosive issues often draws national media attention, local governments find themselves in the spotlight, with the reputation and image of the community at stake. To the subtleties of image, one can add the realities of lives saved or lost, and injuries and property damage suffered or averted, depending upon local government's handling of the explosive issues in the culture-war domain.

Case Selection

The purpose of this article is to explore the various roles, both proactive and reactive, that city governments may play in emergent social conflicts. Ultimately, theoretical development in this area will require explanation of variation in city government responses. Because of the limited attention that these conflicts have received and because of the lack of urban theory concerning them, however, my goal here is more modest—that is, to develop a theoretically rich typology of city government roles in such conflicts. To enhance its theoretical potential, the typology will be based in part on application of concepts from social-movements, political-entrepreneurship, and agenda-setting theory.

However, the typology should also be empirically grounded. In this analysis, that empirical grounding consists of analyzing cases of community controversy involving abortion clinic protest, gay rights, regulation of pornography, protests against judicial handling of sexual assault, and controversy over neo-Nazis. Table 1 lists the cases that will be used. The cases were chosen based upon the availability of published accounts of community controversies and because they most clearly epitomize the issues of sexual morality and religion that are at the heart of contemporary culture wars.[3] The cases constitute a convenience sample rather than a representative random sample. However, the purpose of the analysis is not hypothesis testing and generalization but exploration of the potential diversity of city government roles in social conflicts. Fortunately for this purpose, not only were there cases in each issue area, but the cases involve large and small communities and conservative and liberal-progressive communities; there were cases that received national attention, and cases that did not. The time frames for the cases vary as well, in line with the cycles of activism that have occurred in each issue area.

Finally, there is variation both across the cases and within the cases (i.e., across the various phases of each case) in the amount of conflict and controversy evoked by the issue. Brief descriptions of each of the cases illustrate these variations in level of conflict. In the case of abortion clinic protests in Brookline,

Table 1 Cases of Community Conflict over Culture War Issues

Issue Area	Case Coverage	Source(s)
Abortion clinic protest	Conflict concerning Operation Rescue activities in Brookline, Massachusetts, late 1980s	Hertz (1991)
Abortion clinic protest	Controversy concerning an abortion clinic in Fargo, North Dakota, 1980s	Ginsburg (1989)
Pornography regulation	Conflict concerning an antipornography ordinance with a feminist, civil rights orientation, Minneapolis, Minnesota, 1983	Downs (1989)
Pornography regulation	Events concerning the city's adoption of an antipornography ordinance with a feminist, civil rights, orientation, Indianapolis, Indiana, 1984	Downs (1989)
Gay rights	Conflict concerning a drive for gay rights legislation in New York City, 1970–1971	Marotta (1981)
Gay rights	Conflict concerning the adoption of a gay rights ordinance in Wichita, Kansas, 1977	Various journalistic accounts, assembled by the author
Gay rights	Emergence of a politically mobilized gay community in San Francisco (1960s) and the adoption of a gay rights ordinance in 1977	D'Emilio (1983) and Shilts (1982)
Hate-group regulation	Conflict concerning plans by a Chicago-based Nazi group to march in Skokie, Illinois, 1977	Downs (1985)
Judicial handling of rape	Effort to recall Judge Simonson, Madison, Wisconsin, after his bench comments during a rape case, 1977	Woliver (1993)
Judicial handling of sexual assault	Effort to recall Judge Reinecke, Grant County, Wisconsin, after his bench comments concerning the sexual promiscuity of a five-year-old sexual-assault victim	Woliver (1993)

Massachusetts, there were disruptions over several months as Operation Rescue repeatedly descended upon local abortion clinics, blocking entry when possible and attracting street-side shouting matches between rescuers and pro-choice opponents. Local police were forced to provide extra coverage at a cost of at least $17,000 per day in overtime pay (Hertz 1991, 12). In the Fargo, North Dakota, case, controversy over the scheduled opening of the community's first abortion clinic was initially confined to low-key prayer vigils; then a new pro-life group emerged, which "introduced a confrontational style" (Ginsburg 1989, 115) of protest, bringing ABC television coverage of the activities of the militant group, and a local reaction to the group, culminating in a variety of legal actions against them (pp. 95, 115–119).

In Minneapolis, Minnesota, the city council passed a controversial ordinance that prohibited "discrimination [against women] by trafficking in pornography" and allowed a woman to sue for damages against the purveyors of pornography if she could show a causal link between an assault she suffered and a particular piece of pornography (Downs 1989, 43, 46–47). The ordinance was vetoed by the mayor, but a revised version was enacted at a meeting featuring the arrest of 24 women "for disrupting the council's proceedings" (pp. 62, 65). In Indianapolis, Indiana, an antipornography ordinance modeled on that of Minneapolis was enacted with much less controversy, despite opposition from the Indianapolis Civil Liberties Union, the city's Urban League, its equal opportunity board, and its legal staff (pp. 117–120).

In Madison, Wisconsin, Judge Archie Simonson's comments about the dress of women clashed with the rape reform efforts of women's groups attempting "to change the public's perception of rape from a crime of passion to a crime of violence" (Woliver 1993, 29) and evoked protests and a campaign to recall Simonson. With the support of many governmental organizations, politicians, and groups, Simonson was successfully recalled from the bench (pp. 52, 32). In the Grant County, Wisconsin, case, parents organized to recall Judge Reinecke after his bench comments about the sexual permissiveness or promiscuity of a five-year-old victim of sexual assault. This recall effort was more divisive than that involving Judge Simonson, because law enforcement officers, the county prosecutor, the local bar, and local newspapers rallied to support Judge Reinecke. In a recall election, Reinecke retained his judgeship, capturing 51% of the vote.

Of the cases involving proposed gay rights legislation, two exhibited considerable controversy. The New York City case featured a series of high-profile protest actions by the Gay Activists' Alliance, at least one of which turned into a melee between local police officers and gay activists. The proposed gay rights ordinance ultimately stalled in committee (D'Emilio 1983). In Wichita, Kansas, the proposal for a gay rights ordinance split the community and the city council, which, after heated hearings, passed the ordinance on a split vote. With the support of the local district attorney, a petition drive was mounted to force the ordinance to a referendum, in which it was defeated overwhelmingly. By contrast, a gay rights ordinance was enacted in San Francisco in 1977 on a 10–1 city council vote with only minimal criticism. The ordinance, the "pet project" of Harvey Milk, the first openly gay municipal official in the United States, reflected the substantial electoral muscle of the gay community (Shilts 1982, 199). The sole vote against the ordinance came from Councilman Dan White in an ongoing feud with Milk that culminated in White's assassination of both Milk and Mayor Moscone (Shilts 1982, 199).

In the Skokie, Illinois case, the National Socialist Party of America (NSPA) planned a march in the community, home to large numbers of Holocaust survivors, after the Chicago Park District prevented their demonstration in Marquette Park. In response to threatened violence by the Holocaust survivor community, Skokie officials got an injunction to prevent the march and enacted a series of ordinances to deter the activities of such organizations. With help from the American Civil Liberties Union, the NSPA filed several suits, which were eventually decided against Skokie.

A Taxonomy of Local Government Roles in Social Controversies

Exploration of these cases yields evidence of a variety of different roles that local governments play in social controversies. This section delineates six distinctive roles that were so identified: evasion, repression, hyperactive responsiveness, responsiveness, entrepreneurial instigation, and unintentional instigation.

Initially, it might be expected that local politicians would avoid the volatile issues that evoke culture wars or, when they are raised by citizen activists, evade them as much as possible by referring them to task forces or using other responses that provide access or agenda responsiveness while evading policy responsiveness (Schumaker 1975, 494). After all, the intense minorities that are typically involved in culture-war conflicts can pose problems for political officials, whose constituencies may be alienated by extremist actions or policies that evoke strident protest from opposing single-issue groups. The evasion approach is indeed evident in several of the cases. Skokie officials initially planned to allow the Nazi march, reasoning that it would be best to keep it routine and hope that the event would pass unnoticed and without disturbance. This was precisely the meaning of the "quarantine" policy that major Jewish organizations espoused as a way of preventing anti-Semitic groups from attaining the publicity that they desired (Downs 1985, 23). As I will discuss later, this intentionally low-key approach ultimately backfired for Skokie officials. Evasion also characterizes the response of key New York officials in the case of the failed drive for gay rights legislation in New York in 1971. Although a bill was introduced and many council members gave encouraging responses to activists pressing for the legislation, then-Mayor Lindsay delayed making a public announcement in favor of the ordinance, and without his public support, the legislation remained bottled up in council committee.

Evasion is characterized by symbolic politics and other low-key efforts to maintain the status quo. But, at other times, local governments take more overt and aggressive action to maintain the status quo in the face of challengers. During an intense culture controversy, especially one that imposes substantial costs on local government, local officials may respond in ways that approximate Tarrow's (1994, 95) definition of repression—that is, action to "either depress collective action or raise the cost of its two main preconditions—the organization and mobilization of opinion." In Brookline, for example, city officials filed suit against Operation Rescue under the provisions of the Racketeer Influenced and Corrupt Organizations Act (RICO), ostensibly to recover the roughly $75,000 in police overtime costs that had resulted from the organization's "rescue" effort

(Hertz 1991, 46). However, the repressive purpose of filing the suit is clear from the case. None of the Operation Rescue leaders had monetary resources that the town could have recaptured, and the town counsel did not pursue the litigation once suit was filed. However, the chair of the town council explained that "the RICO suit had done its job, that it had scared off potential rescuers and was largely responsible for the group's dwindling numbers" (p. 227).

Concerned Citizens for Children in Grant County also found itself subject to repression. Judge Reinecke's supporters included law enforcement officials, and the husband of an activist was nearly run off the road by a county police officer in what was considered a "life-threatening situation" (Woliver 1993, 133). There was also a more subtle form of tacit repression, as Woliver (p. 140) explained: "People active in the recall recounted their fears for their families, businesses and futures in Grant County because of their involvement in a controversy against one of only two local judges."

In Fargo, court decisions and city council action generated repressive responses to a relatively militant pro-life group, Save-A-Baby, especially when that group received national television attention. The group, which had established a women's clinic to compete with the community's abortion clinic, had been sued by the abortion clinic for using an imitative clinic name and false advertising to lure women with unwanted pregnancies who presumably had been seeking abortion services. The district court issued a preliminary injunction against the pro-life center, mandating "that they change their name and publicity, and inform callers that they do not perform abortions" (Ginsburg 1989, 120). Ultimately, a county district court jury assessed $23,000 in special damages against the pro-life clinic. The abortion clinic had also sued a leader of the Save-A-Baby group for harassment after he went into the abortion clinic dressed as Santa Claus. The Court ruled in the abortion clinic's favor on this as well, sentencing the Save-A-Baby leader to "two days in jail, a $200 fine, and a year on probation during which he could not be near the abortion clinic" (p. 120). Meanwhile, the city council passed a ban on the picketing of private residences in direct response to the activities of the Save-A-Baby group. Ginsburg (p. 121) argued that these official responses "drew authoritative limits to the range of acceptable behaviors that would be tolerated in the battle over the abortion clinic."

Tarrow (1994) argued that even relatively low-level action, such as a requirement for parade permits, should be conceptualized as a form of repression, because "it gives officials an easy way to keep tabs on their [protestors'] organization and encourages them to resort to legal means" (p. 96). By such standards, the Chicago Park District's requirement that the Nazis obtain $250,000 in liability insurance before being allowed to demonstrate in any Chicago park is clearly an example of repression, as were the Skokie ordinances banning the distribution of hate literature or the wearing of military regalia and the Skokie government's effort to get an injunction barring the neo-Nazis from demonstrating in the community. These efforts to repress an organization whose hate message was offensive to the community were all declared unconstitutional by either the Illinois Supreme Court or the federal district and appeals courts.

There are, in short, substantial legal constraints on the repressive responses that local governments can use, even in dealing with the most disruptive culture-war situations. However, there has also been a wave of innovation in the use of the law in these situations, especially as an instrument to repress hate groups. City governments may, for example, take a cue from civil rights attorney Morris Dees, who pioneered in "bankrupting white extremist groups with extraordinary civil judgments" (Hamm 1993, 210).

But local governments do not necessarily act in ways opposed to the challengers of the status quo. Even when vocal minorities are promoting relatively radical changes, local governments can and do play several kinds of roles in support of status quo challengers; and, sometimes, local officials initiate the movement for radical change.

A number of the cases provide evidence of overt and aggressive action in support of status quo challengers. The hyperactive responsiveness to the agenda of an intense minority is a far cry from the stereotype of local officials studiously hiding from the explosiveness of culture-war issues. Characterizing a response as hyperactive is, of course, a normative judgment, suggesting that officials have gone too far or acted rashly. In several of the case studies, however, evidence is presented to suggest such a characterization—evidence suggesting official action that (a) was relatively precipitous, (b) bypassed normal procedures, (c) disregarded obvious legal or constitutional issues, or (d) was some combination of these. For both the Minneapolis and the Indianapolis cases, Downs (1989) provides evidence that antipornography ordinances were rushed to enactment, some normal procedures that would have provided input from a broader array of stakeholders were bypassed, decision making was swayed by emotional, one-sided hearings, and the constitutional concerns of city legal staff were overlooked. As a result, Downs' interpretation is that the two cases represent "something all too common in political life—the reluctance of elected officials to be found on the wrong side of an emotionally charged issue which partisans have framed as a matter of good versus evil" (p. 91).

The case of abortion clinic protest in Fargo presents another example of government officials making a relatively precipitous decision, apparently as a result of being swept up in the intense emotions of the issue, without due consideration of constitutional issues, at least until their hyperactive responsiveness was reversed by the action of another official. Shortly before the city's first abortion clinic was to open, a local pro-life organization tried to block the clinic's opening by petitioning the city council to revoke its building permit. With the mayor out of town, the remaining city commission members hurried a vote in favor of the petition, but upon his return, the permit was reinstated by the mayor, who declared that the clinic was a legal enterprise and that the use of local regulations to discriminate against it would embroil the city in pointless litigation (Ginsburg 1989, 88).

Local politicians can be responsive to the policy demands of status quo challengers without being hyperactive. This straightforward form of responsiveness is nowhere better illustrated than in the case of Wichita, where the city council passed a gay rights ordinance in 1977. In contrast to the precipitousness, disregard of constitutional issues, and short circuiting of normal procedure that characterize hyperactive responsiveness, city officials in this case took excruciating pains over the ordinance. Before passing the ordinance, Wichita council members heard public comment from both sides at a council meeting, delayed action for a month in order to obtain an opinion from the Kansas attorney general stipulating that the ordinance would not conflict with state law (Stinson 1977), and had nearly seven hours of hearings on the issue before voting 3–2 in favor ("Wichita, Kansas Bans Bias" 1977). After the positive vote on first reading (in Wichita, an ordinance must be endorsed twice), council delayed action on the second reading to get another ruling on the issue of whether the ordinance would affect the school board and other governmental units ("Gay Rights Foes" 1977).

Local politicians are, of course, not limited to responding to culture-war-style conflicts. They can, and sometimes do, play a role in instigating the conflicts, in one of two ways. Conflict can be intentionally instigated if public officials take on the role of issue entrepreneurs, mobilizing the public on symbolic or morals issues. This entrepreneurial instigation is especially evident in the cases involving pornography crusades. In Minneapolis, a veteran city council member, Charlee Hoyt, served as an entrepreneur for the issue of fighting pornography by using the new weapon of an ordinance defining pornography as a violation of women's civil rights (Downs 1989, 57)—an innovative approach that was being promulgated by feminist theorists Andrea Dworkin and Catharine MacKinnon. In Indianapolis, both Mayor Hudnut and the local prosecutor, Steven Goldsmith, were issue entrepreneurs for the city's crusade against pornography. Goldsmith had won the prosecutor's office in 1979 on a campaign emphasizing pornography problems and had immediately initiated pornography raids on local establishments. In the early 1980s, Mayor Hudnut pushed the antipornography issue and directed the local police to escalate their crackdown (p. 99). When Hudnut learned of the innovative ordinance with which Minneapolis had experimented, he established communication between the Indianapolis council and the city council member in Minneapolis who had championed the issue, and he maintained visible and vocal support for passage of the ordinance in Indianapolis (pp. 107–112).

Entrepreneurial instigation sometimes occurs when local officials, who are elected on platforms stressing pornography, gay rights, or abortion-related issues, follow through with policy initiatives in the culture-war genre. In the Indianapolis pornography case just described, for example, electoral politics positioned prosecutor Goldsmith for a role in promoting an aggressive response to pornography. With respect to gay rights, the same is true of Milk, who won election to a San Francisco council seat as a champion of the gay community and made a ban on gay discrimination his first legislative initiative (Shilts 1982, 190).

The category entrepreneurial instigation is meant to be reserved for those instances in which public officials serve as the initial promoters of a culture-war issue, in the process mobilizing citizen groups behind the issue. In practice, it may be difficult to distinguish entrepreneurial instigation from another familiar category—co-optation. Although the term is commonly used to refer to the neutralization of the independent agenda of citizen groups by government, McCarthy and Wolfson (1992, 274) emphasized the possibility that the apparatus of the state can be co-opted by a social movement. The example of entrepreneurial instigation in the Minneapolis case could be interpreted as co-optation of the state by nonstate activists, in this case, Dworkin and MacKinnon. Although there was a history of antipornography efforts in the community, the radical legal departure represented by Dworkin and MacKinnon's ordinance was made possible when Councilwoman Hoyt "opened her office and all its resources to Dworkin, MacKinnon, and their followers" (Downs 1989, 57)—a relatively clear-cut statement of co-optation of a segment of the state. Although it may be empirically difficult to make a clear distinction between issue entrepreneurship that is literally initiated by public officials and issue entrepreneurship that public officials take up as a result of being co-opted by activists within a social movement, the distinction itself may not be conceptually important, because both involve entrepreneurial instigation. As Tarrow (1994, 98) argued, "protesting groups create political opportunities for elites . . . when opportunistic politicians seize the opportunity created by challengers to proclaim themselves tribunes of the people."

At other times, local officials appear to instigate controversy unintentionally—typically by taking actions that spark the emergence of local protest groups and frame a heretofore nonissue in rights-oriented terms. This unintentional instigation is especially apparent in the early history of the gay rights movement. In San Francisco in the 1960s, the emergence of a politically mobilized gay community was in large part the unintended consequence of aggressive police action against the gay community. The San Francisco police "had a long history of harassing gay bars" (D'Emilio 1983, 182–183), and a major scandal in 1959 had revealed that the police had been shaking down a number of gay bar owners for payments, in exchange for which they would be allowed to continue to operate (pp. 182–183). Aggressive police crackdowns on gay bars continued even after this "gayola" episode, and when a group of Protestant clergy instituted a new organization to work with the gay community, local police attempted to force the cancellation of a benefit dance organized by the group. Failing to stop the dance, the police made an aggressive show of force outside the dance and arrested lawyers for the organization who were challenging the police action (pp. 193–194). But the ministers and lawyers "provided a legitimacy to the charges of police harassment that the word of a homosexual lacked" (p. 194). More generally, political agitating for gay rights in San Francisco "came alive through the attacks mounted against it by a hostile city administration and police force" (pp. 195–196).

The case of Judge Simonson's recall in Madison provides yet another example of unintentional instigation if one is willing to construe the concept to include catalytic action for a social movement that is already organized. That is precisely the interpretation offered by Woliver (1993, 45), who noted that "A critical mobilizing event, like Simonson's remarks, can actually help an incipient social movement. Whether mobilization occurs, though, also often depends on the facilitation provided by a preexisting social movement."

Yet another version of unintentional instigation is exemplified by the dilemma of Skokie officials, whose choice of a minimalist strategy in response

Table 2 A Typology of Local Government's Role in Culture Wars

	Supportive of Status Quo Challengers	Not Supportive of Status Quo Challengers
First order	Hyperactive responsiveness Responsiveness Entrepreneurial instigation	Evasion Repression
Second order	Unintentional instigation	Unintentional instigation

to a planned Nazi march turned out to be a miscalculation. Skokie officials had not understood how strong the response of Holocaust survivors would be. Their anger and threats of violence placed officials unexpectedly in the eye of a firestorm, even though evasion was intended to prevent just such controversy (Downs 1985, 44).

This transformation of our interpretation of Skokie's response from one of evasion to unintentional instigation suggests a problem with the typology. If a single behavior or set of behaviors, such as Skokie officials' adoption of a quarantine policy, can be classified in one of two different categories, the typology is not mutually exclusive. The answer to this dilemma lies in recognizing the fact that Skokie officials' unintentional instigation of controversy hinges upon the reaction of nongovernmental groups to local government's action. Similarly, it may be that some local government efforts at repression may instead turn out to be unintentional instigation—for example, if overly aggressive efforts to prevent protest activity by pro-life groups actually sparked a determination on the part of such groups to target the city for high-profile activity. In short, the typology of local government's role in local culture wars perhaps should be conceptualized as including both first-order and second-order responses (see Table 2). First-order responses, such as repression, evasion, responsiveness, and intentional instigation, are primarily based upon the intent of the local decision makers who take the action. A second-order response, such as unintentional instigation, hinges upon the interactive effects of governmental actions and the actions of nongovernmental groups that are a party to the controversial issue. As the foregoing examples suggest, unintentional instigation can either be supportive or nonsupportive of status-quo challengers depending upon who is inadvertently mobilized by governmental action.

Local Governments and Social Controversy

The development of this taxonomy of local government roles in controversies over culture-war issues is only the first step in theory building. Nevertheless, it is a critical first step because existing theories of governmental links to social movements and protest groups are not fully developed for the task and because existing case studies, typically focusing on only one or two cases at a time, have not explored the full range of governmental roles. In this article, my consideration of a varied set of cases of local culture wars yields a taxonomy of local government roles that dovetails with, but that is more wide-ranging than, existing typologies of local governmental responsiveness to social movements.

The cases show that local governments can, like national governments, opt for repressive responses to status quo challengers. Although the specific tactics used for repression may be distinctive for local government, there is a substantial collection of such tactics, ranging from parade permit requirements to disorderly conduct arrests to legal action intended to financially cripple mobilized organizations. For this reason, any theory of local government's role in local culture wars must be anchored at one extreme by the realities of repression—an insight that has been somewhat submerged in recent urban scholarship because of its emphasis upon service delivery or development issues, issue arenas for which the concept of repression is less relevant.

The analysis also suggests that existing typologies of policy responsiveness are limited because they do not include the possibility of hyperactive responsiveness. Indeed, treatments of the extent and character of local government responsiveness to citizen groups have traditionally conceptualized *lack* of responsiveness and co-optation as the only problematic aspects of the responsiveness continuum (Schumaker 1975; Gittell 1980). When emotional, culture-war-style issues are at stake, however, public officials can sometimes be overwhelmed by intense, special interest minorities or themselves committed to moral crusades. The resulting rush to policy, in processes that override procedural safeguards, squelch dissent, and ignore constitutional viability, can be problematic. The concept of hyperactive responsiveness may not be as relevant for the discussion of issues in other policy domains, in which there are material stakes and compromise and coalition building are the key phenomena. To understand governmental responses to culture wars, however, it is necessary to consider the possibility of too much responsiveness.

Theorists of agenda setting have long noted that an *outside initiative* is not the only path for issues to attain agenda status; instead of reacting to popular demands, government officials can be instrumental in mobilizing the public behind issues (Cobb, Keith-Ross, and Ross 1976). When the intense issues that characterize the culture-war domain are at stake, officials who engage in such mobilization are perhaps playing with fire. Strident controversies over abortion, gay rights, pornography, and the like can impose substantial costs on the community, in the form of violence, law enforcement costs, disruptive action, and threats to the community's image nationally. Yet, these cases suggest that public officials do sometimes mobilize the community on culture-war issues. There are at least two reasons for this. Officials may have their own strongly held views about pornography, gay rights, or abortion and may even have won office based upon those views. From a more cynical standpoint, it must be acknowledged that culture-war issues can be excellent raw material for the game of symbolic politics, with its potential advantages for public officials who are skillful players (Edelman 1977).

The intensely held views that are the essence of culture-war issues make yet another form of governmental involvement more important than it would be in other policy domains. As this article has shown, public officials can inadvertently bring about the mobilization of a social movement, either through words or actions that crystallize a grievance, attempts at repression that spark resistance, or any number of other symbolic miscalculations. Unlike the other forms of governmental involvement, however, unintentional instigation is conceptualized here as a second-order phenomenon—that is, the result of reactions to governmental action, regardless of the intent of those actions.

Acknowledgment of this fact suggests yet another possibility: Local government's role in any given culture-war controversy may change several times over the course of the controversy. Perhaps the sequencing of these roles would be of as much interest as are the individual responses or actions that form the building blocks for sequences. Perhaps evasion, for example, is characteristically followed by responsiveness under other circumstances. Perhaps yet another prototypical sequence would involve hyperactive responsiveness after unintentional instigation, as some political leaders take advantage of opportunities inadvertently created by the miscalculation of others. Stated another way, further inquiry into local culture wars may need to take account of various stages in the development of the controversy, from initial agenda setting to the unintended consequences of the policy strategy chosen.

A theory of local government's role in social controversy will, of course, require propositions to account for variation in city governments' adoption of one or the other actions defined here. Variation in institutional arrangements for governance, in the social composition of the community, and many other factors that have long been incorporated into explanations for variation in other spheres of city policy need to be adapted to the task of explaining local governments' role in culture-war issues. For example, the structural arrangements of local government that have been so heavily investigated with respect to their role in shaping economic development policy and service delivery might also be expected to shape local government's role in culture-war controversies. Recent investigations have examined the impact of strong mayors, city managers' offices, and district elections in accounting for the emergence of progrowth and antigrowth entrepreneurs (Schneider and Teske 1993a, 1993b). Similar exploration of the role of these institutional arrangements in the entrepreneurial instigation of culture wars is called for.

Differences in *political* subculture (Elazar 1970) may be significant in explaining the propensity of local governments to engage in hyperactive responsiveness because of the differing expectations of the role of government that are embedded in those subcultural differences. The size and homogeneity of the community may be important predictors of the likelihood of repressive action because smaller, more homogeneous communities may have a stronger sense of community norms being broached by status quo challengers. And Lieske (1993) has recently charted, at a quite localized level, cultural variables that might be used to operationalize broader cultural cleavages between orthodox and progressive (Hunter 1991), materialist and postmaterialist (Inglehart 1990), or biblical and expressive individualist (Bellah et al. 1985) areas. The degree to which these cultural cleavages exist within communities, or perhaps the degree to which a community exhibits a cultural strand that is declining nationally, may be predictive of entrepreneurial instigation because of either status discontents or moral outrages (Wallis 1979, 92–102) that such cleavages provide as the raw material for entrepreneurial instigation.

These are preliminary suggestions of the directions that may be fruitful in the next phase of theory building—the development of propositions to account for variation in local government roles in culture wars. But urban scholars will collectively take up that task only if the phenomenon to be explained is viewed as important and interestingly variegated. It has been the task of this article to contribute to that acknowledgment.

Notes

1. Racial and ethnic conflict is distinctive in that it has a longer history in the United States and played a major role in shaping partisan alignments and other features of national and local politics.

2. In this article, the term *status quo challengers* is used to refer to gay rights activists, abortion clinic protesters, pornography crusaders, feminists critical of judicial permissiveness about rape, and neo-Nazi groups. For the cases and time periods of interest here, those on these sides of various culture-war issues were opposed to the status quo. The status quo for most communities, then and now, is lack of explicit gay rights protections; the existence, or at least the legality, of abortion services; substantial constitutional constraints on the regulation of pornography; and community opposition to and laws limiting the activities of hate groups. Treating feminist groups dealing with judicial treatment of rape as status quo challengers is somewhat less definitive. However, for the cases at issue in this regard, Woliver (1993, 29) argued convincingly that feminist critiques are part of an as-yet-incomplete effort to change prevailing attitudes toward rape.

3. Other controversies, such as those pitting progrowth against antigrowth activists over locational decisions, or conflicts emanating from the environmental justice movement, clearly do involve value conflicts, and just as environmentalism is a component of postmaterialism in Inglehart's (1990) analysis, these growth- and environment-based conflicts arguably are rooted in cultural differences. However, development and land-use conflicts such as these also have features that make them less clearly distinct from the traditional realm of political economy and, hence, less clearly seated in a distinctive realm of cultural conflict. In particular, growth controls, not-in-my-backyard siting, and similar controversies involve substantial material stakes and cultural values for status quo challengers. And, in principle if not in practice, the divisible outcomes at stake in these issues lend themselves to compromise and the politics of coalition formation around compromise solutions (as, for example, around questions of the share of environmental hazards that each neighborhood should bear or the amount of growth that is tolerable). Development, land-use, and environmental issues do not, in this sense, share the uncompromising, all-or-nothing character of culture-war issues such as abortion (i.e., pro-life forces view the occurrence of any abortions as unacceptable).

Bibliography

Bellah, R., R. Madsen, W. Sullivan, A. Swidler, and S. Tipton. 1985. *Habits of the heart*. Berkeley: University of California Press.

Cobb, R., J. Keith-Ross, and M. H. Ross. 1976. Agenda building as a comparative political process. *American Political Science Review* 70:126–38.

D'Emilio, J. 1983. *Sexual politics, sexual communities*. Chicago: University of Chicago Press.

Downs, D. 1985. *Nazis in Skokie: Freedom, community, and the First Amendment*. Notre Dame, IN: University of Notre Dame Press.

——————. 1989. *The new politics of pornography*. Chicago: University of Chicago Press.

Edelman, M. 1977. *Political language*. New York: Academic Press.

Elazar, D. 1970. *Cities of the prairie*. New York: Basic Books.

Gay rights foes reject Miami aid. 1977. *Wichita Eagle*, 15 September, C3.

Ginsburg, F. 1989. *Contested lives: The abortion debate in an American community*. Berkeley: University of California Press.

Gittell, M. 1980. *Limits to citizen participation*. Beverly Hills, CA: Sage Publications.

Green, D. P., and J. A. Cowden, 1992. Who protests: Self-interest and white opposition to busing. *Journal of Politics* 54:471–496.

Hamm, M. 1993. *American skinheads: The criminology and control of hate crime*. Westport, CT: Praeger.

Hawkins, G., and F. Zimring. 1991. *Pornography in a free society*. Cambridge, UK: Cambridge University Press.

Hertz, S. 1991. *Caught in the crossfire*. New York: Prentice Hall.

Hunter, J. D. 1991. *Culture wars*. New York: Basic Books.

——————. 1994. *Before the shooting begins*. New York: Free Press.

Inglehart, R. 1990. *Culture shift*. Princeton, NJ: Princeton University Press.

Lieske, J. 1993. Regional subcultures of the United States. *Journal of Politics* 55 (November): 888–913.

Marotta, T. 1981. *The politics of homosexuality*. Boston: Houghton Mifflin.

McCarthy, J. D., and M. Wolfson. 1992. Consensus movements, conflict movements, and the cooptation of civic and state infrastructures. In *Frontiers in social movement theory*, edited by A. Morris and C. M. Mueller, 273–97. New Haven, CT: Yale University Press.

Peterson, P. 1981. *City limits*. Chicago: University of Chicago Press.

Salisbury, R. 1969. An exchange theory of interest groups. *Midwest Journal of Political Science* 13 (February): 1–32.

Schneider, M., and P. Teske. 1993a. The antigrowth entrepreneur: Challenging the "equilibrium" of the growth machine. *Journal of Politics* 55 (August): 720–736.

——————. 1993b. The progrowth entrepreneur in local government. *Urban Affairs Quarterly* 29 (December): 316–327.

Schumaker, P. 1975. Policy responsiveness to protest-group demands. *Journal of Politics* 37:488–521.

Shilts, R. 1982. *The mayor of Castro street*. New York: St. Martin's.

Stinson, J. 1977. Gay forces win as city OKs law. *Wichita Eagle*, 7 September, C1, C4.

Stone, C. 1989. *Regime politic*. Lawrence: University of Kansas Press.

Tarrow, S. 1994. *Power in movement: Social movements, collective actions and politics*. Cambridge, UK: Cambridge University Press.

Tatalovich, R., and B. Daynes. 1988. *Social regulatory policy: Moral controversies in American politics*. Boulder, CO: Westview.

Wallis, R. 1979. *Salvation and protest*. London: Frances Pinter.

Wichita, Kansas bans bias against homosexuals. 1977. *The New York Times*, 8 September, A18.

Woliver, L. 1993. *From outrage to action: The politics of grass-roots dissent*. Urbana: University of Illinois Press.

Chapter 2

❖❖❖

THE MERCANTILE CITIES

The Culture of Privatism

During the nineteenth century, the Western world underwent urbanization on a scale unprecedented in history. In the United States, the impact of this development was magnified by the fact that the nation was being carved from a wilderness. In just a few decades following the constitutional era, America was transformed from a rural society that defined its national character by reference to the frontier and westward expansion into an urban and industrial culture. Cities were leading symbols of these extraordinary changes. They changed from small, socially homogeneous towns and villages into major trading centers that mushroomed into industrial metropolises by century's end. As the idea of popular government grew, local political leaders struggled to reconcile the pressures of democratic government with the new tensions of emerging capitalism.

The two readings that make up this chapter suggest how this great transformation was reflected in every aspect of urban politics. A system of commercial cities run by merchant elites arose and became the dominant regime prior to the Civil War. These mercantile regimes helped establish what Sam Bass Warner describes as a culture of "privatism" in urban politics and city building. By espousing the notion that cities mainly existed to serve private economic activities, the urban leaders permitted the agenda of local politics and even the physical character of cities to be driven primarily by the market decisions of traders, builders, land speculators, and investors. Warner believes that the culture of privatism made it difficult for public authorities to respond with much effectiveness to the problems of cities as they grew in size and became complex social and political entities. He describes the frustrations that Philadelphia civic leaders faced in their efforts to improve the city's water supply. Although the health of its citizens and even its economic prosperity made a safe and clean supply of water a necessity, the city's political leaders struggled with the notion that the public provision of water should become the norm.

The aristocrats and businessmen who ran the cities considered local economic growth to be the highest municipal priority. Commercial cities could prosper only by gaining a competitive advantage over other cities as trading centers. Consequently, mercantile leaders fought to use public resources to promote canal, railroad, and other transportation improvements in hopes of expanding their trading areas. The spirit of this inter-city rivalry is captured by Richard C. Wade, who portrays the commercial struggles among frontier cities in the first decades of the nineteenth century. In this selection, Wade notes that in these contests, the rewards for winning might be considerable, and the penalties for losing could be devastating: "the economically strongest survived and flourished ... smaller places were trampled in the process, some being swallowed up by ambitious neighbors, others being overwhelmed before they could attain a challenging position." This kind of inter-urban competition continues to be an important feature of urban politics even today.

5

Sam Bass Warner, Jr.

THE ENVIRONMENT OF PRIVATE OPPORTUNITY

American cities have grown with the general culture of the nation, not apart from it. Late eighteenth-century Philadelphia was no exception. Its citizens, formerly the first wave of a Holy Experiment, had been swept up in the tides of secularization and borne on by steady prosperity to a modern view of the world. Like the Puritans of Massachusetts and Connecticut, the Quakers of Pennsylvania had proved unable to sustain the primacy of religion against the solvents of cheap land and private opportunity. Quaker, Anglican, Presbyterian, Methodist, Pietist—each label had its social and political implications—but all congregations shared in the general American secular culture of privatism.[1]

Already by the time of the Revolution privatism had become the American tradition. Its essence lay in its concentration upon the individual and the individual's search for wealth. Psychologically, privatism meant that the individual should seek happiness in personal independence and in the search for wealth; socially, privatism meant that the individual should see his first loyalty as his immediate family, and that a community should be a union of such money-making, accumulating families; politically, privatism meant that the community should keep the peace among individual money-makers, and, if possible, help to create an open and thriving setting where each citizen would have some substantial opportunity to prosper.

To describe the American tradition of privatism is not to summarize the entire American cultural tradition. Privatism lies at the core of many modern cultures; privatism alone will not distinguish the experience of America from that of other nations. The tradition of privatism is, however, the most important element of our culture for understanding the development of cities. The tradition of privatism has always meant that the cities of the United States depended for their wages, employment, and general prosperity upon the aggregate successes and failures of thousands of individual enterprises, not upon community action. It has also meant that the physical forms of American cities, their lots, houses, factories, and streets, have been the outcome of a real estate market of profit-seeking builders, land speculators, and large investors. Finally, the tradition of privatism has meant that the local politics of American cities have depended for their actors, and for a good deal of their subject matter, on the changing focus of men's private economic activities.[2]

In the eighteenth century the tradition of privatism and the social and economic environment of colonial towns nicely complemented each other. Later as towns grew to big cities, and big cities grew to metropolises, the tradition became more and more ill-suited to the realities of urban life. The tradition assumed that there would be no major conflict between private interest, honestly and liberally viewed, and the public welfare. The modes of eighteenth-century town life encouraged this expectation that if each man would look to his own prosperity the entire town would prosper. . . .

The goals of the nineteenth-century municipality remained those of the Revolutionary era. The city was to be an environment for private money-making, and its government was to encourage private business. At the same time the city was to be an equalitarian society; its government should endeavor to maintain an open society where every citizen would have some chance, if not an equal chance, in the race for private wealth. These traditional goals worked upon the settled forms of the municipal corporation; they set the framework of the new municipal institutions, and they directed the attention and the efforts of the city's leaders, both the merchant amateurs and the new professionals.

The enduring effects of the interaction of these traditional goals with the demands of big city life can be summarized in the history of . . . the municipal corporation [and] the waterworks. . . . The history of the municipal corporation is best known and therefore can be sketched briefly. The story of Philadelphia's pioneer municipal waterworks demands more attention since it shows the permanent constraints that the city's tradition of privatism placed upon what was to be a universal public health program. . . .

Municipal Corporation

The Philadelphia municipal corporation grew directly out of the Revolution. The moderate merchant-artisan faction which had resumed control of the city and state at the end of the Revolution wrote the 1789 Philadelphia city charter, the first since independence was gained. It blended the traditional offices of colonial municipal government with the federalist fashion for bicameral legislatures. The taxpayer franchise established in 1776 by the radicals for all of Pennsylvania remained the electoral base of the city. The taxpayers of the city elected at-large both select and common councils which, together, voted appropriations, levied taxes, and enacted local ordinances. The mayor, not popularly elected, but chosen by the councils, as in colonial times, was the chief executive officer. With the approval of the councils he appointed a board of commission-ers and together the mayor and the board carried on the executive business of the city government.

Despite domination by merchants, in the years following the 1789 charter, the demands of radical equalitarianism continued to press upon Philadelphia's corporation and thereby to hold it to a weak executive, to increase local control, and to expand both the franchise and the number of elected offices.[3] Philadel-phia's municipal history, thus, ran directly counter to the trends of centraliza-tion and large-scale activity which characterized the contemporaneous indus-trialization of the city.

The radical fears of strong executives, inherited from the conflicts of the Revolution and continued by the Jacksonians in the nineteenth century, pre-vented the mayor and commissioners of the Philadelphia corporation from exercising much independence of action. When new municipal functions were added, like responsibilities for municipal water and gas, the councils created independent committees which did not report to the mayor but to the councils themselves. The patronage of the new activities, thus, fell to the councilors, not to the mayor, and therefore the effectiveness of the municipal corporation throughout the first half of the nineteenth century depended on the quality of the elected councilors and the volunteers who served on the council's committees.

Localism also gained with successive reforms of the post-Revolutionary Philadelphia and Pennsylvania governments. In 1834, when the basic public school statute for Pennsylvania was enacted it stipulated that three citizens be elected from each ward of Philadelphia to serve as school directors. The colo-nial tradition of having resident tax collectors and assessors in each ward was continued on an elected basis until just before the Civil War. The pressures of neighborhood partisan politics upon these officials produced widely fluctuat-ing assessments and ultimately great confusion in the tax rolls. In 1854, when all the boroughs and districts of Philadelphia County joined into one consoli-dated city, to preserve the strength of past localisms, the select and common councillors were hereafter chosen on a ward basis, not at-large as formerly.

State and municipal election reforms expanded the number of voters and the number of elected offices. In 1838, state judges became elected officials. At the same time the franchise, which had been restricted to all taxpayers, was re-defined to include all white males who had reached the age of twenty-one. This franchise reform, one of the few genuinely popular accomplishments in a deeply divided constitutional convention (1837–1838), reflected an important current in American equalitarianism: an enthusiasm for the uniform political status of whites was often accompanied by a heavy prejudice against Negroes. By the time the state constitutional convention convened in Philadelphia the city had already experienced its first major race riot. In 1841 the mayorality be-came a popularly elected office, while the ballot for Philadelphia county posi-tions grew steadily longer.[4]

By mid-century the city of Philadelphia had grown to a big city and the functions of its government had kept pace with this growth. The cost of half a century of political change which ran against the trends of the city's industrialization now stood out clearly. The committee system of the councils, the extreme localism of politics, and the large number of elected offices appeared as handicaps to effective government. The consolidation of all the county into one municipal corporation in 1854 brought unity of management to the major functions of government, but it did not bring with it imagination or high quality of service.

The authors of the 1854 consolidation charter had voiced concern for effective control over municipal departments and sought devices for protecting the corporation from looting by predatory local political groups. To these ends they considerably enlarged the powers of the mayor at the expense of the councils' committees, and they created new executives in the offices of comptroller and receiver of taxes. So strong was the tradition of elected officials, however, that both these new executives had to be elected, not appointed by the mayor. Altogether, the reforms of 1854 could make but little progress. Bigness and industrialization had already destroyed both the source of competent leadership and the informed community which would have been necessary for the city to have enjoyed a future of strong, efficient, and imaginative government. Instead, a century of weakness and corruption lay ahead.[5]

Development of Waterworks

Philadelphia pioneered in building America's first municipal waterworks and thus operated for forty years an experimental water supply project for all other large cities in the nation. The success of Philadelphia's water program stands as a tribute to its old merchant-led committee system of government. Indeed, in the beginning, its success was as much a product of an aggressive committee as it was the result of sponsorship by the municipal corporation.[6]

The yellow fever epidemic of 1793 forced Philadelphians into their pioneering public water system. In that epidemic, the city's first major plague, one in twelve Philadelphians perished. More than 23,000 persons fled the city, and all business with the outside world ceased for a month.[7] It was clear to those who tasted the well water of different neighborhoods that in crowded blocks the contents of privies penetrated the wells.[8] Although doctors debated repeatedly the causes of the fever, all sides agreed that the cleansing of the streets, yards, and houses of filth and an abundant supply of cool, clear water for drinking were essential requirements if the city was to be preserved.

During these years a private company was digging a canal to connect the Schuylkill River to the Delaware River. It therefore seemed reasonable to add to these transportation plans a branch water supply canal through the center of the city. The canal company, however, soon went bankrupt. In 1797 another serious epidemic of yellow fever struck the city and carried away over 3,000 citizens. Extended negotiations between the canal company and the city were renewed, but satisfactory financial arrangements could not be worked out. The issue then moved to the state legislature, where the company proved a more powerful lobbyist than the municipal corporation. The fever returned in 1798.

In 1799 the immigrant English engineer and architect, Benjamin Latrobe (1764–1820), visited Philadelphia on a commission to design the Bank of Pennsylvania. While in town he heard of the problem and published a pamphlet proposing a quick solution. He suggested, as an alternative to the slow and expensive program of a dam and canals, that the city build two steam pumps, a culvert from the Schuylkill to the edge of the city's dense settlement (then Pennsylvania Square), and a distribution system of wooden pipes and street hydrants. To capture popular support he added the provision of free water to the poor at the street hydrants. The cost of construction and operation of the system, Latrobe maintained, could be met by rents charged to businesses and private homes that were directly connected to the system. Although there had been a steam engine in Philadelphia before the Revolution, Latrobe's scheme was a bold innovation.[9]

At this point, as in the later expansion of Fairmount Dam, the strength of the city's merchant-led committee system of government proved itself. During the years from 1799 to 1837 very able leaders of the city served on the Watering Committee of the City Councils. Henry Drinker, Jr. (1757–1822), son of the well-known Quaker merchant and himself cashier of the Bank of North America, Thomas P. Cope (1768–1854), then at the beginning of his successful merchant career, and Samuel M. Fox (1763–1808) of the Bank of Pennsylvania led the campaign for the Latrobe plan. In subsequent years William Rush (1766–1833), the famous sculptor; Joseph S. Lewis (1778–1836), prominent attorney and son of a wealthy China merchant; and John P. Wetherill (1794–1853), of the old Philadelphia paint manufacturing company Wetherill and Brother, all served on the Watering Committee and directed its aggressive policies.[10]

The city councils and their watering committee fought free of the canal interests and arranged their own financing without state aid. Despite setbacks in construction and periodic shortages of funds which the committee sometimes met by the members' advancing money out of their own pockets, they pushed the project through to completion by 1801. Henceforth Philadelphians enjoyed a reasonably adequate supply of water to cleanse themselves and to fight fires. The trials of the watering committee, however, did not cease. It continued to suffer all the pains of innovation. Engineering problems hampered the Committee until the twenties, financial problems until the thirties. The steam engines for the pumps, though good examples of Watt's low-pressure engine, broke down frequently and consumed mountains of cordwood. After sixteen years of difficulty they were replaced with high-pressure engines but these, though steady and powerful, used even more fuel. The original hydrants rarely shut off completely and in the winter froze solid. After two seasons the hydrants had to be entirely replaced by a new design. The hollow wooden logs used to distribute the water from the tank above the second pump leaked badly and after a few years a program of replacement by cast iron pipe was instituted.[11]

The original Latrobe scheme for financing the works was based on the assumption that many families would want direct water connections to their houses and that these private subscriptions would carry the cost of building and operating the system. Except for the boldest thinkers, however, Philadelphians in 1801 used water sparingly. By 1811 only 2,127 Philadelphians subscribed for water. Most of the city's 54,000 residents (city proper in 1810) depended for water on street hydrants or private wells. There were only two bath-houses in the entire city. As for home bathrooms, American inventors did not turn their attention to sanitary appliances until the 1830's. Thus over the first three decades of operation the watering committee struggled against heavy deficits while continuing to supply its product at a loss in advance of popular usage, for public health reasons.

Having established abundant clear water as part of the city's health services, the watering committee could not turn back even in the face of heavy financial deficits. During the second decade of the nineteenth century the city grew at the rate of about 2,200 persons per year. By 1820 Philadelphia and its immediate environs held a population of 114,000. The lawyer Joseph S. Lewis led the committee to seek a lasting solution to its problems of high operating costs and inadequate supply for the enlarging city. In 1819, in the midst of a severe depression, he proposed, and the City Councils accepted, a plan to invest another $400,000, this time in a dam across the Schuylkill and a series of water-powered pumps to raise the water to adjacent Fairmount Hill, where large reservoirs for a gravity-fed system could be built. The water-powered pumps would cut the operating costs to a mere fraction of the former steam costs. Also, the dam was to be constructed for eight water wheels, although only three would be needed immediately. Thus it was hoped that the Fairmount scheme afforded enough surplus capacity for years to come. Within four years the works were completed.

The Fairmount works met every economic and engineering expectation. They also stand as a lasting memorial to the era of Philadelphia's merchant-led committee government. The watering committee had sufficient taste, standing in the city, and pride in its accomplishment to finish the works and lay out the grounds as a beautiful park. Although only a beginning, like the works themselves, the park was an extremely valuable project. With its 1844 additions, it became the first large urban park in America, and, as such, was an essential link in the chain of outstanding landscapes that included Boston's Mt. Auburn Cemetery, New York's Central Park, and Chicago's lake front. Over the years Philadelphians expanded the original waterworks layout to create the greatest civic monument of Philadelphia, the Fairmount Park system.[12]

The excess capacity of the Fairmount works soon disappeared. Since public waterworks with their abundant supply of water for domestic and commercial users offered a novel product, there was no way to predict its future use. The growth of Philadelphia during the years 1830–1850 exceeded its rate for any other period (1820–1830 38 percent, 1830–1840 37 percent, 1840–1850 58 percent, Philadelphia only). Such a pace of growth, occurring for the first time in large American cities, likewise could not be expected to yield reliable future estimates. Both the sustained, rapid growth in Philadelphia's population and the increase in per capita consumption of water must have surprised contemporaries.[13]

In 1837 the committee issued a triumphant report. It had $100,000 in the bank, six wheels running at the dam, and the number of paying customers had jumped to 20,000. Of equal significance, consumption had begun its rise toward modern levels; doubling since 1823, it now equaled twenty gallons per person per day. The system as a whole—street hydrants, house and commercial connections—served a total population of 196,000. The report noted that 1,500 Philadelphians had installed bathrooms with running water. That critical moment in the history of any social innovation, the time when a fashion of the rich becomes an imperative for the middle class, seemed to have arrived.[14]

Though public enthusiasm for bathing and water closets grew apace, after 1837 the watering committee began to lose the imagination and largeness of view which had characterized its early performance. It seems reasonable to detect in this falling off of the quality of the committee the beginning of the decline in the quality of Philadelphia's municipal officers and a weakening of the committee system of government. Perhaps the very triumph of the Fairmount works in routinizing the water supply of the city, at least for a few years, made the watering committee unattractive to the most imaginative city leaders. Whatever the cause, the committee began to falter and in one way or another failed to keep pace with the growing needs of the city.

During the 1840's, spurred by immigration and industrial expansion, Philadelphia filled up rapidly and the towns and districts outside its boundaries grew at unprecedented rates. Spring Garden, Kensington, and Northern Liberties, districts which had joined the Philadelphia system, now used water in enormous amounts and demanded an equalization of their rates with those of Philadelphia customers. In addition, Spring Garden requested a high-pressure reservoir to give more adequate service on its hills. The watering committee, forgetting the essential public health purpose of its undertaking, now responded like a short-sighted monopolist by refusing to lower its rates. Spring Garden countered by securing legislative authorization to build its own works. Negotiations continued for a time, and ultimately the rates were conceded by the watering committee, but no satisfactory long-term contract could be worked out among Philadelphia and its neighbors. Spring Garden, Northern Liberties, and Kensington joined together to build their own pumping station in 1844. Ironically, they drew their water from behind the Fairmount Dam. In 1850 Kensington set up its own station, drawing from the Delaware River.

By 1850 only Southwark remained connected to the Philadelphia system. Yet such had been the decade's increase in per capita consumption that with all eight wheels working at the dam, and all the reservoirs filled, only three day's supply of water could be stored. In the summer 160,000 people drew forty-four gallons per person per day. Fifteen thousand houses had water closets, and 3,500 had baths. Clearly, the middle class of Philadelphia had adopted modern plumbing as an essential in its standard of living. The modern urban rate of water usage had arrived.

The subsequent history of the Philadelphia Water Works is inglorious. In 1851 inadequate capacity forced the watering committee to refuse West Philadelphia's request for service. The consolidation of all Philadelphia County into one city government in 1854 reunited all the water systems of the city, but union did not revive the old policy of aggressive building to meet future needs and to popularize higher standards of consumption. In the 1870's the city erected new steam pumping stations, but droughts brought shortages. Increasing pollution of the Schuylkill and Delaware rivers destroyed the former quality of the water. Such were the popular priorities of the city that the citizens taxed themselves with disease and dirty drinking water in order to allow private pollution of the rivers to continue unabated. In the years from 1880 to 1910 the typhoid fever rate in Philadelphia exceeded that of New York and Boston. Though filter systems had been demonstrated for over a decade, Philadelphia purchased its filters late and proceeded slowly. As late as 1906, 1,063 persons died of typhoid in Philadelphia in one season. In 1910–1911 filters and chlorine brought relief from these recurrent epidemics.[15]

The early history of Philadelphia's waterworks does more than help to date the mid-nineteenth-century decline in the effectiveness of its municipal government. Its history shows how the city's general culture of privatism stopped a universal public health program short of full realization. Fear of epidemics had created the water system, but once this fear had abated, little or no public support remained to bring the benefits of the new technology to those who could not afford them. The popular goal of the private city was a goal to make Philadelphia a moderately safe place for ordinary men and women to go about conducting their own business; the goal was never to help raise the level of living of the poor.

Notes

1. Quaker historians agree that the Holy Experiment died from materialism and secularization during the eighteenth century. Frederick B. Tolles, *Meeting House and Counting House* (Chapel Hill, 1948), 240–243; Sydney V. James, *A People Among Peoples* (Cambridge, 1963), 37–43, 211–215; and see the charges against his contemporaries in John Woolman, *The Journal of John Woolman* (F. B. Tolles, Introduction, New York, 1961).
2. Howard Mumford Jones, *O Strange New World* (New York, 1964), 194–272, treats with this tradition as a blend of Christian and classical ideas.
3. Philadelphia's experience in these years appears to have been part of a general national trend. Ernest S. Griffith, *Modern Development of City Government in the United Kingdom and the United States* (London, 1927), I, 3–29.
4. The history of the municipal corporation is taken from Edward P. Allinson and Boies Penrose, *City Government of Philadelphia* (Johns Hopkins Studies in Historical and Political Science, Fifth Series, I–11, Baltimore, 1887), 33–61; J. Thomas Scharf and Thompson Westcott, *History of Philadelphia 1606–1884* (Philadelphia, 1884), III, 1703, 1737, 1936.
5. Eli K. Price, *The History of the Consolidation of the City of Philadelphia* (Philadelphia, 1873), 82–89. Compare with Lincoln Steffens, "Philadelphia: Corrupt and Contented," *The Shame of Cities* (New York, 1904, 1957 ed.), 134–161.
6. Public water supplies were established in Philadelphia in 1801, in New York in 1842, Boston 1848, Baltimore, a small private system in 1808, expanded in 1838, and a full public system in 1857.

7. The first U.S. Census returned 44,096 persons for Philadelphia, the Liberties, and South-wark. Therefore the population of the city on the eve of the plague must have been about 48,000. The epidemic is recounted in detail in John H. Powell, *Bring Out Your Dead: The Great Plague of Yellow Fever in Philadelphia in 1793* (Philadelphia, 1949).

8. [Benjamin] Latrobe noted the seepage of wastes through the Philadelphia sand in his journal. Talbot Hamlin, *Benjamin Henry Latrobe* (New York, 1955), 157.

9. Hamlin, Latrobe, 134–135, 157–167; John A. Kouwenhoven, *Made in America* (New York, 1948), 41.

10. For the narrative of the Philadelphia waterworks I have relied on Nelson M. Blake, *Water for the Cities* (Syracuse, 1956), Ch. II, V.

11. There is some evidence that the Philadelphia waterworks may be a case of provincial technological backwardness caused by the imperfect communication of engineering technique in the Atlantic world. W. H. Chaloner, "John Wilkinson, Ironmaster," *History Today,* I (May, 1951), 67, reports shipments of cast iron water pipe from England to Paris in 1780–1781 but does not indicate whether these pipes were for a Paris waterworks or for the Versailles fountain system. Whichever the case it would seem that French engineering and specifications would have saved Philadelphia the grief it experienced with faulty hydrants and fittings. The changeover to cast iron pipe went slowly. Scharf and Westcott claim replacement did not begin until 1818 and that in 1822 there were still thirty-two miles of wooden pipe in the city, *History of Philadelphia,* I, 605.

12. Commissioners of Fairmount Park, *First Annual Report* (Philadelphia, 1869), 6–12; George B. Tatum, "The Origins of Fairmount Park," *Antiques* LXXXII (November, 1962), 502–507.

13. Today planners struggle with the identical problem which faced the Philadelphia Watering Committee. How much extra capacity should be built into the works in the case when capital is in short supply and a city is growing at an indeterminate pace? The size of the Fairmount works, and hence the amount of extra capacity for the entire system, was set by a combination of engineering considerations and prior private property rights. The design of the dam and its wheels followed the plans of an English engineer who had formerly built mills along the nearby Brandywine River. He estimated the possible height of the dam and hence the available power at the site on the basis of contemporary rules of thumb. To guard against an underestimate on his part of the efficiency of the pumps, the Watering Committee purchased additional upstream riparian rights so that the height of the dam could be raised to carry its lake to the Manayunk mills upstream. No further height was possible since to purchase the Manayunk mill rights would have been enormously expensive. Thus the efficiency of the overshot wheels at the Fairmount Dam and the presence of the Manayunk mills determined the capacity of the Philadelphia system for the next thirty years. Thomas Gilpin, "Fairmount Dam and Waterworks, Philadelphia," *Pennsylvania Magazine* XXXVII (October, 1913), 471–479; Select and Common Councils of Philadelphia, *Report of the Watering Committee on the Propriety of Raising the Dam at Fair Mount* (Philadelphia, 1820), 4–6.

14. A great enthusiasm for bathing seized the public at this moment and even suggested to an editorial writer that public bathhouses would improve the moral habits of the poor by lessening the jealousy between classes. *Public Ledger,* July 10, 1838. Purity of the water had not been entirely satisfactory. The same paper complained that the hydrant system meant impure water. It reported an "animal, like a centipede," in a glass of hydrant water. *Public Ledger,* October 6, 1836.

15. Philadelphia Bureau of Water, *Description of the Filtration Works and History of Water Supply 1789–1900* (Philadelphia, 1909), 3–4, 50–51, 70–71; City of Philadelphia, *Third Annual Message of Mayor Harry A. Mackey* (Philadelphia, 1931), 388; Blake, *Water for the Cities,* 97–98, 255–256, 259–261.

6

Richard C. Wade

THE URBAN FRONTIER

Part of Philadelphia's appeal to towndwellers was its leadership among the nation's cities, for nearly every young metropolis . . . coveted a similar primacy in the West. Indeed, one of the most striking characteristics of this period was the development of an urban imperialism which saw rising young giants seek to spread their power and influence over the entire new country. The drive for supremacy, furthermore, was quite conscious, infusing an extraordinary dynamic into city growth, but also breeding bitter rivalries among the claimants. In the ensuing struggles, the economically strongest survived and flourished, while the less successful fell behind. Smaller places were trampled in the process, some being swallowed up by ambitious neighbors, others being overwhelmed before they could attain a challenging position. The contest, however, produced no final victor. In fact, the lead changed three times, and though Cincinnati commanded the field in 1830, Pittsburgh, Louisville, and St. Louis were still in the running.

The rivalries developed very early. Lexington jumped off to a quick start, but by 1810 Pittsburgh, enjoying a commercial and manufacturing boom, forged ahead. The postwar depression undermined its leadership, however, and Cincinnati moved forward to take its place. The fierce competition led to widespread speculation about the outcome. Most of the prophecy was wishful, stemming from the hopes of boosters and involving doubtful calculations. In 1816, for instance, a Pittsburgher summed up many of the elements of this competition in a chart (with ratings presumably on a scale of excellence from one to ten) designed to illustrate the inevitability of the Iron City's supremacy:[1]

	Pittsburgh	Lexington	Cincinnati
Situation for inland trade and navigation	9	2	6
Adaptness for manufacturers	9	3	5
Fertility of surrounding soil	2	7	4
Salubrity	9	7	5
Pleasantness and beauty	.3	1	.6
Elegance of scite [sic] and environs	1	.3	.6
	30.3	20.3	21.2

Reprinted by permission of the publisher from *The Urban Frontier: The Rise of Western Cities*, by Richard C. Wade. Cambridge, Mass.: Harvard University Press. Copyright © 1959 by the President of the Fellows of Harvard College.

Not only did the author work out the estimates in scientific detail, but he also predicted that the totals represented the population (in thousands) which each would reach in 1830.

Before a city could hope to enter the urban sweepstake for the largest prize, it had to eliminate whatever rivals arose in its own area. In many instances the odds in these battles were so uneven that smaller places gave in quickly. In others, a decision came only after a bitter and prolonged struggle. Edwardsville, Illinois, fell easily before St. Louis, but Wheeling's submission to Pittsburgh followed a decade of acrimony. Sometimes defeat meant the end of independence for a town. Louisville, for example, ultimately annexed Shippingport and Portland, while Pittsburgh reached across the river to take in Allegheny. In other cases, the penalty for failure was the lessening of power and prestige. Steubenville and Wheeling, unable to sustain their position against Pittsburgh in the Upper Ohio, had to settle for a much reduced pace of development. The same fate befell Ste. Genevieve, an early challenger of St. Louis's domination of the Mississippi and Missouri. Occasionally a victor reduced its competitor to a mere economic appendage. This is what happened to Jeffersonville and New Albany, Indiana, after Louisville captured the trade of the Falls.

Though struggles for regional primacy characterized the urban growth of the entire West, the most celebrated was Pittsburgh's duel with Wheeling. Both were situated on the Ohio and both hoped to capture its flourishing commerce. Wheeling's great advantage lay in its down-river position, where it outflanked the shoals and rapids which dominated the approach to Pittsburgh. During the late summer, low water made navigation difficult and at times impossible, inducing some merchants to use the Virginia town as a transshipment point to the East. This fact alone made Wheeling a competitor, for in no other department could it match the Iron City. Pittsburgh's detractors saw this situation as early as 1793, when the Army considered establishing a post at Wheeling. Isaac Craig complained that "this new arrangement, . . . has Originated in the Brain of the Gentlemen in Washington who envy Pittsburgh, and . . . have represented to General Knox, that Navigation is practicable from Wheeling in the dry season."[2] The same consideration made Wheeling a stop in the mail route to the West and the Ohio River terminus of the National Road.

Despite these advantages, Wheeling's population barely reached 1,000 by 1815, while Pittsburgh had become the new country's leading metropolis. A serious rivalry seemed almost ridiculous. But the postwar depression, felling the Iron City, gave its smaller neighbor the hope of rising on the ruins. This prospect brightened in 1816, when, after many abortive attempts to change the terminus, the National Road was completed to Wheeling. Optimism about the town's future abounded throughout the valley. A Steubenville editor caught the spirit in verse:

Wheeling has secured her roads,
Come waggoners, come and bring your loads.
Emigrants, come hither, and build a town,
And make Wheeling a place of renown.

By 1822, 5,000 wagons were arriving annually in the booming settlement. "Wheeling is a thriving place," a traveler observed; "it bids fair to rival Pittsburgh in the trade of the Western country."[3]

The Iron City, troubled by a stagnant economy and worried about its future, warily watched the progress of this upstart. Actually, Wheeling's challenge was only a small part of Pittsburgh's total problem, but its very ludicrousness made the situation all the more intolerable. "A miserable Virginia country town, which can never be more than two hundred yards wide, having the mere advantage of a free turnpike road and a warehouse or two, to become rivals of this *Emporium* of the West!" exclaimed the incredulous editor of the *Statesman*. As Wheeling continued to prosper, Pittsburgh accused its competitor of unfair practices, particularly of circulating the rumor that ships could not go up the river to "the Point." "They have taken to lying," the *Statesman* snapped. "We cannot believe this report," the *Gazette* asserted with more charity; "the citizens with whom we are acquainted in that place, are too honorable to countenance such childish, hurtless falsehood," especially since "everybody acquainted with the river knows that the water is as good if not better above than for 100 miles below."[4]

Civic leaders in Wheeling, feeling their oats and certain that the National Road provided a secure base for unlimited growth, continually goaded the stricken giant. "Strange that a 'miserable Virginia Country Town,' a 'mere village,' should have attracted so much attention at the 'emporium of the West,'" the *Northwestern Gazette* observed. Moreover, it asserted that the difficulty of navigation on the Upper Ohio was not mere rumor. "During the drier part of the season the greater part of the Western Merchants order their goods to Wheeling and *not* to Pittsburgh. This fact is a stubborn and decisive one. It speaks volumes. It is a demonstration." A patronizing condescension expressed an increasing confidence. "Pittsburgh may, if she will, be a large and respectable manufacturing town. She may also retain a portion of the carrying trade," the same source graciously conceded. There seemed no limit to Wheeling's assurance. Travelers reported that its residents were "actually doing nothing but walking about on stilts, and stroking their chins with utmost self-complacency. Every man who is so fortunate as to own about 60 feet front and 120 feet back, considers himself . . . snug."[5]

The next few years demonstrated, however, that history was only teasing. Wheeling's hopes for greatness were soon dashed. The National Road proved disappointing as a freight carrier, and Pittsburgh recovered from its depression, once again becoming the urban focus of the Upper Ohio. Though the Virginia town could boast over 5,000 inhabitants in 1830, its rate of growth lagged and its future prospects dimmed. To some shrewd observers the outcome was not unexpected. A Steubenville editor, consoling his readers in 1816 after their efforts to get the National Road had failed, asserted that cities could not be reared on mere highway traffic. "Rely on agriculture and manufactures," he counseled, "and you will do well without the mail or the turnpike bubble—it is not the sound of the coachman's horn that will make a town flourish."[6]

Though Pittsburgh beat back Wheeling's challenge, it could not maintain its Western leadership. Cincinnati, less affected by the postwar collapse, surged by the Iron City and established its primacy throughout the new country. It was not content, however, to win its supremacy by another's injury. Rather it developed its own positive program to widen its commercial opportunities and spread its influence. In fact, the city was so alive with ideas that one visitor referred to it as "that hot bed of projects," and another observed "great plans on foot; whenever two or three meet at a corner nothing is heard but schemes." In broad terms the object of Cincinnati's statesmanship was threefold: to tap the growing trade on the Great Lakes by water links to the Ohio, to facilitate traffic on the river by a canal around the Falls, and to reach into the hinterland with improved roads. Later another canal—this time down the Licking "into the heart of Kentucky"—a bridge across the Ohio, and a railway to Lexington were added.[7] Success would have made the entire valley dependent upon this urban center, and given the Ohio metropolis command of the strategic routes of trade and travel.

This ambitious program caused great concern in Pittsburgh. "We honestly confess," the *Gazette* admitted, that "a canal from the lakes either into the Ohio or the Great Miami . . . adds another item to the amount of our present uneasiness." By tipping the commerce of the valley northward, Cincinnati would substantially reduce the Iron City's importance as the central station between East and West. "Without this trade," the *Statesman* warned, "what can Philadelphia and Pittsburgh become but deserted villages, compared with their great rivals?"[8] Pennsylvania responded to this threat by improving the turnpike between its urban centers and ultimately constructing an elaborate canal across the mountains. In addition, Pittsburgh proposed to head off Cincinnati by building a water route to Lake Erie or tying into the Ohio system below Cleveland.

The challenge to Cincinnati's supremacy, however, came not only from a resurgent Pittsburgh, but also from a booming downriver neighbor, Louisville. As early as 1819 a visitor noted this two-front war. "I discovered two ruling passions in Cincinnati; enmity against Pittsburgh and jealousy of Louisville." In one regard the Falls City was the more serious rival, because as a commercial center it competed directly with the Ohio emporium. In fact, guerilla warfare between the two towns for advantage in the rural market began early in the century.[9] But the great object of contention was the control and traffic on the river—the West's central commercial artery.

In this contest Louisville held one key advantage. Its strategic position at the Falls gave it command of both parts of the Ohio. All passengers and goods had to pass through the town, except during the few months of high water when even large vessels could move safely over the rapids. It was a clumsy system, and from the earliest days many people envisaged a canal around the chutes. Nothing came of these plans until the coming of the steamboat immensely expanded traffic and made the interruption seem intolerable. Though nearly every shipper favored a canal, it was not until Cincinnati, anxious both to loosen river commerce and weaken a rival city, put its weight behind the improvement that any real activity developed.

Cincinnati had a deep stake in this project. A canal would not only aid the town generally but also advance the interests of some powerful groups. The mercantile community was anxious to get freer trade, and many residents had large investments in companies which hoped to dig on either the Kentucky or Indiana side of the Falls.[10] Others owned real estate in the area. William Lytle, for example, had large holdings around Portland of an estimated value of between $100,000 and $500,000.[11] Moreover, ordinary Cincinnatians had come to the conclusion that a canal would serve a broad public purpose. Hence in 1817 a town meeting was called to discuss the issue. An editor provided the backdrop: "No question was ever agitated here that involved more important consequences to this town." And from the beginning Louisville was cast as the villain of the piece. *Liberty Hall* referred to it as "a little town" trying to make "all the upper country tributary to it, by compelling us to deposit our goods in its warehouses and pay extravagant prices for transportation around or over the Falls."[12]

Since the Falls City could frustrate any project on Kentucky soil, Cincinnati's first move was to build on the opposite side. The Indiana legislature incorporated the Jeffersonville Ohio Canal Company in 1817, empowering it to sell 20,000 shares of stock at $50 apiece, and authorizing a lottery for $100,000 more. From the outset it was clear that the scheme stemmed from the Queen City. Not only did that town provide more than half the concern's directors, but also the campaign for funds emphasized its role. "The public may be assured that the wealth, influence, enterprise and talents of Cincinnati are at the head of this measure," *Liberty Hall* declared in 1818. Moreover, advocates underlined the stake of the Ohio metropolis, warning residents that if they did not support the drive they "deserved to be hewers of wood and drawers of water" for Louisville. In May 1819 a prominent Cincinnatian gave the ceremonial address as digging began on the Indiana side.[13]

Louisville hesitated to support any canal. The city had flourished on the transportation break, and many inhabitants felt that facilitating travel over the rapids would destroy the very *raison d'être* of the place. That view was probably extreme, but in the short run no one could deny that certain interests were jeopardized. "It must be admitted that the business of a portion of our population would be affected," the *Public Advertiser* confessed. "The storage and forwarding business would probably be diminished—and there might be less use for hacks and drays."[14] Tavern and hotel owners shared this anxiety, while the pilots who guided the ships through the chutes faced almost certain unemployment.

Unwilling to sacrifice these interests and uneasy about the town's future, Louisville leaders tried to deflect the mounting enthusiasm for a canal. Their first strategy was to suggest a small cut around the Falls which would accommodate keelboats and lesser craft. This expedient found few supporters, and Louisville next tried to reduce the pressure by paving the road to Portland and Shippingport, thus, facilitating the transshipment process.[15] But this, too, was inadequate, and within a few years the clamor for a canal became irresistible.

Yet the city still hoped to salvage something out of defeat, to find some compensation for the loss of its strategic position. In 1824 a local editor laid down the conditions. "It is true that we could feel but little interest in opening a canal merely for the purpose of navigation," he conceded. "A canal to be useful . . . should be constructed to give us ample water power, for various and extensive manufacturing establishments; and a sufficient number of dry docks for the building and . . . repair of nearly all the steamboats employed on western waters, should be constructed as necessary appendages." If the project included these items, he declared, then "the citizens of Louisville will be found among its most zealous advocates."[16]

The Falls City could afford to take its pound of flesh, because building on the Indiana side was much less feasible than the Kentucky route. The engineering problems were immensely more complicated, and the cost was nearly three times as great. In 1819 an official committee, comprised of delegates from Virginia, Pennsylvania, Ohio, and Kentucky, estimated the expense of the northern plan at $1,100,000 and the southern one at $350,000.[17] Hence few people acquainted with the situation took seriously the Jeffersonville Ohio Canal Company's enterprise. Yet the disadvantages of the Indiana route were not insurmountable, and Louisvillians realized that in the long run the Falls would be skirted on one side or the other. If they dragged their feet too much, their opponents would press for action regardless of the cost or difficulty. This possibility ultimately brought the Kentucky emporium to its knees.[18]

While Louisville reluctantly yielded at the Falls, Cincinnati pursued the rest of its expansion program. By 1822 the Miami Canal to Dayton was open, and work had begun on the state system which ultimately connected the Great Lakes with the Ohio River. Though the Queen City could claim less success in the Kentucky area, its economic supremacy in the West was not questioned. The new country's largest urban center, it had corralled the bulk of the region's mounting commerce and become the nexus of trade lines that reached from the Atlantic Ocean to the Gulf of Mexico.

Cincinnati's economic primacy, however, did not yet carry with it cultural leadership. This honor still belonged to Lexington, whose polish and sophistication were the envy of every transmontane town. "Cincinnati may be the Tyre, but Lexington is unquestionably the Athens of the West," *Liberty Hall* conceded in 1820. This admission reflected a sense of inadequacy which constantly shadowed the Queen City and compromised its claim to total supremacy. One resident suggested an ambitious lecture program to overcome the deficiency and "convince those persons at a distance who pronounce us as a *Commercial* people alone, that we have here, both the *Tyre* and the *Athens* of the West." Another observer, though not armed with a remedy, made the same point. "It may be well for us," he counseled, "when we can catch a moment from the grovelling pursuits of commercial operations, to cull and admire the varied sweets of those literary and scientific effusions, which have stamped Lexington as the headquarters of *Science and Letters* in the Western country."[19]

The establishment and success of Transylvania University [in Lexington] aggravated this inferiority complex. Not only did it lend prestige to another place, but it also lured local youths to its classrooms. The *Western Spy* admitted that it was "particularly mortifying to see the College of a neighboring state attract both Students and Professors" from the Ohio metropolis. In the early twenties Cincinnati countered with a medical school which it hoped would become a "powerful rival" and "ultimately go beyond" the Kentucky institution.[20] But it was not until financial difficulties and fire brought down Transylvania that the Queen City could claim cultural parity with its Blue Grass rival.

Lexington's position also bred jealousy in Louisville. Though the larger and more prosperous of the two by 1825, the Falls City had to concede that intellectual primacy rested with its Kentucky neighbor. This admission was not easy to make, because the two towns had been bitter foes for many years. They contended for political leadership in the state; earlier, in fact, each had hoped to become its capital. Moreover, their economic interests often collided, with Lexington depending upon manufacturing and protection and Louisville emphasizing commerce and wanting freer trade. Neither yielded readily to the other on any issue. Yet the cultural leadership of the Blue Grass town was too obvious to be denied, and, from the Falls City viewpoint, it was certainly too important to be permanently surrendered.

There was, however, something of a family quarrel about this rivalry. Despite their differences, both professed love for mother Kentucky, and occasionally one deferred to the other out of filial pride. In 1820, for example, Louisville's *Public Advertiser* supported state aid to Transylvania, explaining that "distinguished institutions of learning in our own state, where education from its cheapness, shall be within the reach of the poor, is the *pivot* on which the grandeur of the state depends." In addition, the Falls City stood to gain by its success. "Louisville cannot be jealous of Lexington," the same newspaper declared; "her future interest is measurably blended with that of Transylvania University; for as that flourishes Lexington will become a more extensive and important customer to her in a commercial point of view." Likewise, when Lexington tried to get money for a hospital, its old foe offered support, but for perhaps less elevated reasons. If the Blue Grass got such an institution, "one of the same kind at this place cannot, consistently, be refused," the editor observed.[21]

And nothing forced the two to discover common interests more quickly than the appearance of a hostile outsider. When Cincinnati planned a medical school to compete with Transylvania, Louisville stood behind the testimony of the university, whose spokesman urged the state to give additional money to the institution. Otherwise, he warned, "in the struggle that must ensue, we of Transylvania will be compelled to enter the lists naked and defenceless, our opponents of Cincinnati being . . . armed. The issue of such a conflict cannot be doubted. We shall certainly be vanquished and your young men will . . . repair to the eastern schools for medical education, or Kentucky must become tributary to the state of Ohio."[22] Lexington reciprocated when the Queen City threatened a canal on the Indiana side of the river.

Kind words were few, however, and mutual aid sporadic. Usually the two communities did little to conceal their animosity. In fact, Louisville had no sooner supported Transylvania's expansion than it began again its vicious barrage on the school and its town. The attack stemmed from a mixture of political, economic, and urban motives, but it centered on the university because it was at once the symbol of Lexington's importance and its most vulnerable spot. The city's economy never recovered from the postwar depression and only its cultural renaissance kept stores and shops open. If the college failed, all failed. This was understood in the Falls City. Indeed, the *Public Advertiser* noted that the "ablest and best citizens" of the Blue Grass metropolis had tried to give a "new impetus" to the place by the encouragement of its "literary establishments."[23] Knowingly, then, Louisville struck at Lexington where it would hurt most.

Nor was there anything gentle about the tactics. In 1816, during the first debate over state assistance to Transylvania, John Rowan from the Falls City argued that the institution ought to be moved elsewhere to keep it from "improper influence" and the "many means of corrupting the morals of youth," which existed in the town. Four years later the criticism had become more barbed. "If you wish to jeopardize every amiable trait in the private character of your son, send him to Lexington," the *Public Advertiser* contended, linking the college to radical politics. "If you wish him to become a Robespierre or a Murat, send him to Lexington to learn the rudiments of Jacobinism and disorganization." By 1829 a Louisville editor was warning parents that at the university their children would be "surrounded by political desperadoes" and that "the very atmosphere of the place has been calculated to pollute the morals and principles of the youth attending it."[24]

Lexington, though an old veteran of urban rivalries, had not anticipated this bitterness. "We thought of all our institutions, it was the pride and boast of the town; and the least calculated to excite the envy, and stir up the opposition of any individual or section of the country." But the assault threatened the city's very life, and it fought back. The defense was generally constructive, detailing the achievements of Transylvania and extolling its influence on students and the new country. Graduates wrote testimonials and local citizens publicized the healthfulness and "literary atmosphere" of the community, while officials dispelled rumors about the snobbery of the college.[25]

The case was good, but Lexington strategists bungled in several respects. In 1829 not a single Jacksonian was appointed to the Board of Trustees, and not enough was done to quiet the uneasiness of either the farmers or the highly religious.[26] As a result, when Transylvania needed support most, it was almost friendless. By 1830 the campaign instituted by Louisville had destroyed Kentucky's brightest ornament and pulled the most substantial prop from Lexington's economy.

Even before Transylvania's demise Lexington felt itself slipping economically, and it tried to steady itself by better connections with the trade of the Ohio River. Canals and roads proved either impractical or inadequate, and in 1829 civic leaders planned a railroad. The act of incorporation in the next year left the northern terminus undecided, with the understanding that it would be either Louisville or Cincinnati. The uncertainty set off a curious kind of competition between those two cities. Neither could foresee the impact that a railroad might have on its own importance, yet they equally feared that it would give their rival a substantial advantage.

Louisville was especially wary. This looked like the canal issue in another form, and many people thought it wise to wait for the results of the first project. Moreover, some of the same local interests seemed to be threatened. The hack and dray owners protested that their $125,000 business would be jeopardized. And since the railroad would pass through the city and continue on to Portland, others feared the growth of a "rival town" on the western end of the Falls. The city council, walking gingerly because of this opposition, appointed a committee to look into the question, and called a public hearing to sound out local opinion. The meeting attracted over three hundred people, and after a lively debate, it voted to keep the tracks out of Louisville.[27]

Very quickly, however, civic leaders realized that any alternative terminus was more perilous to the Falls City than the possible dislocations occasioned by accepting the railroad. Thus "S" wrote that if "we are to have a rival town, the nearer to us the less dangerous," and a "Gentleman in Lexington" warned that its "great rival, Cincinnati," was "straining every nerve" to induce the company to build in that direction. By December 1830 the tide had turned, and the council invited the Lexington and Ohio Railroad to come to Louisville.[28]

Cincinnati, despite its official policy, had many qualms about a railroad from Lexington. "Why should the citizens of Cincinnati be so anxious to create a rival town across the river?" asked the editor of the *Advertiser.* Yet the same logic which drove Louisville to change its mind sustained the Queen City's original decision. On December 7, 1830, a public meeting declared that the project "would conduce to the prosperity of this city, in an eminent degree," and a committee of prominent civic leaders invited the company's directors to come to Cincinnati to discuss details.[29] These events, coupled with Louisville's acceptance, brought great rejoicing to Lexington, for it now looked as though the railroad would bring it a share of the Ohio's commerce and arrest at last the economic decay which had brought the "Athens of the West" to the very brink of disaster.

The struggle for primacy and power—and occasionally survival—was one of the most persistent and striking characteristics of the early urban history of the West. Like imperial states, cities carved out extensive dependencies, extended their influence over the economic and political life of the hinterland, and fought with contending places over strategic trade routes. Nor was the contest limited to the young giants, for smaller towns joined the scramble. Cleveland and Sandusky, for example, clashed over the location of the northern terminus of the Ohio canal, the stakes being nothing less than the burgeoning commerce between the river and the lakes. And their instinct to fight was sound, for the outcome shaped the future of both.

Like most imperialisms, the struggle among Western cities left a record of damage and achievement. It trampled new villages, smothered promising towns, and even brought down established metropolises. Conflicting ambitions infused increasing bitterness into the intercourse of rivals, and made suspicion, jealousy, and vindictiveness a normal part of urban relationships. Yet competition also brought rapid expansion. The fear of failure was a dynamic force, pushing civic leaders into improvements long before they thought them necessary. The constant search for new markets furnished an invaluable stimulus to commercial and industrial enterprise. And, at its best, urban imperialism bred a strong pride in community accomplishment. As one resident put it, "there exists in our city a spirit . . . which may render any man proud to being called a Cincinnatian."[30]

Notes

1. *Pittsburgh Mercury,* February 3, 1816.
2. I. Craig to J. O'Hara, June 15, 1793, MS, Isaac Craig Papers, Carnegie Library of Pittsburgh.
3. C. B. Smith, "The Terminus of the Cumberland Road on the Ohio River" (M.A. Thesis, University of Pittsburgh, 1951), 69; *Western Herald* (Steubenville), April 12, 1816; Smith, "Cumberland Road," 71; Woods, *Illinois Country,* 75.
4. *Pittsburgh Statesman,* June 2, 1821; *Pittsburgh Gazette,* May 4, 1821.
5. *Northwestern Gazette* (Wheeling), June 16, 1821; *Pittsburgh Gazette,* December 18, 1818.
6. Smith, "Cumberland Road," 69; *Western Herald* (Steubenville), September 20, 1816.
7. *Pittsburgh Gazette,* January 22, 1819; February 5, 1819; *Liberty Hall* (Cincinnati), January 21, 1823; November 25, 1825.
8. *Pittsburgh Gazette,* January 22, 1819; *Pittsburgh Statesman,* November 26, 1818.
9. *Pittsburgh Gazette,* February 5, 1819; *Louisville Public Advertiser,* June 21, 1820.
10. For example, see the account of the Ohio Canal Company in *Liberty Hall* (Cincinnati), March 24, 1817.
11. The William Lytle Collection in the Historical and Philosophical Society of Ohio library includes a series of letters which explain his stake in the canal. He owned most of the land in the Portland area through which the canal ultimately passed. For a statement of its value, see D. McClellan to W. Lytle, October 21, 1817, Lytle Collection.
12. *Liberty Hall* (Cincinnati), December 29, 1817; March 26, 1817.
13. *Liberty Hall* (Cincinnati), June 5, 1818; February 26, 1818; May 20, 1818; May 6, 1818; May 14, 1819.
14. *Louisville Public Advertiser,* February 7, 1824.
15. *Liberty Hall* (Cincinnati), March 18, 1816; *Louisville Public Advertiser,* October 16, 1819.
16. *Louisville Public Advertiser,* January 21, 1824.
17. *Louisville Public Advertiser,* November 17, 1819.
18. *Louisville Public Advertiser,* February 7, 1824.
19. *Liberty Hall* (Cincinnati), May 27, 1820; December 17, 1819; May 27, 1820.
20. *Western Spy* (Cincinnati), October 13, 1817; *Liberty Hall* (Cincinnati), January 14, 1823.
21. *Louisville Public Advertiser,* September 20, 1820; September 27, 1820; December 20, 1820.
22. *Louisville Public Advertiser,* November 27, 1820.
23. *Louisville Public Advertiser,* August 23, 1820.
24. *Kentucky Reporter,* February 14, 1816; *Louisville Public Advertiser,* September 9, 1820; October 13, 1829.
25. *Kentucky Reporter,* March 7, 1827; March 10, 1823; February 21, 1827; September 8, 1828.
26. For these problems see, for example, *Louisville Public Advertiser,* October 29, 1829.
27. *Louisville Public Advertiser,* December 8, 1830; November 2, 1830; Louisville, City Journal, October 20, 1830; October 29, 1830; *Louisville Public Advertiser,* November 4, 1830.
28. *Louisville Public Advertiser,* November 3, 1830; November 5, 1830; Louisville, City Journal, December 3, 1830.
29. *Cincinnati Advertiser,* December 11, 1830; *Liberty Hall* (Cincinnati), December 10, 1830.
30. *Liberty Hall* (Cincinnati), January 9, 1829.

Chapter 3

❖❖❖

THE MACHINE POLITICS

The Politics of Clientelism

By the late nineteenth century, a machine system of politics that relied on ethnic solidarity and the distribution of material benefits became the dominant mode of governance in most larger American cities. Machine organizations came together as alliances among politicians from the ethnic wards. Individual politicians could deliver the vote because they had come to know their constituents as friends and neighbors. By cooperating with one another, each of these entrepreneur–politicians could gain control of the levers of power that cities work. But the ethnic voters comprised only the electoral portion of the system. Machine politicians made themselves useful to business by exacting payoffs in exchange for a host of favors ranging from business licenses to construction contracts to monopoly control over streetcars and utilities. Whether the system added up to constituency service or graft and corruption depended on the eye of the beholder.

This style of politics is colorfully rendered in the reading by William L. Riordan about George Washington Plunkett, who climbed out of poverty to become a millionaire during his forty years of service as a Tammany boss in New York City. Note that Plunkett's secret for political success did not depend on winning the minds or appealing to the ideals of the voters, but in gaining the voters' loyalty through petty favors or, when necessary, giving them jobs. Conveying lovable cynicism, Plunkett even saw how it was possible to convert treats to little children into votes on election day!

The United States stands virtually alone among Western industrial democracies in producing machine-style politics. Why did such organizations arise in American cities? Who really benefitted?

The classic answer was formulated by Robert K. Merton decades ago. He asserts that the machines were "functional" in the sense that they satisfied compelling social needs that official governmental institutions neglected. He further argued that the functions that the machines performed were not always obvious because they were "latent" (or unintended) outcomes of the way the machines operated. Merton believed that the machine's ability to centralize power informally served as an antidote to the constitutional dispersal of power that made governing cities difficult. The machine also humanized and personalized assistance to the needy—particularly to immigrants who liked the no-questions-asked help of the ward boss to the impersonal, professional, and frequently paternalistic assistance offered by charity organization workers, who generally disdained the immigrant's ethnicity and religion. The machines also offered businesses, including illicit businesses, with the privileges they needed to survive. Finally, the machines offered the opportunity for upward mobility to many immigrants who found that job discrimination in the private sector limited their prospects.

Over the years, this functionalist explanation of the machine has been challenged by many urban scholars. The selection by Steven Erie questions the idea that the machine provided an important route to social mobility. Even though many machines were dominated by Irish politicians who favored Irish constituents in their distribution of jobs, contracts and other rewards, Erie suggests that the machines actually retarded the upward mobility of Irish-Americans as a group. Party bosses were inclined to spread patronage as thinly as possible as a way to maximize the size of their electoral coalition. This logic lead them to create a multitude of blue-collar and poorly paid public jobs that had no future. To get ahead, an Irish worker was better advised to seek employment in the private sector. Erie also believes that entrenched machine politicians did little to facilitate economic assimilation among southern and eastern Europeans. He points out that in cities where Irish bosses had secure power bases, they found it more advantageous to exclude these newer immigrant groups from voting and participation in the machine to preserve Irish domination. The newer immigrants were incorporated into the machines only in the cases in which exclusionary strategies no longer worked. Erie thinks that the lessons of the Irish machines should give pause to many of today's minority politicians who might believe that a strategy of ethnic group politics—at least if it operates through material inducements—offers their constituents an effective means of political advancement.

7

William L. Riordon

"TO HOLD YOUR DISTRICT: STUDY HUMAN NATURE AND ACT ACCORDIN'"

There's only one way to hold a district: you must study human nature and act accordin'. You can't study human nature in books. Books is a hindrance more than anything else. If you have been to college, so much the worse for you.

In this selection, Riordon is interviewing Plunkitt—Ed.

"To Hold Your District: Study Human Nature and Act Accordin'," from *Plunkitt of Tammany Hall* by William L. Riordon, introduction by Arthur Mann. Copyright © 1963 by E. P. Dutton and Co., Inc., renewed 1991 by Penguin Books USA, Inc. Used by permission of Dutton Signet, a division of Penguin Books USA, Inc.

You'll have to unlearn all you learned before you can get right down to human nature, and unlearnin' takes a lot of time. Some men can never forget what they learned at college. Such men may get to be district leaders by a fluke, but they never last.

To learn real human nature you have to go among the people, see them and be seen. I know every man, woman, and child in the Fifteenth District, except them that's been born this summer—and I know some of them, too. I know what they like and what they don't like, what they are strong at and what they are weak in, and I reach them by approachin' at the right side.

For instance, here's how I gather in the young men. I hear of a young feller that's proud of his voice, thinks that he can sing fine. I ask him to come around to Washington Hall and join our Glee Club. He comes and sings, and he's a follower of Plunkitt for life. Another young feller gains a reputation as a baseball player in a vacant lot. I bring him into our baseball club. That fixes him. You'll find him workin' for my ticket at the polls next election day. Then there's the feller that likes rowin' on the river, the young feller that makes a name as a waltzer on his block, the young feller that's handy with his dukes—I rope them all in by givin' them opportunities to show themselves off. I don't trouble them with political arguments. I just study human nature and act accordin'.

But you may say this game won't work with the hightoned fellers, the fellers that go through college and then join the Citizens' Union. Of course it wouldn't work. I have a special treatment for them. I ain't like the patent medicine man that gives the same medicine for all diseases. The Citizens' Union kind of a young man! I love him! He's the daintiest morsel of the lot, and he don't often escape me.

Before telling you how I catch him, let me mention that before the election last year, the Citizens' Union said they had four hundred or five hundred enrolled voters in my district. They had a lovely headquarters, too, beautiful roll top desks and the cutest rugs in the world. If I was accused of havin' contributed to fix up the nest for them, I wouldn't deny it under oath. What do I mean by that? Never mind. You can guess from the sequel, if you're sharp.

Well, election day came. The Citizens' Union's candidate for Senator, who ran against me, just polled five votes in the district, while I polled something more than 14,000 votes. What became of the 400 or 500 Citizens' Union enrolled voters in my district? Some people guessed that many of them were good Plunkitt men all along and worked with the Cits just to bring them into the Plunkitt camp by election day. You can guess that way, too, if you want to. I never contradict stories about me, especially in hot weather. I just call your attention to the fact that on last election day 395 Citizens' Union enrolled voters in my district were missin' and unaccounted for.

I tell you frankly, though, how I have captured some of the Citizens' Union's young men. I have a plan that never fails. I watch the City Record to see when there's civil service examinations for good things. Then I take my young Cit in hand, tell him all about the good thing and get him worked up till he goes and takes an examination. I don't bother about him any more. It's a cinch that he comes back to me in a few days and asks to join Tammany Hall. Come over to Washington Hall some night and I'll show you a list of names on our rolls marked "C.S." which means, "bucked up against civil service."

As to the older voters, I reach them, too. No, I don't send them campaign literature. That's rot. People can get all the political stuff they want to read—and a good deal more, too—in the papers. Who reads speeches, nowadays, anyhow? It's bad enough to listen to them. You ain't goin' to gain any votes by stuffin' the letter boxes with campaign documents. Like as not you'll lose votes, for there's nothin' a man hates more than to hear the letter carrier ring his bell and go to the letter box expectin' to find a letter he was lookin' for, and find only a lot of printed politics. I met a man this very mornin' who told me he voted the Democratic State ticket last year just because the Republicans kept crammin' his letter box with campaign documents.

What tells in holdin' your grip on your district is to go right down among the poor families and help them in the different ways they need help. I've got a regular system for this. If there's a fire in Ninth, Tenth, or Eleventh Avenue, for example, any hour of the day or night, I'm usually there with some of my election district captains as soon as the fire engines. If a family is burned out I don't ask whether they are Republicans or Democrats, and I don't refer them to the Charity Organization Society, which would investigate their case in a month or two and decide they were worthy of help about the time they are dead from starvation. I just get quarters for them, buy clothes for them if their clothes were burned up, and fix them up till they get things runnin' again. It's philanthropy, but it's politics, too—mighty good politics. Who can tell how many votes one of these fires bring me? The poor are the most grateful people in the world, and, let me tell you, they have more friends in their neighborhoods than the rich have in theirs.

If there's a family in my district in want I know it before the charitable societies do, and me and my men are first on the ground. I have a special corps to look up such cases. The consequence is that the poor look up to George W. Plunkitt as a father, come to him in trouble—and don't forget him on election day.

Another thing, I can always get a job for a deservin' man. I make it a point to keep on the track of jobs, and it seldom happens that I don't have a few up my sleeve ready for use. I know every big employer in the district and in the whole city, for that matter, and they ain't in the habit of sayin' no to me when I ask them for a job.

And the children—the little roses of the district! Do I forget them? Oh, no! They know me, every one of them, and they know that a sight of Uncle George and candy means the same thing. Some of them are the best kind of vote-getters. I'll tell you a case. Last year a little Eleventh Avenue rosebud, whose father is a Republican, caught hold of his whiskers on election day and said she wouldn't let go till he'd promise to vote for me. And she didn't.

8

Robert K. Merton

THE LATENT FUNCTIONS OF THE MACHINE

In large sectors of the American population, the political machine or the "political racket" are judged as unequivocally "bad" and "undesirable." The grounds for such moral judgment vary somewhat, but they consist substantially in pointing out that political machines violate moral codes: political patronage violates the code of selecting personnel on the basis of impersonal qualifications rather than on grounds of party loyalty or contributions to the party war-chest; bossism violates the code that votes should be based on individual appraisal of the qualifications of candidates and of political issues, and not on abiding loyalty to a feudal leader; bribery and "honest graft" obviously offend the proprieties of property; "protection" for crime clearly violates the law and the mores; and so on.

In view of these manifold respects in which political machines, in varying degrees, run counter to the mores and at times to the law, it becomes pertinent to inquire how they manage to continue in operation. The familiar "explanations" for the continuance of the political machine are not here in point. To be sure, it may well be that if "respectable citizenry" would carry through their political obligations, if the electorate were to be alert and enlightened; if the number of elective officers were substantially reduced from the dozens, even hundreds, which the average voter is now expected to appraise in the course of local, county, state and national elections, if the electorate were activated by the "wealthy and educated classes without whose participation," as the not-always democratically oriented [James] Bryce put it, "the best-framed government must speedily degenerate," if these and a plethora of similar changes in political structure were introduced, perhaps the "evils" of the political machine would indeed be exorcized. But it should be noted that these changes are not typically introduced, that political machines have the phoenix-like quality of arising strong and unspoiled from their ashes, that, in short, this structure exhibits a notable vitality in many areas of American political life.

Proceeding from the functional view, therefore, that we should *ordinarily* (not invariably) expect persistent social patterns and social structures to perform positive functions *which are at the same time not adequately fulfilled by other existing patterns and structures*, the thought occurs that perhaps this publicly maligned organization is, *under present conditions,* satisfying basic latent functions. A brief examination of current analyses of this type of structure may also serve to illustrate additional problems of functional analysis.

Some Functions of the Political Machine

Without presuming to enter into the variations of detail marking different political machines—a Tweed, Vare, Crump, Flynn, Hague are by no means identical types of bosses—we can briefly examine the functions more or less common to the political machine, as a generic type of social organization. We neither attempt to itemize all the diverse functions of the political machine nor imply that all these functions are similarly fulfilled by each and every machine.

The key structural function of the Boss is to organize, centralize and maintain in good working condition "the scattered fragments of power" which are at present dispersed through our political organization. By this centralized organization of political power, the boss and his apparatus can satisfy the needs of diverse subgroups in the larger community which are not adequately satisfied by legally devised and culturally approved social structures.

To understand the role of bossism and the machine, therefore, we must look at two types of sociological variables: (1) the *structural context* which makes it difficult, if not impossible, for morally approved structures to fulfill essential social functions, thus leaving the door open for political machines (or their structural equivalents) to fulfill these functions and (2) the subgroups whose distinctive needs are left unsatisfied, except for the latent functions which the machine in fact fulfills.

Structural Context

The constitutional framework of American political organization specifically precludes the legal possibility of highly centralized power and, it has been noted, thus "discourages the growth of effective and responsible leadership. The framers of the Constitution, as Woodrow Wilson observed, set up the check and balance system 'to keep government at a sort of mechanical equipoise by means of a standing amicable contest among its several organic parts.' They distrusted power as dangerous to liberty: and therefore they spread it thin and erected barriers against its concentration." This dispersion of power is found not only at the national level but in local areas as well. "As a consequence," Sait goes on to observe, "when *the people or particular groups* among them demanded positive action, no one had adequate authority to act. The machine provided an antidote."[1]

The constitutional dispersion of power not only makes for difficulty of effective decision and action but when action does occur it is defined and hemmed in by legalistic considerations. In consequence, there develops "a much *more human system* of partisan government, whose chief object soon became the circumvention of government by law. . . . The lawlessness of the extra-official democracy was merely the counterpoise of the legalism of the official democracy. The lawyer having been permitted to subordinate democracy to the Law, the Boss had to be called in to extricate the victim, which he did after a fashion and for a consideration."[2]

Officially, political power is dispersed. Various well-known expedients were devised for this manifest objective. Not only was there the familiar separation of powers among the several branches of the government but, in some measure, tenure in each office was limited, rotation in office approved. And the scope of power inherent in each office was severely circumscribed. Yet, observes Sait in rigorously functional terms, "Leadership is necessary; and *since* it does not develop readily within the constitutional framework, the Boss provides it in a crude and irresponsible form from the outside."[3]

Put in more generalized terms, *the functional deficiencies of the official structure generate an alternative (unofficial) structure to fulfill existing needs somewhat more effectively.* Whatever its specific historical origins, the political machine persists as an apparatus for satisfying otherwise unfulfilled needs of diverse groups in the population. By turning to a few of these subgroups and their characteristic needs, we shall be led at once to a range of latent functions of the political machine.

Functions of the Political Machine for Diverse Subgroups

It is well known that one source of strength of the political machine derives from its roots in the local community and the neighborhood. The political machine does not regard the electorate as a vague, undifferentiated mass of voters. With a keen sociological intuition, the machine recognizes that the voter is primarily a man living in a specific neighborhood, with specific personal problems and personal wants. Public issues are abstract and remote; private problems are extremely concrete and immediate. It is not through the generalized appeal to large public concerns that the machine operates, but through the direct, quasi-feudal relationships between local representatives of the machine and voters in their neighborhood. Elections are won in the precinct.

The machine welds its link with ordinary men and women by elaborate networks of personal relations. Politics is transformed into personal ties. The precinct captain "must be a friend to every man, assuming if he does not feel sympathy with the unfortunate, and utilizing in his good works the resources which the boss puts at his disposal."[4] The precinct captain is forever a friend in need. In our prevailingly impersonal society, the machine, through its local agents, fulfills the important social *function of humanizing and personalizing all manner of assistance* to those in need. Foodbaskets and jobs, legal and extra-legal advice, setting to rights minor scrapes with the law, helping the bright poor boy to a political scholarship in a local college, looking after the bereaved—the whole range of crises when a feller needs a friend, and, above all, a friend who knows the score and who can do something about it—all these find the ever-helpful precinct captain available in the pinch.

To assess this function of the political machine adequately, it is important to note not only the fact that aid is provided but *the manner in which it is provided*. After all, other agencies do exist for dispensing such assistance. Welfare agencies, settlement houses, legal aid clinics, medical aid in free hospitals, public relief departments, immigration authorities—these and a multitude of other organizations are available to provide the most varied types of assistance. But in contrast to the professional techniques of the welfare worker which may typically represent in the mind of the recipient the cold, bureaucratic dispensation of limited aid following upon detailed investigations of *legal* claims to aid of the "client," are the unprofessional techniques of the precinct captain who asks no questions, exacts no compliance with legal rules of eligibility and does not "snoop" into private affairs.

For many, the loss of "self-respect" is too high a price for legalized assistance. In contrast to the gulf between the settlement house workers who so often come from a different social class, educational background and ethnic group, the precinct worker is "just one of us," who understands what it's all about. The condescending lady bountiful can hardly compete with the understanding friend in need. In *this struggle between alternative structures for fulfilling the nominally same functions* of providing aid and support to those who need it, it is clearly the machine politician who is better integrated with the groups which he serves than the impersonal, professionalized, socially distant and legally constrained welfare worker. And since the politician can at times influence and manipulate the official organizations for the dispensation of assistance, whereas the welfare worker has practically no influence on the political machine, they only add to his greater effectiveness. More colloquially and also, perhaps, more incisively, it was the Boston ward-leader, Martin Lomasny, who described this essential function to the curious Lincoln Steffens: "I think," said Lomasny, "that there's got to be in every ward somebody that any bloke can come to—no matter what he's done—and get help. *Help, you understand; none of your law and justice, but help.*"[5]

The "deprived classes," then, constitute one subgroup for whom the political machine clearly satisfies wants not adequately satisfied in the same fashion by the legitimate social structure.

For a second subgroup, that of business (primarily "big" business but also "small") the political boss serves the function of providing those political privileges which entail immediate economic gains. Business corporations, among which the public utilities (railroads, local transportation companies, communications corporations, electric light) are simply the most conspicuous in this regard, seek special political dispensations which will enable them to stabilize their situation and to near their objective of maximizing profits. Interestingly enough, corporations often want to avoid a chaos of uncontrolled competition. They want the greater security of an economic czar who controls, regulates and organizes competition, providing this czar is not a public official with his decisions subject to public scrutiny and public control. (The latter would be "government control," and hence taboo.) The political boss fulfills these requirements admirably.

Examined for a moment apart from any "moral" considerations, the political apparatus of the Boss is effectively designed to perform these functions with a minimum of inefficiency. Holding the strings of diverse governmental divisions, bureaus and agencies in his competent hands, the Boss rationalizes the relations between public and private business. He serves as the business community's ambassador in the otherwise alien (and sometimes unfriendly) realm of government. And, in strict business-like terms, he is well-paid for his economic services to his respectable business clients. In an article entitled, "An Apology to Graft," Steffens suggested that "our economic system, which held up riches, power and acclaim as prizes to men bold enough and able enough to buy corruptly timber, mines, oil fields and franchises and 'get away with it,' was at fault."[6] And, in a conference with a hundred or so of Los Angeles business leaders, he described a fact well known to all of them: the Boss and his machine were an *integral part* of the organization of the economy. "You cannot build or operate a railroad, or a street railway, gas, water, or power company, develop and operate a mine, or get forests and cut timber on a large scale, or run any privileged business, without corrupting or joining in the corruption of the government. You tell me privately that you must, and here I am telling you semipublicly that you must. And that is so all over the country. And that means that we have an organization of society in which, *for some reason,* you and your kind, the ablest, most intelligent, most imaginative, daring, and resourceful leaders of society, are and must be against society and its laws and its all-around growth."[7]

Since the demand for the services of special privileges are built into the structure of the society, the Boss fulfills diverse functions for this second subgroup of business-seeking-privilege. These "needs" of business, as presently constituted, are not adequately provided for by "conventional" and "culturally approved" social structures; consequently, the extra-legal but more-or-less efficient organization of the political machine comes to provide these services. To adopt an *exclusively* moral attitude toward the "corrupt political machine" is to lose sight of the very structural conditions which generate the "evil" that is so bitterly attacked. To adopt a functional outlook on the political machine is not to provide an apologia, but a more solid base for modifying or eliminating the machine, *providing* specific structural arrangements are introduced either for eliminating these effective demands of the business community or, if that is the objective, of satisfying these demands through alternative means.

A third set of distinctive functions fulfilled by the political machine for a special subgroup is that of providing alternative channels of social mobility for those otherwise excluded from the more conventional avenues for personal "advancement." Both the sources of this special "need" (for social mobility) and the respect in which the political machine comes to help satisfy this need can be understood by examining the structure of the larger culture and society. As is well known, the American culture lays enormous emphasis on money and power as a "success" goal legitimate for all members of the society. By no means alone in our inventory of cultural goals, it still remains among the most heavily endowed with positive affect and value. However, certain subgroups and certain ecological areas are notable for the relative absence of opportunity for achieving these (monetary and power) types of success. They constitute, in short, sub-populations where "the cultural emphasis upon pecuniary success has been absorbed, but where there is *little access to conventional and legitimate* means for attaining such success." The conventional occupational opportunities of persons in (such areas) are almost completely limited to manual labor. Given our cultural stigmatization of manual labor, and its correlate, the prestige of white-collar work, it is clear that the result is a tendency to achieve these culturally approved objectives *through whatever means are possible.* These people are on the one hand, "asked to orient their conduct toward the prospect of accumulating wealth [and power] and, on the other, they are largely denied effective opportunities to do so institutionally."

It is within this context of social structure that the political machine fulfills the basic function of providing avenues of social mobility for the otherwise disadvantaged. Within this context, even the corrupt political machine and the racket "represent the triumph of amoral intelligence over morally prescribed 'failure' when the channels of vertical mobility are closed or narrowed *in a society which places a high premium on economic affluence, [power] and social ascent* for all its members."[8] As one sociologist has noted on the basis of several years of close observation in a "slum area":

> The sociologist who dismisses racket and political organizations as deviations from desirable standards thereby neglects some of the major elements of slum life. . . . *He does not discover the functions they perform for the members* [of the groupings in the slum]. The Irish and later immigrant peoples have had the greatest difficulty in finding places for themselves in our urban social and economic structure. Does anyone believe that the immigrants and their children could have achieved their present degree of social mobility without gaining control of the political organization of some of our largest cities? The same is true of the racket organization. *Politics and the rackets have furnished an important means of social mobility for individuals, who, because of ethnic background and low class position,* are blocked from advancement in the "respectable" channels.[9]

This, then represents a third type of function performed for a distinctive subgroup. This function, it may be noted in passing, is fulfilled by the *sheer* existence and operation of the political machine, for it is in the machine itself that these individuals and subgroups find their culturally induced needs more or less satisfied. It refers to the services which the political apparatus provides for its own personnel. But seen in the wider social context we have set forth, it no longer appears as *merely* a means of self-aggrandizement for profit-hungry and power-hungry *individuals,* but as an organized provision for *subgroups* otherwise excluded or restricted from the race for "getting ahead."

Just as the political machine performs services for "legitimate" business, so it operates to perform not dissimilar services for "illegitimate" business: vice, crime and rackets. Once again, the basic sociological role of the machine in this respect can be more fully appreciated only if one temporarily abandons attitudes of moral indignation, to examine with all moral innocence the actual workings of the organization. In this light, it at once appears that the subgroup of the professional criminal, racketeer, gambler, has basic similarities of organization, demands and operation to the subgroup of the industrialist, man of business, speculator. If there is a Lumber King or an Oil King, there is also a Vice King or a Racket King. If expansive legitimate business organizes administrative and financial syndicates to "rationalize" and to "integrate" diverse areas of production and business enterprise, so expansive rackets and crime organize syndicates to bring order to the otherwise chaotic areas of production of illicit goods and services. If legitimate business regards the proliferation of small enterprises as wasteful and inefficient, substituting, for example, the giant chain stores for the hundreds of corner groceries, so illegitimate business adopts the same businesslike attitude, and syndicates crime and vice.

Finally, and in many respects, most important, is the basic similarity, if not near-identity, of the economic role of "legitimate" business and "illegitimate" business. *Both are in some degree concerned with the provision of goods and services for which there is an economic demand.* Morals aside, they are both business, industrial and professional enterprises, dispensing goods and services which some people want, for which there is a market in which goods and services are transformed into commodities. And, in a prevalently market society, we should expect appropriate enterprises to arise whenever there is a market demand for given goods or services.

As is well known, vice, crime and the rackets *are* "big business." Consider only that there have been estimated to be about 500,000 professional prostitutes in the United States, and compare this with the approximately 200,000 physicians and 200,000 nurses. It is difficult to estimate which have the larger clientele: the professional men and women of medicine or the professional men and women of vice. It is, of course, difficult to estimate the economic assets, income, profits and dividends of illicit gambling in this country and to compare it with the economic assets, income, profits and dividends of, say, the shoe industry, but it is altogether possible that the two industries are about on a par. No precise figures exist on the annual expenditures on illicit narcotics, and it is probable that these are less than the expenditures on candy, but it is also probable that they are larger than the expenditure on books.

It takes but a moment's thought to recognize that, *in strictly economic terms*, there is no relevant difference between the provision of licit and of illicit goods and services. The liquor traffic illustrates this perfectly. It would be peculiar to argue that prior to 1920 (when the 18th amendment became effective), the provision of liquor constituted an economic service, that from 1920 to 1933, its production and sale no longer constituted an economic service dispensed in a market, and that from 1934 to the present, it once again took on a serviceable aspect. Or, it would be *economically* (not morally) absurd to suggest that the sale of bootlegged liquor in the dry state of Kansas is less a response to a market demand than the sale of publicly manufactured liquor in the neighboring wet state of Missouri. Examples of this sort can of course be multiplied many times over. Can it be held that in European countries, with registered and legalized prostitution, the prostitute contributes an economic service, whereas in this country, lacking legal sanction, the prostitute provides no such service? Or that the professional abortionist is in the economic market where he has approved legal status and that he is out of the economic market where he is legally taboo? Or that gambling satisfies a specific demand for entertainment in Nevada, where it is one of the largest business enterprises of the largest city in the state, but that it differs essentially in this respect from movie houses in the neighboring state of California?

The failure to recognize that these businesses are only *morally* and not *economically* distinguishable from "legitimate" businesses has led to badly scrambled analysis. Once the economic identity of the two is recognized, we may anticipate that if the political machine performs functions for "legitimate big business" it will be all the more likely to perform not dissimilar functions for "illegitimate big business." And, of course, such is often the case.

The distinctive function of the political machine for their criminal, vice and racket clientele is to enable them to operate in satisfying the economic demands of a large market without due interference from the government. Just as big business may contribute funds to the political party war-chest to ensure a minimum of governmental interference, so with big rackets and big crime. In both instances, the political machine can, in varying degrees, provide "protection." In both instances, many features of the structural context are identical: (1) market demands for goods and services; (2) the operators' concern with maximizing gains from their enterprises; (3) the need for partial control of government which might otherwise interfere with these activities of businessmen; (4) the need for an efficient, powerful and centralized agency to provide an effective liaison of "business" with government.

Without assuming that the foregoing pages exhaust either the range of functions or the range of subgroups served by the political machine, we can at least see that *it presently fulfills some functions for these diverse subgroups which are not adequately fulfilled by culturally approved or more conventional structures.*

Several additional implications of the functional analysis of the political machine can be mentioned here only in passing, although they obviously require to be developed at length. First, the foregoing analysis has direct implications for *social engineering*. It helps explain why the periodic efforts at "political reform," "turning the rascals out" and "cleaning political house" are typically short-lived and ineffectual. It exemplifies a basic theorem: *any attempt to eliminate an existing social structure without providing adequate alternative structures for fulfilling the functions previously fulfilled by the abolished organization is doomed to failure.* (Needless to say, this theorem has much wider bearing than the one instance of the political machine.) When "political reform" confines itself to the manifest task of "turning the rascals out," it is engaging in little more than sociological magic. The reform may for a time bring new figures into the political limelight; it may serve the casual social function of re-assuring the electorate that the moral virtues remain intact and will ultimately triumph; it may actually effect a turnover in the personnel of the political machine; it may even, for a time, so curb the activities of the machine as to leave unsatisfied the many needs it has previously fulfilled. But, inevitably, unless the reform also involves a "reforming" of the social and political structure such that the existing needs are satisfied by alternative structures or unless it involves a change which eliminates these needs altogether, the political machine will return to its integral place in the social scheme of things. *To seek social change, without due recognition of the manifest and latent functions performed by the social organization undergoing change, is to indulge in social ritual rather than social engineering.* The concepts of manifest and latent functions (or their equivalents) are indispensable elements in the theoretic repertoire of the social engineer. In this crucial sense, these concepts are not "merely" theoretical (in the abusive sense of the term), but are eminently practical. In the deliberate enactment of social change, they can be ignored only at the price of considerably heightening the risk of failure.

A second implication of our analysis of the political machine also has a bearing upon areas wider than the one we have considered. The "paradox" has often been noted that the supporters of the political machine include both the "respectable" business class elements who are, of course, opposed to the criminal or racketeer and the distinctly "unrespectable" elements of the underworld. And, at first appearance, this is cited as an instance of very strange bedfellows. The learned judge is not infrequently called upon to sentence the very racketeer beside whom he sat the night before at an informal dinner of the political bigwigs. The district attorney jostles the exonerated convict on his way to the back room where the Boss has called a meeting. The big business man may complain almost as bitterly as the big racketeer about the "extortionate" contributions to the party fund demanded by the Boss. Social opposites meet—in the smoke-filled room of the successful politician.

In the light of a functional analysis all this of course no longer seems paradoxical. Since the machine serves both the businessman and the criminal man, the two seemingly antipodal groups intersect. This points to a more general theorem: *the social functions of an organization help determine the structure (including the recruitment of personnel involved in the structure), just as the structure helps determine the effectiveness with which the functions are fulfilled.* In terms of social status, the business group and the criminal group are indeed poles apart. But status does not fully determine behavior and the interrelations between groups. Functions modify these relations. Given their distinctive needs, the several subgroups in the large society are "integrated," whatever their personal desires or intentions, by the centralizing structure which serves these several needs. In a phrase with many implications which require further study, *structure affects function and function affects structure.*

Notes

1. Edward M. Sait, "Machine, Political," *Encyclopedia of the Social Sciences,* IX, 658b (italics supplied).
2. Herbert Croly, *Progressive Democracy* (New York, 1914), p. 254, cited by Sait, *op. cit.,* 658b.

3. Sait, *op. cit.,* 659a.
4. *Ibid.*
5. *The Autobiography of Lincoln Steffens* (Chautauqua, N.Y.: Chautauqua Press, 1931), 618.
6. *Autobiography of Lincoln Steffens,* 570.
7. *Ibid.,* 572–573.
8. Merton, *op. cit.,* 146.
9. William F. Whyte, "Social Organization in the Slums," *American Sociological Review,* Feb. 1943, 8, 34–39 (italics supplied).

9

Steven P. Erie

BIG-CITY RAINBOW POLITICS: MACHINES REVIVIDUS?

Machines and Ethnic Assimilation

The Pluralist Approach

In the postwar era, social scientists eulogized the dying and much-maligned machine. In the 1940s and 1950s, a new generation of empirically trained sociologists such as William Foote Whyte, Robert K. Merton, and Daniel Bell used the machine as a test case to critique the middle-class Protestant value orientation that had dominated social analysis. Buttressing their claims for a value-neutral, functional approach to social science, the Young Turks argued that the censorious view of machine politics ignored the positive functions performed by lower-class ethnic institutions offering unconventional mobility routes. Finding their career opportunities blocked in the Protestant-controlled business world, the Irish had turned to the machine; the Italians, to the mob. Because it served the material needs of the immigrant working class, machine politics persisted, despite middle-class Protestant opposition.[1]

By the 1960s, political scientists such as [Robert] Dahl, Fred Greenstein, Elmer Cornwell, and Edgar Litt had joined the chorus of machine defenders, arguing that the big-city party bosses had been both ethnic integrators and system stabilizers-transformers.[2] In the hands of the pluralists, the machine became a local precursor to the New Deal ethnic coalition and the welfare state; the boss, a new paradigm of democratic leadership and mass politics.

The pluralist locus classicus was *Who Governs?*, Robert Dahl's 1961 survey of New Haven's political development over two centuries. Dahl's treatment of the Irish party bosses represented part of a larger analysis of successful regime transformation. In nineteenth-century New Haven, an oligarchic system of cumulative inequalities and overlapping privileges (the same hands holding wealth, social standing, and power) gradually and peacefully gave way to a pluralist system of dispersed inequalities and advantages (in which different people controlled different resources).[3]

By the mid-nineteenth century, a new breed of Yankee businessmen-politicians had displaced the "Old Standing Order" of leading Federalist and Congregationalist families. From humble origins, the new self-made entrepreneurs fought to end property restrictions on voting in order to mobilize a new electoral majority of native-born artisans and laborers. But this insurgent elite's primary weapon of victory—the vote—would soon be turned against them. Successfully challenging Yankee leadership at century's end, Irish Democratic politicians naturalized, registered, and claimed the votes of their countrymen in order to forge a new electoral majority.[4]

The Irish bosses then turned to the task of group economic uplift. According to Dahl, politics and city jobs served as "major springboards" for the Irish into the middle class. Controlling the levers of urban power, the Irish traded votes for patronage, accelerating their movement out of the laboring classes. The early machine's patronage cache awaiting capture appeared sizable indeed. In the pre–New Deal era, the big-city machines controlled thousands of public sector and private sector patronage jobs. Tammany Hall, for example, had more than 40,000 patronage jobs at its disposal in the late 1880s. Furthermore, the public sector offered greater social mobility opportunities than did the private sector. In San Francisco at the turn of the century, nearly one-quarter of all public employees were in professional and managerial positions compared with only 6 percent of the privately employed workforce.[5]

Using machine patronage, the Irish supposedly built a middle class with surprising rapidity considering their meager job skills and the discrimination they encountered. In the big cities, the proportion of first- and second-generation Irish in white-collar jobs rose from 12 percent to 27 percent between 1870 and 1900. Among the non-Irish, the white-collar increase was smaller, from 27 percent to 34 percent. As Andrew Greeley has shown, Irish-Americans are now the most affluent of the country's non-Jewish ethnic groups, having translated their apparently early white-collar job gains into a solid middle and upper middle class anchored in business and the professions in the post–World War II era.[6]

Dahl's account of the rise of the Irish "ex-plebes" and the accompanying systemic shift from cumulative to dispersed inequalities is central to a larger pluralist theory of American politics. Placing himself in an Aristotelian-Machiavellian tradition, Dahl highlighted the creative role of political elites such as the Irish party bosses in promoting both change and stability in the modern city-state. In the hands of gifted leaders, the mechanisms of political equality—popular sovereignty, universal suffrage, competitive parties, and the patronage system—could be used to reduce social and economic inequalities.

Our case studies support the pluralist argument regarding the machine's *political* assimilation of the Irish. The English-speaking famine Irish arrived as the competitive second party system was entering its modern or mobilization phase. As the Irish allegiance to the Democratic party solidified, the embryonic machines actively worked to naturalize and enroll Irish voters. Group mobilization allowed the Irish to infiltrate and take over the helm of the big-city Democratic machines.

Yet the machine's *economic* assimilation of the Irish—and its redistributional potential generally—was smaller than pluralists allow. For one thing, early Irish economic progress was slower and more uneven than the growth in white-collar jobholders indicates. As Stephan Thernstrom has carefully shown for Boston, many middle-class gains by first- and second-generation Irish were marginal at best, signaling entry into poorly paid clerical and sales work rather than into business and the professions.[7]

Thernstrom also cautions that it is misleading to compare Irish economic progress with the sluggish performance of the new immigrants. The new immigration was made up of successive waves of impoverished Southern and Eastern Europeans. More instructive is his comparison of the progress of the politically powerful Irish in Boston's labor market relative to that of other early-arriving but politically weaker immigrant groups. First- and second-generation Germans, Scandinavians, and English all climbed the economic ladder more quickly than did their Irish counterparts.

Our case studies of the classic Irish machines suggest that the pluralist model overestimates the magnitude of machine resources and the Irish ability to use them for sizable group economic gain. The Democratic machines of the late nineteenth century offered impressive channels of advancement for *individual* Irish politicians and contractors. But the early machines could do only so much for Irish *group* mobility.

Political and class constraints hampered the early bosses in their search for greater resources. Middle-class Yankee Republicans had not yet migrated to the suburbs. They vigorously contested local elections, demanding fiscal retrenchment. The early Irish bosses like John Kelly also had to contend with opponents in their own ranks: Democratic businessmen-reformers advocating "tight-fisted" economic policies. This bipartisan conservative coalition forced the nascent Celtic machines to pursue cautious fiscal policies, limiting their patronage take.

Republicans dominated state politics during much of this era, reinforcing the fiscal conservatism of the early Irish machines. Republican governors and legislators imposed constitutional restrictions, severely limiting the bosses' ability to raise taxes, increase municipal debts, and reward their working-class ethnic followers. Consequently, . . . only a small minority of the Irish working class in the late nineteenth century could crowd into the machine's patronage enclave.

The twentieth-century machines did a better job of economically aiding the Irish. Political and legal constraints on the bosses' ability to raise and spend money—and thus to create patronage jobs—began to ease as the machine's middle-class Republican and reform opponents moved to the suburbs, as home rule lifted state fiscal restraints, and as the millions of Southern and Eastern Europeans filling the cities demanded new services. Machines directly and indirectly controlled more than 20 percent of post-1900 urban job growth, double their pre–1900 share. In the Irish-run machine cities of New York, Jersey City, and Albany, the Irish were rewarded with more than 60 percent of this newly created patronage. As a result, on the eve of the Depression, at least one-third of the Irish-stock workforce toiled in machine-sponsored jobs.

The second-generation machine's patronage policies appear to support the pluralist argument that politics served as an important conduit of Irish economic advancement. Compared with Yankees, Germans, and Jews, though, the Irish were slow to build a middle class in business and the professions. Today's Irish affluence was latecoming, postdating the heyday of the machine. As even Greeley admits, the Irish middle class was only emerging on the eve of the Depression; its arrival would not occur until after World War II.[8]

In light of Irish political success, why was Irish middle-class status so slow in coming? Was there an *inverse* relation between political success and economic advancement? The Irish crowded into the largely blue-collar urban public sector in the late nineteenth and early twentieth centuries. Yet as low-paid policemen, firemen, and city clerks, the Irish were solidly lower-middle- rather than middle-class. The relative security of blue-collar jobs in public works, police, and fire departments may have hindered the building of an Irish middle class by encouraging long tenure in poorly paid bureaucratic positions. The pluralist machine's apparent cornucopia of resources could turn into a blue-collar cul-de-sac.[9]

It can be argued that by channeling so much of their economic energy into the public sector, the Irish forsook opportunities in the private sector save for industries such as construction that depended on political connections. As Moynihan has accurately observed, the economic rewards of America have gone to entrepreneurs, not to functionaries. Moreover, the Irish public sector job gains were fragile. The Depression forced the cities to cut their payrolls. The 1930s also witnessed the long-awaited revolt of the Southern and Eastern Europeans against their Irish overlords. Thousands of Irish-American payrollers lost their jobs as a result of retrenchment and machine overthrow. Only with lessened job dependence on the machine in the prosperous post–World War II era were the third- and fourth-generation Irish able to move rapidly into business and the professions.

The puzzling question is why the Irish embraced the machine's blue-collar patronage system with such enthusiasm. Dahl has advanced a "blocked mobility" explanation. In his account, the Irish quickly assimilated the American value of upward mobility. However, limited job skills and anti-Catholicism blocked Irish advancement in the private sector. Thus, the Irish, in Dahl's words, "eagerly grabbed the 'dangling rope' [of politics] up the formidable economic slope."[10]

If the Irish so easily assimilated the American success ethic, why did they allow the dangling rope of politics to become a noose? There are both cultural and resource explanations for the Irish overreliance on the patronage system. Moynihan has taken issue with Dahl, arguing that the Irish displayed a "distaste for commerce," valuing security over entrepreneurial success. Seeking safe bureaucratic havens, the Irish settled for marginal advancement through politics.[11]

Borrowing a page from Max Weber, Edward Levine similarly argues that the Irish working class consciously rejected the middle-class Protestant value of economic achievement. Alienated from Protestant values and institutions, the Irish constructed the Democratic party and the Catholic church as mutually reinforcing institutions rooted in working-class Irish Catholic values. For the Irish, power and security, not money or status, represented the highest values. In this scheme of things, social and geographical mobility meant apostasy. Reinforcing their separateness from the Protestant mainstream, politics enveloped the Irish, becoming *the* approved secular career. As the machines have declined, however, the Irish have gradually replaced the values of power and security with those of money and status.[12]

A resource explanation for limited Irish patronage mobility looks to the machine's maintenance needs. To win the jurisdictional battles for working-class support, machines quickly realized the potency of economic appeals. Yet scarce economic benefits had to be spread as widely as possible to realize their full vote-getting value. Thus the Irish bosses stretched patronage, creating large numbers of poorly paid blue-collar positions to maximize the number of working-class voters rewarded. The machine's job growth strategy created ever more blue-collar public employment for the Irish at a time when the cities were moving from a manufacturing to a service economy and when the greatest increases in private sector employment occurred in white-collar ranks.

The party's maintenance needs conflicted with the long-run goal of Irish prosperity. But patronage had short-run economic advantages. The machine's job system allowed unskilled and semiskilled Irish workers to move to the next rung above the working class. In fact, the ready availability of blue-collar patronage helped to *shape* Irish economic horizons, encouraging the values of security, seniority, and slow bureaucratic advancement.

The pluralist view of the machine as an integrator of the immigrants has been applied to the Southern and Eastern Europeans. Elmer Cornwell, for example, argues that the Irish bosses in the northern cities were forced to politically assimilate the second-wave immigrants in order to continue to win elections.[13] Competitive electoral pressures encouraged the Irish bosses to naturalize and register the newer arrivals. Our survey of the classic Irish machines found that the machine's invisible hand did not automatically embrace the newcomers. Mature machines were one-party regimes lacking the political incentive to mobilize the second-wave immigrants. The Irish Democratic bosses had already constructed winning electoral coalitions among early-arriving ethnic groups. The newcomers' political assimilation would only encourage demands for a redistribution of power and patronage.

In entrenched machine cities like New York and Jersey City, naturalization and voter registration rates for the Southern and Eastern Europeans remained quite low until the late 1920s. Electoral participation rates for the second-wave immigrants increased thereafter in response to national candidates and issues rather than to sponsorship by local party bosses.

In competitive party cities, however, the Irish party chieftains worked energetically to mobilize the Southern and Eastern Europeans. The fledgling Democratic machines of Chicago and Pittsburgh most successfully mobilized the newcomers. As the minority party in these cities in the 1920s, the Democrats were forced into actively courting the new ethnics. Chicago's Democratic precinct captains naturalized and registered the new immigrants far more quickly than did their counterparts in one-party New York, Jersey City, and Boston.

Entrenched machines did little to further economic assimilation among the Southern and Eastern Europeans before the latter mobilized in the 1930s. With so much of Irish well-being and group identity dependent on continued control of the machines, Irish politicos were understandably loath to share power and patronage. To preserve their hegemony, the Irish accommodated the slowly mobilizing newcomers in parsimonious fashion, dispensing social services, symbolic recognition, and collective benefits rather than the organization's core resources of power and patronage.

At critical moments the Irish were forced by electoral pressures to enter tactical alliances with some groups for a greater share of the machine's jealously guarded core resources. As Jews flexed their political muscle in New York in the 1920s, the Irish offered them minor offices and a greater share of municipal employment, particularly in the rapidly expanding school system. The Celtic bosses worked as actively to reduce Italian influence by gerrymandering Italian neighborhoods.

Postwar machines such as the Daley organization accommodated the Southern and Eastern Europeans in different and less costly ways than those in which the prewar machines had rewarded the Irish. Wartime and postwar prosperity benefited the second-wave immigrants and their children, propelling large numbers into the property-owning middle class. As homeowners, white ethnics objected to high property taxes to pay for patronage jobs they did not need. The Southern and Eastern Europeans demand a different set of machine policies: low property taxes, the preservation of property values and white neighborhoods, and homeowner rather than welfare services. The postwar Irish-led machines accommodated these taxation and service demands—as long as the Irish maintained control over key party positions and those city offices with major policy-making and patronage-dispensing responsibilities.

Machines did little to assimilate blacks and Hispanics. In the pre-1960 period, black sub-machines to the white machines had emerged in cities such as Chicago and Pittsburgh. Congressman William Dawson, the only black in the Daley machine's inner circle, ran the black sub-machine in the South Side ghetto. To counter the threat of Polish insurgency, Dawson and his lieutenants mobilized the minority vote for Mayor Daley. As the threat of white revolt diminished in the 1960s, the threat of black revolt grew. Using welfare-state benefits, the machine systematically demobilized the black vote.

Contrary to pluralist theory, the big-city machine's political and economic incorporation of ethnic groups was limited. The Irish represent the theory's par excellence case. The nascent Democratic machines actively assisted the Irish in acquiring citizenship, in voting, and in securing patronage jobs. Yet pluralist theory exaggerates the ability of the Irish to turn political into economic success. The economic disadvantages suffered by the Irish could not readily be overcome by politics; they may even have been aggravated. Celtic economic success came *after* the machine's heyday. Failing to consider the class and political constraints on the machine's creation and distribution of resources, pluralists overestimate the old-style party organization's redistributional capacity.

The pluralist case is further weakened when we consider the machine's limited assimilation of other ethnic groups. The entrenched Democratic machines did little to mobilize and reward the new arrivals from Southern and Eastern Europe, the South, the Caribbean, and Latin America. Deprived of machine sponsorship, the newcomers would have to rely on internal group resources to contest urban power. . . .

Today's Big-City Rainbow Politics: Machines Revividus?

In the past twenty years the baton of urban power has slowly been passed to the third- and fourth-generation ethnic arrivals—blacks, Hispanics, and Asians. Black mayors have been elected in Los Angeles, Chicago, Philadelphia, Detroit, Atlanta, Washington, Cleveland, Gary, Newark, and New Orleans. Blacks have also been elected in large numbers to city councils and school boards. The new black power is bureaucratic as well as electoral. In the big cities, black administrators have been appointed to such top policy-making positions as city manager, police chief, and school superintendent.[14]

In the Sunbelt, Hispanics and Asians are beginning to transform urban political life. San Antonio's voters in 1981 elected Henry Cisneros as the first Mexican-American mayor of a major U.S. city. Miami has a Cuban-American mayor and a Hispanic majority on the city council. Reversing a century-old legacy of racism and discrimination against Asians, California's cities are witnessing the first stirrings of Asian-American power. Los Angeles's voters elected Michael Woo to the city council, and San Francisco Mayor Dianne Feinstein appointed Thomas Hsieh to the city's Board of Supervisors.[15]

As the new minorities mobilize, particularly the black and Mexican-American communities with large lower-class populations, they have searched for strategies of group uplift. The viability of the machine model was problematic for the new groups. Before the 1960s, minorities were deliberately kept out of the established system of "city trenches." Except for a few independent politicians such as New York's Adam Clayton Powell, the legacy of the machine era for blacks was "plantation politics" Chicago-style. When the minority assault finally came, the old-style party organizations were in the last stages of decline.[16]

In the postmachine era, the prizes of urban politics seemed hollow indeed. The northern cities where blacks had migrated in massive numbers had experienced economic decline, their treasuries nearing bankruptcy. The rapidly growing Sunbelt cities had small, lean public sectors (the legacy of conservative reformers), limiting government job opportunities. To make matters worse, white civil service commissioners and municipal union stewards zealously guarded the prerogatives of the heavily white public sector workforce, making it difficult for minorities to translate political gains into economic advancement.[17]

Even the means of ethnic capture were more difficult. The new minorities were the victims of reform. In the process of wresting power from the Irish, the Southern and Eastern Europeans had created additional barriers for later-arriving groups. The second-wave ethnics joined Yankee reformers in bringing to the eastern cities the reforms first implemented by progressives in the West and South: at-large city council elections, nonpartisanship, educational requirements for public employment, and expanded civil service coverage. At-large electoral systems, in particular, made it harder for blacks to gain representation on city councils. Designed to prevent the machine's reemergence, reforms also made it more difficult for working-class blacks and Hispanics to gain group influence and benefits.[18]

In this bleak age of reform, a possible return to machine politics didn't seem so bad after all. Black politicians in particular called for the machine's resurrection in part or in toto. During the 1960s, black moderates committed to "working within the system" had embraced the Irish model of group electoral politics to counter radical separatist demands. The radical rhetoric of militant nationalism and community control ultimately proved an empty threat, revealing an incrementalist and patronage core that could be accommodated as the emerging black bourgeoisie took over such community institutions as schools and health clinics. By the 1970s, blacks of diverse ideological inclinations had moved "from protest to politics," emulating the strategy of ethnic group mobilization—registration, turnout, and bloc voting en masse—first perfected by the Irish.[19]

To appeal to both militants and moderates in the minority community, contemporary black politicians disingenuously coupled radical-reformist rhetoric with venerable machine-building techniques designed to enhance group influence and payoffs. Claiming that at-large electoral systems discriminated against racial minorities, followers of rainbow "reformer" Jesse Jackson in cities such as Pittsburgh and Cincinnati have pursued the machine gambit of reviving the ward system. Chicago's "antimachine" Mayor Harold Washington ransacked city hall and special district governments for additional patronage to pay off his supporters and consolidate power. Reformer Washington also vigorously opposed a move to make the city's elections nonpartisan.[20]

Are black politicians correct in looking to the machine past? What lessons could the departed Irish bosses offer today's minorities about group influence, electoral coalition building, and economic advancement through local politics? Moynihan has argued that the twentieth-century black experience needs to be understood in terms of a critical comparison with the nineteenth-century Irish experience.[21]

Both groups have tried their hand at public sector politics, seeking governmental channels of group mobility. The Irish political experience cannot fully be emulated by blacks because the big-city machines—centralized party structures—are unlikely to be revived in anything like their historical form. Yet machine politics—the trading in divisible benefits—has staying power in local politics. The Irish bosses were the undisputed masters of this game. Can their example educate today's minority power brokers about both the possibilities and the limits of ethnic politics?

On the positive side, the Irish experience demonstrates some potential for group economic uplift through the local political process. The votes of the Irish working class could be translated into group power and a major share of city jobs and services. The twentieth-century Celtic municipal engines served as modest redistributional devices, reallocating economic burdens and benefits within the middle of the class structure. To the extent that the Irish bosses were Robin Hoods, they were selective about their victims and beneficiaries. Rather than taking from the very rich and giving to the very poor, the Irish politicos took from the Yankee middle class and gave to the lower-middle-class payroll Irish.

On the negative side, the Irish machines were as much instruments of social control as of economic reward. The nineteenth-century Irish bosses imposed retrenchment on their followers as the price of keeping power. Black mayors are under the same fiscal constraints today. Retrenchment produced ideological-class schisms among the Irish in the 1880s and is doing the same for blacks in the 1980s. The conflict between Tammany's conservative "long-hair" Irish faction and the militant working-class "short-hairs" finds contemporary expression in the tensions between moderate black mayors and militant followers of the Jacksonian rainbow.

The early Irish bosses parsimoniously accommodated later arrivals on the rainbow bandwagon. With limited resources and pressing group demands, black politicians may have to do the same with Hispanics and Asians. The down-side risk of today's slow-growth politics is that the new rainbow coalition may produce a small pot of gold for the black political elite, while browns, yellows, and even the black underclass are left chasing the mirage.

Concluding the Irish-black comparison on an even more pessimistic note, what will urban politics look like at century's end if present trends in conservative national politics and uneven regional economic development continue? Will big-city minority politicians in declining Frostbelt cities be called on to implement an updated "System of '96"—for 1996? Will black leaders soothe the "mixed multitudes" with populist rhetoric while cutting deals with conservative national politicians? And will federally funded "urban enterprise zones" prove to be the newest species of "plantation politics" designed to discipline the have-nots? Big-city minority politicians might have to take a lesson from the Christian Democratic party bosses of stagnant Palermo after all.

Blacks are now emulating the Irish by using political strategies of group uplift. The means employed, however, are different. The Irish used the big-city party organizations; blacks use local and national bureaucracies. The locus of urban power has shifted from political machines to independent and semiautonomous bureaucracies, organized along functional lines. Furthermore, urban politics has been nationalized. In the post–New Deal era, the political access and economic distribution functions once monopolized by local machines now are nationally performed by the Democratic party and federal welfare-state bureaucracies.[22]

Peter Eisinger finds black mayors pursuing a dual strategy of group advancement in this new arena of urban politics. The first prong consists of the politics of public sector bureaucracies. Black leaders in cities such as Detroit and Atlanta have used their appointment powers to name minorities to head city personnel departments and other major agencies. Minority administrators, in turn, have launched aggressive affirmative action programs, producing a dramatic increase in the minority share of public employment. Black mayors are also using affirmative action to award city contracts to minority businesses. Newark's former Mayor Kenneth Gibson, for example, set aside 25 percent of all federal public works project monies for minority contractors.[23]

The second prong consists of a strategy of "trickle down" from private sector economic growth. Black mayors in Los Angeles, Chicago, Detroit, Washington, Atlanta, and Newark have formed alliances with the white business community to promote downtown redevelopment, hoping to create private sector job opportunities for minorities.

The Irish experience suggests the limits of this dual strategy. On the public sector side, the approach has a major down-side risk—retrenchment. The Irish were the principal beneficiaries of city payroll growth from 1900 to 1929; after 1929, however, they were also the victims of retrenchment. Blacks clearly benefited from the halcyon municipal employment growth of the 1960s and early 1970s. The late 1970s, however, brought municipal austerity, threatening to reverse black city payroll gains. As the last hired, minorities were frequently the first victims of budgetary cutbacks. Detroit's black Mayor Coleman Young, for example, was forced by budget-balancing pressures to fire hundreds of minority police, undoing in a single afternoon ten years of hard-fought affirmative action in police hiring.

Black politicians and civil servants may also face a political challenge to their power and prerogatives. In the 1930s and 1940s, the Irish machine's jerry-built rainbow coalition unraveled as the new immigrants countermobilized, jeopardizing the jobs of thousands of Irish payrollers. In the 1990s, Asian-Americans and Hispanics could challenge blacks for control of the big cities, particularly if black politicians are unable or unwilling to share power and patronage. With a large and prosperous middle class, Asian-Americans in particular might assume the broker role, financing and leading an Asian-Hispanic coalition that could threaten today's black municipal workers.

The Irish experience also suggests caution regarding the extent of "trickle-down" to the black masses from publicly subsidized private sector growth. Public investment in urban infrastructure was the early equivalent of today's publicly assisted downtown redevelopment projects. Public works contracts benefited individual Irish contractors while providing temporary low-wage employment for the masses of unskilled and semiskilled Irish workers.

Today, black mayors offer public seed money, tax and zoning abatements, and lease-back arrangements to downtown developers. Ambitious redevelopment projects like Detroit's Renaissance Center and Atlanta's Peachtree Plaza are sold to minorities and the poor on the premise that economic benefits—primarily in the form of job opportunities—will filter down to them. But new convention centers, hotels, and shopping centers are not a viable vehicle of group uplift. Too few jobs are created to make an appreciable dent in inner-city poverty. The limited pool of high-paying professional and managerial positions disproportionately goes to upper-middle-class white suburbanites. Minority "trickle down" has primarily taken the form of a limited number of low-wage service jobs.[24]

There is a vital third element to today's black advancement strategy—federal social programs. Both Irish and black politicians have used the expanding welfare state to consolidate power. The nascent Irish Democratic machines of the 1930s fused with New Deal programs. A generation later, the Great Society served as a catalyst for black power. Studying minority politics in ten northern California cities, Rufus Browning, Dale Marshall, and David Tabb argue that the Great Society programs "provided the functional equivalent of earlier forms of patronage." In the Bay Area cities, federal social initiatives encouraged minority political mobilization, promoted their incorporation into local governing coalitions, and secured greater local governmental responsiveness to minority job and service demands.[25]

The expanding welfare state was more than a vehicle for black assimilation into local politics. It was a primary route of group *economic* advancement. Where the Irish had used machine patronage, blacks now relied on federally funded social programs. In the 1960s and early 1970s, the new black middle class found jobs in the expanding federally funded human services sector—health, education, and welfare. By the late 1970s, nearly half of all black professionals and managers worked in the social welfare sector, compared with less than one-quarter of comparably situated whites.[26]

The welfare state meant more than jobs for the black middle class; it also represented cash and in-kind welfare payments for the underclass. From the mid-1960s onward, the black poor increasingly relied on transfer payments. Two-thirds of poor black families received welfare in the late 1970s, up from one-third in the late 1960s. Economically, blacks were more integrated into the public sector in the late 1970s than the Irish had been during the machine's heyday—but under *federal* and *bureaucratic* auspices.[27]

But black politicians lack integrating mechanisms like the machine that can fuse together the disparate elements of today's urban politics—national versus local, bureaucratic versus electoral. As a result, big-city and minority politics reflect their unreconciled imperatives. The continued flow of welfare-state jobs, transfer payments, and social services, which sustain the black middle class and underclass, depend on group influence and alliance building at the national and state levels where social policy is made and funded. Blacks, however, are not as well organized to press their claims outside the local political arena.

In the absence of local machines capable of mobilizing voters, bureaucratic politics has acted as a depressant on electoral participation. The relationship between the bureaucratic service provider and the recipient differs from the relationship between the party cadre and the voter. Precinct workers are encouraged to mobilize loyal voters on election day. Human service workers, however, have little incentive to politically mobilize their clientele—as long as social programs and budgets grow. In the 1970s, minority service providers increasingly involved themselves in bureaucratic politics within the intergovernmental grant system rather than in mobilizing their clientele in local electoral politics. The expansion of means-tested programs such as AFDC depoliticized welfare recipients by isolating them from the work experiences encouraging political participation.[28]

Whatever the Great Society's initial mobilization effect, it soon acted as a brake on black voter turnout. During the period of welfare-state expansion, from 1964 to 1976, the mass electoral base of black politics in the northern cities eroded. The voting rate for young urban blacks plummeted, from 56 percent to 29 percent, while the rate for unemployed blacks dropped nearly as sharply, from 62 percent to 37 percent. Low turnout hurt big-city black politicians seeking to challenge white-controlled machine and reform regimes.[29]

Welfare-state contraction in the 1980s, however, reversed the bureaucratic expansion–electoral decline cycle. Threatened with job and benefit loss by the Reagan cutbacks, minority social service providers and recipients quickly rediscovered the value of electoral politics. Though primarily generated by national forces, the remobilization drive could be used in local politics. In machine Chicago and reform Philadelphia, black mayoral candidates rode the electoral surge to victory.

It is ironic that the policies of a president who points to his Irish ancestry during campaigns helped to produce the last hurrah for the Irish Democratic machines. Black mayors have ridden the turbulent waves of Reaganite austerity into office. Yet the practitioners of the new ethnic politics are trying to consolidate power with limited local resources and diminished welfare-state largesse. Lacking the tangible benefits demanded by their supporters, the new minority power brokers may discover what was learned the hard way by the now-departed Irish bosses: the real lessons at rainbow's end.

Notes

1. William Foote Whyte, "Social Organization in the Slums," pp. 34–39; William Foote Whyte, *Street Corner Society: The Social Structure of an Italian Slum*, pp. 194–252; Robert K. Merton, *Social Theory and Social Structure*, pp. 125–136; Daniel Bell, "Crime as an American Way of Life," pp. 131–154; Jerome K. Myers, "Assimilation in the Political Community," pp. 175–182.
2. Fred I. Greenstein, "The Changing Pattern of Urban Party Politics," pp. 1–13; Elmer E. Cornwell, "Party Absorption of Ethnic Groups: The Case of Providence, Rhode Island,"

pp. 87–98; Elmer E. Cornwell, "Bosses, Machines, and Ethnic Groups," pp. 27–39; Edgar Litt, *Beyond Pluralism: Ethnic Politics in America*, esp. pp. 60–74, 155–168.

3. Robert A. Dahl, *Who Governs? Democracy and Power in an American City*, pp. 2–86.

4. Ibid., pp. 11–31. In support of his "springboard" thesis, Dahl cites a 1933 sample survey of 1,600 New Haven families conducted by Yale's Institute of Human Relations. Constituting 13 percent of the sample, Irish-Americans held nearly half of the public service jobs. Yet the city's public sector constituted only 5 percent of the local economy and employed only 15 percent of the Irish-stock workforce. The 1930 census reports that blue-collar jobs accounted for nearly half of all public employment. See John W. McConnell, *The Evolution of Social Classes*, pp. 84–85; and U.S. Bureau of the Census, *Fifteenth Census of the United States, 1930*, vol. 4, Table 12, pp. 280–283.

5. Dahl, *Who Governs?* pp. 40–44; Eric L. McKitrick, "The Study of Corruption," pp. 502–514; Steven P. Erie, "Two Faces of Ethnic Power," pp. 262–263.

6. U.S. Census Office, *Ninth Census, 1870*, vol. 1, Tables 29, 32; U.S. Bureau of the Census, *Special Reports: Occupations at the Twelfth Census*, Tables 41, 43; Andrew Greeley, *That Most Distressful Nation: The Taming of the American Irish*, pp. 122–128; Andrew Greeley, *Ethnicity, Denomination, and Inequality*, pp. 54–55.

7. Stephan Thernstrom, *The Other Bostonians*, pp. 132–133, 232.

8. Greeley, *That Most Distressful Nation*, pp. 122–128; Greeley, *Ethnicity*, pp. 54–55.

9. Dennis P. Ryan, *Beyond the Ballot Box: A Social History of the Boston Irish, 1845–1917*, pp. 106, 149.

10. Dahl, *Who Governs?* pp. 33–34, 40–41. Oscar Handlin argues that the acculturated second-generation Irish, not the transplanted first generation, saw politics as a route of personal and group advancement; see Handlin, *The Uprooted*, pp. 201–216.

11. Daniel Patrick Moynihan, "The Irish," in Nathan Glazer and Daniel Patrick Moynihan, *Beyond the Melting Pot*, pp. 229, 259–260.

12. Edward M. Levine, *The Irish and Irish Politicians: A Study of Cultural and Social Alienation*, pp. 134–138.

13. Cornwell, "Bosses."

14. Regarding urban black politics, see Leonard A. Cole, *Blacks in Power: A Comparative Study of Black and White Elected Officials;* William E. Nelson, Jr., and Philip J. Meranto, *Electing Black Mayors: Political Action in the Black Community;* John R. Howard and Robert C. Smith, eds., "Urban Black Politics," pp. 1–150; Peter K. Eisinger, *The Politics of Displacement: Racial and Ethnic Transition in Three American Cities;* Albert Karnig and Susan Welch, *Black Representation and Urban Policy;* and Michael B. Preston et al., eds., *The New Black Politics: The Search for Political Power.*

15. On Hispanic and Asian-American politics, see F. Chris Garcia and Rudolpho de la Garza, *The Chicano Political Experience: Three Perspectives;* Raymond A. Mohl, "Miami: The Ethnic Cauldron," in Richard M. Bernard and Bradley R. Rice, eds., *Sunbelt Cities: Politics and Growth Since World War Two*, pp. 58–99; David L. Clark, "Los Angeles: Improbable Los Angeles," in Bernard and Rice, eds., *Sunbelt Cities*, pp. 268–308; Joan Moore and Harry Pachon, *Hispanics in the United States;* Bruce E. Cain and D. Roderick Kiewiet, *Minorities in California;* and Judy Tachibana, "California's Asians: Power from a Growing Population," pp. 534–543.

16. Martin Kilson, "Political Change in the Negro Ghetto, 1900–1940s," in Nathan Huggins et al., eds., *Key Issues in the Afro-American Experience*, pp. 182–189; Hanes Walton, Jr., *Black Politics: A Theoretical and Structural Analysis*, pp. 56–69.

17. Roger E. Alcaly and David Mermelstein, eds., *The Fiscal Crisis of American Cities;* George Sternlieb and James W. Hughes, "The Uncertain Future of the Center City," pp. 455–572; Marilyn Gittell, "Public Employment and the Public Service," in Alan Gartner et al., eds.,

Public Service Employment: An Analysis of Its History, Problems, and Prospects, pp. 121–142.

18. Leonard Sloan, "Good Government and the Politics of Race," pp. 171–174; Albert Karnig, "Black Representation on City Councils: The Impact of District Elections and Socioeconomic Factors," pp. 223–242; Theodore P. Robinson and Thomas R. Dye, "Reformism and Black Representation on City Councils," pp. 133–142; Richard L. Engstrom and Michael D. McDonald, "The Election of Blacks to City Councils: Clarifying the Impact of Electoral Arrangements on the Seats/Population Relationship," pp. 344–354; Peggy Heilig and Robert J. Mundt, "Changes in Representational Equity: The Effect of Adopting Districts," pp. 393–397.

19. Joyce Gelb, "Blacks, Blocs, and Ballots: The Relevance of Party Politics to the Negro," pp. 44–69; Charles V. Hamilton, "Blacks and the Crisis of Political Participation," pp. 191–193; Robert C. Smith, "The Changing Shape of Urban Black Politics: 1960–1970," pp. 16–28.

20. Linda M. Watkins, "Pittsburgh Blacks' Paucity of Political Clout Stirs Struggle over the City's At-Large Election System," p. 58; Marty Willis, "Jan. 6 Demonstration to Greet All-White City Council," pp. A-1, A-4; Gilbert Price, "Skirmish Begins 'At Large' Battle" [Cincinnati], p. H-8; Larry Green, "Chicago's Mayor Finally Grasps Power and Spoils," pp. 1, 18; Chinta Strausberg, "Mayor Seizes Control of Park Board," pp. 1, 18; Robert Davis and Joseph Tybor, "Mayor Wins Election Ruling," pp. 1, 10.

21. Daniel Patrick Moynihan, "Foreword" to Greeley, *That Most Distressful Nation,* p. xi.

22. Ira Katznelson, "The Crisis of the Capitalist City: Urban Politics and Social Control," in Willis D. Hawley et al., eds., *Theoretical Perspectives on Urban Politics,* pp. 223–226.

23. Peter K. Eisinger, "Black Employment in Municipal Jobs: The Impact of Black Political Power," pp. 380–392; Peter K. Eisinger, "The Economic Conditions of Black Employment in Municipal Bureaucracy," pp. 754–771; Peter K. Eisinger, "Black Mayors and the Politics of Racial Economic Advancement," in William C. McReady, ed., *Culture, Ethnicity, and Identity,* pp. 95–109; John J. Harrigan, *Political Change in the Metropolis,* pp. 129–139. For evidence that minority gains in elective office have not been translated into significant minority policy payoffs, see Susan Welch and Albert Karnig, "The Impact of Black Elected Officials on Urban Social Expenditures," pp. 707–714; and Edmond J. Keller, "The Impact of Black Mayors on Urban Policy," pp. 40–52.

24. Clarence N. Stone, *Economic Growth and Neighborhood Discontent: System Bias in the Urban Renewal Program of Atlanta,* pp. 90–185; Clarence N. Stone, "Atlanta: Protest and Elections Are Not Enough," in Rufus P. Browning and Dale Rogers Marshall, eds., "Black and Hispanic Power in City Politics: A Forum," pp. 618–625; Dennis R. Judd, *The Politics of American Cities: Private Power and Public Policy,* pp. 373–407; John Helyar and Robert Johnson, "Tale of Two Cities: Chicago's Busy Center Masks a Loss of Jobs in Its Outlying Areas," pp. 1, 22.

25. Rufus P. Browning et al., *Protest Is Not Enough: The Struggle of Blacks and Hispanics for Equality in Urban Politics,* pp. 207–238 (quote at p. 214).

26. Michael K. Brown and Steven P. Erie, "Blacks and the Legacy of the Great Society: The Economic and Political Impact of Federal Social Policy," pp. 302–309, esp. Table 3, p. 308; U.S. Equal Employment Opportunity Commission, *Minorities and Women in State and Local Government, 1977,* vol. 1; U.S. Civil Service Commission, *Minority Group Employment in the Federal Government,* 1975.

27. Steven P. Erie, "Public Policy and Black Economic Polarization," pp. 311–315, esp. Table 1, p. 313.

28. Charles V. Hamilton, "Public Policy and Some Political Consequences," in Marguerite R. Barnett and James A. Hefner, eds., *Public Policy for the Black Community,* p. 245; and Charles V. Hamilton, "The Patron-Recipient Relationship and Minority Politics in New York City," p. 224.

29. U.S. Bureau of the Census, *Voter Participation in the National Election, November, 1964,* pp. 11–13, 21–22; U.S. Bureau of the Census, *Voting and Registration in the Election of November, 1976,* pp. 14–23, 61–62.

Bibliography

Alcaly, Roger E., and David Mermelstein, eds. *The Fiscal Crisis of American Cities.* New York: Vintage Books, 1977.

Bell, Daniel. "Crime as an American Way of Life." *Antioch Review* 13 (Summer 1953): 131–154.

Brown, Michael K., and Steven P. Erie. "Blacks and the Legacy of the Great Society: The Economic and Political Impact of Federal Social Policy." *Public Policy* 29, no. 3 (Summer 1981): 299–330.

Browning, Rufus P., Dale Rogers Marshall, and David H. Tabb. *Protest Is Not Enough: The Struggle of Blacks and Hispanics for Equality in Urban Politics.* Berkeley and Los Angeles: University of California Press, 1984.

Cain, Bruce E., and D. Roderick Kieweit. *Minorities in California.* Pasadena, Ca.: California Institute of Technology, 1986.

Clark, David, L. "Los Angeles: Improbable Los Angeles." In *Sunbelt Cities: Politics and Growth Since World War Two,* edited by Richard M. Bernard and Bradley R. Rice, pp. 268–308. Austin: University of Texas Press, 1983.

Cole, Leonard A. *Blacks in Power: A Comparative Study of Black and White Elected Officials.* Princeton: Princeton University Press, 1976.

Cornwell, Elmer E. "Party Absorption of Ethnic Groups: The Case of Providence, Rhode Island." *Social Forces* 38 (March 1960): 205–210.

———. "Bosses, Machines, and Ethnic Groups." *Annals* 353 (May 1964): 27–39.

Dahl, Robert A. *Who Governs? Democracy and Power in an American City.* New Haven: Yale University Press, 1961.

Davis, Robert, and Joseph Tybor. "Mayor Wins Election Ruling." *Chicago Tribune,* September 3, 1986, pp. 1, 10.

Eisinger, Peter K. *The Politics of Displacement: Racial and Ethnic Transition in Three American Cities.* New York: Academic Press, 1980.

———. "Black Employment in Municipal Jobs: The Impact of Black Political Power." *American Political Science Review* 76, no. 2 (June 1982): 380–392.

———. "The Economic Conditions of Black Employment in Municipal Bureaucracy." *American Journal of Political Science* 26, no. 4 (November 1982): 754–771.

———. "Black Mayors and the Politics of Racial Economic Advancement." In *Culture, Ethnicity, and Identity,* edited by William C. McReady, pp. 95–109. New York: Academic Press, 1983.

Engstrom, Richard L., and Michael D. McDonald. "The Election of Blacks to City Councils: Clarifying the Impact of Electoral Arrangements of the Seats/Population Relationship." *American Political Science Review* 75, no. 2 (June 1981): 344–354.

Erie, Steven P. "Public Policy and Black Economic Polarization." *Policy Analysis* 6, no. 3 (Summer 1980): 305–317.

———. "Two Faces of Ethnic Power: Comparing the Irish and Black Experiences." *Polity* 13, no. 2 (Winter 1980): 261–284.

Garcia, F. Chris, and Rudolpho de la Garza. *The Chicano Political Experience: Three Perspectives.* North Scituate, Mass.: Duxbury Press, 1977.

Gelb, Joyce. "Blacks, Blocs, and Ballots: The Relevance of Party Politics to the Negro." *Polity* 3, no. 1 (Fall 1970): 44–69.

Gittell, Marilyn. "Public Employment and the Public Service." In *Public Service Employment: An Analysis of Its History, Problems, and Prospects,* edited by Alan Gartner et al., pp. 121–142. New York: Praeger, 1973.

Glazer, Nathan, and Daniel Patrick Moynihan. *Beyond the Melting Pot.* Cambridge, Mass.: MIT Press, 1964.

Greeley, Andrew. *That Most Distressful Nation: The Taming of the American Irish.* Chicago: Quadrangle, 1972.

――. *Ethnicity, Denomination, and Inequality.* Beverly Hills, Ca.: Sage Publications, 1976.

Green, Larry. "Chicago's Mayor Finally Grasps Power and Spoils." *Los Angeles Times,* August 2, 1986, pt. 1, pp. 1, 18.

Greenstein, Fred I. "The Changing Pattern of Urban Party Politics." *Annals* 353 (May 1964): 1–13.

Hamilton, Charles V. "Blacks and the Crisis of Political Participation." *Public Interest* 34 (Winter 1974): 185–210.

――. "Public Policy and Some Political Consequences." In *Public Policy for the Black Community,* edited by Marguerite R. Barnett and James A. Hefner, pp. 239–255. New York: Alfred Publishing, 1976.

――. "The Patron-Recipient Relationship and Minority Politics in New York City." *Political Science Quarterly* 95 (Summer 1979): 211–227.

Hamilton, Fred. *Rizzo.* New York: Viking Press, 1973.

Handlin, Oscar. *The Uprooted.* New York: Grosset and Dunlap, 1951.

――. *Boston's Immigrants: A Study in Acculturation.* Rev. ed. New York: Atheneum, 1970. Originally published in 1941.

Harrigan, John J. *Political Change in the Metropolis.* Boston: Little, Brown, 1985.

Heilig, Peggy, and Robert J. Mundt. "Changes in Representational Equity: The Effect of Adopting Districts." *Social Science Quarterly* 64, no. 1 (June 1983): 393–397.

Helyar, John, and Robert Johnson. "Tale of Two Cities: Chicago's Busy Center Masks a Loss of Jobs in Its Outlying Areas." *Wall Street Journal,* April 16, 1986, pp. 1, 22.

Howard, John R., and Robert C. Smith, eds. "Urban Black Politics." *Annals* 439 (September 1978): 1–150.

Judd, Dennis R. *The Politics of American Cities: Private Power and Public Policy.* 2d. ed. Boston: Little, Brown, 1984.

Karnig, Albert. "Black Representation on City Councils: The Impact of District Elections and Socioeconomic Factors." *Urban Affairs Quarterly* 12, no. 2 (December 1976): 223–242.

Katznelson, Ira. "The Crisis of the Capitalist City: Urban Politics and Social Control." In *Theoretical Perspectives on Urban Politics,* edited by Willis D. Hawley et al., pp. 214–229. Englewood Cliffs, N.J.: Prentice-Hall, 1976.

Keller, Edmond J. "The Impact of Black Mayors on Urban Policy." *Annals* 439 (September 1979): 40–52.

Kilson, Martin. "Political Change in the Negro Ghetto, 1900–1940s." In *Key Issues in the Afro-American Experience,* edited by Nathan I. Hugins, Martin Kilson, and Daniel M. Fox, pp. 182–189. New York: Harcourt Brace Jovanovich, 1971.

Levine, Edward M. *The Irish and Irish Politicians: A Study of Cultural and Social Alienation.* Notre Dame, Ind.: University of Notre Dame Press, 1966.

Litt, Edgar. *Beyond Pluralism: Ethnic Politics in America.* Glenview, Ill.: Scott, Foresman, 1970.

McConnell, John W. *The Evolution of Social Classes.* Washington, D.C.: American Council on Public Affairs, 1942.

McKitrick, Eric L. "The Study of Corruption." *Political Science Quarterly* 72 (December 1957): 502–514.

Merton, Robert K. *Social Theory and Social Structure.* Rev. ed. New York: Free Press, 1968. Originally published in 1949.

Mohl, Raymond A. "Miami: The Ethnic Cauldron." In *Sunbelt Cities: Politics and Growth Since World War Two,* edited by Richard M. Bernard and Bradley R. Rice, pp. 58–99. Austin: University of Texas Press, 1983.

Moore, Joan, and Harry Pachon. *Hispanics in the United States.* Englewood Cliffs, N.J.: Prentice-Hall, 1985.

Moynihan, Daniel Patrick. "The Irish." In *Beyond the Melting Pot,* by Nathan Glazer and Daniel Patrick Moynihan, pp. 217–287. Cambridge, Mass.: MIT Press, 1964.

Myers, Jerome K. "Assimilation in the Political Community." *Sociology and Social Research* 35 (January–February 1951): 175–182.

Nelson, William E., Jr., and Philip J. Meranto. *Electing Black Mayors: Political Action in the Black Community.* Columbus: Ohio State University Press, 1977.

Preston, Michael B., Lenneal J. Henderson, Jr., and Paul Puryear, eds. *The New Black Politics: The Search for Political Power.* New York: Longman, 1982.

Price, Gilbert. "Skirmish Begins 'At Large' Battle." *Cleveland Call and Post,* February 13, 1986, p. H8.

Robinson, Theodore P., and Thomas R. Dye. "Reformism and Black Representation on City Councils." *Social Science Quarterly* 59, no. 1 (June 1978): 133–142.

Ryan, Dennis P. *Beyond the Ballot Box: A Social History of the Boston Irish, 1845–1917.* Rutherford, N.J.: Fairleigh Dickinson University Press, 1983.

Sloan, Leonard. "Good Government and the Politics of Race." *Social Problems* 17 (Fall 1969): 171–174.

Smith, Robert C. "The Changing Shape of Urban Black Politics: 1960–1970." *Annals* 439 (September 1978): 16–28.

Sternlieb, George, and James W. Huges. "The Uncertain Future of the Center City." *Urban Affairs Quarterly* 18, no. 4 (June 1983): 455–472.

Stone, Clarence N. *Economic Growth and Neighborhood Discontent: System Bias in the Urban Renewal Program of Atlanta*. Chapel Hill: University of North Carolina Press, 1976.

———. "Atlanta: Protest and Elections Are Not Enough." In "Black and Hispanic Power in City Politics: A Forum," edited by Rufus P. Browning and Dale Rogers Marshall. *PS* 19, no. 3 (Summer 1986): 618–625.

Strausberg, Chinta. "Humes, Stroger Trade Blows." *Chicago Defender*, June 3, 1986.

———. "Mayor Seizes Control of Park Board." *Chicago Defender*, June 17, 1986, pp. 1, 18.

Tachibana, Judy. "California's Asians: Power from a Growing Population." *California Journal* 17, no. 11 (November 1986): 534–543.

Thernstrom, Stephan. *The Other Bostonians: Poverty and Progress in the American Metropolis, 1880–1970*. Cambridge, Mass.: Harvard University Press, 1973.

U.S. Bureau of the Census. *Special Reports: Occupations at the Twelfth Census*. Washington, D.C.: Government Printing Office, 1904.

———. *Fifteenth Census of the United States, 1930*. Washington, D.C.: Government Printing Office, 1933.

———. *Voter Participation in the National Election, November, 1964*. Washington, D.C.: Government Printing Office, 1965.

———. *Voting and Registration in the Election of November, 1976*. Washington, D.C.: Government Printing Office, 1977.

U.S. Census Office. *Ninth Census, 1870*. Washington, D.C.: Government Printing Office, 1872.

U.S. Civil Service Commission. *Minority Group Employment in the Federal Government, 1975*. Washington, D.C.: Government Printing Office, 1977.

U.S. Equal Employment Opportunity Commission. *Minorities and Women in State and Local Government, 1977*. Washington, D.C.: Government Printing Office, 1977.

Walton, Hanes, Jr. *Black Politics: A Theoretical and Structural Analysis*. Philadelphia: J. B. Lippincott, 1972.

Watkins, Linda M. "Pittsburgh Blacks' Paucity of Political Clout Stirs Struggle over the City's At-Large Election System." *Wall Street Journal*, April 1, 1986, p. 58.

Welch, Susan, and Albert Karnig. "The Impact of Black Elected Officials on Urban Social Expenditures." *Policy Studies Journal* 7 (Summer 1979): 707–714.

Whyte, William Foote. "Social Organization in the Slums." *American Sociological Review* 8, no. 1 (February 1943): 34–39.

———. *Street Corner Society: The Social Structure of an Italian Slum*. Chicago: University of Chicago Press, 1955. Originally published in 1943.

Willis, Marty. "Jan. 6 Demonstration to Greet All-White City Council." *Pittsburgh Courier*, January 11, 1986, pp. A-1, A-4.

Chapter 4

❖❖❖

REFORM POLITICS

The Contest for Political Control

By the late nineteenth century, the machine politics that was prevalent in most cities began to provoke opposition from upper- and middle-class citizens. At first, the fledgling reform efforts mostly met with failure because they did not succeed in articulating a vision of the city that could unite enough groups behind a compelling cause. During the Progressive Era, however, municipal reform became a national crusade. Although the reformers often attacked the machines by claiming that "boss politics" undermined democracy, they were not necessarily interested in a kind of reform that would actually make cities more democratic. Quite the opposite. The spirit and substance of the reformers' objectives were stated in an unusually candid way in a magazine article reprinted here, which was published in 1890 by Andrew D. White, the first president of Cornell University. White believed that a city could be run like a business, and that its affairs should be nonpartisan in character, having nothing to do with politics. Note that White's advocacy of nonpartisanship was intimately linked to his belief that removing the party label from election ballots could help remove local government from the influence of immigrant voters. The reformers said that they wanted to make local government more efficient, but this claim often served as a useful cover for an antidemocratic attack on the Great Unwashed.

According to the selection by the urban historian Samuel P. Hays, business leaders and the upper class spearheaded reform. The reformers shared a conviction that only they were capable of properly managing the affairs of government. Reformers claimed that they were merely protecting municipal government from corruption, but in reality, they ushered in a centralized style of politics that was much removed from the influence of ordinary voters.

In her selection, Amy Bridges demonstrates that, although it often failed to gain a foothold in the big industrial cities, reform government found a ready home in the newer cities of the Southwest. She argues that reform spread rapidly in southwestern cities because business leaders and civic elites regarded the capture of local government as a necessary step to local economic development. Faced with problems of geographic isolation and threats to the survival of their cities, local elites, in effect, built their own city-states, which they used to develop harbors and rail connections, secure public services and utilities, and lobby the states and Congress for assistance. As an extension of boosters' interest in economic growth, local government became, basically, an extension of the business community. As such, reform in the Southwest became a more thoroughly successful strategy for securing political control than it was in the industrial cities, where reformers were required to compete with political entrepreneurs who were skilled at maintaining the loyalty of immigrant voters. Thus, Bridges' study shows that reform was actually a struggle about who would govern the city more than about sacred principles of efficiency and honest government.

10

Andrew D. White

CITY AFFAIRS ARE NOT POLITICAL

Without the slightest exaggeration we may assert that, with very few exceptions, the city governments of the United States are the worst in Christendom—the most expensive, the most inefficient, and the most corrupt. No one who has any considerable knowledge of our own country and of other countries can deny this. . . .

What is the cause of the difference between municipalities in the old world and in the new? I do not allow that their populations are better than ours. What accounts, then, for the better municipal development in their case and for the miserable results in our own? My answer is this: we are attempting to govern our cities upon a theory which has never been found to work practically in any part of the world. Various forms of it were tried in the great cities of antiquity and of the middle ages, especially in the mediaeval republics of Italy, and without exception they ended in tyranny, confiscation, and bloodshed. The same theory has produced the worst results in various countries of modern Europe, down to a recent period.

What is this evil theory? It is simply that the city is a political body; that its interior affairs have to do with national political parties and issues. My fundamental contention is that a city is a corporation; that as a city it has nothing whatever to do with general political interests; that party political names and duties are utterly out of place there. The questions in a city are not political questions. They have reference to the laying out of streets; to the erection of buildings; to sanitary arrangements, sewerage, water supply, gas supply, electrical supply; to the control of franchises and the like; and to provisions for the public health and comfort in parks, boulevards, libraries, and museums. The work of a city being the creation and control of the city property, it should logi-

---

cally be managed as a piece of property by those who have created it, who have a title to it, or a real substantial part in it, and who can therefore feel strongly their duty to it. Under our theory that a city is a political body, a crowd of illiterate peasants, freshly raked in from Irish bogs, or Bohemian mines, or Italian robber nests, may exercise virtual control. How such men govern cities, we know too well; as a rule they are not alive even to their own most direct interests. . . .

The difference between foreign cities and ours, is that all these well-ordered cities in England, France, Germany, Italy, Switzerland, whether in monarchies or republics, accept this principle—that cities are corporations and not political bodies; that they are not concerned with matters of national policy; that national parties as such have nothing whatever to do with city questions. They base their city governments upon ascertained facts regarding human nature, and upon right reason. They try to conduct them upon the principles observed by honest and energetic men in business affairs. We, on the other hand, are putting ourselves upon a basis which has always failed and will always fail—the idea that a city is a political body, and therefore that it is to be ruled, in the long run, by a city proletariat mob, obeying national party cries.

What is our safety? The reader may possibly expect me, in logical consonance with the statement I have just made, to recommend that the city be treated strictly as a corporate body, and governed entirely by those who have a direct pecuniary interest in it. If so, he is mistaken. I am no doctrinaire; politics cannot be bent completely to logic—certainly not all at once. A wise, statesmanlike view would indicate a compromise between the political idea and the corporate idea. I would not break away entirely from the past, but I would build a better future upon what we may preserve from the past.

To this end I would still leave in existence the theory that the city is a political body, as regards the election of the mayor and common council. I would elect the mayor by the votes of the majority of all the citizens, as at present; I would elect the common council by a majority of all the votes of all the citizens; but instead of electing its members from the wards as at present—so that wards largely controlled by thieves and robbers can send thieves and robbers, and so that men who can carry their ward can control the city—I would elect the board of aldermen on a general ticket, just as the mayor is elected now, thus requiring candidates for the board to have a city reputation. So much for retaining the idea of the city as a political body. In addition to this, in consideration of the fact that the city is a corporation, I would have those owning property in it properly recognized. I would leave to them, and to them alone, the election of a board of control, without whose permission no franchise should be granted and no expenditure should be made. This should be the rule, but to this rule I am inclined to make one exception; I would allow the votes of the board of control, as regards expenditures for primary education, to be overridden by a two-thirds majority of the board of aldermen. I should do this because here alone does the city policy come into direct relations with the general political system of the nation at large. The main argument for the existence of our public schools is that they are an absolute necessity to the existence of our Republic;

that without preliminary education a republic simply becomes an illiterate mob, that if illiterate elements control, the destruction of the Republic is sure. On this ground, considering the public-school system as based upon a national political necessity, I would have an exception made regarding the expenditures for it, leaving in this matter a last resort to the political assembly of the people.

A theory resulting in a system virtually like this, has made the cities of Europe, whether in monarchies or republics, what they are, and has made it an honor in many foreign countries for the foremost citizens to serve in the common councils of their cities. Take one example: It has been my good fortune to know well Rudolf Von Gneist, councilor of the German Empire. My acquaintance with him began when it was my official duty to present to him a testimonial, in behalf of the government of the United States, for his services in settling the north-west boundary between the United States and Great Britain. The Emperor William was the nominal umpire; he made Von Gneist the real umpire— that shows Von Gneist's standing. He is also a leading professor of law in the University of Berlin, a member of the Imperial Parliament and of the Prussian Legislature, and the author of famous books, not only upon law, but upon the constitutional history of Germany and of England. This man has been, during a considerable time, a member of what we should call the board of aldermen of the city of Berlin, and he is proud to serve in that position. With him have been associated other men the most honored in various walks of life, and among these some of the greatest business men, renowned in all lands for their enterprise and their probity. Look through the councils of our cities, using any microscope you can find, and tell me how many such men you discern in them. Under the system I propose, it is, humanly speaking, certain that these better men would seek entrance into our city councils. Especially would this be the case if our citizens should, by and by, learn that it is better to have in the common council an honest man, though a Republican, than a scoundrel, though a Democrat; and better to have a man of ability and civic pride, though a Democrat, than a weak, yielding creature, though a Republican.

Some objections will be made. It will be said, first, that wealthy and well-to-do people do not do their duty in city matters; that if they should, they would have better city government. This is true to this extent, that even well-to-do men are in city politics strangely led away from their civic duties by fancied allegiance to national party men and party issues. But in other respects it is untrue; the vote of a single tenement house, managed by a professional politician, will neutralize the vote of an entire street of well-to-do citizens. Men in business soon find this out; they soon find that to work for political improvement under the present system is time and labor and self-respect thrown away. It may be also said that the proposal is impracticable. I ask, why? History does not show it to be impracticable; for we have before us, as I have shown, the practice of all other great civilized nations on earth, and especially of our principal sister republics.

But it will be said that "revolutions do not go backward." They did go backward in the great cities of Europe when these rid themselves of the old bad system that had at bottom the theory under which ours are managed, and when they entered into their new and better system. The same objection, that revolutions do not go backward, was made against any reform in the tenure of office of the governor and of the higher judiciary in the State of New York; and yet the revolution did go backward, that is, it went back out of doctrinaire folly into sound, substantial, common-sense statesmanship. In 1847 the State of New York so broke away from the old conservative moorings as to make all judgeships elective, with short terms, small pay, and wretched accommodations, and the same plan was pursued as regards the governor and other leading officials; but the State, some years since, very wisely went back to much of its former system—in short, made a revolution backward, if any one chooses to call it so—resuming the far better system of giving our governor and higher judges longer terms, larger salaries, better accommodations, and dignified surroundings. We see, then, that it is not true that steps in a wrong direction in a republic cannot be retraced. As they have been retraced in State affairs, so they may be in municipal affairs.

But it will be said that this change in city government involves a long struggle. It may or it may not. If it does, such a struggle is but part of the price which we pay for the maintenance of free institutions in town, State, and nation. For this struggle, I especially urge all men of light and leading to prepare themselves. As to the public at large, what is most needed in regard to municipal affairs, as in regard to public affairs generally, is the quiet, steady evolution of a knowledge of truth and of proper action in view of it. That truth, as regards city government, is simply the truth that municipal affairs are not political; that political parties as such have nothing to do with cities; that the men who import political considerations into municipal management are to be opposed. This being the case, the adoption of some such system as that which I have sketched would seem likely to prove fruitful of good.

11

Samuel P. Hays

THE POLITICS OF REFORM IN MUNICIPAL GOVERNMENT IN THE PROGRESSIVE ERA

In order to achieve a more complete understanding of social change in the Progressive Era, historians must now undertake a deeper analysis of the practices of economic, political, and social groups. Political ideology alone is no longer

"The Politics of Reform in Municipal Government in the Progressive Era," by Samuel P. Hays, as printed in *Pacific Northwest Quarterly*, Vol. 55, 1964, pp. 157–169. Reprinted by permission of Pacific Northwest Quarterly.

satisfactory evidence to describe social patterns because generalizations based upon it, which tend to divide political groups into the moral and the immoral, the rational and the irrational, the efficient and the inefficient, do not square with political practice. Behind this contemporary rhetoric concerning the nature of reform lay patterns of political behavior which were at variance with it. Since an extensive gap separated ideology and practice, we can no longer take the former as an accurate description of the latter, but must reconstruct social behavior from other types of evidence.

Reform in urban government provides one of the most striking examples of this problem of analysis. The demand for change in municipal affairs, whether in terms of over-all reform, such as the commission and city-manager plans, or of more piecemeal modifications, such as the development of the city-wide school boards, deeply involved reform ideology. Reformers loudly proclaimed a new structure of municipal government as more moral, more rational, and more efficient and, because it was so, self-evidently more desirable. But precisely because of this emphasis, there seemed to be no need to analyze the political forces behind change. Because the goals of reform were good, its causes were obvious; rather than being the product of particular people and particular ideas in particular situations, they were deeply imbedded in the universal impulses and truths of "progress." Consequently, historians have rarely tried to determine precisely who the municipal reformers were or what they did, but instead have relied on reform ideology as an accurate description of reform practice.

The reform ideology which became the basis of historical analysis is well known. It appears in classic form in Lincoln Steffens' *Shame of the Cities*. The urban political struggle of the Progressive Era, so the argument goes, involved a conflict between public impulses for "good government" against a corrupt alliance of "machine politicians" and "special interests."

During the rapid urbanization of the late 19th century, the latter had been free to aggrandize themselves, especially through franchise grants, at the expense of the public. Their power lay primarily in their ability to manipulate the political process, by bribery and corruption, for their own ends. Against such arrangements there gradually arose a public protest, a demand by the public for honest government, for officials who would act for the public rather than for themselves. To accomplish their goals, reformers sought basic modifications in the political system, both in the structure of government and in the manner of selecting public officials. These changes, successful in city after city, enabled the "public interest" to triumph.[1]

Recently, George Mowry, Alfred Chandler, Jr., and Richard Hofstadter have modified this analysis by emphasizing the fact that the impulse for reform did not come from the working class.[2] This might have been suspected from the rather strained efforts of National Municipal League writers in the "Era of Reform" to go out of their way to demonstrate working-class support for commission and city-manager governments.[3] We now know that they clutched at straws, and often erroneously, in order to prove to themselves as well as to the public that municipal reform was a mass movement.

The Mowry-Chandler-Hofstadter writings have further modified older views by asserting that reform in general and municipal reform in particular sprang from a distinctively middle-class movement. This has now become the prevailing view. Its popularity is surprising not only because it is based upon faulty logic and extremely limited evidence, but also because it, too, emphasizes the analysis of ideology rather than practice and fails to contribute much to the understanding of who distinctively were involved in reform and why.

Ostensibly, the "middle-class" theory of reform is based upon a new type of behavioral evidence, the collective biography, in studies by Mowry of California Progressive party leaders, by Chandler of a nationwide group of that party's leading figures, and by Hofstadter of four professions—ministers, lawyers, teachers, editors. These studies demonstrate the middle-class nature of reform, but they fail to determine if reformers were distinctively middle class, specifically if they differed from their opponents. One study of 300 political leaders in the state of Iowa, for example, discovered that Progressive party, Old Guard, and Cummins Republicans were all substantially alike, the Progressives differing only in that they were slightly younger than the others and had less political experience.[4] If its opponents were also middle class, then one cannot describe Progressive reform as a phenomenon, the special nature of which can be explained in terms of middle-class characteristics. One cannot explain the distinctive behavior of people in terms of characteristics which are not distinctive to them.

Hofstadter's evidence concerning professional men fails in yet another way to determine the peculiar characteristics of reformers. For he describes ministers, lawyers, teachers, and editors without determining who within these professions became reformers and who did not. Two analytical distinctions might be made. Ministers involved in municipal reform, it appears, came not from all segments of religion, but peculiarly from upper-class churches. They enjoyed the highest prestige and salaries in the religious community and had no reason to feel a loss of "status," as Hofstadter argues. Their role in reform arose from the class character of their religious organizations rather than from the mere fact of their occupation as ministers.[5] Professional men involved in reform (many of whom—engineers, architects, and doctors—Hofstadter did not examine at all) seem to have come especially from the more advanced segments of their professions, from those who sought to apply their specialized knowledge to a wider range of public affairs.[6] Their role in reform is related not to their attempt to defend earlier patterns of culture, but to the working out of the inner dynamics of professionalization in modern society.

The weakness of the "middle-class" theory of reform stems from the fact that it rests primarily upon ideological evidence, not on a thoroughgoing description of political practice. Although the studies of Mowry, Chandler, and Hofstadter ostensibly derive from behavioral evidence, they actually derive largely from the extensive expressions of middle-ground ideological position, of the reformers' own descriptions of their contemporary society, and of their expressed fears of both the lower and the upper classes, of the fright of being ground between the millstones of labor and capital.[7]

Such evidence, though it accurately portrays what people thought, does not accurately describe what they did. The great majority of Americans look upon themselves as "middle class" and subscribe to a middle-ground ideology, even though in practice they belong to a great variety of distinct social classes. Such ideologies are not rationalizations of deliberate attempts to deceive. They are natural phenomena of human behavior. But the historian should be especially sensitive to their role so that he will not take evidence of political ideology as an accurate representation of political practice.

In the following account I will summarize evidence in both secondary and primary works concerning the political practices in which municipal reformers were involved. Such an analysis logically can be broken down into three parts, each one corresponding to a step in the traditional argument. First, what was the source of reform? Did it lie in the general public rather than in particular groups? Was it middle class, working class, or perhaps of other composition? Second, what was the reform target of attack? Were reformers primarily interested in ousting the corrupt individual, the political or business leader who made private arrangements at the expense of the public, or were they interested in something else? Third, what political innovations did reformers bring about? Did they seek to expand popular participation in the governmental process?

There is now sufficient evidence to determine the validity of these specific elements of the more general argument. Some of it has been available for several decades; some has appeared more recently; some is presented here for the first time. All of it adds up to the conclusion that reform in municipal government involved a political development far different from what we have assumed in the past.

Available evidence indicates that the source of support for reform in municipal government did not come from the lower or middle classes, but from the upper class. The leading business groups in each city and professional men closely allied with them initiated and dominated municipal movements. Leonard White, in his study of the city manager published in 1927, wrote:

> The opposition to bad government usually comes to a head in the local chamber of commerce. Business men finally acquire the conviction that the growth of their city is being seriously impaired by the failures of city officials to perform their duties efficiently. Looking about for a remedy, they are captivated by the resemblance of the city-manager plan to their corporate form of business organization.[8]

In the 1930s White directed a number of studies of the origin of city-manager government. The resulting reports invariably begin with such statements as, "the Chamber of Commerce spearheaded the movement," or commission government in this city was a "businessmen's government."[9] Of thirty-two cases of city-manager government in Oklahoma examined by Jewell C. Phillips, twenty-nine were initiated either by chambers of commerce or by community committees dominated by businessmen.[10] More recently James Weinstein has presented almost irrefutable evidence that the business community, represented largely by chambers of commerce, was the overwhelming force behind both commission and city-manager movements.[11]

Dominant elements of the business community played a prominent role in another crucial aspect of municipal reform: the Municipal Research Bureau movement.[12] Especially in the larger cities, where they had less success in shaping the structure of government, reformers established centers to conduct research in municipal affairs as a springboard for influence.

The first such organization, the Bureau of Municipal Research of New York City, was founded in 1906; it was financed largely through the efforts of Andrew Carnegie and John D. Rockefeller. An investment banker provided the crucial support in Philadelphia, where a Bureau was founded in 1908. A group of wealthy Chicagoans in 1910 established the Bureau of Public Efficiency, a research agency. John H. Patterson of the National Cash Register Company, the leading figure in Dayton municipal reform, financed the Dayton Bureau, founded in 1912. And George Eastman was the driving force behind both the Bureau of Municipal Research and city-manager government in Rochester. In smaller cities data about city government [were] collected by interested individuals in a more informal way or by chambers of commerce, but in larger cities the task required special support, and prominent businessmen supplied it.

The character of municipal reform is demonstrated more precisely by a brief examination of the movements in Des Moines and Pittsburgh. The Des Moines Commercial Club inaugurated and carefully controlled the drive for the commission form of government.[13] In January, 1906 the Club held a so-called "mass meeting" of business and professional men to secure an enabling act from the state legislature. P. C. Kenyon, president of the Club, selected a Committee of 300, composed principally of business and professional men, to draw up a specific proposal. After the legislature approved their plan, the same committee managed the campaign which persuaded the electorate to accept the commission form of government by a narrow margin in June, 1907.

In this election the lower-income wards of the city opposed the change, the upper-income wards supported it strongly, and the middle-income wards were more evenly divided. In order to control the new government, the Committee of 300, now expanded to 530, sought to determine the nomination and election of the five new commissioners, and to this end they selected an avowedly businessman's slate. Their plans backfired when the voters swept into office a slate of anticommission candidates who now controlled the new commission government.

Proponents of the commission form of government in Des Moines spoke frequently in the name of the "people." But their more explicit statements emphasized their intent that the new plan be a "business system" of government, run by businessmen. The slate of candidates for commissioner endorsed by advocates of the plan was known as the "businessman's ticket." J. W. Hill, president of the committees of 300 and 530, bluntly declared: "The professional politician must be ousted and in his place capable businessmen chosen to conduct the affairs of the city." I. M. Earle, general counsel of the Bankers Life Association and a prominent figure in the movement, put the point more precisely: "When the plan was adopted it was the intention to get businessmen to run it."

Although reformers used the ideology of popular government, they in no sense meant that all segments of society should be involved equally in municipal decision-making. They meant that their concept of the city's welfare would be best achieved if the business community controlled city government. As one businessman told a labor audience, the businessman's slate represented labor "better than you do yourself."

The composition of the municipal reform movement in Pittsburgh demonstrates its upper-class and professional as well as its business sources.[14] Here the two principal reform organizations were the Civic Club and the Voters' League. The 745 members of these two organizations came primarily from the upper class. Sixty-five percent appeared in upper-class directories which contained the names of only 2 percent of the city's families. Furthermore, many who were not listed in these directories lived in upper-class areas. These reformers, it should be stressed, comprised not an old but a new upper class. Few came from earlier industrial and mercantile families. Most of them had risen to social position from wealth created after 1870 in the iron, steel, electrical equipment, and other industries, and they lived in the newer rather than the older fashionable areas.

Almost half (48 percent) of the reformers were professional men: doctors, lawyers, ministers, directors of libraries and museums, engineers, architects, private and public school teachers, and college professors. Some of these belonged to the upper class as well, especially the lawyers, ministers, and private school teachers. But for the most part their interest in reform stemmed from the inherent dynamics of their professions rather than from their class connections. They came from the more advanced segments of their organizations, from those in the forefront of the acquisition and application of knowledge. They were not the older professional men, seeking to preserve the past against change; they were in the vanguard of professional life, actively seeking to apply expertise more widely to public affairs.

Pittsburgh reformers included a large segment of businessmen; 52 percent were bankers and corporation officials or their wives. Among them were the presidents of fourteen large banks and officials of Westinghouse, Pittsburgh Plate Glass, U.S. Steel and its component parts (such as Carnegie Steel, American Bridge, and National Tube), Jones and Laughlin, lesser steel companies (such as Crucible, Pittsburgh, Superior, Lockhart, and H. K. Porter), the H. J. Heinz Company, and the Pittsburgh Coal Company, as well as officials of the Pennsylvania Railroad and the Pittsburgh and Lake Erie. These men were not small businessmen; they directed the most powerful banking and industrial organizations of the city. They represented not the old business community, but industries which had developed and grown primarily within the past fifty years and which had come to dominate the city's economic life.

These business, professional, and upper-class groups who dominated municipal reform movements were all involved in the rationalization and systematization of modern life; they wished a form of government which would be more consistent with the objectives inherent in those developments. The most important single feature of their perspective was the rapid expansion of the geographical scope of affairs which they wished to influence and manipulate, a scope which was no longer limited and narrow, no longer within the confines of pedestrian communities, but was now broad and city-wide, covering the whole range of activities of the metropolitan area.

The migration of the upper class from central to outlying areas created a geographical distance between its residential communities and its economic institutions. To protect the latter required involvement both in local ward affairs and in the larger city government as well. Moreover, upper-class cultural institutions, such as museums, libraries, and symphony orchestras, required an active interest in the larger municipal context from which these institutions drew much of their clientele.

Professional groups, broadening the scope of affairs which they sought to study, measure, or manipulate, also sought to influence the public health, the educational system, or the physical arrangements of the entire city. Their concerns were limitless, not bounded by geography, but as expansive as the professional imagination. Finally, the new industrial community greatly broadened its perspective in governmental affairs because of its new recognition of the way in which factors throughout the city affected business growth. The increasing size and scope of industry, the greater stake in more varied and geographically dispersed facts of city life, the effect of floods on many business concerns, the need to promote traffic flows to and from work for both blue-collar and managerial employees—all contributed to this larger interest. The geographically larger private perspectives of upper-class, professional, and business groups gave rise to a geographically larger public perspective.

These reformers were dissatisfied with existing systems of municipal government. They did not oppose corruption per se—although there was plenty of that. They objected to the structure of government which enabled local and particularistic interests to dominate. Prior to the reforms of the Progressive Era, city government consisted primarily of confederations of local wards, each of which was represented on the city's legislative body. Each ward frequently had its own elementary schools and ward-elected school boards which administered them.

These particularistic interests were the focus of a decentralized political life. City councilmen were local leaders. They spoke for their local areas, the economic interests of their inhabitants, their residential concerns, their educational, recreational, and religious interests—i.e., for those aspects of community life which mattered most to those they represented. They rolled logs in the city council to provide streets, sewers, and other public works for their local areas. They defended the community's cultural practices, its distinctive languages or national customs, its liberal attitude toward liquor, and its saloons and dance halls which served as centers of community life. One observer described this process of representation in Seattle:

> The residents of the hill-tops and the suburbs may not fully appreciate the faithfulness of certain downtown ward councilmen to the interests of their constituents. . . . The people of a state would rise in arms against a senator or representative in Congress who deliberately misrepresented their wishes and imperiled their interests, though he might plead a higher regard for national good. Yet people in other parts of the city seem to forget that under the old system the ward elected councilmen with the idea of procuring service of special benefit to that ward.[15]

In short, pre-reform officials spoke for their constituencies, inevitably their own wards which had elected them, rather than for other sections or groups of the city.

The ward system of government especially gave representation in city affairs to lower- and middle-class groups. Most elected ward officials were from these groups, and they, in turn, constituted the major opposition to reforms in municipal government. In Pittsburgh, for example, immediately prior to the changes in both the city council and the school board in 1911 in which city-wide representation replaced ward representation, only 24 percent of the 387 members of those bodies represented the same managerial, professional, and banker occupations which dominated the membership of the Civic Club and the Voters' League. The great majority (67 percent) were small businessmen—grocers, saloonkeepers, livery-stable proprietors, owners of small hotels, druggists—white-collar workers such as clerks and bookkeepers, and skilled and unskilled workmen.[16]

This decentralized system of urban growth and the institutions which arose from it reformers now opposed. Social, professional, and economic life had developed not only in the local wards in a small community context, but also on a larger scale had become highly integrated and organized, giving rise to a super-structure of social organization which lay far above that of ward life and which was sharply divorced from it in both personal contacts and perspective.

By the late 19th century, those involved in these larger institutions found that the decentralized system of political life limited their larger objectives. The movement for reform in municipal government, therefore, constituted an attempt by upper-class, advanced professional, and large business groups to take formal political power from the previously dominant lower- and middle-class elements so that they might advance their own conceptions of desirable public policy. These two groups came from entirely different urban worlds, and the political system fashioned by one was no longer acceptable to the other.

Lower- and middle-class groups not only dominated the pre-reform governments, but vigorously opposed reform. It is significant that none of the occupational groups among them, for example, small businessmen or white-collar workers, skilled or unskilled artisans, had important representation in reform organizations thus far examined. The case studies of city-manager government undertaken in the 1930s under the direction of Leonard White detailed in city after city the particular opposition of labor. In their analysis of Jackson, Michigan, the authors of these studies wrote:

> The *Square Deal*, oldest Labor paper in the state, has been consistently against manager government, perhaps largely because labor has felt that with a decentralized government elected on a ward basis it was more likely to have some voice and to receive its share of privileges.[17]

In Janesville, Wisconsin, the small shopkeepers and workingmen on the west and south sides, heavily Catholic and often Irish, opposed the commission plan in 1911 and in 1912 and the city-manager plan when adopted in 1923.[18] "In Dallas there is hardly a trace of class consciousness in the Marxian sense," one investigator declared, "yet in city elections the division has been to a great extent along class lines."[19] The commission and city-manager elections were no exceptions. To these authors it seemed a logical reaction, rather than an embarrassing fact that had to be swept away, that workingmen should have opposed municipal reform.[20]

In Des Moines working-class representatives, who in previous years might have been council members, were conspicuously absent from the "businessman's slate." Workingmen acceptable to reformers could not be found. A workingman's slate of candidates, therefore, appeared to challenge the reform slate. Organized labor, and especially the mineworkers, took the lead; one of their number, Wesley Ash, a deputy sheriff and union member, made "an astonishing run" in the primary, coming in second among a field of more than twenty candidates.[21] In fact, the strength of anticommission candidates in the primary so alarmed reformers that they frantically sought to appease labor.

The day before the final election they modified their platform to pledge both an eight-hour day and an "American standard of wages." They attempted to persuade the voters that their slate consisted of men who represented labor because they had "begun at the bottom of the ladder and made a good climb toward success by their own unaided efforts."[22] But their tactics failed. In the election on March 30, 1908, voters swept into office the entire "opposition" slate. The business and professional community had succeeded in changing the form of government, but not in securing its control. A cartoon in the leading reform newspaper illustrated their disappointment; John Q. Public sat dejectedly and muttered, "Aw, What's the Use?"

The most visible opposition to reform and the most readily available target of reform attack was the so-called "machine," for through the "machine" many different ward communities as well as lower- and middle-income groups joined effectively to influence the central city government. Their private occupational and social life did not naturally involve these groups in larger city-wide activities in the same way as the upper class was involved; hence they lacked access to privately organized economic and social power on which they could construct political power. The "machine" filled this organizational gap.

Yet it should never be forgotten that the social and economic institutions in the wards themselves provided the "machine's" sustaining support and gave it larger significance. When reformers attacked the "machine" as the most visible institutional element of the ward system, they attacked the entire ward form of political organization and the political power of lower- and middle-income groups which lay behind it.

Reformers often gave the impression that they opposed merely the corrupt politician and his "machine." But in a more fundamental way they looked upon the deficiencies of pre-reform political leaders in terms not of their personal shortcomings, but of the limitations inherent in their occupational, institutional, and class positions. In 1911 the Voters' League of Pittsburgh wrote in its pamphlet analyzing the qualifications of candidates that "a man's occupation ought to give a strong indication of his qualifications for membership on a school board."[23] Certain occupations inherently disqualified a man from serving:

Employment as ordinary laborer and in the lowest class of mill work would naturally lead to the conclusion that such men did not have sufficient education or business training to act as school directors. . . . Objection might also be made to small shopkeepers, clerks, workmen at many trades, who by lack of educational advantages and business training, could not, no matter how honest, be expected to administer properly the affairs of an educational system, requiring special knowledge, and where millions are spent each year.

These, of course, were precisely the groups which did dominate Pittsburgh government prior to reform. The League deplored the fact that school boards contained only a small number of "men prominent throughout the city in business life . . . in professional occupations . . . holding positions as managers, secretaries, auditors, superintendents and foremen" and exhorted these classes to participate more actively as candidates for office.

Reformers, therefore, wished not simply to replace bad men with good; they proposed to change the occupational and class origins of decision-makers. Toward this end they sought innovations in the formal machinery of government, which would concentrate political power by sharply centralizing the processes of decision-making rather than distribute it through more popular participation in public affairs. According to the liberal view of the Progressive Era, the major political innovations of reform involved the equalization of political power through the primary, the direct election of public officials, and the initiative, referendum, and recall. These measures played a large role in the political ideology of the time and were frequently incorporated into new municipal charters. But they provided at best only an occasional and often incidental process of decision-making. Far more important in continuous, sustained, day-to-day processes of government were those innovations which centralized decision-making in the hands of fewer and fewer people.

The systematization of municipal government took place on both the executive and the legislative levels. The strong-mayor and city manager types become the most widely used examples of the former. In the first decade of the 20th century, the commission plan had considerable appeal, but its distribution of administrative responsibility among five people gave rise to a demand for a form with more centralized executive power; consequently, the city-manager or the commission-manager variant often replaced it.[24]

A far more pervasive and significant change, however, lay in the centralization of the system of representation, the shift from ward to city-wide election of councils and school boards. Governing bodies so selected, reformers argued, would give less attention to local and particularistic matters and more to affairs of city-wide scope. This shift, an invariable feature of both commission and city-manager plans, was often adopted by itself. In Pittsburgh, for example, the new charter of 1911 provided as the major innovation that a council of twenty-seven, each member elected from a separate ward, be replaced by a council of nine, each elected by the city as a whole.

Cities displayed wide variations in this innovation. Some regrouped wards into larger units but kept the principle of areas of representation smaller than the entire city. Some combined a majority of councilmen elected by wards with additional ones selected at large. All such innovations, however, constituted steps toward the centralization of the system of representation.

Liberal historians have not appreciated the extent to which municipal reform in the Progressive Era involved a debate over the system of representation. The ward form of representation was universally condemned on the grounds that it gave too much influence to the separate units and not enough attention to the larger problems of the city. Harry A. Toulmin, whose book, *The City Manager,* was published by the National Municipal League, stated the case:

> The spirit of sectionalism had dominated the political life of every city. Ward pitted against ward, alderman against alderman, and legislation only effected by "long-rolling" extravagant measures into operation, molding the city, but gratifying the greed of constituents, has too long stung the conscience of decent citizenship. This constant treaty-making of factionalism has been no less than a curse. The city manager plan proposes the commendable thing of abolishing wards. The plan is not unique in this for it has been common to many forms of commission government. . . .[25]

Such a system should be supplanted, the argument usually went, with city-wide representation in which elected officials could consider the city "as a unit." "The new officers are elected," wrote Toulmin, "each to represent all the people. Their duties are so defined that they must administer the corporate business in its entirety, not as a hodge-podge of associated localities."

Behind the debate over the method of representation, however, lay a debate over who should be represented, over whose views of public policy should prevail. Many reform leaders often explicitly, if not implicitly, expressed fear that lower- and middle-income groups had too much influence in decision-making. One Galveston leader, for example, complained about the movement for initiative, referendum, and recall:

> We have in our city a very large number of negroes employed on the docks; we also have a very large number of unskilled white laborers; this city also has more barrooms, according to its population, than any other city in Texas. Under these circumstances it would be extremely difficult to maintain a satisfactory city government where all ordinances must be submitted back to the voters of the city for their ratification and approval.[26]

At the National Municipal League convention of 1907, Rear Admiral F. E. Chadwick (USN Ret.), a leader in the Newport, Rhode Island, movement for municipal reform, spoke to this question even more directly:

> Our present system has excluded in large degree the representation of those who have the city's well-being most at heart. It has brought, in municipalities . . . a government established by the least educated, the least interested class of citizens.
>
> It stands to reason that a man paying $5,000 taxes in a town is more interested in the well-being and development of his town than the man who pays no taxes. . . . It equally stands to reason that the man of the $5,000 tax should be assured a representation in the committee which lays the tax and spends the money which he contributes. . . . Shall we be truly democratic and give the property owner a fair show or shall we develop a tyranny of ignorance which shall crush him?[27]

Municipal reformers thus debated frequently the question of who should be represented as well as the question of what method of representation should be employed.

That these two questions were intimately connected was revealed in other reform proposals for representation, proposals which were rarely taken seriously. One suggestion was that a class system of representation be substituted for ward representation. For example, in 1908 one of the prominent candidates for commissioner in Des Moines proposed that the city council be composed of representatives of five classes: educational and ministerial organizations, manufacturers and jobbers, public utility corporations, retail merchants including liquor men, and the Des Moines Trades and Labor Assembly. Such a system would have greatly reduced the influence in the council of both middle- and lower-class groups. The proposal revealed the basic problem confronting business and professional leaders: how to reduce the influence in government of the majority of voters among middle- and lower-income groups.[28]

A growing imbalance between population and representation sharpened the desire of reformers to change from ward to city-wide elections. Despite shifts in population within most cities, neither ward district lines nor the apportionment of city council and school board sets changed frequently. Consequently, older areas of the city, with wards that were small in geographical size and held declining populations (usually lower and middle class in composition), continued to be overrepresented, and newer upper-class areas, where population was growing, became increasingly underrepresented. This intensified the reformers' conviction that the structure of government must be changed to give them the voice they needed to make their views on public policy prevail.[29]

It is not insignificant that in some cities (by no means a majority) municipal reform came about outside the urban electoral process. The original commission government in Galveston was appointed rather than elected. "The failure of previous attempts to secure an efficient city government through the local electorate made the business man of Galveston willing to put the conduct of the city's affairs in the hands of a commission dominated by state-appointed officials."[30] Only in 1903 did the courts force Galveston to elect the members of the commission, an innovation which one writer described as "an abandonment of the commission idea," and which led to the decline of influence of the business community in the commission government.[31]

In 1911 Pittsburgh voters were not permitted to approve either the new city charter or the new school board plan, both of which provided for city-wide representation; they were a result of state legislative enactment. The governor appointed the first members of the new city council, but thereafter they were elected. The judges of the court of common pleas, however, and not the voters, selected members of the new school board.

The composition of the new city council and new school board in Pittsburgh, both of which were inaugurated in 1911, revealed the degree to which the shift from ward to city-wide representation produced a change in group representation.[32] Members of the upper class, the advanced professional men, and the larger business groups dominated both. Of the fifteen members of the Pittsburgh Board of Education appointed in 1911 and the nine members of the new city council, none were small businessmen or white-collar workers. Each body contained only one person who could remotely be classified as a blue-collar worker; each of these men filled a position specifically but unofficially designed as reserved for a "representative of labor," and each was an official of the Amalgamated Association of Iron, Steel, and Tin Workers. Six of the nine members of the new city council were prominent businessmen, and all six were listed in upper-class directories. Two others were doctors closely associated with the upper class in both professional and social life. The fifteen members of the Board of Education included ten businessmen with city-wide interests, one doctor associated with the upper class, and three women previously active in upper-class public welfare.

Lower- and middle-class elements felt that the new city governments did not represent them.[33] The studies carried out under the direction of Leonard White contain numerous expressions of the way in which the change in the structure of government produced not only a change in the geographical scope of representation, but also in groups represented. "It is not the policies of the manager or the council they oppose," one researcher declared, "as much as the lack of representation for their economic level and social groups."[34] And another wrote:

> There had been nothing unapproachable about the old ward aldermen. Every voter had a neighbor on the common council who was interested in serving him. The new councilmen, however, made an unfavorable impression on the less well-to-do voters. . . . Election at large made a change that, however desirable in other ways, left the voters in the poorer wards with a feeling that they had been deprived of their share of political importance.[35]

The success of the drive for centralization of administration and representation varied with the size of the city. In the smaller cities, business, professional, and elite groups could easily exercise a dominant influence. Their close ties readily enabled them to shape informal political power which they could transform into formal political power. After the mid–1890s the widespread organization of chambers of commerce provided a base for political action to reform municipal government, resulting in a host of small-city commission and city-manager innovations. In the larger, more heterogeneous cities, whose subcommunities were more dispersed, such community-wide action was extremely difficult. Few commission or city-manager proposals materialized here. Mayors became stronger, and steps were taken toward centralization of representation, but the ward system or some modified version usually persisted. Reformers in large cities often had to rest content with their Municipal Research Bureaus through which they could exert political influence from outside the municipal government.

A central element in the analysis of municipal reform in the Progressive Era is governmental corruption. Should it be understood in moral or political terms? Was it a product of evil men or of particular sociopolitical circumstances? Reform historians have adopted the former view. Selfish and evil men arose to take advantage of a political arrangement whereby unsystematic government offered many opportunities for personal gain at public expense. The system thrived until the "better elements," "men of intelligence and civic responsibility," or "right-thinking people" ousted the culprits and fashioned a political force which produced decisions in the "public interest." In this scheme of things, corruption in public affairs grew out of individual personal failings and a deficient governmental structure which could not hold those predispositions in check, rather than from the peculiar nature of social forces. The contestants involved were morally defined: evil men who must be driven from power, and good men who must be activated politically to secure control of the municipal affairs.

Public corruption, however, involves political even more than moral considerations. It arises more out of the particular distribution of political power than of personal morality. For corruption is a device to exercise control and influence outside the legal channels of decision-making when those channels are not readily responsive. Most generally, corruption stems from an inconsistency between control of the instruments of formal governmental power and the exercise of informal influence in the community. If powerful groups are denied access for formal power in legitimate ways, they seek access through procedures which the community considers illegitimate. Corrupt government, therefore, does not reflect the genius of evil men, but rather the lack of acceptable means for those who exercise power in the private community to wield the same influence in governmental affairs. It can be understood in the Progressive Era not simply by the preponderance of evil men over good, but by the peculiar nature of the distribution of political power.

The political corruption of the "Era of Reform" arose from the inaccessibility of municipal government to those who were rising in power and influence. Municipal government in the United States developed in the 19th century within a context of universal manhood suffrage which decentralized political control. Because all men, whatever their economic, social, or cultural conditions, could vote, leaders who reflected a wide variety of community interests and who represented the views of people of every circumstance arose to guide and direct municipal affairs. Since the majority of urban voters were workingmen or immigrants, the views of those groups carried great and often decisive weight in governmental affairs. Thus, as Herbert Gutman has shown, during strikes in the 1870s city officials were usually friendly to workingmen and refused to use police power to protect strikebreakers.[36]

Ward representation on city councils was an integral part of grass-roots influence, for it enabled diverse urban communities, invariably identified with particular geographical areas of the city, to express their views more clearly through councilmen peculiarly receptive to their concerns. There was a direct, reciprocal flow of power between wards and the center of city affairs in which voters felt a relatively close connection with public matters and city leaders gave special attention to their needs.

Within this political system the community's business leaders grew in influence and power as industrialism advanced, only to find that their economic position did not readily admit them to the formal machinery of government.

Thus, during strikes, they had to rely on either their own private police, Pinkertons, or the state militia to enforce their use of strikebreakers. They frequently found that city officials did not accept their views of what was best for the city and what direction municipal policies should take. They had developed a common outlook, closely related to their economic activities, that the city's economic expansion should become the prime concern of municipal government, and yet they found that this view had to compete with even more influential views of public policy. They found that political tendencies which arose from universal manhood suffrage and ward representation were not always friendly to their political conceptions and goals and had produced a political system over which they had little control, despite the fact that their economic ventures were the core of the city's prosperity and the hope for future urban growth.

Under such circumstances, businessmen sought other methods of influencing municipal affairs. They did not restrict themselves to the channels of popular election and representation, but frequently applied direct influence—if not verbal persuasion, then bribery and corruption. Thereby arose the graft which Lincoln Steffens recounted in his *Shame of the Cities.* Utilities were only the largest of those business groups and individuals who requested special favors, and the franchises they sought were only the most sensational of the prizes which included such items as favorable tax assessments and rates, the vacating of streets wanted for factory expansion, or permission to operate amid antiliquor and other laws regulating personal behavior. The relationships between business and formal government became a maze of accommodations, a set of political arrangements which grew up because effective power had few legitimate means of accomplishing its ends.

Steffens and subsequent liberal historians, however, misread the significance of these arrangements, emphasizing their personal rather than their more fundamental institutional elements. To them corruption involved personal arrangements between powerful business leaders and powerful "machine" politicians. Just as they did not fully appreciate the significance of the search for political influence by the rising business community as a whole, so they did not see fully the role of the "ward politician." They stressed the argument that the political leader manipulated voters to his own personal ends, that he used constituents rather than reflected their views.

A different approach is now taking root, namely, that the urban political organization was an integral part of community life, expressing its needs and its goals. As Oscar Handlin has said, for example, the "machine" not only fulfilled specific wants, but provided one of the few avenues to success and public recognition available to the immigrant.[37] The political leader's arrangements with businessmen, therefore, were not simply personal agreements between conniving individuals; they were far-reaching accommodations between powerful sets of institutions in industrial America.

These accommodations, however, proved to be burdensome and unsatisfactory to the business community and to the upper third of socioeconomic groups in general. They were expensive; they were wasteful; they were uncertain. Toward the end of the 19th century, therefore, business and professional men sought more direct control over municipal government in order to exercise political influence more effectively. They realized their goals in the early 20th century in the new commission and city-manager forms of government and in the shift from ward to city-wide representation.

These innovations did not always accomplish the objectives that the business community desired because other forces could and often did adjust to the change in governmental structure and reestablish their influence. But businessmen hoped that reform would enable them to increase their political power, and most frequently it did. In most cases the innovations which were introduced between 1901, when Galveston adopted a commission form of government, and the Great Depression, and especially the city-manager form which reached a height of popularity in the mid-1920s, served as vehicles whereby business and professional leaders moved directly into the inner circles of government, brought into one political system their own power and the formal machinery of government, and dominated municipal affairs for two decades.

Municipal reform in the early 20th century involves a paradox: the ideology of an extension of political control and the practice of its concentration. While reformers maintained that their movement rested on a wave of popular demands, called their gatherings of business and professional leaders "mass meetings," described their reforms as "part of a world-wide trend toward popular government," and proclaimed an ideology of a popular upheaval against a selfish few, they were in practice shaping the structure of municipal government so that political power would no longer be broadly distributed, but would in fact be more centralized in the hands of a relatively small segment of the population. The paradox became even sharper when new city charters included provisions for the initiative, referendum, and recall. How does the historian cope with this paradox? Does it represent deliberate deception or simply political strategy? Or does it reflect a phenomenon which should be understood rather than explained away?

The expansion of popular involvement in decision-making was frequently a political tactic, not a political system to be established permanently, but a device to secure immediate political victory. The prohibitionist advocacy of the referendum, one of the most extensive sources of support for such a measure, came from the belief that the referendum would provide the opportunity to outlaw liquor more rapidly. The Anti-Saloon League, therefore, urged local option. But the League was not consistent. Towns which were wet, when faced with a county-wide local-option decision to outlaw liquor, demanded town or township local option to reinstate it. The League objected to this as not the proper application of the referendum idea.

Again, "Progressive" reformers often espoused the direct primary when fighting for nominations for their candidates within the party, but once in control they often became cool to it because it might result in their own defeat. By the same token, many municipal reformers attached the initiative, referendum, and recall to municipal charters often as a device to appease voters who opposed the centralization of representation and executive authority. But, by requiring a high percentage of voters to sign petitions—often 25 to 30 percent—these innovations could be and were rendered relatively harmless.

More fundamentally, however, the distinction between ideology and practice in municipal reform arose from the different roles which each played. The ideology of democratization of decision-making was negative rather than positive; it served as an instrument of attack against the existing political system rather than as a guide to alternative action. Those who wished to destroy the "machine" and to eliminate party competition in local government widely utilized the theory that these political instruments thwarted public impulses, and thereby shaped the tone of their attack.

But there is little evidence that the ideology represented a faith in a purely democratic system of decision-making or that reformers actually wished, in practice, to substitute direct democracy as a continuing system of sustained decision-making in place of the old. It was used to destroy the political institutions of the lower and middle classes and the political power which those institutions gave rise to, rather than to provide a clear-cut guide for alternative action.[38]

The guide to alternative action lay in the model of the business enterprise. In describing new conditions which they wished to create, reformers drew on the analogy of the "efficient business enterprise," criticizing current practices with the argument that "no business could conduct its affairs that way and remain in business," and calling upon business practices as the guides to improvement. As one student remarked:

> The folklore of the business elite came by gradual transition to be the symbols of governmental reformers. Efficiency, system, orderliness, budgets, economy, saving, were all injected into the efforts of reformers who sought to remodel municipal government in terms of the great impersonality of corporate enterprise.[39]

Clinton Rodgers Woodruff of the National Municipal League explained that the commission form was "a simple, direct, businesslike way of administering the business affairs of the city. . . . An application to city administration of that type of business organization which has been so common and so successful in the field of commerce and industry."[40] The centralization of decision-making which developed in the business corporation was now applied in municipal reform.

The model of the efficient business enterprise, then, rather than the New England town meeting, provided the positive inspiration for the municipal reformer. In giving concrete shape to this model in the strong-mayor, commission, and city-manager plans, reformers engaged in the elaboration of the processes of rationalization and systematization inherent in modern science and technology. For in many areas of society, industrialization brought a gradual shift upward in the location of decision-making and the geographical extension of the scope of the area affected by decisions.

Experts in business, in government, and in the professions measured, studied, analyzed, and manipulated ever wider realms of human life, and devices which they used to control such affairs constituted the most fundamental and far-reaching innovations in decision-making in modern America, whether in formal government or in the informal exercise of power in private life. Reformers in the Progressive Era played a major role in shaping this new system. While they expressed an ideology of restoring a previous order, they in fact helped to bring forth a system drastically new.[41]

The drama of reform lay in the competition for supremacy between two systems of decision-making. One system, based upon ward representation and growing out of the practices and ideas of representative government, involved wide latitude for the expression of grass-roots impulses and their involvement in the political process. The other grew out of the rationalization of life which came with science and technology, in which decisions arose from expert analysis and flowed from fewer and smaller centers outward to the rest of society. Those who espoused the former looked with fear upon the loss of influence which the latter involved, and those who espoused the latter looked only with disdain upon the wastefulness and inefficiency of the former.

The Progressive Era witnessed rapid strides toward a more centralized system and a relative decline for a more decentralized system. This development constituted an accommodation of forces outside the business community to the political trends within business and professional life rather than vice versa. It involved a tendency for the decision-making processes inherent in science and technology to prevail over those inherent in representative government.

Reformers in the Progressive Era and liberal historians since then misread the nature of the movement to change municipal government because they concentrated upon dramatic and sensational episodes and ignored the analysis of more fundamental political structure, of the persistent relationships of influence and power which grew out of the community's social, ideological, economic, and cultural activities. The reconstruction of these patterns of human relationships and of the changes in them is the historian's most crucial task, for they constitute the central context of historical development. History consists not of erratic and spasmodic fluctuations, of a series of random thoughts and actions, but of patterns of activity and changes in which people hold thoughts and actions in common and in which there are close connections between sequences of events. These contexts give rise to a structure of human relationships which pervade all areas of life; for the political historian the most important of these is the structure of the distribution of power and influence.

The structure of political relationships, however, cannot be adequately understood if we concentrate on evidence concerning ideology rather than practice. For it is becoming increasingly clear that ideological evidence is no safe guide to the understanding of practice, that what people thought and said about their society is not necessarily an accurate representation of what they did. The current task of the historian of the Progressive Era is to quit taking the reformers' own description of political practice at its face value and to utilize a wide variety of new types of evidence to reconstruct political practice in its own terms. This is not to argue that ideology is either important or unimportant. It is merely to state that ideological evidence is not appropriate to the discovery of the nature of political practice.

Only by maintaining this clear distinction can the historian successfully investigate the structure of political life in the Progressive Era. And only then can he begin to cope with the most fundamental problem of all: the relationship between political ideology and political practice. For each of these facets of political life must be understood in its own terms, through its own historical record.

Each involves a distinct set of historical phenomena. The relationship between them for the Progressive Era is not now clear; it has not been investigated. But it cannot be explored until the conceptual distinction is made clear and evidence tapped which is pertinent to each. Because the nature of political practice has so long been distorted by the use of ideological evidence, the most pressing task is for its investigation through new types of evidence appropriate to it. The reconstruction of the movement for municipal reform can constitute a major step forward toward that goal.

Notes

1. See, for example, Clifford W. Patton, *Battle for Municipal Reform* (Washington, D.C., 1940), and Frank Mann Stewart, *A Half-Century of Municipal Reform* (Berkeley, 1950).
2. George F. Mowry, *The California Progressives* (Berkeley and Los Angeles, 1951), pp. 86–101; Richard Hofstadter, *The Age of Reform* (New York, 1955), pp. 131–260; Alfred D. Chandler, Jr., "The Origins of Progressive Leadership," in Elting Morrison *et al.* (eds.), *Letters of Theodore Roosevelt* (Cambridge, 1951–1954), VIII, Appendix III, pp. 1462–64.
3. Harry A. Toulmin, *The City Manager* (New York, 1915), pp. 156–168; Clinton R[odgers] Woodruff, *City Government by Commission* (New York, 1911), pp. 243–253.
4. Eli Daniel Potts, "A Comparative Study of the Leadership of Republican Factions in Iowa, 1904–1914," M.A. thesis (State University of Iowa, 1956). Another satisfactory comparative analysis is contained in William T. Kerr, Jr., "The Progressives of Washington, 1910–12," *PNQ 55* (1964): 16–27.
5. Based upon a study of eleven ministers involved in municipal reform in Pittsburgh, who represented exclusively the upper-class Presbyterian and Episcopal churches.
6. Based upon a study of professional men involved in municipal reform in Pittsburgh, comprising eighty-three doctors, twelve architects, twenty-five educators, and thirteen engineers.
7. See especially Mowry, *The California Progressives*.
8. Leonard White, *The City Manager* (Chicago, 1927), pp. ix–x.
9. Harold A. Stone *et al., City Manager Government in Nine Cities* (Chicago, 1940); Frederick C. Mosher *et al., City Manager Government in Seven Cities* (Chicago, 1940); Harold A. Stone *et al, City Manager Government in the United States* (Chicago, 1940). Cities covered by these studies include: Austin, Texas; Charlotte, North Carolina; Dallas, Texas; Dayton, Ohio; Fredericksburg, Virginia; Jackson, Michigan; Janesville, Wisconsin; Kingsport, Tennessee; Lynchburg, Virginia; Rochester, New York; San Diego, California.
10. Jewell Cass Phillips, *Operation of the Council-Manager Plan of Government in Oklahoma Cities* (Philadelphia, 1935), pp. 31–39.
11. James Weinstein, "Organized Business and the City Commission and Manager Movements," *Journal of Southern History* XXVIII (1962): 166–182.
12. Norman N. Gill, *Municipal Research Bureaus* (Washington, [D.C.,] 1944).
13. This account of the movement for commission government in Des Moines is derived from items in the Des Moines *Register* during the years from 1905 through 1908.
14. Biographical data constitutes the main source of evidence for this study of Pittsburgh reform leaders. It was found in city directories, social registers, directories of corporate directors, biographical compilations, reports of boards of education, settlement houses, welfare organizations, and similar types of material. Especially valuable was the clipping file maintained at the Carnegie Library of Pittsburgh.
15. *Town Crier* (Seattle), Feb. 18, 1911, p. 13.

16. Information derived from the same sources as cited in n. 14.
17. Stone *et al, Nine Cities,* p. 212.
18. *Ibid.,* pp. 3–13.
19. *Ibid.,* p. 329.
20. Stone *et al, City Manager Government,* pp. 26, 237–241, for analysis of opposition to city manager government.
21. Des Moines *Register and Leader,* March 17, 1908.
22. *Ibid.,* March 30, March 28, 1908.
23. Voters' Civic League of Allegheny County, "Bulletin of the Voters' Civic League of Allegheny County Concerning the Public School System of Pittsburgh," Feb. 14, 1911, pp. 2–3.
24. In the decade 1911 to 1920, 45 percent of the municipal charters adopted in eleven home rule states involved the commission form and 35 percent the city manager form; in the following decade the figures stood at 6 percent and 71 percent respectively. The adoption of city manager charters reached a peak in the years 1918 through 1923 and declined sharply after 1933. See Leonard D. White, "The Future of Public Administration," *Public Management* XV (1933): 12.
25. Toulmin, *The City Manager,* p. 42.
26. Woodruff, *City Government,* p. 315. The Galveston commission plan did not contain provisions for the initiative, referendum, or recall, and Galveston commercial groups which had fathered the commission plan opposed movements to include them. In 1911 Governor Colquitt of Texas vetoed a charter bill for Texarkana because it contained such provisions; he maintained that they were "undemocratic" and unnecessary to the success of commission government. *Ibid.,* pp. 314–315.
27. *Ibid.,* pp. 207–208.
28. Des Moines *Register and Leader,* Jan. 15, 1908.
29. Voters' Civic League of Allegheny County, "Report on the Voters' League in the Redistricting of the Wards of the City of Pittsburgh" (Pittsburgh, n.d.).
30. Horace E. Deming, "The Government of American Cities," in Woodruff, *City Government,* p. 167.
31. *Ibid.,* p. 168.
32. Information derived from the same sources as cited in n. 14.
33. W. R. Hopkins, city manager of Cleveland, indicated the degree to which the new type of government was more responsive to the business community: "It is undoubtedly easier for a city manager to insist upon acting in accordance with the business interests of the city than it is for a mayor to do the same thing." Quoted in White, *The City Manager,* p. 13.
34. Stone *et al., Nine Cities,* p. 20.
35. *Ibid.,* p. 225.
36. Herbert Gutman, "An Iron Workers' Strike in the Ohio Valley, 1873–1874," *Ohio Historical Quarterly* LXVIII (1959): 353–370; "Trouble on the Railroads, 1873–1874: Prelude to the 1877 Crisis," *Labor History,* II (1961): 215–236.
37. Oscar Handlin, *The Uprooted* (Boston, 1951), pp. 209–217.
38. Clinton Rodgers Woodruff of the National Municipal League even argued that the initiative, referendum, and recall were rarely used. "Their value lies in their existence rather than in their use." Woodruff, *City Government,* p. 314. It seems apparent that the most widely used of these devices, the referendum, was popularized by legislative bodies when they could not agree or did not want to take responsibility for a decision and sought to pass that responsibility to the general public, rather than because of a faith in the wisdom of popular will.
39. J. B. Shannon, "County Consolidation," *Annals of the American Academy of Political and Social Science* 207 (1940): 168.
40. Woodruff, *City Government,* pp. 29–30.

41. Several recent studies emphasize various aspects of this movement. See, for example, Loren Baritz, *Servants of Power* (Middletown, 1960); Raymond E. Callahan, *Education and the Cult of Efficiency* (Chicago, 1962); Samuel P. Hays, *Conservation and the Gospel of Efficiency* (Cambridge, 1959); Dwight Waldo, *The Administrative State* (New York, 1948), pp. 3–61.

12

Amy Bridges

WINNING THE WEST TO MUNICIPAL REFORM

In the 20 years after 1900, municipal reformers celebrated triumph after triumph as cities across the country adopted commission and city-manager charters. The cities of the Southwest were prominent in the movement for municipal reform. The National Municipal League meetings were held in Los Angeles in 1911; Dallas, Fresno, Los Angeles, and Austin were represented among the league's officers in 1916 ("News and Notes" 1916). Like small and medium-sized cities across the country, cities in the Southwest adopted reform charters in the Progressive Era (Rice 1977; Schiesl 1977).

In this article I show how the Southwest was won to municipal reform. I argue that the adoption of reform charters was not the product of conducive local political culture but, rather, the result of region understood as strategic location. The cities of the Southwest were latecomers to both economic development and national politics, and this had dramatic consequences for local politics. First, the economic well-being of these communities was quite precarious. Any newspaper reader knew that prosperous futures depended on securing resources from outside investors and higher governments (and disaster would surely follow negotiating these relations poorly). A second consequence was the habit of collective action by business leaders in pursuit of resources for growth. When leaders claimed cities required government reform, both the salience of growth issues and the role of elites in negotiating resources for growth with outsiders furthered the reform cause. Reform was also furthered by manipulations of political rules, of which the most important was suffrage restriction, that advantaged advocates of charter revision.

In the first section of the article, I review earlier understandings of the origins of municipal reform. In the succeeding section, I describe the problems of

Author's Note: Richard Kronick, Gary Jacobson, and Roger Lotchin provided helpful comments on earlier drafts. Walter Campbell generously shared unpublished research findings with me. Adrienne Anderson expertly prepared the text.

"Winning the West to Municipal Reform," by Amy Bridges, in *Urban Affairs Quarterly*, June 1992, pp. 494–518. Copyright © 1992 by Amy Bridges. Reprinted by permission of Sage Publications.

southwestern cities at the turn of the century and the efforts of local citizens to solve them. In the third section I describe the political struggle over municipal reform. The concluding discussion accounts for the triumphs of municipal reformers.

Political Science and Municipal Reform

Since Hofstadter (1955) wrote *The Age of Reform*, municipal reform has been associated with the middle class and its discontents. Hofstadter wrote that the mugwumps, squeezed between the many of impoverished immigrant populations and the few of ostentatious wealth, organized to take over municipal government for themselves. "It would be hard to imagine," wrote Hofstadter, "types of political culture more alien to each other than those of the Yankee reformer and the peasant immigrant" (p. 182). Elaborating this thought, Banfield and Wilson (1963, 115–27, 138–50) offered the "political ethos" theory of local political institutions. "Private-regarding" immigrant/working-class values, they argued, supported the creation of political machines, and "public-regarding" Protestant/middle-class values promoted reform regimes. This argument remains the dominant presentation in urban politics textbooks despite many empirical studies raising questions about its validity for both machine politics (Bridges 1987, 1988) and municipal reform. Wolfinger and Field (1966), for example, examined the relationship between political ethos and the structure of city government and found that although, nationwide, there were strong relationships between the presence of middle-class/white Anglo-Saxon Protestant (WASP) voters and reform institutions, these relationships disappeared when the authors controlled for region. Similarly, Bernard and Rice (1975) found that, nationwide, large cities adopting commission or manager charters between 1920 and 1924 were slightly more Protestant, native born, and middle class than large mayor-council cities, but these results were not confirmed within regions (see also Rice 1977, 89).[1] Arguing that "one can do a much better job of predicting a city's political forms by knowing what part of the country it is in than by knowing anything about the composition of the population" (p. 321), Wolfinger and Field (1966) concluded that there was little empirical basis for arguing that institutional form was the product of political ethos.

Unpersuaded by this analysis, Lineberry and Fowler (1967, 701) insisted that "geographical subdivisions are relevant subjects of political inquiry *only because they are differentiated on the basis of attitudinal or socio-economic variables*" (emphasis added). It follows that if western cities are more likely than cities elsewhere to boast reform institutions, the reason must be that their citizens are more public regarding, more conservative, more middle class, or more "WASPy" than urban citizens in other regions (cf. Sale 1976, 159). Anyone attempting to apply the political ethos theory in the Progressive years, however, would be hard pressed to assemble persuasive evidence. Even without European immigrants, the political cultures of the Southwest were complex and diverse at the end of the nineteenth century. Among the WASPs who settled the Southwest were populists, socialists, Wobblies, and militant workers in mines and on docks.

There also are strong theoretical reasons to avoid explanations of political institutions that rely on political culture. Political institutions do not grow from popular values the way oak trees grow from acorns. Among other things, existing political institutions structure the aggregation of preferences so that the relation between popular values and public policy, including choices about future rules and institutions, is a tenuous one (Riker 1982). For example, early in this century in the Southwest, the creation of reform institutions was possible in part because suffrage restrictions limited the expression of preferences.

Region did play an important role in the adoption of municipal reform in the Southwest, but the reason was not the attitudinal or socioeconomic distinction of its residents. Rather, region is better understood as strategic location in the U.S. political economy: Citizens of the Southwest were latecomers to both economic development and the political community. Strategic location denotes two things in particular in the Progressive Era. First, the Southwest was capital poor. Second, the Southwest (with the exception of Texas) was not so closely tied to the party system as the rest of the nation. Each of these aspects of region had enduring effects on local politics.

In 1900 strategic location had obvious concrete referents. Neither employment nor comfort was certain, nor were there resources at hand to secure them. Both the capital and authority needed to secure urban growth were for the most part at distant locales, in the great cities of the East and in the nation's capital. Citizens of southwestern towns had no illusions of living in Adam Smith's universe; here, the conscientious pursuit of individual self-interest would not be assisted by the unseen hand. Rather, collective action was required for individual and collective well-being. The early, persistent, and aggressive organization of business leaders gave local politics much of its distinctive character not only in the Progressive Era but also for decades to come. Although business dominance of local politics is often associated with the company town— F. Hunter's (1963) *Community Power Structure* is the most prominent example— study of the Southwest suggests that business leaders' organization in pursuit of resources and authority also results in their political leadership.

Distance from the political center also influenced the shape of local politics. To explain Progressive successes in the West, Shefter (1983, 459) has argued that the region had a greater "regional receptivity to reform" than the Northeast did because in the West, the third-party system was not well established nor did the issues dividing the Democrats and Republicans have much salience for western voters. Although Shefter did not include New Mexico and Arizona, which were not admitted to the Union until 1912,[2] the same may be said of these territories. Their party systems were created from the top down, because their governments included many patronage appointments from Washington, D.C. (Donnelly 1940; Waltz 1940). Just as voting for the Progressive party and its reform measures may have come more easily in the West because Democratic and Republican party attachments were weaker, so was the region more hospitable to municipal reform. Texas presents a different case but with similar results for reformers. There, cities considering nonpartisanship risked abandoning the Democratic white primary, and although cities were quick in their adoption of municipal reform, often they retained partisan—really one-party—elections.

Region also adds a new dimension to another line of argument about municipal reform. Although political scientists have focused on middle-class values, historians since Hofstadter generally have argued that business leaders were the most prominent advocates of municipal reform. Bridges (1982) and Shefter (1985) have argued for the nineteenth century, and Hays (1964) and Weinstein (1968) have argued for the Progressive Era, that businessmen organized and campaigned for municipal reform to curb the extravagance of machine governments and to centralize political control. These accounts, however, treat cities as wholly autonomous political communities without recognizing their dependence on outside investors and authorities. Weinstein (1968), for example, titled his chapter on municipal reform "The Small Businessman as Big Businessman," capturing his argument that in the city, smaller entrepreneurs could play the creative and directing role that executives of major corporations played in national politics. "Chambers of commerce and other organized business groups," Weinstein argued, "were the decisive element . . . which made the movement a sweeping success" (p. 99).

The account provided here alters this picture. Although I also recognize the crucial role of businessmen, I view their success as a consequence of their capacity to win from outsiders, including state and national government, the investments their communities required. Not only did this distinguish them from competing local elites, but it also provided voters with good reasons to support them, despite the antidemocratic features of reform charters. Like Rice (1977), I recognize that although there was a class character to the struggle over municipal reform, there were voters, workers, and business leaders on both sides.[3]

The account here differs from prior accounts, then, by presenting the complex economic and political tasks of local businessmen in their regional context. In addition, Hays (1964) and Weinstein (1968) provide only cursory accounts of local campaigns for municipal reform and the attendant political struggles. I offer a more complete account of reform rhetoric and opposition arguments, revealing what contemporaries thought was at stake in the adoption of reform charters.

In the discussion that follows, I trace the adoption of municipal reform charters to the strategic location of the Southwest, its distance from economic resources, political authority, and the party system. The discussion begins with a portrait of the dilemmas of southwestern cities and towns in 1900.

Small but Ambitious

At the turn of the century, the cities of the Southwest were small, ambitious, and beset with enormous problems. Everywhere the future was uncertain; nowhere had a strategy been formulated to ensure future prosperity. Austin alone had a firm start with the state capital and the university, although in 1900 it was possible that Austin would try to become an industrial center as well. The largest city, Houston, was locked in intense rivalry with Galveston to the South; Spindletop lay in the future. Phoenix and Albuquerque subsisted on the transshipment of products from agricultural surroundings, and Albuquerque boasted the yards of the Atcheson, Topeka, and Santa Fe Railroad. San Diego, without direct rail connections to the East, had actually suffered population decline in the 1890s.

Everywhere the newspapers provided generous accounts of opportunity and growth, promoting the local economy for an audience of potential investors, consumers, and settlers. A special edition of the *Albuquerque Morning Journal* (25 February 1912) surveyed New Mexico for economic opportunity. The *Journal* boasted of Albuquerque as "The Metropolis of New Mexico," "A City of Present Prosperity," and "A City with a Prosperous Future." Albuquerque was a "modern city with well-graded streets, concrete sidewalks, electric lights, a street railway system, important mercantile and manufacturing establishments, two daily newspapers, and other evidences of great and growing prosperity." Surrounded by "wonderful agricultural opportunities," Albuquerque had direct rail connections to Los Angeles, Topeka, Chicago, and El Paso.

Similarly, San Diego boosters boasted that the city "claims as its true backcountry the entire southwestern region" (Pourade 1965, 9). In the same years, "San Diego Business establishments that want Arizona Trade" advertised regularly in the *Arizona Gazette*. "Del-Mar, The Newport of the Pacific," claimed that "a visit to this terrestrial [sic] paradise" will result in a "departure with regrets or . . . immediate arrangements for your permanent home." Other San Diego advertisers offered merchandising advice for the Mexican market, investment opportunities, legal assistance, life insurance, and accommodations at "Arizona's Seaport" (*Arizona Gazette*, 2 January 1913, 2).

When the written word was inadequate, organized celebration might entice outsiders to come and look. Albuquerque hosted the annual Territorial Fair in the 1890s. From 1899 to 1915 Houston's No-Tsu-Oh (which is Houston spelled backward) Festival, modeled on New Orleans's Mardi Gras, mobilized the city to attract autumn buyers. Segregated but not quiescent, the city's black community organized its own De-Ro-Loc carnival (Sibley 1968, 142; McComb 1981, 190). In 1915, to celebrate the opening of the Panama Canal and to advertise its own port, San Diego hosted the Panama-California Exposition. To finance the exposition the city issued a million dollar bond offering, and a similar amount was raised through private subscription. Total attendance in the exposition's two years topped two million.

The exposition's contribution was not simply a transient one of bringing tourist dollars and national visibility. At the exposition, Joseph Pendleton, a battalion commander of the Marine Corps, convinced Marine Commandant George Barnett to support his vision of a marine advance base on the California coast. San Diego also won the support of then Assistant Secretary of the Navy Franklin D. Roosevelt, who also attended the exposition and who announced placement of a naval dirigible base in San Diego (Pourade 1965, 194–195). An equally enduring legacy was the elegant buildings that were constructed for the exposition and that still form the heart of Balboa Park. Designed by architect Bertram Goodhue, the buildings were praised as a

> superb creation, so Spanish in feeling—yet so rarely equaled in Spain, with its stately approach, its walls springing from the hillside, its welcoming gateway, its soaring tower, and its resplendent dome, foretelling all the southernly privacy and charm of the courts that live beyond. [Here was] constructive imagination, overflowing with the vision of the Orient and South, impatient of rule and convention, free at last to utilize without restraint the exotic setting of a one-time Spanish colony. (Pourade 1965, 187)

The reality was not so bright. As Goodhue himself said of the exposition buildings, many of which were temporary, their purpose was "illusion rather than reality" (Pourade 1965, 199). The same was true of many of the advertisements of southwestern cities and towns. For one thing, they were quite small. Of the cities examined here (see Table 1), the largest, Houston, numbered 44,633 in 1900, and the smallest, Phoenix and Albuquerque, each counted fewer than 6,500. Most communities worried about adequate supplies of water or feared destructive floods; the least fortunate, like Phoenix and Austin, had worries on both counts. Most desired stronger rail connections to the rest of the country and soon sought air mail and air travel connections as well. Utility and mass transit corporations were abusive of their contractual obligations, indifferent to consumers, and exorbitant in their charges.

Local governments were not well positioned to solve these problems. Their financial resources were insufficient for the tasks they faced. Municipal debt was increasing as local systems of assessment and taxation fell behind the needs for paving, grading, and utilities. Flood control, irrigation, and sometimes water supplies required federal assistance. Most utilities were owned by corporations from other states, and federal courts were more sympathetic to investor prerogatives than to municipal authorities when adjudicating disputes between utilities and local governments. Municipal ownership of utilities demanded resources not immediately at hand and so required selling bonds on the national market.

The paucity of local resources for solving local problems provoked organization to secure investment and expertise from elsewhere. Early economic footholds were gained by competing successfully in state or territorial legislatures for institutions like universities, prisons, and asylums, as well as for designation as county or state capital. In 1885 Phoenix's representatives in the Arizona territorial legislature secured an insane asylum (and its $100,000 appropriation), Tempe won a school, Yuma retained its prison, Florence was awarded $15,000 for a bridge (Ehrlich 1981, 236), and Tucson was sorely disappointed to receive only the university (Luckingham 1982, 25).

In the Arizona Territory the site of the capital was in contention from 1864, when it was first placed at Prescott, until it was finally placed in Phoenix more than 20 years later. Tucson mounted campaigns for the capital in 1881 and 1885, Phoenix mounted campaigns in 1879, 1883, 1887, and 1889, and the capital was

Table 1   Population of Southwestern Cities, 1890–1920

City	1890	1900	1910	1920
Albuquerque	5,518	6,238	11,020	26,570
Austin	14,575	22,258	29,860	53,120
Houston	27,557	44,633	78,800	138,276
Phoenix	3,152	5,544	11,134	39,053
San Diego	16,159	16,700	39,578	74,683

Sources: U.S. Bureau of Census (1896, 1902, 1912, 1922).

moved several times. In addition to insisting on the virtues of their respective hometowns, lobbyists had material inducements for legislators. In 1885 a proponent of Tucson complained,

> We are doing all we can. . . . Prescott wines, dines, and "sees" the members of both houses with liberal prodigality and profusion. We have never had a cent to give a supper or treat to a drink. You can readily imagine the great disadvantage under which we labor.
>
> One thousand dollars economically and properly disbursed would have infallibly put the capital at Tucson. . . . Now you can see what is the matter.

Armed with a war chest estimated at $10,000, Phoenix won decisively in 1889 (Ehrlich 1981, 237–38).

More often than the state capital, the nation's capital was a site of urban competition and lobbying. Both San Diego and Houston requested federal assistance in developing port facilities; Phoenix and Austin could not solve their flooding and water supply problems without enormous federal investments in dams. In each case securing assistance followed an elaborate pattern of leadership organization, persuasion of relevant bureaucracies, lobbying Congress, public mobilization, and local-state building. Harbor improvements for Houston and securing the Roosevelt Dam for Phoenix illustrate these processes well.

Houston's efforts to create a harbor pioneered the pattern of leadership organization, attention to bureaucrats, lobbying Congress, popular mobilization, and local-state building. Houston is located on the Buffalo Bayou, about 50 miles inland from the port of Galveston on the Gulf of Mexico. That Houston's ambitions were not nature's intent may be inferred from one visitor's remark: "I yearned to see that seaport, even if I had to employ a detective to hunt it up" (Sibley 1968, 113). Not surprisingly, solving Houston's harbor problems required years of effort. Houston had to present its vision to the Army Corps of Engineers, which doubled the feasibility of Houston's plans. The Rivers and Harbors Committee actually visited Houston in 1897, were feted, and, thanks to a providentially large rainfall, appropriately impressed (Sibley 1968, 116). In the wake of the hurricane that destroyed Galveston, Congress was inclined to look favorably on Houston. In 1902 Congress appropriated $1 million for the bayou, which was dredged to a depth of 18½ feet; a turning basin was added by 1908. This left the channel still inadequate to accommodate the ships commonly plying Gulf waters, but the federal monies were exhausted.

Local leaders then turned from lobbying Washington to local mobilization. For the work to continue, local leaders proposed a county navigation district, and voters approved both the creation of the district and a bond issue to provide matching funds for further federal assistance. In 1909 the mayor proposed a $2 million bond issue to deepen the bayou, and the *Houston Chronicle* (7 January 1909, 4) was quick to editorialize on the stake of the average resident in the success of this effort. Applauding the Houston Labor Council's support for the bond issue, the editors wrote, "In a growing town like Houston the wage-earner's best chance to get ahead financially is to buy a home and reap the benefit of advanced land values"; deepening the bayou meant "Houston's great future growth will be absolutely guaranteed." The chamber of commerce left neither creation of the navigation district nor bond passage to chance, organizing meetings to persuade the public and campaigning in each district (Sibley 1968, 136).

Finally, Houston created a new authority to manage its port. In 1913 the city created a Harbor Board and issued $3 million in bonds to support it (McComb 1981, 65–67). The next year the project was complete, and Houston finally celebrated deep water. The No-Tsu-Oh king, formerly King Nottoc, was rechristened King Retaw. Not to be outdone by fictional rulers, Houston's Mayor Campbell, Governor-elect James Ferguson, and President Woodrow Wilson also participated in the celebration.[4] Because the conclusion of the channel's construction was the beginning of a new era of expanded commerce, young men from the city's leading families chose the celebration to introduce the Red Roosters, an organization dedicated to selling Houston to its environs (Sibley 1968, 142–144).

Albuquerque, Phoenix, San Diego, and Austin all had serious water problems. In Phoenix, flooding and droughts were of concern primarily because the city staked its growth on shipping the agricultural production of its surrounding area, the Salt River Valley. After efforts to secure private sector construction of a dam failed, the reclamation efforts of the federal government (in which Arizona citizens had naturally taken an interest all along) became the sole target of lobbying activity (Krenkel 1978). The federal government—in particular, the U.S. Geological Survey (USGS)—had been considering water reclamation projects for some time. The Agriculture and Interior Departments were also interested in irrigating the Salt River Valley. Phoenix sent Benjamin Fowler to Washington to lobby for the territory's interests and, in concert with George Maxwell (a Californian who had organized the National Irrigation Association), he began campaigning the Department of Interior and the USGS. Equally important, Maxwell and his colleagues lobbied Congress successfully for an amendment to the 1902 Reclamation Act providing that private lands could be included in federal projects (K. L. Smith 1981).

At home in Arizona the next task was to mobilize landowners and to create a new quasi-governmental agency in support of the effort to secure the dam. The Salt River Water Users Association had the purpose of persuading landowners to pledge their lands as collateral to repay the federal government for constructing a dam under the Reclamation Act. By July 1903 more than 200,000 acres had been pledged, and a contract for the Tonto Basin Storage Reservoir—later the Roosevelt Dam—was signed in February 1904 (Krenkel 1978, 88–89). Not only did the Roosevelt Dam create the possibilities for prosperity in the valley, its construction was also an enormous public works project. When the dam was completed eight years later, Theodore Roosevelt himself traveled to the site to participate in the festivities ("Water for Phoenix: Building the Roosevelt Dam" 1977, 286). Roosevelt and the Phoenicians active in the effort to secure the dam (Ben Fowler, Lloyd Christy, Dwight Heard, and William Kibbey) all became local heroes for this accomplishment.

The same story of organization, persuasion, lobbying, mobilization, and local-state building might be told over and over again. San Diego campaigned for two generations for direct rail connections to the East, persuaded the Army Corps of Engineers and the navy of its need for harbor improvements, and sought ever stronger ties to the armed forces. Albuquerque supported the creation of the Bernalillo County (Rio Grande) River Commission, which was empowered to tax residents to provide funds for dikes and dams to protect city and crops from repeated floods. Austin's water problems plagued it for decades. Austin, like Phoenix, watched hopefully as the Army Corps of Engineers surveyed the river and the flood damage it wreaked, lobbied Congress, and railed against federal refusal to supply adequate funds. In 1915 the chamber of commerce formed the Colorado River Improvement Association, and the next year, the association received a $25,000 appropriation from the federal government. This was hardly a down payment, however; solutions to the flooding problems of Austin lay decades ahead (Orum 1987, 85–130).

The urban communities of the Southwest also required utilities and mass transit. By the standards of 1900, a modern community had well-paved and lighted streets, adequate sewers, electricity and water delivered to households, and mass transportation by street railway systems. Initially, these were provided by local firms. San Diego represents the extreme case: In 1900 John D. Spreckels owned a water supply company and the streetcar franchise, promised a railroad east to Yuma, Arizona, and, no doubt to applaud these city-building efforts, owned two of San Diego's three newspapers (Pourade 1965, 15). Undercapitalized and enjoying monopoly franchises in most places, locally owned utilities provided inadequate service to some customers and, unable to keep up with the urban expansion, no service at all to others. Albuquerque's 1914 mayoralty election campaign was waged over whether public or private ownership of the water supply company was preferable, and the sewer system was also troublesome (Schingle 1976, 12). Three years later the city was still attempting to buy the water supply company as well as attempting to force the streetcar company to meet its contractual obligations (Cline 1951, 7).[5]

As a national market in local utilities appeared, street railways, electricity, gas, and telephones were more likely to be provided by national firms. General Electric, for example, organized a holding company for local utilities in order to create a market for its own generating equipment. Pacific Gas and Electric served Arizona as well as California, and Pacific Light and Power, based in Los Angeles, considered acquiring water rights enabling it to control San Diego's water supplies. Utilities in small cities were commonly owned by firms in Chicago, Boston, or New York.

Local consumers and local governments alike believed that these firms delivered precious little service at too high a price. Worse, cities had little reliable legal recourse in their efforts to regulate utilities. The Public Utilities Committee of the Texas League of Municipalities found "the legal situation governing and controlling the right of various cities . . . to exercise the power of rate regulation is in a tangled and dubious condition" ("Proceedings on Public Utilities" 1922, 65).

Outside the courts disputes between cities and utilities might take disruptive forms. Houston suffered the indignity of having the community's lights turned off when the city government threatened Houston Electric Power and Light with competition (Platt 1983, 136). Houston also tried to encourage efficient service delivery by creating competition among street railway companies. Although this had some advantages, competing street railway firms literally tore up the streets in their efforts to establish rights on promising routes (Platt 1983, 132–33). Most often, however, one company simply bought the other's franchise or a third company bought them both. In Albuquerque, too, efforts to create competition among street railway firms collapsed as the erstwhile competitors merged operations (Simmons 1982, 333). Although even brief periods of competition improved service delivery, franchise holders understandably preferred monopoly. Charles B. Holmes, the owner of a Chicago street railway syndicate, argued forcibly that Houston would be boycotted by northern capitalists if her government failed to see the virtues of natural monopolies in public services and urged citizens to "unite with us in developing the interests of the city" (Platt 1983, 128–129).

The conflictual relations between cities and utilities tended toward the resolution Holmes suggested. This happened because firms could create monopolies through the market and because firms could refuse, as Holmes did, to invest if threatened with competition. Although municipal ownership was the answer in some places (often enough because the utilities were unprofitable; see K. L. Smith 1978), monopoly franchises and negotiation were the more common result. Even more than securing harbors, dams, or railroads, providing utilities placed local government at the center of managing growth. This put politicians in the most delicate of positions: If political leaders were too aggressive against outside investors, their cities were threatened with refusal to invest or worse. Houston's Progressive Mayor Samuel Brashear, for example, was forced from office largely because of his very aggressive stance toward utility investors (Platt 1983, 178). If, on the other hand, city government conceded too much to utility owners, voters were likely to reject officeholders as tools of eastern investors. As late as 1933, for example, a handbill circulated in Phoenix denounced "the power and gas barons" who let consumers' money be "shipped to Wall Street Power Barons." "Call each candidate for city commission," the author advised, "and ask how they stand on present light and gas rates" (Irwin 1933). In this setting, negotiating a good franchise contract was an achievement with direct benefits for residents and a political triumph.

Without adequate economic resources or political authority, the cities and towns of the Southwest faced formidable survival problems at the turn of the century. Unable to rely on the unseen hand, local businessmen and political leaders organized to seek aggressively investment and assistance from higher governments and national economic interests. These efforts had widespread salience; their failures meant community tragedy, and their successes meant the possibilities of prosperity and growth.

The immediate result was the creation of dozens of elite organizations. Phoenix's Commercial Club and Civic Federation were founded before 1890; Albuquerque had a Commerce Club, later the chamber of commerce, which began campaigning for investors and residents in the 1890s. There also was a Booster's Association and its journal, the *Albuquerque Booster* (Simmons 1982, 327). Houston boasted a Board of Trade; a Commercial League; Business League; Manufacturers' Association; Merchants' and Business Men's Association; Industrial Club; Bankers', Jobbers' and Manufacturers' Association; the 200,000 Club; Young Men's Business League; and a Junior Chamber of Commerce, as well as the Red Roosters (McComb 1981, 304).

Elite organizations did more than conduct business. The Austin Chamber of Commerce, for example, engaged in a very wide range of activities. In addition to working on Colorado River flooding problems, the chamber commissioned a health survey of the city, worked for creation of a paid fire department, negotiated the merger of the city's competing telephone companies, acquired Barton Springs for the provision of water to the city, and began, in 1917, "educational work for the council-manager form of government" (Austin Chamber of Commerce 1948, 23). These efforts and others constituted "its active program for the growth of Austin" (p. 16). For this and many other things, it often seemed local government was not up to the task.

Building New City-States

Discontent with local government was apparent in the 1890s. Middle-class residents of Houston formed a Good Government League in 1895; in Austin, there were attempts at reform in the 1890s; in Phoenix, the city council itself wrote to the National Municipal League for advice about local government reform. The difficulty was hardly domination of local government by well-organized partisan machines. Although political opponents might denounce one another as *bosses*, none of these cities had strong enough political organizations or strong enough partisan attachments to merit the term *machine*. The problems were of a different sort. Houston's problems, summarized in the *Chronicle* in 1913 (16 October, 4), fairly represent the difficulties of local governments in these years:

> The city owes a large public debt with very little improvement to show for the vast sums of money that have already been spent. Only a small percentage of our streets

are improved, the sewerage and drainage systems are sadly inadequate, while our school facilities are not sufficient to take care of the children should compulsory education be established.

After Galveston adopted commission government in 1901, there was a presumption that any change in local government arrangements would follow Galveston's lead. Galveston was devastated by a hurricane in 1901, and prominent citizens in the Deep Water Committee took the opportunity this created to draft a plan for a new and businesslike administration. Under the auspices of the commission government that the state legislature created, these citizens rebuilt the city. The achievements of Galveston's commission government were trumpeted at the National Municipal League meetings in 1906, in *Harper's Weekly*, *McClure's*, and elsewhere. As Rice (1975, 408) explained, "Galveston's contribution to municipal reform . . . temporarily became the core of urban progressivism."

There were three important elements of commission government: commissioners, citywide elections, and nonpartisanship. Commissioners were to be elected to serve both as heads of departments and as members of the city council. The thought was that these arrangements would centralize administration and simplify lines of authority. Citywide elections and nonpartisanship were as much offensive weapons aimed at machine and party organization as constructive elements for the new scheme. Each was aimed at breaking the ties of voter to officeholder that kept machine politics alive. Later, the addition of a city manager was proposed. Under the city-manager plan, the city council—composed ordinarily of aldermen without administrative responsibilities but in some cases, of commissioners—was meant to vote on matters of policy, and the city manager executed policy and administered the departments of local government.

Proposals for municipal reform provoked heated debate. The dominant themes of reformers' arguments were the substitution of business for politics, government by virtuous citizens, and the promise that reformed local government would be more conducive to municipal growth. Opponents of reform saw in commissions and city managers autocratic arrogations of power and argued for representation and democracy in local government.

Reformers campaigned for commission government by promising "the substitution of business for politics" (*Arizona Gazette*, 22 January 1912, 1). That phrase summarized the purported virtues of the commission and manager forms and the alleged vices of the arrangements they were meant to replace. "Business" signified simplicity, clear lines of responsibility, and efficiency in administration. Efficient administration would put an end to fiscal mismanagement, enable government to retire its debt, and thus lower taxes.

The removal of "politics" from local government meant an end to corruption and "bossism" (*Austin Daily Statesman*, 24 December 1908, 3). San Diego was considered "a concrete case of despotism," a part of California's system of "government of the machine, by the bosses, for the public utility corporations" (Smythe 1907, 456–461). Indeed, argued an Arizona editorial, "many cities had been compelled to adopt [commission government] as a matter of self defense of its citizens against corrupt political machines and grafting politicians. . . . Business and politics will not mix to the advantage of the taxpayer in any municipality. . . . Commission government [will] divorce politics from municipal management, and install business in its stead" (*Arizona Gazette*, 7 October 1913, 4).

Both the installation of businesslike government and the removal of politics from local administration argued for nonpartisan elections (for example, see *Arizona Republican*, 20 August 1913, 4). Theodore Roosevelt had argued that "the worst evils that affect our local government arise from and are the inevitable result of the mixing up of city affairs with the party politics of the nation and state" (Smythe 1907, 461). Nonpartisanship was appropriate for local government because party politics was irrelevant to urban administration. "What had tariff revision or bank guarantees," asked an Austin reformer, "to do with the condition of Austin streets?" (*Austin Daily Statesman*, 29 December 1908, 5). The *Arizona Republican* (2 August 1913, 4) agreed:

> No city can flourish as luxuriantly in the shadow of politics as in the sunshine of nonpartisan cooperation. There is apt to be no civic spirit in politics. When men divide their loyalty between city and party, the former gets a meager share of it.

Nonpartisanship promised to unite all those desiring reform in its pursuit. "There can be no harmony without sacrifice of principle. If there be sacrifice . . . let it be of partisanship rather than patriotism" (*San Diego Union*, 3 January 1909, 10).

In place of self-serving career politicians, commissions would provide "virtuous government by virtuous men." The commission plan would provide "for the employment of the best men we can hire to run this large business, men of capacity and honesty" (*Arizona Republic*, 8 November 1912, 4). Freed from party domination, "The people, on the alert, will always be standing together against the politicians, for good government" (*Arizona Republic*, 20 August 1913, 4).

In some cities local administrators were attacked, but more often care was taken to distinguish between honorable local politicians and objectionable charter arrangements (*Arizona Gazette*, 7 October 1913, 4). Among the systemic causes of inefficiency and disregard for the general good was the election of city council members from wards. Wards were pernicious because "a local alderman will work for his ward against the general welfare of the city." "The typical alderman," argued an Austin professor, "always was, always is, and always will be more anxious to please his little crowd of ward voices and supporters than a commissioner at large" (*Austin Daily Statesman*, 24 December 1908, 2). Even more condemning was the argument that "so long as the town is divided by wards and controlled by politics the growth of the town will be retarded" (Staniszewski n.d., 27). At-large elections would "tend to the best interests of the whole city, and do away with sectional interests" (*San Diego Union*, 10 January 1909, 14). To those who saw in the wards a commitment to democracy, reformers proposed initiative, referendum, and recall (*Arizona Gazette*, 10 October 1913, 4; 7 November 1912, 1).

Taken together, these changes would create an environment conducive to growth. "Business administration," promised reformers in the Texas capital, "would make Austin grow" (*Austin Daily Statesman*, 29 December 1908, 5). In 1913 Houston's voters were urged to adopt amendments to the city charter, because "the present charter . . . is behind the times," and "the proposed amendments are necessary to give Houston what is needed to build for the future" (*Houston Chronicle*, 14 October 1913, 8). In 1912 the *Arizona Republican* (5 November 1912, 4) also linked its arguments for commission and nonpartisan government to growth:

> The city now struggling forward and moving in spite of the charter will continue to be handicapped at a stage of its existence when its form or government ought to be made to encourage and stimulate its growth.

A new charter would "unloose the bonds of the city which have so retarded the growth of Phoenix" (*Arizona Republican*, 5 November 1912, 4).

Opponents of commission government found fault with each of these arguments and proposals. Some opposition was purely practical: Local politicians objected to changes that would likely throw them out of office. In San Diego *The Sun* (11 January 1909, 1) reported that

> "The push"—or in other words, Boss Hardy's local Republican machine—has got the word to vote against the proposed charter amendments. This means that the word has gone out to faithful to vote the charter changes down . . . and keep the city government just as it is now.

The dominant theme of opposition was the desire for democracy and representation, beginning with the process of reform itself. New charters were often drafted by boards of freeholders or specially appointed commissions that were not especially representative.[6]

Commission government was opposed as too centralized, a criticism leveled at the small number of commissioners, citywide elections, and the concentration of responsibilities in the council. Centralization of administration was held to be an autocratic arrogation of power, and the man who drafted Austin's proposed commission charter was charged with "seeking to become the boss of [a local] Tammany" (*Austin Daily Statesman*, 24 December 1908, 4). Similarly, in Albuquerque one ward meeting resolved to oppose the commission charter, believing "it unwise and imprudent to entrust the affairs of the city to the unrestrained control of three men [because] . . . there is no limitation upon the power of the all powerful commission and . . . the proposed form . . . is unrepresentative." (*Albuquerque Morning Journal*, 22 September 1917, 2).

There was opposition everywhere to abolishing wards for electing city council members. In Albuquerque the *Morning Journal* argued that under the mayor-council system, the "working man" could "go to his alderman and secure anything in reason for his ward," whereas under the proposed commission plan, worker and neighborhood would not be represented. For this and other reasons the *Journal* opposed the commission plan, fearing domination by the "'silk stocking' fourth ward" (*Albuquerque Morning Journal*, 21 September 1917, 6). Hispanic politicians in Albuquerque also cautioned their constituents that the influence of Spanish-speaking voters would likely decline under commission government (Schingle 1976, 18). In Austin it was argued that "under the aldermanic system the citizens are assured direct representation in the affairs of the municipality, and direct control over ward improvements. Ward representation is in line with the democratic doctrine of local self-government. Commission government destroys this principle and establishes a centralization in municipal affairs" (*Austin Daily Statesman*, 27 December 1908, 2). Austin's Alderman Cuneo defended himself as "a man who did his duty to his ward every day" (*Austin Daily Statesman*, 24 December 1908, 3).

More broadly, there were objections to the substitution of business for politics. The *Houston Labor Journal* (5 October 1917, 3) editorialized against "hired mayors":

> Let us get back to real representative government and clear the issue of all this "business" buncombe and running municipalities on the "per cent" groove as private corporations are run. Corruption never springs from the gutter. You may find some "thing" in the gutter willing to be tempted, but the source of temptation comes from above—from the so-called business element and the public utility corporations and municipal contractors who have waxed fat off municipal corruption for a half century and longer. And the idea of turning a city government over to this element to reform it is not only preposterous, but absolutely silly. . . . "Per cent" is what they are after; and commission government will never be a success because you can't keep the Big Rich from grafting.

Although those who proposed new charters claimed to be for business administration in place of politics, opponents thought it was more likely that one machine would simply be replaced by another. Commission government in Austin would be "an office holding trust, and . . . enable the trust to so establish itself in power that the people would become powerless to free themselves from the octopus" (*Austin Daily Statesman*, 24 December 1918, 3). Albuquerque's commissioners would be better labeled "kaiser number one, kaiser number two, and kaiser number three" (*Albuquerque Morning Journal*, 22 September 1917, 6). San Diego's proposed manager was denounced as a potential czar (Stone, Price, and Stone 1950, 179).

Although the language of these debates was extravagant, the goals of reformers and fears of opponents were not fanciful. The centralization of authority provided by commission charters facilitated bypassing neighborhood desires and interests. Changes in taxing authority equally threatened neighborhood interests. In the nineteenth century (and, in some places, well into the twentieth century), street paving and other amenities were financed by special assessments. Property owners were assessed for their contribution to improvements immediately affecting them. When cities abandoned this in favor of more general systems of taxation, the means were provided to tax the periphery, as it were, to finance improvements at the center (or deemed by the center as good growth investments).

In Albuquerque the proposed increased taxing power was seen as a direct threat to working-class home owners. Opposing their limited incomes to the situation of two of the proposed charter's well-known supporters, the *Albuquerque Morning Journal* (22 September 1917, 6) editorialized:

Mr. Metcalf can pay for any kind of paving in front of his home, and so can Mr. Coors. But what does it mean to the man of small income who has been able to secure title to a humble home for which he probably still is paying on the install- ment plan?

It would mean ruin.

But Mr. Metcalf and his friends will say that no commission would do such a thing.

Do you want to take that risk? . . .

The ratification of this charter with that provision in it would be the most dis- astrous thing that could occur to Albuquerque.

In addition to denying neighborhoods direct representation by abolishing wards, reform charters proposed making it more difficult to vote and hold of- fice. Although supporters of commission government did not draw attention to the antidemocratic features of their proposals, opponents of commission gov- ernment were quick to point them out. In Phoenix a 1912 charter restricted suf- frage to taxpayers (this was held unconstitutional by the state/territorial gov- ernment) (J. C. Smith 1975, 12, 13). In Austin only property holders were to vote in recall elections, and officials were to post $10,000 bond before taking office (*Austin Daily Statesman,* 29 December 1908, 2). Proposals to cut the pay of pub- lic officials were equally likely to discourage any but the affluent from seeking municipal posts (J. C. Smith 1975, 10, 21). For each of these reasons, opponents of municipal reform argued that although new charters were seductive in their promise of efficient administration, it was nevertheless to be hoped that "our people will not be beguiled into sacrificing their political rights" (*Austin Daily Statesman,* 14 December 1908, 3).

Beguiled they were. Between 1900 and 1922 San Diego, Pasadena, and 20 other cities in California, Albuquerque and Las Vegas in New Mexico, Tulsa, Oklahoma City, and 22 other cities in Oklahoma, Phoenix and Douglas in Ari- zona, and Galveston, Houston, Dallas, Fort Worth, El Paso, Austin, San Anto- nio, and 70 other cities in Texas adopted reform charters (Rice 1977, 113–125).

The Triumphs of Municipal Reform

How may the triumphs of municipal reform be accounted for? In retrospect it can be seen that these outcomes were hardly in doubt. First, suffrage restric- tion, enacted by state legislatures, paved the way for successful municipal re- form campaigns. Since opposition to municipal reform usually came from or- ganized labor and working-class voters (Hays 1964; Rice 1977), suffrage restriction, generally hampering the have-nots, was bound to enhance reform's chances of success. Texas provides the most persuasive evidence. In Texas the poll tax dramatically decreased the eligible electorate; in Houston almost two- thirds of the electorate was disfranchised in 1903, and Houston enacted a city poll tax as well (Platt 1977, 41). The same laws disfranchised many in Austin. Aside from Galveston—which did not vote on its commission charter but was given the charter by the state legislature—there were no successful reform cam- paigns before the poll tax was enacted.[7]

Elsewhere, suffrage restriction was not as dramatic but is suggestive nevertheless. The *Albuquerque Morning Journal* (26 September 1917, 2) reported, in the wake of the adoption of the city-manager plan, that there were "many disfranchised" by faulty registration lists. Since the majority for the charter was 156, and there were reports that as many as 200 may have been disfranchised by efforts in the registration lists, there was room for doubt even though the *Journal* (26 September 1917, 2) declared the election "cleanly and honestly won." As San Diego considered its series of charter changes, California suffered generally declining turnout, spurred in the city by nonpartisanship (required by the state legislature) (Titus 1928). In addition, only freeholders could vote on charter changes (*San Diego Union*, 3 January 1909, 9). California and Arizona each had both literacy tests and registration requirements.

Second, as Shefter (1983) argued, the absence of strong partisan commitments among the electorate eased the way for reform victories. Like suffrage restriction, this weakened the opposition to reform. Strong party organization was also absent among politicians, and their attraction to Progressivism weakened party ties even further.

Third, municipal reform was favored by well-organized local elites. Of course, this was also true in the big cities of the Northeast, where the electoral victories of municipal reform were few and far between ("News and Notes" 1922). Moreover, opposing political leaders often were wealthy too. In the Southwest reformers were distinguished from their opponents by their youth, later arrival in the West, financial connections to the East, opposition to municipal ownership, and successful negotiation with outsiders. In Phoenix the most prominent champions of reform were the men who had secured the federal government's commitment for the Roosevelt Dam, brought the Southern Pacific and Santa Fe railroads to Phoenix, and built the city's outlying neighborhoods (Johnson 1985, 87; G. S. Hunter 1968, 355, 359; K. L. Smith 1978, 177). In Houston the case for reform was pressed by those who organized the navigation district and the harbor board and who, more broadly, led in creating a "new South" strategy for the city (Platt 1977, passim). The author of Austin's new charter was M. M. Shipe, who moved to Austin as a representative of "Kansas City capitalists," was granted a franchise for an electric street railway, and pioneered building suburban communities (Pietzsch et al. 1906, 4; American Historical Society 1931, 233–34; "Shapers of Austin, 1896–1906" 1985; *Austin American Statesman*, 3 July 1990, C1, C2).

San Diego provides support for this argument as a contrary case. In San Diego municipal reform was largely a means for insurgent Republicans to further political goals unrelated to local politics. Municipal reformers resembled their counterparts in other places. Ed Fletcher and William Smythe, for example, came to San Diego from the East and Midwest and invested in land and water development. Smythe was active in the National Irrigation Congress and lobbied in Washington with Benjamin Fowler in support of the National Reclamation Act (Lee 1973). Nevertheless, municipal reform was not a movement of elites who could promise growth and prosperity. Those promises were more effectively made by John Spreckels, who delivered water, street railways, and, eventually, a direct rail line to the East. Spreckels was a staunch Old Guard Republican who opposed reform in every guise. Reformers in San Diego succeeded in winning charter revision but never succeeded in controlling the government. Once-ardent reformers were eventually won away from the cause to pursue politics and growth as usual in the city. In 1915, with reversion to mayor-council government, even the municipal reform charter was abandoned ("News and Notes" 1915). In Los Angeles Progressive Meyer Lissner lamented, "San Diego is a one-man town. . . . That is the whole trouble" (Miller 1976, 129). Former Congressman W. W. Bowers defended San Diego's choice: "I know that all of us were very glad to get the railroad, and with all its extortions we had rather do with it than without. I had rather have water with monopoly than no water and no monopoly" (Pourade 1965, 36).

The mirror side of success with outsiders was the threat of failure. Without investment, federal assistance, public utilities, and a market for bonds, prospects for urban survival were slim. Municipal reform promised to facilitate all of these goals, as some utility owners recognized. For example, Stone and Webster, a Boston firm that eventually owned Houston's street railways, sent George Johnson Baldwin to Galveston in October 1901. Baldwin sent back a long memo praising the commission form. Historian Walter Campbell observed, "Standing alone this [judgment] . . . means little but it is extremely important within the context of Stone & Webster's acquisition and consolidation of street railway and electric companies throughout the nation and the South," including Houston, between 1898 and 1904 (W. E. Campbell, letter to the author, 28 July 1991). From their point of view, a system that insulated city government from neighborhood demands while increasing government's authority and taxing powers was bound to be a more responsive partner in franchise negotiations, as well as a more fiscally sound investment for bankers.

Fourth, all of this suggests that voters had good reasons to support municipal reform and, arguably, better reasons to do so than citizens in the big cities of the Northeast and Midwest. In the nation's older big cities, municipal reformers were seen as agents of the "interests," out to gouge the working classes and contemptuous of immigrants. As the National Municipal Review lamented, municipal reformers in the 1922 campaign in New York were "unable to strike a popular issue, to discredit Tammany, or to convince people that they had no designs on the five-cent fare. [Tammany] talked the old patter about the interests, the traction trust, etc., and . . . won every place" ("News and Notes" 1922). When reformers like Seth Low did win, their administrations bore out the fears of immigrant and working-class voters (Holli 1969, 175). By contrast, local businessmen who promoted municipal reform in the Southwest were seen as courageous Davids fighting the Goliaths of the same trusts, utilities, and interests to secure prosperity, growth, and a fair deal for their communities.

Moreover, pressures and considerations that favored the triumph of municipal reform in the Southwest in the Progressive Era may well have promoted the adoption of reform charters in small cities elsewhere. Small cities everywhere required light, electricity, gas, water, public transportation, and public finance through bond issues. Aggressive promotion of reform charters by the National Municipal League and the testimony of satisfied local public officials and investors increased the visibility and appeal of the commission and, later, the city-manager form of government. It is not surprising, then, that in the Progressive Era, nonpartisanship and commission government became "contemporary political fashion" (Wolfinger and Field 1966, 325).

Early returns on the commission form encouraged those who had campaigned for it. Houston's Mayor Ben Campbell, speaking to the second annual convention of the League of Texas Municipalities in 1914, expressed his satisfaction:

> Our experience is that it brings good results. I do not know that we are any exception to the rule, but I want to tell you now that there is not a business organization in Texas, managed by its president and board of directors, in which there is any more concert of action, uniformity of opinion, solid, strong, undivided effort, for the upbuilding of the whole city, than exists today in the city council of Houston. I believe that the reason for that is . . . our present form of city government. (Campbell 1915, 36)

Not only did cities and towns boast new forms of city government but also an array of special districts, commissions, authorities, and quasi-governmental bodies to market bonds, provide infrastructure, and facilitate growth. Like their counterparts in the great cities of the Northeast, city-builders in the Southwest used these administrative inventions of the Progressive Era to further their economic and political goals. And with more success than municipal reformers in those great cities, leaders in southwestern cities and towns built new local states to meet the challenges of the next generation.

Notes

1. Bernard and Rice (1975) did not test for region. However, age of city—itself highly correlated with region—was a stronger determinant of governmental form than any other variable they tested.
2. Shefter also excluded Utah, Oklahoma, and Texas, all of which I include in the Southwest.
3. Rice (1977, 110) argued that commission government "should be seen as a reform contagion that spread from state to state and city to city. . . . In that context modernization and the affirmation of corporate values, in addition to selfish interests, emerge as important motives for reform." This summary of the argument does not do justice to the many historical insights provided into the values of the reform movement and the complexities of local struggles over municipal reform, for which I and other authors are in his debt.
4. Wilson was not present, but he fired a cannon in Houston by pressing a pearl-topped button in Washington.
5. In the 1890s Houston's locally owned water company exemplified these inadequacies. Unwilling to pay for the installation of meters, the company provided no incentives for customers to conserve water or to fix leaks. As a result, water pressure fell dangerously low, and when a local hospital caught fire, fire fighters could not save it. The city's residents were at risk, and its structures uninsurable (Platt 1993, 137, 141–144).
6. In Phoenix there were protests that despite its claims to represent all the citizens of Phoenix, the committee to draft the charter included no labor representative. The Phoenix

Trades Council demanded "as citizens of the community that the working class be represented in the forming of this charter, and that the working class have representation on the commission," a demand that met with no response. By contrast, representation of the elite women's clubs was agreed to (*Arizona Republic*, 17 April 1913).

7. Rice (1977) listed all commission government adoptions in Texas. There are none between Galveston in 1901 and Houston in 1905. Beaumont provides a good example of a city in which there were several campaigns for reform, none successful until after 1903 (Isaac 1975).

References

American Historical Society. 1931. *American biography, a new encyclopedia.* New York: Author.

Austin Chamber of Commerce. 1948. *Something made Austin grow.* Austin, TX: Author.

Banfield, E., and J. Q. Wilson. 1963. *City politics.* New York, Vintage.

Bernard, R., and B. Rice. 1975. Political environment and the adoption of Progressive municipal reform. *Journal of Urban History* 1:149–174.

Bridges, A. 1982. Another look at plutocracy and politics in antebellum New York City. *Political Science Quarterly* 97:57–71.

———. 1987. *A city in the Republic: Antebellum New York and the origins of machine politics.* Ithaca, NY: Cornell University Press.

———. 1988. Rethinking the origins of machine politics. In *Power, culture, and place,* edited by J. Mollenkopf, 53–71. New York: Russell Sage Foundation.

Campbell, B. 1915. The commission form of government. *Texas Municipalities* 2(2):35–48.

Cline, D. I. 1951. *Albuquerque and the city manager plan.* Albuquerque: University of New Mexico Press.

Donnelly, T. C. 1940. New Mexico: An area of conflicting cultures. In *Rocky Mountain politics,* edited by T. C. Donnelly, 218–51. Albuquerque: University of New Mexico Press.

Ehrlich, K. L. 1981. Arizona's territorial capital moves to Phoenix. *Arizona and the West* 23:231–242.

Hays, S. P. 1964. The politics of municipal reform in the Progressive Era. *Pacific Northwest Quarterly* 55:157–169.

Hofstadter, R. 1955. *The age of reform.* New York: Vintage.

Holli, G. 1969. *Reform in Detroit: Hazen S. Pingree and urban politics.* New York: Oxford University Press.

Hunter, F. 1963. *Community power structure: A study of decision makers.* Garden City, NY: Doubleday.

Hunter, G. S. 1968. The Bull Moose movement in Arizona. *Arizona and the West* 10:343–362.

Irwin, O. 1933. Local power trust getting cold feet. Handbill, clippings file, library of the Arizona Capital.

Isaac, P. E. 1975. Municipal reform in Beaumont, Texas, 1902–1909. *Southwestern Historical Quarterly* 78:409–430.

Johnson, G. W. 1985. Generations of elites and social change in Phoenix. In *Community development in the American West: Past and present nineteenth and twentieth century frontiers,* 79–109. Provo, UT: Brigham Young University.

Krenkel, J. H. 1978. The founding of the Salt River Water Users Association. *Journal of the West* 17(l):82–90.

Lee, L. B. 1973. William E. Smythe and San Diego, 1901–1908. *Journal of San Diego History* 19(2):10–24.

Lineberry, R., and E. Fowler. 1967. Reformism and public policies in American cities. *American Political Science Review* 60:701–716.

Luckingham, B. 1982. The urban southwest: A profile history of Albuquerque—El Paso—Phoenix—Tucson. El Paso: Texas Western Press.

McComb, D. G. 1981. *Houston: A history.* Austin: University of Texas Press.

Miller, G. L. 1976. The San Diego progressive movement, 1900–1920. Master's thesis. University of California, Santa Barbara.

News and notes. 1915. *National Municipal Review* 3:474.

———. 1916. *National Municipal Review* 5(1):171.

———. 1922. *National Municipal Review* 11(1):34.

Orum, A. 1987. *Power, money, and the people.* Austin: Texas Monthly Press.

Pietzsch, L. R., E. D. Phillips, E. D. Sanders, and G. W. Smith. 1906. *The Austin electric street railway system*. Austin: University of Texas Press.

Platt, H. F. 1977. City-building and progressive reform. In *The age of urban reform: New perspectives on the Progressive Era,* edited by H. Ebner and E. M. Tobin, 28–42. Port Washington, NY: Kennikat Press.

————. 1983. *City building in the new South*. Philadelphia, PA: Temple University Press.

Pourade, R. F. 1965. *The history of San Diego.* Vol. 5. San Diego, CA: Union-Tribune.

Proceedings on public utilities. 1922. *Texas Municipalities* 9(4):65–71.

Rice, B. 1975. The Galveston plan of city government by commission: The birth of a Progressive idea. *Southwestern Historical Quarterly* 78:366–408.

————. 1977. *Progressive cities*. Austin: University of Texas Press.

Riker, W. 1982. *Liberalism against populism: A confrontation between the theory of democracy and the theory of social choice.* San Francisco: Freeman.

Sale, K. 1976. *Power shift.* New York: Vintage.

Schiesl, M. J. 1977. *The politics of efficiency, municipal administration, and reform in America: 1880–1920.* Berkeley: University of California Press.

Schingle, M. J. 1976. Albuquerque urban politics, 1891–1955, aldermanic vs. commission government. Senior thesis, University of New Mexico.

Shapers of Austin, l896–1906. 1985. *Austin Magazine* 27:91.

Shefter, M. 1993. Regional receptivity to reform: Legacy of the Progressive Era. *Political Science Quarterly* 98:459–83.

————. 1985. *Political crisis, fiscal crisis: The collapse and revival of New York City.* New York: Basic Books.

Sibley, M. M. 1968. *The port of Houston, a history.* Austin: University of Texas Press.

Simmons, M. 1982. *Albuquerque: A narrative history.* University of New Mexico Press.

Smith, J. C. 1975. The Phoenix drive for municipal reform and charter government. Typescript, Hayden Library, Arizona State University.

Smith, K. L. 1978. From town to city: A history of Phoenix, 1870–1912. Master's thesis, University of California, Santa Barbara.

————. 1981.The campaign for water in central Arizona, 1890–1903. *Arizona and the West* 23:127–148.

Smythe, W. E. 1907. Responsible government for California. *Out West* 26:456–461.

Staniszewski, F. n.d. Ideology and practice in municipal government reform: A case study of Austin. Paper no. 8, Studies in Politics Series 1: Studies in Urban Political Economy. University of Texas at Austin.

Stone, H. A., D. K. Price, and K. H. Stone. 1950. *City manager government in nine cities.* Chicago: Public Administration Service.

Titus, C. J. 1928. Voting in California cities, 1900–1925. *Political and Social Science Quarterly* 8:383–399.

U.S. Bureau of Census. 1896. *U.S. Census of Population, 1890.* Washington, DC: Government Printing Office.

————. 1902. *U.S. Census of Population, 1900. Population,* Part 1, Table 23. Washington, DC: Government Printing Office.

————. 1912. *U.S. Census of Population, 1910.* Part 2, Table 2. Washington, DC: Government Printing Office.

————. 1922. *U.S. Census of Population, 1920.* Part 1, Vol. 3, Table 10. Washington, DC: Government Printing Office.

Waltz, W. E. 1940. Arizona: A state of new-old frontiers. In *Rocky Mountain politics,* edited by T. C. Donnelly, 252–91. Albuquerque: University of New Mexico Press.

Water for Phoenix: Building the Roosevelt Dam. 1977. *Journal of Arizona History* 18:279–286.

Weinstein, J. 1968. *The corporate ideal in the liberal state.* Boston: Beacon.

Wolfinger, R., and J. O. Field. 1966. Political ethos and the structure of city government. *American Political Science Review* 60:306–326.

Chapter 5

❖❖❖

THE SUBURBS

Government Against Government

Throughout American history, there has been a tendency for affluent people to segregate themselves from the less well-off. When these people spilled beyond the boundaries of the central cities and created their own political jurisdictions, an important new dimension was added to the previous pattern of neighborhood segregation that had long existed within the cities. In the late nineteenth century, the development of the suburbs permitted upper-income people to escape the crowded industrial cities. In the twentieth century—and especially after World War II—the white middle class and even substantial numbers of the white working class fled to the suburbs. During the same years, a mass migration of blacks into the older cities was taking place. At every stage, suburbanization involved the construction of enclaves where those who were affluent enough could segregate themselves from the people and problems of the cities and maintain lower wage taxes, higher property values, and superior amenities.

Until recently, most of the literature on suburban development focussed on the sharp socioeconomic differences between suburbs and central cities, so much so that in American culture, almost everyone is accustomed to thinking of urban America in dualisms: rich suburbs/poor cities, white suburbs/black cities, ghetto neighborhoods/affluent subdivisons, crime/safety (Beauregard, 1995). The new urban scholarship questions the accuracy of the stereotypes created by such dualistic thinking, and—just as important—scholars have begun to identify socioeconomic divisions that had been previously overlooked. In her selection, Lynn Appleton maintains that different "gender regimes" have distinguished suburbs from central cities. Although, she says, all cities are patriarchal, in the sense that the families, economic institutions, and governments that make them up are mostly controlled by men, central city neighborhoods have historically provided more opportunities for employment and social interaction for women than have suburbs. The density and heterogeneity and even the housing stock of city neighborhoods have nurtured diverse lifestyles. In these contexts, one finds communities with high proportions of gays, single mothers, and unmarried adults without children. The suburbs, in contrast, historically were hostile to any departure from the narrow norm of the nuclear family. Men, not women, commuted to work, leaving women in relative social isolation. The suburbs segregated men's and women's lives; women were left with the children and worked outside the home far less than did women in cities. Although these patterns have undoubtedly changed substantially in recent years, important vestiges remain.

Patterns of socioeconomic segregation, including the gender regimes noted by Appleton, were created in the years following World War II, when millions of city dwellers moved to the tract housing developments that were springing up everywhere. In the era of the mass-produced suburbs, developers achieved a kind of standardized segmentation that sharply demarcated housing tracts on the basis of income and social class. In his selection, Michael N. Danielson describes the political process by which the social segregation of the suburbs gave rise to political fragmentation. In an effort to protect the privileges that residential segregation bestowed on them, suburbanites tried to assert control over local schools, zoning laws, police enforcement and other local services, and tax policies. The key to such control was the incorporation of local governments. According to Danielson, suburban autonomy was achieved basically as a means of preserving the status quo, and this meant excluding "unwanted neighbors." In the decades following World War II, the exclusionary policies enforced by suburban jurisdictions helped to create a Great Divide that separated suburbs from the central cities, and richer suburbs from poorer ones.

The familiar dualisms that people employ to think of cities and suburbs are becoming less and less descriptive of any substantial reality, because over the past 30 years or so the suburbs have been urbanizing. According to the selection by Joel Garreau, Edge Cities may be harbingers of the urban future. Edge cities are relatively dense nodes at the urban periphery that cluster housing, shopping, employment, and recreation into contained areas close to freeway interchanges. In this selection from his book, Garreau muses that some of the problems associated with the old central cities are becoming replicated in the new edge cities. If this is so, edge cities are just the most recent expressions of a long-term trend in which the suburbs are becoming increasingly differentiated and complex. Over time, the suburbs have become as much different from one another as the suburbs are, as a whole, different from the central cities.

13

Lynn M. Appleton

THE GENDER REGIMES OF AMERICAN CITIES

All cities are patriarchal, but neither all cities nor all patriarchies are the same. Although all patriarchies are systems "of social structures, and practices in which men dominate, oppress and exploit women" (Walby, 1989, p.14), they differ in

"The Gender Regimes of Urban Cities," by Lynn M. Appleton, in *Gender in Urban Research*, Sage Publications, 1994, pp. 44–59. Copyright © 1994 by Lynn M. Appleton. Reprinted by permission of Sage Publications.

their structure, conflicts, and discontents. Cities differ in their "gender regimes" (Connell, 1987): the ways in which their political, economic, and familial systems combine to produce gender inequality. A distinctive gender regime is supported by the low-density, relatively homogeneous style of development in suburban America, prevalent in post-1960s urban growth. Inside this kind of urban place, lives are still shaped by the 19th century's ideology of "separate spheres" (Bose, 1987) for men and women. Struggles over gender are privatized, interpersonal, and intrapsychic. Higher density and more heterogeneous central cities produce a very different gender regime than do suburbs. In these cities, the contradictions of the separate spheres have been heightened and forced into increasingly public and collective realms. Struggles over gender have spilled over into political and workplace struggles, as well as into neighborhood and "lifestyle" politics.

This chapter explores the relationship between variation in urban form and gender relations, drawing on recent work in feminist theory that stresses that there are variations in patriarchal structures. Early feminist work often characterized patriarchy as monolithic and invariant, as if male dominance was the same in medieval France and contemporary Chicago. But feminist scholars recognize that patriarchy varies substantially across time and place as women and "lesser men" respond to the initiatives of privileged men. Not all women are equally oppressed, nor are all men equally oppressors. Degree of male control of women's lives varies substantially (see Kandiyoti, 1988).

Newer work on patriarchy conceptualizes it as a loosely coupled system that produces gender inequality and that is shaped by men's and women's interests, resources, and actions as they negotiate and struggle over power and authority. By incorporating feminist theory on patriarchy into urban studies, we can understand an additional dimension of urban life and politics, including the complex ways in which cities are sites for both reproducing and challenging patriarchy. This research will aid in developing an understanding of the tremendous variation in the ways in which cities maintain the stability of the dominant patriarchal order.

Patriarchal Institutions

To understand the gendered consequences of urban form, the city must be conceptualized as the nexus of three basic institutions that shape patriarchy: the family, the economy, and the state.

The family is a primary site for enacting gender and thereby maintaining patriarchy. The heterosexual family is a strongly gendered institution where only husbands and wives exist, not spouses, and where only mothers and fathers exist, not parents. This family form is not culturally universal. Rather, socially structured resources and opportunities explain men's and women's motivations for and roles in marriage (see Epstein, 1988; Hochschild, 1989), as well as the role of marriage and childbearing in reproducing sex inequality.

Marriage and parenthood have dramatically different consequences for men and women. They contribute to gender inequality because they place a disproportionate burden on women as spouses and parents. These gendered burdens are not solely a consequence of female economic dependence on men. Although individual women's economic resources do have some effect on individual men's participation in housework (see Coleman, 1991), socialized ideas of "women's place" are a more important determinant of the family's division of labor (Cancian, 1987). Regardless of which spouse makes more money, wives consistently carry the greatest burden of child care, household chores, and neighboring activities (Calansanti & Bailey, 1991; Campbell & Lee, 1990; LaRossa & LaRossa, 1989).

Thus research on the family as a gendered and patriarchal institution argues that it is a primary site for our feelings about gender's importance and our ideas about its meaning, an everyday site for the enactment of gender, and an important site of reproduction of sex inequality.

The economy is also a primary site for enacting gender and constructing gender relations. Historically, an increase in gender inequality has been associated with women's exclusion from work that produces exchange value and is performed away from the home. Such exclusion is associated with the assignment of women to the devalued and often invisible work of "secondary production" that is child care, cooking, and cleaning (O'Kelly & Carney, 1986).

In studying industrial societies, research on gendered work focuses on the causes, dynamics, and consequences of women's exclusion from waged work or segregated access to it (Blumberg, 1991; England & McCreary, 1987). When women have paying jobs, their jobs differ from men's in that they are less various, more poorly paid, and offer less opportunity (see Ferree, 1987).

But research on capitalist economies reveals cross-national variation in occupational segregation (see Charles, 1992) and women's average wages (Norris, 1987). These findings suggest that state differences are significant in shaping gender inequality.

Two general theories of the state appear in feminist work (Connell, 1990). One argues that the state is the tool of a patriarchy anchored in family or economy. The other argues that the state itself is patriarchal. The former argument underpins liberal feminism's argument that the state can be captured by feminist interests, whereas the latter suggests that the state is as intractably patriarchal as family or the economy.

Some researchers focus on barriers to women's political activity (Gelb & Gittell, 1986; Matthews, 1992) or on effects of electoral and party systems on gender equality (Norris, 1987). But the largest group of research focuses on how ostensibly "gender neutral" state policies and practices produce gendered outcomes that reproduce sex inequality (see Diamond, 1983).

Institutional Intersections: The City

Urban scholars are accustomed to conceptualizing cities as political and economic systems. But to understand how cities are part of systems of sex stratification, family systems must be included in urban analysis. Each city has a distinctive relationship between its political, economic, and familial systems that constructs its gender regime, its particular version of patriarchy.

I have taken the concept of *gender regime* from the work of theorists who have reconceptualized gender as the product of an ongoing series of struggles within and between social institutions (Connell, 1987). A gender regime is the way that gender is shaped by and shapes a particular social institution or, in the case of the city, a confluence of social institutions. Each city has a gender regime that it shares with similarly constituted cities. Urban gender regimes can be characterized in terms of the prevailing ideologies of how men and women should act, think, and feel, the availability of cultural and behavioral alternatives to those ideologies, men's and women's access to social positions and control of resources, and the relationships between men and women.

Different kinds of cities have different kinds of gender regimes. For example, contemporary New York City has a gender regime that provides an alternative to male/female emotional and economic interdependency. Extensive subcultures of unmarried persons, both heterosexual and homosexual, provide an alternative to heterosexual marriage. Individualist assumptions about adults' lives are a significant counterweight to the familism that is still the dominant American ideology of adulthood.

Such deviant ways of life flourish only in the density and heterogeneity of the urban place (Abrahamson & Sigelman, 1987). Consider New York City's neighbors, the less dense and more homogeneous suburban communities of Long Island. The gender regimes of these cities provide fewer alternatives to heterosexual marriage. The mature adult is expected to be married, and the single-family home is assumed to be an adult's economic goal. No cultural counterweight exists to what Rich (1980) characterizes as "compulsory heterosexuality." These cities have no social space for an oppositional gay subculture (D'Emilio, 1983) or a subculture of female economic independence. In these cities, all adults are expected to marry, and women's primary responsibilities are those of home and family, whereas men's responsibilities are primarily economic.

These two kinds of cities have very different gender regimes: private patriarchy in the Long Island suburbs and a more public patriarchy in the New York central city. Private patriarchy is that set of gender regimes premised on a strongly gendered division of labor inside the home, paid work segregated by and remunerated on the basis of workers' sex, and women's dependence on the income of individual men (Brown 1987). The main site of gender struggle is the family, as spouses contest over scarce resources such as time and money. The hegemony of heterosexuality, parenthood, and marriage are unquestioned.

Public patriarchy is that set of gender regimes premised on women's increasing economic independence of individual men, increasing dependence on the state for income, and decreasing emotional interdependence with men. Paid work continues to be segregated by and remunerated on the basis of workers' gender, but it becomes more central to women's lives. The hegemony of heterosexuality, maternity, and motherhood is challenged when patriarchal ideologies are strained as alternate visions of men's and women's lives develop. Although gender struggle continues inside heterosexual relationships, it increasingly moves to the public realm of women's struggles for better paid jobs, state assistance, and public policies that serve their interests.

The remainder of this chapter will outline the relationship between urban form and these two patriarchal forms. First, I will discuss how the current gender regimes of the central cities were shaped by the urban changes of the 1950s and 1960s. Next, I will discuss the preservation of the private patriarchy in the suburbs of the 1950s and the "uncentered" cities of the most recent spurt of urban growth.

The Public Patriarchy of the Central Cities

Currently, the private patriarchy of the suburbs and uncentered cities is the dominant American patriarchal form: privatized struggles between men and women and a strong culture of separate spheres that define masculinity and femininity (Bose, 1987). In the early 20th century, this was also the patriarchal form that had emerged from the gender struggles of earlier decades (Piess, 1986; Stansell, 1986). But beginning in the 1960s, the central cities have produced a different kind of patriarchy. This "public patriarchy" (Brown, 1987) is characterized by multiple masculinities and femininities open internal dissension in the gender realm, and increasingly public and collective struggles over men's and women's access to resources. It emerged as the composition of the central cities increasingly contrasted with that of the suburbs of the 1950s and, later, of the new cities that emerged from the urban growth in the 1970s and 1980s.

First, because of its demographic composition, the central city contains a disproportionate number of people predisposed to challenge gender inequality. The majority (73% in 1984) of all female householders are central-city dwellers (Cook & Rudd, 1984), and women who live in households without a male wage earner are the most likely to be aware of and want to see change in gender inequality (Davis & Robinson, 1991).

Second, in the 1960s, the leading activists of the second wave of the feminist movement were drawn from the educated elites of these cities (Connell, 1987, p. 271). Third, the central cities produced important challenges to patriarchy from sources that often were unmotivated by conscious criticism of gender inequality, such as the proportion of central-city families that had two wage earners, the proportion of urban women who were single mothers, and the significant proportion of urban dwellers who lived independently of marriage and children. The influence of these groups increased during the 1960s, as industry and more affluent families abandoned the central cities. At this time, patriarchy's most significant "boosters" increasingly abandoned the city to groups that were more critical of the existing system of sex stratification.

Dual-Wage-Earner Families

Despite the prescriptions of the "cult of domesticity" (Bose, 1987), women in the central city of this century were never as much the captives of their homes as were the women of suburbia (Saegert, 1981; Wekerle, 1981). First, even though their income was considered a lesser and "second" income, many urban married women had paying jobs. Although workforce participation varied across decades, city women were more apt to be in the paid workforce than were nonurban women. They found it easier to get work compatible with domestic responsibilities: close to home, part-time, and not requiring additional family investment (e.g., in a second car). In a setting in which many married women worked, spouses found it easier to define wives' paid work as legitimate and "normal." In particular, African American and other minority women found it easy to justify their paid jobs as an essential contribution to family welfare in a racist society (Collins, 1991; Glenn, 1991).

Second, urban density and the structure of public space provided city women with more interactional opportunities than those of suburban women. They had access to extensive networks of family members and, to a lesser extent, women friends. Consequently, their identities were less embedded in husband, children, and home than were those of suburban women.

Third, urban life provided a level of stimulation and challenge that distinguished the urban woman from her suburban counterpart. Thus the central city constructed a more independent wife than did the suburb. Fourth, city homes were smaller and more of their work could be contracted out. City women's housekeeping was a lesser focus of their lives.

Finally, urban husbands were not as dependent on their families for their social and emotional life as were suburban husbands. In the city, same-sex sociability was a normal feature of adult men's lives. Consequently, many urban families differed from private patriarchy's early prescriptions and from the emerging reality of American suburban life.

Single Mothers

In any economy characterized by occupational sex segregation and lower wages for women, most husbandless women are poor. So in the 1960s and 1970s, rates of women's poverty increased as rates of divorce and nonmarital childbearing increased. As McLanahan, Sorensen, and Watson (1989) point out, the increase in women's poverty rates was due mostly to women's responsibility for children. Both men and women became increasingly likely to abandon or not assume spousal roles, but whereas men abandon fatherhood with alacrity, women cling to motherhood.

As the number of husbandless mothers increased, their public benefits declined. Benefit levels failed to keep pace with inflation and more recently, have been directly cut. Current political discourse is dominated by talk about "workfare" and "job training." The clear implication is that mothers should find paid work to support their children. But because nearly half of working women are employed in industries that pay poverty-level wages for full-time work (McLanahan et al., 1989, p. 120), such solutions are unrealistic.

Because most female-headed households are urban households, the feminization of poverty might be a central issue for urban politics. But husbandless women do not mobilize or gain power easily (see West, 1981). Hence their problems are seen as private problems that should be solved by finding a husband or a job.

Unmarried Adults, Often Without Children

In addition to dual-wage-earner families and single mothers, the central city contrasts with the suburbs in its higher proportion of young, single adults. As people married later in life, young men and women worked and lived independently for longer periods of time.

The numbers of women living independently of families were historically unprecedented. They controlled money, made decisions, and negotiated with individual men over the course of a relationship. They were neither daughters, ladies, nor hardworking wives (Piess, 1986). As urban dwellers, they had a distinctive set of preferences for their neighborhoods (Shlay & DiGregorio, 1985). Their emerging subculture subverted the old patriarchal order.

Gay men and lesbians were a second source of challenge to the patriarchal order. During the 20th century, an increasingly large and well-organized gay community developed in major American cities (D'Emilio & Freedman, 1988). By the 1960s, gay men had begun to carve out neighborhoods for themselves, develop elaborate social and economic institutions, and create the basis for a relatively self-contained gay subculture. By mid-century, lesbian communities also emerged in the larger American cities (Faderman, 1991). But trapped in a world of poorly paid women's work, lesbians' limited economic power lessened their ability to create neighborhoods on the scale of those created by gay men.

Initially, lesbians and gay men were a small challenge to private patriarchy. But as the liberation movements of the late 1960s and early 1970s developed, post-Stonewall homosexual communities were an increasingly visible feature of the central city. They challenged assumptions about masculinity and femininity and contributed to the central city's increasingly open debates about the future of patriarchy.

From City to Suburb: Private Patriarchy Preserved

Private patriarchy emerged in the cities of the industrial era, but it found its highest expression in the suburbs of the 1950s and 1960s. In the 1970s and later, it was institutionalized in the new cities of autonomous suburban belts and sunbelt sprawls. It survived in the landscape of the American Dream: a setting of single-family homes, physically separated commercial and residential activities, social class homogeneity, and racial exclusiveness.

Separate Spheres in the Suburbs

Initially, the gender regime of the suburbs was a private patriarchy with a strictly gendered division of labor linked to the heterosexual nuclear family. Men were expected to do paid work, earn a family wage, and support women and children. Women were assigned the unpaid work of social reproduction: "the activities and attitudes, behaviors and emotions, responsibilities and relationships directly involved in the maintenance of a life on a daily basis, and intergenerationally" (Laslett & Brenner, 1989, pp. 382–383). This gender regime had been developed in the early part of the 20th century, survived the challenges of women's changing roles during World War II, and was part of the idealized family sought by the new suburbanites.

Men first embraced the "breadwinner/homemaker" bargain during the latter part of the 19th century (see Laslett & Brenner, 1989). But their ability to achieve breadwinner status required access to the "family wage." Although some men attained this wage through class position, working- and middle-class men's access to it required the successes of the union movement, the protective labor legislation of the 1930s, and a set of national political and economic changes that greatly improved their economic status.[1] The economic prosperity of the 1950s, combined with federal subsidies for home mortgages, made the suburban exodus possible and brought the breadwinner role within reach for a significant proportion of European American men.

Women began their embrace of the "homemaker" role in the late 19th century, although its realization rested on the later economic changes that ensured the family wage for their husbands (Cancian, 1987; Geschwender, 1992; Laslett & Brenner, 1989). They were both pushed and pulled into a primary investment in the work of social reproduction. Child care and housework were less compatible with industrial, paid jobs than with the household production of preindustrial societies. Additionally, "women's jobs" in the industrial economy were generally poorly paid and without intrinsic reward. But the valorization of the separate spheres also has been analyzed as part of women's struggle to justify their withdrawal from waged work, to legitimate a claim on men's income, and to raise their status by creating a new idea of "women's place" (Bose, 1987; Cancian, 1987). By the 1950s, the homemaker role was widely embraced by women migrants to the suburbs (Saegert, 1981). In the suburbs, these relatively affluent and overwhelmingly White women hoped to live out the prescription that "a woman's place is in the home."

Women's Work in the Household

For cultural and practical reasons, suburban houses and yards required more work to decorate, clean, and maintain than did urban rental apartments. They were larger, more elaborate, and prized as a family's only investment. Moreover, by the 1950s, a woman's homemaking was seen as a way to express love for her family and to define her individuality (Cowan, 1983; Laslett & Brenner, 1989). Additionally, although the new "consumerist" ethic rapidly defined women's roles as purchasers of household goods, shopping retreated to "shopping centers" distant from residential neighborhoods. But because of women's lesser access to cars (Salem, 1986, p. 155), shopping was more time-consuming and complicated than in an urban setting.

Even if a woman had been willing to hire household labor, such labor was scarce in the suburbs. The absence of nearby poor women made domestic labor difficult to hire. Even today, poor minority women travel from their urban homes to the suburban ring to do domestic work (Hwang & Fitzpatrick, 1992), but the lack of public transportation makes such commuting difficult. Further, the low density of suburban communities lessened the profitability of businesses that might have decreased household labor (e.g., laundries).

Child care became more labor-intensive in the suburbs. The suburban exodus was at the height of the new child-centered culture of child rearing (Rossi, 1987). Repeatedly, people who moved to the suburbs stressed that they were seeking "a good place to bring up children" (Popenoe, 1977; Saegert, 1981). But low-density neighborhoods and the absence of public transportation limited the pool of potential activities and playmates for children. Because the suburbs provided a range of specialized activities for children (e.g., Little League, dance lessons), "Mom's taxi" emerged as a way of life.

Thus the suburbs segregated men's and women's lives and supported a strongly gendered division of labor.[2] For a short period in American urban history, a new kind of purdah appeared: married women isolated and controlled in the mostly female setting of daytime suburbia while married men ventured into the profane world of work and danger in the central cities. But despite Friedan's (1963) observations in *The Feminine Mystique*, suburban women generally concluded that their lost opportunities for adult interaction and paid work were compensated by their children's and husband's greater pleasure in the new way of life (Popenoe, 1977; Saegert, 1981; Wilson, 1991).

Women's Paid Work

Initially, suburban women's economic dependence on men was ensured by the ideology of the cult of domesticity, adequate husbandly income, and the absence of suburban economic opportunities for women. But the growth of suburban belts in the 1960s soon shifted patterns of industrial and commercial location. As suburbs attracted men's jobs, they also drew complementary jobs in office work. At first, these were reserved for "single girls." But, as these jobs multiplied, two factors changed women's competition for them: a shortage of single girls and a change in norms for working wives and mothers.

Norms for married women's work changed in response to global economic restructuring. In the early 1970s, the income of the average American worker stagnated and then declined. But American families' material desires did neither so, increasingly, married women's paid work was justified as a way of maintaining the family's standard of living (Geschwender, 1992). When they worked, women adopted strategies to define their jobs as "helping out" their husbands rather than as challenges to the separate spheres ideology (Rosen, 1987). Married women with school-age children increasingly sought paid work (Bose, 1987) and, by the late 1980s, about half of the mothers of children under 3 years of age held paying jobs (Ferree, 1987). The change in workforce participation was greatest for White women, because the poverty of minority Americans had long required a dual-wage-earner family.

Although women's and men's jobs differ in the city as well as in the suburbs, women may have less access to good jobs in the suburban setting. First, many of the better paying "women's jobs" are located in the organizational headquarters and government offices of the central city. But because of their household responsibilities, women generally restrict their search for work to jobs near their homes. In low-density settlements that separate residential and commercial areas, opportunities for women's work are severely restricted (Hwang & Fitzpatrick, 1992; Popenoe, 1977; Semyonov & Lewin-Epstein, 1991). Thus suburban working women are unable to close the wage gap in their families.

Paid Work and Household Work

As suburban married women moved into the workforce, new tensions appeared in the private patriarchy. Wives' paid work produced tremendous strain in households in which women still retained almost sole responsibility for child care and housework. Hochschild (1989) estimates that working the "double shift" requires American women with children to work a month per year more than their husbands do. An increasing proportion of American women report that they are overtired, overworked, and overwhelmed by their responsibilities at work and at home (Schor, 1991). Wives' increased earnings and hours of paid work rarely produce comparable increases in husbands' household work (Berk, 1985). In tandem with rising standards of marital happiness, the unequal household burdens of husband and wife have produced high levels of conflict and discontent in American families.

Divorce

Women's marital discontent is likely to increase as their involvement in paid work increases (Booth, Johnson, White, & Edwards, 1984; Hochschild, 1989). When they are discontented, however, women tend to believe that their marital problems are caused by their husbands rather than by external, structural factors. Divorce has become an increasingly frequent solution to marital problems but also a new source of gender inequality. Divorced women's low incomes and primary responsibility for children's support further disadvantages them relative to men (Goldberg, 1990; Weitzman, 1985). Generally, they are poor (McLanahan et al., 1989), and the suburbs have few places for them to live and few jobs that permit them to support their families.

Female-Headed Households in the Suburbs

The suburbs and low-density cities assume that a married couple is the normal household. Newly divorced women supporting children have trouble finding a job that pays a family wage and affordable rental property that permits children. Despite their increased need for the support and shared resources of a network of friends or kin, suburban single mothers are likely to be more socially isolated than mothers in an urban setting.

In denser and more heterogeneous central cities, the range of housing options is greater. More and better jobs are available to women. Public transportation and a wide range of social services are available, and urban women are better able to live near networks of friends and kin. Additionally, poor urban women with children have a greater likelihood of seeking public or collective solutions to their problems than do poor suburban women. The tradition of stronger state presence and collective action in the cities stands in stark contrast to the tradition of minimal government in the suburbs and uncentered cities.

Conclusion

Although most Americans live in urbanized areas, most do not live in densely settled and heterogeneous central cities. Most live in low-density and relatively homogeneous urban places that are the linear descendants of the first suburban explosion. Therefore, most live in settings that support a private patriarchy that originated in but migrated from the central city. And if trends in American urbanization continue unabated, the dominance of the private patriarchy is likely to continue.

But in this chapter, I have argued that the dominance of private patriarchy is neither assured nor uniform. Cities vary in their gender regimes, with consequences for the degree and legitimacy of sex stratification. For example, cities vary in their zoning regulations and support for public transportation, and their policies have significant effects on women's access to paid work. Cities vary in their proportion of unmarried adults, and this variation affects their residents' perceptions of what constitutes "normal" adult life. Interurban variation in gender relations is as significant as the ways in which cities differ in their class composition or system of racial/ethnic relations. The higher density and more heterogeneous central cities offer challenges to the dominant system of sex stratification that are absent in the gender regimes of lower density and more homogeneous urban places. An understanding of changing patterns of gender struggle requires an understanding of urban change and, because urban change has been shaped by gendered ideals of personal and family life, urban analysis requires an analysis of gender struggles.

Notes

1. In this, I include a range of phenomena: in the 1920s, the dramatic decrease in immigration; the American post–World War II economic boom; the federal government's willingness to subsidize private home ownership through low mortgages and tax deductions. Note, however, that these changes disproportionately benefited White men and excluded men of color.
2. Nancy Chodorow (1978), leading theorist of the sociological psychoanalytic approach to gender, argues that contemporary American masculine and feminine character are consequences of infancy in the gendered world of separate spheres, characteristic of the suburbs.

Bibliography

Abrahamson, M., & Sigelman, L. (1987). Occupational sex segregation in metropolitan areas. *American Sociological Review, 52,* 588–597.

Berk, S. F. (1985). *The gender factory: The apportionment of work in American households.* New York: Plenum.

Blumberg, R. L. (1991). Introduction: The "triple overlap" of tender stratification, economy, and the family. In R. L. Blumberg (Ed.), *Gender, family, and economy: The triple overlap* (pp. 7–34). Newbury Park, CA: Sage Publications.

Booth, A., Johnson, D. R., White, L., & Edwards, J. N. (1984). Women, outside employment, and marital instability. *American Journal of Sociology, 90,* 567–583.

Bose, C. (1987). Dual spheres. In B. B. Hess & M. M. Ferree (Eds.), *Analyzing gender: A handbook of social science research* (pp. 267–285). Newbury Park, CA: Sage Publications.

Brown, C. (1987). The new patriarchy. In C. Bose, R. Feldberg, & N. Sokoloff (Eds.), *Hidden aspects of women's work* (pp. 137–159). New York: Praeger.

Calansanti, T. M., & Bailey, C. A. (1991). Gender inequality and the division of household labor in the United States and Sweden: A socialist-feminist approach. *Social Problems, 38,* 34–53.

Campbell, K., & Lee, B. A. (1990). Gender differences in urban neighboring. *Sociological Quarterly, 31,* 495–512.

Cancian, F. (1987). *Love in America: Gender and self-development.* New York: Cambridge University Press.

Charles, M. (1992). Cross-national variation in occupational sex segregation. *American Journal of Sociology, 57,* 493–502.

Chodorow, N. (1978). *The reproduction of mothering.* Berkeley: University of California Press.

Coleman, M. T. (1991). The division of household labor: Suggestions for future empirical consideration and theoretical development. In R. L. Blumberg (Ed.), *Gender, family, and economy: The triple overlap* (pp. 245–260). Newbury Park, CA: Sage Publications.

Collins, P. H. (1991). *Black feminist thought: Knowledge, consciousness, and the politics of empowerment.* New York: Routledge.

Connell, R. W. (1987). *Gender and power: Society, the person and sexual politics.* Stanford, CA: Stanford University Press.

Connell, R. W. (1990). The state, gender, and sexual politics: Theory and appraisal. *Theory and Society, 19,* 507–544.

Cook, C., & Rudd, N. M. (1984). Factors influencing the residential location of female householders. *Urban Affairs Quarterly, 20,* 78–96.

Cowan, R. S. (1983). *More work for mother: The ironies of household technology from the open hearth to the microwave.* New York: Basic Books.

Davis, N. J., & Robinson, R. V. (1991). Men's and women's consciousness of gender inequality: Austria, West Germany, Great Britain, and the United States. *American Sociological Review, 56,* 72–84.

D'Emilio, J. (1983). Capitalism and gay identity. In A. Snitow, C. Stansell, & S. Thompson (Eds.), *Powers of desire: The politics of sexuality* (pp. 100–116). New York: Monthly Review Press.

D'Emilio, J., & Freedman, E. B. (1988). *Intimate matters: A history of sexuality in America.* New York: Harper & Row.

Diamond, I. (Ed.). (1983). *Families, politics, and public policy: A feminist dialogue on women and the state.* New York: Longman.

England, P., & McCreary, L. (1987). Gender inequality in paid employment. In B. B. Hess & M. M. Ferree (Eds.), *Analyzing gender: A handbook of social science research* (pp. 286–321). Newbury Park, CA: Sage Publications.

Epstein, C. F. (1988). *Deceptive distinctions: Sex, gender, and the social order.* New Haven, CT: Yale University Press.

Faderman, L. (1991). *Odd girls and twilight lovers: A history of lesbian life in twentieth-century America.* New York: Penguin.

Ferree, M. M. (1987). She works hard for a living: Gender and class on the job. In B. B. Hess & M. M. Ferree (Eds.), *Analyzing gender: A handbook of social science research* (pp. 322–347). Newbury Park, CA: Sage Publications.

Friedan, B. (1963). *The feminine mystique.* New York: Dell.

Gelb, J., & Gittell, M. (1986). The role of activist women in cities. In J. Boles (Ed.), *The egalitarian city: Issues of rights, distribution, access, and power* (pp. 93–109). New York: Praeger.

Geschwender, J. A. (1992). Ethgender, women's waged labor, and economic mobility. *Social Problems, 39,* 1–15.

Glenn, E. N. (1991). Racial ethnic women's labor: The intersection of race, gender, and class oppression. In R. L. Blumberg (Ed.), *Gender, family, and economy: The triple overlap* (pp. 173–200). Newbury Park, CA: Sage.

Goldberg, G. S. (1990). The United States: Feminization of poverty amidst plenty. In G. S. Goldberg & E. Kremen (Eds.), *The feminization of poverty: Only in America?* (pp. 17–58). New York: Greenwood.

Hochschild, A. R. (1989). *The second shift.* New York: Avon.

Hwang, S., & Fitzpatrick, K. M. (1992). The effect of occupational sex segregation and the spatial distribution of jobs on commuting patterns. *Social Science Quarterly, 73,* 550–564.

Kandiyoti, D. (1988). Bargaining with patriarchy. *Gender and Society, 2,* 274–290.

LaRossa, R., & LaRossa, M. M. (1989). Baby care: Fathers vs. mothers. In B. J. Risman & P. Schwartz (Eds.), *Gender in intimate relationships: A microstructural approach* (pp. 138–154). Belmont, CA: Wadsworth.

Laslett, B., & Brenner, J. (1989). Gender and social reproduction: Historical perspectives. *Annual Review of Sociology, 15,* 381–404.

Matthews, G. (1992). *The rise of public woman: Woman's power and woman's place in the United States, 1630–1970.* New York: Oxford University Press.

McLanahan, S. S., Sorensen, A., & Watson, D. (1989). Sex differences in poverty, 1950–1980. *Signs, 15,* 102–122.

Norris, P. (1987). *Politics and sexual equality: The comparative position of women in Western democracies.* Boulder, CO: Rienner.

O'Kelly, C. G., & Carney, L. S. (1986). *Women and men in society: Cross-cultural perspectives on gender stratification.* Belmont, CA: Wadsworth.

Piess, K. (1986). *Cheap amusements: Working women and leisure in turn-of-the-century New York.* Philadelphia, PA: Temple University Press.

Popenoe, D. (1977). *The suburban environment: Sweden and the United States.* Chicago: University of Chicago Press.

Rich, A. (1980). Compulsory heterosexuality and the lesbian continuum. *Signs, 5,* 631–660.

Rosen, E. I. (1987). *Bitter choices: Blue-collar women in and out of work.* Chicago: University of Chicago Press.

Rossi, A. S. (1987). Parenthood in transition: From lineage to child to self-orientation. In J. B. Lancaster, J. Altmann, A. S. Rossi, & L. R. Sherrod (Eds.), *Parenting across the life span: The biosocial dimension* (pp. 31–84). New York: Aldine de Gruyter.

Saegert, S. (1981). Masculine cities and feminine suburbs: Polarized ideas, contradictory realities. In C. R. Stimpson, E. Dixler, M. J. Nelson, & K. B. Yatrakis (Eds.), *Women and the American city* (pp. 93–108). Chicago: University of Chicago Press.

Salem, G. (1986). Gender equity and the urban environment. In J. Boles (Ed.), *The egalitarian city: Issues of rights, distribution, access, and power* (pp. 152–161). New York: Praeger.

Schor, J. B. (1991). *The overworked American: The unexpected decline of leisure.* New York: Basic Books.

Semyonov, M., & Lewin-Epstein, N. (1991). Suburban labor markets, urban labor markets, and gender inequality in earning. *Sociological Quarterly, 32,* 611–620.

Shlay, A. B., & DiGregorio, D. A. (1985). Same city, different worlds: Examining gender- and work-based differences in perceptions of neighborhood desirability. *Urban Affairs Quarterly, 21,* 66–86.

Stansell, C. (1986). *City of women: Sex and class in New York, 1789–1860.* New York: Alfred A. Knopf.

Walby, S. (1989). Theorizing patriarchy. *Sociology, 23,* 213–234.

Weitzman, L. (1985). *The divorce revolution: The unexpected consequences for women and children.* New York: Free Press.

Wekerle, G. R. (1981). Women in the urban environment. In C. R. Stimpson, E. Dixler, M. J. Nelson, & K. B. Yatrakis (Eds.), *Women and the American city* (pp. 185–211). Chicago: University of Chicago Press.

West, G. (1981). *The NWRO: The social protest of poor women.* New York: Praeger.

Wilson, E. (1991). *The sphinx in the city: Urban life, the control of disorder, and women.* Berkeley: University of California Press.

14

Michael N. Danielson

SUBURBAN AUTONOMY

Suburbia is essentially a political phenomenon. Political independence is the one thing the increasingly diversified settlements beyond the city limits have in common. Local autonomy means that suburban communities seek to control their own destiny largely free from the need to adjust their interests to those of other local jurisdictions and residents of the metropolis. Since local governments in the United States bear the primary responsibility for the provision of basic public services such as education, police and fire protection, as well as the regulation of housing and land use, independence provides suburbs with considerable control over the vital parameters of community life, including the power to exclude unwanted neighbors. In the differentiated and fragmented metropolis, these powers are exercised by suburban governments which are usually responsive to the interests of their relatively homogeneous constituencies. The result, as Robert C. Wood notes, is the division of the metropolitan population into "clusters homogeneous in their skills and outlook which have achieved municipal status and erected social and political barriers against invasion."[1]

With few exceptions, political autonomy affords suburbanites a potential for exclusion which exceeds that usually available to the resident of the central city. Through zoning, building codes, and other planning powers, suburban communities to a far greater degree than city neighborhoods are able to protect the local turf from undesirable housing and residents. Independence also means that the formal consent of local government must be obtained before most state or federal housing programs for the poor can be initiated, a power rarely delegated by city hall to its neighborhoods. In addition, exclusionary policies are more easily pursued in small and relatively cohesive political systems than in large ones with diverse constituency interests. To protect itself from unwanted developments, a city neighborhood must keep an eye on a variety of agencies and possess substantial clout in complex political arenas.

By living in a smaller, more homogeneous, and less complex polity, the resident of an autonomous suburb tends to be insulated from unwanted change. Local actions are far less likely to threaten him with lower-income neighbors or other disturbing developments in a jurisdiction where both fellow citizens and public officials share his frame of reference. As a consequence, political independence reduces the chances that suburban dwellers will face the sorts of issues concerning race, status, property values, and community character that frequently confront blue-collar and middle-class neighborhoods in the central city. When suburbanites cannot avoid such challenges, they are more likely to enlist the support of a local government that is closely tuned to their interests and values than is commonly the case in the large and heterogeneous central city.

Because of these considerations, the use of local powers over land, housing, and urban development to promote local social values and protect community character are widely viewed as the most important functions of local governments in suburbia. Residents of upper- and middle-class suburbs in the Philadelphia area ranked maintenance of their community's social characteristics—defined in terms of keeping out "undesirables" and maintaining the "quality" of residents—as a more important objective for local government than either the provision of public services or maintenance of low tax rates. In suburbs of lower social rank, maintenance of social characteristics was considered more important than the provision of local services and amenities, and almost as important as keeping down local tax rates.[2]

Exclusionary considerations, of course, are neither the sole nor the most important factor underlying the exodus to the suburbs. Most urban Americans have moved outward in search of better housing, nicer surroundings, social status, and separation from the inner city and its inhabitants. Increasingly, however, political separation has come to be an essential element of the appeal of the suburbs. In the words of a local leader in a blue-collar suburb in the Detroit area, "the most important thing to many people in Warren is just the simple fact that it isn't Detroit."[3] Speaking of the blacks who flocked to East Cleveland during the 1960s, the suburb's black city manager notes that "they feel that at least they are not living in the inner city."[4] Regardless of their reasons for moving outward, most suburbanites quickly discover the utility of local autonomy as a means of protecting their neighborhood, their social standing, their

Table 1 Attitudes of Residents of 16 Suburbs in the Philadelphia Area Toward the Importance of Various Objectives of Local Government

	Social Rank Grouping of Municipalities (percent judging objective very important)		
Attitude	Upper	Middle	Lower
Keep undesirables out	62.0	79.5	75.0
Maintain "quality" of residents	69.0	47.0	43.0
Maintain improved public services	44.8	41.2	35.7
Provide aesthetic amenities	50.0	38.2	32.1
Acquire business and industry	8.6	23.5	50.0
Keep tax rate down	56.9	79.5	82.0

Source: Oliver P. Williams, et al., *Suburban Differences and Metropolitan Policies: A Philadelphia Story* (Philadelphia: University of Pennsylvania Press, 1965), pp. 217–219.

property values, and the racial integrity of the local schools from outside threats. As Daniel J. Elazar notes: "People sought *suburbanization* for essentially private purposes, revolving around better living conditions. The same people sought *suburbs* with independent local governments of their own for essentially public ones, namely the ability to maintain these conditions by joining with like-minded neighbors to preserve those life styles which they sought in suburbanization."[5] In the process, local autonomy and exclusion have become closely intertwined. Political independence greatly strengthens the suburban community's ability to exclude, while the desire to exclude both enhances the attractions of local autonomy and reinforces the suburban commitment to the preservation of local control over the vital parameters of community life.

The Scope of Local Autonomy

In its simplest form, suburban autonomy involves a ring of unincorporated communities lying beyond the city limits, with local governmental services provided by town or county governments. The largest of these "doughnut" types of metropolitan political systems is found in the Baltimore area. Baltimore County, whose 610 square miles and 616,000 inhabitants surround the city of Baltimore and its 895,000 residents, has no incorporated municipalities or elected local officials except for a county executive and a seven-member council.[6] While approximately half of all suburbanites in the United States live in unincorporated areas, arrangements typically are more complex than those in Baltimore County. Rarely does the entire suburban portion of a metropolitan area consist of unincorporated territory. Instead, municipalities are usually scattered amidst the unincorporated neighborhoods. Public services for unincorporated areas tend to be provided by a melange of authorities, school districts, county governments, and state agencies. Regulatory and planning activities affecting land use and housing normally are the responsibility of county governments in unincorporated areas.

Greater control over land, housing, and other key local functions is exercised by suburban communities which have incorporated as municipalities under state law. Municipal governments have more extensive authority than local governments in unincorporated areas to tax, to borrow, to provide services, and to regulate urban development. Another attraction of incorporation is the protection it provides a suburb against absorption into other local jurisdictions. In most states, incorporation guarantees the political independence of a community, since territory in a municipality cannot be annexed by another local government. On the other hand, incorporation usually means more extensive and expensive local services. As a result, many suburbanites prefer unincorporated status, particularly when essential public services are available from other public agencies and when state law protects unincorporated areas from the territorial ambitions of adjacent municipalities.

Incorporation also provides suburbanites with a local government more responsive to community desires than is the case with unincorporated areas. Responsiveness results primarily from size and spatial differentiation. Most suburban municipalities are quite small. In 1967, two-thirds of all incorporated local jurisdictions in metropolitan areas had fewer than 5,000 inhabitants. And half of all suburban municipalities encompassed less than a square mile of land area.[7] Superimposing these small governmental units on the spatially differentiated population of the metropolis commonly results in relatively homogeneous local constituencies. Within these jurisdictions, local government tends to be highly responsive to the wishes of residents, particularly on sensitive issues such as housing and community development. By contrast, constituencies are larger and more diverse in most unincorporated areas in suburbia. In these larger local units, governments generally are less concerned about particular neighborhoods than is the typical small-scale incorporated suburban government.

The desire to secure local control over land use, housing, and urban development has been a common motivation for the incorporation of suburban municipalities. Local land owners, builders, and developers have employed incorporation to secure control over planning and zoning in order to advance or protect their economic interests. On the other hand, residents, particularly in newly suburbanizing areas, have frequently sought to incorporate their communities in order to transfer planning responsibilities and land-use controls from the hands of county and township officials to those of local residents, elected to office by their neighbors. Often with good reason, these larger units of suburban local government are considered to be too sympathetic to development interests and insufficiently concerned with the interests of individual communities. As the leader of a homeowner's group seeking to incorporate a suburban neighborhood in the Chicago area explains: "Our main goal in trying to incorporate is to protect our residents from improper zoning. Present restrictions by the county, which . . . controls zoning within our boundaries, is rather loose."[8]

Another common but usually unvoiced concern which has stimulated incorporation efforts is the desire to exclude blacks and subsidized housing. In the San Francisco area, John H. Denton believes "that one of the principal purposes (if not the entire purpose) of suburban incorporations is to give their populations control of the racial composition of their communities."[9] Municipal status substantially enhances the capability of a suburban community to exclude subsidized housing, and the blacks who might live in such units. Incorporation permits local officials to decide whether the community will participate in subsidized housing programs. It also provides local residents with control over zoning and other powers which can prevent the construction of subsidized housing.

An illustration of the creation of a suburban municipality to foreclose the construction of subsidized housing is provided by the incorporation of Black Jack, a community of 2,900 in the St. Louis area.[10] Late in 1969, a nonprofit group organized by church organizations in the St. Louis area took an option on a twelve-acre site in an unincorporated section of St. Louis County known as Black Jack. The land in question was part of 67 acres which had been zoned by the county government for multiple-family dwellings; and over 300 apartments already had been constructed by private developers on fifteen of the acres. The church group planned to construct 210 apartments for rental to families earning between $5,700 and $10,200 under the federal government's Section 236 program for moderate-income housing. The site was chosen by the church groups because they "wanted to determine the feasibility of providing subsidized housing for people—black and white—just beginning to climb above the poverty line but still too poor to move to the suburbs."[11]

For residents of the area, almost all of whom were white, middle-income, and living in single-family homes costing between $25,000 and $45,000, the notion of subsidized and integrated housing for lower-income families in their community was not at all feasible. Their reaction was vehement and their actions swift. With local neighborhood associations leading the opposition, circulars were distributed, mass meetings held, and public officials contacted. In addition, a delegation was dispatched to Washington to present petitions to top officials of the Department of Housing and Urban Development. In opposing the project, residents emphasized the lack of public services, overcrowded local schools, poor transportation links with the rest of the metropolis, and the absence of jobs in Black Jack's portion of St. Louis County. Concern also was expressed over the impact on property values and community character if lower-income families, and particularly poor blacks, were to live in Black Jack.

Dissatisfaction with county housing and land-use policies in the Black Jack area had stirred thoughts of incorporation before the subsidized housing project materialized. With the announcement of the project, local residents moved quickly to seek incorporation in order to deny the development of the site for apartments. Two weeks after the federal government agreed to finance the project, over 1,400 residents of the area petitioned the St. Louis County Council for incorporation of 2.65 square miles encompassing the proposed housing. At the request of the county council, the incorporation proposal was evaluated by the county planning department, which opposed the creation of a new municipality "on fiscal, planning, and legal grounds."[12] Far more influential with the county council, however, was the strong local support for incorporation. Black Jack's advocates successfully linked opposition to incorporation with support for subsidized housing. Suburbanites throughout the northern portion of the county were warned by the Black Jack Improvement Association that approval of the project "could open the door to similar projects being located almost anywhere in the North County area. By stopping this project, you would lessen the chance of one perhaps appearing in your neighborhood."[13] Obviously, the way to stop the project was to permit incorporation. Framing the issue in these terms, as one observer notes, rendered the council members "powerless. The housing issue which precipitated the incorporation was too politically sensitive to allow the council to turn down the petition, and thus indirectly sanction" the construction of subsidized housing.[14]

The result was approval by the county council of the creation of the city of Black Jack, the first new municipality in St. Louis County in over a decade. With incorporation, control over land use within Black Jack was transferred from the county to the new municipality. Less than three months after incorporation, Black Jack's City Council enacted a zoning ordinance which prohibited the construction of apartments within the municipality, thus blocking the proposed subsidized housing.[15]

While the powers available to independent local governments provide suburban communities such as Black Jack with the capability to exclude, local autonomy is relative rather than absolute. Local control over land use, housing, and related matters, like all local powers in the United States, is derived from state governments. Autonomy of suburban governments is limited by municipal charters which are granted by the state and by delegation of responsibilities to other units of local government, such as townships and counties by the state constitution or legislature. The states oversee a wide range of local activities and provide local governments with substantial financial assistance, particularly for public education. They also construct most of the major roads and regulate sewer development, a pair of activities which greatly influence the accessibility of land for development. State actions may constrain suburban autonomy, as in the establishment of public agencies empowered to supersede local land-use controls, such as New Jersey's Hackensack Meadowlands Development Commission or New York's Urban Development Corporation.[16] On the other hand, the state may expand the powers of residents of independent suburbs, as have those states which require that public housing proposals be approved by local voters in a referendum.

Local autonomy in the suburbs also is affected by activities of metropolitan and federal agencies, as well as by intervention from the courts. A wide variety of metropolitan agencies exercise responsibility for area-wide planning, major public works, and other activities which affect housing and development patterns within local jurisdictions in the metropolis. The federal government supports housing, highway, water, sewer, planning, and other programs which influence the ability of suburban governments to shape the nature and timing of development within their boundaries. The federal government also has substantial powers to prevent local governments from discriminating against minorities in the development, sale, and rental of housing. In addition, all local authority is subject to review in state courts, and the exercise of many local powers raise issues which fall within the jurisdiction of federal courts.

In the policy areas of greatest importance for exclusion, however, local autonomy tends to be particularly broad. As Richard F. Babcock notes: "Local control over use of private land has withstood with incredible resilience the centripetal political forces of the last generation."[17] State governments typically have delegated virtually all responsibility for planning, zoning, building codes, and related activities to local governments. Few states even maintain an administrative machinery to oversee local land-use and housing controls. Only in response to environmental problems and pressures have states begun to develop plans and regulatory mechanisms which seek to guide or supercede the land-use activities of local governments. Almost all of these state efforts, however, are limited to areas of critical ecological concern, such as coastal zones and floodplains.[18]

Most states also have done little to enlarge the scale of land-use control in suburbia. County governments usually are limited to regulating unincorporated areas, with few states providing counties with a significant land-use role within suburban municipalities. When states provide for county agencies or regional bodies to review local zoning actions, the review power typically, as Coke and Gargan note, "is advisory only; the reviewing agency has no authority unilaterally to overrun the zoning action."[19] Nor have states necessarily permitted metropolitan governments, in the few areas where they have been created, to exercise land-use controls throughout their jurisdiction. In Miami, as the National Commission on Urban Problems pointed out, "the metropolitan government has zoning authority only in unincorporated territory. In Nashville-Davidson County, several small suburban municipalities continued in existence after the creation of the metropolitan government and retained their zoning powers."[20] The state law creating Unigov in the Indianapolis area also permitted suburban municipalities to continue to control land use.

Local autonomy over housing and land use is bolstered further by the absence of a direct federal role in zoning and other development controls. Moreover, local rather than federal officials determine the location of housing units supported by national subsidy programs.[21] A final factor enhancing the ability of suburban governments to use their autonomy to foster exclusion has been the reluctance of most courts to impose significant constraints on the exercise of local land-use powers.[22]

As a result of these developments, suburban governments have been able to use their autonomy to influence housing opportunities with relatively little outside interference. And because land-use patterns strongly affect local taxes and public services, community character, and the quality of local schools, zoning has become the essence of local autonomy for most suburbanites.

Using Local Autonomy

Local autonomy, of course, does not guarantee success to suburbanites in their efforts to control development. Great variations exist in the use of local controls. A few suburbs permit almost any kind of development, others seek to exclude practically everything. Most, however, pursue more selective policies which result from the concerns and values of local residents, fiscal realities, environmental constraints, and the pressures for growth and change which constantly test the effectiveness of local controls. Some suburbs are highly skilled in their use of the means available to influence settlement patterns, employing sophisticated planning techniques and acting in a timely fashion to shape the forces of change. Others are far less skillful, and their tardy and piecemeal efforts tend to be overwhelmed by private developers.

Size is a major barrier to the acquisition of planning and zoning expertise in many suburbs. In his analysis of suburban land development in three northeastern metropolitan areas, Marion Clawson emphasizes that:

> Most of these local governments are . . . too small in most instances to engage any full-time employees for any of these functions. Those which do hire usually pay low wages. Only the largest of the local governments have top-ranking jobs that pay enough to attract and hold well-trained professional or technical people. Staffing levels in planning and land-use-related activities are low in relation to numbers of persons engaged in the construction activities affected by their work.[23]

Many suburbs, however, have overcome the handicaps posed by small size and limited resources. Mounting suburban concern over the implications of unregulated development during the 1960s increased local willingness to invest in the acquisition of sophisticated planning capabilities. The financial burdens imposed by these activities were eased by assistance from federal and state planning programs. And the shortage of skilled local employees was offset by the availability of advice from private planning consultants.

Acquisition of planning skills, however, cannot insure that local efforts will strongly influence development. Accessibility, topography, land values, and other physical and market factors play a major role in shaping settlement patterns in suburbs. So do the decisions of metropolitan, state, and federal agencies concerning roads, water supply, sewers, and other major public facilities. Control over land use, the primary power available to local government, is essentially negative. Zoning, subdivision regulation, building codes, and other planning devices may prevent undesirable development, but by themselves cannot induce desired change. Zoning vacant land in a working-class suburb for two-acre estates may foreclose the construction of more tract houses on small lots. In the absence of excellent schools, attractive surroundings, and separation from lower-status neighbors, however, such local actions is unlikely to result in construction of expensive housing for an upper-income clientele. Similarly, creation of a commercial or industrial district within a suburb will not attract developers unless the site is desirable in terms of the availability of an adequate tract of land at a competitive price, its proximity to highways and other transportation facilities, and its accessibility to markets, suppliers, and labor force.

The ability of suburban governments to shape urban development is frequently undermined by the very factors which afford growing suburbs an opportunity to influence settlement patterns. Having vacant land and being in the path of development in the decentralizing metropolis often means that growth overwhelms the capacity of small and amateur local governments to cope with the complexities of suburbanization. For some fiscally hard-pressed suburban jurisdictions, the perceived tax benefits of growth outweigh the advantages of effective controls, at least during the crucial initial phases of the development process. Local planning controls often fail to check the private sector because of the dominant influence in newly developing areas of large land owners, real-estate operators, bankers, and related interests. Local officials frequently are closely tied to those who are profiting from suburbanization. In Santa Clara County in California, as in many rapidly developing areas, local "officials and the greedy land speculators and developers . . . were never really opposing interests. With few exceptions the local officials were also involved in real estate speculation, had other vested interests in the rapid development of the valley, or . . . simply were unable to make a strong stand against the powerful development interests and their allies in local government."[24]

Outright corruption also subverts the suburban plans and zoning regulations. The high financial stakes of land development combines with the importance of local land-use controls to produce offers which some suburban officials cannot resist. Illustrative is the experience of Hoffman Estates, a suburb in the Chicago area where three officials were convicted of bribery, conspiracy, and tax evasion in 1973 after taking bribes from Kaufman & Broad Homes, one of the nation's largest homebuilding firms. As Ed McCahill has pointed out, the rewards in this instance were high for both local officials and the developer:

> For about $90,000 in bribes, Kaufman & Broad nearly were able to plop an entire town of 25,000 residents right in the middle of a community which had no hospital or industry to speak of, an inadequate transportation system, and schools filled to capacity. The rezoning proposal allowed 33 housing units per acre when Hoffman Estates had no zoning specifications other than "residential." The $90,000 in bribes paid during the 1960s, when the village had only recently been incorporated and was unaccustomed to planning for subdivisions. One of the incidents that tipped off Hoffman Estates homeowners that something was amiss was when their showers went dry in 1970, as 2,500 new neighbors started tapping into the inadequate water system.[25]

As more and more people move to suburbs residential interests are less likely to be compromised by local governments in contests involving developers. With growth constantly augmenting the ranks of those who seek to use local autonomy to preserve and protect their local community from unwanted change, residents have become increasingly active participants in the politics of suburban development. Doubts, often well founded, concerning the ability or desire of local officials to withstand the pressures and other blandishments of developers has stimulated a great deal of political activity at the grass roots. Neighborhood organizations have been created or politicized to bring pressure to bear on local governments, and to fight adverse land-use actions in the courts.[26] An official of a neighborhood civic organization opposed to more apartment construction in East Brunswick, New Jersey, explains the evolution of his group's political activities as follows: "We were a loose social organization that met for July 4 neighborhood picnics before this zoning dilemma blew up. That action pulled us into legal action, with each of the families contributing money to legally fight the variance before the Zoning Board."[27] To check the discretionary power of local officials, suburbanites in some jurisdictions have sought direct public participation in land-use questions. Voters in East-lake, a suburb in the Cleveland area, approved an amendment to the local charter in 1971 which required approval of all rezoning sections by 55 percent of those voting in a public referendum. Residential interests supporting the provision "wanted to get the power back to the people" by making it neces-sary for "a developer to convince the voters he's bringing something good into the city."[28]

Local officials who fail to respond to these residential pressures increas-ingly face retribution at the polls. In many suburbs, a new generation of office holders is emerging dedicated to using local autonomy to protect residential interests rather than to facilitate developers and land owners. As Fred P. Bossel-man notes:

> The most important manifestation of the new mood is the changing character of suburban political leaders. Traditionally suburban governments have been domi-nated by the local businessmen, especially real estate brokers, many of whom owned substantial tracts of vacant land. They naturally saw growth as good for business—as long as it didn't attract "undesirables," of course.
>
> This is changing. . . . [In] many parts of the country in the past few years . . . voters have ousted the incumbents and replaced them with a new type of local official. They are housewives, junior executives, engineers, mechanics, truck drivers—in short, typi-cal suburban homeowners who's only contact with the community is to live in it, not to make money off it. This might be characterized . . . as "suburbia for the suburbanites."[29]

As a consequence of these developments, more and more public officials in suburbia reflect the values of the relatively homogenous constituencies which elect them or hire them. Zoning and planning boards increasingly are com-posed of members sympathetic to the interests of local residents. In Greenwich, Connecticut, as in thousands of suburbs, "no one can get elected unless he swears on the Bible, under the tree at midnight, and with a blood oath to up-hold zoning."[30] Suburban city managers, planning directors, and the consul-tants who provide much of the technical and planning advice in many suburbs commonly adjust their attitudes, proposals, and actions to the limited horizons of the suburban jurisdiction which hires them. As a former suburban mayor emphasizes, "the officials they elect understand that their responsibility is to keep the community the way the people here want it."[31]

Of course, the growing influence of residents in suburban politics does not mean that local controls over housing and land use always are employed to ad-vance residential interests. Residents are not cohesive on every development issue, especially in the larger and more heterogeneous suburban jurisdiction. Moreover, landowners and developers retain considerable influence, particu-larly in areas in the path of suburbanization where residents often are outnum-bered by those who seek to profit from development. Nor does local autonomy protect residents of suburbs from losing battles with state highway depart-ments and other outside agencies which are able to alter the pattern of subur-ban development without the consent of the affected localities.

Despite these limitations, local autonomy constitutes an effective shield against social change in many suburban jurisdictions. As residential influence mounts, autonomy offers most suburbanites local governmental institutions responsive to their interests. Equally important, political independence provides the legal means to pursue these objectives through the exercise of local planning, land-use, and housing controls. In the typical community, the purposes of local autonomy tend to be defined by the widespread suburban preoccupation with home and school, class and status concerns, racial separation, and the desire to be insulated from the problems of the inner city. Internal consensus on the uses of local autonomy, particularly in smaller and relatively homogeneous suburban jurisdictions, is likely to be high when property values, educational quality, community character, or the influx of blacks or lower-income residents are at issue. The result, in the words of one suburban political leader, is "the politics of the territorial imperative . . . [which] means opposing new housing and new people, anything that might change the status quo."[32]

Notes

1. *Suburbia: Its People and Their Politics* (Boston: Houghton Mifflin, 1958), p. 128.
2. See Oliver P. Williams et al., *Suburban Differences and Metropolitan Policies: A Philadelphia Story* (Philadelphia: University of Pa. Press, 1965), pp. 217–219.
3. See Walter S. Mossberg, "A Blue Collar Town Fears Urban Renewal Perils Its Way of Life," *Wall Street Journal,* Nov. 2, 1970.
4. Gladstone L. Chandler, Jr., city manager, East Cleveland, O., quoted in Paul Delaney, "The Outer City: Negroes Find Few Tangible Gains," *New York Times,* June 1, 1971; reprinted as "Negroes Find Few Tangible Gains," in Louis H. Masotti and Jeffrey K. Hadden, eds., *Suburbia in Transition,* (New York: Franklin Watts, 1974), p. 278. East Cleveland had no black residents in the mid–1950s; by 1970, 60 percent of its population was black.
5. "Suburbanization; Reviving the Town on the Metropolitan Frontier," *Publius 5,* (Winter, 1975), p. 59.
6. The Baltimore standard metropolitan statistical area contains four additional counties—Anne Arundel, Carroll, Harford and Howard—which lie beyond Baltimore County.
7. See Allen D. Manvel, "Metropolitan Growth and Governmental Fragmentation," in A. E. Kier Nash, ed., *Governance and Population: The Governmental Implications of Population Change,* Vol. 4, Research Reports, U.S. Commission on Population Growth and the American Future (Washington: U.S. Government Printing Office, 1972), p. 181.
8. Robert Poltzer, Prospect Heights Improvement Association, quoted in Dan Egler, "Prospect Heights Seeks to Incorporate," *Chicago Tribune,* Oct. 1, 1972.
9. "Phase I Report" to the National Committee Against Discrimination in Housing, U.S. Department of Housing and Urban Development Project, No. Cal. D–8 (n.d.), pt. 3, p. Jc–11.
10. For a summary of the events leading to the incorporation of Black Jack, see Ronald F. Kirby, Frank de Leeuw, and William Silverman, *Residential Zoning and Equal Housing Opportunities: A Case Study in Black Jack, Missouri* (Washington: Urban Inst., 1972), pp. 17–27.
11. See B. Drummond Ayres, "Bulldozers Turn Up Soil and Ill Will in a Suburb of St. Louis," *New York Times,* Jan. 18, 1971.

12. See *Park View Heights Corporation v. City of Black Jack,* 467 F.2d 1208 (1972) at 1211.

13. See William K. Reilly, ed., *The Use of Land: A Citizens' Policy Guide to Urban Growth,* A Task Force Report Sponsored by The Rockefeller Brothers Fund (New York: Thomas Y. Crowell Company, 1973), p. 90.

14. Jerome Pratter, "Dispersed Subsidized Housing and Suburbia: Confrontation in Black Jack," *Land-Use Controls Annual* (Chicago: American Society of Planning Officials, 1972), p. 152.

15. Black Jack's actions were challenged in court by the sponsors of the project, other organizations, and the federal government; see *United States v. City of Black Jack, Missouri,* 372 F. Supp. 319 (1974); *United States v. City of Black Jack, Missouri,* 508 F.2d 1179 (1974); *Park View Heights Corporation v. City of Black Jack,* 467 F.2d 1208; and the discussion of the Black Jack litigation in chapter 7.

16. Suburban opposition to this grant of power to the Urban Development Corporation led the New York legislature to rescind it in 1973; see chapter 10 for a discussion of the New York Urban Development Corporation's turbulent efforts to open the suburbs.

17. *The Zoning Game: Municipal Practices and Policies* (Madison: University of Wis. Press, 1966), p. 19.

18. State land-use activities and their impact on suburban exclusion are discussed in detail in chapter 10.

19. James G. Coke and John J. Gargan, *Fragmentation in Land-Use Planning and Control,* Prepared for the consideration of the National Commission on Urban Problems, Research Report No. 18 (Washington: U.S. Government Printing Office, 1969), p. 6.

20. *Building the American City,* Report of the National Commission on Urban Problems to the Congress and President of the United States, 91st Cong., 1st sess., House Doc. No. 91–34 (Washington: U.S. Government Printing Office, 1968), p. 209.

21. The federal role in suburban exclusion is examined in chapter 8.

22. Judicial attitudes concerning exclusionary zoning and housing policies began to shift in the late 1960s; see chapter 7 for an analysis of the role of the courts in opening the suburbs.

23. *Suburban Land Conversion in the United States: An Economic and Governmental Process* (Baltimore: Johns Hopkins University Press, 1971), pp. 65–66.

24. Leonard Downie, Jr., *Mortgage on America* (New York: Praeger Publishers, 1974), p. 111.

25. "Stealing: A Primer on Zoning Corruption," *Planning* 39 (Dec., 1973), p. 6.

26. For a discussion of suburban neighborhood associations, and their role in land-use politics, see R. Robert Linowes and Don T. Allensworth, *The Politics of Land Use: Planning, Zoning, and the Private Developer* (New York: Praeger Publishers, 1973), pp. 114–142.

27. George Post, vice president, Prides Wood Civic Association, East Brunswick, N.J., quoted in Ruth Ann Burns, "Apartment Proposal Stirs a Dispute in East Brunswick," *New York Times,* Oct. 8, 1972.

28. See "Eastlake Is Upheld on Requiring Vote in Rezoning Cases," *Cleveland Plain Dealer,* Oct. 31, 1972, Eastlake's ordinance was overturned four years later by the Supreme Court of Ohio; see *Forest City Enterprises, Inc. v. City of Eastlake,* 41 Ohio St. 2d 187, 324 N.F.2d, 740 (1975).

29. "The Right to Move, the Need to Grow," *Planning* 39 (Sept., 1973), pp. 10–11.

30. See Ralph Blumenthal, "Pressures of Growth Stir Zoning Battles in Suburbs," *New York Times,* May 29, 1967.

31. Harry J. Butler, Wayne, N.J., quoted in Richard Reeves, "Land Is Prize in Battle for Control of Suburbs," *New York Times,* Aug. 17, 1971; reprinted as "The Battle Over Land," in Masotti and Hadden, *Suburbia in Transition,* p. 310.

32. John F. English, former chairman of the Democratic Party, Nassau County, N.Y., quoted in *ibid.,* p. 304.

15

Joel Garreau

EDGE CITY

For all its newness, Edge City is in some ways more faithful to city traditions than the old downtown. Believe it or not, one of the founding premises of cities—from the beginning of fixed settlements eight thousand years ago—was that you were safer inside one than out. First, people clustered around leaders with a successful track record against wolves, alligators, and big cats. "The archetypal chieftain in Sumerian legend is Gilgamesh: the heroic hunter, the strong protector, not least significantly, the builder of the wall around Uruk," writes Lewis Mumford in *The City in History*. Those evolved into the medieval walls of Vienna, raised against the Turks, as well as walled cities from Avignon to Fez. Walled cities with gates that closed at night existed in China in this century. In America, the walled city was immortalized by frontier stockades like Fort Laramie, Wyoming.

Edge City functions very similarly. "The bedrock attribute of a successful city district is that a person must feel personally safe and secure on the street among all these strangers," writes Jane Jacobs, stressing the importance of safety in her very first chapter. For better or for worse, there is not an endless number of such places today in America. Two that come to mind are our sports stadiums and Edge City's village square—the enclosed shopping mall.

Actually, William Jackson [a mall developer] is not so sure about the sports stadiums. "Only when they're winning," he says, thinking of the last time he was at a Giants game at the Meadowlands. "And only when you're in the stadium." Jackson is the senior project manager . . . of Bridgewater Commons [a mall in New Jersey], the man who oversaw its design and construction. "I've walked from the parking lot to the stadium and not felt safe at all. When you walk across the turnpike, there's a very narrow crossover bridge. It's like when you get off the subway in New York and all of a sudden everybody's on the staircase. You don't know who's behind you and who's beside you and what he's going to pull out of your pocket and what he's going to pull out of his pocket. You just kind of go with the flow and hope that nothing happens."

Jackson's professional analysis is germane because state-of-the-art Edge City design pays overwhelming homage to one principle: making women—specifically women—feel safe. In fact, that concern has evolved beyond "safe" and into the art and science of "comfortable," and how people can be made to feel that.

That it works at a place like Bridgewater Commons is unquestionable. Women don't wear their purses in the cross-chest, football-carry, urban-guerrilla mode unless they're doing it for fashion reasons. That's downtown behavior. One crowded Sunday afternoon, toddlers could be seen straggling from their parents much farther than would be comfortable even outdoors in a park, much less a supermarket.

This is not for lack of crime. Shoplifting is always an issue, and some of the mall rats without question deal drugs. One mother recently reported a pair of people at Bridgewater Commons attempting, unsuccessfully, to snatch her stroller with her child and her purse still in it. However, this foiled attempt was viewed as sufficiently unusual to merit major newspaper attention. In such places, there is generally not much violence. Nine million people a year come through the doors of Bridgewater Commons. In the first two years of its existence, the number of assaults reported to the police was two.

This is because Edge Cities have privatized the domains in which large numbers of strangers come together. Edge Cities grew up in the midst of what originally had been residential suburbia. No matter how heterogeneous the population is becoming, the values of the territory's settlers survive. Sociologists who lamented the flight to suburbia claimed the middle class had abandoned the concept of city. They were wrong. The middle class simply built a new kind of city that functions in a Spanish style. It brought its quasi-public spaces in behind high walls, into the atria, open to the sun streaming through the skylights of the courtyards. There, patrol and control can operate at a high level.

"It's pretty hard to walk on my property without seeing some sort of highly visible security," says Jackson. Guards wear uniforms that look like those of the Marines. "I don't want them to be shy and subtle. I want them to be very overt." The gumball-machine lights on the patrol trucks go on at the drop of a lug nut. Even if these paladins are only helping somebody change a flat tire, they do it with stark orange flashers. A local Explorer Scout unit occasionally scans the place from the roof with binoculars. At Christmas, the mall is patrolled on horseback. That's good community relations: the horse is a former member of the Philadelphia Police Department owned by the local animal-control officer who likes to keep his mount's skills sharp by working him amid people and cars. It's also beautiful public relations: children want to pet the horse. The horse patrol has tremendous visibility: the officer sits up so high that he can see and be seen for great distances. The pair can cruise real slow if that seems right. And they are intimidating—it's a big horse.

"You're in a toughie situation," says Jackson. "We're not police and we'll never usurp the police power." But Jackson gladly does everything he can to blur the line. He wants the township's police to have "a knowledge of the center that is very intimate." The chief of police is encouraged to lunch in the food court. The patrol officers are encouraged to park their cruisers in the deck, get out, and walk around. Even the normally desk-bound dispatchers are wooed with awards plaques and private tours. "There's definitely a symbiotic relationship. The police have a substation here. In the mall, sure. I'm trying to encourage that coordination to the nth degree. We have a police liaison who just happens to be the juvenile officer for the high schools and the township. Most high school kids, they're very good and well behaved. You will only have a small segment with problems. We recognize them by sight and we ban them. We are private property. Arrest them for trespass and ban them.

"Kids on average will have in their pockets $25 apiece when they walk in the door. We know that. When they leave they are much better than their parents because they leave almost to the penny with nothing. When you stop and think about it, that is very strong economics. You don't want to just arbitrarily throw them out. But being private property, that does give me a lot of rights. High-spirited youth can be escorted off. Quietly, subtly, but out of the picture."

"Sharper Image controls who they let in their store," Richmond picks up. "They have somebody watching who's coming in. Sometimes they have a greeter at the door say 'There's a limit. You can't go in until somebody leaves because there's too many people in there.' Kids get bored and leave. It's their sales philosophy—they want their salespeople to be able to meet, greet, and sell. And they're looking for shoplifters."

Yet no matter how insidious and sophisticated are the methods by which issues of safety are addressed, Richmond and Jackson see it as only part of a much larger issue—what it takes to make people feel comfortable.

They play that game at a very high level. "See that marble floor there?" Richmond asks. "We used to give it a very high, very bright gloss, but we've toned it down." Why, I ask; did women think they were going to slip? Not that, he says. "We found that it brought out feelings of inadequacy. We brought it down to the level of shine on their own floors."

Richmond had earlier given me a serious market segmentation by mall floor. On the floor for the affluent, he said, prime customers on weekdays were wives of those senior executives who were in their late fifties. On Saturday and Sunday, it became the territory of women who were thirty-eight, had 2.3 kids, and were working. I thought he was pulling my leg with data that precise and started to josh him. He cut me off. "I've got my marketing staff if you'd like to talk to them," he said stiffly. They do *not* kid about anything that offers them control.

They take equally seriously the goal of "comfortable." The range of custom-crafted lighting systems for the mall, for example, can be manipulated to create an enormous range of moods, varying according to the time of day, the season, and the crowds. That task is so important that it is handled on a daily basis by Richmond, the manager, himself, not by some flunky. And this devotion to "comfort levels" is not peculiar to Bridgewater Commons or even to malls. In Edge City hotels, offices, and commercial areas, glass elevators and glass stairwells are rarely there for the view out. They are there for the view in. Rape is unlikely in a glass elevator.

Another effort at comfort: the hot trend is to have parking decks with roofs at expensive, "wasted," warehouselike heights, with light levels appropriate to night baseball. Again, the highest goal is to make women feel safe. The older, more "logical" design, with roofs just tall enough for a car antenna, and lights only bright enough to show car keys, has Alfred Hitchcock overtones.

Similarly, the lawn designs of Edge City office campuses also broadcast their values. One can see a stranger approaching for a quarter of a mile. The inside of a soaring glass office lobby is about as public a place as is ever built in Edge City.

Designers who wish to make Edge City more humane frequently advocate that public parks and public places be added to match the great piazzas of the cities of old. That sounds great. But George Sternlieb of the Center for Urban Policy at Rutgers, points out the reason that there's no equivalent of the old urban parks in Edge City. "They don't want the strangers. If it is a choice between parks and strangers, the people there would sooner do without the parks." In Edge City, about the closest thing you find to a public space—where just about anybody can go—is the parking lot. In Edge City, no commercial center could survive if it had as poor a reputation for safety as do the streets of most downtowns. In Edge City, there are no dark alleys.

In the course of my travels, I never did find any sound, practical, financial, technical, physical, or legal reasons why we could not build more nineteenth-century-style downtowns out at 287 and 78 or anywhere else—if we chose. Yet we do not. Edge City is frequently accused of being the result of no planning. Yet a close examination demonstrates that quite the opposite is the case. The controls exercised in the name of "safety" and "comfort" in Edge City are the result of vast amounts of planning. Also design, money, thought, premeditation, listening to people, and giving them exactly what they say they want.

There are homeless people in Edge City, for example. But they are not found sleeping outside the centers of commerce and industry. Our planning, design, and control of public spaces that are really private property make sure of that. Every Christmas there is a national flap over whether malls will allow the Salvation Army into their domains. But it isn't just a question of charity. It's a question of how much we value safety and comfort. In Edge City there is very little truly "public" space. On purpose.

Chapter 6

❖❖❖

THE CENTRAL CITIES

Keeping the Peace: Governance

The governance of central cities in the United States has undergone a fundamental transformation in recent decades. The regimes in these cities have coped with huge changes in their populations, their economies, and in their political processes. Minority mayors have been swept into office in virtually all of the big cities and in scores of smaller ones. And yet the benefits of incorporation are far from clear. The essay by Christopher Howard, Michael Lipsky, and Dale Rogers Marshall assesses the growth of political participation among minority groups, including the poor, that has occurred during recent decades in most large cities. As substantial minority participation has become routinized, this new fact of urban life has not always yielded the results that were expected by those who struggled for it. Indeed, the authors conclude that "The difficulties of developing political coalitions that give priority to the challenge of poverty and the plight of American cities must not be underestimated." They point out that winning in electoral politics often gives minority officeholders a false victory. The grim fiscal realities of unbalanced budgets, the flight of middle-class taxpayers to suburbia, and abandonment of central cities by state and federal governments are among the constraints that discourage all mayors from mounting costly governmental offensives to overcome inner-city social problems. Furthermore, increasing ethnic and racial diversity within many cities often complicates building a consensus on important programs or around minority candidates for office.

The authors also assess the rise of grass roots neighborhood organizations as an alternative to conventional forms of political participation, such as through party politics. They conclude that this new "Urban Populism" is not without problems. The movement usually underrepresents the poor, and particular groups often promote parochial views (such as NIMBYism) or are more interested in collaborating with government agencies than in changing the status quo on policy. Nevertheless, Howard, Lipsky, and Marshall conclude that increasing citizen participation is the most valuable resource available to the poor for gaining material benefits and, in particular, for gaining a place at the political table.

The selection from William Sites extends the Howard, Lipsky, and Marshall analysis by tracing policy changes through the Koch, Dinkins, and Giuliani administrations in New York City. What makes Sites's articles so interesting is that these mayors won office on widely divergent political platforms; Koch promised fiscal austerity, Dinkins (the city's first African American mayor) emphasized a new link between city hall and the neighborhoods through a community-based housing strategy, and Giuliani campaigned on themes emphasizing support for business and a withdrawal from social commitments. But what Sites finds is that the policies pursued by each of these mayors were remarkably similar; all of them ended up emphasizing a rather conventional pro-growth approach that involved providing subsidies for business. Sites explains this result by reference to the importance of factors such as changes in the real estate market and in national policies—factors that, he says, have been relatively neglected by scholars relying upon urban regime theory.

The trend toward increasing political participation has also included cities of the Sunbelt, according to Carl Abbott's survey of the enormous urban political and economic changes in that region during the past forty years. Traditionally, Sunbelt cities were ruled by closed business-dominated regimes that excluded most groups, especially minorities, from exerting a political voice. Over time, however, the political and economic systems of the Sunbelt cities have come to resemble more closely those of northern cities. Metropolitan politics has changed as well. Suburban development has occurred beyond the reach of and at the expense of many central cities in the Sunbelt. Equally important, the growth and increasing diversity of their populations have forced local governments to become more inclusive of blacks, Latinos, women, and other groups, though businessmen and civic notables still operate at the center of Sunbelt regimes.

Almost all urban scholars grant that new groups have begun to participate in urban politics in recent decades. But does increased political participation change urban policy, or does it merely fragment power? All of the selections making up this chapter should be read with this important question in mind.

16

Christopher Howard, Michael Lipsky, and Dale Rogers Marshall

CITIZEN PARTICIPATION IN URBAN POLITICS: RISE AND ROUTINIZATION

Electoral Politics

The rise of minority mayors has often been cited as the best evidence that disadvantaged groups have made gains in urban politics over the last 30 years. The change has indeed been dramatic. Whereas there were no black or Latino mayors of cities with populations greater than 50,000 in 1960, there were 27 black and three Latino mayors of cities this size by 1985. By 1991, there were 33 black mayors in cities this size (Joint Center for Political and Economic Studies 1992). They became the elected leaders of some of America's largest cities—New York, Chicago, Los Angeles, Detroit, Atlanta, San Antonio, Newark, and Denver, among others. Some, like Newark's Kenneth Gibson and Atlanta's Andrew Young, were veterans of the civil rights movement and the War on Poverty.

The total number of black elected officials, who far outnumber Latino officials nationally, grew 138 percent between 1970 and 1975, 40 percent from 1975 to 1980, and 23 percent between 1980 and 1985. Part of the explanation for the declining rate of growth lies in demographics. The 1970–75 surge came primarily in cities with large black populations. Comparable data for Latino officials are unavailable. What is clear is that between the early 1970s and 1990, the total number of elected officials grew at a faster rate than the rate of growth of Latino populations in Arizona, California, Florida, New Mexico, New York, and Texas (Pachon and DeSipio 1992).

By the 1980s, there were few cities left with large minority populations that had not elected a black or Latino official. As rapid as these changes have been, continued growth in the number of minority elected officials is likely to be less rapid. Minorities are currently declining as a percentage of population in many urban areas as white professionals return to the central cities. Faster growth can be expected for Latino officials than black officials, principally because of faster growth in the (naturalized) Latino population. Of course, minority population size does not fix a ceiling on the potential number of minority elected officials, but the clear (not perfect) split of recent urban elections along racial or ethnic lines indicates that this factor is important (Browning, Marshall, and Tabb 1990; Pachon and DeSipio 1992; Williams 1987).

As one might expect with such a large increase, no one model of political organization predominated. Based on an investigation of 10 northern California cities over 20 years, Browning, Marshall, and Tabb (1984) produced a study that identified four general patterns of minority mobilization and incorporation in urban electoral politics. In descending order of minority influence, these patterns are biracial electoral alliance, cooptation, protest and exclusion, and weak mobilization. The key to higher levels of responsiveness—the degree to which minority demands are translated into public policy—is not simply representation but incorporation into the governing coalition. Election to city council, for instance, is less meaningful if the council member represents the minority party or is excluded from the dominant faction of the majority party. A tradition of protest and activism helped to accelerate the process of incorporation, but was not in itself sufficient to produce tangible benefits to the minority community. Blacks and Latinos achieved the highest levels of incorporation in those cities in which they formed alliances with liberal whites.

Incorporation brought tangible shifts in public policy. Cities where it occurred not only experienced a sharper increase in city minority employment and in the percentage of city contracts awarded to minority businesses but appointed more minorities to city boards and commissions, established many more minority programs, created police review boards, and were in general more responsive in delivering services than cities in which minority representation was either negligible or was coopted (Browning et al. 1984, 1990; Button 1989; Eisinger 1982).

A number of scholars have questioned the significance of these findings because the sample communities came from a relatively prosperous region of the country with a reputation for liberal views and included only two major cities, San Francisco and Oakland. Subsequent testing of the thesis that "protest is not enough" has borne out the primary finding, with several important qualifications. First, inclusion in a dominant coalition does assure a much stronger minority position than does just representation, but the value of political incorporation will be tempered by the larger context of the urban political economy. In a context of fiscal crisis, the need for economic development constrains the kinds of redistributive policies that blacks and Latinos might have been expected to favor. Second, entrenched party machines have created barriers to incorporation in cities such as New York and Chicago. Third, as New York City and Miami demonstrate, blacks and Latinos cannot be assumed to be natural political allies; they have at times worked at cross-purposes. Mollenkopf (1986) warns of a possible rollback of minority gains in New York City. Thus, even incorporation may not be enough to provide minorities with meaningful control over urban public policy (see essays in Browning et al. 1990).

These qualifications bring into question the impact that minority electoral participation has had on the black and Latino communities. Students of urban politics have divided sharply in their assessments of how effectively minority officials have worked within these constraints. Most would agree that incorporation seems to have increased levels of political participation and trust in government among minorities (Bobo and Gilliam 1990). Their disagreements relate to the size and distribution of material benefits. Among the optimists, Bette Woody has argued that

> black mayors . . . blended a sophisticated mix of managerial reform principles, good government and grass roots participation, designed to compete in regional and national arenas for a larger slice of the social and economic pie. . . . The black mayors thus proved some of the more successful practitioners of an amalgamation of populist and socially responsive goals on the one hand and on the other, leaders of the fight for management reform and sound government operation. (1982: 3)

Less-sanguine observers have emphasized the degree to which benefits have accrued disproportionately to more-upwardly mobile blacks and Latinos, leaving behind a significant underclass. In their view, the election of minority officials and federal initiatives like the War on Poverty have helped to create a black middle class of government employees but failed to alleviate poverty. William Nelson, Jr., offered a typical judgment of this group:

> The upsurge in the election of "new breed" black politicians to public office has been most effective in the promotion of the social and economic interest of upwardly mobile, elite sectors of the black community.

> Elected on reform platforms that promised profound changes in the policy-making process, black mayors have almost uniformly embraced corporate-centered strategies that have virtually precluded the redistribution of major benefits to broad segments of the black community. (1987: 172, 174)

A third perspective—and in our view the most persuasive—has emphasized the numerous obstacles to reform common to black, Latino, and white officials. Decentralized and overlapping authority, the product of "good government" reforms, has lowered the potential for any one city official, including the mayor, to affect public policy. Weak political organizations and candidate-centered elections have depressed voter turnout and produced officials who owe sustained allegiance to no group. Where urban machines have dominated, competing views have been ignored and new actors discouraged from participating. Perhaps most important, city officials, regardless of race or ethnic background, have come under increasing pressure to make economic development their overriding policy objective. The combination of slower rates of economic growth, the exodus of more-affluent residents to the suburbs (and, hence, declining tax bases of many cities), public resistance to tax increases, and the increasing mobility of capital has limited cities' ability to engage in redistribution (Reed 1988; Stone 1989). Meanwhile, the national government, a prime sponsor of programs for disadvantaged groups in the 1960s and 1970s, has reduced aid to the cities—a policy some have termed "fend-for-yourself federalism" (Altshuler and Howard 1991; Kirschten 1989).

As a result, many mayors who campaigned on a progressive or populist platform have actively pursued corporate investment once in office. Coleman Young of Detroit and Tom Bradley of Los Angeles are the most-commonly cited recent examples; Andrew Young of Atlanta, Federico Peña of Denver, and Lionel Wilson of Oakland also fit this pattern (Judd 1986). These same pressures have changed the types of candidates likely to run for office, the tenor of their campaigns, and the substance of their message. Referring to the second generation of minority mayors (e.g., Wilson Goode of Philadelphia, Kurt Schmoke of Baltimore), one observer has written: "More pragmatists than pioneers, professionals than preachers, coalition builders than confrontationists, they came to power during a period of drastic cutbacks in federal money for cities, and they are hawking economic progress and managerial expertise" (Moore 1988: 373).

Moreover, minority officials have faced an additional set of constraints. Their core constituency has become a smaller portion of the electorate as affluent whites and other racial and ethnic immigrants have moved to the cities. As the black middle class has grown, its participation in civic matters has declined or dispersed over a larger metropolitan area. Traditional black organizations like the NAACP have lost membership and support. In this third view, then, black and Latino officials on the whole have been as constrained, or as ineffective, in addressing the poverty-related problems of their constituents as their white counterparts. Ironically, the process of generating real benefits for the black middle class may have undercut political support for minority officials and reoriented urban politics more along income and class divisions than along racial lines (Nelson 1987; Rich 1987; Williams 1987).

Looking back over the last quarter century of minority participation in electoral politics, we foresee three issues becoming more important in the near future. The first is that of growing income disparities and class divisions within the minority community. Although these disparities are most obvious within the black electorate, Miami and Los Angeles provide comparable evidence for Latinos. These schisms are most evident in Atlanta, Chicago (since Harold Washington's death in 1987), Cleveland, and Philadelphia. According to Carolyn Adams, "it is increasingly difficult for a single black candidate to appeal to the disparate socioeconomic groups within the black community."

A second and related issue is that of generational succession. The mature generation of minority officials, which grew up with the civil rights movement and various federal antipoverty programs in the 1960s, succeeded in replacing more conservative businessmen, politicians, and civil rights leaders because they better represented the views of a population coming of age. There is some evidence, still mostly anecdotal, that this process is repeating. In New York City, for instance, black leaders divided sharply over their responses to racial incidents such as the Howard Beach murders and Washington Heights riots. A younger generation of ministers and lawyers has gained visibility in characterizing these incidents as the most obvious signs of a profoundly racist society and has challenged city leaders, regardless of color, to be more open and aggressive in confronting racism. These leaders regularly question the wisdom of working through the Democratic party to achieve their goals, and sometimes advance independent candidates and policy platforms. Alternatively, pragmatic mayors like Goode and Schmoke may represent the future generation. James Jennings (1993) suggests that neither set of leaders will alone speak for the black community. They will instead share power, and ideally will discover ways to combine their respective resources to effect meaningful policy change (see also Morris 1992).

The extent to which the next generation adopts the politics of confrontation will have a profound effect on the third issue in minority electoral politics, the growing importance of multiethnic electoral coalitions. Demographic changes will continue to force minority officials, even in cities where minorities now outnumber whites, to develop closer alliances with white constituencies. The increasing racial and ethnic diversity of cities will create the potential for many different types of coalitions. Obviously it will be difficult to forge such alliances if the parties view each other more as the problem than as the solution. At such a moment of political flux, the side that expands its constituency by mobilizing disadvantaged citizens who currently refrain from participation may well tip the balance of power in its favor.

Urban Populism

Most scholars use the term "neighborhood movement" or "citizen movement" to capture the diversity of grass-roots organizing and protest that emerged during the 1970s and 1980s. One 1978 survey identified over 1,000 community and neighborhood groups organized around 40 different issues. Gary Delgado (1986) estimated the number of these groups at over 8,000 by the mid-1980s. Neither of the terms for these activities, however, is adequate. Although neighborhoods did reemerge as important actors in urban politics, considerable activity took place elsewhere. Statewide organizations like Massachusetts Fair Share and national organizations such as the Associated Communities Organized for Reform Now (ACORN) were central actors. Nor is it clear whether "neighborhood" refers to a geographic entity, type of organization, or a particular set of values. "Citizen movement" is a catchall phrase whose vagueness seems designed to capture as many developments as possible under one heading. Those who use this term tend to highlight the more progressive organizations and ignore the more conservative and even reactionary elements. Further, the inclusion of "movement" in both terms overstates the unity of these organizations.

A different conceptual framework is needed. The richness and ambiguity of these efforts may be better understood through the concept of "urban populism": urban because the majority of these organizations operate in cities; populism because, like the agrarian populists of the late 19th century, they are openly suspicious of concentrated power, whether in the form of big business or big government. Urban populists stress local solutions to local problems and build upon the strength of community churches, ethnic associations, and similar organizations. They work through and around existing institutions, much as their 19th-century counterparts did. Their membership also cuts across traditional political divisions of left and right, liberal and conservative. This term also captures a central tension. Whereas many urban populists affirm the highest democratic ideals, others demand local control to preserve their communities racially and culturally—a reminder of the racism that tainted populism a century ago.

The analogy to agrarian populism should not be taken too far, however: urban populism of the 1980s and 1990s has been geographically fragmented and oriented toward short-term goals; urban populists have devoted little attention to fundamental critiques of capitalist democracy and have created nothing like the Farmers Alliance or the People's party. Still, the similarities appear close enough to make the analogy useful.

The roots of urban populism are as numerous as its branches. All of the protest movements of the 1960s appear to have influenced it (Boyte 1980; Delgado 1986; Fisher 1984; Perlman 1976; Piven and Cloward 1977; Rosenbloom 1979). The combination of Nixon's reelection, the end of the Vietnam War, and the winding down of civil rights/black power compelled many activists to rethink their approaches to social change. Some began to focus on tangible issues in their local communities. A 1976 poll of leaders in 32 grass-roots organizations found that 12 traced their roots to the civil rights movement, 6 to the National Welfare Rights Organization (NWRO), 6 to Saul Alinsky's Industrial Areas Foundation (IAF), and 6 to the Students for a Democratic Society (SDS) or to the antiwar movement (Perlman 1976).

Because the predecessor movements had different goals and used different strategies, the community organizations that emerged were remarkably diverse. Some of the activists who came through the civil rights movement and SDS favored the creation of alternative institutions such as food co-ops and credit unions. Welfare rights advocates argued for mass protests leading to systemic breakdown. Organizations like ACORN, a descendant of NWRO, emphasized grass-roots organizing around local issues. Some SDS veterans preferred to use the media to mobilize the population around long-term goals. And many organizations have employed any number of combinations of these strategies.

Admittedly, some elements of urban populism did not spring from the protest movements. Many white, working-class neighborhood groups originated as a response to major development projects (e.g., highways and stadiums). These projects either displaced working-class whites directly or displaced blacks who moved into white working-class neighborhoods. These groups were essentially conservative; they wanted to shield their neighborhoods from outsiders. They were less interested in organizing for more political power or a better distribution of goods and services than in being left alone to determine the character and composition of their neighborhoods. Some of the best-known groups, such as Restore Our Alienated Rights (ROAR) in South Boston and BUSTOP in Los Angeles, developed in opposition to court-ordered school busing. Although these organizations used the same rhetoric of community control as other urban populists, their motive was racism and their politics were the politics of exclusion (Ackerman 1977; Davis 1978; Fisher 1984; Perlman 1976; Thomas 1986). Whereas some of these organizations are truly inclusive and progressive, a "parochial and reactive 'Not in My Backyard' stance" appears to have become more prevalent over time (Boyte 1991: 60).

Perhaps the least well-understood element of urban populism has been the growth of alternative organizations providing goods and services. Examples of typical organizations that spread rapidly in the 1970s and 1980s include community development corporations (CDCs), which promoted economic development, affordable housing, and job training in particular neighborhoods; rape crisis centers; battered women's shelters; food co-ops; and housing co-ops. Despite their diversity, all of these groups originated out of a desire to meet basic human needs in a decentralized, democratic, face-to-face setting. Their brand of urban populism may have been less confrontational than the practice of ACORN and ROAR, but distrust of big government and big business runs through all of them. Such an attitude would seem to create conflicts between many of the new nonprofit social service agencies and the government whose funds support them. The relationship persists because of mutual need: alternative organizations need to survive and governments need to develop flexible mechanisms to deliver public services in the wake of new service demands, fiscal constraints, and widespread public dissatisfaction with the results of established agencies and approaches (Smith and Lipsky 1993).

Pressure to create these kinds of alternative organizations has increased in recent years. Spurred by the decrease in national funding for cities and the increasing mobility of capital, many neighborhood groups have created local development organizations to fill in the gaps left by state and market.

"It's been a remarkable transformation," says Norman Krumholz, professor of urban planning at Cleveland State University and former city planning director under three Cleveland mayors. "What began in the early '70s as a group of grass-roots activist organizations, very strident in style and confrontational in expression, has been transformed into a set of enormously competent community development corporations that are now doing economic development, housing, and commercial development." (quoted in Katz 1990: 49)

Many of these goods and services are desperately needed, and the involvement by community organizations signals an expansion of their influence in urban politics. On the other hand, participation has forced these same organizations to stress collaboration over confrontation. Their housing and development projects often require a coalition of public and quasi-public agencies, churches, foundations, and private banks, none of which is legally required to cooperate. Put simply, "the era of 'baiting the establishment' is ending" (Katz 1990: 48). "While LDCs [local development corporations] offer a route to community preservation and autonomy, their search for funding restricts their usefulness as independent neighborhood advocates and produces inherently co-optative tendencies" (Fainstein 1987: 330). Thus, urban populism provides further evidence of the rise and routinization of citizen participation.

Not surprisingly, the strengths of urban populism are also its basic weaknesses. First, alternative organizations that develop and remain outside existing structures of economic and political power can provide citizens with new avenues of political participation; such organizations are also by definition incapable of affecting the larger questions of public policy. To date, many of these organizations have eschewed electoral politics. Those representing less-affluent citizens fear cooptation by local governments and middle-income groups. They also believe that no matter how populist the rhetoric, elected officials will ultimately emphasize economic development without sufficient attention to redistribution. Many of those concerned with consumer and environmental issues claim that nonpartisanship is a key to their credibility. Other organizations steer clear of partisan politics to preserve their tax-exempt status (Paget 1990). Unless these organizations find some means of influencing traditional arenas of politics, they will be forced to continue reacting to decisions made elsewhere. And to the extent that they are financially dependent on government, they may be reluctant to advocate significant change.

Second, although the range of strategies and tactics has given urban populism tremendous flexibility in achieving local objectives, this same diversity has hindered its ability to transcend local issues and become a unified, national movement. Urban populists have succeeded to the extent they have previously because of their emphasis on short-term goals. There is no inherent reason why tenant groups in New York City cannot forge alliances with environmental activists in Seattle. But so long as the democratic ideal of urban populism gives priority to values of community over values of justice and equality, the conservative and clannish tendencies of urban populism will persist.

Finally, urban populism has yet to succeed in incorporating the urban poor. With few exceptions, the majority of populist organizations operate in working-class and middle-class neighborhoods. So far, the principal unifying force of urban populism has been the Reverend Jesse Jackson, whose broad democratic vision recognizes the value of community and places it within a larger framework of justice and equality. Whether Reverend Jackson (or anyone) can accommodate urban populism's conservative tendencies, and mobilize those who consider electoral politics pointless, remains to be seen.

Conclusion and Discussion

In trying to understand the larger meaning of citizen participation in urban politics over the last quarter century, it may be helpful to draw a few analogies to the Progressive era. Scholars have frequently commented upon the paradox of Progressivism—the simultaneous expansion and contraction of mass democracy (for a recent statement, see McDonagh 1993). The introduction of the referendum, recall, and initiative enabled ordinary citizens to have more influence over the timing and content of public debate, as well as more control over elected officials. Women gained the right to vote toward the end of the era. In theory the Seventh Amendment requiring direct election of U.S. senators opened the political process, as did direct primaries. On the other hand, personal registration requirements placed the burden on voters to make themselves eligible to participate in elections. Council-manager forms of city government permitted some measure of popular representation while shifting daily operation of the city to appointed professionals. Most important, the shift from ward to at-large representation diluted the influence of ethnic and working-class voters who had recently emerged as important actors in urban politics.

Recent changes in citizen participation have similarly moved in opposing directions. It seems clear that the political system is more open than it was in the 1950s. This expansion would not have happened without [the] civil rights movement. Blacks developed multiple modes of political protest as a substitute for traditional electoral activity, which had been ineffectual in producing equal rights for blacks. The national government, at least for a time, provided direct support to disadvantaged groups attempting to gain a better distribution of public goods and services and sometimes even political power. These relatively modest efforts helped to institutionalize some of the gains made by political protest. For example, bureaucracies that once were closed to political input now routinely mandate and seek citizen involvement. Members of minority groups have been elected mayors of many of America's largest cities. Thousands of community groups have sprung up around the country and engaged in debates over every imaginable area of urban policy.

Yet each of these gains has been accompanied by corresponding constraints on citizen participation. The national government no longer tries to mobilize disadvantaged groups; local circumstances are allowed to determine the appropriate level of citizen participation. Citizens may have been incorporated into the decision-making process of public agencies, but primarily in ways that produce small, incremental changes in public policy. In a cruel twist of fate, minorities have reached city hall "precisely at the moment when the real power to deliver jobs, money, education, and basic services is migrating to higher levels of government and the private sector" (Williams 1987: 129). And many community groups have eschewed the larger questions of urban policy and failed to address the needs of the poorest neighborhoods.

One way to resolve this paradox, for both the Progressive era and the recent past, is to examine exactly who has benefited from these changes. Progressive-era reforms were explicitly designed to regain control of municipal government from ethnic immigrants by limiting the power of urban machines and "ward heelers." The cumulative effect of these reforms increased the political power of the middle class, especially professionals, at the expense of ethnic immigrants. Although it is impossible to explain the most recent reorganization of citizen participation with reference to explicit strategies of disfranchisement, the effect has been distressingly familiar. Middle- and upper-income groups have more of the political resources needed to be effective in routine modes of participation. While routinization has limited the potential for significant changes in urban policy, such changes are at the same time almost totally closed off to disadvantaged groups. Routine modes of political participation exhibit the same skew toward better-educated and higher-income groups as electoral politics. While absolute gains have been made since the 1950s, disadvantaged groups remain relatively powerless in urban politics. It does not seem too severe to conclude that racial minorities and the poor have once again lagged behind all other groups in reaping the benefits of change in urban politics.

If there is one lesson to be drawn from the last quarter century of urban politics, it is that political mobilization is a precondition to any meaningful approach to the problems of the urban poor. The most politically active groups of the last few decades have consistently done better, in terms of political power and distribution of public goods and services, than groups who were simply the targets of government programs. Disadvantaged groups have found ways to compensate partially for their lack of traditional political resources via political mobilization. Spontaneous protest has produced immediate results for disadvantaged groups[,] but not on issues of the magnitude of chronic poverty; those require political organization and the capability to participate effectively in electoral, administrative, and protest politics. Participation by disadvantaged groups in these different political arenas has become far more legitimate and open than it was in the 1950s. This is perhaps the most positive development in urban politics over the last few decades. Nevertheless, major changes in citizen participation have not been matched by fundamental shifts in public policy.

The difficulties of developing political coalitions that give priority to the challenge of poverty and the plight of American cities must not be underestimated. It seems unlikely but not impossible that the current generation of elected officials will genuinely attempt to address these problems. If so, these officials will undoubtedly make disadvantaged groups the targets of government action rather than providing them with the political resources needed to bargain as political equals. A more promising but less likely scenario would involve an alliance between the next generation of minority elected officials or urban populist groups and the disadvantaged. Together they could constitute a governing coalition in some cities and form a crucial swing bloc in state and national politics.

There is an additional reason for emphasizing the need for greater political participation by the urban poor, besides material benefits. Politics is more than an instrumental activity, more than a working out of who gets what and when, though this is a crucial dimension. Politics is also a process of becoming, a means for individuals to establish themselves in their own eyes and those of their neighbors as equal citizens. Equal citizenship is a precondition of self-respect for individuals in any society (Bowles and Gintis 1987; Gutmann 1988). Lacking the resources needed to participate as equals, low-income urban citizens are much less likely to be engaged politically than more-affluent citizens. Although signs of hope can be found (Berry, Portney, and Thomson 1993), considerable evidence indicates that the urban poor have become alienated (Cohen and Dawson 1993). After decades of neglect, it has increasingly become rational for the urban poor to sever their ties to the body politic. To make the American polity whole, this calculus must be changed.

To those who are unmoved by our vision of democracy, we appeal to self-interest. Urban poverty, drugs, and crime will not yield even to enlightened policy intervention unless the urban poor are able to mobilize to change destructive community patterns. For this reason, the entire society may be said to have a stake in increasing the scope and substance of citizen participation in American cities. Otherwise, we can fully expect disadvantaged citizens to again practice the politics of disruption, perhaps even on the scale of 1967 and 1992.

References

Ackerman, Frank. 1977. "The Melting Snowball: Limits of the 'New Populism' in Practice." *Socialist Revolution* 7 (5, September–October): 113–124.

Altshuler, Alan, and Christopher Howard. 1991. "Local Government and Economic Development in the United States." Paper presented at the Organization for Economic and Comparative Development–Kennedy School conference on "Local Development in Multi-Party Democracies," July 8–10, Paris.

Berry, Jeffrey M., Kent E. Portney, and Ken Thomson. 1993. *The Rebirth of Urban Democracy.* Washington, D.C.: Brookings Institution.

Bobo, Lawrence, and Franklin D. Gilliam, Jr. 1990. "Race, Sociopolitical Participation, and Black Empowerment." *American Political Science Review* 84 (2, June): 377–393.

Bowles, Samuel, and Herbert Gintis. 1987. *Democracy and Capitalism.* New York: Basic Books.

Boyte, Harry C. 1980. *The Backyard Revolution.* Philadelphia: Temple University Press.

———. 1991. "Democratic Engagement: Bringing Populism and Liberalism Together." *The American Prospect* 6 (Summer): 55–63.

Browning, Rufus P., Dale Rogers Marshall, and David H. Tabb. 1984. *Protest Is Not Enough: The Struggle of Blacks and Hispanics for Equality in Urban Politics.* Berkeley: University of California Press.

———, eds. 1990. *Racial Politics in American Cities.* White Plains, N.Y.: Longman.

Button, James W. 1978. *Black Violence.* Princeton, N.J.: Princeton University Press.

———. 1989. *Blacks and Social Change.* Princeton, N.J.: Princeton University Press.

Cohen, Cathy J., and Michael C. Dawson. 1993. "Neighborhood Poverty and African-American Politics." *American Political Science Review* 87 (2, June): 286–302.

Davis, Mike. 1978. "Socialist Renaissance or Populist Mirage? A Reply to Harry Boyte." *Socialist Review* 8 (4–5, July–October): 53–63.

Delgado, Gary. 1986. *Organizing the Movement: The Roots and Growth of ACORN.* Philadelphia: Temple University Press.

Eisinger, Peter K. 1982. "Black Employment and Municipal Jobs: The Impact of Black Political Power." *American Political Science Review* 76: 380–392.

Fainstein, Susan S. 1987. "Local Mobilization and Economic Discontent." In *The Capitalist City: Global Restructuring and Community Politics,* edited by Michael Peter Smith and Joe Feagin (323–342). Oxford: Basil Blackwell.

Fisher, Robert. 1984. *Let the People Decide: Neighborhood Organizing in America.* Boston: Twayne Publishers.

Gutmann, Amy, ed. 1988. *Democracy and the Welfare State.* Princeton, N.J.: Princeton University Press.

Jennings, James. 1993. *The Politics of Black Empowerment.* Detroit: Wayne State University Press.

Joint Center for Political Economic Studies. 1992. *Black Elected Officials: A National Roster, 1991.* Washington, D.C.: Joint Center for Political and Economic Studies Press.

Judd, Dennis R. 1986. "Electoral Coalitions, Minority Mayors, and the Contradictions in the Municipal Policy Agenda." In *Cities in Stress,* edited by M. Gottdiener (145–70). Beverly Hills, Calif.: Sage Publications.

Katz, Jeffrey L. 1990. "Neighborhood Politics: A Changing World." *Governing* 4 (2, November): 48–54.

Kirschten, Dick. 1989. "More Problems, Less Clout." *National Journal* (August 12): 2026–2030.

McDonagh, Eileen L. 1993. "The 'Welfare Rights State' and the 'Civil Rights State': Policy Paradox and State Building in the Progressive Era." *Studies in American Political Development* 7 (2, Fall): 225–274.

Mollenkopf, John. 1986. "New York: The Great Anomaly." *PS* 19 (3, Summer): 591–597.

Moore, W. John. 1988. "From Dreamers to Doers." *National Journal* 20 (7, February 13): 372–377.

Morris, Aldon. 1992. "The Future of Black Politics: Substance versus Process and Formality." *National Political Science Review* 3: 168–174.

Nelson, William E., Jr. 1987. "Cleveland: The Evolution of Black Political Power." In *The New Black Politics,* 2nd ed., edited by Michael B. Preston, Lenneal J. Henderson, Jr., and Paul L. Puryear (172–199). New York: Longman.

Pachon, Harry, and Louis DeSipio. 1992. "Latino Elected Officials in the 1990s." *PS* 25 (2, June): 212–217.

Paget, Karen. 1990. "Citizen Organizing: Many Movements, No Majority." *The American Prospect* 2 (Summer): 115–128.

Perlman, Janice. 1976. "Grassrooting the System." *Social Policy* 7 (2, September–October): 4–20.

Piven, Frances Fox, and Richard Cloward. 1971. *Poor People's Movements.* New York: Pantheon.

Reed, Adolph, Jr. 1988. "The Black Urban Regime: Structural Origins and Constraints." In *Power, Community, and the City,* vol. 1, edited by Michael Peter Smith. New Brunswick, N.J.: Transaction Books.

Rich, Wilbur C. 1987. "Coleman Young and Detroit Politics: 1973–1986." In *The New Black Politics,* 2nd ed., edited by Michael B. Preston, Lenneal J. Henderson, Jr., and Paul L. Puryear (200–221). New York: Longman.

Rosenbloom, Robert A. 1979. "The Politics of the Neighborhood Movement." *South Atlantic Urban Studies* 4: 103–120.

Smith, Steven Rathgeb, and Michael Lipsky. 1993. *Nonprofits for Hire: The Welfare State in the Age of Contracting.* Cambridge, Mass.: Harvard University Press.

Stone, Clarence N. 1989. *Regime Politics.* Lawrence: University Press of Kansas.

———. 1990. "Race and Regime in Atlanta." In *Racial Politics in American Cities,* edited by Rufus P. Browning, Dale Rogers Marshall, and David H. Tabb (125–139). White Plains, N.Y.: Longman.

Thomas, John Clayton. 1986. *Between Citizen and City.* Lawrence: University Press of Kansas.

Williams, Linda. 1987. "Black Political Progress in the 1980s: The Electoral Arena." In *The New Black Politics,* 2nd ed., edited by Michael B. Preston, Lenneal J. Henderson, and Paul L. Puryear (197–235). New York: Longman.

Woody, Bette. 1982. *Managing Crisis Cities: The New Black Leadership and the Politics of Resource Allocation.* Westport, Conn.: Greenwood Press.

17

William Sites

THE LIMITS OF URBAN REGIME THEORY
New York City Under Koch, Dinkins, and Giuliani

Does local politics still matter? Many urban scholars of the past two decades have shifted their focus from a traditional concern with local politics to the relationship between cities and the larger economic environment (Peterson 1981; Tabb and Sawers 1984; Smith and Feagin 1987; Sassen 1991; Savitch and Kantor 1995). Yet, a number of recent contributions suggest, if not a *localist* revival, at least the emergence of a substantial body of work devoted to examining the ways in which local political actors shape the development of cities. The most promising approaches have been those drawn from urban regime theory, which claims that local policy is shaped by particular regimes or political coalitions (Shefter 1985; Elkin 1987a; Stone and Sanders 1987; Stone 1989; Mollenkopf 1992; Turner 1992; DiGaetano and Klemanski 1993). Regime theorists emphasize political factors of causation, especially the importance of public officials (in the United States, they are usually mayors) who, in their role as coalition leaders, fashion distinctive development policies to induce economic growth and sustain electoral support.

Among other reasons, the urban regime approach remains analytically attractive because the historical evolution of cities is reinterpreted as the product of a contingent relationship between urban development and political action. Inasmuch as urban governance is constructed by coalitions, local conditions remain relatively open to diverse policy priorities, including those that do not favor market-oriented growth. The regime perspective also suggests that the different ways in which this room-for-maneuver is exploited have been shaped principally by the strategies of political leaders, especially by their use of the considerable resources of local government. Particular development strategies to build and sustain coalitions have been categorized into three basic types. *Progrowth* regimes encourage market-oriented development, using incentives or public subsidies to promote the kind of economic growth favored by downtown interests. *Progressive* regimes (also referred to as social-reform or growth-management regimes) seek to limit downtown expansion in favor of more community-oriented development. *Caretaker* (or maintenance) regimes tend to avoid development issues altogether, concentrating instead on fiscal stability and improvements in the provision of routine services.

The case of New York City might be expected to illustrate the strong explanatory power of a regime analysis. Mollenkopf (1992, 199) has argued that contemporary New York offers strong support for a coalition-oriented analysis premised on the "autonomy of urban politics." Certainly, New York has had a long history of public-sector involvement in development and housing provision. Over that time, public officials have amassed a fairly extensive array of local-state resources with which to influence development and disburse benefits to constituent groups (Caro 1974; Danielson and Doig 1982). Electoral competition recently has been keen, with mayoral challengers defeating incumbents in the last two races. Applying a regime approach, one might argue that the city's three most recent mayoral administrations exemplify the three types of regimes. In this scenario, Mayor Edward Koch (1978-1989) would represent the prototypical progrowth entrepreneur; Mayor David Dinkins (1990-1993), the progressive leader of a multiracial community-oriented coalition; and . . . , Rudolph Giuliani, the caretaker executive stressing budgetary stability and service improvements. Despite its superficial fit, however, this characterization actually serves to dramatize several major weaknesses inherent in the application of a regime approach.

In this article, I evaluate the urban regime perspective by examining the evolution of local policy in New York City during a 20-year period between the mid-1970s and the present. Tracing significant continuities in policy over the course of two decades, I argue that local development and housing programs have been strongly oriented toward market interests irrespective of political administration. This market orientation is explained by the impact of economic restructuring and federal retrenchment as well as by direct pressures on the local state by privileged economic actors. I also examine in some detail certain key moments during the 20-year span when shifts in policy resulted in real or apparent concessions to nonmarket actors but failed to constitute a sustained challenge to the standard growth orientation. These policy shifts—both their occurrence and their limited nature—are explained not simply by changes in political strategy or leadership but also by changes in the local real estate market, changes in the kinds of pressures exerted by economic elites, and changes in community mobilization. I conclude that regime theory's emphasis on political leadership and policy form, at the expense of other aspects of urban analysis, underestimates the downtown orientation of many growth alternatives as well as the obstacles to genuinely progressive, community-oriented urban development. In short, local politics does matter, but there is much about it that is neither local nor the product of a political arena centered on public officials, state resources, and electoral outcomes.[1]

Regime Theory

The urban regime perspective emerged in the wake of broader debates over theories of the state. Rejecting Marxian tendencies to impute an economically derived logic to state policy (Cockburn 1977; Castells 1979), theorists using a state-centered perspective argued for the autonomy of the state, or of the local state, and the primacy of political factors of causation (Evans, Rueschemeyer and Skocpol 1985; Gurr and King 1987). Urban regime theorists move beyond the polarities of this debate by asserting that a *division of labor* (Elkin 1987a, 18; DiGaetano and Klemanski 1993, 57) exists between state and market in democratic capitalist societies such as the United States. Political power lies in the hands of the state, which, in turn, is accountable ultimately to the electorate, whereas private economic actors control the market resources necessary to generate economic growth and state revenues. Public officials, lacking direct economic control but needing to promote market activity, develop characteristic strategies for using the capacities of the state—and especially, in the case of the local state, its powers that influence urban development (such as taxation, regulation, subsidy, and service provision)—to induce economic activity and elicit political support. Particular development strategies tend to build and sustain different kinds of political coalitions, or regimes, and theorists have elaborated various typologies that attempt to categorize the range of approaches (see Stone 1987; Turner 1992; DiGaetano and Klemanski 1993). In different ways, most typologies distinguish between progrowth, progressive, and caretaker regimes.[2]

The major strength of the regime perspective is that urban development is conceptualized as an active, volitional process rather than as simply the residual effect of urbanization or economic accumulation. Public officials *can* alter local development, and electoral coalitions may play a role in shaping regime priorities. Yet, the regime approach presents serious shortcomings. To begin with, its categories of policy orientation (progrowth, progressive, caretaker) run the risk of mistaking shifts in the *form* of policy (which may be fairly frequent) for shifts in the major *beneficiaries* of policy (which are less frequent). A progrowth regime, for example, can launch new policy initiatives or significant re-allocations of public resources that nevertheless continue to deliver benefits primarily to downtown interests. Policy innovation—or even significant increases in concessionary benefits to lower-income groups—does not necessarily indicate a shift in the growth paradigm.

Furthermore, the theory's central focus on local-state actors results in a serious underestimation of the social (nonstate) pressures that influence urban development. First, the larger economic and political environment confronts local officials with distinctive opportunities and constraints that have changed over time. The effect, at any given moment, has been to encourage certain local strategies and discourage others. Second, municipal officials have also been forced to respond to direct pressures from local development actors—financial organizations, real estate developers, community groups—as they emerge at different moments in the evolution of local policy and urban change. These actors, as well as public officials, need to be foregrounded in any analysis of urban politics.

Local governments within a market-driven society such as the United States invariably depend on both economic activities and state resources that they do not control. The nature and effects of these dependencies have varied historically. But through much of the second half of the twentieth century, corporate location decisions and federal policy have fueled suburbanization and the growth of newer regions at the expense of older cities (Smith 1988; Markusen et al. 1991). Over time, the state system of the post-World War II era also evolved significant federal-local government programs to promote downtown rebuilding (such as urban renewal) and, during the 1960s, anti-poverty efforts in response to social-movement demands (Piven 1984). By the 1970s, however, corporate and federal response to economic stagnation, coupled with a decline in popular mobilization, did little to contravene the process of urban deconcentration in older areas. Greater vulnerability of cities to market forces, reinforced by federal policies that reduced urban commitments and actively spurred corporate mobility, strongly encouraged leaders in most locales—by the late 1970s or early 1980s—to adopt or sustain some version of a *neoliberal* growth strategy oriented around business subsidy and popular austerity (Fainstein and Fainstein 1989; Levine 1989; Krauskopf 1989). Of course, the impact of this process of economic and political restructuring on localities has varied over time and place, and cities have formulated distinctive policy responses to broader trends (Fainstein et al. 1983; Clavel and Kleniewski 1990). However, even in New York City, which had aggressively expanded public-sector capacities, first under administrator Robert Moses and then under Mayor John Lindsay, new parameters established during the 1970s retailored policy more exclusively around corporate revival in the urban core. Since that time, persistent characteristics of the broader environment—especially capital mobility, neoliberal economic and social policy at the federal level, and fragmentation and demobilization of broad-based social movements (labor, civil rights)—continue to operate as constraints on local alternatives to standard progrowth approaches (Goldsmith and Blakely 1992; Gaffikin and Warf 1993; Fisher 1993).

In addition to the constraints and opportunities presented by the larger environment, local-state officials also experience more direct or immediate pressures from local actors with important stakes in the development process. Market actors—such as bondholders and financial institutions, real estate developers, property owners—operate at different moments as pressure groups with distinct or particularistic interests in policy. Community actors—neighborhood associations, tenant groups, community-based service providers—also can emerge as significant interest-group participants in policy making. Local economic conditions (and especially the local real estate market) can vary year by year, leading to sudden revisions in policy. Also, changes in local politics, as regime theorists emphasize, can generate new constituency groups to be appeased or new leaders to push for new policies. At different moments, one or more of these actors or changes in conditions may emerge as particularly influential with respect to a city's development. A fundamental question is whether, and under what circumstances, these changes result in policy initiatives that genuinely depart from standard progrowth strategies.

Continuity and Change in New York City

In the following analysis of New York's development and housing policies since the 1970s, I examine the ways in which the broader environment, as well as a variety of local forces, tended to reinforce a consistently downtown-oriented progrowth approach. Beginning in the mid-1970s, fiscal-crisis measures to spur economic development, rationalize retrenchment in public services, and routinize intervention by fiscal elites served to anchor local policy firmly around a public-sector mission to promote market stimulus. Since that time, New York has undergone four major "moments" of policy innovation that, in different ways, appeared to promise significant departures from this market-oriented development agenda: a sudden endorsement of community-based revival strategies by Mayor Koch in 1978, the creation of a 10-year housing plan in 1986, strong public support for lower-income housing and community development from newly elected Mayor Dinkins in 1990, and a new focus on fiscal stability through privatization by Mayor Giuliani following his election in 1993. Each policy shift has been the product of a distinctive set of circumstances, and each initiative exhibits elements that depart from, or represent an evolution in, the neoliberal growth model produced by the fiscal crisis of the 1970s. In each case, however, policy innovation failed to constitute a major shift in the city's growth strategy.

Fiscal Crisis and Neoliberal Growth

New York's fiscal crisis of 1975-1977 marked a pivotal point in local development policy, serving to reorient local policy around a flexible, ad hoc transformation of the city to promote and sustain corporate expansion (Temporary Commission on City Finances 1978). As a philosophy of public action, this neoliberal approach hinged on the argument that market-oriented policies would lead eventually to the city's revival and distribute its long-term benefits broadly. This approach, particularly in New York, guided local-state efforts to favor market actors—mobile, financial and service-sector corporations, real estate developers, and professional/managerial workers in the central business districts (CBDs) and property owners, developers, and gentrifiers in CBD-accessible residential areas. It was a strategy that also relied heavily on tax subsidies, incentive zoning, and deregulation, rather than reinvestment in public services, human capital, and neighborhood stabilization, which might be the emphasis in more community-oriented approaches. Moreover, these policy parameters were enforced by newly created, elite-dominated fiscal monitors. These agencies would soon withdraw from active roles in policy formation but not before institutional mechanisms were in place that would automatically trigger fiscal intervention in the event of future budget imbalances.

New York had long relied, even more than most U.S. cities, on a combination of public- and private-led initiatives to shape local economic growth. In the immediate postwar period, public agencies played a central role in developing the kinds of infrastructure expansion and housing construction deemed critical for economic modernization (Jackson 1984; Caro 1974). Prodded into a more inclusive mode by the urban political mobilizations of the 1960s, local officials in the liberal city combined market-stimulus policies (such as zoning incentives) with the community-oriented programs supported by federal antipoverty agencies (Fainstein and Fainstein 1984). *Urban crisis,* formerly understood as physical and economic decay, was briefly defined in ways that focused on racial exclusion, social inequality, and community disintegration as well. By the mid-1970s, however, growing budget deficits and questionable accounting procedures raised the specter of municipal default, and urban crisis was now retranslated into *fiscal crisis.*

Neoliberal resolution to this crisis was undergirded by the thesis that budgetary burdens were driven by poor people, municipal workers, racial minorities, community groups, and the liberal politicians who supported them (Auletta 1979; Morris 1980). Less often blamed were developers who had overbuilt (Fainstein and Fainstein 1984), financial institutions that encouraged and profited from irresponsible municipal borrowing (Tabb 1982), or planners who disregarded secular industrial decline (Netzer 1990), let alone the corporate decisions and federal policies that long favored suburbanization at the expense of older urban centers (Smith 1988). Guided by principles of triage and planned shrinkage (see Fried 1976), city government reduced spending on services (Horton and McCormick 1980), shed much of its commitment to community development, and explicitly encouraged the poor to move elsewhere (Starr 1976).

The late 1970s also saw a flurry of new or expanded tax-incentive programs oriented toward CBD businesses and the core land market. The Industrial and Commercial Incentives Board, created in 1976 (and later renamed the Industrial and Commercial Incentives Program [ICIP]), began offering tax abatements to major corporations and builders for development projects primarily in the Manhattan CBD (Leichter 1985). Amendments to a tax-subsidy program called 421a, which had been designed originally to offer tax breaks to increase the stock of middle-income housing, instead stimulated luxury residential construction (Sternlieb and Listokin 1985). State regulations governing cooperative conversion were loosened. Tax abatements for residential rehabilitation—especially the J–51 program, which had been enacted in the 1950s to upgrade cold-water flats—were retailored in 1975 to stimulate privately financed condominiums, cooperatives, and residential conversions (Kaiser 1976). In addition, a series of major Manhattan redevelopment projects (South Street Seaport, Battery Park City, Javits Convention Center, and a Times Square redevelopment project) were launched or sustained by a combination of public (federal, state, and local) and private developers, despite free-market rhetoric and apparent fiscal constraints (Mollenkopf 1983). None of these initiatives wrenched New York out of its economic doldrums. Over time, however, and taken together, they would eventually give shape to the city's future expansion.

This combination of budgetary austerity and developmental stimulus was facilitated by a de facto suspension of formal democratic processes during the crisis period. As a condition for avoiding municipal default, much local authority over spending and revenue collection was removed from local elected officials and vested in a group of business leaders and state and national officials acting through newly created bodies such as the Emergency Financial Control Board (EFCB) and the Municipal Assistance Corporation (Alcaly and Bodian 1976; Pecorella 1987). As budgets stabilized by the late 1970s, these fiscal monitors took a less directive role; yet, their survival was assured when the U.S. Congress demanded a long-term function for the EFCB (renamed, accordingly, the Financial Control Board) as a condition for federal loans (Bailey 1984). Even when inactive, oversight institutions remained an ongoing incentive for elected officials to shape policy priorities in ways that would discourage new interventions by fiscal monitors.

Enacted in ad hoc fashion amid an often-chaotic political climate, the various measures of the fiscal-crisis period—development incentives, triage, and the institutionalization of elite intervention—established new and consistent policy norms firmly orienting public-sector activity around market stimulus. It would be difficult to interpret these changes as local-state-led policy innovations to induce economic activity from otherwise passive or disorganized market actors. Instead, the new measures were clearly imposed on New York's public officials by a combination of economic and (nonlocal) political elites. Changes in economic and political conditions over the next two decades would test the endurance of these norms by creating a series of opportunities for challenge.

The Brief Embrace of Community-Based Revival

The development priorities of the crisis period were soon pressed by events early in the tenure of Mayor Koch. Shortly after taking office in 1978, Koch was confronted by strong pressures to respond to the near-collapse of New York's lower income housing market. The new mayor answered with a surprising endorsement of community-based housing initiatives and, by the end of his first year, had set up programs to support neighborhood rehabilitation, tenant-run cooperatives, and community-managed housing ("HPD's 'child' matures" 1978; Department of Housing Preservation and Development 1979). Almost immediately thereafter, however, the administration began to retreat from its initial commitment. Over subsequent years, the community-oriented housing programs that did survive came to occupy a relatively minor part of the city's revival strategy (Department of Housing Preservation and Development 1986).

Koch's brief embrace of community-based initiatives (and subsequent disengagement from them) was propelled by a combination of economic and political pressure that had little to do with endorsement or abandonment of an alternative growth strategy. Instead, its catalyst was the problem of stagnation in the local real estate market, which, still mired in a decade-long slump, was failing to deliver on crisis-resolution promises that market vitality would pull New York out of its economic morass. As housing abandonment and arson spread through the city's poorest areas, the political sway of triage actively discouraged large-scale public intervention to combat the destruction of these neighborhoods. Yet, New York's fiscal preoccupations also had led to passage of a new law that obligated local government to seize the properties of owners who were no longer paying taxes on them (DeRienzo and Allen 1985). Intended to force owners to pay up, and thus boost revenues, the measure instead made the city titleholder to thousands of run-down properties once their owners fled the collapsing market in slum housing. Efforts by city officials to resell the properties met with failure, and by early 1978, as Mayor Koch took office, administrative chaos and allegations of corruption in the auction sales program led to its suspension (Kifner 1978; Baldwin 1978). Koch, now under considerable public pressure to devise a new approach to the housing crisis, began to tout the kind of community-rehabilitation strategies to which he had paid little attention during his mayoral campaign. This political conversion was also encouraged by a similar move by President Jimmy Carter, who pushed forward new federal support for neighborhood self-help housing rehabilitation (Lawson 1986).

Just as prolonged failures in the local real estate market had created pressures for alternative policies, economic revival in 1979 provided the administration with an opportunity to trim the sails of the new neighborhood-based programs. Major construction resumed in the Manhattan business districts, and there were unmistakable signs that neighborhood gentrification was on the rise in areas adjacent to the CBD (Real Estate Board of New York 1985; Chall 1983-1984). Critics pointed out that growth was highly uneven and that the residential displacement induced by market gentrification made this process a poor substitute for community-based revival, but Koch successfully ignored them. Community groups were unable to mobilize pressure sufficiently to hold the city to its original programmatic commitments, let alone push a neighborhood strategy to the top of the city's development agenda (Brower 1982).

Koch's policy shifts had not been driven by community pressure nor by an interest in forging new coalitions. The flirtation with community development was an act of political expediency in the face of economic pressures and unanticipated increases in governmental responsibility. Economic expansion in the Manhattan core may not have ameliorated the housing crisis, but it certainly gave the mayor an opportunity to reembrace neoliberal market solutions. And over the remainder of his first term, Koch's willingness to enforce austerity and subsidize economic development was rewarded by fiscal monitors, who facilitated the city's renewed access to the credit markets, and by real estate developers, who gave generously to his subsequent campaigns (Shefter 1985; Bellush 1990). It is possible that if local stagnation had continued, pressure for a more prolonged community embrace might have grown. However, the combination of economic circumstances and reigning political forces did not favor a genuine commitment to neighborhood development even during this short moment in the sun.

Shifting Ground, Building Housing

After two terms of office had built him a reputation as the nation's preeminent free-market mayor, Koch began his third term in 1986 by unveiling a $5-billion housing plan that promised to build or rehabilitate 250,000 apartments over 10 years. Despite its ambitious scope, the 10-Year Housing Plan, which might appear to signal a dramatic departure from market-based priorities, represented more of a policy shift in means than in ends. The plan was indeed crafted to be a political vehicle by which the mayor hoped to extend his mayoralty into a fourth term (thereby supporting a regime perspective's emphasis on political strategy), but the necessity for a shift in strategy was spurred on by the new kinds of pressures and opportunities generated by the city's economic revival.

New York's economic boom seemed for a time to vindicate crisis-resolution promises. By the mid-1980s, however, it had shifted the public agenda onto new terrain. One result was that austerity became an increasingly hard sell in an era of budget surpluses (Shefter 1985, 206). Another result was that the very uneven nature of the revival itself—not only spatially and socially but *sectorally*—became a political issue: Despite all the commercial development changing the Manhattan skyline, there was a growing consensus that, in the words of one economic observer (quoted in Berger 1985, A1), "the strongest real-estate market maybe in the world can't deliver more than a handful of housing units." But this newest housing crisis meant different things to different groups. Community advocates focused criticism on growing homelessness and the shrinking supply of lower-income housing, whereas business analysts feared that inflated land values and housing shortages among the upper-middle class might short-circuit the city's economic machine (Hayes 1985; Tobier 1989; DePalma 1985). After a coalition of community-based nonprofit groups unveiled its own housing proposal for the city in early 1986, the Koch administration countered with a press conference announcing the first sketchy version of the 10-Year Housing Plan (Purnick 1986). As the plan took shape over the course of Koch's third and final term, corporate calls for additional housing for higher-level professional workers, as well as the administration's own political priorities, kept pressure on the plan to target upper-income beneficiaries (Lueck 1987a, 1987b). Brower (1989) concluded that as of 1989, Koch's last year in office, roughly two-thirds of the housing slated for production under the plan was targeted toward market-rate and upper-middle-income housing consumers, with the remainder earmarked for the poor.

There is no question that the new plan ushered in an expanded public role in the production of housing and that the plan's provisions to develop subsidized housing for the poor represented a major advance beyond the prior decade's neglect. There is also little evidence that the business community, in spite of its concern for the housing needs of professionals, actively pressured public officials to create a housing program of the magnitude of the 10-Year Housing Plan. Although the timing of the plan suggests a desire to ward off more radical alternatives, the plan does represent an instance in which public officials and their strategic political designs—the kinds of factors favored by a regime approach—emerge as a major agent of policy change. It is important, however, to emphasize the economic conditions that encouraged this emergence as well as the limited nature of the policy change itself: On [the] one hand, strong local growth opened new space for policy innovation; on the other hand, policy reform driven by growth leaders, rather than by sustained community mobilization, did not decisively depart from preexisting growth priorities or beneficiaries.

For all the focus on housing, it is also noteworthy that reliance on market-oriented development incentives, especially the ICIP and J–51 tax subsidies, actually accelerated during Koch's third term (Department of Finance 1993; City of New York 1990). To the extent that New York's robust economy permitted a major shift toward community-based development and redistributive housing policy, it was an opportunity that was not pursued.

New Hopes, Old Story

After 12 years of market-oriented policy under Koch, Dinkins was elected New York's first African-American mayor in 1989. Uniting blacks, Hispanics, and liberal whites, the Dinkins victory was attributable in no small measure to strong support from community groups and the city's more progressive municipal employees' unions. As a candidate, Dinkins had promised to end the racial divisiveness of the Koch years, and expectations ran high for a new relationship between city hall and the neighborhoods. The new mayor's first moves appeared to bear out these hopes, but they were soon extinguished by a combination of external constraints and self-imposed political weaknesses.

Early in his term, Dinkins modified New York's 10-Year Housing Plan in ways that promised to increase affordability and economic integration, to benefit more homeless individuals, and to rely more on community-based nonprofit housing providers (Terry 1990). The mayor's housing commissioner envisioned "a tremendous and growing commitment" ("On the Record" 1990, 8) to community-based housing, noting that "you can't expect the not-for-profits to assume the burden without also understanding that you have to create a financial foundation for them" (p. 9). Community groups responded with enthusiasm, as long-stalled plans to produce subsidized housing in abandoned properties began to be implemented. Yet, even early on, before the onset of acute fiscal strains, the mayor dismayed community advocates by giving final approval to a rash of Koch-negotiated development deals, some of which Dinkins himself had earlier questioned (Neuwirth 1990). By the second year of his term, Dinkins began to waver on his promise to eliminate or reform the ICIP tax-incentive program. Developers, led by the Real Estate Board of New York, announced that the administration's position on ICIPs would be viewed as a litmus test of the mayor's attitudes toward the market and, correspondingly, his future relationship with business (Breznick 1990; Seifman 1991). In response, the ICIP program was renewed in early 1992, with the number of projects granted benefits climbing yet again, and a freeze on corporate taxes was declared (McKinley 1992a, 1992b; Department of Finance 1993). Meanwhile, severe funding cuts were stalling community-based projects and estranging the mayor from key elements of his electoral base. Housing and community-development spending was reduced 9.4% in fiscal year 1992, and publicly sponsored housing starts that same year fell to fewer than half their number in 1989, Koch's final year (Department of City Planning 1993).

By the end of its four-year term, the Dinkins administration showed few signs of having pursued a policy agenda much different from that of its predecessor, let alone having forged a progressive regime. This failure stemmed, in part, from circumstances beyond the mayor's control. Elected two years after the October 1987 stock market crash, Dinkins inherited a declining local economy that would only worsen as most of the country slid into recession. Prolonged stagnation, along with major funding reductions from federal and state governments, brought severe budgetary pressures and the reemergence of fiscal monitoring agencies as direct arbiters of local spending and policy (McKinley 1991).

Under such conditions, a determinedly progressive administration would have faced an uphill task in hewing to its program. From its inception, however, the Dinkins coalition had mobilized a community base behind a leadership core heavy with former Koch aides, advised by policy centrists, and funded by a campaign chest well-stocked by developer contributions (Lynn 1989; Roberts 1989). The candidate's campaign message of "racial healing" was short-term succor to a divided city, but the coalition had not articulated an alternative vision of development and community renewal. The mayor's political response to deteriorating economic conditions and to the accompanying interest-group pressures from the financial and development sectors was, therefore, in the words of one ambivalent supporter, to "demobiliz[e] the coalition that elected him" (Roberts 1991, B1). Standing for reelection in 1993, Dinkins was unable to generate the grassroots enthusiasm that had carried him to victory four years earlier.

It is quite possible that a more conservative administration experiencing the same conditions would have pursued policies with more devastating effects on public services and lower-income New York residents. It is also true that the severe economic stagnation that Dinkins inherited was partly a consequence of the development policies of the Koch years. Yet, the fact that Dinkins did not administer austerity with relish hardly qualifies the administration's policies as progressive or community-oriented—let alone socialist (Wriston 1994)—nor does it make them fundamentally different in kind from those of his predecessor.

Caretaking: Taking Care of Business

In 1993, Giuliani defeated Dinkins to become New York's first Republican mayor in two decades. Although it may be too soon to develop a measured assessment of the city's most recent administration, a regime approach might suggest that Giuliani has shown many of the signs—in terms of personal temperament, party affiliation, electoral base, and professed philosophy of governance—associated with leaders of a caretaker coalition. Enjoying few long-standing ties to the city's economic elite or to community groups and minority constituencies, the new mayor's electoral support is rooted in antitax middle-class home owners and white working-class residents of New York's outer boroughs. Giuliani, a former federal prosecutor, has not highlighted a broader vision of development, focusing instead on budget issues and improved services. Responding to fiscal pressures with a pragmatic zeal for privatization and cutting bureaucratic waste, Giuliani could be seen to be piecing together the mix of constituencies and policy issues distinctive of a caretaker regime.

Upon closer examination, however, Giuliani actually appears to be pursuing an aggressively market-oriented development policy, one shorn of some of the secondary concessions to community interests that had been meted out during the late Koch and early Dinkins years. From the beginning, the new mayor's planning director (quoted in Dunlap 1994, 1) went out of his way to signal a clear development agenda: "No one is looking to unravel necessary and appropriate community protections, but there is no question that this is an administration that is sympathetic to the role of development in the economy." The Giuliani administration moved quickly in its first year to expand the city's tax-subsidy development programs, giving out a record $300 million in property tax breaks alone (Lueck 1995). To assist developers who had overbuilt in the Lower Manhattan financial district, the mayor also proposed an estimated $230 million in exemptions from property and commercial rent taxes (Lower Manhattan Task Force 1994). Other development projects moved forward with significant public subsidies, including the extension of the Midtown Manhattan CBD into the Times Square area. Meanwhile, a 30% cut in subsidized housing starts and a refusal to take title to abandoned lower-income properties suggested an implicit return to the mid-1970s policy of triage (Department of City Planning 1994).

There is no question that Giuliani, like Dinkins before him, has been forced to cope with serious fiscal constraints as the New York City economy fails to rebound strongly from the recession of the early 1990s (Office of the State Comptroller 1995c). Conservative priorities at both state and federal levels have resulted in further cuts in aid and threaten to impose new budgetary burdens. These pressures serve to highlight a problem with the notion of a caretaker (or maintenance) regime that supposedly concentrates on service provision and fiscal stability: Under most circumstances, public officials today, regardless of intentions, have little choice but to pursue aggressively some version of development, whether community- or market-oriented. In response, Giuliani's own political themes have vividly echoed many of the priorities of New York's corporate agenda, including greater subsidies to the financial sector and to the Downtown and Midtown Manhattan CBDs, weaker public oversight in land use, retrenchment and less equitable disbursement of education funding, selective privatization, and the removal of homeless people from publicly visible areas (New York City Partnership 1989, 1990; New York Chamber of Commerce and Industry and the New York City Partnership Privatization Task Force, n.d.; Port Authority of New York and New Jersey 1988).

Conceptual Tools and Urban Analysis

In this study, I have argued that, over the course of two decades and three political administrations, local policy in New York has followed a growth strategy consistently oriented toward the interests of powerful market actors. At various times, city officials have sounded fresh ideological themes, modified programs, and launched new initiatives, but the central thread of public policy has closely followed the development and fiscal goals set by corporate visions of urban revival. The analysis presented here suggests that a regime perspective, with its focus on public leadership and local-state initiative, fails to emphasize many of the economic and political forces that have reinforced this downtown orientation as well as the frequently reactive role of New York's political officials. The characteristic factors of a regime approach do help explain the relatively modest policy shifts that occurred in New York during the past 20 years but only when combined with other factors such as changes in the local real estate market and resurgent interest-group pressures.

Beyond year-by-year fluctuations, the general economic and policy trends shaping New York City remain quite clear. Since the 1970s, the local economy has registered significant profit growth, long-term decline in aggregate income growth, and an increasing disparity between incomes and employment growth, with employment growth remaining stubbornly low (Office of the State Comptroller 1995b). Local government's reliance on tax incentives for development remains stronger than ever in the face of perenially weak evidence that incentives actually deliver on job creation and in spite of the generally poor prospects for employment growth in the city's most favored industries (Leichter 1990; Office of the State Comptroller 1995a; Citizens Budget Commission 1995). On the other hand, for residents left behind by the city's economy, declines in local spending for public assistance (excluding Medicaid) have been calculated at 20%, in real terms, between 1975 and 1992 (Citizens Budget Commission 1994). In short, neither market nor policy has distributed benefits equitably.

Emerging in the wake of studies focused on the economic structure of the city, the urban regime literature led analysts to pay greater attention to policy, politics, coalition building, and public leadership. As an exhortation to move beyond economic reductionism, regime theory still remains a useful corrective. Instead of leading to more complex understandings, however, analysts too often err the other way—either by isolating the political process from social and economic pressures or by counterposing a dynamic politics to a static notion of economic growth. A central implication of the regime perspective is that alternative local policies are more achievable today, and perhaps even more commonly achieved, than observers might expect. Yet, this depends in part on whether such "progressive" regimes that do emerge actually strive for qualitative shifts in local power or, instead, accept quite limited—and often temporary—concessions to lower-income residents within a standard progrowth orientation. This distinction remains critical to separating those alternatives that remain modestly beneficial or, worse, largely symbolic—*neoprogressive* regimes (Reed 1987)—from those that, however flawed or short-lived, aggressively pursue social equity, community participation, and democratic accountability (Clavel and Wiewel 1991). Furthermore, an excessive emphasis on local possibilities downplays the need for major changes in direction in national policy and risks lending support, however unwittingly, to current fashionable claims that localities will do better free of federal interference.

A significant gap in the conceptual framework of many regime analyses is the role of social movements or community mobilization in urban politics. Although the impact of popular mobilization on cities has varied significantly over time and place, the current weaknesses of community actors need to be examined (rather than assumed) and related to the ongoing changes in the national state that, as indicated earlier, the regime approach also tends to slight. Furthermore, the changing nature of community organization may powerfully affect the resources of political leaders: Reform-minded officials, for example, may pursue a neighborhood agenda under various circumstances, but unless they lead (or are carried by) strong social movements, these politicians will have a hard time lifting their own bootstraps to implement such an agenda. Over the past two decades, New York has seen isolated instances of community mobilization gain significant concessions with respect to particular programs, development projects, and neighborhoods, even in the face of relatively hostile administrations (Savitch 1988; Hirsch 1993; Abu-Lughod 1994). Community groups have not created a powerful political alliance capable of generating a sustained challenge to neoliberal growth priorities at the citywide level, and it is not clear under what conditions they might do so.

To theorize the relationship between local policy and urban power, and to be able to recognize genuine innovations in policy approach and the conditions under which they emerge, requires a perspective that links policy change and continuity to broader social forces as well as to market pressures and political conflicts within distinctive locales. The favored conceptual tools of the urban regime literature continue to be useful in this task but by themselves result in analyses that are focused too insistently on public-sector actors, local-state initiative, and coalition building at the expense of market and community pressures, economic restructuring, and national-state retrenchment.

Notes

1. Not all of the studies referred to herein were constructed explicitly from a regime framework or terminology (see, e.g., Mollenkopf 1992); even among those that were, there are considerable differences in emphasis over such issues as the centrality of state actors, the relative power of business, and the importance of electoral coalitions. I believe that there are sufficient affinities in conceptualization and analysis to warrant treating the works cited here as a singular framework for the study of urban politics. For a more theoretical discussion, see Stoker (1995), who also attempted to distinguish regime theory from other approaches used in those studies that, in his view, employ regime-theory discourse but not its conceptual framework. My concern is to evaluate whether the central claims of a regime perspective orient the analysis of an important case to yield a persuasive explanation.

2. Studies of local policy are often difficult to compare because of differences in basic definitions, approaches, and time periods, rendering the value of typologies uncertain. For example, an attempt to categorize regimes in cities analyzed in some of the more prominent studies would suggest that progrowth coalitions have been dominant in Atlanta (Stone 1989), Dallas (Elkin 1987b), Houston (Feagin 1988), Baltimore (Levine 1987), Detroit and Philadelphia (Clavel and Kleniewski 1990), and Tampa and Jacksonville (Turner 1992), and progressive coalitions have ruled—at least for a time—in Boston (Swanstrom 1988),

San Francisco (Keating 1986), Chicago (Mier, Moe, and Sherr 1986), Santa Monica (Capek and Gilderbloom 1992), Orlando (Turner 1992), and Minneapolis (Nickel 1995). Caretaker regimes, although less often noted, have been suggested in analyses of New Orleans (Whelan 1987), Fort Lauderdale (Turner 1992) and Kalamazoo (Stone and Sanders 1987). For reasons that are advanced later in this article, I remain skeptical about the value of this kind of typology. See Walton (1990) for a perceptive commentary on the methodological pitfalls of comparative urban politics.

References

Abu-Lughod, J. L. 1994. *From urban village to East Village: The battle for New York's Lower East Side.* Cambridge, MA: Blackwell.

Alcaly, R. E., and H. Bodian. 1976. New York's fiscal crisis and the economy. In *The fiscal crisis of American cities: Essays on the political economy of urban America with special reference to New York,* edited by R. E. Alcaly and D. Mermelstein, 30–58. New York: Vintage.

Auletta, K. 1979. *The streets were paved with gold.* New York: Vintage.

Bailey, R. W. 1984. *The crisis regime: The MAC, the EFCB, and the political impact of the New York City financial crisis.* Albany: State Uniersity of New York Press.

Baldwin, S. 1978. City's auction sales: Going, going, gone? *City Limits* 3 (September): 1.

Bellush, J. 1990. Clusters of power: Interest groups. In *Urban politics, New York style,* edited by J. Bellush and D. Netzer, 296–338. Armonk, NY: M. E. Sharpe.

Berger, J. 1985. Failure of plan for homelessness reflects city housing crisis. *New York Times,* 19 February, A1.

Breznick, A. 1990. Dinkins nears revision of ICIP program. *Crain's New York Business,* 17 December.

Brower, B. 1982. Requiem for a housing policy: Selling alternative management. *City Limits* 7 (October): 21.

———. 1989. *Missing the mark: Subsidizing housing for the privileged, displacing the poor.* New York: Association of Neighborhood and Housing Development and the Housing Justice Campaign.

Capek, S., and J. Gilderbloom. 1992. *Community and commodity: Tenants and the American City.* Albany: State University of New York Press.

Caro, R. A. 1974. *The power broker: Robert Moses and the fall of New York.* New York: Vintage.

Castells, M. 1979. *The urban question: A Marxist approach.* Cambridge, MA: MIT Press.

Chall, D. E. 1983–1984. Neighborhood changes in New York City during the 1970s: Are the "gentry" returning? *Federal Reserve Bank of New York Quarterly Review* (Winter): 38–48.

Citizens Budget Commission. 1994. Poverty and public spending related to poverty in New York City. New York: Author.

———. 1995. *Professional business services in the New York City economy.* New York: Author.

City of New York. 1990. *J–51 Tax Exemption/Tax Abatement Program.* Fiscal year 1990. Annual report. New York: Author.

Clavel, P., and N. Kleniewski. 1990. Space for progressive local policy: Examples from the United States and the United Kingdom. In *Beyond the city limits: Urban policy and economic restructuring in comparative perspective,* edited by J. R. Logan and T. Swanstrom, 199–234. Philadelphia: Temple University Press.

Clavel, P., and W. Wiewel, eds. 1991. *Harold Washington and the neighborhoods: Progressive city government in Chicago, 1983–1987.* New Brunswick, NJ: Rutgers University Press.

Cockburn, C. 1977. *The local state: Management of cities and people.* London: Pluto.

Danielson, M. N., and J. W. Doig. 1982. *New York: The politics of urban regional development.* Berkeley: University of California Press.

DePalma, A. 1985. Will shortage of housing crimp economic growth? *New York Times,* 18 August, sec. 4, 20.

Department of City Planning. 1993. *Annual report on social indicators.* New York: Author.

———. 1994. *Annual report on social indicators.* New York: Author.

Department of Finance. 1993. *Finance New York: Industrial and Commercial Incentive Program.* Annual report. New York: Author.

Department of Housing Preservation and Development. 1979. *The in rem housing program: First annual report, September 1978 to September 1979.* New York: Author.

———. 1986. *The in rem housing program: Annual report, FY 1985 and FY 1986.* New York: Author.

DeRienzo, H., and J. B. Allen. 1985. *The New York City in rem housing program: A report.* New York: New York Urban Coalition.

DiGaetano, A., and J. S. Klemanski. 1993. Urban regimes in comparative perspective: The politics of urban development in Britain. *Urban Affairs Quarterly* 29 (1): 54–83.

Dunlap, D. W. 1994. Taking city planning in a new direction. *New York Times,* 24 April, sec. 10, 1.

Elkin, S. 1987a. *City and regime in the American republic.* Chicago: University of Chicago Press.

———. 1987b. State and market in city politics: Or, the "real" Dallas. In *The politics of urban development,* edited by C. N. Stone and H. T. Sanders, 25–51. Lawrence: University Press of Kansas.

Evans, P. B., D. Rueschemeyer, and T. Skocpol, eds. 1985. *Bringing the state back in.* London: Cambridge University Press.

Fainstein, N. I., and S. S. Fainstein. 1984. The politics of urban development: New York City since 1945. *City Almanac* 17 (6): 1–26.

Fainstein, S. S., and N. Fainstein. 1989. The ambivalent state: Economic development policy in the U.S. federal system under the Reagan administration. *Urban Affairs Quarterly* 25 (1): 41–62.

Fainstein, S. S., N. I. Fainstein, R. C. Hill, D. R. Judd, and M. P. Smith. 1983. *Restructuring the city: The political economy of urban redevelopment.* New York: Longman.

Feagin, J. R. 1988. Tallying the social costs of urban growth under capitalism: The case of Houston. In *Business elites and urban development,* edited by S. Cummings, 205–234. Albany: State University of New York Press.

Fisher, R. 1993. Grass-roots organizing worldwide: Common ground, historical roots, and the tension between democracy and the state. In *Mobilizing the community: Local politics in the era of the global city,* edited by R. Fisher and J. Kling, 3–27. Newbury Park, CA: Sage Publications.

Fried, J. 1976. City's housing administrator proposes "planned shrinkage" of some slums. *New York Times,* 3 February, 35.

Gaffikin, F., and B. Warf. 1993. Urban policy and the post-Keynesian state in the United Kingdom and the United States. *International Journal of Urban and Regional Research* 17 (1): 67–84.

Goldsmith, W. W., and E. J. Blakely. 1992. *Separate societies: Poverty and inequality in U.S. cities.* Philadelphia: Temple University Press.

Gurr, T. R., and D. S. King. 1987. *The state and the city.* Chicago: University of Chicago Press.

Hayes, R. 1985. The mayor and the homeless poor. *City Limits* 10 (August/September): 6–9.

Hirsch, E. L. 1993. Protest movements and urban theory. *Research in Urban Sociology* 3: 159–180.

Horton, R. D., and M. McCormick. 1980. Services. In *Setting municipal priorities, 1981,* edited by C. Brecher and R. D. Horton, 85–112. Montclair, NJ: Allanheld, Osmun.

HPD's "child" matures: Rehabs set to start. 1978. City Limits 3 (November): 12.

Jackson, K. T. 1984. The capital of capitalism: The New York metropolitan region, 1890–1940. In *Metropolis 1890–1940,* edited by A. Sutcliffe, 319–354. Chicago: University of Chicago Press.

Kaiser, C. 1976. "J–51" a way to save failing properties. *New York Times,* 1 February, sec. 8, 1.

Keating, W. D. 1986. Linking downtown development to broader community goals. *Journal of the American Planning Association* 52 (2): 133–141.

Kifner, J. 1978. Property seizures in city are chaotic. *New York Times,* 19 March, 36.

Krauskopf, J. A. 1989. Federal aid. In *Setting municipal priorities, 1990,* edited by C. Brecher and R. D. Horton, 117–37. New York: New York University Press.

Lawson, R. 1986. Tenant responses to the urban housing crisis. 1970–1984. In *The tenant movement in New York City, 1904–1984,* edited by R. Lawson, 209–276. New Brunswick, NJ: Rutgers University Press.

Leichter, F. S. 1985. The NYC Industrial and Commercial Incentive Program: Every day is Christmas. An investigative report by State Senator Franz S. Leichter, 28th S.D., Manhattan. Photocopy.

———. 1990. It's still Christmas every day: The NYC Industrial and Commercial Incentive Program. A report by State Senator Franz S. Leichter, 28th S.D., Manhattan. Photocopy.

Levine, M. V. 1987. Downtown redevelopment as an urban growth strategy: A critical reappraisal of the Baltimore renaissance. *Journal of Urban Affairs* 9 (2): 103–124.

———. 1989. The politics of partnership: Urban redevelopment since 1945. In *Unequal partnerships: The political economy of urban redevelopment in postwar America,* edited by G. D. Squires, 12–34. New Brunswick, NJ: Rutgers University Press.

Lower Manhattan Task Force. 1994. *A plan for the revitalization of Lower Manhattan.* New York: Author.

Lueck, T. J. 1987a. As housing costs mount, New York companies move away. *New York Times,* 3 March, sec. 2, 1.

———. 1987b. Retraining and housing called keys to growth. *New York Times,* 5 March, sec. 2, 1.

———. 1995. Pared budgets don't cut the flow of tax breaks. *New York Times,* 5 July, sec. 1, 1.

Lynn, F. 1989. Dinkins team: Old hands join a few newcomers. *New York Times,* 4 November, 29.

Markusen, A., P. Hall, S. Campbell, and S. Deitrick. 1991. *The rise of the gunbelt: The military remapping of industrial America.* New York: Oxford University Press.

McKinley, J. C., Jr. 1991. Dinkins shifts on fiscal plan under pressure. *New York Times,* 13 November, B1.

———. 1992a. Dinkins pledges four-year corporate tax freeze. *New York Times,* 20 October, B9.

———. 1992b. Tax incentive for builders is extended. *New York Times,* 26 February, B1.

Mier, R., K. J. Moe, and I. Sherr. 1986. Strategic planning and the pursuit of reform, economic development and equity. *Journal of the American Planning Association* 52: 299–309.

Mollenkopf, J. 1983. Economic development. In *Setting municipal priorities, 1984,* edited by C. Brecher and R. D. Horton, 131–157. New York: New York University Press.

Mollenkopf, J. H. 1992. *A phoenix in the ashes: The rise and fall of the Koch coalition in New York City politics.* Princeton, NJ: Princeton University Press.

Morris, C. R. 1980. *The cost of good intentions: New York City and the liberal experiment, 1960–1975.* New York: Norton.

Netzer, D. 1990. The economy and the governing of the city. In *Urban politics, New York style,* edited by J. Bellush and D. Netzer, 27–59. Armonk, NY: M. E. Sharpe.

Neuwirth, R. 1990. A development fire sale: The rush is on at the Board of Estimate. *Village Voice,* 21 August, 15–18.

New York Chamber of Commerce and Industry and the New York City Partnership Privatization Task Force. N.d. [1993]. *Putting the public first: Making New York work through privatization and competition.* New York: Author.

New York City Partnership. 1989. Meeting the challenge: Maintaining and enhancing New York City as the world financial capital. A report by the Financial Services Task Force of the New York City Partnership. New York. Photocopy.

———. 1990. *From schools to skyscrapers: Building an effective development process for New York City.* New York: Author.

Nickel, D. R. 1995. The progressive city? Urban redevelopment in Minneapolis. *Urban Affairs Review* 30 (3): 355–377.

Office of the State Comptroller. 1995a. *New York City Economic Development Corporation: Improvements needed to strengthen Industrial Development Agency program.* New York: Office of the State Deputy Comptroller for the City of New York.

———. 1995b. *Recent trends in the New York City economy.* New York: Office of the State Deputy Comptroller for the City of New York.

———. 1995c. *Review of the financial plan of the City of New York for fiscal years 1996 through 1999.* Report 4–96. New York: Office of the State Deputy Comptroller for the City of New York.

On the record: Housing Commissioner Felice Michetti. 1990. *City Limits* 15 (October): 8–11.

Pecorella, R. F. 1987. Fiscal crisis and regime change: A contextual approach. In *The politics of urban development,* edited by C. N. Stone and H. T. Sanders, 52–72. Lawrence: University Press of Kansas.

Peterson, P. E. 1981. *City limits.* Chicago: University of Chicago Press.

Piven, F. F. 1984. Federal policy and urban fiscal strain. *Yale Law & Policy Review* 2: 291–321.

Port Authority of New York and New Jersey. 1988. *The homeless: The impact on the transportation industry.* New York: Author.

Purnick, J. 1986. Koch to announce plan for 250,000 apartments. *New York Times,* 30 April, B3.

Real Estate Board of New York. 1985. *Rebuilding Manhattan: A study of new office construction.* New York: Real Estate Board of New York Research Department.

Reed, A., Jr. 1987. A critique of neo-progressivism in theorizing about local development policy: A case from Atlanta. In *The politics of urban development,* edited by C. N. Stone and H. T. Sanders, 199–215. Lawrence: University Press of Kansas.

Roberts, S. 1989. Dinkins gaining support among business executives. *New York Times,* 26 September, B1.

———. 1991. Gadflies of today parcel the blame among old allies. *New York Times,* 1 July, B1.

Sassen, S. 1991. *The global city: New York, London, Tokyo.* Princeton, NJ: Princeton University Press.

Savitch, H. V. 1988. *Post-industrial cities: Politics and planning in New York, Paris and London.* Princeton, NJ: Princeton University Press.

Savitch, H. V., and P. Kantor. 1995. City business: An international perspective on marketplace politics. *International Journal of Urban and Regional Research* 19 (4): 495–512.

Seifman, D. 1991. Inside City Hall. *New York Post,* 28 September, 9.

Shefter, M. 1985. *Political crisis/fiscal crisis: The collapse and revival of New York City.* New York: Basic.

Smith, M. P. 1988. *City, state, and market: The political economy of urban society.* New York: Blackwell.

Smith, M. P., and J. R. Feagin, eds. 1987. *The capitalist city: Global restructuring and community politics.* New York: Blackwell.

Starr, R. 1976. Making New York smaller. *New York Times Magazine,* 14 November, 32.

Sternlieb, G., and D. Listokin. 1985. Housing. In *Setting municipal priorities, 1986,* edited by C. Brecher and R. D. Horton, 382–411, New York: New York University Press.

Stoker, G. 1995. Regime theory and urban politics. In *Theories of urban politics,* edited by D. Judge, G. Stoker, and H. Wolman, 54–71. Thousand Oaks, CA: Sage Publications.

Stone, C. N. 1987. Summing up: Urban regimes, development policy, and political arrangements. In *The politics of urban development,* edited by C. N. Stone and H. T. Sanders, 269–290. Lawrence: University Press of Kansas.

———. 1989. *Regime politics: Governing Atlanta, 1946–1988.* Lawrence: University Press of Kansas.

Stone, C. N., and H. T. Sanders, eds. 1987. *The politics of urban development.* Lawrence: University Press of Kansas.

Swanstrom, T. 1988. Urban populism, uneven development, and the space for reform. In *Business elites and urban development,* edited by S. Cummings, 121–152. Albany: State Uniersity. of New York Press.

Tabb, W. K. 1982. *The long default: New York City and the urban fiscal crisis.* New York: Monthly Review Press.

Tabb, W. K., and L. Sawers, eds. 1984. *Marxism and the metropolis: New perspectives in urban political economy,* 2d ed. New York: Oxford University Press.

Temporary Commission on City Finances. 1978. *The city in transition: Prospects and policies for New York.* Final report. New York: Arno.

Terry, D. 1990. Dinkins expands housing plan to assist the poor. *New York Times,* 17 May, B3.

Tobier, E. 1989. The homeless. In *Setting municipal priorities, 1990,* edited by C. Brecher and R. D. Horton, 307–338. New York: New York University Press.

Turner, R. S. 1992. Growth politics and downtown development: The economic imperative in sunbelt cities. *Urban Affairs Quarterly* 28 (1): 3–21.

Watson, J. 1990. Theoretical methods in comparative urban politics. In *Beyond the city limits: Urban policy and economic restructuring in comparative perspective,* edited by J. R. Logan and T. Swanstrom, 243–257. Philadelphia: Temple University Press.

Wriston, W. 1994. Advice for the new mayor. *City Journal* 4 (1): 8–9.

Whelan, R. 1987. New Orleans: Mayoral politics and economic development policies in the postwar years, 1945–1986. In *The politics of urban development,* edited by C. N. Stone and H. T. Sanders, 216–229. Lawrence: University Press of Kansas.

18

Carl Abbott

THE POLITICAL TRANSFORMATION OF SUNBELT CITIES

Two recent overviews of politics in the emerging Sunbelt confirm the importance of [the] postwar transformation. For the broadly defined Southwest from Texas to California, political scientist Amy Bridges emphasizes that the agitation and

"The Political Transformation of Sunbelt Cities" pp. 248–262 in *The New Urban American: Growth and Politics in Sunbelt Cities* by Carl Abbott. Rev. ed. Chapel Hill: The University of North Carolina Press. Copyright © 1987 by The University of North Carolina Press. Reprinted by permission of The University of North Carolina Press.

adoption of formal governmental changes in a wide range of cities constituted an effective "refounding" of city governments. Reform regimes that matched textbook models replaced factional politics and personal nonpartisan machines. Focusing on the traditional South, Richard Bernard distinguishes between the G.I. revolts, whose intent was to replace older political cliques with younger leadership, and the more systematic efforts at structural reform that followed in the late 1940s and 1950s. From Oklahoma City to New Orleans, however, the results reflected a common interest in economic growth without social change.[1]

If the immediate aim of postwar reformers was to throw the rascals out and to stencil new names on the doors at city hall, their broader goal was to define and implement a single set of policies to guide the development of the entire metropolitan area. The frequently expressed worries about the disease of decentralization arose from an early concern about possible development of intrametropolitan conflict. Ambitious mayors and planners in the optimistic years of the later forties and early fifties therefore offered programs of annexation and regional planning in order to preserve the dominant role of the central city in local decisions and to block the development of independent political influence in suburban areas. Business and political leaders in city halls and downtown clubs also expected that rapid economic growth under central city leadership would prevent the emergence of dissatisfaction in peripheral areas by bringing prosperity to individual suburbanites and an expanding tax base to suburban governments.

A decade of reform campaigns, charter review commissions, and charismatic candidates gave way in the 1950s to the urban renewal era in sunbelt cities. As postwar reformers consolidated their hold on city governments, they implemented their agenda of administrative modernization and economic development. Businesslike government meant new budgeting, purchasing, and personnel practices, the restructuring of operating departments, and the recruitment of professional workers from a national pool. It also meant the creation of businesslike housing and redevelopment agencies whose semi-independent status made it easy to provide public services without worrying about the satisfaction of specific interests. Government partnership with the private sector meant new freeways, port and airport improvements, downtown office space, and enticements to new manufacturing industries.

The men in the foreground during the 1950s and 1960s were the same people who could be found in the Chamber of Commerce board room or at the monthly meetings of the Jaycees, for the sunbelt reform movements operated with the assumption that leadership should come from certain groups within the local business community. In the Virginia of Jefferson and Washington, the gentleman freeholders who owned the large plantations took it as a matter of course that their stake in the economy entitled them to control public decisions. Two centuries later, local market businessmen in Norfolk and Richmond drew the same conclusion, stepping from private to public offices as naturally as the Lees and Randolphs had accepted the call to Williamsburg. From one ocean to the other, it was difficult to distinguish the members of the Good Government League in San Antonio, the Charter Government Committee in Phoenix, or the Myers Park clique in Charlotte from the crowd in the country club lounge.

The natural allies of the downtown businessmen were the municipal bureaucrats. Programs of economic growth promised a large tax base with which to implement new initiatives, while the promotion of administrative efficiency allowed opportunities to establish reputations among their professional peers. Along with Cincinnati and Kansas City, the showcases for ambitious city managers were large sunbelt cities like San Diego, Dallas, Fort Worth, Richmond, and Norfolk, where an organized business community offered a stable base of support. The same years were also a golden age for the planners, housing experts, public health specialists, and redevelopment officials who filled the operating bureaus and agencies. As Lester Salamon has stated, urban planning on a broad scale "has never been more effective than when it was harnessed to the goals of that powerful coalition of progressive business elements and activist chief executives that took shape in city after city following the Second World War and that exploited the potent planning tools made available by the federal urban renewal and highway programs to lay claim to the decaying urban core for the administrative activities required in an increasingly technological society."[2]

The sunbelt states in the 1950s and 1960s easily offered more than a score of examples of booster governments. The homogeneous, middle-American populations of most western cities made it easy for civic leaders to construct agreement around the related goals of population growth and a white-collar economy. New residents had moved to San Jose, Albuquerque, and Denver precisely because of their range of high-status jobs, while established businessmen enjoyed the resulting booms in retailing and real estate. The tightly guarded political systems of many southern cities achieved the same consensus by excluding dissident voices and admitting minorities on carefully defined terms. Indeed, one of the significant differences between the booming cities of the economic Sunbelt during the urban renewal era and the less successful cities of the Mid-South lies in the area of political accommodation between whites and blacks. Particularly prosperous cities such as Norfolk, Charlotte, and Atlanta developed a tacit contract that traded white backing for substantial public housing programs and expanded municipal jobs in return for black acceptance of downtown renewal and freeway programs that often disrupted black neighborhoods. San Antonio and other Texas cities also managed voluntary desegregation of public facilities with minimal white resistance. The white business communities in deep South cities like Little Rock, Memphis, New Orleans, and Birmingham, however, were unwilling or unable to offer black residents the same sort of accommodation until the end of the 1960s.[3]

Despite its importance, the postwar reform era in sunbelt cities received relatively little attention from contemporary observers. For most urban experts, references to a modern "civic renaissance" brought to mind a list of cities in the old industrial belt. The editors of Fortune in 1957 and 1958 defined what is still a commonly accepted list of cities that benefited from reinvigorated leadership after 1945. One article described a "new breed" of big-city mayors who were not so much politicians as public entrepreneurs interested in the promotion of economic growth. Examples included Richard Daley of Chicago, Richardson Dilworth of Philadelphia, David Lawrence of Pittsburgh, Robert Wagner of New York, Charles Taft of Cincinnati, Raymond Tucker of Saint Louis, and Frank Zeidler of Milwaukee. Another editorial called attention to the "businessman's city," with particular reference to the Greater Philadelphia Movement and Saint Louis Civic Progress. *Fortune* also cited Cincinnati, New York, Philadelphia, Milwaukee, Pittsburgh, Baltimore, Detroit, and San Francisco as evidence that large cities were among the best-run organizations in the country.[4]

Historians and political scientists who examined the civic renaissance of the 1950s tended to start with general propositions and to end with examples drawn from the Northeast and Middle West. In 1964, for instance, Robert Salisbury argued that a "new convergence of power" was reshaping American urban politics as strong mayors, professional planners, and businessmen combined their efforts to promote economic growth. His cases in point were Chicago, Saint Louis, Pittsburgh, and New Haven. Three years later, Jeanne Lowe argued that New York, New Haven, Pittsburgh, Philadelphia, and Washington were the cities that were winning their "race with time."[5] Several studies in the 1970s summarized the experience of the same sorts of cities. New Haven, Boston, Chicago, Pittsburgh, Philadelphia, Saint Louis, and New Orleans appear on every list; Wilmington, Newark, Syracuse, Baltimore, Cleveland, and San Francisco appear on occasion.[6]

If the postwar decades in fact brought a "burst of civic reform activity not seen since the progressive era," the focus of change was more properly the emerging Sunbelt than the Northeast. In the first place, the spirit of civic optimism in the Northeast scarcely survived the 1960 census of population and the 1963 censuses of business and manufacturers. In combination with the high unemployment of the 1959 recession, population losses or minimal gains in the older cities were a painful shock to their activist leadership. Data on business locations similarly showed that heroic revitalization programs in cities like Pittsburgh had failed to modernize the economic base or to counteract the national tilt toward the South and West.[7]

In the second place, reform-minded businessmen in many northern cities were as much front men for regular political organizations as they were independent actors. In Chicago, Richard Daley was not a representative of a new breed of civic leaders but a canny politico who reinvigorated the Democratic party with the assistance of businessmen and establishment institutions like the University of Chicago. Mayor [Richard] Lee of New Haven similarly used the local Democratic machine as a tool for urban redevelopment and as an independent power base for negotiations with business interests. In Pittsburgh and Saint Louis, the civic renaissance involved a sometimes uneasy partnership between regular party politicians and central city business interests. Pittsburgh's Mayor David Lawrence and his Democratic organization worked as senior partners with the Allegheny Conference on Community Development, which represented Richard Mellon and other major industrialists. Without the same tight central control, progressive government in Saint Louis depended on constant negotiations between the "good government" mayor and the professional politicians based in county offices and ward committees.[8]

The "renaissance coalition" in the North also involved the customary mobilization of labor unions and European ethnic groups. No matter how shiny the new buildings looked to a visitor or how new the rhetoric sounded in *Harpers* or *Fortune*, local residents viewed urban redevelopment as another manifestation of traditional city politics. Scholars generally agree that urban machines and politicians from the 1930s to the 1960s were able to use the new programs of state and federal aid to preserve their own influence. Certainly Richard Lee and Richard Daley sold their programs to the voters not in terms of general issues but as a way of satisfying a package of specific interests. In short, the new progressivism in northern cities with strong ethnic communities and established party organizations was an effort to use new tools to assemble the same sort of investment coalition that historians associate with turn-of-the-century bosses.

The postwar reform movements in sunbelt cities as described in this study differ from those of the northern cities on each of the points described. . . . [S]unbelt cities on the average have smaller European ethnic communities and weaker unions. They are also likely to have city manager administrations and nonpartisan elections. Both characteristics helped the civic-minded businessmen who had assumed control after 1945 to make their decisions without worrying about other interests within the city. Indeed, if the editors of *Fortune* had really wanted to find the "businessman's city" in its pure form in 1957, they should have looked to Dallas, San Antonio, Norfolk, Denver, and San Jose.

The third stage in the cycle of urban reform in the postwar Sunbelt was the gradual weakening or breakup of the businessmen's coalitions between 1965 and 1980. In part, the decline stemmed from problems among the reformers themselves. The neoprogressives in many cities by the 1970s were as tired as the original Progressives had been in 1920. A decade or two decades of political control had allowed the reformers to achieve many of their goals in restructuring city administrations, installing modern management practices, and rebuilding sections of downtowns. More and more of the old leaders preferred a graceful exit from the public arena to further years of strenuous effort to accomplish a dwindling list of reforms. Most of the reform efforts also failed to recruit successors as the original leaders dropped out of politics or moved to new jobs. Even the highly organized Good Government League forgot to replace sixty-year-old and seventy-year-old members with men and women in their thirties and forties. As a consequence, younger businessmen and lawyers with political ambitions tended to develop new issues and to build careers outside the reform context.

The rapid growth of suburbs relative to central cities offered a direct challenge to the business-oriented conditions in many metropolitan areas. Tentatively during the 1950s and more strongly during the 1960s, governments within the suburban ring raised the basic question of equity in the allocation of the benefits and burdens of local government. Indeed, the same rapid growth that demonstrated the success of central city reform movements also exacerbated intrametropolitan conflict by forcing quick decisions and quick action on the service needs of new suburbs. With little time for careful debate and inadequate institutions for areawide decision making, residents of each metropolis had to apportion limited public resources between the competing demands of suburban development and urban redevelopment. The result, with growing frequency, was a politics of confrontation between older and newer areas over taxes and services led by increasingly self-sufficient suburban governments. Because of the rapid sorting of metropolitan population by socioeconomic status, conflicts between older and newer areas were often conflicts as well between poorer and richer communities. Both city and suburban officials scrambled to make sure that decisions on highway construction, bus routes, sewers, and other metropolitan service networks met the specific needs of their own constituents. Suburbs looked jealously at water systems and other physical services that remained under control of city agencies at the same time that they worked to fend off annexation and the extension of city school districts. Residents on both sides of the boundary markers argued loudly that they were being gouged by the tax collectors but short-changed on the services that their taxes purchased.

The suburbanization of retailing, recreation, and construction also had a direct impact on the downtown-oriented administrations of the 1950s by opening a gap between businessmen dependent on inner-city markets and real estate values and those whose prosperity was tied to peripheral growth. In San Antonio, the split among locally oriented businesses was a major element in the collapse of the Good Government League. In Charlotte, a similar split helped to defeat a city-county consolidation proposal in 1971. The new charter was developed and supported by the Chamber of Commerce and the downtown business interests that had pushed urban renewal and economic development programs in the later fifties and sixties. It mobilized the opposition of suburban voters who feared the creation of a single school system and of suburban businessmen who saw it as a tool for maintaining downtown dominance of local growth patterns. Across the continent, the rise of San Jose's sprawling suburbanized electronics industry had similar effects. Represented through the Santa Clara Manufacturing Group, the new industrialists diluted the remaining influence of an already weak downtown elite in the 1970s. In the rebalanced political system, "downtown San Jose has simply not been a serious concern for the major corporate interests who have built their low-rise headquarters in Silicon Valley cities to the north such as Mountain View, Sunnyvale, Santa Clara, and Palo Alto."[9]

Fragmentation of the reform consensus also involved the definition and legitimation of geographically localized interests within central cities themselves, bringing the replacement of the simple city-suburb dichotomy by a complex pattern of spatial politics based on the particular interests of numerous subareas.

The unexpected defection of portions of the central city middle class was rooted in the growth histories of sunbelt cities themselves. The first members of the 1940s baby boom (which was intensified in the Sunbelt by the extraordinary wartime and postwar migration of people in their twenties and thirties) reached voting age in the 1960s. Reduction in the average age of the urban electorate brought pressures for younger leadership and changes in service demands, such as an increased emphasis on urban environmental amenities. Rapid expansion of downtown professional and managerial employment also brought in new migrants with no loyalties to the power brokers of the 1950s. These new voters supported the preservation of older centrally located neighborhoods for the middle class. One result in cities like Seattle, Portland, and Denver was the incorporation of neighborhood interests into both political rhetoric and the bureaucratic decision process.[10]

Greater long-range impact on local politics came from the empowerment of geographically concentrated minority populations. The Voting Rights Act of 1965, which was extended to Hispanic voters in 1975 and renewed in 1982, provided an essential tool for minority representation. Richmond, Houston, San Antonio, Fort Worth, Albuquerque, Oakland, Stockton, Sacramento, San Jose, and San Francisco were a few of the cities that shifted to full or partial ward systems for city council elections during the 1970s and early 1980s. Overall, one-third of the cities in the Confederate South with significant black populations made the same shift. The result has been substantial and presumably permanent increases in minority representation within city governments.[11]

Trends in the 1980s have reflected both the changing environment of national politics and the continuing logic of political development within sunbelt cities. The most predictable extension of the trends of the 1970s has been the maturing of suburban political independence. In the 1960s and 1970s, suburbs were increasingly able to block central city growth agendas. By extension, the 1980s have brought greater prominence for suburb-focused development agendas in direct competition with central cities.[12] Metropolitan Miami provides a good example of such active promotional suburban governments. Coral Gables (42,000 population in 1980) has declared itself the "Global City of the Future." Local business interests and the city government have cooperated to make Coral Gables an international banking center for Latin American trade. A few miles to the north, Hialeah (145,000) has captured and facilitated much of the peripheral industrial growth associated with Miami International Airport. Bellevue (74,000) has planned and promoted an alternative downtown across Lake Washington from Seattle. DeKalb and Cobb counties function as full-service governments that help Atlanta's booming northern suburbs turn their back on the central city.[13] Other supersuburbs that view themselves as full peers of their regional centers include Long Beach; Arlington, Texas; and Virginia Beach.[14]

Even without the governmental support of a supersuburb, new suburban business interests have emerged in many sunbelt cities to directly challenge the redevelopment schemes of the old downtown elite with their own programs for investment in suburban services and promotion of suburban growth. In the 1980s Portland's west suburban electronics industry began to veto the central city's public service strategy and to argue effectively its own contradictory needs. In Phoenix, "Los Angeles–like urban sprawl resulted in the creation of multiple power centers throughout the Salt River Valley" from the late 1960s. Peripheral development created new, localized sets of business and investment interests different from those of the postwar city elite. New centers with their own groups of economic and civic leaders include the independent suburbs of Scottsdale and Mesa-Tempe-Chandler and the growing northwest and Camelback-Biltmore regions.[15]

The full impacts of suburban independence can be seen in Denver. The eastern suburb of Aurora (159,000) has dealt with Denver as an equal since the early 1970s. The city has invested heavily in the infrastructure for economic growth, including a joint water supply system with Colorado Springs that frees Aurora of its dependence on the transmountain pipelines of the Denver Water Board. The city markets itself intensively as an office and industrial location. It has annexed aggressively at the same time that state law has largely locked Denver within its boundaries. Arvada (85,000) and Lakewood (114,000), on the other side of Denver, have plans for major territorial expansion and employment growth. Fort Collins, the core city of a separate metropolitan area adjacent to Denver on the north, rejected a "slow-growth" regulation in 1979 and rode a high-tech boom to a population of 53,000 by 1985.

The political and economic power of suburban Colorado was sufficient during the last decade to block Governor Richard Lamm's efforts to maintain planning controls on sprawling metropolitan growth. The decision to build a modified form of Interstate 470 through the southwest suburbs, with its inevitable stimulation of population development, was an early defeat for Lamm's campaign platform of controlled growth. A set of "Human Settlement Policies," adopted by executive order in 1979 and designed to mitigate and guide urban growth, foundered within months on suburban legislative resistance. Lamm's citizen-based Front Range Project produced broad policy goals rather than specific growth controls. According to political scientist Dennis Judd, the result was inevitable, for "business and political leaders promoting controls tended to reside in or near Denver City proper: their motivation was to prevent competition with the downtown and to promote 'compatible' development outside the city. In contrast, suburban officials and developers were quite anxious to develop their own economic bases, and they cared little if this was compatible or competitive with Denver."[16]

In the face of aggressive suburban development, many central cities themselves have shown renewed interest in "businesslike," growth-oriented local government.[17] The reaction is in part a response to the shrinking of available resources. Portland and some other cities have been trying to shake off the effects of the depression of the early 1980s in the resource-extraction industries. The shifting of national priorities and cuts in federal urban programs have directly limited city budgets, increased competition for available discretionary funds, and provided support for policies and coalitions that promise local investment and jobs.[18] At the same time, the shift to the center can be seen as a logical synthesis of postwar political trends. Quality-of-life liberals have become middle-aged quality-of-life consumers and yuppies have replaced granola-eaters. More important, newly empowered minorities are pressing for a fair share of an expanding pie. The political rebalancing of the 1970s now means that there are strong pressures to assure that the benefits and burdens of growth are more equitably distributed than in the 1950s and 1960s.

Andrew Young's administration as mayor of Atlanta is representative. Elected in 1981 following a temporary downturn in local business, he cemented relations with the white business community and helped the city out of its economic doldrums. His day-to-day support and his overwhelming reelection margin in 1985 reflect an effective coalition of the white commercial-civic elite and the black middle class. Young sided with the business community on specific issues including a sales tax increase and a controversial parkway to the Carter presidential library that threatened neighborhoods reprieved from freeway construction in the 1970s. More broadly, Young has embraced the development program of Central Atlanta Progress. "A large measure of cooperation and good will" between the city administration and major business interests, argues Clarence Stone, "marks the emergence of a revamped but apparently stable urban regime, as in the past devoted mainly to promoting economic development especially in Atlanta's central business district."[19]

Other southern cities in the 1980s have shown similar biracial coalitions around economic growth. Like Andrew Young, Birmingham's Mayor Richard Arrington has built his success on a simultaneous appeal to blacks and to white professionals. The replacement of civil rights activist Henry Marsh as mayor of Richmond by Roy West in 1981 marked a sharp return to the downtown development and pro-business policies formed by that city's white establishment— an approach that West himself defines as building Richmond's "New South image." Mayor Ernest Morial of New Orleans was described in 1983 as a "new breed" executive who took an aggressive role in business recruitment and promotion of downtown development. As the city's first black mayor, however, he also seemed to the white establishment to play to racial tensions. Sidney Barthelemey, a black council member, defeated Morial in 1986 with a conciliatory racial style that won about a quarter of the black voters and nearly all of the white.[20]

Successful local politicians in western cities in the mid-1980s have tended to emphasize the importance of economic growth while retaining a commitment to values of livability. Seattle's Charles Royer placed his first emphasis on the city's economic health in contrast to the neighborhood orientation of Wes Uhlman. Harvey Kinney won the mayor's office in Albuquerque by running against his predecessor's "environmentalism," but he adopted many of the same policies without the rhetoric. Portland's Bud Clark, elected in 1985, had political roots in neighborhood organizations and an informal personal style but stressed economic development and the need to try "anything you can do to bring business to Portland." In San Francisco, Mayor Diane Feinstein has followed the factionalized neighborhood- and minority-based politics of the 1970s with an administration that promotes closer ties to major economic interests. As journalist Francis Fitzgerald has recently written, "Feinstein had urged a return to citywide elections for the Board of Supervisors, and the city supported her. Now that she had an electoral system in which the neighborhoods could not prevail over the downtown . . . she could proceed to steer the city back to a more conservative, pro business course. Though she was a liberal Democrat, she would not be out of step in the eighties."[21]

Denver and San Antonio may offer the clearest examples of administrations that have tried to bring together newly mobilized constituencies of the 1970s and the downtown establishment around programs of diversified and planned economic expansion. In each case, a young Hispanic politician has brought new ideas into city government. Henry Cisneros of San Antonio defeated a representative of the downtown establishment in 1981. Federico Peña ousted crusty, fourteen-year incumbent Bill McNichols from Denver's city hall in 1983 with the help of thousands of volunteers. If the campaigns had come in 1976 or 1978, they might well have produced deep community divisions. In the 1980s, however, Peña and Cisneros were able to run on positive platforms as advocates of a new generation of urban growth that would avoid the unnecessary costs of the urban renewal era and make jobs available for all segments of the community.

Peña took the reins in a city with a public leadership vacuum reminiscent of 1947. Like Ben Stapleton a generation before, Bill McNichols had run an administration marked by age, croneyism, and indifference to any but routine services. The energy industry building boom of the late 1970s and early 1980s was largely guided by the private Denver Partnership, representing the major actors in downtown development, rather than by the city. Peña's campaign in 1983 tapped neighborhood activism that had been stifled under McNichols but also enlisted major businesses and developers at the start. His slogan of "Imagine a Great City" could appeal to both groups, as can his theme of growth in the context of long-range planning. Although Peña retained broad popularity, his first major defeat came in October 1985, when voters decisively rejected a $138 million convention center proposed for the northern fringe of downtown. Opposition was based on specific objections to the site, which obviously benefited some landowners more than others, and on a general unwillingness to undertake major new commitments in the midst of the city's lingering recession.[22]

Henry Cisneros has given San Antonio a new political center after the collapse of the Good Government League, the rise of Hispanic influence, and the city-suburban battles of the 1970s. A pragmatic liberal with experience in Washington, he had a record of attention to economic development issues as a city council member from 1975 to 1981. His comfortable election as mayor with 62 percent of the vote in 1981 and his overwhelming reelections in 1983 and 1985 gave him the opportunity to develop a systematic growth strategy first outlined in his own report on "San Antonio's Place in the Technology Environment: A Review of Opportunities and a Blueprint for Action." This "orange book" defined five areas for growth and served as a springboard for Target '90, a consensus goals document involving several hundred civic leaders. Cisneros is described as a "state of the art civic entrepreneur" trying to link government and business and to build a national and international reputation for the city, especially in the area of biotechnology. In a manner analogous to Andrew Young, his essential strategy is to meet the needs of Hispanic residents by expanding job opportunities and building the middle class. However, booming growth on the far north side has yet to create many new jobs downtown or elsewhere in core areas easily accessible to inner neighborhoods. Indeed, the income gap between rich and poor districts widened in the early 1980s.[23] Even in the most up-to-date cities, neighborhoods and suburbs remain essential variables for metropolitan policy and politics.

The history of metropolitan politics in the Sunbelt since 1940 confirms the importance of underlying patterns of social geography. Spatial politics in southern and western cities has meant the development of metropolitan pluralism. A wide range of groups, defined variously by ethnicity, social class, or residential location, have developed the capacity and willingness to pursue parochial goals through formal and informal political entities that are considerably smaller than the metropolis as a whole. The common element in the political geography of many SMSAs is therefore the complexity of competition among central cities, their neighborhoods, and their suburbs. The same metropolitan area may illustrate the problems of neighborhood rivalries, intersuburban competition, sectoral disputes within regional agencies, and traditional city-suburban conflicts.

An irony of sunbelt growth is the convergence of metropolitan politics and problems on northern patterns. The South and West may continue to be centers for economic change, but their systems of metropolitan governance increasingly mirror the divisions of a Chicago or Philadelphia. The Sunbelt's cities emerged from the challenges of World War II with exciting opportunities to build new metropolitan communities without the accumulated mistakes and hostilities that burdened older cities. Their first generation of postwar leaders matched the opportunities with strong ambitions for metropolitan growth under unified direction. Nevertheless, the theme of the last two decades has been the ineffectiveness of integrative institutions, whether the focus is the fate of reform administrations or the rise of intrametropolitan conflict. Despite the promise of common goals, the trend in sunbelt SMSAs has been toward increasing variety and fragmentation in governmental structure. Efforts to sell the entire metropolis on common policies have failed to prevent the proliferation of concern for small areal units. Regional planning, annexation, and deference to core city leadership have all been weakened by the outward tide of population that advanced the status of suburban rings and by smaller eddies that created socioeconomic differences among neighborhoods and among suburbs.

In consequence, the residents of sunbelt SMSAs can expect to face increasingly difficult problems of urban maturity. Their special circumstance of growth gave them a postponement but not an exemption from the defining characteristics of American urban society. Although the urban renewal era lasted longer in the South and West than in the Northeast, the closing years of the century do not necessarily promise the same distinctiveness for the central cities of the Sunbelt that characterized the first postwar generation. Southern and western cities which have lost their battle for continued territorial growth will increasingly find themselves faced with the same problems of obsolescence that haunt New York and Chicago. It is too early to predict the replication of the South Bronx or Chicago's Woodlawn in the Gulf and Pacific cities, but it is not too early to worry about the results of blocked growth for cities such as Atlanta, Richmond, Miami, and New Orleans. Even Los Angeles looks more and more like an older rather than younger city. While the suburban world of Orange and Ventura counties has continued to grow, Los Angeles itself has experienced net outmigration, increasing population densities, a shift toward multifamily housing, and a rising proportion of minority residents.[24] In a symbolic indication of the relative fortunes of the city and its suburbs, the Los Angeles Rams announced a move to Orange County only two years after the New York Giants skipped from the Bronx to New Jersey.

The response of many city dwellers and city politicians to their loss of special status within the metropolis has been to turn in on themselves. Residents defend their own wards and neighborhoods from rapid change while city officials scramble to locate new housing or new factories on remaining parcels of vacant land within the city limits. Unfortunately, the well-publicized return to the city, which was widely hailed in South Atlantic cities such as Baltimore, Washington, Richmond, Charleston, and Savannah and western cities such as Seattle, Portland, and Denver will not have significant long-range impact on the aging process. Beyond the admitted aesthetic attractions of older neighborhoods, the rediscovered advantages of the central city are the availability of housing suitable for one- and two-member households and convenience to downtown office jobs. The former can be supplied just as easily in wellplanned suburbs. The latter in itself furnishes a limited market in most cities. In addition, the new rapid-transit systems in Washington, Atlanta, San Francisco, Miami, Portland, and other cities are reducing the competitive advantage of older neighborhoods by enhancing the access of suburbanites to downtown business districts and simultaneously building up rival suburban office nodes.

More broadly, sunbelt citizens can expect that increasing political fragmentation of their metropolitan areas will continue to erode their advantages over older cities and to exacerbate inequities in the intrametropolitan allocation of the benefits of growth and government. When entire SMSAs are considered, sunbelt cities still have resources to provide decent jobs and adequate public services. They can expect another generation of economic prosperity to attract new residents with high levels of education and skills. However, governmental fragmentation and suburban independence will mean that many metropolitan resources will be unavailable for the central cities of these same SMSAs.

Over the past generation, the most exciting aspects of metropolitan politics in the Sunbelt have been the inclusive vision of the 1940s and the willingness to accommodate new interests in the 1970s. In contrast, the 1980s have brought a diminished political vision focused on shorter-term economic development programs for suburbs and central cities. The development efforts themselves have merit, for prosperity is a precondition for effective planning and inclusive public services. However, the underlying economic and political strategies have become increasingly separate and self-interested. The need that remains is to tie the isolated agendas into unified visions of just and prosperous cities.

244   The Political Transformation of Sunbelt Cities

Before the current pattern of intrametropolitan parochialism or conflict becomes a permanent habit, sunbelt cities can continue to seek the institutions and the leadership to build true metropolitan communities.

Notes

1. Bridges, Amy. "Municipal Reform in the Southwest." Paper delivered at conference on "The Sunbelt: A Region and Regionalism in the Making," Miami, Florida, November 1985; Bernard, Richard. "Municipal Politics in the Sunbelt South." Paper delivered at conference on "The Sunbelt: A Region and Regionalism in the Making," Miami, Florida, November 1985.
2. Salamon, Lester. "Urban Politics, Urban Policy, Case Studies, and Political Theory." *Public Administration Review* 37 (August 1977): 418–428.
3. Jacoway, Elizabeth. "Civil Rights and the Changing South." In *Southern Businessmen and Desegregation,* edited by Elizabeth Jacoway and David Colburn, p. 11. Baton Rouge: Louisiana State University Press, 1982; Goldberg, Robert A. "Racial Change on the Southern Periphery: The Case of San Antonio, Texas, 1960–65." *Journal of Southern History* 49 (August 1983): 373; Jennings, M. Kent. *Community Influentials: The Elites of Atlanta.* New York: The Free Press, 1964; Wright, William E. *Memphis Politics: A Study in Racial Bloc Voting.* New York: McGraw-Hill Book Co., 1962.
4. "New Strength in City Hall." *Fortune* 56 (November 1957): 156–159, 251–264; "The Businessmen's City." *Fortune* 57 (February 1958): 93–96.
5. Lowe, Jeanne. *Cities in a Race with Time.* New York: Random House, 1967; Salisbury, Robert. "Urban Politics: The New Convergence of Power." *Journal of Politics* 26 (November 1964): 775–797.
6. Gelfand, Mark. *A Nation of Cities: The Federal Government and Urban America, 1933–65.* New York: Oxford University Press, 1975, pp. 158–164; Miller, Zane. *The Urbanization of America.* New York: Harcourt, Brace, Jovanovich, 1973, pp. 181–197; Mollenkopf, John. "The Post-War Politics of Urban Development." *Politics and Society* 5 (1975): 273–280; Barnekov, Timothy, and Rich, Daniel. "Privatism and Urban Development: An Analysis of the Organized Influence of Local Business Elites." *Urban Affairs Quarterly* 12 (June 1977): 431–460.
7. Adrian, Charles. "Metropology: Folklore and Field Research." *Public Administration Review* 21 (Summer 1961): 148–153; Miller, *Urbanization of America,* pp. 196–197.
8. Lubove, Roy. *Twentieth Century Pittsburgh: Government, Business, and Environmental Change.* New York: John Wiley, 1969; Wolfinger, Raymond. *The Politics of Progress.* Englewood Cliffs, N.J.: Prentice-Hall, 1974.
9. Trounstine, Philip J., and Christensen, Terry. *Movers and Shakers: The Study of Community Power.* New York: St. Martin's Press, 1982.
10. Judd, Dennis. "From Cowtown to Sunbelt City: Boosterism and Economic Growth in Denver." In *Restructuring the City: The Political Economy of Urban Development,* edited by Susan Fainstein et al., pp. 167–201. New York: Longman, 1983.
11. San Francisco returned to elections at large in 1980 after experimenting with districts for the 1977 and 1979 elections. Denver modified its electoral system to add "black" and "Hispanic" districts in 1971. San Jose's adoption of districts was pushed more strongly by neighborhood groups than by minorities. Browning, Rufus; Marshall, Dale Rogers; and Tabb, David. *Protest Is Not Enough: The Struggle of Blacks and Hispanics for Equality.* Berkeley: University of California Press, 1984, pp. 19–24, 46–69, 202; Muñoz, Carlos, Jr., and Henry, Charles. "Rainbow Coalitions in Four Cities: San Antonio, Denver, Chicago, and Philadelphia." *PS* 19 (Summer 1986): 604; Heilig, Peggy, and Mundt, Robert J.

"Changes in Representational Equity: The Effect of Adopting Districts." *Social Science Quarterly* 64 (June 1983): 393–397; Davidson, Chandler, and Korbel, George. "At Large Elections and Minority Group Representation." *Journal of Politics* 43 (November 1981): 982–1005.

12. Bernard, Richard, and Rice, Bradley R., eds. *Sunbelt Cities: Politics and Growth since World War II*. Austin: University of Texas Press, 1983, pp. 20–26; Bridges, "Municipal Reform."

13. Rice, Bradley R. "If Dixie Were Atlanta." In *Sunbelt Cities*, edited by Bernard and Rice, pp. 53–54; Mohl, Raymond. "Miami: The Ethnic Cauldron." In *Sunbelt Cities*, edited by Bernard and Rice, pp. 58–99.

14. The city of Norfolk managed the first steps toward downtown economic revitalization with a successful waterfront festival market, which opened in 1984. However, fears of white population loss to suburban Virginia Beach and Chesapeake prompted the recent controversial recision of a city-wide plan for school integration through busing that had operated since 1971. The School Board's decision in the spring of 1986 capped six years of political debate and court challenges. The result was a school year that opened in the fall of 1986 with projected enrollment in a quarter of the city's elementary schools over 95 percent black. Such is the indirect political influence of suburban prosperity.

15. Johnson, G. Wesley. "Generations of Elites and Social Change in Phoenix." In *Community Development in the American West*, edited by Jessie Embry and Howard Christy, pp. 98–105. Provo: Charles Redd Center for Western Studies, 1985; Louv, Richard. *America II.* New York: Penguin Books, 1985.

16. Judd, "Cowtown to Sunbelt City," p. 195; Gottlieb, Robert, and Wiley, Peter. *Empires in the Sun.* New York: Putnam, 1982.

17. The stages of political change described here are similar to the model posited by Susan and Norman Fainstein, "Regime Strategies, Communal Resistance, and Economic Forces." In *Restructuring the City*, edited by Fainstein, pp. 245–282. The Fainsteins describe stages of "directive" municipal politics (before 1965), "concessionary" politics (1965 to 1975), and "conservative" politics (1975 to 1981 or later). Their periodization is somewhat different than mine, however, and the basis of their analysis is class rather than place.

18. Browning, Rufus, and Marshall, Dale Rogers. "Is Anything Enough?" *PS* 19 (Summer 1986): 635–640.

19. Stone, Clarence. "Atlanta: Protest and Elections Are Not Enough." *PS* 19 (Summer 1986): 618–625.

20. *Nation's Cities*, 13 June 1983; New Orleans *Times-Picayune*, 3 March 1986; *Wall Street Journal*, 2 and 25 November 1983.

21. *Nation's Cities*, 25 January 1982; Browning et al., *Protest Is Not Enough*, p. 58; Fitzgerald, Francis. "The Castro." *The New Yorker*, 21 July 1986, pp. 47–48.

22. Foster, Richard. "In Downtown Denver, a Civic Group Calls the Shots." *Planning* 49 (January 1983): 18–21; Wittenauer, Cheryl. "Federico Peña: From Dark Horse to Driving Force." *Hispanic Business* 6 (February 1984): 20–23; Muñoz and Henry, "Rainbow Coalitions," p. 606; *Washington Post*, 18 October 1985.

23. Fulton, William. "Henry Cisneros: Mayor as Entrepreneur." *Planning* 51 (February 1985): 4–10; Muñoz and Henry, "Rainbow Coalitions"; Broder, David. "San Antonio's Uneven Growth Reflected in Wider Income Gap." *Washington Post*, 11 March 1986.

24. Stanley, David T. *Cities in Trouble.* Columbus, Ohio: Academy for Contemporary Problems, 1976, pp. 1–5; Nathan, Richard, and Adams, Charles. "Understanding Central City Hardship." *Political Science Quarterly* 91 (Spring 1976): 51–62; Nelson, Howard J., and Clark, William A. V. *The Los Angeles Metropolitan Experience: Uniqueness, Generality, and the Goal of the Good Life.* Cambridge, Mass.: Ballinger Publishing Co., 1976.

Chapter 7

❖❖❖

ENTREPRENEURIAL CITIES

The Politics of Growth

The economic restructuring of local economies, the new economic competition among cities, and the withdrawal of the federal government from urban affairs have precipitated the rise of entrepreneurial cities. These communities are engaged in an economic rivalry with one another in a fashion that has some resemblance to the fierce competition of the railroad-building era, when cities fought place wars for economic survival. Within the cities, the priority placed on economic growth has triggered contests over the costs and benefits of particular policies.

The readings in this chapter provide various perspectives on the possibilities and problems of top-down versus bottom-up development strategies. As the authors of the first two selections point out, top-down, corporate-led development is problematic for local democracy because the private sector tends to call the shots. But what are the alternatives? In his selection, Lemann is skeptical about the results of economic development programs in the poverty areas, although he supports their social-services impacts. In their selection, Kantor and Savitch argue that some local governments have considerable room for maneuvering in bargaining with business, thus providing the opportunity for local politics to influence development policies.

Richard Fogelsong's brief story of the coming of Disney World to Winter Park, Florida, describes how the transformation of that community by one of America's most famous entertainment giants was dominated by private purposes and unexpected public consequences. Although Disney promised to build a model residential community, what eventually materialized was a mega-complex entertainment center that is run purely as a business. This was possible in part because the Disney corporation managed to win the legal right to incorporate itself as a virtual city-state controlled by the company, but enjoying regulatory powers and privileges normally reserved by law to popularly elected local governments. Without a resident citizen population, the government of Epcot became—to use Fogelsong's phrase—"a Vatican with mouse ears." As such, company executives could make key decisions without having to answer to any local residents other than a handful of their own employees.

Peter Eisenger argues that urban governments in the United States have devoted enormous public resources to the construction of large entertainment projects such as stadiums, convention centers, entertainment districts, and festival malls. Most of the critics of these projects have focused on their economic benefits, and they have often found them to be of questionable value. But Eisenger directs our attention, instead, to the political and social implications of the fact that these projects are often oversold or misrepresented, that they are often financed in questionable ways, and that they often seem intended more for visitors than for local residents. The implication is that the building of the tourism and entertainment city may be skewing the municipal agenda away from fundamental urban services and may be straining the bonds of trust between local political leaders and the citizenry.

For many years, government officials have been casting about for a strategy to assist the poor who live in decaying inner-city neighborhoods and ghettos. The most recent turn in policy has been the idea of revitalizing the economies of inner-city areas—rather than providing these residents with old-fashioned social services and other forms of conventional assistance, such as better housing and improved schools. Indeed, the Empowerment Zone program signed into law by President Clinton in 1993 (also supported by many Republicans in previous administrations) embodies this very approach. The reading by Nicholas Lemann argues that there is abundant evidence that community development programs for the inner-city actually have a long history of repeated failure, and often replace social programs that might do more good.

Why do the advocates of community development not give up and try something better? Lemann asserts that the community development approach satisfies powerful political constituencies who benefit even when the programs fail. This includes: geographic areas that receive program dollars no matter what happens; the philanthropic foundations who need a program that fits their small organizational reach; the businesses and grass roots activists who are glorified as city saviors; and the fiscal needs of public officials seeking cheap programs in order to meet tight budgets. Most compelling, the community development approach avoids racial integration, leaving racial minorities as segregated as ever. In contrast, programs that might really change life for those in the ghetto fail to attract political support because they might threaten these constituencies.

Paul Kantor and H.V. Savitch demonstrate how local officials need not always be junior partners in the urban development process, chasing after footloose business. In their comparative analysis of cities in the United States and Western Europe, Kantor and Savitch show that the ability of city officials to influence the local capital investment process depends on their bargaining advantages relative to business. These authors describe how cities can gain leverage by improved market conditions, changes in local political systems, and programs that regulate investment.

For example, some city governments have the advantage of a favorable local market environment for attracting or keeping business. This may be because there are businesses that have large sunk investments there or because the community has such a diversified economy that jobs that are lost are easily replaced. Similarly, cities that have highly participatory political systems and have access to national grant-in-aid and regulatory programs are better able to extract concessions out of business investors in the city-building process. The bottom line is that cities are not all equal when it comes to bargaining with business for investment. In general, however, U.S. cities are in a more dependent position than are their counterparts in Western Europe—largely because the national government in the United States does much less than do the governments of Europe to support local governments.

19

Richard Foglesong

WHEN DISNEY COMES TO TOWN

"It was as though they'd put a gun to our head," said the director of tri-county planning. "They were offering to invest $600 million. And there was the glamour of Disney. You could hardly say no to that. We were all just spellbound."

They had come from around the state to hear, finally, what Disney's new East Coast theme park would look like. The new Republican governor and most of his cabinet were there. So was half the legislature. Bankers, developers and a planeload of reporters filled out the audience. Everyone was clamoring to hear Disney's proposal, but the politicians, in particular, were anxious to know what the giant entertainment company would demand of the state legislature.

The project was Walt Disney World; the year was 1967; the place was Winter Park, Fla., outside Orlando, where the pooh-bahs had gathered to hear Disney's plans for a regional theme park. There are significant differences between 1960s Florida and 1990s Virginia, of course—Floridians were relatively untutored in the consequences of urban growth, while Virginians today are not so naive—yet the odd familiarity of the Winter Park scene highlights some of the more striking parallels between Disney's Orlando project and its present-day plans for a park in Haymarket. Then, as now, Disney's proposal was accompanied by hardball lobbying from the company, hoopla from business interests, enthusiastic support from a Republican governor and a struggle over the financing of roads. Then—as now—the Walt Disney Co. proved more powerful than local critics or media skeptics, hiring the right lobbyists and nurturing the right legislators. Then—as now—Disney got what it wanted from the state.

Given these similarities, it's instructive to consider the disparity between the plan that Disney laid out on that heady day in Winter Park and what actually transpired in Central Florida. Simply put, the California company proposed one kind of development, which it used to gain special governmental powers, and then built something else. And yet Floridians, blinded by the pixie

"When Disney Comes to Town," by Richard Foglesong, as appeared in *The Washington Post Magazine*, May 15, 1994. Richard Foglesong is Professor of Politics at Rollins College in Florida. Reprinted by permission of the author.

dust, hardly noticed. Then—as now?—people were mesmerized by the Disney mystique.

   The big news about the Florida project, initially, was its much-vaunted plan for a model city where ordinary people would make their homes and go about their lives in an idealized setting. This was a concept that had been brewing for some time: Two years before the Winter Park presentation, Walt Disney, speaking at a Florida press conference, rhapsodized about building a "City of Tomorrow." In the following months, the City of Tomorrow became an obsession with Walt, according to Disney biographer Bob Thomas. The company already knew how to build an amusement park, Walt insisted; so he focused his attention on what he was soon calling "an experimental prototype community of tomorrow"—or Epcot.

   But the company's commitment to Epcot depended on the creative leadership of one man—Walt himself. In the fall of 1966, Orlando banker and power broker Billy Dial flew to California to meet with the 64-year-old Disney. Worried about the showman's health, he asked over lunch: "Mr. Disney, if you walked out of this restaurant and were hit by a truck, what would happen to the Orlando project?" Walt responded: "Absolutely nothing. My brother runs this company, I just piddle around."

   Dial was unpersuaded, and with good reason: Three weeks later, he was in New York at the Bankers Trust Co. when he received a hurried phone call from Disney executive Donn Tatum, who said simply, "Walt is dead." It was December 15, 1966, and Walt Disney had died from lung cancer before almost anyone realized he was ill. His death left the company directionless—creatively at least—and Epcot, which had existed mostly in his head, in a state of flux. Roy Disney, the company's financial mastermind and Walt's older brother, was 73 and had already announced his plans to retire.

   Roy agreed to stay on and, after polling senior executives, gave the East Coast project his blessing and directed that it be called *Walt* Disney World as a tribute to his brother. Disney execs knew little of Walt's Epcot plans, however, so they focused instead on building a Disneyland-type amusement park; as Disney Vice President Card Walker would later observe, "It was the thing we knew best."

   Indeed, Walt's comments on a May 23, 1966, memo suggest that he himself had privately backed away from the model city vision before he died. In the memo, which was found in Walt's desk and is now kept at the Disney Archives in Burbank, Calif., Florida attorney Paul Helliwell sketched out the problem of allowing permanent residents at Epcot. If people lived there, they would vote there, diluting the company's political control of the property. It seems that Walt's thoughts were headed in a similar direction: On the memo, every time Helliwell referred to "permanent residents," Walt crossed it out and substituted "temporary residents/tourists."

   Yet the company persisted in hyping Epcot as the centerpiece of Walt Disney World. When, shortly after Walt's death, Roy addressed that SRO crowd in Winter Park, he touted Epcot. The highlight of the press conference was a 25-minute color film, Walt's last screen appearance, in which he described Epcot as the "heart" of the Florida project, a vibrant community where people would "live and work and play." In the film and in the accompanying press release, the company said Epcot would "serve a new population of 20,000."

Following the Winter Park press conference, Roy and Republican Gov. Claude Kirk flew to Jacksonville, where they filmed a joint presentation that was shown along with the Epcot film on statewide television. Floridians thus saw Walt, in a posthumous appearance, describing Epcot as a working community that would always be on the cutting edge of technology and urban design. The film was unequivocal in this depiction; yet, a decade later, a Disney spokesman would state that the model city concept was "only one visual presentation of one way to go." The film was likewise shown to the Florida legislature as it began work on the Disney legislation.

If, after Walt's death, the company was uncommitted to building a true residential community, why did company officials present this as the crux of their proposal? In part it was because the Epcot film was so visually compelling—with Walt alive on screen, offering his futuristic vision of Epcot and appealing for lawmakers' support. But it was also for legal reasons best explained in the Helliwell memo.

In that memo, Helliwell expressed concern about state and local laws that might limit the company's "freedom of action" in developing its 43-square-mile property. He proposed a Disney-controlled government with regulatory powers "superseding to the fullest extent possible under law state and county regulatory authorities." There was just one hitch: Under Florida law, as Helliwell explained, planning and zoning authority could only be exercised by a popularly elected government. To escape external land-use controls, the company had to submit to control by voters. Disney attorneys, however, found a clever way to avoid this fate.

Their proposed legislation called for a two-tier system of government. The top tier, embracing an area twice the size of Manhattan, was the Reedy Creek Improvement District. It would be controlled by the landowner, its board of supervisors elected on the principle of one acre equals one vote. Since Disney owned the land, Disney would elect the board. The bottom tier consisted of two municipalities, Bay Lake and Lake Buena Vista, each having a handful of residents who would be trusted Disney employees living in company housing. Officially, planning and zoning authority was vested in these two municipalities. Their residents would elect a government and then—ingeniously—transfer administrative responsibility for planning and zoning to the Reedy Creek District.

By this legal magic, the company was able to comply with the law and still enjoy regulatory immunity. The charter made it possible for the Reedy Creek government to regulate land use, provide police and fire services, license the manufacture and sale of alcoholic beverages, build roads, lay sewer lines, construct waste-treatment plants, carry out flood projects—even build an airport or nuclear plant, all without local or state approval. The company was creating a sort of Vatican with Mouse ears: a city-state within the larger state of Florida, controlled by the company yet enjoying regulatory powers reserved by law for popularly elected governments.

To acquire such powers, the company had to convince the Florida legislature that Epcot would be a bona fide community. Paul Helliwell, acting as lobbyist, frequently used the term "resident" in describing the company's plans. Disney lobbyists also told lawmakers that Disney would include "public school sites and other public needs in their two cities," according to an April 22, 1967, article in the Orlando Sentinel-Star. And Helliwell told legislators, few of whom had read the thick Reedy Creek charter, that the company was not asking for anything "that had not been done before." At best the statement was half-true: The charter combined the powers available in three kinds of special districts. But Florida had not combined those powers in one district before.

In persuading the legislature to adopt this legislation, the California company ably plied the old-boy system. A good example is a meeting between J. J. Griffin, a former state representative who became a Disney lobbyist, and the powerful president of the Senate, Verle Pope. Griffin had started a long-winded explanation of the weighty Reedy Creek charter when Pope stopped him. "J. J.," he said, "I just have one question. Is this good for Florida?" Griffin answered, "Yes, sir, I believe it is." Whereupon Pope said, "Well, that's good enough for me." (The anecdote is recounted by Griffin in the film "Florida's Disney Decade," produced by Disney.)

With Pope's blessing, the legislation sailed through the Senate, passing unanimously and without debate. In the House there was one dissenting vote, from Miami. Less than an hour after the vote, the State Road Board approved emergency funding for Disney's road requests. And finally, the Florida Supreme Court ruled in 1968 that the Reedy Creek District was legally entitled to issue tax-free municipal bonds. The bonding power would "greatly aid Disney interests" but would nevertheless benefit the "numerous inhabitants of the district," the court ruled.

What about those "numerous inhabitants" today? How fares the city where 20,000 would "live and work and play"? Sure enough, in 1982, 11 years after the turnstiles began spinning at Disney World, the company opened something called Epcot. Yet today, there are more hotels than homes on Disney property. Between the two cities of Bay Lake and Lake Buena Vista, there are 43 residents living in 17 mobile homes—all nonunion Disney supervisors and their families, who safeguard the company's political control of its property.

Disney is also designing a huge mixed-use development called "Celebration," billed as a further realization of Walt's urban vision. While some permanent housing is scheduled for Celebration, it will be de-annexed from the Reedy Creek District—making it impossible for homeowners to vote in Disney elections. Celebration will also have time-share units, whose temporary occupants will not have voting rights. The model city described by Walt, promoted by Roy and dangled before Florida lawmakers by Disney lobbyists has never come about; the promises of 1967 are the stuff of history.

20

Peter Eisinger

THE POLITICS OF BREAD AND CIRCUSES
Building the City for the Visitor Class

"I feel like a Roman emperor. I can't give decent city services, I want to close [city] health centers, and I want to cut back on library hours, and here I am giving bread and circuses to the people."

Philadelphia Mayor Edward Rendell on the occasion of the opening of the
Pennsylvania Convention Center, 1993 (Bissinger 1997, 202)

During the period of rapid urbanization in the late nineteenth century, the great task of American municipal governments was to manage the politics of city building for a burgeoning populace by providing the public services essential to health, safety, and civic education. A century later, city governments are consumed by a very different task. City regimes now devote enormous energies and resources not simply to the basic and traditional municipal functions but also to the task of making cities, in the words of Judd and Fainstein (1999), "places to play." This undertaking entails the construction of expensive entertainment amenities, often in partnership with private investors, designed to appeal primarily to out-of-town visitors, including the suburban middle classes. This is true even in the nation's poorest, most decrepit cities, such as Detroit and Newark. Putting the best face on this urban obsession, Sharon Zukin (1995, 2) noted that "culture is more and more the business of cities." But another way to view this development is to say that increasingly, the urban civic arena is preoccupied by a politics of bread and circuses.

Building a city as an entertainment venue is a very different undertaking than building a city to accommodate residential interests. Although the former objective is often justified as a means to generate the resources to accomplish the latter aim, the two are not easily reconciled. For example, one feature that distinguished the development of municipal services in the late nineteenth century was their fundamental democratic nature. These were not just for the well-to-do but also for the common people. Indeed, as Jon Teaford (1984) pointed out,

"The Politics of Bread and Circuses" by Peter Eisinger, *Urban Affairs Review*, Vol. 35, No. 3, January 2000, pp. 316–333. Copyright © 2000 by Sage Publications. Reprinted by permission of Sage Publications.

American city dwellers of all classes had greater access to clean water, free schools, public libraries, parks, and public health facilities than did even the comfortable urban middle classes in the great cities of Europe. Today, however, the city as a place to play is manifestly built for the middle classes, who can afford to attend professional sporting events, eat in the new outdoor cafés, attend trade and professional conventions, shop in the festival malls, and patronize the high- and middlebrow arts. Many, if not most, of these are visitors to the city, and in the view of local leaders, they must be shielded from the city's residents. The city is no longer regarded as the great melting pot, the meeting place of diverse classes and races. Thus, for example, the proposal for a "Yankee Village" surrounding Yankee Stadium in the Bronx would involve increasing parking capacity and constructing a new mass-transit station within the confines of the stadium to ensure that no matter how they travel to the ball game, "fans will not come into contact with Bronx locals" (Fainstein and Stokes 1998, 160).

It is not surprising that political and civic leaders increasingly are intent on spending their political and fiscal resources to support such entertainment facilities.[1] Such amenities not only offer literally monumental evidence of mayoral achievement, but more important, local leaders believe that they hold out the prospect of economic revival by bringing the middle class back into the cities from which it fled long ago, not as resident taxpayers but at least as free-spending visitors. Thus city leaders make entertainment projects a keystone of their urban economic development strategy, hoping that they will generate ancillary investment, high employment multipliers in the hospitality and retail sectors, and local tax revenues.

A substantial literature, however, suggests that such expectations are generally misplaced (Swindell and Rosentraub 1998). The economic effects of stadium investments, casino projects, convention centers, and other entertainment amenities generally show up on the negative side of the balance sheet, and in the few cases when they do not, their effects are highly localized. Cost overruns in the construction phase, high public subsidies for operating expenses and debt service, sweetheart deals for professional sports team owners, overoptimistic job creation projections, the unlikelihood of stimulating ancillary development beyond the immediate neighborhood, and the absence of evidence that new entertainment venues actually increase total regional entertainment spending mean that such projects almost never pay for themselves (Rosentraub 1997; Sanders 1998; Gross 1998).

Although a great deal of attention has been paid to the issue of economic impacts of entertainment amenities, little effort has been made to consider the broader consequences for cities of pursuing a politics of bread and circuses. What does it mean for cities to spend their money and their political capital in pursuit of the discretionary entertainment spending of visitors rather than the tax payments of a resident middle class? Does courting the middle class as visitors mean the creation of a different sort of city than one designed either to bring the middle class back as residents or to serve the diverse and often poorer resident population?

Urban Entertainment Amenities in the Late Twentieth Century

Despite the need to build the basic infrastructure of urban settlements and to provide for public health and safety in the late nineteenth century, local governments in the United States did not entirely ignore the recreational and cultural interests of their populations. The creation of New York's Central Park in 1857 and Chicago's Jackson Park in 1893 bracketed a period of great urban public park building. In the 1860s, Philadelphia created the first public zoo in the United States (Teaford 1984). City playgrounds for children, with swings and slides and climbing frames, appeared around the turn of the century (Sessoms 1984). Milwaukee built the first public indoor swimming pool in the late 1890s, located, incidentally, in a working-class neighborhood (Orum 1995). After World War II, leisure time expanded, and cities responded by building municipal golf courses and softball fields (Herson and Bolland 1998). The construction of stadiums paid for by local taxpayers began in the 1920s, when several cities—Chicago, Los Angeles, and Cleveland—built facilities to accompany bids for the Olympic games (Danielson 1997). Thus the expenditure of local public resources for entertainment and recreational amenities is not entirely new. Nevertheless, the current pattern of local government entertainment investment is different from that in the earlier period in several ways:

1. The pace and variety of construction have markedly increased
2. The demographic and economic context is different
3. The intended patron base has shifted from the city's residents to visitors
4. The scale of entertainment construction is significantly greater

Pace and Variety

Annual state and local expenditures for sports facilities and convention centers rose from about $700 million in the mid-1970s to more than $2 billion in the early 1990s (Sanders 1995). Table 1 shows the decade-by-decade record of construction of major-league professional sports facilities for football, baseball, basketball, and hockey. The boom in stadiums and arenas began in the 1960s as professional sports franchises expanded into the sunbelt states. By the 1990s, however, cities in all regions of the country were building facilities for major-league teams. Over the same period, cities invested heavily in convention centers and exhibition halls. In 1970, only 15 cities in the United States had a facility to host a trade show for 20,000 people. By 1985, the number of cities that could accommodate such large crowds had increased tenfold (Frieden and Sagalyn 1989). By David Laslo's count, there were 409 convention halls in 1997 in cities of all sizes with more than 55-million square feet of exhibition space, up from 24-million square feet in 120 cities at the end of the 1960s (Laslo 1998).

Cities also began to invest with private partners in festival malls, riverfront walks, and urban entertainment districts. Boston's subsidy of the Faneuil Hall–Quincy Market complex in the mid-1970s served as the prototype urban festival mall project, in which developers, with city assistance, combined architec-

Table 1 Number of Urban Professional Sports Facilities Constructed with 50% Public Financing or More, by Decade

1920–1929	3[a]
1930–1939	—
1940–1949	1
1950–1959	2
1960–1969	10
1970–1979	16
1980–1989	7
1990–1998	19

Source: Rafool (1997).
Note: Professional sports facilities include baseball and football stadiums and basketball and hockey arenas. Publicly financed suburban facilities, such as the New Jersey Meadowlands complex, are not included here.
[a]Although each of these three stadiums was built originally to bid for the Olympic games, all were eventually used by professional sports teams.

tural renovation, high-end retailing, and a wide array of restaurants and cafés as a way of drawing people into the heart of the city. Quincy Market was so successful economically and aesthetically that nearly 250 communities were prompted to copy the model in one way or another over the following dozen years (Walters 1990). One variant of these developments occurred along urban riverfronts, often in decaying industrial districts. Cleveland, Chattanooga, Columbia (South Carolina), and Louisville are among the cities in which planners have sought to transform these wasteland areas by combining parkland, mixed-use commercial and residential development, and entertainment venues to create a riverside version of the festival mall (Jordan 1997). Yet another type of city gathering place in the 1990s is the downtown urban entertainment district, typified in some cities by a high concentration of multiplex movie theaters, sports complexes, bars and cafés, and "theme" retailing, such as Disney and Nike stores. Downtown Phoenix and New York City's Times Square are the pioneer models (Fulton 1997). In other cities, the entertainment is more sedate: Newark's New Jersey Center for the Performing Arts and Philadelphia's Avenue of the Arts complex are examples of the approximately 60 officially designated arts-based cultural districts in cities across the country (Strom 1998; *New York Times*, 18 November 1997).

Context

The era in which cities began to build public parks, the most common sort of nineteenth-century recreational amenity, was a time of rapid urban population and economic growth. Later, when cities first began in earnest to finance professional sports facilities, it was primarily the new and prosperous cities of the South and West that did so. Prior to 1970, of the 14 cities that built publicly financed sports facilities, 10 (71%) were growing in population.

After 1970, however, municipal investment in entertainment amenities became a universal urban undertaking. Of the 30 cities that undertook stadium or arena construction in the next quarter century, only 57% were growing. Thirteen of the cities were experiencing population losses, some of drastic dimensions, such as Detroit and St. Louis. Even more striking is that 26 of the 30 cities that built sports facilities after 1970 were experiencing an increase in the number of people living in high-poverty neighborhoods—that is, census tracts in which 40% or more of the population lives below the federal poverty line (Jargowsky 1997, 222–232). In Houston, for example, the number of people in high-poverty tracts rose from slightly over 4,000 in 1970 to more than 119,000 in 1990. In Detroit, the increase was from just over 64,000 to 363,000, and in Cincinnati, it was from 2,200 to almost 20,000. In short, in the contemporary period, many local governments have been making large public investments in entertainment facilities at the same time that the municipal tax base is declining and social welfare needs are rising.

Patron Base

In the nineteenth century, urban recreational facilities were designed for the urban populace. Although the great city parks built after the Civil War were often far from the immigrant quarters and thus beyond the easy reach of slum dwellers too poor to pay the carfare, for "middle-class urbanites and their working-class cousins . . . the great parks were accessible refuges from the drabness of the city, and thousands flooded the municipal preserves each weekend" (Teaford 1984, 257–258). Even exceptional events such as world's fairs relied heavily on local visitors. Cronon (1991, 343) noted that of all the people who came to Chicago's Columbian Exposition of 1893, "the largest share undoubtedly came from Chicago itself." Writing about what were at the turn of the nineteenth century admittedly largely privately financed ballparks, midways, dance halls, vaudeville theaters, and movie palaces, Nasaw (1993, 2) stated that "the world of 'public' amusements was . . . where the city's peoples came together to have a good time in public."

In contrast, today's entertainment facilities, marketed vigorously by tourism promoters, are designed to bring visitors into the city (Kotler, Haider, and Rein 1993). Tourism is a way of importing spending and exporting the tax burden. These are the obvious objectives behind the construction of convention centers. An estimated 80% to 95% of convention-goers stay overnight in the host city, paying hefty room taxes in the process. They represent a highly desirable type of visitor because they tend to spend considerably more per day than ordinary tourists or attendees at cultural performances or sporting matches (Petersen 1996, 6). These latter events are aimed at other sorts of out-of-town visitors besides convention-goers. For example, New Jersey's Performing Arts Center, located in the heart of Newark, drew 70% of its audience in its first year from suburban counties around Newark (New York Times, 6 July 1998). Even in a city as large as New York, the fan base at sporting events is heavily suburban: 85% of those who go to Yankee baseball games are suburbanites (Fainstein and

Stokes 1998, 159). In fact, baseball teams justify new stadiums in part on the grounds that such facilities will increase out-of-town fan attendance. In making the case for a new stadium for the Milwaukee Brewers baseball team, consultants pointed out that Minnesota Twins and the Toronto Blue Jays built new facilities and promptly saw their nonmetropolitan attendance grow by 47% and 52%, respectively. The consultants predicted a similar effect of a new Brewer stadium (Arthur Andersen & Co. 1995, 9). In short, the objective of the new politics of entertainment amenities is primarily to attract visitors.

Scale

Facilities built today are more expensive and bigger than in the past. Soldier Field in Chicago, built in 1924, cost the equivalent of only $20 million in 1995 dollars. Baltimore's Memorial Stadium of 1950 cost only $38 million, adjusted to 1995 dollars. The generation of stadiums from the 1960s—for example, Candlestick in San Francisco, Jack Murphy in San Diego, and RFK Stadium in Washington, D.C.—rarely cost more than $125 million in 1995 dollars (Rafool 1997). Contemporary stadiums, however, with their retractable roofs, elaborate concession areas, luxury boxes, closed-circuit television transmission, and high-tech scoreboards, begin at well over $200 million and range to a projected $1 billion or more for a proposed new Yankee stadium on Manhattan's congested West Side.

For certain classes of entertainment facilities, size has also increased. Convention centers built in the late 1960s in Atlanta and Denver had 70,000- and 100,000-square feet of exhibition space, respectively. Replacement facilities built in those cities more recently have 950,000- and 300,000-square feet, and they must compete with Chicago's upgraded McCormick Place with its 2.2-million square feet of space (it was originally only one-seventh that size) and New York City's 750,000-square-foot Javits Center (Kotler, Haider, and Rein 1993; Sanders 1998).

Building a City for Visitors

The amount of fiscal and political resources and the level of energy that local elites must devote to the realization of large entertainment projects are so great that more mundane urban problems and needs must often be subordinated or ignored. In pursuing big entertainment projects, local elites create a hierarchy of interests in which the concerns of visitors to cities—including commuters, day-trippers, tourists, and business travelers—take precedence over those of the people who reside in the city. Visitors must not only have easy transportation access to the city, but once there, they must at least have parking or mass-transit access to the city's attractions, police protection, clean and well-lit streets in tourist districts, sanitary restaurants, honest taxi service, and fireproof hotels. Proponents of big entertainment projects justify the allocation of public resources and civic energies to big projects and the services that support them on the grounds that the projects themselves generate big economic development gains for residents of the city in the form of jobs and tax revenues. It is this claim that has attracted the attention of analysts. Yet the effects on cities of the mobilization of resources to build big entertainment amenities are likely to extend well beyond economic development outcomes. One of the potential unexplored effects of entertainment projects is that they threaten to strain the bonds of trust and accountability between citizens and their leaders. A second possible effect is that the effort to realize these projects can easily skew or distort the civic agenda.

Straining the Links Between Leaders and the Led

In seeking to build publicly subsidized entertainment projects to attract visiting spenders, local elites risk deepening distrust of government, creating deep polarities, and breeding cynicism among residents in the city. Consider first the democratic challenges of public financing of huge capital projects for entertainment purposes. Because these efforts are both so costly and so important to local elites, the preference is to shield the funding decision from the uncertain outcome of a public vote. Sometimes a bond or tax referendum is unavoidable if the project requires a levy on local taxpayers, however. This is a minor risk for local elites because more than half the time, voters refuse to pass such referenda. However, a negative outcome is rarely a permanent obstacle to the eventual commitment of public subsidies. It simply delays the project as leaders search for ways to detour around voter disapproval. In such cases, if resorting to means other than a public vote to use public funds does not stoke the fires of voter frustration, then other factors associated with large capital expenditures for entertainment amenities are likely to do so. These include the high opportunity costs associated with making such large investments, the potential for driving up the cost of public borrowing for other projects, and the diminution of local fiscal flexibility.

Referenda on whether to commit public funds to the construction of big entertainment amenities are not in fact the norm. Although the National Council of State Legislatures has determined that public financing was used for the construction of major-league sports facilities in 71 cases through 1996, there was no public vote in 54 of these (Rafool 1997). When referenda are held, they result, more often than not, in negative votes. The same is true of votes on convention and civic centers. Herson and Bolland (1998, 352) noted that in the late 1980s, voter support for bond issues for these sorts of projects fell, on average, below 44%. By way of comparison, support for bond issues for water and sewer systems in the same period ranged from 69% to 77%.

A negative referendum outcome does not always lay the issue to rest. As the mayor of Chandler, Arizona, once commented on an approaching referendum on whether to provide public funds to build a new spring training site for a major-league ball club, "If the voters pass this, we'll move forward. If the voters don't pass this, we'll still move forward" (quoted in Fort 1997, 146). There were at least 30 sports-facility-funding referenda between 1984 and 1997, of which 19 produced negative votes in 14 different cities (Sekwat 1996; Fort 1997). However, in 7 of the 14 cities—Chicago, Cleveland, Milwaukee, Phoenix, Pittsburgh, San Jose, and Seattle—new stadiums or arenas were subsequently initiated using public funds other than simply local levies.

State legislatures in Wisconsin, Arizona, Pennsylvania, and Washington provided funding packages for the stadiums in Milwaukee, Phoenix, Pittsburgh, and Seattle, thus essentially bypassing local electorates. In a typical scenario, the state of Pennsylvania came to the rescue of stadium proponents when Pittsburgh-area voters in 1997 resoundingly defeated a ballot measure that would have imposed a half-percentage-point sales tax for seven years to finance two new stadiums for the baseball and football teams, expand the convention center, and pay for projects in Pittsburgh's cultural district. In the wake of the defeat, state and local politicians and team officials immediately began to meet privately to work out what came to be called Plan B. This involved committing public funds through a bond sale backed by a county sales tax already in place and a hotel tax, as well as securing $150 million from the state of Pennsylvania. Stadium construction is going forward. In the state of Washington, voters turned down an increase in the state sales tax to fund a new stadium for the Seattle Mariners, but the state legislature, declaring an "emergency" to block another public referendum, passed an alternative public financing plan in a special session called by the governor.

The sales tax in the Pennsylvania case, although county based, is administered by the Allegheny County Regional Asset District, a special authority created in 1994 to raise tax revenues for the present stadium, the zoo, and local libraries. The use of special authorities to administer taxes and borrow money for stadium financing and operations is widespread. Major-league sports facilities are managed by special authorities in at least 14 other cities besides Pittsburgh (Rafool 1997). Although stadium and other big-asset projects are not always controversial, one virtue of special authorities, from the point of view of project proponents, is that their governing boards are typically insulated from the voters. For example, the mayor of Pittsburgh and the members of the Allegheny County Commission select the seven members of the Allegheny County Regional Asset District, one of whom must be chosen from a list of nominees supplied by the private development community. Likewise, the King County executive and the governor of the state of Washington appoint the seven members of the Washington State Major League Baseball Stadium Public Facilities District, and in Michigan, the Wayne County executive alone chooses the six members of the Detroit Stadium Authority.

The sums involved in financing big entertainment projects, particularly stadiums, are so large that they inevitably raise issues of the apparent opportunity costs in voters' minds. The irony of spending hundreds of millions of public dollars to fund a sports facility that will be used a few times a year is not lost on proponents of greater social spending. As New York residents began to debate the construction of a stadium on Manhattan's West Side, with an estimated cost promising to top $1 billion, parents' organizations made the case that this was enough money to build sufficient classroom space to end the city's chronic school overcrowding (*New York Times*, 22 May 1998). Because education is a municipal responsibility in New York City, the opportunity-cost equation does not pose a merely hypothetical guns-or-butter choice: Money raised for the stadium would not be available for the schools. In other cities, the schools are run by separate school districts and financed by a dedicated property tax. Voters may or may not be entirely aware of the existence of two separate revenue streams, but the symbolism of spending for a stadium in a city with an impoverished and effective school system, such as in Cleveland, is not lost on parents' groups. Cleveland's mayor has defended the investment of $280 million in a football stadium: "The income for the stadium couldn't be used for the schools," he says, "so we're not robbing children to pay for football. Far more important is keeping a community mosaic" (*New York Times*, 2 September 1998).

Even if money spent for a big entertainment project could not legally be spent for other purposes, a commitment to a large local capital expenditure may greatly constrain the degree of fiscal flexibility that a city has over time. Furthermore, it could conceivably drive up the cost of borrowing for other purposes. Both of these effects are conjectural. It is known that local taxpayers have a finite tax tolerance or willingness to pay. Even very small exactions, such as the one-tenth of 1% sales tax levied on residents of metropolitan Milwaukee for the new Brewer stadium, can elicit intense opposition. Given citizen tax resistance, it is possible that cities that nevertheless commit to expensive capital projects may eventually find that the taxpayers are "tapped out," unwilling to permit tax increases for other less glamorous services or emergencies.

We also know that various sorts of government bonds must compete for buyers. Particularly large bond issues, such as those to finance a stadium, may so dominate the bond market for a period that they force other borrowers to raise the interest rates on their securities to attract buyers. The result is that taxpayers will end up paying more to retire school bonds or highway bonds than they would have if those borrowing authorities had not had to compete with the stadium bonds.

Where fiscal matters are concerned, the potential for strains between large segments of the electorate and local political elites is clearly high. What is not known is whether voters in those cities where there is significant opposition to public spending for large entertainment projects hold public officials accountable at election time. Memories are often short, and support for such spending in some cities balances opposition. (Indeed, supporters may overwhelm opponents in cities where a team's fortunes flourish, as was the case in San Diego and Denver, where stadium referenda coincided with Padres and Broncos championship seasons.) But other sources of tension besides simply fiscal issues may arise to produce strains between the electorate and its leaders.

Consider what might be called the problem of taxpayer bait and switch. The public is promised a stadium at a certain price, and this is the figure on which a referendum is held or around which the public debate revolves. Once construction is under way, however, the price inevitably rises. The cost of Coors Field in Denver rose from $141 million, the estimate on which the 1990 voter referendum was based, to $215 million when the stadium was finished. Jacobs Field in Cleveland went from an initial cost of $128 million to more than $170 million. The new football stadium for the Browns was running $33 million over budget in 1998, and the project had not yet even been completed. The Bank One Ball Park in Phoenix came in at $110 million over budget. In Wisconsin, a state government audit estimated the final cost of Miller Park in Milwaukee at $398 million, up from the $250 million figure that set the initial public debate. Referring to the memo of understanding signed by state and local officials and ball club executives who acknowledged the initial cost at $250 million, a Wisconsin state legislator commented, "We were told to rely on that . . . [but now] I have to ask, 'Is your word any good?'" (*Milwaukee Journal Sentinel*, 13 November 1997).

Another issue has to do with the politics of fantastic expectations. Projections of benefits or economic activity by development proponents are almost always exaggerated. New York City Mayor Rudolph Giuliani claimed that a new Yankee Stadium in Manhattan would generate $1 billion worth of economic activity in the city each year. An independent consulting firm, however, estimated the impact at $100 million. Stadium and other big entertainment projects almost never actually deliver the magnitude of economic benefits promised. New York's Times Square entertainment district has indubitably revitalized that formerly seedy neighborhood, but developers apparently overestimated the real estate market and consumer demand for theme retailing. Rent speculation quickly outpaced the market, driving many retail and restaurant businesses away and leaving significant commercial space empty (*New York Times*, 8 February 1999). Proponents of gambling casinos paint an incomplete and unrealistically optimistic picture of their economic impact by emphasizing the gains but almost never the costs. Indeed, Gazel (1998, 83) concluded, "Many state and local economies in the United States have, most likely, experienced net monetary losses due to casino gambling in their jurisdictions."

Stadiums generally fail to generate a significant number of jobs after the construction phase (Baade and Sanderson 1997). Even when such projects do result in employment gains, the cost in public subsidies per job created is extremely high compared to other economic development programs (Baade and Sanderson 1997; Rosentraub 1997). The Congressional Research Service once calculated, for example, that each job created by the construction of a football stadium for the Baltimore Ravens would cost $127,000 in public funds, far above the $6,250 per job created spent on average by the state of Maryland economic development fund for business and industrial projects (Peirce 1996).

The source of fantastic or exaggerated expectations is not simply the rhetoric of persuasion by local political and development elites bent on gaining public support for building a stadium or convention center. The rhetoric itself is usually based on consultant projections about the economic impact of these amenities that use inflated spending and employment multipliers. Although the application of multipliers by neutral economic analysts is generally informed by empirical research or by reference to U.S. Department of Commerce standards, consultants hired by project proponents often seem to pull their multipliers out of thin air. Baade and Dye (1988) showed, for example, that economic impact projections for stadium projects have used multipliers that range from 1.2 to 3.2, although no objective factors can explain either the values selected by the consultants or the variation among them. As Rosentraub (1997, 163) stated, "If abused or misrepresented, the multiplier can produce estimates of impact that are nothing more than a mythical expectation of growth."

What are the effects on a local electorate of perfunctory referenda, disembodied special authorities, enormous public expenditures to subsidize wealthy team owners, chronic cost overruns for capital projects, minuscule job creation, and disappointing levels of spin-off economic activity? First, it is important to acknowledge that many residents will not in fact be disaffected, for they take pride in their professional sports teams and various cultural amenities and are willing to pay to keep them (Swindell and Rosentraub 1998). Many of these people will support local elites as they seek to build entertainment amenities. Indeed, Austrian and Rosentraub (1997) observed that elected officials in Cleveland were returned to office by the voters despite high stadium and arena cost overruns, although the executive director of the project lost the confidence of his board and his job as well. Nevertheless, many citizens—sometimes a minority, although rarely a small one, and often a majority—are opposed to public subsidies of huge entertainment projects, perhaps even offended at the expenditure of funds for games and tourism when more pressing social needs go unsatisfied. In Wisconsin, angry voters mounted the first successful recall campaign in state history to remove the state senator who cast the deciding vote in the legislature to impose a sales tax to finance the new Brewer stadium. Whether the Wisconsin case is an anomaly or a sign of things to come is not clear, but the ways in which opposition is played out more broadly in local politics bear watching.

When local elites build big entertainment projects with public help, they run the risk not only of breeding cynicism but also of polarizing their community. The issue lends itself to stark, if oversimplified, contrasts—stadiums for millionaires or schoolrooms for poor children. When sports facilities are concerned, it holds out the potential for driving a wedge between the young and the old and between men and women. When the issue is a convention or performing arts center, the wedge is likely to divide social classes and perhaps the races. When local elites push to support casino gambling, the cleavage falls along religious lines. No other type of major capital expenditure—not for roads, schools, wastewater treatment facilities, public buildings, jails, or sewers—has the potential to generate such intense divisions in local politics.

Skewing the Civic Agenda

Big entertainment projects may be regarded as spongelike in character: They often have a tendency to absorb a disproportionate share of resources that might go to other projects or other places in the city. When Houston Mayor Bob Lanier refused to accede to the demands by the Oiler football team for a new city-financed stadium, he framed the issue in either-or terms for a U.S. Senate subcommittee: "Sure, sports are important to a city's image, but in my judgment it's more important to have parks, police, water, and youth programs" (*Texas Monthly* 1996). All politics is about making choices, of course, but the allocation of such great amounts of money, energy, and attention to entertainment amenities carries with it a special harsh irony in poor big cities with competing needs. Mayor Lanier claimed to be speaking for "working-class taxpayers" who would never be able to afford to sit in the luxury boxes their tax dollars would help to finance. In reality, the deepest line of cleavage created by the pursuit of entertainment projects is often that between downtown interests and residential neighborhoods, a conflict that subsumes a whole set of mutually reinforcing racial, class, big business–small business, and even city-suburban divisions. As a critic of the New Jersey Performing Arts Center (NJPAC) in Newark complained, "It is being built by nonresidents for nonresidents. They will come and get dumped off at the front, see the show, and then leave without having any impact on the community" (*Newark Star-Ledger*, 2 March 1997). This "dumping" function is essentially the rationale for Detroit's showcase mass-transit facility built during the late 1970s, the People Mover monorail. It plies a two-mile loop around the downtown to serve hockey fans, who drive in from the suburbs, and out-of-town visitors to the Detroit auto show. Riders use the People Mover to visit the downtown restaurant area (Greektown) and then travel to their events in Joe Louis Arena or Cobo Hall. Detroit has no other light- or heavy-rail mass transit to serve residential commuters to the downtown coming from the far reaches of the city. During ordinary weekdays, the People Mover, one of the most costly mass-transit projects in its time, rarely carries more than a few thousand residents a day.

The clearest illustrations of how the civic agenda is skewed in favor of downtown interests lie in the realms of public safety and development priorities. Tourist attractions cannot succeed unless visitors are made to feel safe. Shortly after the NJPAC opened in downtown Newark, the director expressed relief that there had been no "Bonfire of the Vanities" incidents, referring to the Tom Wolfe novel in which white suburbanites become lost and then get terrorized in a South Bronx ghetto (Strom 1998). Cities go to great lengths to provide reassurance. Fort Worth prominently advertises its Sundance Square entertainment district as "one of the . . . safest downtown districts in America," but city leaders do more than proclaim the safety of their attractions. They allocate hard dollars to protect the space around tourist attractions, which necessitates shifting resources from or denying new resources to other parts of the city. Thus, in Newark, the city has built a new police substation across the street from the Performing Arts Center, and the state constructed a highway ramp to make it easier for visitors to drive directly from out of town into the adjacent state-financed parking garage. In Detroit, city officials project the need to hire an additional 300 officers to protect visitors to the casinos. On days that the Yankees play in the Bronx, there are more police in the borough than on other days. Understanding the need to shift police resources to the stadium locale on game days, the mayor of Providence, Rhode Island, demanded that if the city were to help build a new stadium for the New England Patriots, the team itself would have to come up with special payments for the extra police services required

(Mahtesian 1998). The team owner saved himself those costs, choosing instead to stay in Foxboro.

Big entertainment projects are often so large that they absorb all of a city's public development resources. Although the NJPAC, Coors Field in Denver, and the Gateway project in Cleveland do seem to have stimulated considerable ancillary development in the downtowns of their respective cities, there is still a question of whether such development has spillover effects in the residential neighborhoods. Baltimore's investment in the Inner Harbor festival market-place in the 1970s certainly did not spontaneously stimulate development in adjacent poor residential areas, nor did it generate surplus revenues that the city could use for neighborhood development projects. As a result, Baltimore has become "two cities: a city of developers, suburban professionals, and 'back to the city' gentry . . . and a city of impoverished blacks and displaced manu-facturing workers, who continue to suffer from shrinking economic opportuni-ties, declining public services and neighborhood distress" (Levine 1987, 103). A similar result is unfolding in Detroit. Until the city embraced plans to partici-pate in building two downtown stadiums and three gambling casinos, its Downtown Development Agency made a practice of concentrating on small commercial and housing projects. Now, however, the city has committed huge sums to land acquisition, site clearance, and infrastructure improvements for the big entertainment amenities. Would-be loft, office tower, and housing de-velopers and small business entrepreneurs complain not only that no public money is left over for their projects but also that city officials do not even re-turn their phone calls (*Detroit Free Press*, 28 September and 6 October 1998).

Balancing Urban Priorities

Few people would argue with the proposition that facilities that bring high or even mass culture, sports, and recreational opportunities to a city may enhance the quality of urban life. Stadiums and performing arts centers and festival malls help to transform places that would otherwise simply be markets or dor-mitories or, to remember George Sternlieb's (1971) phrase, "sandboxes" into destinations. Thus a case can be made that at some level, public encourage-ment and facilitation of these entertainment amenities are a legitimate govern-mental function in a generally affluent society.

The issue, then, is not whether to spend public money; rather, the issue is a matter of balance or proportionality. When the public costs of building a sta-dium, convention center, or festival mall compromise the basic services pro-vided to residents of the city, exhaust the municipality's fiscal flexibility, or con-sume its political energies, the priorities have become unbalanced. The principle might be reduced to the simple, though rarely observed, injunction that entertainment amenities should be subsidized by the public only in those places that can afford it. In judging how much of a city's resources to commit to entertainment amenities, at least two rules of thumb should be kept in mind. One is that most entertainment projects are highly profitable to their investors, at least eventually, and many could be—indeed, would be—built without much public support at all. A second is that most of these projects provide quite low economic returns to the city in the way of jobs and tax revenues.

The problem, of course, is that few cities are bold enough to call the bluff of a team owner seeking a new stadium or the hotel industry seeking a new convention center. And then to justify their accession to the demands of these developers, city officials exaggerate the returns to the city. Thus it is all too common for a city to use its scarce resources not to build infrastructure, fund youth recreation programs, subsidize homeless shelters, or enrich the schools but to help wealthy investors construct entertainment facilities for well-off visitors who produce few payoffs for residents. When local leaders fail to calibrate public expenditures to public returns and speak instead of creating a "big-league" image or a "world-class" city as a way of justifying expenditures on entertaining amenities, then it is fair to conclude that they are offering their constituents not the best basic services that have long been core municipal responsibilities but rather the thin sustenance of bread and circuses.

Note

1. *Entertainment facilities* include sports stadiums and arenas, festival malls, performing arts centers, entertainment districts, casinos, and convention centers. The latter do not technically provide entertainment. Nevertheless, I include them in this category because, like those amenities designed explicitly for the entertainment of large numbers of people, they receive public subsidies primarily because they promise to import dollars that will recirculate in the local retail and hospitality sectors and that can be tapped through various tourism taxes, such as hotel room and car rental taxes. Another common term used to refer to stadiums, arenas, and convention centers is *public assembly facilities,* preferred by the Urban Land Institute, but this seems to exclude art museums, entertainment districts, casinos, and festival malls (see Petersen 1996).

References

Arthur Andersen & Co. 1995. *Economic impact report: Proposed Milwaukee Brewers Stadium.* Milwaukee, WI: Author.

Austrian, Z., and M. Rosentraub. 1997. Cleveland's gateway to the future. In *Sports, jobs & taxes,* edited by R. Noll and A. Zimbalist, 355–384. Washington, DC: Brookings Institution.

Baade, R., and R. Dye. 1988. Sports stadiums and area development: A critical review. *Economic Development Quarterly* 2:265–275.

Baade, R., and A. Sanderson. 1997. The employment effect of teams and sports facilities. In *Sports, jobs & taxes,* edited by R. Noll and A. Zimbalist, 92–118. Washington, DC: Brookings Institution.

Bissinger, B. 1997. *A prayer for the city.* New York: Random House.

Cronon, D. 1991. *Nature's metropolis: Chicago and the great West.* New York: Norton.

Danielson, M. 1997. *Home team.* Princeton, NJ: Princeton University Press.

Fainstein, S., and R. J. Stokes. 1998. Spaces for play: The impacts of entertainment development on New York City. *Economic Development Quarterly* 12:150–165.

Fort, R. 1997. Direct democracy and the stadium mess. In *Sports, jobs & taxes,* edited by R. Noll and A. Zimbalist, 146–177. Washington, DC: Brookings Institution.

Frieden, B., and L. Sagalyn. 1989. *Downtown, Inc.* Cambridge: MIT Press.

Fulton, W. 1997. Planet downtown. *Governing* 10:22–26.

Gazel, R. 1998. The economic impacts of casino gambling at the state and local levels. *Annals* 556:66–84.

Gross, M. 1998. Legal gambling as a strategy for economic development. *Economic Development Quarterly* 12:203–213.

Herson, L., and J. Bolland. 1998. *The urban web.* Chicago: Nelson-Hall.

Jargowsky, P. 1997. *Poverty and place.* New York: Russell Sage.

Jordan, A. 1997. River of dreams. *Governing* 10:26–30.

Judd, D., and S. Fainstein, eds. 1999. *The tourist city.* New Haven, CT: Yale University Press.

Kotler, P., D. Haider, and I. Rein. 1993. *Marketing places.* New York: Free Press.

Laslo, D. 1998. Proliferating convention centers: Issues in community, equity and efficiency and the case of St. Louis' convention center expansion. Paper presented at the annual meeting of the American Political Science Association, Boston, September.

Levine, M. 1987. Downtown redevelopment as an urban growth strategy: A critical appraisal of the Baltimore renaissance. *Journal of Urban Affairs* 9:103–123.

Mahtesian, C. 1998. The stadium trap. *Governing* 11:26.

Nasaw, D. 1993. *Going out.* New York: Basic Books.

Orum, A. 1995. *City-building in America.* Boulder, CO: Westview.

Peirce, N. 1996. Calling time on sports tax breaks. *National Journal,* 20 July: 1592.

Petersen, D. 1996. *Sports, convention, and entertainment facilities.* Washington, DC: Urban Land Institute.

Rafool, A. 1997. *Playing the stadium game: Financing professional sport in the 90s.* Denver, CO: National Council of State Legislatures.

Rosentraub, M. 1997. *Major league losers.* New York: Basic Books.

Sanders, H. 1995. Public works and public dollars: Federal infrastructure aid and local investment policy. In *Building the public city,* edited by D. Perry. Thousand Oaks, CA: Sage Publications.

———. 1998. Convention center follies. *The Public Interest* (summer): 58–72.

Sekwat, A. 1996. The cost of major sports franchises relocation. *PA Times* 19:4, 20.

Sessoms, H. D. 1984. *Leisure services.* Englewood Cliffs, NJ: Prentice Hall.

Sternlieb, G. 1971. The city as sandbox. *The Public Interest* (fall): 14–21.

Strom, E. 1998. The New Jersey Performing Arts Center: Will it save Newark? Paper presented at the Urban Affairs Association Annual Meeting, Fort Worth, TX, April.

Swindell, D., and M. Rosentraub. 1998. Who benefits from the presence of professional sports teams? The implications for public funding of stadiums and arenas. *Public Administration Review* 58:11–20.

Teaford, J. 1984. *The unheralded triumph.* Baltimore, MD: Johns Hopkins University Press.

Walters, J. 1990. After the festival is over. *Governing* 3:26–34.

Zukin, S. 1995. *The cultures of cities.* Cambridge, MA: Blackwell.

21

Nicholas Lemann

THE MYTH OF COMMUNITY DEVELOPMENT

Inner-city revitalization is a phrase so familiar that it's part of the unexamined background noise of society. In fact, it requires some explanation. The most obvious solution to poverty is simply to provide for poor people's material needs, through cash grants, vouchers like food stamps and services like Medicaid. But

"The Myth of Community Development" by Nicholas Lemann, as appeared in *New York Times Magazine,* January 9, 1994.

for 100 years—roughly since the publication of Jacob Riis's "How the Other Half Lives"—American reformers have felt that the problems of poor urban slums went beyond just a lack of income. The slums were unhealthful and physically dangerous, and people there didn't seem to behave in a way that would put them on the track out of poverty. Therefore it was necessary to make some special efforts to improve conditions in the slums.

Traditionally these efforts involved what used to be called "social uplift": education, counseling, improvement of the housing stock, crime control. In recent decades, though, the idea of social uplift has become thoroughly disreputable among both the poor (who see it as patronizing) and the not-poor (who see it as expensive and ineffective). But what all parties have found they can live with is the idea that the way to cure the special ills of the slums is to generate a lot of home-grown business activity there. This would not only give poor people jobs and therefore money; it would create in them a whole new spirit of self-reliance. They would be able to build independent communities that control their own resources and destiny; from the standpoint of middle-class voters, creating a job base in the ghettos would be hardheaded and unwasteful. Hence the emergence of "economic development" or "community revitalization"—as opposed to straight income support, or old-fashioned social services—as a supposed panacea.

The problem is that on the whole, urban slums have never been home to many businesses except for sweatshops and minor neighborhood provisioners. The slums are usually near downtown, and the residents, when they can find work, have usually found it downtown. Also, poor neighborhoods are usually transitional: rather than being stable, self-sufficient communities on the model of a village in Vermont, they tend to be home to people who plan to move out as soon as they make a little money. The standard model of progress for poor people living in urban slums, repeated millions and millions of times over the decades, is to get a good job outside the neighborhood and then decamp for a nicer part of town.

So to try to create a lot of new economic activity in poor neighborhoods is to swim against the great sweeping tide of urban life in America. Inside the ghetto, it usually does no harm—but it doesn't help much either. Outside the ghetto, though, it does a great deal of harm. Attempts at economic revitalization often take the place of other efforts that would do much more good (especially improving schools, housing and police protection), and they establish a public mission that can't be accomplished. Nothing does more to feed the public perception that antipoverty programs—in fact, Government programs generally—don't work than the poor physical appearance of the ghettos; the more the Government claims it's going to revitalize them, the harder it becomes politically to take on the problem in the future.

The story of how America got to this point is not so much about urban poverty itself as it is about *perceptions* of urban poverty. Cities rose during the first half of the 20th century and have fallen during the second half. In the early years of their rise, as Americans flocked to them, respectable opinion often found cities horrifying, partly because of their squalid immigrant slums and corrupt political machines, and partly because virtue was thought to reside in the countryside. Theodore Roosevelt, the only President born on Manhattan Island, created a Commission on Country Life to revitalize a depopulating rural America. (It was unsuccessful.)

Not many years after cities ceased to be alarming, they began to appear to need saving. By the late 1940's, it was clear that the mass migration to the suburbs was depleting urban America of population and retailing base, and the arrival of a new wave of poor newcomers (this time African-Americans from the South) led to a fresh round of concern about slum conditions. In 1949, the Truman Administration created Urban Renewal, the first Federal program to make a commitment to restoring cities to some kind of past glory.

But Urban Renewal quickly became unpopular, especially among liberals. The rap on it, wholly justified, was that it bulldozed neighborhoods, especially black neighborhoods (hence its nickname, "Negro Removal") and replaced them with highways, sterile housing developments and municipal office complexes that looked wonderful when planners presented them at Chamber of Commerce meetings but, when built, only hastened the city's decline. In the late 50's and early 60's, books like Herbert J. Gans's "Urban Villagers" and Jane Jacobs's "Death and Life of the Great American Cities" enshrined the view that city neighborhoods, including poor ones, are precious, vibrant organisms with a complex life that planners don't understand.

When the next round of urban programs began, in the Kennedy Administration, they were animated by a backlash against urban renewal. A related line of thinking about slums that emerged at about the same time was hostility to the "ladies bountiful" who had been operating settlement houses and otherwise providing social services for many years. Both these oppositions to urban renewal and to social work, led to the same conclusion—an elevation of the role that poor people themselves should play in the improvement of the slums.

The early 1960's, then, were the starting point for the current phase of thinking about ghettos. For fully 30 years, the reigning ideas about Government policy in poor city neighborhoods have been essentially the same—even though these ideas are still being referred to as new. They were first tried in the early 1960's, in small, foundation-financed efforts like the Gray Areas Project in New Haven and Mobilization for Youth on the Lower East Side (both underwritten by the Ford Foundation); then they were introduced into the Federal bloodstream through the work of the President's Council on Juvenile Delinquency, which was run by Attorney General Robert F. Kennedy; finally, in 1964, they became the basis for the centerpiece of the War on Poverty, the Community Action program. These are the ideas:

Bottom Up, Not Top Down. The people who know the most about the needs of poor neighborhoods are the residents; therefore, poverty programs should be designed and implemented by them, not imposed from above by mayors, members of Congress, social workers, intellectuals, Federal bureaucrats or other authority figures.

Comprehensive and Coordinated. Antipoverty programs are a confusing morass, run by competing, byzantine bureaucracies. Rather than being operated "categorically" by different agencies in Washington (welfare and Medicaid are examples of "categorical" antipoverty programs because each addresses a single problem in isolation), these programs should be, on a local level, housed under one roof and reorganized so that all the problems of poor people are addressed together systematically.

Revitalize the Neighborhood. Ultimately, the theory goes, the health of a neighborhood depends on its economic base. The only real long-term answer to the problems of an inner-city ghetto is for good jobs to be available there. Anyone interested in helping poor neighborhoods must primarily focus on economic development.

It took only a few months for the War on Poverty to start being perceived as a failure. In retrospect, the poverty warriors were always swimming upstream against public opinion and politics. As long as the economy was growing rapidly and the poverty rate was decreasing, newly prosperous middle-class voters were willing to tolerate some governmental generosity. But they never pressed their representatives to finance programs they perceived as benefiting disadvantaged minorities. Also, the "bottom up" idea in the War on Poverty found its expression in a provision that directed Federal funds to community groups without the advice and consent of local elected officialdom; so mayors, senators and representatives, deprived of the pork-barrel opportunities embedded in virtually every other Federal program, were generally unfriendly to the War on Poverty.

But in a way, these political weaknesses only served to solidify the ideas about neighborhood revitalization that underlay the War on Poverty: everyone was too busy fighting enemies to re-examine its theoretical basis. Even as it became clear that the War on Poverty itself was never going to become a large, successful Federal program, succeeding antipoverty programs usually accepted the War on Poverty paradigm. Model Cities, the Johnson Administration's last major antipoverty initiative, was supposed to correct the political shortcomings of the War on Poverty by dropping the exclusion of mayors and members of Congress—but the idea was still to revitalize poor neighborhoods. Robert Kennedy, by then Senator from New York and Johnson's archenemy, was contemptuous of Model Cities. His ambitious antipoverty program was the Bedford-Stuyvesant Restoration Corporation, which was different from Model Cities in crucial respects. But it was also driven by the idea of economically revitalizing the ghetto.

The 1970's saw a succession of programs, like Community Development Block Grants during the Ford Administration and Urban Development Action Grants during the Carter Administration, which were sold as being different from the failed programs of the past while resting on the same assumptions: bottom-up planning, coordination of programs, neighborhood redevelopment.

During the 1980's, the dominant new antipoverty idea in Washington was creating Enterprise Zones: ghetto areas that would be given special tax breaks to encourage business. Their most prominent advocate was . . . Jack F. Kemp, who first proposed legislation to create them back in 1980, when he was a Congressman from Buffalo. The Reagan and Bush Administrations regularly called for legislation to establish Enterprise Zones, as did Kemp when he was Secretary of Housing and Urban Development [HUD] under Bush. Kemp has a sincere and boundless faith that miracles can result from tax cuts; in his HUD days, which coincided with the collapse of Communism, he would tell visitors that the ghettos were "akin to a third-world socialist economy" and capitalism would make them blossom.

The antipoverty talk in the Bush Administration was, as usual, full of the notion of rejecting the failed programs of the past in favor of new ideas, but the new ideas had a certain familiarity: Enterprise Zones were another revitalize-the-ghetto scheme. Many of the slogans used to promote Enterprise Zones—"empowerment," "a hand up, not a handout," "teach a man to fish and he'll eat for a lifetime"—were, consciously or not, verbatim appropriations of language that was used to sell the War on Poverty.

Kemp was well known to be frustrated with Bush's level of commitment to the enterprise zone idea—insufficient to get a bill passed. Then came the Los Angeles riots, and, as one Government expert puts it, "the only thing on the shelf was Enterprise Zones." Their previous failure to become Federal policy suddenly became a virtue because they appeared to be a fresh approach. The Administration and Congress quickly put together legislation that landed on President Bush's desk in October 1992, in the heat of the presidential race. The bill also contained a few tiny technical adjustments that would increase Government revenues, like a change in the tax-accounting procedure for securities dealers. Afraid he would be accused of again breaking his "no new taxes" pledge, Bush announced he would veto the bill.

Why has the Federal Government consistently backed economic revitalization efforts in the ghettos? The answer to this question is not the one you'd expect—that these efforts have been successful. Ghettos aren't very attractive locations for businesses. As Andrew Cuomo puts it, "It's misleading to say, once I.B.M. moves to the South Bronx everything's going to be rosy. One, I.B.M. isn't going to the South Bronx, because the other cost of doing business outweighs the tax incentives. Also if I.B.M. did show up, the people in the zone aren't in a position to show up. They need training, and services like day care—a comprehensive strategy."

In addition, the era of Government ghetto-revitalization programs has coincided with a major flow of population out of the areas that were supposedly being revived. Just during the 1970's, the peak decade of ghetto outmigration, Bedford-Stuyvesant lost one-third of its population. So did Central Harlem. The two community districts that make up the poorest part of the South Bronx lost two-thirds.

In New York City, most of these neighborhoods have stopped losing population—primarily because of immigration, not Government revitalization efforts—but in many other cities, the outflow has continued. A recent series of articles in The Miami Herald, for example, reported that all of Miami's traditional black neighborhoods are still heavy population losers: "In Liberty City, 27 percent of the population is gone. In the black section of Coconut Grove, 35 percent. In Overtown, where highway construction helped spur decline, 76 percent of the population is gone." The Herald also cited black-population-loss figures of 100,000 for Chicago, 124,000 for Atlanta and 224,000 for Washington.

It's no tragedy when people leave ghettos. They're just following the standard American pattern by moving to the outer city—places like Queens—or to the suburbs. Today, minorities are suburbanizing more rapidly than whites. A recent Urban Institute paper calculates that just during the 1980's, the black population of the suburbs in the 39 largest metropolitan areas increased by 38 percent. Jobs have followed people to the suburbs, and that makes it even more difficult to create an employment base in poor inner-city neighborhoods.

It is therefore extremely difficult to find statistical evidence that any inner-city neighborhood in the country has been economically revitalized. One often hears anecdotal revitalization success stories, but they usually involve either the building of a "festival marketplace," like South Street Seaport in New York, or the shoring up of an area that is blue-collar rather than poor and residential rather than industrial, like South Shore in Chicago, which President Clinton often mention[ed] in speeches. An Urban Institute report produced after the Los Angeles riots said, "There are virtually no examples of success in restoring strong economic activity and job creation to an inner-city area the size of South-Central Los Angeles, as is being attempted in the wake of the riots." Rebuild L.A., the much-publicized local civic effort to revitalize South-Central, has been unable to induce businesses to locate major facilities there, which is one reason that its first director, Peter V. Ueberroth, resigned.

So then why is inner-city revitalization attractive to policy makers? One reason is that although Americans move around a lot, and poor people are especially mobile, politicians represent geographical areas and so naturally think of the welfare of people in terms of the welfare of places. Schemes to revive places are always popular with politicians, and with politicians' lobbies like the United States Conference of Mayors. The Model Cities program, to cite a famous example, was in early discussions supposed to be a demonstration project in a handful of cities. But in order to get it through Congress the Johnson Administration expanded it to 150 sites (and thus vastly diluted its chances of success)—which gave the program an automatic base of 150 votes in the House.

Philanthropic foundations also like revitalization. The idea that foundations wield great power might sound strange to people outside of fields like education, foreign affairs and social policy, but within their orbit, what they do matters tremendously. In poverty-fighting, during periods when the Federal Government isn't rolling out large, centrally administered programs, foundations become, by default, the key players. The foundations' strong attachment to revitalization comes partly from the natural tendency to believe that the thing you *can* do is the essential thing *to* do. Foundations don't have enough money or power to take control of inner-city public education, or impose work requirements on welfare recipients or send poor people money and food. But they can foster community-development efforts, which are relatively cheap because they're so localized and which don't require the wielding of Government authority. For decades, the Ford Foundation has invested heavily in inner-city economic development, and in recent years, other big foundations have followed suit. The heads of the two most important foundations involved in antipoverty work are both alumni of ghetto revitalization efforts: Franklin

A. Thomas of the Ford Foundation previously ran Bedford-Stuyvesant Restoration, and Peter C. Goldmark, Jr., of the Rockefeller Foundation as a young man worked for the Federal Community Action Program. Most conclaves devoted to devising solutions to the problems of ghettos are dominated by foundation people, and they usually end with ringing endorsements of economic revitalization.

Two other disparate constituencies are able to dwell comfortably under the theoretical roof of revitalization. Business groups—a city's local Chamber of Commerce, for example—like revitalization because it glorifies small business and presents itself as a practical alternative to the big-Government approach. Ghetto revitalization projects often have the word "corporation" in their name in order to enhance their appeal to business contributors.

At the other end of the spectrum, grass-roots inner-city community groups like revitalization because it puts them at center stage as saviors of their neighborhoods (and recipients of funds), provides administrative jobs and operates from a flattering set of assumptions about the hidden "strengths" of areas that are usually defined solely in terms of their poverty, crime rates, poor schools, dilapidated housing and other problems.

Finally, revitalization is bureaucratically appealing to White House staff members. In Administration after Administration, these people suffer the same frustrations: it's too difficult to get action at a reasonable cost, and the Cabinet departments are lumbering and intransigent. So when an Administration sets up a White House task force or working group on concentrated inner-city poverty, as has nearly every Administration of the past three decades, what usually happens is that the departments submit ideas for expensive programs to be run by them, and the White House, frustrated, looks for a cheaper and higher-impact alternative. The next step—in the Bush Administration, no less than in the Kennedy Administration—is that the White House becomes entranced with the idea that community development efforts should be run locally rather than by Federal bureaucrats. That is both the cheapest and the most dramatic-sounding option.

Given that the residents of many of the poorest urban neighborhoods are African-American, a final political advantage of community development is that it neatly avoids what is perhaps the most perilous of all issues for elected officials—racial integration. Scholars, policy analysts and journalists have been moving in recent years toward the view that "hypersegregation" of the black poor causes great harm. But politicians simply can't afford to embrace this view wholeheartedly. A good example is the position of Henry G. Cisneros, the Secretary of Housing and Urban Development. When Cisneros took office, he developed a list of four fundamental "commitments" driving all HUD activities—and then became so impassioned about integration that he added a fifth commitment, to, in his words "consistently working to deconcentrate the poorest of the poor, giving people a lift up and out" of the ghetto. At Cisneros's urging, President Clinton . . . decided to issue . . . a tough new executive order banning housing discrimination against people who want to leave all-minority neighborhoods. But Cisneros still loyally (though with noticeably less fervor) endorses developing the ghetto economically, which would seem to be exactly the opposite approach.

During the 1992 campaign, Bill Clinton came out for Enterprise Zones—in a more careful and less breezily optimistic way than Kemp, but for them nonetheless. In a long interview with the staff of *The Atlantic Monthly* (including me) just before the Democratic Convention, he said, "I agree with Kemp about Enterprise Zones, but . . . I think it's a very narrow view of what needs to be done to . . . re-create that sort of economy there." And a little later: "I think they will be of limited impact unless you also have . . . the national initiatives I've called for on education, health care and the economy."

Besides his personal convictions about Enterprise Zones, Clinton had good political reasons to support them. Because they are primarily based on tax cuts, they don't have to be proposed in the form of new-spending legislation, which is unpopular. Enterprise Zones have a tough-minded, economic growth–oriented "new Democrat" aura of promoting the work ethic as a solution to poverty, rather than welfare and Government programs of the "throwing money at problems" variety. They tap into a longing for the restoration of community that seems to be at large in the country right now. They generate good will inexpensively among the urban lobbying groups. After the election, Clinton put his new National Economic Council in charge of fulfilling the Enterprise Zones campaign promise, and the Council wound up, in effect, revising the Republicans' abandoned Enterprise Zones Bill.

State and local experiments with Enterprise Zones (which, admittedly, don't involve tax breaks on the scale that the Federal Government can provide) haven't produced impressive results. Enterprise Zones don't directly attack essential problems like poor education and crime, which act like a "tax" on businesses that often outweighs whatever actual tax break they have reaped. By targeting only certain places, Enterprise Zones are, in the words of one report, "a means of redistributing investment and employment, not a means of achieving more of each."

. . . The Administration's optimism about Empowerment Zones [the Empowerment Zone/Enterprise Communities Program, funded in 1993] is extremely limited. Paul Diamond, who is probably the leading Empowerment Zones enthusiast, says he believes that if the zones are located near existing facilities with job-generating potential, like universities and hospitals (a Harlem zone, for example, could abut Columbia University and the Columbia-Presbyterian medical complex) and in cities that are drawing immigrants, they could substantially improve conditions. Other Administration officials predict that perhaps one of the six zones could end up a visible economic success, while the rest can only hope to be somewhat safer and less deteriorated-looking.

And this is the optimistic view. As an example of the pessimistic (though still Democratic) view, Lawrence F. O'Donnell Jr., staff director of the Senate Finance Committee and a protégé and soul mate of Moynihan's, says: "My own belief is this bill will represent a net harm to Empowerment Zone communities. I wouldn't be surprised if three years from now, you have an Empowerment Zone in which no employer of significance has moved in, because employers are not so concerned with the tax picture as the safety and service and transportation picture. . . . There's going to be *tremendous* chicanery around this. . . . What if the guy from the South Bronx who gets a job does what every guy does, which is move? He's no longer a tax break. Do you fire him? What he's going to end up doing is lying about his address. It completely ignores one of the most obvious phenomena of this century—people do not *want* to live near their work."

All over urban America, hundreds, even thousands of local organizations are engaged in efforts to revitalize neighborhoods. Much of this activity is extremely impressive, not least because of the dedication of the people involved. The War on Poverty set up more than 500 local community action agencies. Today, more than a decade after the last desiccated vestige of the Johnson-era Office of Economic Opportunity, a little-known agency called the Community Services Administration, was eliminated as an independent body by the Reagan Administration, hundreds of community action agencies still exist. An overlapping category, descended from Robert Kennedy's Bedford-Stuyvesant project, is Community Development Corporations, which are heavily supported by foundations and exist in poor neighborhoods in every big city.

It's unscientific and unfair to single out one of these local organizations as the best in the country—but if the title were being handed out it would, by common assent of people in the field, probably go to the New Community Corporation in Newark. Founded a year after the 1967 Newark riots, New Community became a substantial enterprise during the 1980's, under the direction of a rumpled, unassuming Catholic priest, William J. Linder. Today it operates 2,500 housing units that are home to 6,000 people; seven day-care centers; an elementary school; a shopping center anchored by a new Pathmark supermarket; a nursing home; a job-placement center; a newspaper and a restaurant. It has 1,266 employees and a $95 million annual budget. The neighborhood where New Community operates feels organized and safe. Right next to it, a private developer has built market-rate housing, which is a vote of confidence in New Community's ability to stabilize the area.

It would be a mistake, however, to make the leap from the impressive work of New Community, or that of other Community Development Corporations, to the conclusion that ghetto economic revitalization can work—although making that leap has become routine for journalists, foundation executives and Government officials. A strict unwritten code among Community Development Corporation people dictates that they must insist economic development is their primary mission. Linder certainly does. To the naked eye, though, economic development is hardly the most striking feature of Community Development Corporations. In the neighborhood where New Community operates, there is almost no private-sector economic activity. New Community, an imaginative and energetic harvester of grants, loans, subsidies and tax abatements from Government, foundations and business, owns outright almost everything there.

Its main activity—and the main activity of most other Community Development Corporations—is creating and operating housing for the poor. Because there are so many Community Development Corporations and other local efforts, and because these organizations are often run by inexperienced people, many are incompetent or even corrupt; they fizzle out, or limp along for years. The most impressive thing about the hundreds of good Community Development Corporations, though, is almost always their housing work.

Subsidized housing is the spiritual center of antipoverty work. In the dawning days of urban social reform, Jacob Riis and his allies believed that the key to solving the problems of the slums was building "model tenements." By the mid-1960's, the pandemic violence and social deterioration at big public-housing projects was the main evidence for the view (which still prevails) that Government antipoverty programs had failed. To visit successful Community Development Corporations is to see that subsidized housing for the poor can work—in fact, there seems to be a consistent model that works from neighborhood to neighborhood. The key points in common are heavy emphasis on security (New Community has a private security force of 120 people, almost one-tenth of its payroll); keeping the size of each development manageably small; creating some economic mix of tenants; screening prospective tenants and expelling tenants who commit crimes or otherwise break the rules. Subsidized housing of this kind tends to be run by a single strong leader. For example, the deputy borough president of the Bronx, Genevieve Brooks, started out as head of a Community Development Corporation called the Mid-Bronx Desperadoes.

The implications of an existing replicable formula for running subsidized housing for the poor are immense. It raises the hope of making some significant dent in problems like homelessness and inner-city dilapidation. Success stories in housing might well make the public more willing also to support Government efforts in education, child care, health, public safety and job training that would address what everyone knows is an intolerable crisis in the ghettos.

But the people who are doing good work in poor urban neighborhoods—who have significantly improved horrific conditions by figuring out how to deliver traditional social services well—almost always say that they are engaged in "economic development" or "grass-roots community development," rather than trumpeting their real story. (The most comprehensive national study of Community Development Corporations does admit, slightly through gritted teeth, that housing is "the C.D.C.'s' largest single program area," and that their "record in housing is stronger than it is in the development of commercial property or business enterprises.") The idea of poor people being ministered to today has a creepy, Kiplingesque feeling to it; everyone in the field finds the idea that poor people are being "empowered" much more comfortable. In a way, the whole notion of economic revitalization functions as a kind of code: it's a formulation that isn't taken literally and one that worked wonderfully well to bring all the antipoverty players together in a period when their cause wasn't receiving much attention from the general public or the Federal Government.

Now things are changing. An Administration interested in antipoverty programs was in the White House. Bill Clinton made it obvious that he understood and was tormented by how bad things are in the ghettos. It is also his natural inclination to look to the Federal Government to do something about it. But what? Economic revitalization efforts pass every test but one, the reality test. They are popular among all the key players in antipoverty policy; they sound good; they have bipartisan appeal; they are based on tax breaks rather than on spending and so are easier to pass. The only problem is that so far they haven't worked—which creates a larger problem.

Think for a minute about *why* most people believe that the Great Society was a failure. What's the evidence? It is the enduring physical and social deterioration of poor inner-city neighborhoods. The Government promised to turn these places around, and instead they got worse; ipso facto, Government can't do anything right. This is exactly the button that Marlin Fitzwater press secretary to President George [Herbert] Bush tried to push . . . when he blamed the Great Society for the Los Angeles riots. It's all too easy to imagine the Republican nominee in 1996 staging a press conference in one of the Clinton Administration's Empowerment Zones, waving a hand expressively at the scenery and saying: "See? They told us that by spending billions here they were going to create a nice place." All this will be hypocritical, of course, because the Republican nominee will probably be someone who supported a quite similar Bush plan, but it will be effective.

On the other hand, programs to make daily life in the ghettos decent and to put inner-city residents on the track to something better are problematic for Washington. Voters are absolutely certain that social services cost a lot and don't work, so political support for them is hard to come by. Meanwhile, there is considerable evidence that out in the ghettos, people are finding ways to deliver social services, especially housing and day care, effectively. Everybody involved in antipoverty work knows this, which is the reason that, on the ground, community efforts focus primarily on housing, safety, education and job training—and the reason that Washington tries regularly to sneak more financing for these social services into legislation. What the people who know won't do, at the moment, is state these goals directly. They fear that public hostility to Government social-service programs is too strong. It's a tragedy. What is gained in the short run by making a promise that sounds more appealing—economic development—is far outweighed by what is lost in the long run when the dream doesn't come true.

22

Paul Kantor and H. V. Savitch

CAN POLITICIANS BARGAIN WITH BUSINESS? A THEORETICAL AND COMPARATIVE PERSPECTIVE ON URBAN DEVELOPMENT

In the summer of 1989, United Air Lines announced it was planning a new maintenance hub that would bring nearly a billion dollars in investment and generate

"Can Politicians Bargain with Business?" by Paul Kantor and H. V. Savitch in *Urban Affairs Quarterly*, December 1993, pp. 230–255. Copyright © 1992 by Paul Kantor and H. V. Savitch. Reprinted by permission of Sage Publications.

over 7,000 jobs for the region lucky enough to attract it. Within a few short months, officials in over 90 localities were competing for the bonanza and were tripping over one another in an effort to lure United. Denver offered $115 million in incentives and cash, Oklahoma City sought to raise $120 million, and localities in Virginia offered a similar amount. The competition for United was so keen that cities began to bid against one another and asked that their bids be kept secret.

United was so delighted at the level of bidding that it repeatedly delayed its decision in anticipation the offers would get even better. Nearly two years later, city officials in nine finalists were enhancing their incentives, courting United executives, and holding their breaths. Reflecting on the competition, Louisville Mayor Jerry Abramson quipped, "We haven't begun to offer up our firstborn yet, but we're getting close. Right now we are into siblings."[1]

Except for the extremity of the case, there is nothing new about cities questing for private capital. Cities compete with one another for tourism, foreign trade, baseball franchises, and federal grants. Yet, there is another side to this behavior. Although 93 cities competed for the United hub, many others did not, and some cities would have resisted the corporate intrusion (Etzkowitz and Mack 1976; Savitch 1988). When United stalled and raised the ante, Kentucky's governor angrily withdrew, complaining that he would "not continue this auction, this bidding war. There is a point at which you draw the line" ("Governor turns down UAL," *Courier-Journal*, 18 October 1991). In Denver, the legislature's majority leader protested, saying, "United has a ring and is pulling Colorado by the nose." With those remarks and heightening resentment, public opinion began to pull the state away from the lure of United ("UAL bidding goes on," *Courier-Journal*, 22 October 1991).

Such cases do not seem uncommon. Although many cities are willing to build sports stadia, others have turned down the opportunity. For instance, when Fort Wayne, Indiana, declined to go beyond its offer of a short-term low-interest loan to obtain a minor-league baseball team, the franchise was taken elsewhere (Rosentraub and Swindell 1990). Although officials in some cities trip over one another in efforts to attract business by lowering taxes, officials in others raise them. Over the last three years, Los Angeles, New York, and Denver have increased business taxes. Notwithstanding high taxes and locational costs, business continues to seek out such cities as San Francisco, Tokyo, London, Toronto, and Frankfurt.

Nevertheless, the literature on urban politics has not systematically examined such "nondecisional" cases (Bachrach and Baratz 1962) to probe the precise circumstances under which local governments can influence the capital investment process. . . .

. . . We propose that questions of how, when, and why local government can influence economic development are best answered by treating political control as something that springs from bargaining advantages that the state has in political and economic exchange relationships with business. Variations in local-government influence are strongly tied to the ways in which the larger political economy distributes particular bargaining resources between the public and private sectors.

Following Lindblom (1977), we find that it is useful to regard this context as a liberal-democratic system in which there is a division of labor between business and government (Kantor 1988; Elkin 1987). The private sector is responsible for the production of wealth in a market system in which choices over production and exchange are determined by price mechanisms. For its part, the public sector is organized along polyarchal lines (Dahl 1971; Dahl and Lindblom 1965) in which public decisions are subject to popular control. Public officials may be viewed as primarily responsible for the management of political support for governmental undertakings; business leaders can be considered essentially managers of market enterprises.

This perspective suggests that even though public and private control systems are theoretically separate, in reality they are highly interdependent. So far as government is concerned, the private sector produces economic resources that are necessary for the well-being of the political community—including jobs, revenues for public programs, and political support that is likely to flow to public authorities from popular satisfaction with economic prosperity and security. For business, the public sector is important because it provides forms of intervention into the market that are necessary for the promotion of economic enterprise but that the private sector cannot provide on its own. Such interventions include inducements that enable private investors to take risks (tax abatements and tax credits), the resolution of private conflicts that threaten social or economic stability (courts, mediation services), and the creation of an infrastructure or other forms of support (highways, workforce training).

Configuring Bargaining Advantages

Conceptualized in this manner, business and government must engage in exchange relationships (bargaining) to realize common goals. This is done by using bargaining advantages that derive from three dimensions or spheres of interdependence: market conditions, popular-control systems, and public-intervention mechanisms.

Market conditions consist of the circumstances or forces that make cities more or less appealing to private investors. The market position that results is a source of bargaining advantages or disadvantages for government. Market conditions may be site specific, as when localities find they are desirable because of innate features that have become critical (e.g., Washington, D.C., as an important organizational locale or Singapore as a gateway for investment in Asia). Market conditions are also reflected in larger economic fluctuations that put urban investment at a premium (e.g., the office-building boom of the 1980s) or put urban investment at risk (e.g., the savings-and-loan bust of the 1990s). We posit that cities with strong market positions obtain influence over the capital investment process.

Popular-control systems are the polyarchal processes through which public-sector decisions that affect urban development are legitimized. Such processes may vary along several dimensions, including the scope of public participation, the extent to which participation is organized, and the effectiveness of electoral mechanisms in ensuring accountability in the process of legitimization. We posit that popular-control systems that motivate and enable elected political leaders to exercise influence over the process of legitimizing economic development decisions enhance local-government control over business investment.

Public-intervention mechanisms are relationships and methods used by state institutions to regulate the marketplace. The kinds of policy instruments available to government and the way in which it uses them can affect the distribution of bargaining advantages between business and government. We posit that governmental systems that centralize or coordinate power as well as financial support are better able to regulate economic development and shape the marketplace. These systems enhance local governmental influence over investment.

Although we are unable to test all of these propositions systematically, we seek to illustrate their reality in the pages that follow. Our analysis suggests that there is substantial variation among local governments in their ability to bargain. We also suggest that bargaining advantages tend to be cumulative— that is, the more advantages a city holds, the greater its ability to bargain. Finally, we suggest that because bargaining is a product of political and economic circumstance, so is urban development. Although it may not be possible for a city to manipulate all the variables affecting its bargaining position, most cities can manipulate some and thereby shape its own future.

Table 1 describes how differences in market conditions, popular-control systems and public-intervention mechanisms furnish bargaining advantages

Table 1 System Characteristics

	Characteristics Determining Governmental Bargaining Advantages	
Sphere of Activity	**Low**	**High**
Market condition	Competitive	Noncompetitive
	Nondiversified	Economic diversity
	Company towns	Economics of agglomeration
	Flexible capital	Fixed capital
	Mobile investment	Sunk investments
Popular control	Low party competition	Competitive parties
	Unstable partisanship	Stable partisanship
	Low ideological cohesion	High ideological cohesion
	Nonprogrammatic parties	Programmatic parties
	Fragmented party organization	High party discipline
	Few channels for citizen participation	Multiple channels for citizen participation
Public intervention	Particularistic policies	General market regulation
	Side payments	Spending on infrastructure, subsidies
	Decentralized	Centralized
	Local borrowing	National borrowing
	Finance: dependence on private investment	Finance: autonomous investment

or disadvantages to cities. Each of these bargaining components are examined here. In our analysis, public-sector influence over capital investment is indicated by distinct kinds of outcomes. When bargaining relationships put local government at a persistent disadvantage, the public sector tends to absorb greater costs and risks of private enterprise (Jones and Bachelor 1986). Cities in a weak position also are more inclined to accommodate private-sector demands, even at the cost of maintaining or expanding programs that serve non-business groups.

When bargaining relationships put local governments at a persistent advantage, an altogether different set of outcomes are likely (Logan and Molotch 1987; Capek and Gilderbloom 1992). Public actors tend to impose costs for the privilege of doing business in the locality or to place other demands on the private investor. They may levy differential taxes on businesses located in high-density commercial districts, charge linkage fees on downtown development (which can be invested elsewhere), demand amenity contributions that are applied toward the enhancement of city services, or impose inclusionary zoning, requiring developers to set aside a number of low- or moderate-income rental units in market-rate housing. More often than not, cities will be somewhere between such bipolar situations of a weak or strong bargaining position. Table 2 indicates the kinds of outcomes that are related to the three kinds of bargaining components.

Markets and Public Control of Urban Development

There is little doubt that businesses' greatest bargaining resource in urban development is its control over private wealth in the capital investment process. It is this dimension of business-government relations that Peterson's (1981) market-centered model of local politics describes. The logic of this model is that cities compete for capital investment by seeking to attract mobile capital to the community; failure to meet the conditions demanded by business for investment leads to the "automatic punishing recoil" (Lindblom 1982) of the marketplace as business disinvests. This notion has been variously interpreted to suggest that business inherently holds a dominant position (Fainstein et al. 1986; Mollenkopf 1983; Logan and Molotch 1987; Jones and Bachelor 1986; Kantor 1988).

Although the market-centered model is a powerful tool for analyzing development politics, it does not fully capture the bargaining relationships that logically derive from it. Specifically, the market perspective tends to highlight only those advantages that accrue to business. Yet, the marketplace works in two directions, not one. If we look at specific market conditions and bargaining demands, it becomes apparent that government also can use the market to obtain leverage over business. Thus we will present a number of common market-centered arguments and show their other side.

Table 2 Bargaining Components

	Bargaining Yields
Market conditions	
Unfavorable	Inducement to business:
	Cash outlays, tax exemptions, aid to capital projects, loan guarantees, free land, large-scale condemnation
Favorable	Demands on business:
	Development fees (linkage), public amenities (refurbished train stations, bus shelters, pedestrian walkways), higher business taxes, stiffer architectural (building setbacks), restrictive zoning requirements
Mixed	Negotiations with business:
	Extent of tax abatements, public-private contributions to capital projects, payments for land, capital improvements to land
Popular control	
Weak	Acquiescent, uninvolved public—bargaining takes place exclusively between elites—increasing number of side payments, low accountability, exclusionary zoning
Strong	Institutionalized land-use review policies, employment concessions for local residents and minorities, contract set-asides for local firms or minority contractors, rent control or stabilization laws, inclusionary zoning
[Public] intervention	
Dispersed	Absence of zoning or loose zoning laws, tax code enforcement, intense competition between localities, significant sublocal disparities
Integrated	Highly restrictive zoning laws, strict code enforcement, extensive infrastructure investments, frequent public-private compacts

The Cities-Lose-If-Business-Wins Argument

In the market model, public and private actors represent institutions that compete to achieve rival goals. Business pursues public objectives only insofar as they serve private needs; if important business needs are not met, local government experiences the discipline of the marketplace as capital and labor seek alternative locations.

Yet, in this description of market dynamics, cases in which local government and business may also share the same goals (as distinct from the same interests) are ignored; in such instances the market model no longer indicates business advantage in the development process. Thus a local government may have an interest in raising public revenue by increasing retail sales while shopkeepers and investors have an interest in maximizing profits. Though their interests are different, they may share the common goal of bringing about higher sales through expanded development. When this happens, bargaining between government and business shifts from rivalry over competing goals to settling differences over how to facilitate what already has been agreed on. This kind of scenario enhances the value of bargaining resources that are mostly owned by the public sector. Development politics focuses on such things as the ability to amass land, grant legal privileges and rights, control zoning, provide appropriate infrastructure, and—not least—enlist public support. Because alternative means of promoting growth are important choices (Logan and Swanstrom 1990), substantial bargaining leverage over development outcomes is placed in the hands of those who manage the governmental process, a point that Mollenkopf (1983) underscored in his study of urban renewal politics.

Yet, this partial escape from the market often is not recognized. Peterson (1981) considered the sharing of interests and goals to be one and the same. Other scholars have often assumed that there is an inherent conflict between private and public goals (Stone and Sanders 1987; Logan and Swanstrom 1990; Swanstrom 1986). However, a strong case can be made that business and government often share common goals. Although they cannot logically share interests, public officials, motivated by different stakes, frequently choose to pursue economic objectives that are also favored by business (Cummings 1988). Although some critics reject progrowth values, these values tend to be supported broadly by local electorates (Logan and Molotch 1987, 50–98; Vaughn 1979; Crenson 1971).

To take a different tack on former head of General Motors Charles Wilson's aphorism, scholars may be too anxious to suggest that if it is good for General Motors, it must be bad for Detroit. Yet, local officials and their publics do not always share this logic. When government and business perceive common goals, such perceptions can have a powerful effect on opportunities for political control over the urban economy. Under these conditions, the ability of political authorities to create political support for specific programs and their willingness to use public authority to assist business can become important bargaining resources for achieving their own interests. At the very least, the extent to which agreement between business and local government is a by-product of political choice rather than of economic constraint should be a premise for empirical investigation instead of an a priori conclusion.

The Capital Mobility Argument

This argument encompasses an assumption that bargaining advantages accrue to business as it becomes more mobile. Historically, private capital was more dependent on the local state than it is today (Kantor 1988). Technological advances in production, communications, and transportation have enhanced the ability of business to move more easily and rapidly. Changes in the organization of capital, especially the rise of multilocational corporations, have increased business mobility and made urban locations interchangable. Automation, robotics, and the postindustrial revolution are supposed to enhance capital mobility. Fixed capital has been nudged aside by a new postindustrial technology of flexible capital (Hill 1989; Parkinson, Foley, and Judd 1989).

It would seem to follow that increasing capital mobility must favor business interests. Yet, this conclusion does not always follow, if one considers specific cities and businesses that are caught up in this process of economic globalization. Capital is, in fact, not always very portable. Although cities are frequently viewed as interchangeable by some corporations, many cities retain inherent advantages of location (e.g., Brussels), of agglomeration (e.g., New York), of technological prowess (e.g., Grenoble), or of political access (e.g., Washington, D.C.). The dispersion of capital has triggered a countermovement to create centers that specialize in the communication, coordination, and support of far-flung corporate units. Larger global cities have captured these roles. Much of postindustrial capital has put enormous sunk costs into major cities. One of the more conspicuous examples is the Canadian development firm of Olympia and York, which has invested billions of dollars in New York, London, Ontario, and a host of other cities. As Olympia and York teeters on the edge of collapse, banks, realty interests, and mortgage brokers are also threatened. It is not easy for any of these interests to pull up stakes.

There has been a fairly stable tendency for corporate headquarters operations, together with the ancillary services on which headquarters depend, to gravitate to large cities that have acquired the status of world business centers (Sassen 1988; Noyelle and Stanback 1984). New York's downtown and midtown, London's financial district and its docklands, Paris's La Defense, and Tokyo's Shinjuku are some outstanding examples of postindustrialism that [have] generated billions in fixed investments. Movement by individual enterprises away from such established corporate business centers is unlikely for various reasons, including that this kind of change imposes costs on those owning fixed assets in these locations and disrupts established business networks.

Cities that have experienced ascendant market positions have not been reluctant to cash in on this. When property values and development pressures rose in downtowns, local politicians used the advantage to impose new planning requirements and demand development fees. In San Francisco, a moratorium on high-rise construction regulates the amount and pace of investment (Muzzio and Bailey 1986). In Boston and several other large cities, linkage policies have exacted fees on office development to support moderate-income housing (Dreier 1989). In Paris, differential taxes have been placed on high-rise development and the proceeds used to support city services (Savitch 1988). One should also recognize that market conditions are not immutable.

Local governments may be subject to the blandishments of business at an early stage of development, when there is great eagerness for development and capital has wide investment choices. However, once business has made the investment, it may be bound for the long term. Thus bargaining does not stop after the first deal is struck, and the advantages may shift.

This occurred in Orlando, Florida, where Disney World exacted early concessions from the local governments, only to be faced with new sets of public demands afterward (Foglesong 1989). Prior to building what is now a vast entertainment complex near Orlando, Disney planners capitalized on their impending investment and won huge concessions from government (including political autonomy, tax advantages, and free infrastructure). However, as Disney transformed the region into a sprawling tourist center, local government demanded that the corporation relinquish autonomy and pressured it to pay for physical improvements. Disney struggled to defeat these demands but eventually conceded. With huge sunk investments, Disney executives had little choice but to accommodate the public sector.

So although some industries have grown more mobile, others have not. The issue turns on the relative costs incurred by business and by government when facilities, jobs, and people are moved. How relative costs are assessed and the likelihood that businesses will absorb them influence the respective bargaining postures of business and government.

The City-Cannot-Choose Argument

In the market model, business makes investment choices among stationary cities; because cities cannot move, powerful bargaining advantages accrue to business in the urban development process and supposedly this enables them to exact what they want from local governments. Although this is sometimes the case, it is also true that local communities may have investment choices as well. Some local governments can make choices among alternative types of business investment. In particular, economic diversification enables local political authorities to market the community in a particular economic sector (e.g., as a tourist city, as a research or technical center, or as a sound place in which to retire). Further, economic diversification enhances a locality's ability to withstand economic pressure from any particular segment of the business community. This has occurred in cities as far ranging as Seattle, Singapore, and Rome, enabling them to maintain powerful market positions for years, despite profound changes in the world and national economies.

Experience teaches city officials to sense their vulnerabilities and develop defenses against dominance by a single industry. Through diversification, these cities can gain a good deal of strength, not only in weathering economic fluctuations but in dealing with prospective investors. Houston's experience after oil prices crashed moved city leaders to develop high-technology and service industries (Feagin 1988). Pittsburgh's successful effort to clean its air gave that city a new economic complexion. Louisville's deindustrial crisis was followed by a succession of new investments in health services, a revival in the transportation industry, and a booming business in the arts (Vogel 1990). Diversification, which was so instrumental in strengthening the public hand, was actually made possible by government coalitions with business.

The advantages of diversification are most apparent when these cities are compared to localities that are prisoners of relatively monopolistic bargaining relations with business. Officials in single-industry towns are strongly inclined to accommodate business demands on matters of development because they lack alternative sources of capital investment. Crenson (1971) found this pattern in Gary, Indiana, where local officials resisted proposals for pollution control because they feared that U.S. Steel would lay off workers. Similarly, Jones and Bachelor (1986) described how Detroit leaders weakened their market position when they sought to preserve the city's position as a site for automobile manufacturing. When worldwide changes in the auto industry eroded Detroit's traditional competitive advantages, political leaders fought to subsidize new plants and to demolish an otherwise viable residential neighborhood.

Neither Gary's steel-centered strategy nor Detroit's auto-centered strategy has stemmed their economic decline. The lesson for urban politicians is clear: Instead of vainly hanging on to old industry, go for new, preferably clean business. More than most politicians, big-city mayors have learned well and are fast becoming major economic promoters (Savitch and Thomas 1991).

The City-Maximizes-Growth Argument

Although the market model is built on the supposition that it is in the interest of cities to promote economic growth, not all localities seek to compete in capital markets. To the extent that communities ignore participation in this market, they do not have to bargain with business over demands that they might choose to bring to the bargaining table. Santa Barbara, Vancouver, and Stockholm are cities that have insisted growth and instituted extensive land-use controls. These cities are in enviable positions as they deal with business and developers.

Aside from major cities, there are smaller communities that do not seek to compete for capital investment such as suburban areas and middle-size cities that after years of expansion, now face environmental degradation. Even if these localities have a stake in maintaining competitive advantages as bedroom communities or steady-state mixed commercial/residential locales, their bargaining relationship with business is more independent than in relatively growth-hungry urban communities (Danielson 1976). University towns, in which a self-sustaining and alert population values its traditions, have managed to resist the intrusions of unwanted industry. Coastal cities, which seek to preserve open space, have successfully acquired land or used zoning to curtail development.

Moreover, there are cities in which governmental structures reduce financial pressure and are able to resist indiscriminate development. Regionalism and annexation have enabled cities to widen their tax nets, so that business cannot easily play one municipality off against another. Minneapolis–St. Paul, Miami-Dade, and metro Toronto furnish examples of localities banding together to strengthen their fiscal positions and turn down unwanted growth. In

Western European and other non-American nations, cities are heavily financed by central government, thereby reducing and sometimes eliminating the pressure to attract development. For these cities, growth only engenders liabilities.

Popular-Control Systems and Urban Development

Democratic political institutions not only provide means of disciplining public officials, but they constrain all political actors who seek governmental cooperation or public legitimation in the pursuit of their interests. The reality of this is suggested by the fact that business development projects frequently get stopped when they lack a compelling public rationale and generate significant community opposition. This has occurred under varying conditions and in different types of cities. In Paris, neighborhood mobilization successfully averted developers (Body-Gendrot 1987); in London, communities were able to totally redo urban renewal plans (Christensen 1979); in Amsterdam and Berlin, local squatters defied property owners by taking over abandoned buildings; after the recent earthquake in San Francisco, public opinion prevailed against the business community in preventing the reconstruction of a major highway. The existence of open, competitive systems of elections and other polyarchal institutions affords a means by which nonbusiness interests are able to influence, however imperfectly, an urban development process in which business power otherwise looms large.

But do institutions of popular control afford political authorities with a valuable bargaining resource in dealing with business? Are democratic institutions loose cannons that are irrelevant to political bargaining over economic development? From our bargaining perspective, it would appear that these institutions can provide a resource upon which political leaders can draw to impose their own policy preferences when the three conditions described in the following paragraphs are satisfied.

First, public approval of bargaining outcomes between government and business must be connected to the capital-investment process. This is often not the case because most private-sector investment decisions are virtually outside the influence of local government. Even when the characteristics of private projects require substantial public-sector cooperation, many decisions are only indirectly dependent on processes of political approval. Economic-development decisions have increasingly become insulated from the mainstream political processes of city governments as a result of the proliferation of public-benefit corporations (Walsh 1978; Kantor 1993). As power to finance and regulate business development has been ceded to public-benefit corporations, the ability of elected political leaders to build popular coalitions around development issues has shrunk because it makes little sense to appeal to voters on matters that they cannot influence.

On the other hand, the importance of this bargaining resource increases as issues spill over their ordinary institutional boundaries and into public or neighborhood arenas. When this occurs, elected political authorities gain bargaining advantages by putting together coalitions that can play a vital role in the urban development game. Consequently, even the most powerful public and private developers can be checked by politicians representing hostile voter coalitions.

In New York, Robert Moses's slide from power was made possible by mounting public discontent with his later projects and by the intervention of a popular governor who capitalized on this to undercut Moses's position (Caro 1974); Donald Trump's plans for the Upper West Side of Manhattan incurred defeats by a coalition of irate residents, local legislators, and a hostile mayor (Savitch 1988); a major highway (Westway) proposal, sponsored by developers, bankers, and other business interests, was defeated by community activists who skillfully used the courts to question the project's environmental impact.

Second, public authorities must have the managerial capability to organize and deliver political support for programs sought by business. Credible bargaining requires organizing a stable constituency whose consent can be offered to business in a quid pro quo process. However, political authorities clearly differ enormously in their capacity to draw on this resource. In the United States, the decline of machine politics, the weakening of party loyalties and organizations, and the dispersal of political power to interest groups have weakened the capacity of elected political authorities. To some extent, this has been counterbalanced by grassroots and other populist-style movements that have provided a broad base for mayors and other political leaders (Swanstrom 1986; Dreier and Keating 1990; Savitch and Thomas 1991; Capek and Gilderbloom 1992).

In contrast, in Western European cities, the stability and cohesion displayed by urban party systems more frequently strengthen political control of development. In Paris, extensive political control over major development projects is related to stable and well-organized political support enjoyed by officials who dominated the central and local governments (Savitch 1988). In London, ideological divisions between Conservative and Labour parties at the local and national levels limit the ability of business interests to win a powerful role, even in cases involving massive redevelopment such as Covent Garden, the construction of motorways, and the docklands renewal adjacent to the financial city. For example, changes in planning the docklands project were tied to shifts in party control at both the national and local levels. Given the political significance of development issues to both major British parties, it was difficult for nonparty interests to offer inducements that were capable of splitting politicians away from their partisan agendas (Savitch 1988).

Similarly, even highly fragmented but highly ideological political party systems seem capable of providing a powerful bargaining resource to elected governmental authorities. In Italy, many small parties compete for power at the national and local levels. Although this is sometimes a source of political instability, the relatively stable ideological character of party loyalties means that elected politicians are assured of constituency support. Consequently, this base of political power offers substantial bargaining advantages in dealing with business. According to Molotch and Vicari (1988), this enables elected political authorities to undertake major projects relatively free from business pressure. In Milan, officials planned and built a subway line through the downtown commercial district of the city with minimal involvement of local business.

Third, popular-control mechanisms are a valuable bargaining resource when they bind elected leaders to programmatic objectives. If political authorities are not easily disciplined for failure to promote programmatic objectives in development bargaining, business may promote their claims by providing selective incentives (side payments), such as jobs, campaign donations, and other petty favors, to public officials in exchange for their cooperation. When this happens, the bargaining position of city governments is undermined by splitting off public officials from their representational roles—and the process of popular control becomes more of a business resource.

In America, where partisan attachments are weak and where ethnic, neighborhood, and other particularistic loyalties are strong, political leaders are inclined to put a high value on seeking selective benefits to the neglect of programmatic objectives. Although populist mayors have sometimes succeeded in overcoming these obstacles (Swanstrom 1986; Dreier and Keating 1990), the need to maintain unstable political coalitions that are easily undermined by racial and ethnic rivalries limits programmatic political competition. For example, in Detroit and Atlanta, black mayors have relied heavily on economic development to generate side payments that are used to minimize political opposition; this is facilitated by the symbolic importance that these black mayors enjoy among the heavily black electorates in the two cities. Consequently, they have been able to hold on to power without challenging many business demands (Stone 1989; Hill 1986). In contrast, in Western Europe, where political-party systems more frequently discipline public officials to compete on programmatic grounds, bargaining with business is less likely to focus on side payments. As suggested earlier, in France, Italy, and Britain, votes are more often secured by partisan and ideological loyalties and reinforced by programmatic competition than by generating selective incentives for followers.

In sum, city governments vary enormously in their capacity to draw on the popular-control process in bargaining over development. The proximity of electoral competition to development, the capability of officials to organize voter support, and the extent of competition over programmatic objectives are crucial factors that weaken or enhance the resources of city governments.

State Intervention and Urban Development

From our bargaining perspective, public policy can be a valuable resource in dealing with business as long as two conditions are present: (1) Government proposals are either desired by business or can be imposed without choking off business performance, and (2) public authorities can threaten to withhold the benefits of public intervention to secure other demands. In reality, it is not always easy for local governments to meet these two conditions. Tax abatements, loans, grants, and other business incentives often are not sufficiently enticing to influence investment behavior. Further, such subsidies may be easily replaced by competing local and state governments (Eisinger 1989).

Still, there are valuable resources that politicians can use to enhance their bargaining posture. Most valuable are forms of public intervention that are not easily replaceable by the private sector, programs that arise from market failure, particularly land-use regulations and investments in public works that support or enhance private-sector activities, such as highways and bridges.

The history of zoning suggests how government can shape private investment via land-use regulation. In New York City, the rise of zoning legislation occurred in response to the needs of businesses to find a means of preventing land values from plummeting. In 1916, retail merchants along New York's fashionable Fifth Avenue were threatened by encroachments from factories and warehouses in the nearby garment district, and reformers capitalized on business needs by promoting a zoning ordinance. At the same time, reformers went a step beyond business and seized the opportunity to build public support for a broader zoning law. They adopted a system that protected residential, as well as commercial, areas and initiated a system of public scrutiny of commercial, industrial, and residential land-use changes (Makielski 1966).

Ironically, integrated national governmental systems appear to enhance local governmental control of urban development, and political structures that decentralize the regulation of market failures afford less local governmental influence. Political systems that accord a powerful urban regulatory role for the national government limit local political authority in urban planning, of course. Yet, these more centralized systems can often work to enhance local governmental bargaining power with the private sector; they do this by making it easier for governments to contain capital movement (overriding private decision making), as well as by permitting localities to draw on the resources, regulatory apparatus, and political support of higher levels of government.

Contrasts between American and some Western European cities illustrate the different bargaining implications of each system. The United States is unique in the degree to which urban public capital investment is highly decentralized. Although the national government provides grants to support highway and other capital projects, this aid is spotty and unconnected to any system of national urban planning. Most important, responsibility for financing most local infrastructure is highly decentralized. Consequently, local and state governments have little choice but to find an administrative means of extracting revenues from the private sector that gives priority to satisfying investor confidence. To market long-term debt, public corporations must contend with investor fears that borrowed funds might be diverted to satisfy political pressures, rather than used for debt repayment. Consequently, major urban infrastructure development is in the hands of public corporations that are only indirectly accountable to urban electorates. These corporations are well known for courting private investors and treating them as constituents rather than as bargaining rivals (Caro 1974; Walsh 1978).

The European experience is quite different. There, most capital expenditures are supported by the central government. In France, upwards of 75% of local budgets are financed by central government; in Holland, the figure is 92%. This relieves some of the pressure on local authorities to compete with one another for capital investment to finance basic services. Local governments in Europe are capable of dealing with business from a position of greater strength. Beyond this, national government is not as dependent on private capital as local government is and can turn to vast financial and regulatory powers to reinforce public bargaining on the part of national and local governmental authorities.

The case of La Defense, just outside of Paris, is instructive of how state-business relations have been managed in Western Europe. During the 1960s, the national government planned to build another central business district for Paris on the vacant fields of La Defense. Despite skepticism by private investors, funds were allocated by the national government. Just as the project was launched, it was confronted by a fiscal crisis. French business looked on as La Defense reeled from one difficulty to another, and the enterprise was mocked as a "white elephant." The national government responded quickly, infusing the project with funds from the treasury, from nationalized banks, and from pensions. To buttress these efforts, the government clamped down on new office construction within Paris and used other carrots and sticks to persuade corporations that La Defense was the wave of the future. The effort worked, and La Defense became a premier site as an international business headquarters.

La Defense was not built in unique circumstances. To the contrary, it demonstrates the cumulative effect of centralized policy intervention on urban development. It is not unusual for governments throughout Western Europe to pour infrastructure into a particular development area, to freeze the price of surrounding land to prevent speculation, to construct buildings in the same area by relying on public corporations, and to design all the structures in the development site. The last public act is usually to invite private investors to compete for the privilege of obtaining space. Only then does bargaining begin. . . .

Comparison of . . . two antipodal cities [—Amsterdam and Detroit—] permits us to illustrate the cumulative consequences of differences in bargaining resources for political control of business development. To begin with market conditions, Amsterdam has a highly favorable market position because it is at the center of Holland's economic engine—a horseshoe shaped region called the Randstad. The cities of the Randstad (Amsterdam, Utrecht, Rotterdam, and the Hague) form a powerful and diversified conurbation that drives Holland's economy, its politics, and its sociocultural life. Amsterdam itself is the nation's political and financial capital. It also holds light industry, is a tourist and historic center, and is one of northern Europe's transportation hubs. Although Amsterdam has gone through significant deindustrialization (Jobse and Needham 1987) and has lost 21% of its population since 1960, it has transformed its economy to residential and postindustrial uses and is attractively positioned as one of the keystones of a united Europe.

Detroit's market conditions are dramatically less favorable. It is situated in what was once America's industrial heartland and what is now balefully called the Rustbelt. Known as America's Motor City, its economy revolved around automobile manufacture. Deindustrialization and foreign competition have taken a devastating toll. In just three decades, Detroit lost more than half its manufacturing jobs and 38% of its population (Darden et al. 1987). Nearly half the population lives below the poverty line, and one quarter is unemployed (Nethercutt 1987). Detroit has tried to come back to its former prominence by rebuilding its downtown and diversifying its economy for tourism and banking. But those efforts have not changed the city's market posture. Jobs and the middle class continue to move to surrounding suburbs, and any possible conversion of the Rustbelt economy appears slim when viewed against more attractive opportunities elsewhere.

The differences in popular control of these two cities are equally stark. Amsterdam is governed by a 45-member council that is elected by proportional representation (the council also elects a smaller body of aldermen) and is well organized and easily disciplined by the voters. Political parties have cohesive programs geared to conservative, social democratic, centrist, and left-wing orientations. Political accountability is reinforced by a system of elected district councils that represent different neighborhoods of the city. These councils participate in a host of decentralized services including land use, housing, and development.

In contrast, Detroit's government is poorly organized in respect to promoting popular control of economic development. A nine-member city council is elected at large and in nonpartisan balloting. Detroit's mayor [in 1993], Coleman Young, has held power for 16 years and has based his administration on distributing selective benefits, especially city jobs and contracts, while focusing on downtown project development (Hill 1986; Rich 1991). The system affords scant opportunity for neighborhood expression, and the city's singular ethnic composition (Detroit is 75% black) is coupled to a politics of black symbolism that impedes programmatic accountability and pluralist opposition. Indeed, one scholar has described Detroit as ruled by a tight-knit elite (Ewen 1978); two other researchers believed that the city's power was exercised at the peaks of major sectors within the city (Jones and Bachelor 1986).

The two cities also differ dramatically in respect to modes of policy intervention. Like many European cities, Amsterdam is governed within an integrated national planning scheme. The Dutch rely on three-tier government, at the national, regional, and municipal levels. Goals are set at the uppermost levels, master plans are developed at the regional level, and allocation plans are implemented at the grass roots. A municipalities fund allocates financial support based on population, and over 90% of Amsterdam's budget is carried by the national treasury.

By contrast, Detroit stands very much alone. While "golden corridors" (drawn from Detroit's former wealth) have sprung up in affluent outskirts, the suburbs now resist the central city. Attempts at creating metropolitan mechanisms to share tax bases or to undertake planning have failed (Darden et al. 1987). Over the years, federal aid has shrunk and now accounts for less than 6% of the city's budget (Savitch and Thomas 1991). State aid has compensated for some of Detroit's shortfalls, but like most states, Michigan is at a loss to do anything about the internecine struggles for jobs and investment.

Given the cumulative differences along all three dimensions, the bargaining outcomes for each city are dramatically opposite. Under the planning and support of national and regional authorities, Amsterdam has managed its deindustrialization—first by moving heavy industry to specific subregions (called *concentrated deconcentration*) and later by locating housing and light commerce in abandoned wharves and depleted neighborhoods. The Dutch have accomplished this through a combination of infrastructure investment, direct subsidies, and the power to finance and build housing (Levine and Van Weesop 1988; Van Weesop and Wiegersma 1991). Amsterdam's capacity to construct housing is a particularly potent policy instrument and constitutes a countervailing alternative to private development. Between 50% and 80% of housing in Amsterdam is subsidized or publicly built. This puts a considerable squeeze on private developers, who face limitations of land availability as well as zoning, density, and architectural controls. As a condition of development, it is not uncommon for commercial investors to agree to devote a portion of their projects toward residential use (Van Weesop and Wiegersma 1991).

Indeed, the bargaining game in Holland is tilted toward the public sector in ways that seem unimaginable in the United States. Freestyle commercial development in Amsterdam has been restricted, so that most neighborhoods remain residential. Because of massive housing subsidies, neighborhoods have lacked the extremes of wealth or poverty. Even squatting has been declared legal. Abandoned buildings have been taken over by groups of young, marginal, and working-class populations—thus leading to lower-class gentrification (Mamadouh 1990).

All this compares very differently to the thrust of development outcomes in Detroit. The case of Poletown provides a stark profile of Detroit's response to bargaining with the private sector (Fasenfest 1986). When General Motors announced that it was looking for a new plant site, the city invoked the state's "quick take" law, allowing municipalities to acquire property before actually reaching agreement with individual owners. To attract the plant and an anticipated 6,000 jobs, the city moved more than 3,000 residents and 143 institutions (hospitals, churches, schools, and businesses) and demolished more than 1,000 buildings. To strike this bargain, Detroit committed to at least $200 million in direct expenditures and a dozen years of tax abatements. In the end, the bargaining exchange resulted in one lost neighborhood and a gain of an automobile plant—all under what one judge labeled as the "guiding and sustaining, indeed controlling hand of the General Motors Corporation" (Jones and Bachelor 1986).

In many respects, Poletown reflects a larger pattern of bargaining. The city is now trying to expand its airport. At stake are 3,600 homes, more than 12,000 residents, and scores of businesses. The city and a local bank also have their sights set on a venerable auditorium called Ford Hall. The arrangement calls for razing Ford Hall and granting the developers an $18 million no-interest loan, payable in 28 years. When citizen protests stalled the project, developers threatened to move elsewhere. Since then, Detroit's city council approved the project (Rich 1991).

The polar cases of Amsterdam and Detroit reveal something about the vastly different development prizes and sacrifices that particular cities experience as a result of their accumulated bargaining advantages. Amsterdam is able to use public investment to extract concessions from investors and enforce development standards in a process conducted under public scrutiny. Detroit offers land, money, and tax relief to attract development in a process managed by a tight circle of political and economic elites.

Political Control of Urban Development

By examining urban development from a state-bargaining perspective, we are able to identify some critical forces that influence local governmental control over this area of policy. From this vantage point, public influence over urban development appears to be tied to differences in market conditions, popular control mechanisms, and public policy systems because these interdependent spheres powerfully affect the ability of politicians to bargain with business. . . .

By using our bargaining perspective, future researchers may be able to overcome the limitations of extant theory and better understand the actual political choices of local communities in economic development.

Note

1. Urban Summit Conference, New York City, 12 November 1990.

References

Almond, G. 1988. The return to the state. *American Political Science Review* 82:853–874.

Bachrach, P., and M. Baratz. 1962. The two faces of power. *American Political Science Review* 56:947–952.

Body-Gendrot, S. 1987. Grass roots mobilization in the Thirteenth Arrondissment: A cross national view. In *The politics of urban development,* edited by C. Stone and H. Sanders, 125–143. Lawrence: University Press of Kansas.

Capek, S., and J. Gilderbloom. 1992. *Community versus commodity.* Albany: State University of New York Press.

Caro, R. 1974. *The power broker.* New York: Vintage.

Christensen, T. 1979. *Neighborhood survival.* London: Prism Press.

Crenson, M. 1971. *The un-politics of air pollution.* Baltimore, MD: Johns Hopkins University Press.

Cummings, S., ed. 1988. *Business elites and urban development.* Albany: State University of New York Press.

Dahl, R. 1971. *Polyarchy.* New Haven, CT: Yale University Press.

Dahl, R., and C. E. Lindblom. 1965. *Politics, economics, and welfare.* New Haven, CT: Yale University Press.

Danielson, M. 1976. *The politics of exclusion.* New York: Columbia University Press.

Darden, J., R. C. Hill, J. Thomas, and R. Thomas. 1987. *Race and uneven development.* Philadelphia: Temple University Press.

Dreier, P. 1989. Economic growth and economic justice in Boston. In *Unequal partnerships,* edited by G. Squires, 35–58. New Brunswick, NJ: Rutgers University Press.

Dreier, P., and W. D. Keating. 1990. The limits of localism: Progressive housing policies in Boston, 1984–1989. *Urban Affairs Quarterly* 26:191–216.

Eisinger, P. 1989. *Rise of the entrepreneurial state*. Madison: University of Wisconsin Press.

Elkin, D. 1987. State and market in city politics: Or, the real Dallas. In *The politics of urban development*, edited by C. Stone and H. Sanders, 25–51. Lawrence: University Press of Kansas.

Etzkowitz, H., and R. Mack. 1976. Emperialism in the First World: The corporation and the suburb. Paper presented at the Pacific Sociological Association meetings, San Jose, CA, March.

Ewen, L. 1978. *Corporate power and the urban crisis in Detroit*. Princeton, NJ: Princeton University Press.

Fainstein, S. S., N. I. Fainstein, R. C. Hill, D. Judd, and M. P. Smith. 1986. *Restructuring the city*. 2nd ed. New York: Longman.

Fasenfest, D. 1986. Community politics and urban redevelopment. *Urban Affairs Quarterly* 22:101–123.

Feagin, J. 1988. *Free enterprise city*. New Brunswick, NJ: Rutgers University Press.

Foglesong, R. 1989. Do politics matter in the formulation of local economic development policy: The case of Orlando, Florida. Paper presented at the annual meeting of the American Political Science Association, Atlanta, GA, September.

Governor turns down UAL. 1991. *Courier-Journal*, 18 October, 1.

Hill, R. C. 1986. Crisis in the Motor City: The politics of urban development in Detroit. In *Restructuring the city*. 2d ed., by S. S. Fainstein, N. I. Fainstein, R. C. Hill, D. Judd, and M. P. Smith. New York: Longman.

———. Industrial restructuring, state intervention, and uneven development in the United States and Japan. Paper presented at conference: The Tiger by the Tail: Urban Policy and Economic Restructuring in Comparative Perspective, State University of New York, Albany, October.

Jobse, B., and B. Needham. 1987. The economic future of the Randstad, Holland. *Urban Studies* 25: 282–296.

Jones, B., and L. Bachelor. 1986. *The sustaining hand*. Lawrence: University Press of Kansas.

Kantor, P. 1993. The dual city as political choice. *Journal of Urban Affairs* 15 (3): 231–244.

Kantor, P. (with S. David). 1988. *The dependent city*. Boston, MA: Scott, Foresman/Little, Brown.

Levine, M., and J. Van Weesop. 1988. The changing nature of urban planning in the Netherlands. *Journal of the American Planning Association* 54:315–323.

Lindblom, C. 1977. *Politics and markets*. New Haven, CT: Yale University Press.

———. 1982. The market as a prison. *Journal of Politics*. 44:324–336.

Logan, J., and H. Molotch. 1987. *Urban fortunes*. Berkeley: University of California Press.

Logan, J., and T. Swanstrom, eds. 1990. *Beyond the city limits*. Philadelphia: Temple University Press.

Makielski, S. 1966. *The politics of zoning*. New York: Columbia University Press.

Mamadouh, V. 1990. Squatting, housing, and urban policy in Amsterdam. Paper presented at the International Research Conference on Housing Debates and Urban Challenges, Paris, July.

Mollenkopf, J. 1983. *The contested city*. Princeton, NJ: Princeton University Press.

Molotch, H., and S. Vicari. 1988. Three ways to build: The development process in the United States, Japan, and Italy. *Urban Affairs Quarterly* 24:188–214.

Muzzio, D., and R. Bailey. 1986. Economic development, housing, and zoning. *Journal of Urban Affairs* 8:1–18.

Nethercutt, M. 1987. *Detroit twenty years after: A statistical profile of the Detroit area since 1967*. Detroit, MI: Center for Urban Studies, Wayne State University.

Noyelle, T., and T. M. Stanback. 1984. *Economic transformation of American cities*. New York: Conservation for Human Resources Columbia University.

Parkinson, M., B. Foley, and D. Judd. 1989. *Regenerating the cities*. Boston, MA: Scott, Foresman.

Peterson, P. 1981. *City limits*. Chicago: University of Chicago Press.

Rich, W. 1991. Detroit: From Motor City to service hub. In *Big city politics in transition*, edited by H. V. Savitch and J. C. Thomas, 64–85. Newbury Park, CA: Sage Publications.

Rosentraub, M., and D. Swindell. 1990. "Just say no"? The economic and political realities of a small city's investment in minor league baseball. Paper presented at the 20th annual meeting of the Urban Affairs Association, Charlotte, NC, April.

Sassen, S. 1988. *The mobility of capital and labor*. Cambridge: Cambridge University Press.

Savitch, H. V. 1988. *Post-industrial cities: Politics and planning in New York, Paris, and London*. Princeton, NJ: Princeton University Press.

Savitch, H. V., and J. C. Thomas, eds. 1991. *Big city politics in transition*. Newbury Park, CA: Sage Publications.

Stone, C. 1989. *Regime politics.* Lawrence: University Press of Kansas.

Stone, C., and H. Sanders, eds. 1987. *The politics of urban development.* Lawrence: University Press of Kansas.

Swanstrom, T. 1986. *The crisis of growth politics.* Philadelphia: Temple University Press.

UAL bidding goes on. 1991. *Courier-Journal,* 22 October, 1.

Van Weesop, J., and M. Wiegersma. 1991. Gentrification in the Netherlands. In *Urban housing for the better-off: Gentrification in Europe,* edited by J. Van Weesop and S. Musterd, 98–111. Utrecht, Netherlands: Bureau Stedellijke Netwerken.

Vaughn, R. 1979. *State taxation and economic development.* Washington, DC: Council of State Planning Agencies.

Vogel, R. 1990. The local regime and economic development. *Economic Development Quarterly* 4:101–112.

Walsh, A. 1978. *The public's business.* Cambridge: MIT Press.

Chapter 8

❖❖❖

THE NEW INEQUALITIES

The Divided Metropolis

Even casual observers of American cities cannot fail to notice the vast inequalities that separate rich from poor. Sprawling ghettos beset by poverty, crime, and physical decay are located in the shadows of gleaming skyscrapers and guarded condominium buildings. On downtown streets, the homeless wander amid tourists and affluent white-collar workers. The readings that make up this chapter reveal that these inequalities have historically been associated with three responses. The first is the everpresent possibility of urban violence, expressed not only as crime but also as riots and disorders. Urban riots are nothing new in urban America. The first of the major riots of the 1960s, the 1965 riot in the Watts area of Los Angeles, was followed by major rioting in the summers of 1966, 1967, and 1968. In 1967, a commission appointed by President Lyndon Johnson issued its *Report of the National Advisory Commission on Civil Disorders*. The report caused a sensation when its authors blamed the riots on extreme racial segregation and discrimination and famously noted that, "The nation is rapidly moving toward two . . . separate Americas." In the selection taken from the report, the commission recommended a complex and controversial set of policies designed to end discrimination.

In his selection, Mike Davis asserts that urban inequalities and social tensions have resulted in the militarization of urban space in Los Angeles. The construction of monumental and corporate fortresses downtown and the multiplication of defended residential enclaves are a means by which the affluent respond to urban tensions. The militarization of space has taken various forms. There has been, first, the destruction of public spaces where people can mingle without restrictions. Second, "mean streets" have become sharply segregated from the privatized spaces hidden behind facades and walls. Third, minority populations and the poor have been subjected to high-tech police enforcement and a pervasive surveillance, creating a "carceral city" that is, for marginalized populations, not unlike a prison. For those readers who think Davis's piece seems far-fetched, it may be helpful to remember that Los Angeles supplied many of the images for the futuristic movie, *Bladerunner*. If it were possible to do so, we would incorporate a selection from that movie into this book.

The selection by Dennis R. Judd describes how new walls have been enclosing four principal activities that compose urban life: residence, consumption, work, and leisure. Home and residence are becoming incorporated into gated communities in both cities and suburbs, enclosed shopping malls now compete with business streets, corporate office complexes bring affluent office workers into defended fortresses, and tourists and suburbanites who visit the central cities spend much of their time within "tourist bubbles" that are expressly designed to provide an environment removed from everyday city life. Although Judd argues that the building of public spaces for specialized activities may help bring the urban community together, when such segmentation takes the form of privatized and walled enclosures, these spaces merely segregate and divide.

William Julius Wilson proposes a specific political strategy for challenging urban inequalities. He argues that many, if not most, of the major social issues that concern poor and minority residents of central cities also compromise the quality of life for other urban residents. Low wages, unemployment, urban sprawl, health, and social insecurity are among several issues that cut across racial and social-class divisions. Consequently, Wilson suggests that race-neutral governmental programs supported by multi-racial coalitions are the only viable political strategy for helping disadvantaged urban residents, especially in the current political environment.

23

REPORT OF THE NATIONAL ADVISORY COMMISSION ON CIVIL DISORDERS

The summer of 1967 again brought racial disorders to American cities, and with them shock, fear and bewilderment to the nation.

The worst came during a two-week period in July, first in Newark and then in Detroit. Each set off a chain reaction in neighboring communities.

On July 28, 1967, the President of the United States [Lyndon Baines Johnson] established this Commission and directed us to answer three basic questions:

What happened?
Why did it happen?
What can be done to prevent it from happening again?

To respond to these questions, we have undertaken a broad range of studies and investigations. We have visited the riot cities; we have heard many witnesses; we have sought the counsel of experts across the country.

This is our basic conclusion: Our nation is moving toward two societies, one black, one white—separate and unequal.

Report of the National Advisory Commission on Civil Disorders. 1968, by Tom Wicker. Pp. 1, 9–11, and 21–29. New York: Bantam Books.

Reaction to last summer's disorders has quickened the movement and deepened the division. Discrimination and segregation have long permeated much of American life; they now threaten the future of every American.

This deepening racial division is not inevitable. The movement apart can be reversed. Choice is still possible. Our principal task is to define that choice and to press for a national resolution.

To pursue our present course will involve the continuing polarization of the American community and, ultimately, the destruction of basic democratic values.

The alternative is not blind repression or capitulation to lawlessness. It is the realization of common opportunities for all within a single society. . . .

The Basic Causes

In addressing the question "Why did it happen?" we shift our focus from the local to the national scene, from the particular events of the summer of 1967 to the factors within the society at large that created a mood of violence among many urban Negroes.

These factors are complex and interacting; they vary significantly in their effect from city to city and from year to year; and the consequences of one disorder, generating new grievances and new demands, become the causes of the next. Thus was created the "thicket of tension, conflicting evidence and extreme opinions" cited by the President.

Despite these complexities, certain fundamental matters are clear. Of these, the most fundamental is the racial attitude and behavior of white Americans toward black Americans.

Race prejudice has shaped our history decisively; it now threatens to affect our future.

White racism is essentially responsible for the explosive mixture which has been accumulating in our cities since the end of World War II. Among the ingredients of this mixture are:

- *Pervasive discrimination and segregation* in employment, education and housing, which have resulted in the continuing exclusion of great numbers of Negroes from the benefits of economic progress.
- *Black in-migration and white exodus,* which have produced the massive and growing concentrations of impoverished Negroes in our major cities, creating a growing crisis of deteriorating facilities and services and unmet human needs.
- *The black ghettos* where segregation and poverty converge on the young to destroy opportunity and enforce failure. Crime, drug addiction, dependency on welfare, and bitterness and resentment against society in general and white society in particular are the result.

At the same time, most whites and some Negroes outside the ghetto have prospered to a degree unparalleled in the history of civilization. Through television and other media, this affluence has been flaunted before the eyes of the Negro poor and the jobless ghetto youth.

Yet these facts alone cannot be said to have caused the disorders. Recently, other powerful ingredients have begun to catalyze the mixture:

- *Frustrated hopes* are the residue of the unfulfilled expectations aroused by the great judicial and legislative victories of the Civil Rights Movement and the dramatic struggle for equal rights in the South.
- *A climate that tends toward approval and encouragement of violence* as a form of protest has been created by white terrorism directed against nonviolent protest; by the open defiance of law and federal authority by state and local officials resisting desegregation; and by some protest groups engaging in civil disobedience who turn their backs on nonviolence, go beyond the constitutionally protected rights of petition and free assembly, and resort to violence to attempt to compel alteration of laws and policies with which they disagree.
- *The frustrations of powerlessness* have led some Negroes to the conviction that there is no effective alternative to violence as a means of achieving redress of grievances, and of "moving the system." These frustrations are reflected in alienation and hostility toward the institutions of law and government and the white society which controls them, and in the reach toward racial consciousness and solidarity reflected in the slogan "Black Power."
- *A new mood* has sprung up among Negroes, particularly among the young, in which self-esteem and enhanced racial pride are replacing apathy and submission to "the system."
- *The police are not merely a "spark" factor.* To some Negroes police have come to symbolize white power, white racism and white repression. And the fact is that many police do reflect and express these white attitudes. The atmosphere of hostility and cynicism is reinforced by a widespread belief among Negroes in the existence of police brutality and in a "double standard" of justice and protection—one for Negroes and one for whites.

To this point, we have attempted to identify the prime components of the "explosive mixture." . . . We seek to analyze them in the perspective of history. Their meaning, however, is clear:

In the summer of 1967, we have seen in our cities a chain reaction of racial violence. If we are heedless, none of us shall escape the consequences. . . .

The Future of the Cities

By 1985, the Negro population in central cities is expected to increase by 68 percent to approximately 20.3 million. Coupled with the continued exodus of white families to the suburbs, this growth will produce majority Negro populations in many of the nation's largest cities.

The future of these cities, and of their burgeoning Negro populations, is grim. Most new employment opportunities are being created in suburbs and outlying areas. This trend will continue unless important changes in public policy are made.

In prospect, therefore, is further deterioration of already inadequate municipal tax bases in the face of increasing demands for public services, and continuing unemployment and poverty among the urban Negro population:

- We can maintain present policies, continuing both the proportion of the nation's resources now allocated to programs for the unemployed and the disadvantaged, and the inadequate and failing effort to achieve an integrated society.
- We can adopt a policy of "enrichment" aimed at improving dramatically the quality of ghetto life while abandoning integration as a goal.
- We can pursue integration by combining ghetto "enrichment" with policies which will encourage Negro movement out of central city areas.

The first choice, continuance of present policies, has ominous consequences for our society. The share of the nation's resources now allocated to programs for the disadvantaged is insufficient to arrest the deterioration of life in central city ghettos. Under such conditions, a rising proportion of Negroes may come to see in the deprivation and segregation they experience, a justification for violent protest, or for extending support to now isolated extremists who advocate civil disruption. Large-scale and continuing violence could result, followed by white retaliation, and, ultimately, the separation of the two communities in a garrison state.

Even if violence does not occur, the consequences are unacceptable. Development of a racially integrated society, extraordinarily difficult today, will be virtually impossible when the present black central city population of 12.1 million has grown to almost 21 million.

To continue present policies is to make permanent the division of our country into two societies; one, largely Negro and poor, located in the central cities; the other, predominantly white and affluent, located in the suburbs and in outlying areas.

The second choice, ghetto enrichment coupled with abandonment of integration, is also unacceptable. It is another way of choosing a permanently divided country. Moreover, equality cannot be achieved under conditions of nearly complete separation. In a country where the economy, and particularly the resources of employment, are predominantly white, a policy of separation can only relegate Negroes to a permanently inferior economic status.

We believe that the only possible choice for America is the third—a policy which combines ghetto enrichment with programs designed to encourage integration of substantial numbers of Negroes into the society outside the ghetto.

Enrichment must be an important adjunct to integration, for no matter how ambitious or energetic the program, few Negroes now living in central cities can be quickly integrated. In the meantime, large-scale improvement in the quality of ghetto life is essential.

But this can be no more than an interim strategy. Programs must be developed which will permit substantial Negro movement out of the ghettos. The primary goal must be a single society, in which every citizen will be free to live and work according to his capabilities and desires, not his color.

Recommendations for National Action

Introduction

No American—white or black—can escape the consequences of the continuing social and economic decay of our major cities.

Only a commitment to national action on an unprecedented scale can shape a future compatible with the historic ideals of American society.

The great productivity of our economy, and a federal revenue system which is highly responsive to economic growth, can provide the resources.

The major need is to generate new will—the will to tax ourselves to the extent necessary to meet the vital needs of the nation.

We have set forth goals and proposed strategies to reach those goals. We discuss and recommend programs not to commit each of us to specific parts of such programs but to illustrate the type and dimension of action needed.

The major goal is the creation of a true union—a single society and a single American identity. Toward that goal, we propose the following objectives for national action:

- Opening up opportunities to those who are restricted by racial segregation and discrimination, and eliminating all barriers to their choice of jobs, education and housing.
- Removing the frustration of powerlessness among the disadvantaged by providing the means for them to deal with the problems that affect their own lives and by increasing the capacity of our public and private institutions to respond to these problems.
- Increasing communication across racial lines to destroy stereotypes, to halt polarization, end distrust and hostility, and create common ground for efforts toward public order and social justice.

We propose these aims to fulfill our pledge of equality and to meet the fundamental needs of a democratic and civilized society—domestic peace and social justice.

Pervasive unemployment and underemployment are the most persistent and serious grievances in minority areas. They are inextricably linked to the problem of civil disorder.

Despite growing federal expenditures for manpower development and training programs, and sustained general economic prosperity and increasing demands for skilled workers, about two million—white and nonwhite—are permanently unemployed. About ten million are underemployed, of whom 6.5 million work full time for wages below the poverty line.

The 500,000 "hard-core" unemployed in the central cities who lack a basic education and are unable to hold a steady job are made up in large part of Negro males between the ages of 18 and 25. In the riot cities which we surveyed, Negroes were three times as likely as whites to hold unskilled jobs, which are often part time, seasonal, low-paying and "dead end."

Negro males between the ages of 15 and 25 predominated among the rioters. More than 20 percent of the rioters were unemployed, and many who were employed held intermittent, low status, unskilled jobs which they regarded as below their education and ability.

The Commission recommends that the federal government:

- Undertake joint efforts with cities and states to consolidate existing manpower programs to avoid fragmentation and duplication.
- Take immediate action to create 2,000,000 new jobs over the next three years—one million in the public sector and one million in the private sector—to absorb the hard-core unemployed and materially reduce the level of underemployment for all workers, black and white. We propose 250,000 public sector and 300,000 private sector jobs in the first year.
- Provide on-the-job training by both public and private employers with reimbursement to private employers for the extra costs of training the hard-core unemployed, by contract or by tax credits.
- Provide tax and other incentives to investment in rural as well as urban poverty areas in order to offer to the rural poor an alternative to migration to urban centers.
- Take new and vigorous action to remove artificial barriers to employment and promotion, including not only racial discrimination but, in certain cases, arrest records or lack of a high school diploma. Strengthen those agencies such as the Equal Employment Opportunity Commission, charged with eliminating discriminatory practices, and provide full support for Title VI of the 1964 Civil Rights Act allowing federal grant-in-aid funds to be withheld from activities which discriminate on grounds of color or race.

The Commission commends the recent public commitment of the National Council of the Building and Construction Trades Unions, AFL-CIO, to encourage and recruit Negro membership in apprenticeship programs. This commitment should be intensified and implemented.

Education

Education in a democratic society must equip children to develop their potential and to participate fully in American life. For the community at large, the schools have discharged this responsibility well. But for many minorities, and particularly for the children of the ghetto, the schools have failed to provide the educational experience which could overcome the effects of discrimination and deprivation.

This failure is one of the persistent sources of grievance and resentment within the Negro community. The hostility of Negro parents and students toward the school system is generating increasing conflict and causing disruption within many city school districts. But the most dramatic evidence of the relationship between educational practices and civil disorders lies in the high incidence of riot participation by ghetto youth who have not completed high school.

The bleak record of public education for ghetto children is growing worse. In the critical skills—verbal and reading ability—Negro students are falling further behind whites with each year of school completed. The high unemployment and underemployment rate for Negro youth is evidence, in part, of the growing educational crisis.

We support integration as the priority education strategy; it is essential to the future of American society. In this last summer's disorders we have seen the consequences of racial isolation at all levels, and of attitudes toward race, on both sides, produced by three centuries of myth, ignorance and bias. It is indispensable that opportunities for interaction between the races be expanded.

We recognize that the growing dominance of pupils from disadvantaged minorities in city school populations will not soon be reversed. No matter how great the effort toward desegregation, many children of the ghetto will not, within their school careers, attend integrated schools.

If existing disadvantages are not to be perpetuated, we must drastically improve the quality of ghetto education. Equality of results with all-white schools must be the goal.

To implement these strategies, the Commission recommends:

- Sharply increased efforts to eliminate de facto segregation in our schools through substantial federal aid to school systems seeking to desegregate either within the system or in cooperation with neighboring school systems.
- Elimination of racial discrimination in Northern as well as Southern schools by vigorous application of Title VI of the Civil Rights Act of 1964.
- Extension of quality early childhood education to every disadvantaged child in the country.
- Efforts to improve dramatically schools serving disadvantaged children through substantial federal funding of year-round compensatory education programs, improved teaching, and expanded experimentation and research.
- Elimination of illiteracy through greater federal support for adult basic education.
- Enlarged opportunities for parent and community participation in the public schools.
- Reoriented vocational education emphasizing work-experience training and the involvement of business and industry.
- Expanded opportunities for higher education through increased federal assistance to disadvantaged students.
- Revision of state aid formulas to assure more per student aid to districts having a high proportion of disadvantaged school-age children.

The Welfare System

Our present system of public welfare is designed to save money instead of people, and tragically ends up doing neither. This system has two critical deficiencies:

First, it excludes large numbers of persons who are in great need, and who, if provided a decent level of support, might be able to become more productive and self-sufficient. No federal funds are available for millions of unemployed and underemployed men and women who are needy but neither aged, handicapped nor the parents of minor children.

Second, for those included, the system provides assistance well below the minimum necessary for a decent level of existence, and imposes restrictions that encourage continued dependency on welfare and undermine self-respect.

A welter of statutory requirements and administrative practices and regulations operate to remind recipients that they are considered untrustworthy, promiscuous and lazy. Residence requirements prevent assistance to people in need who are newly arrived in the state. Searches of recipients' homes violate privacy. Inadequate social services compound the problems.

The Commission recommends that the federal government, acting with state and local governments where necessary, reform the existing welfare system to:

- Establish, for recipients in existing welfare categories, uniform national standards of assistance at least as high as the annual "poverty level" of income, now set by the Social Security Administration at $3,335 per year for an urban family of four.
- Require that all states receiving federal welfare contributions participate in the Aid to Families with Dependent Children—Unemployed Parents program (AFDC-UP) that permits assistance to families with both father and mother in the home, thus aiding the family while it is still intact.
- Bear a substantially greater portion of all welfare costs—at least 90 percent of total payments.
- Increase incentives for seeking employment and job training, but remove restrictions recently enacted by the Congress that would compel mothers of young children to work.
- Provide more adequate social services through neighborhood centers and family-planning programs.
- Remove the freeze placed by the 1967 welfare amendments on the percentage of children in a state that can be covered by federal assistance.
- Eliminate residence requirements.

As a long-range goal, the Commission recommends that the federal government seek to develop a national system of income supplementation based strictly on need with two broad and basic purposes:

- To provide, for those who can work or who do work, any necessary supplements in such a way as to develop incentives for fuller employment;
- To provide, for those who cannot work and for mothers who decide to remain with their children, a minimum standard of decent living, and to

aid in the saving of children from the prison of poverty that has held their parents.

A broad system of supplementation would involve substantially greater federal expenditures than anything now contemplated. The cost will range widely depending on the standard of need accepted as the "basic allowance" to individuals and families, and on the rate at which additional income above this level is taxed. Yet if the deepening cycle of poverty and dependence on welfare can be broken, if the children of the poor can be given the opportunity to scale the wall that now separates them from the rest of society, the return on this investment will be great indeed.

Housing

After more than three decades of fragmented and grossly underfunded federal housing programs, nearly six million substandard housing units remain occupied in the United States.

The housing problem is particularly acute in the minority ghettos. Nearly two-thirds of all non-white families living in the central cities today live in neighborhoods marked with substandard housing and general urban blight. Two major factors are responsible.

First: Many ghetto residents simply cannot pay the rent necessary to support decent housing. In Detroit, for example, over 40 percent of the non-white occupied units in 1960 required rent of over 35 percent of the tenants' income.

Second: Discrimination prevents access to many non-slum areas, particularly the suburbs, where good housing exists. In addition, by creating a "back pressure" in the racial ghettos, it makes it possible for landlords to break up apartments for denser occupancy, and keeps prices and rents of deteriorated ghetto housing higher than they would be in a truly free market.

To date, federal programs have been able to do comparatively little to provide housing for the disadvantaged. In the 31-year history of subsidized federal housing, only about 800,000 units have been constructed, with recent production averaging about 50,000 units a year. By comparison, over a period only three years longer, FHA insurance guarantees have made possible the construction of over ten million middle- and upper-income units.

Two points are fundamental to the Commission's recommendations:

First: Federal housing programs must be given a new thrust aimed at overcoming the prevailing patterns of racial segregation. If this is not done, those programs will continue to concentrate the most impoverished and dependent segments of the population into the central-city ghettos where there is already a critical gap between the needs of the population and the public resources to deal with them.

Second: The private sector must be brought into the production and financing of low and moderate rental housing to supply the capabilities and capital necessary to meet the housing needs of the nation.

The Commission recommends that the federal government:

- Enact a comprehensive and enforceable federal open housing law to cover the sale or rental of all housing, including single family homes.
- Reorient federal housing programs to place more low and moderate income housing outside of ghetto areas.
- Bring within the reach of low and moderate income families within the next five years six million new and existing units of decent housing, beginning with 600,000 units in the next year.
- Expansion and modification of the rent supplement program to permit use of supplements for existing housing, thus greatly increasing the reach of the program.
- Expansion and modification of the below-market interest rate program to enlarge the interest subsidy to all sponsors and provide interest-free loans to nonprofit sponsors to cover pre-construction costs, and permit sale of projects to nonprofit corporations, cooperatives, or condominiums.
- Creation of an ownership supplement program similar to present rent supplements, to make home ownership possible for low-income families.
- Federal writedown of interest rates on loans to private builders constructing moderate-rent housing.
- Expansion of the public housing program, with emphasis on small units on scattered sites, and leasing and "turnkey" programs.
- Expansion of the Model Cities program.
- Expansion and reorientation of the urban renewal program to give priority to projects directly assisting low-income households to obtain adequate housing.

Conclusion

One of the first witnesses to be invited to appear before this Commission was Dr. Kenneth B. Clark, a distinguished and perceptive scholar. Referring to the reports of earlier riot commissions, he said:

> I read that report . . . of the 1919 riot in Chicago, and it is as if I were reading the report of the investigating committee on the Harlem riot of '35, the report of the investigating committee on the Harlem riot of '43, the report of the McCone Commission on the Watts riot.
>
> I must again in candor say to you members of this Commission—it is a kind of Alice in Wonderland—with the same moving picture re-shown over and over again, the same analysis, the same recommendations, and the same inaction.

These words come to our minds as we conclude this report.

We have provided an honest beginning. We have learned much. But we have uncovered no startling truths, no unique insights, no simple solutions. The destruction and the bitterness of racial disorder, the harsh polemics of black revolt and white repression have been seen and heard before in this country.

It is time now to end the destruction and the violence, not only in the streets of the ghetto but in the lives of people.

24

Mike Davis

FORTRESS LOS ANGELES: THE MILITARIZATION OF URBAN SPACE

The city bristles with malice. The carefully manicured lawns of the Westside sprout ominous little signs threatening "ARMED RESPONSE!" Wealthier neighborhoods in the canyons and hillsides cower behind walls guarded by gun-toting private police and state-of-the-art electronic surveillance systems. Downtown, a publicly subsidized "urban renaissance" has raised a forbidding corporate citadel, separated from the surrounding poor neighborhoods by battlements and moats. Some of these neighborhoods—predominately black or Latino—have in turn been sealed off by the police with barricades and checkpoints. In Hollywood, architect Frank Gehry has enshrined the siege look in a library that looks like a Foreign Legion fort. In Watts, developer Alexander Haagen has pioneered the totally secure shopping mall, a latter-day Panopticon, a prison of consumerism surrounded by iron-stake fences and motion detectors, overseen by a police substation in a central tower. Meanwhile in Downtown, a spectacular structure that tourists regularly mistake for a hotel is actually a new federal prison.

Welcome to post-liberal Los Angeles, where the defense of luxury has given birth to an arsenal of security systems and an obsession with the policing of social boundaries through architecture. This militarization of city life is increasingly visible everywhere in the built environment of the 1990s. Yet contemporary urban theory has remained oddly silent about its implications. Indeed, the pop apocalypticism of Hollywood movies and pulp science fiction has been more realistic—and politically perceptive—in representing the hardening of the urban landscape. Images of prison-like inner cities (*Escape from New York, Running Man*), high-tech police death squads (*Bladerunner*), sentient skyscrapers (*Die Hard*), and guerrilla warfare in the streets (*Colors*) are not fantasies, but merely extrapolations from the present.

Such stark dystopian visions show how much the obsession with security has supplanted hopes for urban reform and social integration. The dire predictions of Richard Nixon's 1969 National Commission on the Causes and Prevention of Violence have been tragically fulfilled in the social polarizations of the

Reagan era.[1] We do indeed now live in "fortress cities" brutally divided into "fortified cells" of affluence and "places of terror" where police battle the criminalized poor. The "Second Civil War" that began during the long hot summers of the late 1960s has been institutionalized in the very structure of urban space. The old liberal attempts at social control, which at least tried to balance repression with reform, have been superseded by open social warfare that pits the interests of the middle class against the welfare of the urban poor. In cities like Los Angeles, on the hard edge of post-modernity, architecture and the police apparatus are being merged to an unprecedented degree.

The Destruction of Public Space

The universal consequence of the crusade to secure the city is the destruction of any truly democratic urban space. The American city is being systematically turned inward. The "public" spaces of the new megastructures and supermalls have supplanted traditional streets and disciplined their spontaneity. Inside malls, office centers, and cultural complexes, public activities are sorted into strictly functional compartments under the gaze of private police forces. This architectural privatization of the physical public sphere, moreover, is complemented by a paralleled restructuring of electronic space, as heavily guarded, pay-access databases and subscription cable services expropriate the invisible *agora*. In Los Angeles, for example, the ghetto is defined not only by its paucity of parks and public amenities, but also by the fact that it is not wired into any of the key information circuits. In contrast, the affluent Westside is plugged—often at public expense—into dense networks of educational and cultural media.

In either guise, architectural or electronic, this polarization marks the decline of urban liberalism, and with it the end of what might be called the Olmstedian vision of public space in America. Frederick Law Olmsted, the father of Central Park, conceived public landscapes and parks as social safety-valves, *mixing* classes and ethnicities in common (bourgeois) recreations and pleasures: "No one who has closely observed the conduct of the people who visit [Central] Park," he wrote, "can doubt that it exercises a distinctly harmonizing and refining influence upon the most unfortunate and most lawless classes of the city—an influence favorable to courtesy, self-control, and temperance."[2]

This reformist ideal of public space as the emollient of class struggle is now as obsolete as Rooseveltian nostrums of full employment and an Economic Bill of Rights. As for the mixing of classes, contemporary urban America is more like Victorian England than the New York of Walt Whitman or Fiorello La Guardia. In Los Angeles—once a paradise of free beaches, luxurious parks, and "cruising strips"—genuinely democratic space is virtually extinct. The pleasure domes of the elite Westside rely upon the social imprisonment of a third-world service proletariat in increasingly repressive ghettos and barrios. In a city of several million aspiring immigrants (where Spanish-surname children are now almost two-thirds of the school-age population), public amenities are shrinking radically, libraries and playgrounds are closing, parks are falling derelict, and streets are growing ever more desolate and dangerous.

Here, as in other American cities, municipal policy has taken its lead from the security offensive and the middle-class demand for increased spatial and social insulation. Taxes previously targeted for traditional public spaces and recreational facilities have been redirected to support corporate redevelopment projects. A pliant city government—in the case of Los Angeles, one ironically professing to represent a liberal biracial coalition—has collaborated in privatizing public space and subsidizing new exclusive enclaves (benignly called "urban villages"). The celebratory language used to describe contemporary Los Angeles—"urban renaissance," "city of the future," and so on—is only a triumphal gloss laid over the brutalization of its inner-city neighborhoods and the stark divisions of class and race represented in its built environment. Urban form obediently follows repressive function. Los Angeles, as always in the vanguard, offers an especially disturbing guide to the emerging liaisons between urban architecture and the police state.

Forbidden City

Los Angeles's first spatial militarist was the legendary General Harrison Gray Otis, proprietor of the *Times* and implacable foe of organized labor. In the 1890s, after locking out his union printers and announcing a crusade for "industrial freedom," Otis retreated into a new *Times* building designed as a fortress with grim turrets and battlements crowned by a bellicose bronze eagle. To emphasize his truculence, he later had a small, functional cannon installed on the hood of his Packard touring car. Not surprisingly, this display of aggression produced a response in kind. On October 1, 1910, the heavily fortified *Times* headquarters—the command-post of the open shop on the West Coast—was destroyed in a catastrophic explosion, blamed on union saboteurs.

Eighty years later, the martial spirit of General Otis pervades the design of Los Angeles's new Downtown, whose skyscrapers march from Bunker Hill down the Figueroa corridor. Two billion dollars of public tax subsidies have enticed big banks and corporate headquarters back to a central city they almost abandoned in the 1960s. Into a waiting grid, cleared of tenement housing by the city's powerful and largely unaccountable redevelopment agency, local developers and offshore investors (increasingly Japanese) have planted a series of block-square complexes: Crocker Center, the Bonaventure Hotel and Shopping Mall, the World Trade Center, California Plaza, Arco Center, and so on. With an increasingly dense and self-contained circulation system linking these superblocks, the new financial district is best conceived as a single, self-referential hyperstructure, a Miesian skyscape of fantastic proportions.

Like similar megalomaniacal complexes tethered to fragmented and desolate downtowns—such as the Renaissance Center in Detroit and the Peachtree and Omni centers in Atlanta—Bunker Hill and the Figueroa corridor have provoked a storm of objections to their abuse of scale and composition, their denigration of street life, and their confiscation of the vital energy of the center, now sequestered within their subterranean concourses or privatized plazas. Sam Hall Kaplan, the former design critic of the *Times*, has vociferously denounced the antistreet bias of redevelopment; in his view, the superimposition of "hermetically sealed fortresses" and random "pieces of suburbia" onto Downtown has "killed the street" and "dammed the rivers of life."[3]

Yet Kaplan's vigorous defense of pedestrian democracy remains grounded in liberal complaints about "bland design" and "elitist planning practices." Like most architectural critics, he rails against the oversights of urban design without conceding a dimension of foresight, and even of deliberate repressive intent. For when Downtown's new "Gold Coast" is seen in relation to other social landscapes in the central city, the "fortress effect" emerges, not as an inadvertent failure of design, but as an explicit—and, in its own terms, successful—socio-spatial strategy.

The goals of this strategy may be summarized as a double repression: to obliterate all connection with Downtown's past and to prevent any dynamic association with the non-Anglo urbanism of its future. Los Angeles is unusual among major urban centers in having preserved, however negligently, most of its Beaux Arts commercial core. Yet the city chose to transplant—at immense public cost—the entire corporate and financial district from around Broadway and Spring Street to Bunker Hill, a half-dozen blocks further west.

The underlying logic of this operation is revealing. In other cities, developers have tried to harmonize the new cityscape and the old, exploiting the latter's historic buildings to create gentrified zones (Faneuil Market, Ghirardelli Square, and so on) as supports to middle-class residential colonization. But Downtown Los Angeles's redevelopers considered property values in the old Broadway core as irreversibly eroded by the area's status as the hub of public transportation primarily used by black and Mexican poor. In the wake of the 1965 Watts Rebellion, whose fires burned to within a few blocks of the old Downtown, resegregated spatial security became the paramount concern. The 1960–64 "Centropolis" masterplan, which had envisioned the renewal of the old core, was unceremoniously scrapped. Meanwhile the Los Angeles Police Department (LAPD) abetted the flight of business from the Broadway–Spring Street area to the fortified redoubts of Bunker Hill by spreading scare literature about the "immigrant gang invasion" by black teenagers.[4]

To emphasize the "security" of the new Downtown, virtually all the traditional pedestrian links to the old center, including the famous Angels' Flight funicular railroad, were removed. The Harbor Freeway and the regraded palisades of Bunker Hill further cut off the new financial core from the poor immigrant neighborhoods that surround it on every side. Along the base of California Plaza (home of the Museum of Contemporary Art), Hill Street functions as the stark boundary separating the luxury of Bunker Hill from the chaotic life of Broadway, now the primary shopping and entertainment street for Latino immigrants. Because gentrifiers now have their eye on the northern end of the Broadway corridor (redubbed Bunker Hill East), the redevelopment agency promises to restore pedestrian access to the Hill in the 1990s. This, of course, only dramatizes the current bias against any spatial interaction between old and new, poor and rich—except in the framework of gentrification. Although a few white-collar types sometimes venture into the Grand Central Market—a popular emporium of tropical produce and fresh foods—Latino shoppers or Saturday *flaneurs* never ascend to the upscale precincts above Hill Street. The occasional appearance of a destitute street nomad in Broadway Plaza or in front of the Museum of Contemporary Art sets off a quiet panic, as video cameras turn on their mounts and security guards adjust their belts.

Photographs of the old Downtown in its 1940s prime show crowds of Anglo, black, and Mexican shoppers of all ages and classes. The contemporary Downtown "renaissance" renders such heterogeneity virtually impossible. It is intended not just to "kill the street" as Kaplan feared, but to "kill the crowd," to eliminate that democratic mixture that Olmsted believed was America's antidote to European class polarization. The new Downtown is designed to ensure a seamless continuum of middle-class work, consumption, and recreation, insulated from the city's "unsavory" streets. Ramparts and battlements, reflective glass and elevated pedways, are tropes in an architectural language warning off the underclass Other. Although architectural critics are usually blind to this militarized syntax, urban pariah groups—whether young black men, poor Latino immigrants, or elderly homeless white females, read the signs immediately.

Extreme though it may seem, Bunker Hill is only one local expression of the national movement toward "defensible" urban centers. Cities of all sizes are rushing to apply and profit from a formula that links together clustered development, social homogeneity, and a perception of security. As an article in *Urban Land* magazine on "how to overcome fear of crime in downtowns" advised:

> A downtown can be designed and developed to make visitors feel that it—or a significant portion of it—is attractive and the type of place that "respectable people" like themselves tend to frequent. . . . A core downtown area that is compact, densely developed and multifunctional, [with] offices and housing for middle- and upper-income residents . . . can assure a high percentage of "respectable," law-abiding pedestrians. Such an attractive redeveloped core area would also be large enough to affect the downtown's overall image.[5]

Mean Streets

This strategic armoring of the city against the poor is especially obvious at street level. In his famous study of the "social life of small urban spaces," William Whyte points out that the quality of any urban environment can be measured, first of all, by whether there are convenient, comfortable places for pedestrians to sit. This maxim has been warmly taken to heart by designers of the high corporate precincts of Bunker Hill and its adjacent "urban villages." As part of the city's policy of subsidizing the white-collar residential colonization of Downtown, tens of millions of dollars of tax revenue have been invested in the creation of attractive "soft" environments in favored areas. Planners envision a succession of opulent piazzas, fountains, public art, exotic shrubbery, and comfortable street furniture along a ten-block pedestrian corridor from Bunker Hill to South Park. Brochures sell Downtown's "livability" with idyllic representations of office workers and affluent tourists sipping cappuccino and listening to free jazz concerts in the terraced gardens of California Plaza and Grand Hope Park.

In stark contrast, a few blocks away, the city is engaged in a relentless struggle to make the streets as unlivable as possible for the homeless and poor. The persistence of thousands of street people on the fringes of Bunker Hill and the Civic Center tarnishes the image of designer living Downtown and betrays the laboriously constructed illusion of an urban "renaissance." City hall has retaliated with its own version of low-intensity warfare.

Although city leaders periodically propose schemes for removing indigents *en masse*—deporting them to a poor farm on the edge of the desert, confining them in camps on the mountains, or interning them on derelict ferries in the harbor—such "final solutions" have been blocked by council members' fears of the displacement of the homeless into their districts. Instead the city, self-consciously adopting the idiom of cold war, has promoted the "containment" (the official term) of the homeless in Skid Row, along Fifth Street, systematically transforming the neighborhood into an outdoor poorhouse. But this containment strategy breeds its own vicious cycle of contradiction. By condensing the mass of the desperate and helpless together in such a small space, and denying adequate housing, official policy has transformed Skid Row into probably the most dangerous ten square blocks in the world. Every night on Skid Row is Friday the 13th, and, unsurprisingly, many of the homeless seek to escape the area during the night at all costs, searching safer niches in other parts of Downtown. The city in turn tightens the noose with increased police harassment and ingenious design deterrents.

One of the simplest but most mean-spirited of these deterrents is the Rapid Transit District's new barrel-shaped bus bench, which offers a minimal surface for uncomfortable sitting while making sleeping impossible. Such "bumproof" benches are being widely introduced on the periphery of Skid Row. Another invention is the aggressive deployment of outdoor sprinklers. Several years ago the city opened a Skid Row Park; to ensure that the park could not be used for overnight camping, overhead sprinklers were programmed to drench unsuspecting sleepers at random times during the night. The system was immediately copied by local merchants to drive the homeless away from (public) storefront sidewalks. Meanwhile Downtown restaurants and markets have built baroque enclosures to protect their refuse from the homeless. Although no one in Los Angeles has yet proposed adding cyanide to the garbage, as was suggested in Phoenix a few years back, one popular seafood restaurant has spent $12,000 to build the ultimate bag-lady-proof trash cage: three-quarter-inch steel rods with alloy locks and vicious out-turned spikes to safeguard moldering fishheads and stale french fries.

Public toilets, however, have become the real frontline of the city's war on the homeless. Los Angeles, as a matter of deliberate policy, has fewer public lavatories than any other major North American city. On the advice of the Los Angeles police, who now sit on the "design board" of at least one major Downtown project, the redevelopment agency bulldozed the few remaining public toilets on Skid Row. Agency planners then considered whether to include a "free-standing public toilet" in their design for the upscale South Park residential development; agency chairman Jim Wood later admitted that the decision not to build the toilet was a "policy decision and not a design decision." The agency preferred the alternative of "quasi-public restrooms"—toilets in restaurants, art galleries, and office buildings—which can be made available selectively to tourists and white-collar workers while being denied to vagrants and other unsuitables. The same logic has inspired the city's transportation planners to exclude toilets from their designs for Los Angeles's new subway system.[6]

Bereft of toilets, the Downtown badlands east of Hill Street also lack outside water sources for drinking or washing. A common and troubling sight these days is the homeless men—many of them young refugees from El Salvador—washing, swimming, even drinking from the sewer effluent that flows down the concrete channel of the Los Angeles River on the eastern edge of Downtown. The city's public health department has made no effort to post warning signs in Spanish or to mobilize alternative clean-water sources.

In those areas where Downtown professionals must cross paths with the homeless or the working poor—such as the zone of gentrification along Broadway just south of the Civic Center—extraordinary precautions have been taken to ensure the physical separation of the different classes. The redevelopment agency, for example, again brought in the police to help design "twenty-four-hour, state-of-the-art security" for the two new parking structures that serve the Los Angeles Times headquarters and the Ronald Reagan State Office Building. In contrast to the mean streets outside, both parking structures incorporate beautifully landscaped microparks, and one even boasts a food court, picnic area, and historical exhibit. Both structures are intended to function as "confidence-building" circulation systems that allow white-collar workers to walk from car to office, or from car to boutique, with minimum exposure to the public street. The Broadway–Spring Center, in particular, which links the two local hubs of gentrification (the Reagan Building and the proposed Grand Central Square) has been warmly praised by architectural critics for adding greenery and art to parking. It also adds a considerable dose of menace—armed guards, locked gates, and ubiquitous security cameras—to scare away the homeless and the poor.

The cold war on the streets of Downtown is ever escalating. The police, lobbied by Downtown merchants and developers, have broken up every attempt by the homeless and their allies to create safe havens or self-governed encampments. "Justiceville," founded by homeless activist Ted Hayes, was roughly dispersed; when its inhabitants attempted to find refuge at Venice Beach, they were arrested at the behest of the local council member (a renowned environmentalist) and sent back to Skid Row. The city's own brief experiment with legalized camping—a grudging response to a series of deaths from exposure during the cold winter of 1987—was abruptly terminated after only four months to make way for the construction of a transit maintenance yard. Current policy seems to involve perverse play upon the famous irony about the equal rights of the rich and poor to sleep in the rough. As the former head of the city planning commission explained, in the City of the Angels it is not against the law to sleep in the street per se—"only to erect any sort of protective shelter."[7] To enforce this proscription against "cardboard condos," the police periodically sweep the Nickel, tearing down shelters, confiscating possessions, and arresting resisters. Such cynical repression has turned the majority of the homeless into bedouins. They are visible all over Downtown, pushing their few pathetic possessions in stolen shopping carts, always fugitive, always in motion, pressed between the official policy of containment and the inhumanity of Downtown streets.

Sequestering the Poor

An insidious spatial logic also regulates the lives of Los Angeles's working poor. Just across the moat of the Harbor Freeway, west of Bunker Hill, lies the MacArthur Park district—once upon a time the city's wealthiest neighborhood. Although frequently characterized as a no-man's-land awaiting resurrection by developers, the district is, in fact, home to the largest Central American community in the United States. In the congested streets bordering the park, a hundred thousand Salvadorans and Guatemalans, including a large community of Mayan-speakers, crowd into tenements and boarding houses barely adequate for a fourth as many people. Every morning at 6 A.M. this Latino Bantustan dispatches armies of sewing *operadoras*, dishwashers, and janitors to turn the wheels of the Downtown economy. But because MacArthur Park is midway between Downtown and the famous Miracle Mile, it too will soon fall to redevelopment's bulldozers.

Hungry to exploit the lower land prices in the district, a powerful coterie of developers, represented by a famous ex-councilman and the former president of the planning commissions, has won official approval for their vision of "Central City West": literally, a second Downtown comprising 25 million square feet of new office and retail space. Although local politicians have insisted upon a significant quota of low-income replacement housing, such a palliative will hardly compensate for the large-scale population displacement sure to follow the construction of the new skyscrapers and yuppified "urban villages." In the meantime, Korean capital, seeking *lebensraum* for Los Angeles's burgeoning Koreatown, is also pushing into the MacArthur Park area, uprooting tenements to construct heavily fortified condominiums and office complexes. Other Asian and European speculators are counting on the new Metrorail stations, across from the park, to become a magnet for new investment in the district.

The recent intrusion of so many powerful interests into the area has put increasing pressure upon the police to "take back the streets" from what is usually represented as an occupying army of drug-dealers, illegal immigrants, and homicidal homeboys. Thus in the summer of 1990 the LAPD announced a massive operation to "retake crime-plagued MacArthur Park" and surrounding neighborhoods "street by street, alley by alley." While the area is undoubtedly a major drug market, principally for drive-in Anglo commuters, the police have focused not only on addict-dealers and gang members, but also on the industrious sidewalk vendors who have made the circumference of the park an exuberant swap meet. Thus Mayan women selling such local staples as tropical fruit, baby clothes, and roach spray have been rounded up in the same sweeps as alleged "narcoterrorists."[8] (Similar dragnets in other Southern California communities have focused on Latino day-laborers congregated at streetcorner "slave markets.")

By criminalizing every attempt by the poor—whether the Skid Row homeless or MacArthur Park vendors—to use public space for survival purposes, law-enforcement agencies have abolished the last informal safety-net separating misery from catastrophe. (Few third-world cities are so pitiless.) At the same time, the police, encouraged by local businessmen and property owners, are taking the first, tentative steps toward criminalizing entire inner-city communities. The "war" on drugs and gangs again has been the pretext for the LAPD's novel, and disturbing, experiments with community blockades. A large section of the Pico-Union neighborhood, just south of MacArthur Park, has been quarantined since the summer of 1989; "Narcotics Enforcement Area" barriers restrict entry to residents "on legitimate business only." Inspired by the positive response of older residents and local politicians, the police have subsequently franchised "Operation Cul-de-Sac" to other low-income Latino and black neighborhoods.

Thus in November 1989 (as the Berlin Wall was being demolished), the Devonshire Division of the LAPD closed off a "drug-ridden" twelve-block section of the northern San Fernando Valley. To control circulation within this largely Latino neighborhood, the police convinced apartment owners to finance the construction of a permanent guard station. Twenty miles to the south, a square mile of the mixed black and Latino Central-Avalon community has also been converted into Narcotic Enforcement turf with concrete roadblocks. Given the popularity of these quarantines—save amongst the ghetto youth against whom they are directed—it is possible that a majority of the inner city may eventually be partitioned into police-regulated "no-go" areas.

The official rhetoric of the contemporary war against the urban underclasses resounds with comparisons to the War in Vietnam a generation ago. The LAPD's community blockades evoke the infamous policy of quarantining suspect populations in "strategic hamlets." But an even more ominous emulation is the reconstruction of Los Angeles's public housing projects as "defensible spaces." Deep in the Mekong of Delta of the Watts-Willowbrook ghetto, for example, the Imperial Courts Housing Project has been fortified with chain-link fencing, RESTRICTED ENTRY signs, obligatory identity passes—and a substation of the LAPD. Visitors are stopped and frisked, the police routinely order residents back into their apartments at night, and domestic life is subjected to constant police scrutiny. For public-housing tenants and inhabitants of narcotic-enforcement zones, the loss of freedom is the price of "security."

Security by Design

If the contemporary search for bourgeois security can be read in the design of bus benches, megastructures, and housing projects, it is also visible at the level of *auteur*. No recent architect has so ingeniously elaborated or so brazenly embraced the urban-security function as Los Angeles's Pritzker Prize laureate Frank Gehry. His strongest suit is his straightforward exploitations of rough urban environments, and the explicit incorporation of their harshest edges and detritus as powerful representational elements. Affectionately described by colleagues as an "old socialist" or "street-fighter with a heart," Gehry makes little pretense at architectural reformism or "design for democracy." He boasts instead of trying "to make the best with the reality of things."[9] With sometimes chilling effect, his work clarifies the underlying relations of repression, surveillance, and exclusion that characterize the fragmented landscape of Los Angeles.

An early example of Gehry's new urban realism was his 1964 solution of the problem of how to insert luxurious spaces—and high property values—into decaying neighborhoods. His Danziger Studio in Hollywood is the pioneer instance of what has become an entire species of Los Angeles "stealth houses," which dissimulate their opulence behind proletarian or gangster facades. The street frontage of the Danziger is simply a massive gray wall, treated with a rough finish to ensure that it would collect dust from the passing traffic and weather into a simulacrum of the nearby porn studios and garages. Gehry was explicit in his search for a design that was "introverted and fortresslike," with the silent aura of a "dumb box."[10]

Indeed, "dumb boxes" and screen walls form an entire cycle of his work, ranging from the American School of Dance (1968) to his Gemini GEL (1979)—both in Hollywood. His most seminal design, however, was his walled town center for Cochiti Lake, New Mexico (1973): here ice-blue ramparts of awesome severity enclose an entire community, a plan replicated on a smaller scale in his 1976 Jung Institute in Los Angeles. In both of these cases architectural drama is generated by the contrast between the fortified exteriors, set against "unappealing neighborhoods" (Gehry) or deserts, and the opulent interiors, opened to the sky by clerestories and lightwells. Gehry's walled-in compounds and cities, in other words, offer powerful metaphors for the retreat from the street and the introversion of space that has characterized the design backlash to the urban insurrections of the 1960s.

Gehry took up the same problem in 1984 in his design for the Loyala Law School in MacArthur Park district. The inner-city location of the campus confronted Gehry with an explicit choice: to create a genuine public space, extending into the community, or to choose the security of a defensible enclave, as in his previous work. Gehry's choice, as one critic explained, was a neoconservative design that was "open, but not *too* open. The South Instructional Hall and the chapel show solid backs to Olympic Boulevard, and with the anonymous street sides of the Burns Building, form a gateway that is neither forbidding nor overly welcoming. It is simply there, like everything else in the neighborhood."[11] This description considerably understates the forbidding qualities of the campus's formidable steel-stake fencing, concrete-block ziggurat, and stark frontage walls.

But if the Danziger Studio camouflages itself, and the Cochiti Lake and Loyala designs are dumb boxes with an attitude, Gehry's baroquely fortified Goldwyn Branch Library in Hollywood (1984) positively taunts potential trespassers "to make my day." This is probably the most menacing library ever built, a bizarre hybrid of a drydocked dreadnought and a cavalry fort. With its fifteen-foot-high security walls of stuccoed concrete block, it's anti-graffiti barricades covered in ceramic tile, its sunken entrance protected by ten-foot-high steel stakes, and its stylized sentry boxes perched precariously on each side, the Goldwyn Library (influenced by Gehry's 1980 high-security design for the U.S. Chancellery in Damascus) projects nothing less than sheer aggression.

Some of the Gehry's admirers have praised the Library as "generous and inviting,"[12] "the old-fashioned kind of library," and so on. But they miss the point. The previous Hollywood library had been destroyed by arson, and the Samuel Goldwyn Foundation, which endows this collection of filmland memorabilia, was understandably preoccupied by physical security. Gehry's commission was to design a structure that was inherently vandalproof. His innovation, of course, was to reject the low-profile high-tech security systems that most architects subtly integrate into their blueprints, and to choose instead a high-profile, low-tech approach that foregrounds the security function as the central motif of the design. There is no dissimulation of function by form here—quite the opposite. How playful or witty you find the resulting effect depends on your existential position. The Goldwyn Library by its very structure conjures up the demonic Other—arsonist, graffitist, invader—and casts the shadow of its own arrogant paranoia onto the surrounding seedy, though not particularly hostile streets.

These streets are a battleground, but not of the expected kind. Several years ago the *Los Angeles Times* broke the sordid story of how the entertainment conglomerates and a few large landowners had managed to capture control of the local redevelopment process. Their plan, still the focus of controversy, is to use eminent domain and higher taxes to clear the poor (increasingly refugees from Central American) from the streets of Hollywood and reap the huge windfalls from "upgrading" the area into a glitzy theme-park for international tourism.[13] In the context of this strategy, the Goldwyn Library—like Gehry's earlier walled compounds—is a kind of architectural fire-base, a beachhead for gentrification. Its soaring, light-filled interiors surrounded by barricades speak volumes about how public architecture in America is literally turning its back on the city for security and profit.

The Panopticon Mall

In other parts of the inner city, however, similar "fortress" designs are being used to recapture the poor as consumers. If the Goldwyn Library is a "shining example of the possibilities of public- and private-sector cooperation," then developer Alexander Haagen's ghetto malls are truly stellar instances. Haagen, who began his career distributing jukeboxes to the honkytonks of Wilmington, made his first fortune selling corner lots to oil companies for gas stations—sites since recycled as minimalls. He now controls the largest retail-development empire in Southern California, comprising more than forty shopping centers, and has become nationally acclaimed as the impresario of South-Central Los Angeles's "retail revival."

Haagen was perhaps the first major developer in the nation to grasp the latent profit potential of abandoned inner-city retail markets. After the Watts Rebellion in 1965, the handful of large discount stores in the South-Central region took flight, and small businesses were closed down by the banks' discriminatory redlining practices. As a result, 750,000 black and Latino shoppers were forced to commute to distant regional malls or adjacent white neighborhoods even for their everyday groceries. Haagen reasoned that a retail developer prepared to return to the inner city could monopolize very high sales volumes. He also was well aware of the accumulating anger of the black community against decades of benign neglect by City Hall and the redevelopment agency; while the agency had moved swiftly to assemble land for billionaire developers Downtown, it floundered in Watts for years, unable to attract a single supermarket to anchor a proposed neighborhood shopping center. Haagen knew that the Bradley regime, in hot water with its South-Central constituents, would handsomely reward any private-sector initiative that could solve the anchor-tenant problem. His ingenious solution was a comprehensive "*security-oriented* design and management strategy."[14]

Haagen made his first move in 1979, taking title to an old Sears site in the heart of the ghetto. Impressed by his success there, the redevelopment agency transferred to him the completion of its long-delayed Martin Luther King, Jr., Center in Watts. A year later Haagen Development won the bid for the $120 million renovation of Crenshaw Plaza (a pioneer 1940s mall on the western fringe of the ghetto), as well as a contract from Los Angeles County to build another shopping complex in the Willowbrook area south of Watts. In each case Haagen's guarantee of total physical security was the key to persuading retailers and their insurers to take up leases. The essence of security, in turn, was a site plan clearly derived from Jeremy Bentham's proposed Panopticon—the eighteenth-century model prison to be constructed radially so that a single guard in a central tower could observe every prisoner at all times.

The King Shopping Center in Watts provides the best prototype of this commercial Brave New World for the inner city:

> The King Center site is surrounded by an eight-foot-high, wrought-iron fence comparable to security fences found at the perimeters of private estates and exclusive residential communities. Video cameras equipped with motion detectors are positioned near entrances and throughout the shopping center. The center, including parking lots, can be bathed in bright [lights] at the flip of a switch.
>
> There are six entrances to the center: three entry points for autos, two service gates, and one pedestrian walkway. . . . The service area . . . is enclosed with a six-foot-high concrete-block wall; both service gates remain closed and are under closed-circuit video surveillance, equipped for two-way voice communications, and operated by remote control from a security "observatory." Infrared beams at

the bases of light fixtures detect intruders who might circumvent video cameras by climbing over the wall.[15]

The observatory functions as both eye and brain of this complex security system. It contains the headquarters of the shopping-center manager, a substation of the LAPD, and a dispatch operator who both monitors the video and audio systems and maintains communication "with other secure shopping centers tied into the system, and with the police and fire departments." At any time of day or night, there are at least four security guards on duty—one at the observatory, and three on patrol. They are trained and backed up by the regular LAPD officers operating from the observatory substation.[16]

The King Center and its three siblings (all variations on the Panopticon theme), as expected, have been bonanzas, averaging annual sales of more than $350 per leasable square foot, as compared to about $200 for their suburban equivalents.[17] Moreover, Haagen has reaped the multiple windfalls of tax breaks, federal and city grants, massive free publicity, subsidized tenants, and sixty- to ninety-year ground leases. No wonder he has been able to boast, "We've proved that the only color that counts in business is green. There are huge opportunities and huge profits to be made in these depressed inner-city areas of America that have been abandoned."[18]

High-Rent Security

The security-driven logic of contemporary urban design finds its major "grassroots" expression in the frenetic efforts of Los Angeles's affluent neighborhoods to physically insulate their real-estate values and life-styles. Luxury developments outside the city limits have often been able to incorporate as "fortress cities," complete with security walls, guarded entries, private police, and even private roadways. It is simply impossible for ordinary citizens to enter the "cities" of Hidden Hills (western San Fernando Valley), Bradbury (San Gabriel Valley), Rancho Mirage (low desert), or Palos Verdes Estates (Palos Verdes Peninsula) without an invitation from a resident. Indeed Bradbury, with nine hundred inhabitants and ten miles of gated private roads, is so obsessed with security that its three city officials will not return phone calls from the press, since "each time an article appears, . . . it draws attention to the city, and the number of burglaries increases."[19]

Recently, Hidden Hills, a Norman Rockwell painting behind walls, has been bitterly divided over a Superior Court order to build forty-eight units of seniors' housing on vacant land outside the city gates. At meetings of the city's powerful homeowners' association (whose members include Frankie Avalon, Neil Diamond, and Bob Eubanks) opponents of compliance have argued vehemently that the old folks "will attract gangs and dope."[20]

Meanwhile, older high-income cities like Beverly Hills and San Marino have restricted access to their public facilities, using byzantine layers of regulations to build invisible walls. San Marino, which may be the richest and most Republican city in the country (85 percent), now closes its parks on weekends to exclude Latino and Asian families from adjacent communities. An alternative plan, now under discussion, would reopen the parks on Saturdays, but only to those with proof of residence or the means to pay daunting use fees. Other upscale areas (including thirty-seven Los Angeles neighborhoods) have minted similar residential privileges by restricting parking to local homeowners. Predictably such preferential parking ordinances proliferate mainly neighborhoods with three-car garages.

Affluent areas of the City of Los Angeles have long envied the autonomy of fortress enclaves like Hidden Hills and Palos Verdes. Now, with the cooperation of a pliant city council, they are winning permission to literally wall themselves off from the rest of the city. Since its construction in the late 1940s, Park La Brea has been Los Angeles's most successful experiment in mixed-income, high-rise living. Its urbane population of singles, young families, and retirees has always given a touch of Manhattan to the La Brea Tarpits area of Wilshire Boulevard. But its new owners, Forest City Enterprises, hope to "upgrade" the project image by sealing it off from the surrounding neighborhoods with security fencing and NO TRESPASSING signs. As a spokesperson for the owners blandly observed, "It's a trend in general to have enclosed communities."[21]

A few miles north of Park La Brea, above the Hollywood Bowl, the wealthy residents of Whitley Heights have won the unprecedented privilege of withdrawing their streets from public use. Eight high-tech gates will restrict access to residents and approved visitors using special electronic codes. An immediate byproduct of "gatehood" has been a dramatic 20 percent rise in local property values—a windfall that other residential districts are eager to emulate. Thus in the once wide-open tractlands of the San Fernando Valley—where a decade ago there were virtually no walled-off communities—homeowners are rushing to fortify their equity with walls and gates. Brian Weinstock, a leading local contractor, proudly boasts of the Valley's more than one hundred newly gated neighborhoods, and reports insatiable demand for additional security. "The first question out of [every buyer's] mouth is whether there is a gated community. The demand is there on a three-to-one basis."[22]

Meanwhile the very rich are yearning for unassailable high-tech castles. Where gates and walls will not suffice, the house itself is redesigned to incorporate state-of-the-art security. An important if unacknowledged motive for the current "mansionizing" mania on the city's Westside—the tearing down of $3 million houses to build $30 million supermansions—is the search for "absolute security." To achieve it, residential architects are borrowing design secrets from overseas embassies and military command posts. For example, one of the features currently in high demand is the "terrorist-proof security room" concealed in the houseplan and reached by hidden sliding panels or secret doors. Merv Griffin and his fellow mansionizers are hardening their palaces like banks or missile silos.

But technology is not enough. Contemporary residential security in Los Angeles—whether in the fortified mansion or the average suburban bunker—depends upon the extensive deployment of private security services. Through their local homeowners' associations, virtually every affluent neighborhood from the Palisades to Silver Lake contracts its own private policing; hence the thousands of lawns displaying the little ARMED RESPONSE warnings. A recent

Times want-ads section contained over a hundred ads for guards and patrol-men, mostly from firms specializing in residential protection. Within greater Los Angeles, the security-services industry is a Cinderella sector that has tripled its sales and workforce—from 24,000 to 75,000 guards—over the last decade. "It is easier to become an armed guard than it is to become a barber, hairdresser, or journeyman carpenter," reports Linda Williams in the *Times*. Al-though the patrolmen are mostly minority males earning close to minimum wage, their employers are often multinational conglomerates offering a daz-zling range of security products and services. As Michael Kaye, president of burgeoning Westec, a subsidiary of Japan's Secom, Ltd., explains: "We're not a security-guard company. We sell a *concept* of security."[23]

What homeowners' associations contract from Westec—or its principal rival, Bel-Air Patrol (part of Borg-Warner's family of security companies, which in-clude Burns and Pinkerton)—is a complete "systems package": alarm hardware, monitoring, watch patrols, personal escorts, and, of course, "armed response" as necessary. Although law-enforcement experts debate the efficiency of such sys-tems in foiling professional criminals, there is no doubt that they are brilliantly successful in deterring unintentional trespassers and innocent pedestrians. Any-one who has tried to take a stroll at dusk through a neighborhood patrolled by armed security guards and signposted with death threats quickly realizes how merely notional, if not utterly obsolete, is the old idea of "freedom of the city."

The LAPD as Space Police

This comprehensive urban security mobilization depends not only on the incor-poration of the police function into the built environment, but also on the grow-ing technopower of the police themselves. Undoubtedly the LAPD's pioneering substitution of technology for manpower was in part a necessary adaptation to the city's dispersed form; but it also expresses the department's particular rela-tionship to the community. Especially in its self-representation, the LAPD ap-pears as the progressive antithesis to the traditional big city police department with its patronage armies of patrolmen grafting off their beats. The LAPD, as reformed in the early 1950s by the legendary Chief Parker (who admired, above all, the gung-ho elitism of the Marines), would be incorruptible because unap-proachable, a "few good men" doing battle with a fundamentally evil city. *Dragnet's* Sergeant Friday precisely captured the Parkerized LAPD's prudish alienation from a citizenry composed of fools, degenerates, and psychopaths.

Technology helped foster this paranoid esprit de corps, and virtually estab-lished a new definition of policing, where technologized surveillance and re-sponse supplanted the traditional patrolman's intimate folk knowledge of a spe-cific community. Thus back in the 1920s the LAPD had pioneered the replacement of the flatfoot or mounted officer with the radio patrol car—the be-ginning of dispersed, mechanized policing. Under Parker, ever alert to spinoffs from military technology, the LAPD introduced the first police helicopters for systematic aerial surveillance. After the Watts Rebellion of 1965, this airborne effort became the cornerstone of a policing strategy for the entire inner city. As part of its Astro program LAPD helicopters maintain an average nineteen-hour-per-day vigil over "high-crime areas." To facilitate ground-air coordination, thousands of residential rooftops have been painted with large, identifying street numbers, transforming the aerial view of the city into a huge police grid.

The fifty-pilot LAPD airforce was recently updated with French Aerospatiale helicopters equipped with futuristic surveillance technology. Their forward-looking infrared cameras are extraordinary night eyes that can easily form heat images from a single burning cigarette a mile away, while their 30-million-candle-power spotlights, appropriately called "Night Suns," can turn night into day. Meanwhile the LAPD retains another fleet of Bell Jet Rangers capable of delivering SWAT units anywhere in the region. Their training, which sometimes includes practice assaults on Downtown high-rises, anticipates some of the spookier Hollywood images—as in *Blue Thunder* or *Running Man*—of airborne police terror.

But the decisive element in the LAPD's metamorphosis into a Technopolice has been its long and successful liaison with the military aerospace industry.[24] Just in time for the opening of the 1984 Los Angeles Olympics, the department acquired ECCCS (Emergency Command Control Communications Systems), the most powerful police communications system in the world. First conceptualized by Hughes Aerospace between 1969 and 1971, ECCCS's design was refined and updated by NASA's Jet Propulsion Laboratory, incorporating elements of space technology and mission-centered communication.

Bunkered in the earthquake-proof security-hardened fourth and fifth sublevels of City Hall East (and interconnecting with the police pentagon in Parker Center), the Central Dispatch Center coordinates all the complex itineraries and responses of the LAPD using digitalized communication to eliminate voice congestion and guaranteed the secrecy of transmission. ECCCS, together with the LAPD's prodigious information-processing assets, including ever-growing databases on suspect citizens, have become the central neural system for the vast and disparate security operations, both public and private, taking place in Los Angeles.

The Carceral City

All these technologically advanced policing strategies have led to an invisible Haussmannization of Los Angeles. No need to clear fields of fire when you control the sky; no need to hire informers when surveillance cameras ornament every building. But the police have also reorganized space in far more straightforward ways. We have already seen their growing role as Downtown urban designers, indispensable for their expertise in "security." In addition they lobby incessantly for the allocation of more land for such law-and-order needs as jail space for a burgeoning inmate population and expanded administrative and training facilities for themselves. In Los Angeles this has taken the form of a *de facto* urban-renewal program, operated by the police agencies, that threatens to convert an entire section of Downtown and East LA into a vast penal colony.

Nearly 25,000 prisoners are presently held in six severely overcrowded county and federal facilities within a three-mile radius of City Hall—the largest single incarcerated population in the country. Racing to meet the challenge of the "war on drugs"—which will double detained populations within a decade—authorities are forging ahead with the reconstruction of a controversial state prison in East Los Angeles as well as a giant expansion of County Jail near Chinatown. The Immigration and Naturalization Service, meanwhile, has been trying to shoehorn privatized "microprisons" into unsuspecting inner-city neighborhoods. Confronting record overcrowding in its regular detention centers, the INS has commandeered motels and apartments for operation by private contractors as auxiliary jails for detained aliens—many of them Chinese and Central American political refugees.

The demand for more law-enforcement space in the central city, however, will inevitably bring the police into conflict with developers. The plan to add two high-rise towers with 2,400 new beds to County Jail on Bauchet Street, Downtown, has already raised the ire of developers hoping to make nearby Union Station the hub of a vast complex of skyscraper hotels and offices. One solution to the increasing conflict between carceral and commercial redevelopment is to use architectural camouflage to insert jail space into the skyscape. Ironically, even as buildings and homes become more like prisons or fortresses, prisons are becoming aesthetic objects. Indeed, carceral structures are the new frontier of public architecture. As an office glut in most parts of the country reduces commissions for corporate high-rises, celebrity architects are designing jails, prisons, and police stations.

An extraordinary example, the flagship of the emergent genre, is Welton Becket Associates' new Metropolitan Detentions Center in Downtown Los Angeles. Although this ten-story Federal Bureau of Prisons facility is one of the most visible new structures in the city, few of the hundreds of thousands of commuters who pass by every day have even an inkling of its function as a holding center for what has been officially describe[d] as the "managerial elite of narco-terrorism." This postmodern Bastille—the largest prison built in a major U.S. urban center in decades—looks instead like a futuristic hotel or office block, with artistic flourishes (for example, the high-tech trellises on its bridge-balconies) that are comparable to Downtown's best-designed recent architecture. In contrast to the human inferno of desperately overcrowded County Jail a few blocks away, the Becket structure appears less a detention center than a convention center for federal felons—a "distinguished" addition to Down-town's continuum of security and design.

The Fear of Crowds

In actual practice, the militarization of urban space tends to race far ahead of its theoretical representations. This is not to say, however, that the fortress city lacks apologists. Charles Murray, ideologue *par excellence* of 1980s antiwel-farism, has recently outlined ambitious justifications for renewed urban segregation in the 1990s. Writing in the *New Republic* (increasingly, the theoretical journal of the backlash against the urban poor), Murray argues that *landlords*— "one of the greatly maligned forces for social good in this country"—*not cops* are the best bet for winning the war on drugs.[25] Given the prohibitive cost of building sufficient prison space to warehouse the country's burgeoning population of inner-city drug users, Murray proposes instead to isolate them socially and spatially. In his three-prong strategy, employers would urine-test and fire drug-tainted workers at will; parents would use vouchers to remove their children from drug-ridden public schools; and, most importantly, landlords would maintain drug-free neighborhoods by excluding the "wrong kind of person."

Murray advocates, in other words, the restoration of the right of employers and landlords to discriminate—"without having to justify their arbitrariness." Only by letting "like-minded people . . . control and shape their small worlds," and letting landlords pursue their natural instinct "to let good tenants be and to evict bad ones," can the larger part of urban America find its way back to a golden age of harmonious, self-regulating communities. Murray is undoubtedly proud of all the Los Angeles suburbanites rushing to wall off their tract-home *gemeinschafts*.

At the same time, he unflinchingly accepts that the underclass—typified, in his words, by the "pregnant teenage[r] smoking crack" and the "Uzi-toting young male"—will become even more outcast: "If the result of implementing these policies is to concentrate the bad apples into a few hyperviolent, antisocial neighborhoods, so be it." Presumably it will be cheaper to police these pariah communities—where *everyone*, by definition, is a member of the dangerous class—than to apprehend and incarcerate hundreds of thousands of individuals. "Drug-free zones" for the majority, as a logical corollary, demand social-refuse dumps for the criminalized minority. Resurrected Jim Crow legislation, euphemistically advertised as "local self-determination," will insulate the urban middle classes (now including the Cosby family as well) from the New Jack City at their doorstep.

In this quest for spatial discrimination, the aims of contemporary architecture and the police converge most strikingly around the problem of crowd control. Cothinkers of Murray doubtless find the heterogeneous crowd a subversive anathema to their idyll of "like-mindedness." As we have seen, the designers of malls and pseudopublic space attack the crowd by homogenizing it. They set up architectural and semiotic barriers that filter out the "undesirables." They enclose the mass that remains, directing its circulation with behaviorist ferocity. The crowd is lured by visual stimuli of all kinds, dulled by Muzak, sometimes even scented by invisible aromatizers. This Skinnerian orchestration, if well conducted, produces a veritable commercial symphony of swarming, consuming nomads moving from one cash-point to another.

Outside in the streets, the task is more difficult. The LAPD continues to restrict the rights of public assembly and freedom of movement, especially of the young, through its mass sweeps and "Operation Hammer," selective juvenile curfews, and regular blockades of popular "cruising" boulevards. Even gilded white youth suffer from the strict police regulation of personal mobility. In the former world capital of adolescence, where millions overseas still imagine Gidget at a late-night beach party, the beaches are now closed at dusk, patrolled by helicopter gunships and police dune buggies.

A watershed in the local assault on the crowd was the rise and fall of the "Los Angeles Street Scene." Launched in 1978, the two-day annual festival at the Civic Center was intended to publicize Downtown's revitalization as well as to provide Mayor Bradley's version of the traditional Democratic barbecue. The LAPD remained skeptical. Finally in 1986, after the failure of the Ramones to appear as promised, a youthful audience began to tear up one of the stages. They were immediately charged by a phalanx of 150 police, including mounted units. In the two-hour melee that followed, angry punks bombarded the police cavalry with rocks and bottles; fifteen officers and horses were injured. The producer of the Street Scene, a Bradley official, suggested that "more middle-of-the-road entertainment" might attract less "boisterous crowds." The prestigious *Downtown News* counterattacked: "The Street Scene gives Downtown a bad name. It flies in the face of all that has been done here in the last thirty years." The paper demanded "reparations for the wounded 'reputation of Downtown.'" The Mayor canceled the Scene.[26]

The demise of the Scene suggested the consolidation of an official consensus about crowds and the use of space in Los Angeles. Once the restructuring of Downtown eliminated the social mixing of groups in normal pedestrian circulation, the Street Scene (ironically named) remained one of the few occasions or places (along with redevelopment-threatened Hollywood Boulevard and the Venice boardwalks) where Chinatown punks, Glendale skinheads, Boyle Height lowriders, Valley Girls, Marina designer couples, Slauson rappers, Skid Row homeless, and gawkers from Des Moines could still mingle together in relative amity. Moreover, in the years since the Battle of the Ramones, relentless police intimidation has ignited one youthful crowd after another into pandemonium, producing major riots in Hollywood on Halloween night in 1988, and in Westwood Village in March 1991 (during the premiere of *New Jack City*). Each incident, in turn, furnishes new pretexts for regulating crowds and "preventing the invasion of outsiders" (as one Westwood merchant explained in a TV interview). Inexorably, Los Angeles moves to extinguish [its] last public spaces, with all of their democratic intoxications, risks, and undeodorized odors.

Notes

1. National Committee on the Causes and Prevention of Violence. *To Establish Justice, to Ensure Domestic Tranquility* (Final Report. Washington D.C.: USGPO, 1969).
2. Quoted in John F. Kasson, *Amusing the Million* (New York: Hill and Wang, 1978), p. 15.
3. *Los Angeles Times*, Nov. 4, 1978.
4. Ibid., Dec. 24, 1972.
5. N. David Milder, "Crime and Downtown Revitalization," *Urban Land*, Sept. 1987, p. 18.
6. Tom Chorneau, "Quandary over a Park Restroom," *Downtown News*, August 25, 1986.
7. See "Cold Snap's Toll at 5 as Its Iciest Night Arrives," *Los Angeles Times*, Dec. 29, 1988.
8. Ibid., June 17, 1990.
9. "The old socialist" quote is from Michael Rotundi of Morphosis. Gehry himself boasts: "I get my inspiration from the streets. I'm more of a street fighter than a Roman scholar." (Quoted in Adele Freedman, *Progressive Architecture*, Oct. 1986, p. 99.)

10. The best catalogue of Gehry's work is Peter Arnell and Ted Bickford, eds., *Frank Gehry: Buildings and Projects* (New York: 1985).
11. Milfred Friedman, ed., *The Architecture of Frank Gehry* (New York: 1986), p. 175.
12. Pilar Viladas, "Illuminated Manuscripts," *Progressive Architecture,* Oct. 1986, pp. 76, 84.
13. See David Ferrell's articles in the *Los Angeles Times,* Aug. 31 and Oct. 16, 1987.
14. Ibid., Oct. 7, 1987.
15. Jane Bukwalter, "Securing Shopping Centers for Inner Cities," *Urban Land,* Apr. 1987, p. 24.
16. Ibid.
17. Richard Titus, "Security Works," *Urban Land,* Jan. 1990, p. 2.
18. Buckwalter, "Securing," p. 25.
19. *Los Angeles Daily News,* Nov. 1, 1987.
20. Interview, Fox News, Mar. 1990.
21. *Los Angeles Times,* July 25, 1989.
22. Jim Carlton, quoted in *Los Angeles Times,* Oct. 8, 1988.
23. Quoted in *Los Angeles Times,* Aug. 29, 1988.
24. Interviews with LAPD personnel; also Don Rosen, "Bleu Thunder," *Los Angeles Herald Examiner,* May 28, 1989.
25. Charles Murray, "How to Win the War on Drugs," *New Republic,* May 21, 1990, pp. 19–25.
26. *Los Angeles Times,* Sept. 22 and 25, 1986.

25

Dennis R. Judd

ENCLOSURE, COMMUNITY, AND PUBLIC LIFE

Over the past four decades, the material enclosure of urban space in the United States has been proceeding at an accelerating pace. Peter Marcuse has identified an intensified "turf allegiance," sharply defended "turf barricades and turf battles," and "the subsuming of the public interest under the private" as three of several features that distinguish the divided cities of the late twentieth century (Marcuse 1993, p. 358). Of New York City he says: "The prevalence of barbed wire, and indeed . . . razor-edge wire . . . is a graphic and frightening symbol of the cleavages running through the city." He goes on to add:

> And not only in New York City. My current and limited exposure to southern California suggests that walls and fences are, not metaphorically but actually, an increasing part of the accepted landscape. . . . New private cities are built with walls

around them, policed by private security patrols whose permission is needed for access. Even in the public city, fences around developments are ubiquitous... (Marcuse 1993, p. 361).

The construction of monumental corporate fortresses and the multiplication of defended residential enclaves constitute the most compelling images from Mike Davis's book on Los Angeles, *City of Quartz*. Here is his description of an urban landscape fractured into defended enclaves:

> The carefully manicured lawn of Los Angeles's Westside sprout forests of ominous little signs warning: 'Armed Response!' Even richer neighborhoods in the canyons and hillsides isolate themselves behind walls guarded by guntoting private police and state-of-the-art electronic surveillance. Downtown, a publicly subsidized 'urban renaissance' has raised the nation's largest corporate citadel, segregated from the poor neighborhoods around it by a monumental architectural glacis.... In Watts, developer Alexander Haagen demonstrates his strategy for recolonizing inner-city markets: a panoptican shopping mall surrounded by staked metal fences and a substation of the LAPD in a central surveillance tower... (Davis 1992, p. 223).

A chorus of voices provided back-up support for Marcuse and Davis, all raising alarms about the effects of enclosing urban space. Among social scientists and in the popular press as well, the prevailing view is that enclosure represents a secession from the larger society (McKenzie 1994), that it is a means of exerci[s]ing surveillance and control over marginalized people (Davis 1992a), that it is inspired by and inspires fear of crime and social disorder (Judd 1995), and that it signals a withdrawal from public space and public life (Sorkin 1992). Except for builders and developers, it is difficult to find anybody who identifies positive aspects to the proliferation of enclaves. Yet it may be a mistake to dismiss the idea out-of-hand that enclosure may have positive as well as negative effects on urban life and urban culture.

From the Greek city-states until at least the late eighteenth century, enclaves were essential features of the European notion of the "ideal city." The designers of ancient and medieval cities incorporated such features as town squares, marketplaces, and residential districts into their town plans as a means of protecting the interactions and institutions of community and public life (Rosenau 1983). Thus, "the medieval city was the quintessential city of discrete enclaves, where each corporate entity—church, monastery, university, guild, and so on—each political authority and even each extended family had its identifiable district, each of which frequently functioned as an autonomous 'city within a city'" (Plattus 1993, p. 79). In this interpretation, both communities based on kinship ("each extended family") and the institutions of civic culture ("each corporate entity") were nurtured by enclaves. Even when walls were built for defensive purposes they could, simultaneously, promote richer human interactions than otherwise would have occurred within the city:

> ... city walls could play a ... two-sided role. For the crafts and trading community within the city, the use of walls for military defense was accompanied by the use of those same walls for economic benefit, for they permitted the dominant guilds to

control entry, to regulate commerce, to set the rules for business activity within their precincts. If they were an unwelcome necessity for defense, they were a very useful instrument of control and enrichment when they were built (Marcuse 1994, p. 44).

Especially in the United States, twentieth-century urban development tended to eliminate enclaves, and in the process, public space. As Richard Sennett has pointed out, cities planned around "humane civic spaces" gave way to a grid pattern of development that flattened everything out so that places lost their particular character and their relationship to the larger city (1990, p. 49). Lewis Mumford and other critics of the 1950s style of suburbanization painted a portrait of a stultifying environment of conformity. In his book *The Great Good Place*, Ray Oldenburg has traced the decline of public places—places where people can mingle freely—to suburban grid development (Oldenburg 1989). The builders of today's enclaves claim that they are recreating the spaces for community and public life. Victor Gruen, the architect of the first enclosed mall (opened in Edina, Minnesota in 1956), hoped it would be "an antidote to suburban sprawl" and a "mechanism for creating community centers where there were none" (Kowinski 1985, p. 120). The builders of gated residential housing projects have made similar claims; even considering themselves "community builders" rather than mere housing developers (Weiss 1987).

Sociologists, historians, and others have long been mourning the "loss of community" in American cities, proclaiming that it died sometime late in the eighteenth century or (depending upon the author) at some critical juncture in the nineteenth century (Bender 1978). Urbanization and/or industrialization have been most often named as the culprits in the tragic demise of community. Sometime in the twentieth century the corpse must have been exhumed because it appears it has been murdered all over again by a new generation of villains, this time by the modern corporation, the automobile, television, and (most recently) by computers and electronic communications. And dare we neglect to mention architects and developers? In his *The Geography of Nowhere*, James Howard Kunstler aims his eloquent scorn at modernist architects and their corporate sponsors who, he says, killed small-town life sometime after World War II when corporate franchise stores and shopping malls undermined locally operated businesses (Kunstler 1993, p. 186).

Thomas Bender has asked the sensible question, "How many times can community collapse in America?" (Bender 1978, p. 46). He attributes the wildly varying estimates of its demise to imprecise definitions and to a nostalgia for the intimate interactions that allegedly once characterized small-town and village life. Bender challenges the idea that community has actually disappeared, asserting that scholars have been looking in the wrong places. Obviously, he grants, towns and cities no longer bound entire communities based on kinship and familial networks, as they perhaps did as late as the seventeenth century. Instead, the "close, often intimate, and usually face to face" relationships that compose community necessarily embraces "a limited number of people in a somewhat restricted social space or network . . . (Bender 1978, p. 7).

This formulation raises an intriguing question about whether the enclosure of space may facilitate a revival of community, or at least of public life, in cities of the late twentieth century. As Sennett has persuasively argued, community and public life are not the same things; they can exist simultaneously and one can exist without the other being present at all. In making this point, Sennett has also argued that the myth of the loss of community denigrates the value of public life which was the "essence of urbanity," the arena within which people "can act together, without compulsion to be the same" (Sennett 1977, p. 255). The affective and emotional ties that define family and kinship relationships are not much like the complex interactions that occur in public places like, say, Times Square. Thus, in this paper I entertain the premise that the recent enclosure of urban space may nurture community and/or public life.

The Four Enclosures

By the mid-1990s, walls or their functionally equivalent[1] barriers had begun to enclose the four principal venues and activities that compose urban life: residence, consumption, work, and leisure. Home and residence are becoming incorporated into the gated residential communities springing up in the Sunbelt and in suburbs all over the United States. Since the mid-1960s enclosed shopping malls have sprouted like mushrooms near freeway interchanges and more recently they have invaded the downtown areas of central cities. Enclosure also has begun to encompass work and leisure. In central cities a downtown corporate office complex is developing within perimeters that segregate affluent office workers within a defended space. And, finally, tourists and suburbanites who visit cities spend much of their time within "tourist bubbles" that are expressly constructed to provide a specialized environment for play.

Gated Communities

The number of "New Towns," cooperative apartments, condominiums, and single-family housing developments constructed by a single developer and enclosed by defended perimeters exploded from about 1,000 in the early 1960s to well over 80,000 by 1984 (Rosenberry 1989, p. 69). These developments intensify the segregation that has always characterized the suburbanization process in the United States, and in that sense they may logically be regarded merely as the latest expression of a logic of urban growth that has been unfolding for decades. What makes them different from the typical suburb, however, is that they are privatized and walled; usually they are surrounded by physical walls, but sometimes laser perimeters or patrols accomplish the same thing. Entry is generally restricted; visitors often must present identification or proof that they have been invited. In these respects the new gated communities are remarkably like the walled cities of medieval Europe, constructed to keep the hordes at bay.

The promise of security is nestled at the center of all advertisements for the new walled cities. Typical are these two ads from *The New York Times:*

> The new Southwinds Ocean House offers apartments of 3,000 sq. ft. with all the advantages of a single family home. A resident manager and security gate ensure care-free living. You may laze by the pool/gazebo, exercise in the lap pool, or stroll the miles of sandy beaches at your doorstep. . .

On another page of the same day's paper:

> Sailfish Point is an idyll celebrating your achievements. Its numbers add up to a guarded gate and 24-hour security patrols (*NYT* 1990, p. 13).

Common Interests Developments (CIDs) describe "a community in which the residents own or control common areas or shared amenities" (Louv 1985, p. 85). By virtue of buying into the developments, residents also agree to abide by a variety of covenants, conditions, and restrictions (CC&Rs). The CC&Rs and common properties, amenities, and services are administered by a homeowners' association, to which all deed holders belong. The fact that homeowners and condominium associations elect their own governing boards led the executive director of the leading national organization representing CIDs, the Community Association Institute, to proclaim homeowners' associations to be a "classic form of democratic government. It's right out of Civics 1" (Stevens 1988, p. A18). Surely such a rebirth of local democracy would have to be regarded as an important development in the public life of cities. One political scientist has asserted that CID associations are superior to voluntary neighborhood associations outside CIDs because they last longer and possess superior resources (Rich 1980). Across the nation there are at least 750,000 CID residents serving on the boards of 150,000 associations (Barton and Silverman 1994, p. 37).

In investigating claims that CID homeowners' associations may signal a rebirth of local democracy, it is important to note that they are invariably established not by the residents through voluntary agreement, but by a developer who sets up a residential association and all of its governing procedures and bylaws before the first piece of property is sold. Indeed, even the Community Association Institute itself, which purports to represent all the homeowners' associations in the country, was established by the National Association of Home Builders and the Urban Land Institute in 1973 as a means of marketing CIDs to the public (McKenzie 1994, pp. 110–114). Typically developers retain direct control of the homeowners' associations' membership and policies until a project is well along to completion (Scott 1994, pp. 23–24). Homeowners cannot buy property in a development without becoming a member of the residents' association or without, by virtue of owning property, agreeing to abide by its rules. Further, most associations cannot be dissolved or their bylaws changed without a unanimous vote of all the association members.

The CC&Rs enforced by residents' associations may be extraordinarily detailed and may even not be available to residents. They may dictate, for example, the minimum and maximum permissible ages of residents, hours and frequency of visitors, color of paint on a house, style and color of draperies hung in windows, size of pets and number of children (if either is allowed), parking rules, patio and landscaping—the list can be staggering in its length and detail.

Because they are not required to observe rights of self expression, free association, and free speech, residents' associations can and often do become dictatorial. The residents of CIDs often bridle at the rules, and lawsuits against developers or community associations over their enforcement are frequent. One study of 600 homeowners' associations found that more than 44 percent of the boards had been threatened with lawsuits in a year's time (Winokur 1989, p. 88). Homeowners almost always lose their cases. The courts generally uphold the right of association boards to enforce property contracts and their accompanying restrictions on the ground that buyers voluntarily accepted the terms when they signed a deed.

As one would expect in these circumstances, the residents of CIDs express a high level of discontent with their community associations, and attendance at meetings is very low (Winokur 1993, p. 115). A study of associations in suburbs outside Phoenix found that most people had never attended a meeting, nor did they evince any interest in or knowledge of the issues that might arise if they did (Alexander 1994, p. 159). Instead, distrust of their associations was the order of the day, no doubt because their boards were often enough used as a weapon when one resident became involved in a dispute with another (Alexander 1994, p. 161). It seems clear from this evidence that the version of the democratic life practiced in CIDs is likely to undermine not only participation, but the social relationships within these new walled cities as well.[2]

Enclosed Shopping Malls

Shopping malls are the earliest and the best known enclosed spaces to be constructed in contemporary American cities. Jesse Clyde Nichols built the nation's first modern shopping center, Country Club Plaza, in Kansas City in 1923 (Jackson 1985, p. 123). Country Club Plaza artfully romanticizes the architecture of Seville, which Nichols loved, and sets apart its miniature cityscape from surrounding areas with walls inset with multicolored tile mosaics, red-tile roofs, towers, and gables. The first enclosed mall in the nation, Southdale, opened on October 8, 1956, in Edina, Minnesota. Today thousands of them are sprinkled across the urban landscape. Unlike the first generation of shopping malls, many of the newer ones constitute more than a mere collection of stores. The larger of them interconnect shopping, recreation, hotels, restaurants, office towers, and, sometimes, condominiums and apartments. These "sealed realms" (Boddy 1992, p. 125) engulf and centralize activities that were formerly spread throughout the urban community-at-large. Many of the enclosed malls built in big cities have accreted block-by-block, with tubes and skyways connecting atriums, arcades, food courts, and hotels. In Minneapolis the downtown mall has grown by eating away the insides of the historic buildings, leaving only their facades intact. In Montreal and Dallas veritable underground cities have formed through a network of tunnels. The mall's assault on Atlanta has been much more direct: a huge enclosed complex has been built on the rubble of the historic downtown.

It is not difficult to find claims that the modern mall is the functional equivalent of the medieval marketplace. There is considerable symbolic resonance connected to such a claim. The marketplace was an extraordinarily important space for the public life of medieval cities. It was the scene of the feasts, fairs, and carnivals that occurred throughout the year, the occasions when "the unofficial folk culture of the Middle Ages and even of the Renaissance" found expression (Bakhtin 1968, p. 154). The marketplace provided a space within which normal social hierarchies and relationships were generally suspended, in part because many of the traders came from various locations outside a particular city, and thus they were marginal to its everyday life and customs (Agnew 1986). An image similar to this spontaneous mixture is superficially projected in modern shopping malls. The writer Tom Wolfe has referred to John Portman's Peachtree Center in downtown Atlanta as "Great theater" (Oney 1987, p. 184). To achieve this effect, Portman sprinkles his lobbies with Japanese streamers, giant mobiles, bronze and glass elevators outlined in lights, a variety of kitsch touches, such as a Liberace-style grand piano situated on an elevated bandstand. Many of the plazas and atriums in Peachtree seem remarkably like carnival midways. A similar carnival atmosphere pervades all of James Rouse's festival malls. In Rouse's case, the effect is achieved by mixing specialty shops, clothing stores, restaurants and food stands, and bars; and by employing musicians, jugglers, and comedian fudge makers to entertain shoppers.

It perhaps goes without saying that mall developers contrive to create an atmosphere of fun and spectacle not to create the setting for a spontaneous public life, but to sell merchandise as efficiently and profitably as possible. Malls are constructed by the same calculus that produces advertising—"pure imageability" (Sorkin 1992a, p. xiv). The environment of malls is regulated to ensure absolute predictability. Each type of mall is defined by its mix of shops, design features, and clientele. There are a few standard variations: the luxury hotel/tourist/office and restaurant complexes such as Peachtree; the festival market like Rouse's; malls that concentrate on exclusive, upscale, high fashion stores; malls that cater to the "typical" middle-class family; and major brand discount malls (this type is rarely enclosed because it tends to be situated along interstates at the edge or beyond urban areas. In every region of the country and from city to city, within these themes the activities, the mix of tenant stores, the atmosphere, and the customer profile are remarkably uniform. The uniformity is not a result of enclosure per se. It occurs because a few architectural firms and developers dominate the market.

Malls are convenient for developers because they make the total control of a commercial space possible. Malls are expressly designed *not* to be venues for free, unrestricted interactions. "Undesirable" characters and activities are prohibited. Obvious non-customers, such as bagladies, the homeless, or in some cases, teenagers, may be asked to move on or will be thrown out. As a reminder that it is a private space, the sign at the entrance to the Lerner Company's mall reads:

Areas . . . used by the public are not public ways, but are for the use of the tenants and public transacting business with them. Permission to use said areas may be revoked at any time.

Since malls are privately owned, their corporate sponsors are not bound to respect the constitutional rights guaranteed in public places. The courts have generally agreed with this interpretation. In 1968 the Warren Court ruled that there was a right to free speech in spaces that were essentially public, though privately owned ("if it walks like a duck, quacks like a duck . . . ") (*Food Employees Local v. Logan Valley Plaza, Inc.,* 391 US 1 308). Only eight years later, however, the Burger Court overruled that decision (*Hudgens v. NLRB,* 424 US 507). In 1979 the California Supreme Court, citing language in the state constitution, ruled that malls in California were required to allow restricted rights to speak, picket, and distribute leaflets (*Robins v. Pruneyard Shopping Center,* 23 Cal. 3d. 899). That decision was affirmed by the U.S. Supreme Court (*Pruneyard Shopping Center v. Robins,* 100 Ct. 2035). Five states allow some political expression in malls; for most of the country they are regarded, before the law, as strictly private places (Glaberson 1992, p. A10).

These characteristics do not mean that malls are unpopular with shoppers. In Britain, for example, they are perceived as cleaner and safer than downtown shopping districts (Utley 1995, p. 7). In the United States they are popular with local shoppers and tourists as well (Greenfield 1986, p. 33). Does this mean that despite (or because of) their status as corporate-controlled spaces they provide a setting for the interactions that sustain public life? Before any definitive answers are possible, studies are necessary to examine that question specifically. One must, however, express doubts. Malls are marketplaces that sell goods made and distributed by multinational corporations, in a setting that strictly regulates the competition among providers and that maximizes the impact of merchandising. They are, in other words, a means of unifying "international investment, production, and consumption" into one controlled space (Zukin 1991, p. 51). If malls contribute to a sense of public life, they surely do so on the same terms as the mass advertising and the electronic media. The stimulation provided in the encompassing environments of malls is precisely like television: the consumer is the passive object of a kaleidoscope of images and impressions. Rather than providing a space that enhances the public city, it is likely that this version of the new walled cities overwhelms its users with an overwhelming corporate presence whose message is singular: buy, buy!

Downtown, Inc.

The downtown office-corporate complex of large cities is becoming increasingly demarcated and defended from surrounding land uses (Sassen 1994; Zukin 1991). Enclosure provides a defensible space for corporate executives and affluent office workers who commute from the suburbs or from gentrified neighborhoods and condominiums within the city. The design of the individual buildings is an important line of defense. Perhaps because it is such an automobile-oriented city, the fortifications of downtown Los Angeles are hostile to street life of any kind; bare concrete walls sweep down to the edges of the sidewalks, and street entry is difficult or uninviting. In a pedestrian city like New York, the prevailing mode of defense takes a different form. High-rise buildings sometimes have courtyards or spaces accessible to the street (developers receive bonuses from the city if they provide them), and imposing facades punctuated by revolving doors. Step inside and there is typically a lobby with a guard (or "help") station that screens all visitors, thus accomplishing the defense of the interior space.

In addition to the design of the buildings themselves, clustering office towers densely into a well-defined office district helps to create a space reserved primarily for the affluent white-collar workers commuting downtown. In many cities a variety of physical barriers bound the downtown corporate enclave. In St. Louis, for example, a huge stadium/convention center complex anchors the north side of the downtown and a baseball stadium and an elevated freeway anchors the south. To the east is a freeway and the grounds of the Gateway Arch. Only the west side is lacking in physical barriers of some sort. For pure defense of downtown corporate enclaves, however, physical walls are more efficient than porous barriers. Atlanta and Detroit have shown the way by moving a large proportion of their downtown office workers into comprehensive sealed realms. In Atlanta's Peachtree Center and Detroit's Renaissance Center workers drive into parking garages and then enter a city-within-a-city where they can work, shop, eat lunch, and find a variety of diversions after work, if they wish (perhaps a tryst in one of the several luxury hotels connected via skytubes). They never have to step outside.

Sharon Zukin has called the corporate office-gentrification complex of contemporary cities an important example of "landscapes of power" (Zukin 1991). The new downtowns present a microcosm of the social and economic relations of the postindustrial economy. First in global cities but increasingly also in cities further down the urban hierarchy, high-level professional operations and information industries have become clustered into "strategic nodes with a hyperconcentration of facilities" (Sassen 1994, p. 2) supporting layer upon layer of highly educated, technologically sophisticated professionals offering specialized services—corporate managers, management consultants, legal experts, accountants, computer specialists, financial analysts, media and public relations consultants, and the like. This army of white-collar workers are supported by an expensive, substantially sealed-off public and private infrastructure supporting their employment. When the downtown complex supporting these corporate workers become sufficiently elaborated, they become surrounded by gentrified neighborhoods and high-rise luxury housing developments. In such cities the downtown becomes primarily devoted to corporate power, personal wealth, luxury consumption, and tourism.

According to Zukin, the form of urban development that ensues in the wake of this transformation is itself an expression of a corporate logic that centralizes and standardizes:

> Superstar architects create a standardized form that they move from place to place. They also create buildings that look stupendous from a distance—on the city's

skyline—but fail to fit in with a local 'context.' This makes an architecture that is less risky for investors but also less evocative of a sense of place (Zukin 1991, p. 47).

The new downtowns are not, essentially, local at all; rather they make a city habitable by the employees of national and international corporations. This is why they are standardized, and it is also why they are increasingly segregated from the cities in which they temporarily reside. Christine Boyer has observed that they "come to represent a *kind* of place," a set of well-defined images that not only deny locality, but suggest a "virtual urbanism," and set-piece tableaux: "The series of well-designed spatial nodes in cities around the world being produced within the context of global capitalism can also be thought of as theatrical stage sets" (Boyer 1995, p. 94). Insofar as a public life is generated in such settings, it is certain to be part of a global rather than urban (local) culture.

The Tourist Space

The fourth realm of enclosure in American cities embraces leisure and tourism. For more than two decades U.S. cities have been investing in an elaborate, costly infrastructure to support tourism. Between 1976 and 1986 250 convention centers, sports arenas, community centers, and performing halls were constructed or started, at a cost of more than $10 billion (*U.S. News and World Report* 1986, p. 45). Since the early 1980s the downtowns of American cities have experienced a conversion of land use that approaches, in its scale, the restructuring of downtown economies and land use wrought by the massive urban renewal clearance projects of the 1950s and 1960s. In their attempts to attract tourists, cities have been aggressively reconstructing their physical environments.

The mix that comprises the corporate/entertainment complex is remarkably standardized from city to city, so much so that it constitutes a virtual template for economic revitalization, copied by cities all over the United States. Tourist and entertainment facilities coexist in symbiotic relationship with the corporate towers, and there is some overlap: shopping malls, restaurants, and bars cater to tourists as well as to the daytime professionals who work downtown. Bernard Frieden and Lynn Sagalyn have referred to the various components making up the new downtowns as every mayor's "trophy collection." Typically the trophies include an atrium hotel, festival mall, a convention center, a restored historic neighborhood, a domed stadium, an aquarium, new office towers, and a redeveloped waterfront (1990, pp. 43–47). In the 1990s a casino gambling facility might have to be added to make the set complete.

Several of the facilities composing the tourist space are enclosed, and frequently a well-defined perimeter surrounds the entire complex. This is particularly the case in older port and industrial cities, where urban decay and social problems have made substantial areas inhospitable to visitors. These tourist spaces look so similar from one city to the next that sometimes it seems as if they come from a factory manufacturing just a few standardized models. Baltimore provides perhaps a dramatic (though by now quite typical) example of a pure tourist space carved out of urban decay. Called the "Cinderella city of the

1980s" (Peirce, Guskind, and Gardner 1983). Baltimore has transformed its harbor by replacing the abandoned, desolate buildings that once lined its waterfront with open vistas and tourist amenities. The Harbour Place area is bounded on all sides by broad plazas which lend themselves to constant surveillance. The millions of visitors a year are conveniently protected from seeing the Baltimore beyond the tourist enclave, the other part of the city of what has been labeled "the two Baltimores" (Hula 1990, pp. 191–215).

The downtown corporate complex overlaps and shares some of the space of the specialized tourist districts that have sprung up in older cities. Without doubt these tourist spaces are substantially occupied by corporate environments that vary little from city to city—the Rouse malls, renovated harbors, and perfectly replicated Hard Rock Cafes and their ilk appear as so many "variations on a theme park" (Sorkin 1992a). They are carefully constructed "tourist bubbles" meant to reduce the anxiety of the visitor:

> At its most extreme 'tourist bubbles' can envelop the traveler so that he/she only moves inside secured, protected and normalized environments. It is possible for the tourist to visit a foreign country but within a 'bubble' where the learnt defense responses of home will still apply to everything from personal security to food. Even if we wish to risk something in a strange city there are still packaged control strategies on offer for us: for example, if we hire a car in Miami we will be given a map showing the dangerous areas to avoid . . . (Bottoms and Wiles 1995, p. 42).

Despite their isolating effects, tourist bubbles could, in principle, become the site for the kind of community-wide celebrations and rituals that nurture a sense of local identity and patriotism. Benjamin McRee has commented on the "social wholeness" that communal celebrations brought to medieval society:

> In otherwise stratified and faction-ridden communities, men and women put their differences aside long enough to share communal meals, engage in neighborhood games, and march through the streets shoulder to shoulder in processional demonstrations of fraternity (McRee 1994, p. 189).

McRee's comment brings to mind some of the communal celebrations held in contemporary cities—such events as July 4th fireworks and St. Patrick's Day parades. Other events may also become a venue for gathering the urban community into one place. For example, home and garden shows held in convention centers may be occasions where locality is not only expressed but, in a sense, made comprehensible—the rows of displays by home builders, renovation contractors, window manufacturers, garden shops, and appliance and furniture retailers create the effect of a miniature city. In quite a few cities sports stadiums are located adjacent or within the tourist space. At least in principle, professional sports franchises may overcome differences and provide an occasion for expressions of local patriotism and pride, even though professional sports is probably a media phenomenon more than a local industry. Fan loyalty is also, undoubtedly, undermined by the velocity with which teams now move from city to city (Euchner 1993).

The construction of specialized spaces set aside for tourism and leisure is as likely to contribute to racial, ethnic, and class divisions as to any impulse toward local patriotism. In medieval cities, public ceremonies sometimes fomented discord and division rather than unity. They "could be insidiously divisive, drawing attention to the lines separating different social groups within the community rather than working to erase those lines" (McRee 1994, p. 189). Such was the case when fraternal organizations and other groups organized celebrations meant to reaffirm their special status within local society. This is also likely to be the case when tourist spaces exclude significant segments of the urban population.

Even for the affluent middle class who can regularly use them, the tourist bubbles are unlikely sites for the expression of community spirit or civic solidarity. Instead, like malls and theme parks, they are sites of consumption. As an expression of their purpose, the activities defined as fun and leisure are normally carefully organized and closely managed. The events surrounding the opening of the World Financial Center in New York City in October 1988 provides an example. The advertising agents for the developer, Olympia & York, staged five days of celebrations, all intended to convey (in the advertising firm's language) "a progressive understanding of the uses of public space" (Boyer 1994, p. 468). As it transpired, the celebrations were tied closely to the marketing needs of the businesses located in the World Financial Center. The activities defined, and strictly limited, the recreation and leisure that those attending could "consume." In this respect, the idea that the celebration was a community event was advertising copy more than anything else.

Enclaves as Expressions of International Circuits of Capital

There can be little doubt that enclaves have the potential for providing the spaces necessary for nurturing community and public life. Examples of such spaces abound. In the early years of the nineteenth century Times Square in New York City became one such space. Perhaps because its emergence as a public space was not much orchestrated by business and political elites, "Times Square established a new kind of public space in whose vaudeville halls, legitimate theaters, and winter gardens different social classes mingled with near abandon" (Zukin 1995, p. 116). Times Square constituted a public space that nurtured the impersonal interactions that Sennett thought necessary for the public life of a city (Sennett 1977).

The new enclosures blur the boundaries between public and private space. The managers of these enclosed spaces are free to define them either way, depending upon context and circumstance. As Sharon Zukin shows, there is an ongoing, often fluid negotiation over the use of public space managed under public auspices—such venues as parks, markets, and city streets and squares (Zukin 1995). The rules change fundamentally when such space becomes privatized. The four enclosures are means of asserting authoritarian domination and control. The community associations of CIDS are put in place by developers solely to protect property values, and to do this they, in effect, secede from the larger urban community (Scott 1994, pp. 25–26). Malls are designed as encompassing environments so that the developer can gain control of all aspects of shopping and merchandising. The new downtowns and the tourist bubbles are emerging as local nodes in international circuits of capital and culture (Zukin 1991). The four enclosures are devoted entirely to private purposes, but they masquerade as the neighborhoods, town squares, and marketplaces of our time. They are part of "the strange and alarming process by which technologies of connection, through the monumentalization of transportation and the ephemeralization of communication, have become the agents of extreme disjunction and the displacement, if not the death, of the public realm" (Plattus 1993, p. 81). Their walls encompass not community and public life, but corporate culture.

Notes

1. Though current theories emphasizing the material, political, cultural, symbolic, and even electronic dimensions of space may render such an approach unfashionable (Liggett and Perry 1995), for the purposes of this paper I define enclosure literally, as space bounded by physical barriers or their technological or functional equivalents (such as laser beams, surveillance cameras, intensified security perimeters, and the like).
2. Of course there may be (and undoubtedly are) social relationships in CIDs outside the context of formal participation in association governance bodies. Particularly in developments for the elderly, there may be high participation rates in organized recreational activities and in informal networks. Survey data is needed to document such participation.

Bibliography

Agnew, J. 1986. *Worlds Apart: The Market and the Theater in Anglo-American Thought, 1550–1750.* New York: Cambridge University Press.

Alexander, G.S. 1994. "Conditions of 'Voice,' Passivity, Disappointment, and Democracy in Homeowner Associations." In *Common Interest Communities: Private Governments and the Public Interest,* edited by S. E. Barton and C.J. Silverman. Berkeley: Institute of Governmental Studies Press, University of California.

Bakhtin, M. 1968. *Rabelais and His World.* Cambridge, MA: The MIT Press.

Barton, S.E., and C.J. Silverman (eds.). 1994. *Common Interest Communities: Private Governments and the Public Interest.* Berkeley: Institute of Governmental Studies Press, University of California.

Bender, T. 1978. *Community and Social Change in America.* New Brunswick, NJ: Rutgers University Press.

Boddy, T. 1992. "Underground and Overhead: Building the Analogous City." In *Variations on a Theme Park: The New American City and the End of Public Space,* edited by M. Sorkin. New York: Hill and Wang.

Bottoms, A., and P. Wiles. 1995. "Crime and Insecurity in the City." Unpublished paper, The University of Sheffield, U.K.

Boyer, M.C. 1994. *The City of Collective Memory: Its Historical Imagery and Architectural Entertainments.* Cambridge, MA: The MIT Press.

———. 1995. "The Great Frame-Up: Fantastic Appearances in Contemporary Spatial Politics." In *Spatial Practices: Critical Explorations in Social Spatial Theory,* edited by H. Liggett and D.C. Perry. Thousand Oaks, CA: Sage Publications.

Davis, M. 1992. *City of Quartz: Excavating the Future in Los Angeles.* New York: Vintage Books.

Euchner, C. 1993. *Playing the Field: Why Sports Teams Move and Cities Fight to Keep Them.* Baltimore: The Johns Hopkins University Press.

Frieden, B.J., and L.B. Sagalyn. 1990. "Downtown Malls and the City Agenda." *Social Science and Modern Society* 27 (5): 43–47.

Glaberson, W. 1992. "In Malls, Protest and Politics Are as Welcome as Crime." *The New York Times,* April 21: A10.

Greenfield, N.R. 1986. "Why Everyone Goes to the Mall." *The New York Times,* December 21: 33.

Hula, R.C. 1990. "The Two Baltimores." In *Leadership and Urban Regeneration: Cities in North America and Europe*, edited by D. Judd and M. Parkinson. Thousand Oaks, CA: Sage Publications.

Jackson, K. 1985. *Crabgrass Frontier: The Suburbanization of the United States*. New York: Oxford University Press.

Judd, D.R. 1995. "The Rise of the New Walled Cities." In *Spatial Practices: Critical Explorations in Social/Spatial Theory*, edited by H. Liggett and D.C. Perry. Thousand Oaks, CA: Sage Publications.

Kowinski, W.S. 1985. *The Malling of America: An Inside Look at the Great Consumer Paradise*. New York: William Morrow.

Kunstler, J.H. 1993. *The Geography of Nowhere: The Rise and Decline of America's Man-Made Landscape*. New York: Simon & Schuster.

Liggett, H. and D.C. Perry (ed.). 1995. *Spatial Practices: Critical Explorations in Social/Spatial Theory*. Thousand Oaks, CA: Sage Publications.

Liggett, H. 1995. "City Sights/Sites of Memories and Dreams." In *Spatial Practices: Critical Explorations in Social/Spatial Theory*, edited by H. Liggett and D.C. Perry. Thousand Oaks, CA: Sage Publications.

Louv, R. 1985. *America II: The Book That Captures Americans in the Act of Creating the Future*. New York: Penguin Books.

Marcuse, P. 1993. "What's So New About Divided Cities?" *International Journal of Urban and Regional Research* 17 (3): 355–365.

———. 1994. "Walls as Metaphor and Reality." In *Managing Divided Cities*, edited by S. Dunn. Keele, Staffordshire, U.K.: Keele University Press.

McKenzie, E. 1994. *Privatopia*. Yale University Press.

McRee, B.R. 1994. "Unity or Division? The Social Meaning of Guild Ceremony in Urban Communities." In *City and Spectacle in Medieval Europe*, edited by B.A. Hanawalt and K.L. Reyerson. Minneapolis: University of Minnesota Press.

The New York Times Magazine 1990. Advertising supplement, November 18: 13.

Oldenburg, R. 1989. *The Great Good Place*. New York: Paragon.

Oney, S. 1987. "Portman's Complaint." *Esquire* (June): 182–189.

Peirce, N., R. Guskind, and J. Gardner. 1983. "Politics Is Not the Only Thing That is Changing America's Big Cities." *National Journal* (November 26): 2480.

Plattus, A. 1993. "At the Edge of the Urban Millennium." In *The Edge of the Millennium*, edited by S. Yelavich. New York: Whitney Library of Design.

Rich, R.C. 1980. "A Political-Economy Approach to the Study of Neighborhood Organizations." *American Journal of Political Science* 24 (4): 559–592.

Rosenberry, K. 1989. "Condominium and Homeowner Associations: Should They Be Treated Like 'Mini-Governments?'" Pp. 69–73 in *Residential Community Association: Private Governments in the Intergovernmental System*. Washington, DC: Advisory Commission on Intergovernmental Relations.

Rosenau, H. 1983. *The Ideal City: Its Architectural Evolution in Europe*. New York: Methuen.

Sassen, S. 1994. *Cities in a World Economy*. Thousand Oaks, CA: Pine Forge Press.

Scott, S. 1994. "The Homes Association: Will 'Private Government' Serve the Public Interest?" In *Common Interest Communities: Private Governments and the Public Interest*, edited by S.E. Barton and C.J. Silverman. Berkeley, CA: Institute of Governmental Studies Press, University of California.

Sennett, R. 1977. *The Fall of the Public Man*. New York: Alfred Knopf.

———. 1990. *The Conscience of the Eye: The Design and Social Life of Cities*. New York: W. W. Norton & Co.

Sorkin, M. 1992a. "Introduction: Variations on a Theme Park." Pp. xi–xv in *Variations on a Theme Park: The New American City and the End of Space*, edited by M. Sorkin. New York: The Noonday Press.

———. 1992b. "See You in Disneyland." Pp. 205–232 in *Variations on a Theme Park: The New American City and the End of Space*, edited by M. Sorkin. New York: The Noonday Press.

Stevens, W.K. 1989. "Condominium Owners Grapple With Governing Themselves." *The New York Times*, September 1: A18.

U.S. News and World Report. 1986. "Convention Centers Spark Civic Wars" (February): 45.

Utley, A. 1995. "Shopping Malls Win Youth Vote." *The Times Higher*. London, U.K.

Weiss, M.A. 1987. *The Rise of the Community Builders: The American Real Estate Industry and Urban Land Planning*. New York: Columbia University Press.

Winokur, J.L. 1989. "Association-Administered Servitude Regimes: A Private Property Perspective." Pp. 85–89 in *Residential Community Associations: Private Government in the Intergovernmental System*. Washington, DC: Advisory Commission on Intergovernmental Relations.

———. 1994. "Choice, Consent, and Citizenship in Common Interest Communities." In *Common Interest Communities: Private Governments and the Public Interest,* edited by S.E. Barton and C.J. Silverman. Berkeley, CA: Institute of Governmental Studies Press, University of California.

Zukin, S. 1991. *Landscapes of Power: From Detroit to Disney World.* Berkeley: University of California Press.

———. 1995. *The Cultures of Cities.* Cambridge, MA: Blackwell Publishers.

26

William Julius Wilson

BUILDING A FOUNDATION FOR MULTIRACIAL COOPERATION

As the new global economy creates growing inequality in the labor market and increasing economic and emotional stresses for ordinary families, including those where the working mother is the only parent, many of the policies and actions of the government do more to aggravate than alleviate their economic woes. I have in mind trade policies that facilitate the pursuit of cheap labor in the global marketplace, monetary policies that elevate real interest rates and thereby lower employment rates, tax policies that favor the truly wealthy, and partisan opposition to programs of public investment and national health insurance.

The University of Texas economist James K. Galbraith reminds us of the more enviable position of workers vis-à-vis the government that existed several decades ago:

> From 1945 through 1970, the state maintained a wide range of protections for low-wage, less educated, more vulnerable workers, so that a broadly equal pattern of social progress was sustained despite, even in those distant years, rapid technological change. These protections were held in place by a stable macroeconomic policy that avoided sharp or prolonged disruptions to economic growth, and in particular by a monetary policy that was subordinated to these larger objectives. In those years, the government *as a whole* was committed to the pursuit of full employment, price stability, and high rates of economic growth. Following 1970, technological change continued, but the protections were withdrawn, and at the same time macroeconomic policy became much more unstable. The state shifted its support from the economy in general, the macroeconomy, to specific leading sectors of the economy—in fact, to the firms and industries most devoted to technological change. Monetary policy led the way, by declaring its independence from the larger objectives of economic policy, and its responsibility for the defeat of inflation above all other economic goals.[1]

Moreover, the "Reagan experiment" operated under the assumption that in order to increase productivity and economic growth and reduce prices, unemployment, and poverty, the government should avoid active interventions in domestic policies. This experiment resulted in historic and profound changes in tax and transfer policies in the 1980s. The rapid inflation of the 1970s had already eroded the real value of many transfer benefits and pushed lower- and middle-income wage earners into higher marginal tax brackets. To make matters worse, the tax structure became even more regressive, featuring an increase in Social Security taxes, on top of regressive taxes on wages, and a diminished progressivity of the taxes on total income.[2]

"Given the large increase in market inequality in the 1980s," state the economists Sheldon Danziger and Peter Gottschalk, "government tax and transfer policies would have had to become more redistributed than they were in the 1970s just to keep post-tax, post-transfer inequality constant. Instead, tax and transfer policy changes became less effective in reducing market inequality. As a result, post-tax and transfer inequality increased by even more than market inequality."[3] Although the Tax Reform Act of 1986 and the Omnibus Budget Reconciliation Act of 1990 represent attempts to redistribute income progressively, the changes "were barely noticeable."[4]

There have been other recent government efforts to ease the burdens on vulnerable families, such as the expansions of the earned income tax credit (EITC) in 1986, 1990, and 1993, and the Family and Medical Leave Act of 1993 (FMLA). The EITC is a wage subsidy for the working poor, and its expansions reflected a recognition, even under the Bush and Reagan administrations, of the erosion of wages for low-paid work and the weakening of other policies to help the working poor, such as the minimum wage. The FMLA was designed to partially alleviate the conflicts involving family and work experienced by a growing number of Americans. Under the FMLA, workers are allowed to take up to twelve weeks of unpaid leave for the birth or adoption of a child and for illness, including the illness of a spouse or parent. However, even these modest proposals have been hotly debated in Congress. The traditional bipartisan support for the EITC has begun to erode in the Republican-controlled Congress, so much so that the Senate passed a budget resolution in 1995 that assumed cuts in the EITC by roughly 21 billion dollars over seven years. And the FMLA was initially vetoed by President Bush.*

---

*Francine D. Blau, Marianne A. Ferber, and Anne E. Winkler point out in this connection that opponents of the FMLA "tended to ignore or minimize the potential benefits of leaves for employers and were particularly concerned about the cost imposed on them, since they continue to pay for health insurance for workers on leave and must bear the costs of training replacement workers. Pay for replacement workers, however, is not an added cost because workers on leave do not draw a paycheck. Moreover, there are benefits. . . . Family leave lowers the cost of turnover, which can be quite substantial when training and moving expenses are considered. Also, it may enhance workers' commitment to the firm and hence their productivity. In fact, a recent study found that providing such unpaid leaves to employees is less expensive for employers than replacing workers who are forced to resign because such leaves are not available. This suggests that the cost of providing short, unpaid family leave is not likely to be unduly onerous for business. International evidence also indicates that, at least thus far, parental leave has not caused the severe problems for firms that had been anticipated by some critics" (Francine D. Blau, Marianne A. Ferber, and Anne E. Winkler, The Economics of Women, Men, and Work, 3d ed. [Upper Saddle River, N.J.: Prentice-Hall, 1998], 315).

A multiracial political coalition could generate an earnest national debate on Congress's current approach to domestic policies and prompt public officials to consider seriously the effects of their action or inaction on a broad range of issues that impact vulnerable families. Take, for example, the issue of trade liberalization policies. Although the overall impact of trade liberalization legislation continues to be debated by economists, it appears to me to be an ideal issue around which to organize a national dialogue on policies that may adversely affect ordinary families.

It is true that liberalized trade has increased exports in areas such as the aerospace industry, with beneficial effects for highly skilled workers. At the same time, increasing imports that compete with labor-intensive industries (such as apparel, textile, toys, footwear, and some manufacturing industries) hurt low-skilled labor.[5] This is one of the issues raised by House Democrats who in 1997 and again in 1998 voted overwhelmingly against President Clinton's "fast-track" proposal on free trade. The legislation that the president introduced was written to attract Republican support. It therefore did not include the labor and environmental protection standards demanded by Democrats and their allies—union leaders and environmentalists.[6]

The Democrats were not persuaded by Clinton's argument that Americans stand to gain from an economy dominated by high technology and an educated workforce. The House Democrats argued instead that blue-collar workers would be forced into a "race to the bottom" through competition with developing countries that lack the labor laws and environmental protections that have evolved in the United States. As House Minority leader Richard Gephardt put it, the question is not *whether* to trade, since we all know that trade is important for the overall health and growth of the economy. The question is *how* to trade. Moreover, union leaders, often branded as protectionist, indicated that they would not have opposed the fast-track legislation if it had guaranteed workplace and environmental rights. As Frank Borgers, a professor of labor relations at the University of Massachusetts, put it: "If you raise labor standards in low-wage countries, that's good for them and good for us. It would slow the exodus of jobs."[7]

During debates on the fast-track trade bill in 1997, the vast majority of Democrats in the House of Representatives told Clinton that "American trade policy is skewed in the wrong direction. They sought to equalize the terms of competition between workers in the United States and other countries rather than focus on protecting intellectual property rights or other corporate interests."[8]

An intergroup coalition of organized labor, environmental groups, and Hispanic organizations, including the Hispanic caucus in the House of Representatives, fought against the president's bill on free trade. Black leaders such as Maxine Waters, John Lewis, and Jesse Jackson were involved in this debate, but their efforts were not highly visible. If the proposed fast-track legislation of trade would increase the displacement of low-skilled labor in this country, it would create enormous problems for the large proportion of unskilled African American workers.

Issues that are defined explicitly in racial terms understandably attract more attention from black leaders. But it is important that black leaders expand their vision and address race-neutral issues that significantly affect the African American community with the same degree of attention they give to race-specific issues.

The displacement problems associated with free trade are a race-neutral issue that ought to bring together the swelling ranks of have-not Americans—that is, the low- to moderate-income groups of any race—in an important and constructive dialogue on national economic policy. At the time of this writing, the fast-track trade bill has once again been defeated in the House of Representatives, but the pressure to open U.S. markets to goods produced cheaply in countries that lack reasonable safety, wage, and environmental standards for their workers is unlikely to abate.

As we think about other issues of national economic policy that affect low- to moderate-income families and that ought to engage different racial groups in a national dialogue, one issue immediately comes to mind: the need to generate national support for achieving and maintaining tight labor markets—in other words, full employment.

Such a goal by definition challenges the monetary policies supported by Wall Street, policies by which the Federal Reserve Board, concerned with keeping inflation in check, keeps labor markets from tightening by maintaining or creating high interest rates: as interest rates rise, unemployment rates climb.

In a critical assessment of this approach, Galbraith points out that the principal causes of the rising inequality in the wage structure

> lie in the hard blows of recession, unemployment, and slow economic growth, combined with the effects of inflation and political resistance to rising real value of the minimum wage. These are blows that, when once delivered, are not erased in any short period of economic recovery. They can be reversed, and in American history have been reversed, only by sustained periods of full employment alongside controlled inflation and a determined drive toward social justice. We last saw such a movement in this country in the 1960s, and before that only during World War II.[9]

However, Galbraith goes on to point out that beginning in 1970 the government's goal of full employment was abandoned in favor of fighting inflation. The only instrument deemed suitable for this purpose was high interest rates produced by the Federal Reserve. Unfortunately for the average worker, high interest rates elevate unemployment.[10]

As the economic analyst Jeff Faux has pointed out, this is a value issue. The Federal Reserve Board "protects the value of financial assets over the value of jobs by consistently overestimating the level of unemployment necessary to retain price stability."[11] Economists are not sure what constitutes the right level of unemployment to stabilize prices. But in the last few years, when tighter labor markets have failed to trigger inflation, the opinions of the financial pundits have consistently been wrong on this question.[12]

A powerful multiracial coalition that included the swelling ranks of the low- to moderate-income have-nots could, as a part of its national agenda, demand that the president appoint, and Congress approve, members to the Federal Reserve Board who will ensure that it upholds "its mandate to pursue both high employment and price stability by probing much more forcefully the limits of the economy's capacity to produce without inflation."[13] Policies that are effective in promoting full employment and controlling inflation would likely draw the support of the more advantaged, higher-income members of society as well. Currently, the discussion of how to control inflation is a complex one that involves mainly intellectual and financial elites. But I think that Jeff Faux is absolutely correct when he argues that "Americans are more likely to participate in a national debate over what it takes to achieve full employment than in the current dispiriting argument over how many people must be denied work in order to make the bond market comfortable."[14]

Such a debate over employment policies would be greatly facilitated if we were able to overcome our racial divisions and develop and coordinate local grassroots organizations that could join established national leaders—or generate new ones—in a powerful political coalition. This coalition could pursue policy issues relevant to all members of the large have-not population. But issues pursued by such a coalition do not have to be limited to those that address the problems of lower- to moderate-income groups. A standing coalition would also be poised to join forces with other groups to address particular issues that affect broader segments of population across race and class lines.

Let me give a quick example. It is generally recognized that public investment in core infrastructure improvements in roads, transit, sewers, and utilities is important for private investment. Indeed, private investment relies heavily on core infrastructure maintenance and improvement.[15] What is not generally recognized is that core infrastructure investments, in turn, are dependent on factors of density and distance for their initial feasibility and efficient operation. However, urban sprawl has made public investment in core infrastructure more costly and difficult. From 1970 to 1990, the urbanized area of American metropolitan regions expanded from eight to fifteen times as fast as population growth. From 1973 to 1996, as sprawl intensified, the growth in the value of core infrastructure plummeted.[16]

The strains that urban sprawl places on the core infrastructure are felt in many ways. As industrial and residential development sprawls across an ever-broadening geographical area, it creates a situation in which the urban economy is inadequately supported, as more transportation costs and inefficiency are imposed on business, more urban minorities are further removed from access to jobs, and more pollution and destruction of natural resources occur over a wider area.[17]

In Portland, Oregon, public discussion of the adverse effects of urban sprawl on the quality of metropolitan life led to the passage of zoning laws to control urban sprawl. It seems to me that an ongoing public discussion of the effects of urban sprawl on families, institutions, and neighborhoods could bring together groups not only from different racial backgrounds, but from different economic class backgrounds as well.

Generating Interracial Cooperation and Coalition Building

Given the complex national and international economic changes that affect broad segments of the American population, the development of a progressive multiracial political coalition is more important now than ever. As long as groups affected by global economic changes reject or fail to consider or envision the need for mutual political cooperation, they stand little chance of generating the political muscle needed to ease their economic burdens. The case for a progressive multiracial political coalition has to be made in political messages that resonate with broad segments of the American population. And the effectiveness of these messages will depend in part upon how we define the issues to be addressed.

The political message calling for change and outlining the need for a multiracial coalition ought to emphasize the benefits that would accrue to all groups who are struggling economically in America, not just poor minorities. The message should encompass the idea that changes in the global economy have enhanced social inequality and created situations that have heightened antagonisms between different racial and ethnic groups, and that although these groups are seen as social adversaries, they are potential allies in a reform coalition. Why? Because they are all negatively affected more or less by impersonal global economic changes.

Given the racial friction that has marred intergroup interaction in urban America, the formation of a multiracial reform coalition presents a challenge. Indeed, the contemporary emphasis on racial division and racial ideology makes it difficult to promote the idea of a multiracial political coalition to develop and pursue a mass-based economic agenda. Beginning with the riots in Los Angeles in 1992, and especially after the 1995 O.J. Simpson murder trial, media attention to racial matters has highlighted those factors that divide us.

Although it is important to acknowledge the racial divisions in America so that they can be meaningfully addressed, the incessant attention given to these gaps has obscured the following fact: black, white, Latino, Asian, and Native Americans share many concerns, are besieged by many similar problems, and have important norms, values, and aspirations in common. Take the issue of values. An analysis of the responses to questions that were variously asked in the national surveys conducted by National Opinion Research Center's General Social Survey since 1982 reveals only marginal racial differences in core values pertaining to work, education, family, religion, law enforcement, and civic duty. For example, in a 1982 survey 90 percent of whites and 89 percent of blacks felt that one's own family and children are very important; in a 1984 survey 88 percent of whites and 95 percent of blacks felt that the obligation of

Table 1 Are the Problems of People Like You (or Families Like Yours) Getting Worse?

	Percent Saying "Worse" or "Harder"			
Problem	Whites (N = 802)	African Americans (N = 474)	Latinos (N = 252)	Asian Americans (N = 353)
To maintain quality public schools	55	57	45	47
To get good jobs	56	60	50	56
To find decent, affordable housing	55	49	55	48
To stay together as a family	45	48	40	34
To get decent health care	44	39	30	30

Source: Adapted from Jennifer Hochschild and Reuel Rogers, "Race Relations in a Diversifying Nation," in *New Dimensions: African Americans in a Diversifying Nation,* ed. James Jackson (forthcoming), based on data from the Washington Post/Kaiser Foundation/Harvard Survey Project 1995.

American citizens to do community service is very or somewhat important; and in a 1993 survey 95 percent of whites and 92 percent of blacks felt that hard work in achieving life outcomes is either important or very important, and 97 percent of blacks and 88 percent of whites supported the view that being self-sufficient was either very important or one of the most important things in life.*

Also consider the perception of problems. As revealed in Table 1, questions about whether problems pertaining to public schools, jobs, affordable housing, families, and health care were getting worse or harder for the people with whom the respondents identify ("people like you or families like yours") elicited considerable agreement across racial and ethnic groups.

Furthermore, consider views on major policy issues. As seen in Table 2, except for affirmative action and abortion, there are no notable differences across racial and ethnic groups on reported strong preferences for congressional action—with overwhelming support for balancing the budget and changing the welfare system, less enthusiasm for cutting personal income taxes and reforming Medicare, and even less for business tax breaks. Finally, as Jennifer

*Findings from the General Surveys of the National Opinion Research Center of the University of Chicago. Considering the prevailing stereotypes, the findings on self-sufficiency are counterintuitive. Although there is a 9 percent racial gap, an overwhelming majority of respondents from both races strongly supported the idea of self-sufficiency. The only other finding that should be mentioned pertains to views on the importance of being married. Whereas 43 percent of the black respondents felt that being married was very important or one of the most important things in life, 53 percent of the white respondents felt this way.

Table 2 Policy Preferences for Congressional Action

Policy Issue	Whites (N = 802)	African Americans (N = 474)	Latinos (N = 252)	Asian Americans (N = 353)
	Percent Saying "Strongly Feel Congress Should Do"			
Limit tax breaks for business	39	41	41	30
Balance the budget	82	79	75	75
Cut personal income taxes	52	50	55	46
Reform the welfare system	83	73	81	68
Reform Medicare	53	58	59	58
Put more limits on abortion	35	32	50	24
Limit affirmative action	38	25	30	27

Source: Adapted from Jennifer Hochschild and Reuel Rogers, "Race Relations in a Diversifying Nation," in New Directions: African Americans in a Diversifying Nation, ed. James Jackson (forthcoming), based on data from the Washington Post/Kaiser Foundation/Harvard Survey Project 1995.

Hochschild and Reuel Rogers point out, there is considerable convergence in views across racial and ethnic groups with regard to policy preferences for solving particular problems, including education, crime, gang violence, and drugs.[18]

The development and articulation of an ideological vision that captures and highlights commonalities in basic core values and attitudes is paramount in establishing the case for a progressive multiracial political coalition and defusing the opposition of pessimists who promote the more limited advantages of group-specific political mobilization.[19]*

Social psychological research on interdependence reveals that when people believe that they need each other they relinquish their initial prejudices and stereotypes and join programs that foster mutual interaction and cooperation. Moreover, when people from different groups do get along, their perceptions about and behavior toward each other undergo change.[20] Under such circumstances, not only are efforts made by the participants in the research experiment to behave in ways that do not disrupt the interaction, but they also make

---

*However, Lani Guinier and Gerald Torres argue that the most effective way to involve minorities in racially inclusive coalitions is to organize them first around political issues that are explicitly race-specific. They assert that racial minorities are less likely to respond to calls for coalition building if their leaders do not first speak to and organize them around matters that relate to their racial experiences. Only then, it is argued, would it be possible to get racial minorities to expand their concerns and embrace issues that interest all groups. This claim is reasonable, but there is little systematic evidence to support it. Indeed, none of the successful multiracial coalitions discussed later in this chapter used this two-step process of minority involvement. (See Lani Guinier and Gerald Torres, "Critical Race Theory Revisited," the second of three Nathan I. Huggins Lectures, Harvard University, Cambridge, Massachusetts, April 20, 1999.)

an effort to express consistent and similar attitudes and opinions about an issue that confronts and concerns them.[21]

These conclusions are based mainly on David W. Johnson, Roger Johnson, and Geoffrey Maruyama's review and analysis of ninety-eight experimental studies of goal interdependence and interpersonal attraction. They revealed support in the research literature for the idea that interpersonal attraction among different racial and ethnic groups is enhanced by cooperative experiences. One reason for enhanced cooperation is that "within cooperative situations participants benefit from encouraging others to achieve, whereas in competitive situations participants benefit from obstructing others' efforts to achieve."[22] Accordingly, promotive interaction is greater within situations that are cooperative than in those that are competitive. The research reported considerably more interaction across ethnic lines in cooperative situations, and more cross-ethnic helping in such situations as well. In addition, the research indicated that cooperative situations enhance *social perspective taking*, "the ability to understand how a situation appears to another person and how that person is reacting cognitively and emotionally to it."[23] Finally, the research revealed that within cooperative situations "participants seemed to have a differentiated view of collaborators and tended to minimize perceived differences in ability and view all collaborators as being equally worthwhile, regardless of their performance level or ability."[24]

This research suggests the need for effective leadership to develop and articulate an ideological vision that not only highlights common interests, norms, values, aspirations, and goals, but also helps individuals and groups appreciate the importance of interracial cooperation to achieve and sustain them. This does not mean that group differences are not acknowledged in this vision. As the Harvard sociologist Marshall Ganz has pointed out, "acknowledging differences is essential to collaborating around common interest. . . . It is important not to pretend that we are all the same." He notes that racial and ethnic groups have important differences, "but these become resources rather than liabilities if we come up with ways to [build] on our commonalities."[25]

Visionary group leaders, especially those who head strong community organizations, are essential for articulating and communicating this vision, as well as for developing and sustaining this multiracial political coalition. According to the political scientist Raphael J. Sonenshein, the most effective coalitions are those that begin building in communities with strong political organizations already in place.[26]

Nonetheless, there is a common perception that given America's history of racial division and its current racism, it is naive to assume that a national multiracial coalition with a mass-based economic agenda could ever materialize. Many who share this perception do not consider seriously the possibility of creating the conditions of perceived interdependence needed to promote interracial cooperation and coalition building. Nor do they entertain the idea that given the right social circumstances, including the presence of creative, visionary leaders, such conditions could emerge.

However, there are cases from historical and contemporary America that cast doubt on such pessimism. A comprehensive study of interracial unionism during the Great Depression, for example, reveals that the United Auto Workers in Detroit, the primarily Pennsylvania-based Steel Workers Organizing Committee, and the similarly based United Mine Workers were "able to organize a racially mixed labor force in settings where past racial antagonisms and minority strike-breaking had been sources of labor defeat."[27] The interracial solidarity was facilitated by a number of factors that relate to general principles about perceived interdependence and that represent structural conditions conducive to interracial cooperation. These factors include racial convergence of orientations toward the labor market, a favorable political context featuring legislation (for example, the Wagner Act) that facilitated organizing activities, and changes in organizing tactics "that institutionalize racial inclusiveness in the union structure."[28]

Moreover, multiracial grassroots community organizations whose institutions, actions, and belief systems exemplify the very conditions of perceived interdependence do in fact exist today in this country. These groups benefit from the presence of forward-looking leaders who have effectively mobilized groups in their communities to achieve local goals. A notable example is the Living Wage Campaign. In a number of cities coalitions of local labor leaders, community-based organizations, religious leaders, and student groups, with multiracial participation, have prompted the passage of "living wage" ordinances. These ordinances require employers with municipal contracts or subsidies to raise the hourly minimum wage substantially above the federal minimum of $5.15. Living wage campaigns have been successful in sixteen cities, including Baltimore, Boston, Los Angeles, Milwaukee, Minneapolis, and New York. In addition, living wage campaigns are currently underway in seventeen other municipalities, including Albany, Chicago, Denver, Detroit, Philadelphia, Pittsburgh, and St. Louis.

The Living Wage Campaign movement is an excellent example of what can happen when local leaders are able to forge coalitions to rally behind an issue that concerns all races, in this case economic justice. With direct access to city legislators, leaders of these coalitions have been able to demonstrate the importance of mutual cooperation in achieving desired political goals.

The movement's first victory was in Baltimore in 1997, when a living wage ordinance was passed that required contractors doing business with the city to pay their workers a minimum of $6.10 an hour. Today they must pay $7.70 an hour, which is indexed to the rate of inflation. Los Angeles requires companies doing business with the city to pay a minimum wage of $7.25 an hour plus health benefits and twelve days of paid vacation. The city council in San Jose recently passed the highest living wage ordinance in the country, requiring businesses that receive city service contracts to pay their workers a minimum of $9.50 an hour with health benefits, or $10.75 an hour if employees do not receive health benefits. Reflecting on this legislation, Harry Kelber of *Sweat Labor Magazine* writes: "Although living-wage ordinances are limited to workers whose employers have contracts or other economic relationships with the city, they will put pressure on other employers to upgrade the wages of their workers."[29]

The Living Wage Campaign is gaining momentum, and whether it will expand to embrace other issues of economic and social justice remains to be seen. If it does, perhaps it might benefit from the lessons and experiences of a longer standing and very effective multiracial political coalition at the local level—namely, the national community organization networks of the Industrial Areas Foundation.[30]

A Case Study of an Effective Multiracial Political Coalition at the Grassroots Level: The Industrial Areas Foundation

More than fifty years ago, Saul Alinsky founded the Industrial Areas Foundation in conjunction with his efforts to organize Chicago's marginalized poor. Alinsky envisioned the IAF as a team of professional organizers who could identify committed individuals, assemble them for group action, and instruct them in effective methods of community improvement. Through this method, the IAF could help individuals organize into potentially powerful coalitions; IAF professionals could move from place to place in their mission of education and development, while the work of community development and improvement could be carried out by the people with the greatest stake in its success.

Today there is a national network of dynamic IAF organizations in forty communities from California to Massachusetts. To achieve this success, IAF professional organizers have worked within faith-based organizations—in most cases, Christian churches—to identify experienced leaders and to assemble them into nonsectarian coalitions devoted to community development. An important feature of the IAF approach is that even though the members of the coalition are drawn from faith communities, the IAF assembly constitutes an independent organization that is not tied to the participants' respective churches.

IAF organizations are known by many names, such as the Greater Boston Interfaith Organization (GBIO), Tying Nashville Together (TNT), East Brooklyn Churches (EBC), Baltimoreans United in Leadership Development (BUILD), and Valley Organized Community Efforts (VOICE), in Los Angeles County. Each organization reflects the distinctive needs of its community, because the agenda of each is determined by its leaders and members, not by the IAF.

Some of the IAF's most successful organizations are in Texas, where eleven IAF institutions are active across the state. Included among these is the San Antonio–based Communities Organized for Public Service (COPS), the largest, longest-standing IAF institution in the country and generally regarded as one of the strongest community organizations in the nation. COPS initiatives have resulted in hundreds of millions of dollars of infrastructure improvements in poor inner-city neighborhoods of San Antonio, through the upgrading or repair of streets, sidewalks, public lighting, and sewer drainage and the establishment or construction of parks and libraries. In addition, COPS has been responsible for the construction or rehabilitation of thousands of housing units.[31]

In Texas the IAF has created a model statewide network that has effectively influenced political decisions in municipal governments, the state legislature, and the governor's mansion. Furthermore, the network has brought together whites, African Americans, Mexican Americans, Catholics, and Protestants for mutual support in addressing matters of common concern and interest.

In mobilizing leadership in Texas, the IAF has generated and sustained interracial cooperation in three related ways. First, in initially establishing its multiracial organization, the Texas IAF relied on its members' shared commitment to broad religious principles to generate trust and a sense of common identity. Second, Texas IAF issues originate from local consensus and thus are consensual, not divisive; in addition, these issues are always framed in a race-neutral manner. And third, Hispanic, African American, and white leaders are united in local IAF organizations but retain significant autonomy by also serving in other organizations or enterprises that address race- and neighborhood-specific issues that are not part of the Texas IAF agenda, "as long as they remain within the broad unitary framework of the IAF." In other words, members of the IAF are allowed "to participate in race-oriented campaigns separately from their IAF involvement." Thus, the IAF follows a race-neutral strategy, "defining issues in a nonracial manner and emphasizing the potential benefit of its campaigns to all Americans."[32]

Although the IAF has been criticized for not explicitly addressing racial issues,[33] Mark Warren points out that such criticisms "miss the larger significance of the IAF's experience." He goes on to state:

> The IAF does indeed take up very many "issues of race," like poor schools, neighborhood neglect, health care shortages, and lack of economic opportunity. But it frames these issues in nonracial terms, emphasizing the interest of the whole community in addressing them. The IAF follows a local version of universalistic public policy, developing programs potentially open to all but with special benefit to low income, minority communities. . . . The Texas IAF has often proven adept at redefining issues that many perceive as racial, such as the poor state of education in inner-city African-American neighborhoods.[34]

The importance of the IAF's use of religious institutions in developing and sustaining interracial organizations should not be underemphasized. The fundamental worldview common to the Catholic clergy, Protestant ministers, and other active practitioners of Judeo-Christian creeds provides a foundation that allows for trust as its starting point. Seeing their common identity as "children of God," the leaders of the different racial or ethnic groups in the Texas IAF more readily perceive the commonality of their economic and political interests. Working to better the community for all can be seen as a matter of faith, hope, and charity. The IAF's consensual political strategy builds on this intersection of faith and action to frame issues within a larger context of religious and family values.[35] "What IAF has found is that when people learn through politics to work with each other, support one another's projects," claims Ernesto Cortes (head of the Southwest IAF), "a trust emerges that goes beyond the barriers of race, ethnicity, income, and geography; we have found that we can rebuild community by reconstructing society."[36]

However, as political writer William Greider has argued, in order to maximize political strength, it is important that a coalition attempt to build bridges not only across the racial divide, but across the class divide as well. In this connection he points out:

> IAF organizations are already at work on the [class] bridge building. Some of the Texas organizations, for instance, are truly diverse, with memberships that leap across the usual lines of race and class. Many white middle-class members, drawn by their Christian or Jewish faith and progressive civic values, have a conscience-driven commitment to their communities and a sense that this is the only politics that produces anything meaningful. . . . Cortes does not think that the IAF Texas network will achieve full status as a major power in the state until it succeeds at creating a presence among the white blue-collar workers in East Texas and elsewhere—people who have common economic interests but are in social conflict with blacks and Hispanics. The organizers are looking for such openings.[37]

In its successes in fostering influential community groups, the IAF provides a model for the development of a multiracial political coalition that would address *national* issues. Recall that social psychological research reveals that people who believe that they need each other go beyond their initial prejudices and stereotypes to join programs that foster mutual interaction and cooperation. And when groups are motivated to get along, their perceptions about and behavior toward each other undergo change. The research indicates that not only does each group make an effort to behave in ways that do not disrupt the interaction, but the groups also make an effort to express consistent and similar attitudes and opinions about an issue that confronts them.

The activities of the IAF support these research findings on mutual group interaction and cooperation. Effective leadership from visionary organizers such as Ernesto Cortes has created an awareness of common interests, goals, and values that can be enhanced by multiracial cooperation. IAF organizations clearly demonstrate that, despite America's strife-ridden racial history, effective leadership can overcome obstacles to foster sustained interracial cooperation. And I believe that IAF groups such as COPS in San Antonio provide a reference point for the proponents of social equality who feel that the development of a multiracial political coalition to address national issues, rather than purely local or regional issues, is feasible and desirable.

A key aspect of IAF successes, however, is also one that garners the groups' major criticism: they do not pursue issues as race-specific problems. Affirmations of racial solidarity are seen as incompatible with the organizations' commitment to build "whenever possible community organizations made up of diverse racial, ethnic and religious groups."[38] For example, in San Antonio, when the Hispanic south and west sides of San Antonio were plagued with floods, the local IAF organization, COPS, did not define the problem as a "Latino issue" or an issue of race; rather, the issue was presented as one of "poor drainage and disgraceful neglect of the lives of citizens of San Antonio."[39] In Fort Worth, Texas, the local IAF's efforts to increase parental involvement in the predominantly African American school were not described in terms of confronting racial discrimination in education; rather, the issue was discussed as one of neglect and failure in the local educational institutions.[40]

In San Antonio, COPS initially fought for improved sidewalks, better drainage systems, and comprehensive street pavings. After succeeding in these pursuits, COPS focused on upgrading housing, improving police protection, pursuing education reform, and promoting economic development. Many of these issues were also effectively pursued by the United Neighborhood Organization (UNO), the IAF chapter in Los Angeles, "along with a successful effort to increase the minimum wage in California."[41] Although both the UNO and COPS are heavily represented by Mexican Americans, issues such as bilingual education and immigration were conspicuously absent from the political agenda.[42] Finally, Texas IAF organizations have not called for municipal affirmative action to increase minority hiring or promotion. Nor have they endorsed political candidates on the basis of their race or ethnicity.[43]

In short, the IAF believes that racially defined issues are divisive and therefore counterproductive.[44] It is possible that defining an issue as a *Latino* issue or as a *black* issue runs the risk of provoking marginalization: if this is a black (Latino) problem, let African American (Mexican American) citizens solve it. But by presenting social and economic problems within the larger framework of support for San Antonio citizens or for Texans (or, given my hope for a nationwide IAF model, even for Americans), IAF-type organizations lay the groundwork for a discussion that shares resources across all groups. And, in fact, although IAF groups are careful to define issues in race-neutral terms, they do address issues of race by confronting the problems of the poor and the overlooked—persons who, in American society, are often racial minorities.

Even though the IAF has been successful in building an effective multiracial coalition by ignoring or avoiding explicit racial issues, would such a strategy be viable in the long run for a national multiracial coalition? If a progressive multiracial coalition is trying to build support for a mass-based economic agenda, a race-neutral strategy makes sense for the most part. Why? Because the goal is to attract wide segments of the population with messages that resonate across racial groups. "Both survey and case study evidence suggests that the more a multiracial coalition focuses on issues of racial and ethnic equality per se, the less stable it will be and the more likely it will be to fragment into competitive factions," state Jennifer Hochschild and Reuel Rogers. "Conversely, the same evidence shows that the more a multiracial coalition focuses on issues that are not ostensibly about race, and that have the potential to involve a wide range of people of all identities, the greater its chance of persistence and success."[45]

However, given the focus on basic economic issues, what about affirmative action? In the context of race-neutral agitation for social change, is affirmative action a divisive, racially explicit issue? Because many Americans view affirmative action programs as central to the continuing quest for economic racial justice in America, can it really be in any multiracial coalition's best interest to exclude such programs from its agenda?

A strategy that avoids explicitly racial issues has not been fatal to the IAF grassroots networks, bound together by a background of religious faith and the work of visionary community leaders who have been able to explain the merits of such a strategy to their constituents. This approach, however, may not work at the national level. For African Americans, affirmative action as national policy is seen as crucial for addressing American racial injustice that ranges from persistent institutional racism to overt racial discrimination. Accordingly, only an extraordinary appeal for a purely race-neutral strategy in employment would attract a significant segment of the black population to the coalition. Just as the coalition is weaker if it cannot attract large segments of the dominant white population, so too is it less powerful if only a fraction of the minority population is involved or interested.

Notes

1. Galbraith, 1998, 10.
2. Sheldon Danziger and Peter Gottschalk, introduction to *Uneven Tides: Rising Inequality in America*, ed. Sheldon Danziger and Peter Gottschalk (New York: Russell Sage Foundation, 1993).
3. Ibid., 15.
4. Edward M. Gramlich, Richard Kasten, and Frank Sammartino, "Growing Inequality in the 1980s: The Role of Federal Taxes and Cash Transfers," in *Uneven Tides: Rising Inequality in America*, ed. Sheldon Danziger and Peter Gottschalk (New York: Russell Sage Foundation, 1993), 245.
5. Schwartzman, 1997.
6. John M. Broder, "Party Spurned, Repays Clinton with Rebellion," *New York Times*, November 11, 1997, pp. A1 and A6.
7. Frank Borgers quoted in Steven Greenhouse, "Business and Labor Struggle with Globalization," *New York Times*, August 2, 1998.
8. David Sanger, "A Handicap for Clinton, but U.S. Still Dominates," *New York Times*, November 11, 1997, p. A6.
9. Galbraith, 1998, 8–9.
10. Ibid.
11. Faux, 1997, 32.
12. Ibid.
13. Ibid.
14. Ibid.
15. Richmond, 1997.
16. Ibid.
17. Ibid.
18. Jennifer Hochschild and Reuel Rogers, "Race Relations in a Diversifying Nation," in *New Directions: African Americans in a Diversifying Nation*, ed. James Jackson (forthcoming).
19. Raphael J. Sonenshein, "Biracial Coalitions in Big Cities: Why They Succeed, Why They Fail," in *Racial Politics in American Cities*, ed. Rufus P. Browing, Dale Rogers Marshall, and David H. Tabb (New York: Longman, 1990), 193–211.
20. For a good discussion and summary of this research, see D.W. Johnson, R. Johnson, and G. Maruyama, "Goal Interdependence and Interpersonal Attraction in Heterogeneous Classrooms: A Meta-Analysis," in *Groups in Contact: The Psychology of Desegregation*, ed. N. Miller and M.B. Brewer (Orlando, Fla.: Academic Press, 1984), 187–212. Also see Susan T. Fiske, "Stereotyping, Prejudice, and Discrimination," in *The Handbook of Social Psychology*, 4th ed., ed. D.T. Gilbert, S.T. Fiske, and G. Lindzey (New York: McGraw Hill, 1998).
21. Johnson, Johnson, and Maruyama, 1984.
22. Ibid., 199.

23. Ibid., 200.
24. Ibid., 202.
25. Marshall Ganz, private communication, October 16, 1998, Cambridge, Mass.
26. Sonenshein, 1990, 203.
27. John Brueggemann and Terry Boswell, "Realizing Solidarity: Sources of Interracial Union-ism during the Great Depression," *Work and Occupations* 25 (November 1998): 437.
28. Ibid., 442.
29. Harry Kelber, "Start a 'Living Wage' Campaign," http://sweatmag.org/livstart.htm.
30. Other successful multiracial enterprises have been identified and described as promising practices by President Clinton's Initiative on Race. See "One America, Promising Practices: The President's Initiative on Race," http://www.whitehouse.gov/Initiatives/OneAmerica/OneAmerica_Links.html.
31. Ernesto Cortes Jr., "Reweaving the Social Fabric," *Boston Review* (June–September, 1994): 12–14.
32. Mark R. Warren, "Creating a Multi-Racial Democratic Community: Case Study of the Texas Industrial Areas Foundation" (paper prepared for the conference on Social Networks and Urban Poverty, Russell Sage Foundation, New York, New York, March 1–2, 1996).
33. See, for example, James Jennings, "The Politics of Black Empowerment in Urban America: Reflections on Race, Class and Community," in *Dilemmas of Activism*, ed. Joseph M. Kling and Prudence S. Posner (Philadelphia: Temple University Press, 1990).
34. Warren, 1996.
35. Ibid.
36. Cortes, 1994.
37. William Greider, *Who Will Tell the People: The Betrayal of American Democracy* (New York: Simon and Schuster, 1992), 235.
38. Peter Skerry, *Mexican Americans: An Ambivalent Minority* (New York: The Free Press, 1993), 157.
39. Warren, 1996.
40. Ibid.
41. Skerry, 1993, 157.
42. Ibid.
43. Warren, 1996.
44. Ibid.
45. Hochschild and Rogers, 6–7.

Chapter 9

❖❖❖

NATIONAL POLICY AND LOCAL GOVERNMENTS

Cities in a Federal System

Reassessment of the appropriate roles for the various governments within our federal system has become a major policy issue. For more than two decades, federal policy-makers have shed their responsibilities in favor of grant-in-aid approaches that leave more discretion to local and state governments. During recent years, the conservative political tide and growing antigovernmental sentiments have fueled demands for further limitations on federal responsibility. The arrival of a Republican administration in 2000 dedicated to containing federal power continues this trend.

The selections in this chapter scrutinize this drift in national urban policy and probe what the different levels of government should do and what policies they ought to pursue. Both essays raise sobering questions about the social and political consequences of assigning less responsibility to the federal government. In Essay 27, Paul E. Peterson argues that there is an inescapable division of domestic policy roles in our federal system of government. He asserts that the local and state governments have historically taken the main responsibility for managing the nation's physical infrastructure (development policy), while the national government has been the dominant provider of social services for the elderly, the disabled, the poor, and other disadvantaged groups (redistributive programs). This division of responsibility is growing more pronounced despite political pressures to shed federal responsibilities for aiding the poor and disadvantaged citizens. He believes that it will continue no matter what officials might otherwise wish.

Peterson reasons that economic competition among states and localities tends to make them efficient providers of developmental programs. Yet this is not true in the case of redistributive activities, because the economic pressures discourage and even punish (through the flight of taxpayers and businesses) generosity to the down-and-out. In contrast, the federal government is far less affected by these kinds of economic pressures, which enables national officials to bear the costs of redistributive programs more easily. Consequently, Peterson concludes that proposals to shift responsibility from Washington to the states and local governments are bound to lead to growing inequalities, although they may succeed in the area of economic development. "One may regret that states and localities no longer seem capable of caring for the sick and needy," he suggests, "but it is a price a federal system must pay in an ever more integrated society."

Peter Eisinger (Essay 28) highlights the interdependency of local, state and national politics. He examines the fiscal link between the federal government and municipal governments after years of devolution, and concludes that a New Federal Order has emerged. He argues that changes in intergovernmental relations have forced mayors to focus more on making the most of the limited resources they have, making city hall less likely to attend to social, racial, and economic issues. Urban politics increasingly is focused on the political consequences of the cities' inability to solve many of their most pressing problems. Not surprisingly, in recent years many cities, such as New York, Los Angeles, Philadelphia, Indianapolis, and others, have witnessed the election of conservative mayors who stress public order and quality of life issues (such as clean streets) that are amenable to limited government.

27

Paul E. Peterson

WHO SHOULD DO WHAT? DIVIDED RESPONSIBILITY IN THE FEDERAL SYSTEM

The newly elected Republican-controlled congress arrived in Washington in January [1995] determined to turn a great deal of national policymaking over to the states. The Republicans' twin goals are to cut federal spending on state and local programs and to allow states to design public programs to fit their particular needs.

Many of their proposals—giving states more responsibility for transportation, job training, education, crime control, and other policies that affect economic development—are promising. A number are rightly winning the support of the Clinton administration. Indeed, President Clinton proposes to finance a tax cut by means of substantial reductions in federal spending on roads, housing, education, and flood control. For example, money is to be saved by combining 30 separate grants for construction and repair of mass transit systems, highways, airports, and railroads into a modest, if unified, transportation grant to states and localities.

The convergence of interest between the Republicans and President Clinton results partly, of course, from the enormous pressure exerted on federal spending by demands for tax cuts, the rising cost of senior-citizen entitlements, and the budget deficits piled up during the 1980s. But it also reflects an important trend in American federalism as it has been developing over the

"Who Should Do What?" by Paul Peterson, from *The Brookings Review*, Spring 1995, pp. 6–11. Copyright © 1995 *The Brookings Institution*. Reprinted by permission of The Brookings Institution.

past two decades—a shift in economic development responsibilities from the national to the state and local level. Despite partisan infighting, it is entirely possible that some version of these proposals will be enacted and that the shift will continue.

But Republican leaders are also proposing to delegate to the states responsibility for a broad range of social policies that serve low-income citizens. Early in March, for example, the House Ways and Means Committee approved legislation eliminating Aid to Families with Dependent Children [AFDC], an entitlement program, and replacing it with a fixed block grant that, unlike AFDC, would not increase or decrease depending on the number of welfare recipients. Under the proposed block grant program, states could set, within limited guidelines, their own eligibility standards and benefit levels.

Unlike the Republicans' proposals to increase the state role in economic development policy-making, transferring redistributive policy from Washington to the states would be a mistake. It would defy the logic of the existing division of responsibility between the national and state levels of government and give states responsibility for a policy role for which they are unsuited.

Dividing Public Responsibilities

As relations between state and national governments have evolved over this century, the two levels of government have—for very good reasons, as I shall explain shortly—taken distinctively different domestic policy roles. Traditionally, states and localities have taken responsibility for managing the country's physical and social infrastructure—roads, education, mass transit systems, public parks, police and fire services, and sanitation systems—necessary for the country's economic growth. I shall call these kinds of policies *developmental* because without them economic progress would be retarded. The national government, by contrast, has taken responsibility for transferring economic resources from those who have gained the most from economic development to those who have gained the least—the elderly, the disabled, the unemployed, the sick, the poor, families headed by single parents, and others lacking in material resources. I shall refer to these policies as *redistributive* because they shift resources from the "haves" to the "have-nots."

Since 1962, developmental spending at the state and local level has been more than double that at the national level. In 1962, state and local spending was 9.4 percent of gross national product as compared with 4.2 percent for national spending (Figure 1 on the facing page). Despite growth in the size of the domestic responsibilities of the national government in subsequent decades, Washington still spends less than half as much on development at the lower tiers. In 1990, the states and localities were spending 10.8 percent of GNP [Gross National Product] on the country's developmental infrastructure, while the national government was spending only 5.2 percent of GNP.

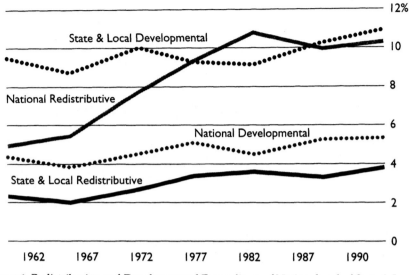

Figure 1 Redistributive and Developmental Expenditure of National and of State & Local Governments as a Percentage of the Gross National Product, 1962–1990.

With regard to redistributive expenditure, the story is entirely different. Since 1962, the state and local share of the country's spending on the elderly, the poor, and the needy has steadily declined. While national government redistributive spending more than doubled, from 4.9 percent of GNP in 1962 to 10.3 percent in 1990, state and local redistributive spending edged up only slightly, from a very low 2.2 percent of GNP in 1962 to only a slightly higher 3.5 percent in 1990. The modest increment at the state and local levels is particularly striking, inasmuch as this was the period when the civil rights movement awakened the country to problems of poverty, the Great Society was introduced, and entitlements became an entrenched part of American social policy. Yet the percentage of state spending devoted to redistribution increased only from 28.9 percent to 33.0 percent. And at the local level the increase was barely detectable, from 13.5 percent to 14.1 percent.

State and local reluctance to participate in the redistributive movement can hardly be attributed to the political climate. Over most of this period Democrats controlled at least part of state government in most states, and they held unified control over both houses of the state legislature as well as the gubernatorial chair in many. And despite the intent of today's congressional Republicans to transfer welfare policy to the states, there is no indication that states are becoming either more suited for or more capable of such policy.

To the contrary, the division of responsibility between national and state governments is growing more pronounced, as each level of government has learned to concentrate its spending on the things it does best. States and localities, ever more constrained by market forces, are increasingly competent at making choices affecting state and community development. But state and local capacities to care for the needs of poor and disadvantaged citizens have been diminishing.

Economic Development Engine

Local governments are efficient mechanisms for supplying most of the physical and social infrastructure needed for economic development. In providing roads, schools, sanitation systems, and public safety to their residents, local governments must be sensitive to local businesses and residents. If they ignore them, people will vote with their feet and move to another town. Since 17 percent of the population changes its residence each year, the effects of locational choices on property values can be quickly felt. Moreover, if a locality makes a poor policy choice, its failure will soon become apparent and will be ignored by other communities. If it chooses wisely, its policy will be copied—and thus be disseminated throughout the federal system.

Not all local policies will be identical, of course. People vary in their tastes and preferences. Some towns will provide sex education in their schools; others will not. Some towns will ban smoking in stores and restaurants; others will be more permissive. Some towns will emphasize country lanes for walkers and joggers; others will concentrate on playgrounds and baseball diamonds. Part of what makes local government efficient is the variety it provides for people choosing a place to live.

Developmental policy cannot be an exclusively local prerogative, however. For example, major systems of transportation, air and water pollution control, and some forms of higher education must be coordinated across a substantial geographical area. Thus state governments, too, are significant participants in economic development.

The national government, on the whole, is the least efficient provider of economic development. Unlike states and localities, it operates under few market-like constraints. It need not fear that a series of poor economic investments will cause citizens to move to another country. But without market signals to help guide policy choices, development easily degenerates into political "pork" that does little to spur national economic growth. Proposals to create a national industrial policy have generally gone nowhere—in good part because proponents cannot convince policymakers that national bureaucracies can allocate scarce economic resources wisely.

Washington did enlarge its developmental responsibilities during the 1970s, largely through grants to state and local governments. Federal dollars were given to cities and towns to help build roads, fight crime, improve schools, and redevelop deteriorating central business districts. Members of Congress delighted in taking credit for securing federal dollars that helped build bridges, dams, tunnels, and colliders. Joe McDade of Scranton, Pennsylvania, ranking Republican on the House Appropriations Committee, may have been one of the all-time winners. He secured federal monies to help build a center for the performing arts and fund a microbiology institute for cancer research at the University of Scranton (even though it has no medical school and few research scientists), restore an antique aqueduct, construct McDade Park (including a tourist-friendly museum on the history of coal mining), turn the home of second-rate author Zane Grey into a national monument, finance a flood-control project, and convert a railroad station into a fancy hotel and restaurant.

This kind of developmental pork prospered during the sixties and seventies partly because Congress was organized into subcommittees that focused member attention on narrow issues and interests. But it was also facilitated by the fact that the revenues of the national government increased automatically by means of inflation-induced bracket creep within a steeply progressive income tax. Members of Congress could enjoy increasing tax revenues without ever passing a tax increase. Indeed, it was possible to claim that taxes were being cut even when inflation was causing them to increase. (The famous Kennedy tax cut of 1963, for example, was in fact nothing other than an offset against bracket increase.)

But in 1981 income taxes were sharply reduced, brackets were indexed to inflation, and fiscal deficits mounted. In subsequent years, every new federal program had to be paid for with a new tax. Even existing programs were endangered by the squeeze created by the pressing demand for tax cuts and the rising cost of senior-citizen entitlements. Developmental pork lost its allure. The size of the intergovernmental grant program dropped precipitously, and the percentage of the remaining grants that were developmental (as distinct from redistributive) declined from a high of 59.5 in 1977 to 43.1 in 1990. Far from being a radical departure from past practice, the recent cuts in developmental spending proposed by both Republican leaders and the Clinton administration are just the latest in a decade-long series of like-minded decisions.

Not that Washington should play no role in economic development. Some policies, such as investment in scientific research, have such broad and far-reaching consequences that they must be carried out by the national government. Others, such as certain components of the communication and transportation system, must be coordinated in Washington to achieve a desired degree of national integration. Still other development aid to states and localities allows the national government to minimize the adverse effects of economic development on the environment.

Nevertheless, the national role in economic development has dwindled in recent years under the pressure of fiscal deficits, anti-tax pressures, and senior-citizen entitlements, and it will probably continue to do so.

Redistributing the Wealth

For the same reason that local governments are best suited to providing economic development—the mobility of labor and capital—they are not effective at redistributing wealth. Local governments, for example, avoid progressive income taxes. No more than 3 percent of local revenues comes from this source. Any locality making a serious attempt to tax the rich and give to the poor will attract more poor citizens and drive away the rich. No amount of determination on the part of local political leaders can make redistributive efforts succeed. If no other force is able to stop their efforts, bankruptcy will.

The smaller the territorial reach of a local government, the less its capacity for redistribution. Most small suburbs in metropolitan areas have almost no capacity to meet the special needs of low-income citizens, because the effects of such actions would be immediately felt in the suburb's tax rate, property values, and attractiveness to business. Big cities are somewhat better able to undertake redistribution because of their greater geographical reach and their control over extremely valuable land at the heart of the nation's transportation system.

The greater territorial reach of states also makes them better at redistribution than most local governments. The costs of moving across state lines is more substantial than changing residence within a metropolitan area. As against the 17 percent of the population who change residence every year, only 3 percent move across a state line. Even so, labor and capital can and do move, and states must take that possibility into account in their policymaking. Since 1970, for example, states have been in something of a race to lower welfare benefits for fear that high benefits could attract poor people to the state—thus raising social spending and perhaps triggering an exodus of taxpayers.

The bulk of the responsibility for income redistribution falls to the national government. It levies higher taxes on the well-to-do than on the poor, then carries out redistribution through pensions, welfare, health care, and other programs aimed at the needy, the old, the sick, the disabled, and the disadvantaged. The largest and most successful redistributive programs in the United States—Social Security and Medicare—are designed and administered in Washington. And again the explanation is capital and labor mobility—or rather comparative *im*mobility. Washington is best suited to engage in redistribution because it can prevent the in-migration of labor from foreign countries and need not worry as much about the outward flow of capital. If any state or local government had attempted to mount programs like Social Security by itself, it would have gone bankrupt long before becoming a haven for the aged.

The increasing integration of the world economy has begun to erode some of the national government's redistributive capacities. Information and products can move globally at low cost. Capital also flows freely. Nevertheless, as long as the U.S. political economy remains healthy and stable, the national government will continue to have the capability of redistributing substantial amounts of the national income.

Current economic trends are having a considerably more powerful effect at state and local levels. The improvements in transportation and communication systems that have produced an increasingly integrated world economy are also at work among states and localities within the United States itself. Capital, entrepreneurial activity, and skilled labor have become ever more mobile. State and local governments now face increasingly competitive relationships with each other and must attend ever more strictly to economic development. The result is that they are growing ever more reluctant to provide for the needy within their ranks.

Making the Best of Federalism

The Republican proposals for wholesale policy shifts from Washington to the states and localities have grabbed their share of headlines, and many are likely to be signed, sealed, and delivered. Plans to transfer economic development functions to the states are not only politically feasible but also smart policy, for they place economic development in the hands of those policymakers best able to manage it.

But the Republican plans to move welfare policymaking to the nation's statehouses are more dubious, if for no other reason than that state and local officials have become increasingly reluctant to pay for the cost of social policy. It is my (perhaps reckless) prediction that any policy enacted in the forthcoming Congress that dramatically shifts the responsibility for welfare downward to states and cities will prove unworkable and short-lived, simply because such shifts run at odds with the underlying structure of the federal system. If I am wrong and welfare policy is permanently turned over to the states, the well-being of the most marginal members of society, including large numbers of children living in poverty, will be adversely affected in serious ways.

States have demonstrated that they are increasingly incapable of sustaining welfare benefits in an ever more integrated economy. State AFDC benefits are jointly funded by the national and state governments but set at the state level. For the first 33 years after AFDC was established in 1937, states raised the real value of this benefit program steadily. The mean benefit paid to a family in the average state was $287 in 1940, $431 in 1950, $520 in 1960, and $608 in 1970 (all figures are in 1993 dollars).

But in 1970 welfare benefits began to decline, partly because states became more fearful that high benefit levels were attracting and retaining poor people within their states. In 1969 the Supreme Court decided, in *Shapiro v. Thompson*, that newcomers could not be denied access to state welfare benefits. Over the next 20 years evidence accumulated that high benefit levels acted as a (low-strength, but nonetheless detectable) welfare magnet. The debate over the welfare magnet intensified and, after 1970, welfare benefits began to fall—to $497 in 1975, $437 in 1980, $409 in 1985. In 1990 they reached $379, and in 1993 they dropped to $349, not much more than they were in 1940!

In the earliest days of this century, states often led the way to innovative social policies (Wisconsin had an unemployment compensation system before the national government did). But in recent years state proposals to reform welfare have generally taken the form of reductions in welfare assistance. In

1988 the Family Support Act explicitly gave states the opportunity to experiment with Aid to Families with Dependent Children. The first three proposals submitted to the Department of Health and Human Services all proposed new restrictions on welfare. Wisconsin and New Jersey petitioned, among other things, to withhold the increase in benefits that typically comes with the birth of an additional child. California proposed an immediate 25 percent reduction in benefits, a second further reduction for all families remaining on welfare after six months, and a restriction that limited benefit levels to new arrivals to California to the level they were receiving in their previous state of residence. What began in a few states is now spreading nationwide.

Although AFDC has been the major target of state welfare cuts, other redistributive programs have proven to be politically unpalatable as well. State general assistance programs have all but disappeared. State supplementary benefits to the long-term unemployed and to disabled persons have also been dramatically reduced, even while national benefits have kept pace with increases in the cost of living. State contributions to unemployment insurance programs have fallen far short of what is necessary to maintain their viability.

Looking to the Future

Intensified state and local opposition to redistribution is understandable in an economy that has become increasingly integrated and a society that has become ever more mobile. States and localities can no longer make policy choices as if they were living in isolation from other parts of the country. The decisions they take are noticed by people elsewhere, and the impact on their economic and fiscal situation will be felt sooner rather than later. One may regret that states and localities no longer seem capable of caring for their sick and needy, but it is a price a federal system must pay in an ever more integrated society.

Because states and localities are unequipped to finance social welfare programs, their role in any welfare reform should be carefully circumscribed. The legislation approved in March [1995] by the House Ways and Means Committee to abolish AFDC gives states far too much latitude to set policy and is almost certain to worsen the "welfare magnet" problem. As some states tighten eligibility standards and reduce benefit levels, states with more generous benefits will become more powerful welfare magnets than ever before and yet will receive no commensurate increase in federal funding, as now happens, if poor people move to take advantage of the more generous benefits. And states are already making strenuous efforts to avoid losing the "race to the bottom."

The state of Wisconsin reported last summer that about 20 percent of new AFDC applicants in Milwaukee county came from new residents, many of whom were arriving from Illinois, a state with lower welfare benefits. To respond to these pressures, Wisconsin asked the national government for permission to try an experiment in which recent migrants would for six months only receive a level of benefits equal to that of the state from which they were migrating. In the past, courts have declared such discriminatory treatment of newcomers as unconstitutional, but the Supreme Court announced last fall that it would be willing to revisit this issue. If discrimination against newcomers to a state is given constitutional blessing, a new round of state welfare cuts can be anticipated.

Time has shown that national government has a different sphere of competence than that of state and local governments. The new breeze blowing through Washington should capitalize on this increasingly well-known fact and return to states and localities most of the responsibility for maintaining the nation's physical and social infrastructure necessary to sustain economic growth. But some things, namely programs for the sick, the poor, the needy, and the elderly, remain a Washington responsibility. To turn these responsibilities over to the states is to turn the clock backward.

28

Peter Eisinger

CITY POLITICS IN AN ERA OF FEDERAL DEVOLUTION

The effort that began more than 25 years ago to construct what might be called a New Federal Order is still very much a work in progress. President Clinton and most members of Congress . . . clearly embraced some of the elements that differentiate this federal arrangement from its New Deal-Great Society predecessor such as diminishing federal intergovernmental aid, block grants, and formal devolution of federal responsibilities. But the scope and details of implementation of this latest iteration of the federal arrangement are not yet fully worked out. The bare walls of the edifice have been erected, but there is little interior decoration.

As members of the tripartite federal partnership that came to its fullest expression in the Great Society and the years immediately following, local governments have a deep interest in the process and outcomes of federal realignment. As the outlines of the New Federal Order of the 1990s have taken shape, it is clear that the implications for urban government are manifold. Nevertheless, even though many of the problems and issues that are reshaping federalism are concentrated in urban areas, much is uncertain about what precise role the cities will play in the emerging intergovernmental environment. Curiously, city representatives and city interests have been, according to Weir (1996, 1), "conspicuously absent from the congressional debate about devolution."

"City Politics in an Era of Federal Devolution" by Peter Eisinger, *Urban Affairs Review*, Vol. 33, No. 3, January 1998, pp. 308–325. Copyright © 1998 by Sage Publications. Reprinted by permission of Sage Publications.

Certain developments in national politics make this an appropriate moment to take stock and to speculate about the future of the cities in the New Federal Order. In summer 1996, Congress passed, and the president signed, the new welfare law, converting cash support for the poor from an open-ended federal entitlement to a fixed block grant to the states. Devolution through block granting is the focus of debate in other areas of public policy, from law enforcement to highway funding and from job training to housing, all policy domains in which the local government role is clearer and more formalized than in the welfare realm. Not only is there now broad interest in devolving power though block grants but the intergovernmental aid reductions put in place in Republican Washington in the 1980s are no longer resisted by deficit-averse Democrats. In this article, then, I explore what is known about cities in the New Federal Order, what their future role might be, and what the effects on cities of the changes in the federal arrangement have been.

I suggest that to the extent that cities are increasingly cut off from federal aid and program initiatives, mayors must focus more and more on making the most of the resources they control. Thus the arts of public management are becoming the primary tasks of local political leadership. This represents an important change in the moral climate of local politics, because city hall is far less likely to be used these days as the bully pulpit from which mayors once sought to exercise leadership on major social, racial, and economic issues.

The New Federal Order

I define the New Federal Order as that rearrangement of federal relationships that began with President Richard Nixon's efforts to devolve authority from Washington to subnational governments through block grants and general revenue sharing and continues today as Congress, the president, and the governors combine to contract the role of the federal government in domestic policy. Although the initial efforts in the 1970s to transform the New Deal-Great Society federal system were seen as partisan attempts to diminish Washington's influence, both parties seem to agree today not only that the era of big government is over but that the proper locus of policy invention and administration is at the state and local level, For example, even before the passage of the welfare reform bill of 1996, the Clinton administration had approved 78 state welfare demonstration projects. More generally, the president's urban policy, according to his assistant secretary of the Department of Housing and Urban Development (HUD) at the time, "recognizes that the most pressing problems facing older cities can no longer be addressed through countercyclical grant-in-aid programs" (Stegman 1996). Where do the cities fit, then, in the New Federal Order?

It is important to begin by distinguishing several different aspects of the process of creating the New Federal Order. One aspect is simply the contraction of federal intergovernmental aid. This trend represents the devolution by default of fiscal responsibility to states and localities. A second aspect is the formal devolution of power from Washington to subnational government, a re-arrangement of responsibilities that, for the most part, has not yet greatly increased the powers and responsibilities that, for the most part, has not yet greatly increased the powers and responsibilities of city governments. A third feature concerns the indirect consequences of devolution to the states. These spin-off fiscal and political effects are manifold, and they affect the cities in important ways.

Fiscal Contraction

Federal assistance to cities is much diminished since the late 1970s. The contraction of aid has been so dramatic that the federal government's loss of interest in urban affairs is one of the signal stories of the great transformation to the New Federal Order. Yet a focus on the big picture alone may be somewhat misleading: Cities have not been entirely cut adrift fiscally to live on their own resources.

In 1977, the year before federal aid contraction began, municipal governments looked to Washington for 15.9% of their total revenues. By 1992, federal assistance had decreased to only 4.7% of local revenues (Chernick and Reschovsky 1997; see also Wallin 1996). In 1991, combined federal grants in aid to state and local governments regained their high watermark of 1978 (in constant dollar terms), but the functional distribution of intergovernmental fiscal assistance had changed in ways particularly disadvantageous to the cities. Although grants for education, job training, and social services, many of which are allocated to local governments, accounted for 23.9% of federal intergovernmental aid in 1980, the figure had decreased to 15.8% by 1994. Community development assistance decreased during this period from 7.1% to 2.9% of federal aid, and grants for sewer and water construction and environmental cleanup went from 5.9% to 2.0%. Meanwhile, health-related grants, mainly Medicaid, which is channeled through the states to individuals, rose from 17.2% of all federal intergovernmental assistance to 42.1% (Advisory Commission on Intergovernmental Relations 1994, 31). In short, a much smaller proportion of federal aid is devoted to urban programs than was true just a decade and a half ago.

An analysis by the U.S. Conference of Mayors ([USCM] 1994) of funding of key urban programs shows how severe the cuts have been from the perspective of the cities. Between 1981 and 1993, funding of community development block grants, urban development action grants, general revenue sharing, mass transit aid, employment and training programs, clean-water construction, assisted housing, and the various programs of the Economic Development Administration decreased by 66.3% in real dollar terms (see Table 1).

State governments did little to make up for the evaporation of federal monies for their municipalities. Reeling from the losses of federal aid that they themselves were experiencing, especially with the end of the state portion of general revenue sharing in 1980, state governments significantly reduced the rate of growth of aid to their local governments. Altogether, state aid to local

Table 1 Federal Funds for Cities, 1981–1993 (in billions of constant 1993 dollars)

Program	FY 1981 ($)	FY 1993 ($)	% Real Cut
Community Development Block Grant	6.3	4.0	–36.5
Urban Development Action Grant	0.6	0.0	–100.0
General revenue sharing	8.0	0.0	–100.0
Mass transit	6.9	3.5	–49.3
Employment and training	14.3	4.2	–70.6
Economic Development Administration	0.6	0.2	–66.7
Assisted housing	26.8	8.9	–66.8
Clean-water construction	6.0	2.6	–56.7

Source: U.S. Conference of Mayors (1994).

governments as a proportion of local revenues decreased from 25.4% to 21.2% of local revenues between 1977 and 1992 (Chernick and Reschovsky 1997).

Although urban-oriented federal aid had dropped substantially by the mid-1990s, the federal government in the Clinton era has not abandoned the cities. Beginning with fiscal year 1995, the USCM began tracking federal funding of a range of specific "municipal programs."[1] Of the 80 programs tracked over the three-year period by the USCM, 27 showed decreases, 8 were unchanged, and 45 received increases in funding. Of those 45, however, only 26 received funding increases that equaled or exceeded the inflation rate.

The data indicate, however, that with a few exceptions, municipal programs did not experience the huge cuts in the middle Clinton years that they had suffered in the earlier decade. Federal funding of programs that benefit cities could be described as approaching a steady state, with substantial changes only at the tails of the distribution. One implication for the cities is that although they do not stand to lose even more federal dollars, it is unlikely that a return to the patterns of the pre-Reagan era will occur. Nothing in the patterns of federal aid in the 1990s suggests that city governments will be able to relax their habits of fiscal self-reliance.

Formal Devolution

The principal definition of the term devolution in the context of U.S. federalism is the reallocation of specific responsibilities and authority from Washington to subnational governments. Since 1980, devolution has primarily involved a shift from national to state government. Such a rearrangement lay at the heart of President Reagan's New Federalism, one of the elements of which involved a failed proposal to carry out the so-called Great Swap: Washington would assume full responsibility for Medicaid in return for complete state takeover of the Aid to Families with Dependent Children (AFDC) and Food Stamps programs.

Reagan's effort to shape the New Federal Order was not entirely in vain, however: He did succeed in persuading Congress to consolidate 77 categorical grants-in-aid into 10 broad block grants to the states. The consequence was to strip Congress of the authority to designate specific uses of federal assistance for a variety of mainly health and education programs. State governments could now establish their own priorities within the broad boundaries of these new block grants. As in the current era, however, the interests of cities were scarcely considered in this federal reordering. Indeed, the new state power came directly at the expense of the cities: Of the categorical programs consolidated into block grants to the states, 47 had previously delivered funds directly to local governments (Ladd 1994, 219).

The Reagan federalism reforms failed to stem the growth of categorical grants, the number of which had reached an all-time high of 618 by 1995. Yet, contrary to the legislative trend, interest in devolution has remained high, both in Washington and in the state houses, fueled by the increasingly bipartisan conviction that in most matters of domestic policy, government closest to the people governs best. For proponents of devolution, the decade of the 1990s began in a promising way with the passage of the Intermodal Surface Transportation Efficiency Act (ISTEA), which greatly expands the ability of state and local governments alike to reallocate transportation funds among specific modes. Thus, in 1995, for example, more than $800 million was shifted by subnational governments from one purpose to another, such as the New York City Transit Authority's transfer of money initially designated for highways to mass transit projects, including station upgrades and signal modernization.[2]

Another significant devolutionary initiative during the Clinton years was the 1996 Personal Responsibility and Work Opportunity Reconciliation Act, better known as welfare reform, which created the Temporary Assistance to Needy Families (TANF) block grant. Henceforth, states will receive a fixed amount of funding from which to provide income support and work programs. State governments will now be responsible for establishing eligibility requirements and time limits. The shift of welfare responsibility to the states creates no formal local role, however, although there are clearly indirect implications for the cities that will be discussed later.

In no analysis of the urban implications of the changing distribution of responsibilities and authority in the federal system can one ignore two other initiatives of the mid-1990s: the Empowerment Zone and Enterprise Cities Act of 1993 and the Unfunded Mandates Reform Act of 1995. Neither devolves specific powers to subnational governments that they did not have before, but unlike most earlier devolutionary reforms, they both promise to expand the scope of local self-determination.

Along with providing some tax and regulatory relief, the Empowerment Zone and Enterprise Cities Program offers selected communities grants under the Title XX Human Services block grant program that may be used for an expanded range of social services and economic development. The Title XX block grant is made to the states, which in turn pass the funds onto their winning communities. In the first round, the few big winners received grants of $100 million each over a 10-year period, and a larger number of cities won smaller grants.

The program does not represent a devolution of new programmatic authority and responsibility in the field of economic and community development;
these already rest primarily at the subnational level. Rather, the empowerment
zone program devolves additional *capacity* to facilitate initiatives devised at the
local level. Indeed, HUD is explicit in its implementation guidelines that programs are to be the product of strategic plans developed in the neighborhoods
rather than in Washington (U.S. Government Accounting Office 1996, 3, 5).

The Unfunded Mandates Reform Act of 1995 has less obvious consequences but holds out the potential for curbing the growth rate of federal intergovernmental regulation and oversight and the imposition on states and localities of enforceable duties, as they are called in the act. The relief from mandates
provided by Congress is oblique: The purpose of the act is to "assist congress in
its consideration of proposed legislation ... containing Federal mandates ...
by providing for development of information about the nature and size of
mandates, [by promoting] informed and deliberate decisions by Congress on
the appropriateness of Federal mandates in any particular instance, [and by re-
quiring] that Congress consider whether to provide funding" to help subnational governments comply with the mandates (Unfunded Mandate Reform
Act of 1995, P.L. 104-4). Member of Congress may be called upon to vote explicitly to include a mandate in a new program. The act is thus designed not so
much to bar unfunded mandates as to discourage Congress by making the decision to impose a new mandate a thoroughly self-conscious and transparent
action. If the intent of the act is realized, state and local governments may find
over time that they may exercise unregulated governance over a slightly larger
range of functions.

Although it is evident that little formal devolution from Washington to the
cities has yet occurred, there are various proposals on the political agenda that
would expand the urban role in the New Federal Order. During his term as the
head of HUD, Secretary Henry Cisneros recommended creating a block grant
through the consolidation of existing programs that would go to local governments to serve the homeless. Cisneros was said to believe that "homelessness is
a local problem that is best solved ... at the local level. ... The most Washington can do is show the way" (Rapp 1994, 80). There has also been talk in Washington of consolidating 60 current HUD programs into three block grants for
housing assistance, housing production, and community development. Another proposal, put forth by congressional Republicans after they won control
of the House in the 1994 elections, was to eliminate the Community Oriented
Policing Services program and substitute a $10 billion block grant to localities
for law enforcement purposes, but President Clinton vetoed the appropriations
bill that threatened to transform this signature program.

As these examples make clear, devolution is increasingly a shared goal of
both political parties. Unlike the devolution of the Reagan years, the expansion
of state authority is not the sole focus of federal reform. Although little formal
authority has yet been transferred to local governments, some of the groundwork has been laid by forcing city governments to rely more heavily on their
own resources. City governments may anticipate playing an even more central
role in the federal rearrangement in the future.

Indirect Consequences of Devolution

As federal devolution proceeds at the end of the century, cities are increasingly subjected to a variety of indirect effects. Some of these are a function of the increased burdens on state governments; others stem from the cities' growing fiscal self-reliance. There are at least three categories of indirect consequences. First, there are the looming fiscal effects of welfare devolution. Second, there will be some shifting of burdens in a variety of functional areas as federal aid reductions force cities to provide services now supported by shared funding. Finally, there are a number of consequences, already evident, for the nature of local politics and political leadership. In particular, political reputation and success increasingly rest on public management skills rather than on the ability to exercise moral suasion on matters of social policy or to promote a racial agenda. These latter effects, already strongly in evidence, are signs of a deep change in the texture of urban politics.

Fiscal Effects Weir (1996) offered the general prediction that states will adjust to reductions in federal funding by poaching on local revenue sources, although how widespread this might become and the particular forms it might take are not yet apparent. There is one modest fiscal challenge to local government revenues, however, and it derives from the new welfare law. Certain provisions of the bill are likely to reduce municipal tax collections, increase local government costs by creating greater demand for local public service jobs and education, and harm the consumer economy in high-poverty neighborhoods by reducing the disposable income of the poor.

The new law provides that after a maximum of two years on TANF, recipients must leave the welfare rolls and engage in some sort of work. Some will succeed, finding unsubsidized jobs in the private sector. Others, however, will not. Indeed, this outcome is the more likely in many cities, because there are simply not enough entry-level jobs to absorb the number of adults that will come off the welfare rolls. For example, if all the unemployed adults in Chicago—those on public assistance as well as those who are not—were to look for work, there would be six workers for every available entry-level job (Weir 1996, 4). In New York City, there are currently approximately 470,000 able-bodied adults on welfare. They will join the roughly 271,000 unemployed people not on welfare in the job search. These roughly three-quarters of a million people will be competing for employment in a local economy that is producing about 20,000 new jobs per year, and many of these require substantial skills and education (Finder 1996).

Of those who do not find work in the private sector, some will migrate from the state and others will fall back on relatives or friends. In either case, they will no longer have the steady, even if modest, spending power provided by cash welfare assistance. Pagano, Lobenhofer, and Dudas (1996) argued that one result of this loss of cash assistance by people otherwise not gainfully employed will be to lower the city's property and sales taxes and the local excise tax base by reducing both rental housing demand and consumer spending. With less cash—and fuel or food stamp benefits—flowing into poor urban communities, retail sales and employment dependent on welfare clients will suffer. Using an economy-wide model developed at the U.S. Department of Agriculture, Smallwood et al. (1995, 10) found that even a modest cut in food assistance will lead to more than 100,000 lost jobs in food processing, retail, and non-food sectors.[3]

Those who exhaust their welfare eligibility but who cannot find work in the private sector and who do not vanish from administrative view by moving in with relatives or leaving the state have several options, according to the law. They may seek subsidized employment in either the public sector or community service programs; they may seek job skills training directly related to employment; or, for high school dropouts, they may return to high school.[4] Although the block grant to the states may fund some of these options, it is also likely that local government resources may be called into play to create public service jobs or classroom training and education. This is so in large part because the new law does not provide enough funding to finance subsidized work and training. The Congressional Budget Office estimates the shortfall in support of the work requirement at $12 billion over the next six years (Super et al. 1996, 14). States may pick up some of these costs, but they are likely to push some of them onto the cities. The 1996 welfare reform, then, will not be free of cost for the cities.

Service Shifting of Burdens Some welfare recipients who reach their time limits will find neither work nor shelter with relatives or friends. Some will no doubt find themselves literally on the streets. Homeless programs that are funded locally will certainly feel the impact. Other unsuccessful job seekers will resort to crime, increasing the burden on the local criminal justice system.

Although anyone who would have been eligible for welfare on 16 July 1996 remains eligible for Medicaid, there is no guarantee that congress will not change the entire Medicaid program. The House and the Senate were near agreement late in 1995 to create a Medicaid block grant to the states that would have provided reduced funding over the next seven years. If such a proposal is successfully revived, one effect on cities will surely be an increase in demand on public hospital emergency services (see Center on Budget and Policy Priorities 1996).

Public Management as Urban Politics The most important impact on the cities of the shifting balance in the federal arrangement has been to change what could be called the moral tenor of urban politics. In short, good public administration has displaced the urban social and racial agendas that had dominated local politics since the 1960s. By increasingly forcing local leaders to make do with less intergovernmental aid and by making them husband what resources can be raised locally, the New Federal Order has placed a premium on local public management skills and discouraged grand visions of social and racial reform. As an official from the USCM explained, "In the last few years, our attention has shifted from trying to increase aid to cities in any form to trying to streamline it and make it more effective. *Let's talk about how we can make better use of what we're getting*" (Stanfield 1996, 1802, emphasis added).

Some scholars see this simply as part of a broad national trend toward conservatism, one that, as Sonenshein, Schockman, and DeLeon (1996, 1) put it, reaches down "even into the generally safe Democratic and minority reaches of urban leadership." Others see a more complex phenomenon taking place; for example, Clark (1994, 23) argued that a New Political Culture has emerged in the cities, one that features lifestyle and consumption concerns (especially lower taxes) rather than redistribution and material issues like housing and community development for the disadvantaged. He traced the crystallization of this middle-class urban politics to the decline of federal and state grants, many of which were targeted to poverty clienteles. Thus the contraction of federal aid has not only meant less money for the cities, but less policy guidance.

In a political climate in which the fear of taxpayer revolts is always present and the continuing flight of the middle class is a constant threat to urban health, leaders must first and foremost demonstrate skills in managing scarce resources. Social issues may or may not be present on current mayoral agendas, but if they are a matter of concern, the new mayors make clear that they can best be addressed by better management. This set of management tasks contrasts significantly with the mayoral challenge of the 1960s and 1970s, the dimensions of which were laid out most clearly by the Kerner Commission (National Advisory Commission on Civil Disorders 1968, 298): "Now, as never before, the American city has need for the personal qualities of strong democratic leadership" to address racial polarization, slum clearance, housing, police misconduct, poverty, and unemployment.

The prototype mayors of this earlier period were people like John Lindsay of New York, Jerome Cavanagh of Detroit, Kevin White of Boston, and Richard Lee of New Haven. They excelled in grantsmanship, and they understood how to use city hall as a bully pulpit in their efforts to bridge racial and class divisions. As Sonenshein, Schockman, and DeLeon (1996, 5) described, "Sympathetic to the urban poor, supported by private philanthropy and federal aid, seeking redevelopment, these liberal mayors redefined the mayoral role." In the political climate of the 1990s, however, mayors seek guidance to accomplish their leadership tasks not first by reference to the moral compass of liberal reform but rather from the more neutral market. According to Gurwitt (1994, 26), Mayor Steven Goldsmith of Indianapolis, who exemplifies the new mayoral type, argues that market forces and competition ultimately serve the citizens of his city better than the government monopoly. Mastery of the market, he believes, requires the ingenuity of the entrepreneur and the management skills of a corporate executive officer (CEO).

The new mayors seem at ease with their fiscal self-reliance. The mayor of Nashville, quoted in an editorial in *The Wall Street Journal* ("Cities Discover Federalism" 1995), professed that "it's not all bad [that] Washington is busy extricating itself from . . . responsibility for well-being [in the cities]." Cities now have more freedom to experiment. John Norquist, mayor of Milwaukee, made a similar point about the freeing effects of federal divestment: Federal grants, he says, "are only costing us more money, because they force us to . . . do things we wouldn't otherwise do" (quoted in Osborne 1992, 63).

The new mayors speak the language of modern public management and run their administrations accordingly. They believe in reinvention, innovation, privatization, competition, strategic planning, and productivity improvements. They favor economic development and low taxes, partnership with the business sector, and good housekeeping. As Mayor Norquist reportedly said ("A Genuine New Democrat" 1996), his success is a function of performance, not ideology.

The issue of privatization illustrates how the commitment to the new public management crosses partisan and racial boundaries. Although Mayor Goldsmith, a Republican who once declared that he wanted to become the CEO of Indianapolis, is noted for his leadership in privatizing public services, the same policies have been pursued with equal fervor by Mayor Richard Daley, Jr. of Chicago, a Democrat, and by successive black mayoral administrations in Detroit (see Smith and Leyden 1996; Jackson and Wilson 1996). Daley has been particularly vigorous in contracting formerly public responsibilities to private firms, including, among others, the parking garage at O'Hare Airport, sewer cleaning, office janitorial services, the management of public golf courses, water customer billing, abandoned automobile collection, parking ticket enforcement, and tree stump removal.

The change in the moral tenor of urban politics is perhaps nowhere more evident than in the cities governed by black mayors. "'New black leaders,'" such as Michael White of Cleveland, Kurt Schmoke of Baltimore, Marc Morial of New Orleans, and others, are characterized as "technopoliticians" in contrast to such "champions of the race" as Coleman Young of Detroit and Marion Barry of Washington (Barras 1996, 20). According to Barras (p. 19), "They have moved beyond rallies and protest marches, replacing talk with action and ushering in a new era of competent, professional stewardship in cities."

Young's successor in Detroit provides an example. Peirce (1993, 3013) wrote that Mayor Dennis Archer's agenda is to fashion a "reinvented" city government "that pays its bills on time," improves its low bond rating, and "picks up garbage on time and keeps the streetlights on all night." Archer, who established close ties to the white business establishment in pursuit of economic development objectives, is contrasted with Young for "rejecting the politics of class and race." Similarly, Barras (1996) compared Bill Campbell, mayor of Atlanta, to the civil rights giants Maynard Jackson and Andrew Young, who preceded him in city hall.[5] Although Campbell is a strong supporter of affirmative action, he reportedly sees himself

> as the vanguard of a new generation of black leaders who embrace a less conspicuous brand of racial politics. . . . His agenda is less about the fight for black empowerment than about paving potholes, encouraging job growth, making neighborhoods safer and building downtown housing. (Sack 1996)

Two decades ago, the social agendas of both black and white mayors captured the attention of the news media and urban observers, but today, the public spotlight is on the new public managers. Eggers (1993) claimed that "America's boldest mayors" were Edward Rendell of Philadelphia, Milwaukee's Norquist, and Indianapolis's Goldsmith. What was bold about these urban leaders was their management initiatives: Rendell's Private Sector Task Force on Management and Productivity, which saved the city more than $150 million; Norquist's strategic budget process; and Goldsmith's introduction of competitive bidding between city service providers and private firms.

Leadership as public management is what urban electorates apparently want in this age of local fiscal self-reliance. In fact, America's boldest mayors hardly stand out from their colleagues in other cities. Mayor Richard Riordan of Los Angeles, a businessman turned politician, runs his city in the style of a CEO—nonideological, managerial, eschewing the "arts of political leadership and public appeals" (Sonenshein, Schockman, and DeLeon 1996, 15). Even Rudolph Giuliani of New York, an aggressive and brash former public prosecutor, came to office promising to "reinvent" city government by cutting and streamlining its massive size (Gurwitt 1995, 23).

The New Federal Order Brings New City Limits

In the New Federal Order, the fiscal links between Washington and the cities have become significantly attenuated. More than at any time since the early Great Society years, city governments can spend only what they can raise. It is possible to imagine several responses to this local fiscal autonomy. One response is to raise taxes to maintain the array of service responsibilities that people have come to expect. To some modest extent, this is what city governments have done. Beginning in 1982 and continuing through the decade, city governments increased per capita tax revenues to offset rising expenditure burdens (Bahl et al. 1991, Table 7). Another response is to engage vigorously in economic development activities, seeking to raise additional revenues by growing the indigenous tax base. There is strong evidence that this has been done in cities too (Clarke and Gaile 1989).

Another response, ever sensitive to citizen resistance to higher taxes, is to husband the resources that cities control through more careful management strategies characterized by contracting out, strategic planning, downsizing, and reorganizing. There is strong evidence that this, too, has been a major response in the cities to the New Federal Order.

The resultant emergence of a public management agenda in place of a social reform platform—what Sonenshein, Schockman, and DeLeon (1996) called the platform of multiethnic liberalism— might be seen as a narrowing of political vision. In a different light, better, more innovative management of the scarce resources under local control may be seen as simply a realistic response to a fiscal world very different from that of a quarter of a century ago. In a sense, the absence of a growing stream of federal dollars has meant that city political leaders cannot afford, fiscally or politically, to push an agenda of social and racial reform financed by local taxpayers alone. Nor can municipal leaders find much encouragement for defying these realities: Left to confront the great urban racial and economic polarities, few elected officials would be so foolhardy as to risk inevitable failure by initiating solutions based solely on the modest and limited resources that they themselves can raise. It is far easier—and the outcome more certain—to lower taxes, reduce government employment, and fill potholes. City limits have never been more in evidence.

Notes

1. The definition of municipal is somewhat broad. In its analysis, the USCM included Food Stamps, AFDC, Headstart, and National Endowment for the Arts grants, none of which, by any account, would be regarded as particularly municipal in character. But it also included various homeless assistance grants, a broad range of assisted housing programs, mass transit, community policing, and other such programs that have a strong urban component. Prior to 1995, the USCM tracked funding for a mix of specific programs and general categories of programs (see Table 1).
2. Testimony of Secretary of Transportation Federico Peña in the *Reauthorization of ISTEA* hearings before the Committee on Transportation and Infrastructure, U.S. House of Representatives, 2 May 1996.
3. A $5 billion cut in federal food assistance would reduce food spending by $750 million per year, a .10% decrease. Smallwood et al. (1995) calculated that 3,600 farm jobs would be lost, as well as 14,000 jobs in food processing and another 103,000 jobs that are generated indirectly.
4. An excellent comparison of the features of the new welfare law with the old Aid to Families with Dependent Children program is contained in Burke (1996).
5. In a national survey of 1,211 black Americans conducted in 1992 for the *Detroit News*, researchers found that 94% of the respondents believed that the people who came to power during the civil rights era were out of touch with the real concerns of ordinary African-Americans. Such leaders continue to cite racism as the most pressing issue facing blacks, but the black citizenry is concerned about crime, employment, and economic prospects (Barras 1996, 19).

Bibliography

Advisory Commission on Intergovernmental Relations. 1994. *Significant features of fiscal federalism, 1994.* Vol. 2. Washington, DC: Government Printing Office.

Bahl, R., J. Martinez, D. Sjoquist, and L. Williams. 1991. The fiscal conditions of U.S. cities at the beginning of the 1990s. Paper presented at the Urban Institute Conference on Big City Governance and Fiscal Choices, Southern California University, Los Angeles, June.

Barras, J. R. 1996. From symbolism to substance: The rise of America's new generation of black political leaders. *New Democrat* 8 (November-December): 19–22.

Burke, V. 1996. New welfare law: Comparison of the new block grant program with Aid to Families with Dependent Children. Congressional Research Service Report to Congress, 26 August.

Center on Budget and Policy Priorities. 1996 (22 March). The NGA Medicaid Proposal will shift costs onto local governments. Washington, DC: Author.

Chernick, H., and A. Reschovsky. 1997. Urban fiscal problems: Coordinating actions among governments. In *The urban crisis: Linking research to action,* edited by B. Weisbrod and J. Worthy, 131–176. Evanston, IL: Northwestern University Press.

Cities discover federalism. 1995. *The Wall Street Journal,* 8 December.

Clark, T. N. 1994. Race and class versus the New Political Culture. In *Urban Innovation,* edited by T. N. Clark, 21–78. Thousand Oaks, CA: Sage Publications.

Clarke, S., and G. Gaile. 1989. Moving toward entrepreneurial economic development policies: Opportunities and barriers. *Policy Studies Journal* 17 (spring): 574–598.

Eggers, W. D. 1993. City lights: America's boldest mayors. *Policy Review* (summer): 67–74.

Finder, A. 1996. Welfare clients outnumber jobs they might fill. *The New York Times,* 25 August. A genuine new democrat. 1996. *The Wall Street Journal,* 21 March.

Gurwitt, R. 1994. Indianapolis and the Republican future. *Governing* 7 (February): 24–28.

———. 1995. The trials of Rudy Giuliani. *Governing* 8 (June): 23–27.

———. 1996. Detroit dresses for business. *Governing* 8 (April): 38–42.

Jackson, C., and D. Wilson. 1996. Service delivery in Detroit, Michigan. Paper presented at the annual meeting of the Midwest Political Science Association, Chicago, IL, April.

Ladd, H. 1994. Big-city finances. In *Big-city politics, governance, and fiscal constraints,* edited by G. Peterson, 201–66. Washington, DC: Urban Institute.

National Advisory Commission on Civil Disorders. 1968. *Report of the National Advisory Commission on Civil Disorders.* New York: Bantam.

Osborne, D. 1992. John Norquist and the Milwaukee experiment. *Governing* 5 (November): 63.

Pagano, M., J. Lobenhofer, and A. Dudas. 1996. Cities and the changing federal system: Estimating the impacts of the Contract with America. Department of Political Science, Miami University of Ohio. Typescript.

Peirce, N. 1993. Motor City's "Mayor Realtor." *National Journal,* 18 December, 3013.

Rapp, D. 1994. A program for Billy Yeager. *Governing* 7 (July): 80.

Sack, K. 1996. Mayor finds old issue emerging in new way. *The New York Times,* 15 July.

Smallwood, D., B. Kuhn, K. Hanson, S. Vogel, and J. Blaylock. 1995. Economic effects of refocusing national food-assistance efforts. *Food Review* 18 (January-April): 2–12.

Smith, D., and K. Leyden. 1996. Exploring the political dimension of privatization: A tale of two cities. Paper presented at the annual meeting of the Midwest Political Science Association, Chicago, IL, April.

Sonenshein, R., E. Schockman, and R. DeLeon. 1996. Urban conservatism in an age of diversity. Paper presented at the 1996 annual meeting of the Western Political Science Association, San Francisco, California, March.

Stanfield, R. 1996. Mayors are the soul of the new machine. *National Journal* 28 (24 August): 1801–1802.

Stegman, M. 1996. Speech presented at Rutgers University, Princeton, NJ, 28 February.

Super, D., S. Parrott, S. Steinmetz, and C. Mann. 1996. The new welfare law. Policy brief. Washington, DC: Center on Budget and Policy Priorities.

U.S. Conference of Mayors (USCM). 1994. *The federal budget and the cities.* Washington, DC: Government Printing Office.

———. 1995–1997. Funding levels for key municipal programs. Annual releases. Washington, DC: Author.

U.S. Government Accounting Office. 1996. Community development: Status of urban empowerment zones. Report to the chair of the Subcommittee on Human Resources and Intergovernmental Relations, Committee on Government Reform and Oversight, House of Representatives, Washington, DC, December.

Wallin, B. 1996. Federal retrenchment and state-local response: Lessons from the past. Paper presented at the annual meeting of the American Political Science Association, San Francisco, 30 August.

Weir, M. 1996. Big cities confront the New Federalism. Paper presented at Columbia University, New York, 12 April.

Chapter 10

❖❖❖

THE NEW REGIONAL POLITICS

Regional Politics in the Twenty-First Century

The dawn of the millennium finds metropolitan America to be a sprawling and tangled landscape. Decades of suburban growth accompanied by the dispersal of jobs and populations have created massive economic regions of almost uninterrupted development, but these regions lack governmental coherence. The political fragmentation of metropolitan areas into hundreds of jurisdictions forms a pattern of checkerboard governance. A few places, such as Miami-Dade County, Florida, and Minneapolis-St. Paul, Minnesota, have forged metropolitan-wide political institutions that coordinate service delivery. Portland, Oregon, stands alone as a region with a growth boundary that curbs sprawl. Cooperation is actually commonplace in urban areas as a means of coordinating such services as 911-dialing and county-wide parks and recreational and library services (Teaford, 1997). But effective regional coordination of land use and development is rare. The pressures for a more effective regional governance are building. The problems are many: traffic congestion; unequal employment opportunities; disparities in fiscal health between poorer central cities and wealthier suburbs; lack of investment in mass transit; inequalities in educational resources; the loss of open space to sprawled development; air and water pollution. These problems require solutions that go beyond the borders of particular local governments.

The essays that follow provide a profile of the new regionalism. William R. Barnes and Larry C. Ledebur (Essay 29) alert the reader to what they call the "New Economic Commons." They point out that urban areas are single economies (or commons) characterized by interdependence; the fact that these regions are overlaid with multiple political jurisdictions does not change this fact. Regional economic interdependence means that the long-term economic and civic health of citizens depends on the ability of urban areas to adapt and change, at least sometimes, as regions. Otherwise, vital regional economic interests are overlooked as cities and suburbs look out only for themselves.

John C. Teaford, *Post-Suburbia: Government and Politics in the Edge Cities* (Baltimore: The Johns Hopkins University Press, 1997).

Although Barnes and Ledebur assert that there are regional interests that deserve political expression, they do not explain how this can be achieved. The essay by Myron Orfield describes how some degree of coordination has been achieved in the Minneapolis-St. Paul region. Orfield, who is a state legislator, acknowledges that regional reform is difficult and controversial, but, he claims it is possible because of the emergence of a new political center of gravity in urban politics. In the past, attempts to build regional political coalitions in Minneapolis-St. Paul were built on weak foundations—notably leaders dedicated to good government ideals. Their initial success in building regional political institutions was short-lived because they neglected to mobilize powerful interests sufficiently. In contrast, practitioners of the New Regionalism persuaded central-city interests to join with older suburbs who shared similar problems of decaying neighborhoods, sagging tax bases, and a retrenching local economy. The Twin Cities' success in building regional cooperation was enabled by this new political coalition— a coalition that potentially exists in other metropolitan areas around the country.

Although many critics concede that greater regional cooperation sounds fine in the abstract, its practice is another story. Pietro S. Nivola's essay (Essay 31) claims that there are good reasons why metropolitan areas in the United States are so different from most of Europe, where urban sprawl is more contained and people live in higher densities. He says that in the United States people spread out in order to enjoy the advantages afforded by cheap gasoline prices: detached single family homes, private auto travel (rather than reliance on mass transit), abundant land, and scattered but cost-efficient shopping and services. According to Nivola's somewhat unconventional view, urban sprawl reflects American lifestyle and tastes, and he therefore does not think that governmental reform is likely to rein in sprawl.

In his selection, Fred Siegel says that sprawl is . . . "not some malignancy to be summarily excised, but, rather, part and parcel of prosperity." Siegel says that fragmented government offers abundant advantages. It enables people who live in badly governed central cities to escape to other jurisdictions by providing an array of alternative places to live, shop, and conduct business. Most of all, Siegel believes that fragmented government avoids the dead hand of a single, powerful, regional government that restricts choice. Although Siegel concedes that there may be cases of successful regional governments, as in Portland, Oregon, time will tell if such examples can be copied elsewhere. In the meantime, he prefers to address common regional issues through one-off measures like tax sharing and the prohibition of public policies that favor suburbs over central cities.

These perspectives undoubtedly are only the beginning of the debate over finding an urban policy for the new century. As experience with managing mature metropolitan areas grows, there will surely be more experiments with new forms of regional governance and cooperation.

29

William R. Barnes and Larry C. Ledebur

THE REGIONAL ECONOMIC COMMONS

Debate about the relationships of cities and suburbs has too often degenerated into an unproductive "either/or" controversy serving narrow political and social interests. Much of metropolitan politics and public discourse are at an apparent dead end on this issue.

Current infatuation with the image of economic autonomy and fragmentation has bolstered claims of suburban economic, social, and cultural independence from their greater regions. Such claims echo those of an earlier age and very different circumstances of the "independence" of central cities from their regions and, hence, their suburbs. Both views, current and past, deny the commonality and economic interdependence of jurisdictions within the economic region. Each is dangerously incorrect.

Cities and suburbs are political jurisdictions astride a single regional economy. Jurisdictions within a regional economy are, therefore, economically interdependent. The nature and dimensions of this interdependence vary from place to place, but interdependence is nonetheless an economic reality. Denial of this essential reality fosters the seeds of the spatial suicide occurring in many of our nation's urban areas.

The damage wrought by this image of economic fragmentation and autonomy must be repaired. To do so requires a clear vision of the integral nature of political economy of economic regions. Achieving this vision again necessitates separating economies from polities, and economics from politics, before subsequently rejoining them as a new political economy of regions.

The Dilemma of Local "Statism"

The modified nationalist or local statist paradigm with its simple and appealing sense of symmetry and orderliness, provides the foundation of the image of jurisdictional autonomy and independence. Political boundaries and economies appear congruent. Each rectangle or square in Figure 10.1 represents a separate political jurisdiction, and the larger rectangle represents the central city of the region. Through the lens of modified nationalism, each jurisdiction is a separate economy competing with other jurisdictional economies within (and beyond) their region.

In this view, each jurisdiction is, for all practical purposes, an autonomous unit of government bound only by the state authorities or restrictions under

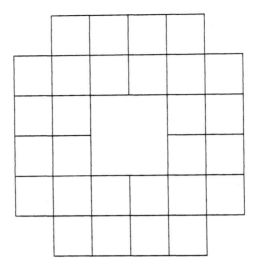

Figure 10.1 Statist Perspective of the Urban Political Economy

which it operates. Each has its own tax base. Each makes specific policies and investment decisions and provides a specific mix of services, amenities, and taxes ostensibly preferred by their citizens.

In the eyes of "public choice" advocates, this pattern of governmental "fragmentation" permits all citizens of the region to choose the jurisdiction that provides their preferred "mix" of services, amenities, and tax obligations. This choice permits individuals and families to maximize their locational advantage subject only to the constraints of income or wealth.

Critics of the public choice perspective counter that the outcome of this system of government is sharp disparities in tax bases among jurisdictions across urban areas with disturbing differences in the quality of life, services, and amenities and relative tax burdens experienced by citizens across the region. In other words, this model of locational choice underlies the pattern of income and, therefore, racial and social segregation that prevails in most metropolitan areas.

The jurisdictionally focused blinders of this perspective inevitably encourage competitive actions to promote local tax bases without consideration of any consequences to other jurisdictions or the regional economy. Incentives for interjurisdictional cooperation are limited, by and large, to economies of scale in the provision of some services, significant spillover effects, responses to external threats posed by actions of state and federal governments, or, in rare cases, federal or state programs to promote some form of cooperative action.

The Achilles' heel of the statist perspective at the local level is that using this paradigm makes it exceedingly difficult for jurisdictionally based politicians and citizenry to correctly perceive the true nature of the economy held in common and the costs of misperceiving or ignoring its interdependence. It also makes coordinating actions among two or more jurisdictions extraordinarily difficult.

The Region as an Economy

The regional paradigm provides a very different view of reality. To understand this perspective, the reader is asked to mentally and visually roll up the lattice-work of jurisdictions overlaying the regional economy and, for the present, set this rolled lattice aside. Doing so permits examination of the regional economy unimpeded by the vision-narrowing blinders of the jurisdictional framework.

In attempting to understand the economy without jurisdictions, it is important to keep sight of the grounding of the economy in all its facets in social contexts that must be viable if the economic components are to be successful, just as the economy must succeed if these social environments are to be viable. The concept of the urban system—the social, political, institutional, and economic system of the region—captures this broader context.

Figure 10.2 presents a visual representation of the regional economy. It assumes hexagonal form. At the spatial center of this economy is the historical

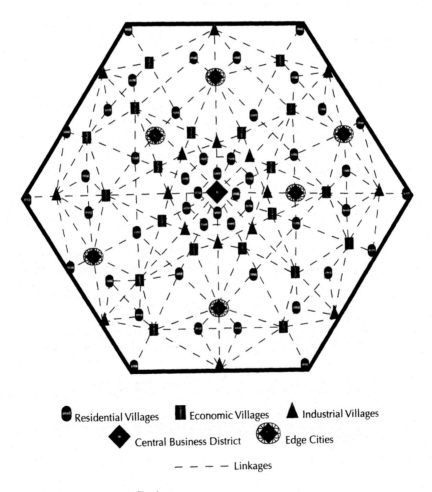

Figure 10.2 Local Economic Region

central business district around which many or most regional economies grew. Arrayed across the plane of this economy are activity centers: residential villages (neighborhoods), economic villages (clusters of retail, commercial, and service activities), and industrial villages (clusters of manufacturing, warehousing, shipping, wholesale, etc.).

Dispersed throughout the region are a set of edge cities that include the central business districts of other central cities in the region (e.g., Dearborn and Pontiac in the greater Detroit region) and the recent edge cities. In *Edge City*, Joel Garreau achieved a glimpse of the organizational form of the metropolitan economic region.[1] Garreau's insight was that, in suburbs, there is no single urban center or hub. Rather, the development pattern in suburban areas is characterized by multiple clusters of development and economic activity. In the jargon of urbanologists, the suburbs and metropolitan area as a whole are polycentric (multiple-centered or "multinodal") rather than monocentric (organized around a single central core as in the traditional view of the city).

This economic region is a complex, integrated, highly interdependent system—a complex network of clusters of economic, social, institutional, and residential activities. It consists of multiple clusters or nodes of development and economic activity that are linked and interdependent. Each cluster of specialized activities, including residential, is part of an economically integrated whole. This linked, interdependent system of development nodes is the organizational form of the economic region. Neither edge cities nor central cities, nor any other parts of the local economic region, are economically autonomous and independent.

The view of the economic region as a complex, interdependent nodal system emphasizes the critical role of the linkages or functional relationships (dashed lines in Figure 10.2) that create and sustain the system. Edgar Dunn argues that urban systems can be described by classifying actors, places, and physical linkages and by detailing these functional relationships among these actors, places, and linkages.[2]

The most obvious of these linkages are the regional networks of physical infrastructure, such as the transportation and communications networks that connect the urban system. The greater the efficiency of these linkages—that is, the lower the time and money cost of sustaining economic and social activity patterns—the greater the productivity and interdependence of the system.

Although physical infrastructure is the linkage that is most easily visualized and that, perhaps, serves best to communicate the image of functional relationships among nodes, other nonphysical linkages are no less important. Among these are service delivery systems such as health, education, and safety; regional financial systems; intergovernmental linkages; and human resource systems.

The economic region is also the regional labor market. The productivity of this local economy will be directly affected by the efficiency of the linkages between workers and jobs. The more regional this system—the more it transcends jurisdictions and proximity—the more productive the local economy will be, with the labor market becoming less exclusionary.

In this intraurban system, the central business district of the central city historically was, and often remains, a crucial center of functionally specialized economic, social, and institutional activity. It also is true that these central areas are most often the locus of governance functions as well as more specialized business, cultural, health, entertainment, and recreational activities that serve a wider regional audience.

Clearly, the degree of influence or dominance of this central node varies among metropolitan regional economies. In some, particularly economic regions that are international centers, the role of the central business is greater. In others, the role and regional influence of the central business district are weaker. Regardless, in an interdependent regional economy, core cities play an important role that has not been supplanted by edge cities.

The isolated, point-in-time image of Figure 10.2 obscures two key characteristics of the regional economy. First, this complex, interdependent regional economic system is not static or unchanging. It is a dynamic, evolving system continuously adapting to changing local imperatives and external demands. The long-term economic vitality, productivity, and social health of each regional economic system will depend on its ability to change, to adapt, and to reconfigure its spatial form and patterns of economic activity.

Second, the regional economic system is neither self-contained nor autonomous. An essential characteristic of the economic region is that it is an open system, inextricably linked to other economic regions, and thus its welfare is interdependent with other economic regions. Just as the destinies of components within an urban system are "interwoven,"[3] the fates and futures of economic regions are interdependent because of the openness of these urban systems.

The Regional Economic Commons

In the regional paradigm, the economic (the economic region) and the political (local jurisdictions) must be re-fused into the political economy of the region. This is shown in Figure 10.3 in which the lattice of political jurisdictions (Figure 10.1) overlays the regional economy (Figure 10.2). In this political economy, the boundaries of the economy and boundaries of the polities are not the same. No single jurisdiction lays claim to the whole of the economy or, as represented here, incorporates a major portion of the economic base of the region.

Figure 10.3 is a generic representation of the map of almost any urban region. Economic and residential clusters or nodes are found, in greater or lesser degree, within the boundaries of each jurisdiction. In many cases, these activity nodes fall completely within a jurisdiction. In others, however, these clusters spill across jurisdictional boundaries and are part of what is perceived to be the economic base of two or more jurisdictions. Linkages and functional relationships of the economic system are not constrained by jurisdictional boundaries,

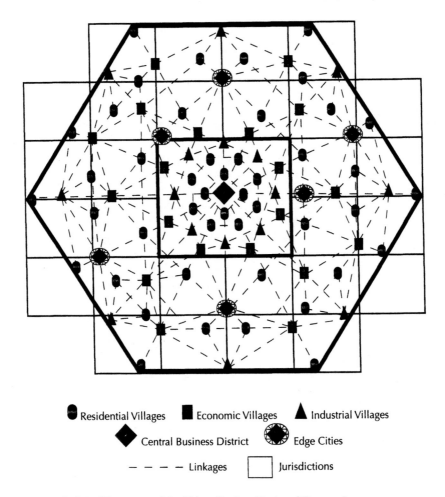

Figure 10.3 Political Economy of the Urban Region: Regional Economic Commons

although jurisdictions have powers to promote or diminish the efficiency of these systems linkages and relationships through their investment decisions and regulations.

Policies and uncoordinated investment patterns that are driven by narrowly construed jurisdictional interests can erode economic linkages and functional relationships, diminishing the productivity of the economic system as a whole. This is apparent in urban transportation systems that are not region-wide but are provided by jurisdictions that often make it difficult and costly to move throughout the system. This issue is also important in relation to significant differences in regulations, environmental standards, and so on and in the quality and availability of basic utilities and services such as public education, public safety, and open housing.

David Rusk, in *Cities Without Suburbs,* argues that cities that are "elastic" or able to expand their jurisdictional boundaries through annexation fare far better than those with tax bases limited by inelastic boundaries.[4] This argument can be expanded in the context of the regional paradigm. Increasing the proportion of the regional economy and tax base within a single political jurisdiction both reduces the barrier effects of jurisdictional boundaries on linkages and functional relationships and increases the possibility of making policies and investment decisions that promote the productivity of the regional economy. Visually this is seen in Figure 10.4, which differs from Figure 10.3 in the share of the regional economy falling within the jurisdictional boundaries of the central city.[5]

Under the regional paradigm, the regional economy is held in common. The blurred boundaries of the regional economy and the sharply defined jurisdictional boundaries of the polities are not aligned—not congruent. In almost

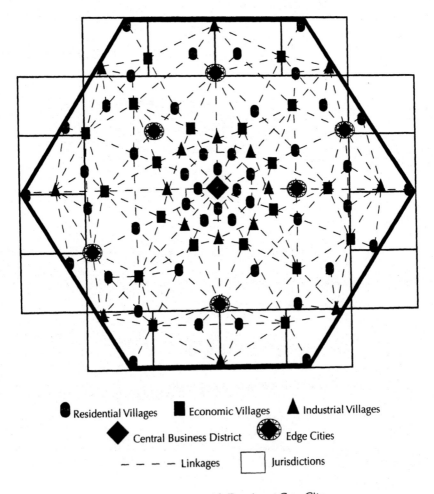

● Residential Villages   ■ Economic Villages   ▲ Industrial Villages

◆ Central Business District   ◉ Edge Cities

— — — — Linkages   ☐ Jurisdictions

Figure 10.4 Regional Economic Commons with Dominant Core City

every place, the regional economy is latticed with many local political jurisdictions and many stakeholders.

A single local economy with multiple jurisdictional stakeholders raises fundamental questions of local economic governance and local economic policy making. It poses the dilemma of the commons. Who tends the regional economic commons when no single jurisdiction holds exclusive rights? Who nurtures the economy held in common?

This regional economy is a "collective good" in the classic sense. If one unit of government were congruent with the local economy, the benefits (and costs) of economic policies would accrue within that jurisdiction. In the economy held in common, however, public action to promote the economy creates benefits that cannot be entirely captured by the investing jurisdiction. The local government undertaking the action bears the cost but cannot capture all the benefits. Absent collective action, therefore, local governments inevitably will underinvest in the nurturing of the regional economy because of these spillover effects.

The defining characteristic of the regional economic commons, therefore, is interdependence. This stands in stark contrast to the misleading sense of economic autonomy derived from the statist paradigm.

The interdependence of the commons has two key dimensions, one economic and one political. Economic interdependence arises from the very nature of the economic region as a complex interdependent system. What affects any element or dimension of the system affects the whole and, directly or indirectly, each of the parts.

Political interdependence arises from the nature of the economic commons. The regional economy is held in common by many jurisdictions and many stakeholders. Households live in one jurisdiction, shop in another, and work in another. The welfare of each jurisdiction within the region, therefore, will be affected by the actions of other jurisdictions through their effects on the economic commons as a whole.

There is also vertical economic and political interdependence in the political economy of the regional paradigm. Each local economic commons is an interdependent part of the national common market. Actions that affect the common market affect each economic commons. In turn, local actions that affect a single economic commons directly or indirectly impact all others in the common market. Local governments, therefore, have an important stake in what federal and state governments do that affect the common market and any one of its economic commons. In turn, federal and state governments have important stakes in local actions that affect the regional economic commons. Recognition of these vertical and horizontal dimensions of economic and political interdependence in the economy is critical to effective policy making at each level of government in our federal system.

Recognition that the region is a single economy, an economic commons, overlaid with multiple political jurisdictions provides a radically different perspective for policy and policy making. If interdependence is a signature economic characteristic of the region, collaboration becomes a key to success in economic governance of the commons. In other words, if economic interdependence is a fact, collaboration is a defining political challenge. A region's success in responding to this challenge may be a critical determinant of its economic future.

Growing the Regional Economy

This view of the regional economy, absent the lattice of jurisdictions, provides an important perspective on "growing the economy." If the singular goal of a region is to enhance the economic productivity of the economic region, in what should we invest? What would be the appropriate level of investment in each area or function? How would we prioritize these investments?

Some answers to this difficult question are obvious. Investments would be made in continuously upgrading the quality of the regional workforce and other important factors of production as well as sustaining and enhancing critical economic development infrastructure. Strategic investments would be made in ensuring that essential economic functions are performed well and efficiently while avoiding wasteful duplication of capacity and facilities. Investments would be made in social service networks of efficient scales. Investments would be targeted to developing clusters of specialized economic activities and residential patterns and transportation systems that facilitate the economic functions of these clusters while minimizing time, money, and disamenity costs of transporting workers, materials, and products.

This perspective of the economy is also useful in identifying improbable and potentially inefficient investments and investment patterns. If there is a focus on the growth and productivity of the regional economy,

It is highly unlikely that investments would be made that create sharp disparities in the quality of schools across the regional economy that adversely impact the quality of the regional workforce.

It is highly unlikely that investments would be made in spatially fragmented transportation systems.

It is highly unlikely that infrastructure investments would be made that facilitate economically inefficient and wasteful accelerated turnover in housing and building stock.

It is highly unlikely that letting parts of the economy's critical infrastructure fall into disrepair would be viewed as effective stewardship of the economy's scarce competitive resources.

It is highly unlikely that investments would be undertaken that simply move economic activity around within the region without contributing to regional productivity.

It is highly unlikely that segregating households by income class or race would be viewed as efficient or rational economic development policies.

This litany of productive and unproductive investments makes clear that a line of sight to the regional economy from each jurisdiction both clarifies needed actions and highlights the economic irrationality of many current policies and investment patterns.

Disparities in the Commons

This perspective on the regional commons brings focus to a critical issue at the heart of many of our nation's metropolitan areas: Do sharp economic disparities within the region matter?

Clearly, there are important social and political reasons why persistent disparities within the regional commons matter. Widening disparities between cities and suburbs will inevitably undermine social cohesion and political legitimacy.[6]

Do economic disparities, however, matter to the productivity and growth of the economic commons? Do these disparities matter to suburbs and more prosperous segments of the economic commons? Do they matter to other regional economic commons in the U.S. common market?

The core issue is whether the regional economic commons or the U.S. common market can prosper if large segments of each are impaired and unable to contribute to system maintenance, productivity, and growth. It is unfortunate that the debate surrounding this issue is almost always in terms of cities and suburbs. Political dynamics of multijurisdictional metropolitan areas frame the debate in these terms. The fact that almost all social and economic data are collected and reported by jurisdictions compounds the inclination to view the issue in city-suburban terms. It is very difficult to address the issue of the effects of disparities on economic performance outside this restrictive city-suburb framework.

A substantial decline in the economic welfare of cities relative to their suburbs has been occurring since at least 1960 (Figure 10.5). In 1960, per capita income was slightly greater in central cities of metropolitan areas than in their

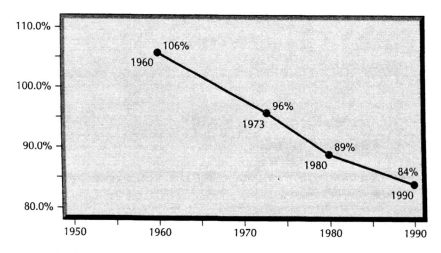

Figure 10.5 Central City and Suburban Income Disparities, 1960–1990. Reprinted with permission from Ledebur, L. C., & Barnes, W. R. (1992, September). *City distress, metropolitan disparities and economic growth: Combined revised edition* (p. 2). Washington, DC: National League of Cities.

suburbs. By 1973, per capita income in central cities had fallen to 96% of their suburbs. By 1980, this ratio had fallen to 89%. This decline in the economic welfare of cities relative to suburbs continued in the 1980s. By 1990, per capita income in central cities was down to 84% of suburban income.

A great deal of attention has focused on the polarization of incomes in the United States in the past decade. The *1994 Economic Report of the President* devoted a prominent subsection to this topic, calling it a "threat to the social fabric."[7] The data in these figures suggest a spatial dimension to this issue. Quality of life is directly related to geographical places and the economic vitality of these places. The long-term trend toward increasing disparities between per capita incomes in cities and their suburbs means that the issue of economic inequality must also be addressed in this spatial context.

Evidence of a relationship between disparities and metropolitan economic performance is strong, although additional research remains to be done. Figure 10.6 examines the average rate of employment growth from 1988 to 1991 for the largest 85 metropolitan areas, categorized by the per capita income disparities between cities and their suburbs.

As Figure 10.6 shows, there is a direct relationship between city-suburban disparities and rates of employment growth. Metropolitan areas with lower disparities tend to have higher rates of employment growth. Those with lower employment gains tend to have higher disparities and those with higher employment gains tend to have lower disparities.

The tendency for lower disparities and higher rates of employment growth to go together is apparent in Figure 10.7, which presents rates of employment growth for individual metropolitan areas ranked by levels of disparities in per

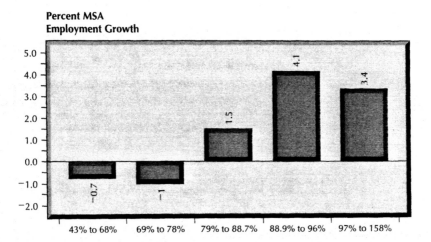

Figure 10.6 City and Suburban Economic Disparities and Metropolitan Growth. Calculated for the 85 largest MSAs with central cities in 1990. Per capita income ratios are for 1989. Employment growth rates are for the period January 1988 to August 1991. Bars represent average rates of employment growth for 85 cities divided into quintiles (17 cities per quintile).

Source: U.S. Bureau of the Census, 1990 Census; Bureau of Labor Statistics, Washington, D.C.

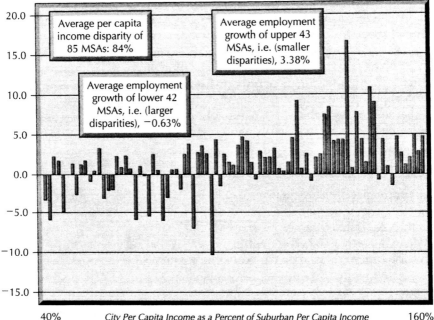

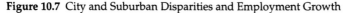

40%   *City Per Capita Income as a Percent of Suburban Per Capita Income*   160%

Figure 10.7 City and Suburban Disparities and Employment Growth

Source: U.S. Bureau of the Census, 1990 Census; Bureau of Labor Statistics, Washington, D.C.
Note: Calculated for the 85 largest MSAs with central cities in 1990. Per capita income ratios are for 1989. Employment growth rates are for the period January 1988 to August 1991. Bars represent average rates of employment growth for 85 cities divided into quintiles (17 cities per quintile).

capita income. There are exceptions to this generalization. A few metropolitan areas with relatively higher income disparities experienced relatively high rates of employment growth. These exceptions may be due to the size of these cities relative to their suburbs, unique characteristics of their economic bases and other particular local or regional characteristics, or they may simply be exceptions to the general trend.

Other research has corroborated this finding.[8] In a study for the National Bureau of Economic Research, Roland Benabou explored the relationships among education, income distribution, and growth at the local level.[9] On the basis of data for 14 metropolitan areas, he identified "a strong positive relationship between the lack of economic segregation, measured by the ratio of central city to suburban mean incomes, and the area's growth in both per capita income (1969–1989) and total employment (1973–1988)."[10] This he terms a "striking stylized fact" that does not permit any inference about causality but does suggest that city-suburban stratification and metropolitan economic performance are interdependent processes that require systematic economic analysis to identify the underlying mechanisms.

Benabou develops what he refers to as an integrated framework for analyzing the determinants of inequality and growth and starting to untangle the lines of causality.[11] On the basis of this analysis, he concludes that "minor differences in educational technologies, preferences, or wealth can lead to a high degree of income stratification," and that "stratification makes inequality in education and income more persistent across generations." Furthermore, he finds that "the polarization of urban areas resulting from individual residential decisions can be quite inefficient both from the point of view of aggregate growth and in the Pareto sense, especially in the long run." Finally, he notes that "because of the cumulative nature of the stratification process, it is likely to be much harder to reverse once it has run its course than to arrest it at an early stage."

Within the framework of the regional economic commons, we believe that sharp and pervasive disparities create a drag on and impair the productivity and performance of the regional economy. In a complex, highly interdependent economic system, therefore, widening disparities do matter to all parts of the regional economic commons.

There is a critical need for further research that focuses on the effects of sharp disparities within regional economic commons on the economic performance of the region. To address this issue effectively, research must focus on the region as an economic system rather than a mosaic of jurisdictions with jurisdictions as the unit of analysis. This is a difficult task, particularly with the limitations of jurisdictionally organized data.

The view through the lens of the economic commons strongly suggests that sharp disparities will adversely affect economic productivity and performance of the individual regional economic commons. Because the U.S. common market is a highly interdependent system, what affects one regional economy ripples out to the system as a whole. The concern about disparities in the commons is not singular to that economy but to the national economic system as a whole.

Notes

1. Garreau, J. (1991). *Edge City: Life on the new frontier.* New York: Doubleday.
2. Dunn, E. S., Jr. (1980). *The development of U.S. urban systems.* Baltimore, MD: The Johns Hopkins University Press.
3. Cisneros, H. G. (Ed.). (1993). *Interwoven destinies: Cities and the nation.* New York: Norton.
4. Rusk, D. (1993). *Cities without suburbs.* Washington, DC: Woodrow Wilson Center Press.
5. Weak support for the elasticity hypothesis is found in Blair, J. P., Staley, S. R., & Zhang, Z. (1996, Summer). The central city elasticity hypothesis: A critical appraisal of Rusk's theory of urban development. *Journal of the American Planning Association, 62*(3), 346–353. On the basis of their statistical analysis the authors argue that the economies of states have a stronger influence on changes in poverty rates and income than central city elasticity (p. 351). Implicit in this argument is the thesis that the state is an economy or meaningful economic unit rather than a political jurisdiction astride a set of regional economies. We believe that measurements of economic performance of states are an outcome of the performance of regional economies, not of a separate state economy. The authors' findings do suggest, however, the importance of understanding the functional relationships and linkages among local economic regions and their effects on economic performance of linked regional economies.

6. Swanstrom, T. (1996, May). Ideas matter: Reflections on the new regionalism. *Cityscape,*
    2(2). Swanstrom argues that the greatest weakness of the new regionalism debate is that it
    is "trapped in the terms of the liberal/conservative debate between more government or
    freer markets" (p. 15) and "between a new layer of regional governments or governmental
    fragmentation" (p. 13). We believe that this characterization and generalization is not cor-
    rect. Regional government or even more government is not the solution that fall naturally
    from the recognition that the regional economy is a collective good or commons. Rather,
    it is the growing awareness of the need for governance, not government restructuring: col-
    laboration among new jurisdictions, not metropolitan government. The issue is not liberal
    or conservative, not more or less government, but rather how existing governments can
    work together to tend the economic commons.
7. *1994 Economic Report of the President* (1994). Washington, DC: Government Printing Of-
    fice. (p. 26).
8. See, for example, Savitch, H. V., Sanders, D., & Collins, D. (1992). The regional city and
    public partnerships. In R. Berkman et al. (Eds.), *In the national interest: The 1990 urban
    summit* (pp. 65–77). New York: Twentieth Century Fund Press. See also studies discussed
    in Chapter 3.
9. Benabou, R. (1994). *Education, income distribution and growth: The local connection*
    (Working Paper No. 4798). Cambridge, MA: National Bureau of Economic Research.
10. Benabou, R. (1994). *Education, income distribution and growth: The local connection*
    (Working Paper No. 4798, p. 3). Cambridge, MA: National Bureau of Economic Research.
11. Benabou, R. (1994). *Education, income distribution and growth: The local connection* (Work-
    ing Paper No. 4798, pp. 28–29). Cambridge, MA: National Bureau of Economic Research.

30

Myron Orfield

CONFLICT OR CONSENSUS?
Forty Years of Minnesota Metropolitan Politics

Skeptics tell me that regional equity reform will never happen in America's
metropolitan regions because the suburbs are now in charge of American politics. It may be true that the suburbs are in charge of American politics. But the
politics of metropolitan reform is not about cities versus suburbs or, for that
matter, about Democrats versus Republicans.

The suburbs are not a monolith, economically, racially, or politically. Surrounding America's central cities, with their high social needs and low per
capita tax wealth, are three types of suburbs. First are the older suburbs, which
comprise about a quarter of the population of U.S. metropolitan regions. These
communities are often declining socially faster than the central cities and often
have even less per household property, income, or sales tax wealth. Second are

"Conflict or Consensus?" by Myron Orfield, *The Brookings Review*, Fall 1998, pp. 31–34.
Copyright © 1998 *The Brookings Institution.* Used with permission.

the low tax-base developing suburbs, which make up about 10–15 percent of U.S. metropolitan regions. They are growing rapidly in population, especially among school-age children, but without an adequate tax base to support that growth and its accompanying overcrowded schools, highway congestion, and ground water pollution. Both the central city and these two types of suburbs have small tax bases, comparatively high tax rates, and comparatively low spending. Median household incomes are also comparatively low: $25,000–30,000 in central cities in 1990, $25,000–40,000 in older suburbs, and $35,000–50,000 in low tax-base developing suburbs. Families in these communities are thus extremely sensitive to property tax increases. A third type of suburb is the high tax-base developing community. These affluent communities, with the region's highest median incomes, never amount to more than 30 percent of a region's population. They have all the benefits of a regional economy—access to labor and product markets, regionally built freeways and often airports—but are able to externalize the costs of social and economic need on the older suburbs and the central city.

Suburbs and cities can also be surprisingly diverse in their electoral results. Not all suburbs are Republican—or all cities Democratic. In Philadelphia, Republicans control almost all the suburbs and even the white working-class parts of the city. In Pittsburgh, Democrats control virtually all suburban seats except the highest property-wealth areas. In San Francisco, almost all suburbs are represented by Democrats, while in Los Angeles and Southern California, most of the white suburbs are represented by Republicans. In general, Democrats build their base in central cities, move to the older and low tax-base suburbs, and, if they are very effective, capture a few of the high tax-base suburbs. Republicans do just the opposite. In many states the balance of power rests on electoral contests in a few older suburbs or low tax-capacity developing suburbs.

Minnesota has been engaged in the politics of metropolitan regional reform for almost 40 years. Over the decades, three types of metropolitan coalitions have sought to move policy reforms through the state legislature. The first, a Republican-led bipartisan coalition, engaged in some bitter legislative fights; the second, a consensualist-led coalition, eschewed controversy; the third, a Democratic-driven bipartisan group, revived the real-world reform political style of their Republican predecessors. The following short history of metropolitanism in Minnesota suggests the complexity of coalition politics—and my own conviction that, while compromise and accommodation is the necessary essence of politics, regional reform, like all other real reform movements in U.S. history, necessarily involves some degree of controversy.

The Progressive Republican Vanguard

In the 1960s and 1970s, metropolitan reform efforts in Minnesota's legislature were led by "good government" Rockefeller Republicans and reform Democrats—in a sense the progressives that Richard Hofstader wrote of in his *Age of*

Reform. Joined by leaders of local corporations, they took aim at waste in government and set out to plan and shape a more cohesive, cost-effective, efficient, and equitable region. Though they sought rough metropolitan-wide equity in Minnesota's Twin Cities, they were not typical practitioners of class warfare. They valued equity because they knew from hard-headed calculation the costs of inequity and of destructive competition for development among municipalities in a single metropolitan region.

In some ways progressive Republican regionalism was an elegant, direct, limited-government response to growing sprawl and interlocal disparity. Joining Minnesota's Governor LeVander were Oregon's Tom McCall, Michigan's Miliken and Romney, and the great Republican mayor of Indianapolis, Richard Lugar. Had the country heeded their far-sighted strategy, the 1980s and 1990s might have been much different for the central cities and older suburbs.

In Minnesota the progressive Republicans and reform Democrats created regional sewer, transit, and airport authorities for the Twin Cities, as well as a Metropolitan Council of the Twin Cities with weak supervisory powers over these authorities. (Making the Met Council an elected body was a top goal, but it failed in a tie vote in 1967.) They also created a metropolitan land use planning framework and enacted Minnesota's famous tax-base sharing, or fiscal disparities, law, which, since 1971, has shared 40 percent of the growth of our commercial and industrial property tax base among the 187 cities, 49 school districts, and 7 counties in our region of some 2.5 million people.

The battle to pass the fiscal disparities act was brutal. Though the legislation, introduced in 1969, had its origins in the ethereal world of good government progressivism, its political managers were shrewd vote counters who made sure that two-thirds of the Twin City region's lawmakers understood that the bill would both lower their constituents' taxes and improve their schools and public services. Some of the progressives' key allies were populists who did not hesitate to play the class card with blue-collar voters in the low property-value suburbs. Probably not coincidentally, the populists collected most of the votes. The progressives pragmatically swallowed their compunctions.

The fiscal disparities bill that passed in 1971 was supported by a coalition of Democratic central-city legislators and Republicans from less wealthy suburbs—essentially the two-thirds of the region that received new tax base from the act. A few more-rural Republicans who had a strong personal relationship with the bill's Republican sponsor went along. The opposition was also bipartisan—Democrats and Republicans representing areas in the one-third of the region that would lose some of their tax base. Debate over the bill was ugly. Republican Charlie Weaver, Sr., the bill's sponsor, was accused of fomenting "communism" and "community socialism" and of being a "Karl Marx" out to take from "the progressive communities to give to the backward ones." One opponent warned that "the fiscal disparities law will destroy the state." "Why should those who wish to work be forced to share with those who

won't or can't help themselves?" demanded a representative of the high property-wealth areas. Amid growing controversy, after two divisive failed ses-
sions, the bill would pass the Minnesota Senate by a single vote.

Not until 1975—after court challenges that went all the way to the U.S.
Supreme Court (which refused to hear the case)—did the fiscal disparities law
finally go into effect. The last legal challenge to the law came in 1981, a decade
after passage. High property-wealth southern Twin Cities suburbs were finally
rebuffed in the Minnesota Tax Court. But representatives and state senators
from high property-wealth Twin Cities suburbs have tried to repeal the statute
in virtually every legislative session for the past 25 years.

A New Approach

The tough progressive reformers were followed by consensus-based regionalists whose preferred approach, it has often been joked, was to convene leaders
from across metropolitan Twin Cities in the boardroom of a local bank to hum
together the word "regionalism." Highly polished professional policy wonks,
the new generation of leaders leaned more to touring the country extolling the
virtues of regional reform, which many had no part in accomplishing, than to
gritty work in city halls and the legislature to make it happen. To make matters
worse, business support for regionalism began to erode. The rise of national
and multinational companies created a cadre of rotating, frequently moving executives who, facing a more competitive business environment, eschewed controversy in favor of political action that would boost the bottom line.

By the 1980s, proponents of the regional perspective in Minnesota had
dwindled to the chairman of the Citizens League, a local policy group financially supported by the region's big businesses; a half-dozen legislators; two
or three executives of declining power; and the editorial board of the Minneapolis paper.

Meanwhile, some suburbs, particularly the high property-wealth developing ones that saw no gain but plenty of loss coming from metropolitan action,
rebelled. Over the course of the 1980s, as the Twin Cities region rapidly became
more like the rest of the nation—more racially and socially segregated—and as
fundamental divisions hardened, those suburbs hired high-priced lobbyists
and prepared for a fight to dismantle "regional socialism." Metropolitanism's
opponents, tough and organized, began to control the regional debate.

During 1980–90, state lawmakers gradually dismantled the metropolitan authority that had been put in place in the 1960s and 1970s. They stripped the Met
Council of its authority over major development projects: the downtown domed
stadium, a new regional race track, and even the Mall of America—a local landmark that by its sheer size had a thunderous effect on the retail market in central
Minneapolis and St. Paul and the southern suburbs. They severely weakened the
land use planning statute by giving supercedence to local zoning. They also overturned the Met Council system of infrastructure pricing, abandoned a regional af-

fordable housing system, and shelved well-conceived regional density guide-lines. And they took a hard, well-financed run at the fiscal disparities system.

Sometimes the consensus-based regionalists would oppose the changes, but more often they seemed unable to stomach controversy. Their general response to the newly assertive high property-wealth suburbs was to seek accommodation. Meanwhile, developers in the high property-wealth suburbs and their lawyers obtained coveted seats on the Met Council itself.

The first generation of regionalists had fought bloody fights for land use planning, the consolidation of regional services, and tax equity. A decade later, the consensus-based regionalists were reduced to building regional citizenship through a proposal for a bus that looked like a trolley car to connect the state capital to downtown St. Paul. Times, and tactics, had clearly changed.

The proud legacy of the first-generation regionalists was in shambles. In 1967, the Twin Cities had created a regional transit system with a tax base that encompassed seven regional counties and 187 cities. By 1998, what had been one of the most financially broad-based transit systems in the nation was struggling with below-average funding per capita. The Met Council, now in thrall to developers, allocated virtually all federal resources to its large highway building program. Finally, the Citizens League and the consensus-based regionalists, perhaps to curry favor with the rebellious high property-wealth suburbs, used their influence both to defeat the development of a fixed-rail transit service and to fragment and privatize the transit system. By the early 1980s, the southwestern developing suburbs, the most prosperous parts of the region and those that benefited most from the development of a regional sewer and highway system, were allowed to "opt out" of funding the transit system that served the region's struggling core.

In 1991, the Met Council was on the verge of being abolished. A measure to eliminate the Council passed on the House floor, and the governor opined that the Council should either do something or disappear. The consensus-based regionalists, frustrated after a decade of difficulty, were not even grousing about legislative roadblocks. They had moved on to champion school choice and had joined the business community in an effort to cut comparatively high Minnesota business property taxes.

The Third Generation

Out of this state of affairs emerged a new type of regionalist, of which I count myself one. Most of us were new to politics in the 1990s, and we were spurred to action by worrisome conditions in the Twin Cities, where concentrated poverty was growing—at the fourth fastest rate in the nation.

To address the growing concentration of poverty in the central cities, we began to investigate reforms, particularly in fair housing, at a metropolitan level. We began to wonder, in particular, whether the sprawl at the edge of the Twin Cities area was undermining the stability at the core and whether the older suburbs, adjacent to the city, were having equally serious problems. As we learned more about the region's problems, we came to appreciate the metropolitan structure that had been put in place 20 years before—a structure severely out of fashion and irrelevant in liberal circles. "What does land use planning in the suburbs have to do with us?" asked our central-city politicos. "We need more of a neighborhood-based strategy," they said. We were also received as fish out of water when we went to the Met Council and the Citizens League to discuss our regional concerns. "This is not what the Met Council is about," they said. "It is about land use planning and infrastructure, not about urban issues or poverty."

In addition to the concentration of poverty at the core, we grew interested in the subsidies and governmental actions supporting sprawl. We were inspired by the land use reforms in Oregon and the work of Governor Tom Mc-Call, Henry Richmond, and 1,000 Friends of Oregon. We read the infrastructure work of Robert Burchell at Rutgers. We became aesthetically attached to New Urbanism and Peter Calthorpe, its proponent of metropolitan social equity and transit-oriented development.

Our third-wave regionalism gradually became broader based. We added environmentalism and the strength of the environmental movement to what had heretofore been a sterile discussion of planning and efficiency. We also brought issues of concentrated poverty and regional fair housing into an equity discussion that had previously been limited to interlocal fiscal equity. The dormant strength of the civil rights movement and social gospel also readied itself for metropolitan action and activism. In only a few years, hundreds of churches joined the movement for regional reform.

We also mobilized the rapidly declining, blue-collar suburbs—angry places unattached to either political party—to advance regional reform. Blue-collar mayors, a few with decidedly hostile views toward social and racial changes in their communities, united with African-American political leaders, environmentalists, and bishops of the major regional churches to advance a regional agenda for fair housing, land use planning, tax equity, and an accountable elected regional governance structure.

In fact, probably the most important element of the new regional coalition was the older, struggling, fully developed suburbs—the biggest prospective winners in regional reform. To them, tax-base sharing means lower property taxes and better services, particularly better-funded schools. Regional housing policy means, over time, fewer units of affordable housing crowding their doorstep. As one older-suburban mayor put it, "If those guys in the new suburbs don't start to build affordable housing, we'll be swimming in this stuff."

Winning over these suburbs was not easy. We had to overcome long-term, powerful resentments and distrust, based on class and race and fueled by every national political campaign since Hubert Humphrey lost the White House in 1968. But after two years of constant cajoling and courting and steady reminders of the growing inequities among the suburbs, the middle-income, working-class, blue-collar suburbs joined the central cities and created a coalition of great political clout in the legislature.

In 1994 this coalition of central-city and suburban legislators passed the Metropolitan Reorganization Act, which placed all regional sewer, transit, and land use planning under the operational authority of the Metropolitan Council of the Twin Cities. In doing so, it transformed the Met Council from a $40-million-a-year planning agency to a $600-million-a-year regional government operating regional sewers and transit, with supervisory authority over the major decisions of another $300-million-a-year agency that runs the regional airport. That same year, in the Metropolitan Land Use Reform Act, our coalition insulated metro-area farmers from public assessments that would have forced them to subdivide farm land for development.

In both 1993 and 1994 the legislature passed sweeping fair housing bills (both vetoed); in 1995 a weakened version was finally signed. In 1995 the legislature passed a measure that would have added a significant part of the residential property tax base to the fiscal disparities pool. While the measure passed strongly, it too was vetoed. In 1996 a statewide land use planning framework was adopted, and a regional brownfields fund created. Throughout the process, we restored to the Council many of the powers and prerogatives that had been removed from it during the 1980s in the areas of land use planning and infrastructure pricing. In each area of reform—land use planning, tax equity, and regional structural reform—we were initially opposed by the consensus-based regionalists as "too controversial," only to have our ideas adopted by them a few years later as the political center of gravity began to change.

Worth Fighting For

Like all real reform, regional reform is a struggle. From the fight against municipal corruption and the fight against the trusts to the women's movement, the consumer movement, the environmental movement, and the civil rights movement, reform has involved difficult contests against entrenched interests who operated against the general welfare. Today, we are told that the Age of Reform is over. We are in an age of consensus politics, when calmer words—"collaboration," "boundary crossing," "win-win" strategies—carry more promise than "assertive" ones.

In every region of this nation, [roughly] 20–40 percent of the people live in central cities, 25–30 percent in older declining suburbs, and 10–15 percent in low tax-base developing suburbs. These communities, representing a clear majority of regional population, are being directly harmed by an inefficient, wasteful, unfair system. Studies indicate that the regions in the nation that have the least economic disparity have the strongest economic growth and those with most disparity are the weakest economically. The social polarization and wasteful sprawl that are common in our nation take opportunity from people and businesses, destroy cities and older suburbs, waste our economic bounty, and threaten our future.

Those who care about these problems must "assert" themselves to reverse these trends. We must engage in a politics that is free of personal attacks and sensationalism, that is conducted with a smile and good manners—like the progressives. At each roadblock, we must seek a compromise that moves equity forward, before we entrench unproductively. We must achieve the broadest possible level of good feeling, gather for our cause as many allies as we can from all walks of life and from all points of the compass. We must educate and persuade. However, if there are those who stand in our path utterly—who will permit no forward movement—we must fight. We must fight for the future of individuals, for the future of communities, and for the future of our country.

In the end, the goal is regional reform, not regional consensus.

31

Pietro S. Nivola

FAT CITY

Understanding American Urban Form from a Transatlantic Perspective

Urban settlements grow in three directions: up into high-rise buildings, in by crowding, or out into the suburbs. Although cities everywhere have developed in each of these ways at various times, nowhere in Europe has the outward dispersal of people and jobs matched the scope of suburbanization in the metropolitan areas of the United States. Here, less than a quarter of the nation's population lived in suburbia in 1950. Now more than 60 percent does. Why have most European cities remained compact compared with the sprawling American metropolis?

Misconceptions

At first glance, the answer seems elementary. The urban centers of Europe are older, and the populations of their countries did not increase as rapidly in the postwar period. In addition, stringent national land use laws slowed suburban development, whereas the disjoined jurisdictions in U.S. metropolitan regions encouraged it.

But on closer inspection, this conventional wisdom does not suffice. The contours of most major urban areas in the United States were formed to a great extent by economic and demographic expansion after the Second World War. The same was true in much of Europe, where entire cities were reduced to rubble by the war and had to be rebuilt from the ground up. Consider Germany, the European country whose cities were carpet bombed. Many German cities today are old in name only, and though Germany's population as a whole grew much less quickly than America's after 1950, West German cities experienced formidable economic growth and in-migrations. Yet the metropolitan population density of the United States is still about one-fourth that of Germany. New York, our densest city, has approximately one-third the number of inhabitants per square mile of Frankfurt. Moreover, the dispersed U.S. pattern of development has continued apace even in places where population has increased little or not at all. From 1970 to 1990, the Chicago area's population rose by only 4 percent, but the region's built-up land increased 46 percent. Metropolitan Cleveland's population actually declined by 8 percent, yet 33 percent more of the area's territory was developed.

Nor can our extreme degree of decentralization necessarily be imputed to the fragmented jurisdictional structure of U.S. metropolitan areas, wherein every suburban town or county presumably has autonomous control over the use of land. Actually, many urban regions in the United States are less fragmented than are those in much of Europe. Since 1950 about half of America's central cities have at least doubled their territory by annexing new suburbs. Houston covered 160 square miles in 1950. By 1980, exercising broad powers to annex its environs, it incorporated 556 square miles. In the same 30-year period, Jacksonville went from being a town of 30 square miles to a regional government enveloping 841 square miles—two-thirds the size of Rhode Island. True, the tri-state region of New York contains some 780 separate localities, some with zoning ordinances that permit only low-density subdivisions. But the urban region of Paris—Île de France—comprises 1,300 municipalities, all of which also have considerable discretion in the consignment of land for development.

The fact that central agencies in countries like France may exert influence on these local decisions through national land use statutes is not an especially telling distinction either. Think of the relationship of U.S. state governments to their local communities as roughly analogous to that of Europe's unitary regimes to their respective local entities. Not only are the governments of some of our states behemoths (New York state's annual expenditures, for example, approximate Sweden's entire national budget), but also a significant number have enacted territorial planning legislation reminiscent of European guidelines. Indeed, from a legal standpoint, local governments in this country are mere "creatures" of the states, which can direct, modify, or even abolish their localities at will. Frequently, European municipalities, with their ancient independent charters, are less subordinated.

Different Strokes

The more interesting contrasts between the formative influences on urban spatial structures in America and Europe lie elsewhere. With three and a half million square miles of territory, the United States has had much more space over which to spread its settlements. And on this vast expanse, the diffusion of decentralizing technologies—motor vehicles, for example—commenced decades earlier than in other industrial countries. (In 1921, 1 in 12 Americans owned an automobile. Germany did not reach that ratio until 1960.) But besides such fundamentals, the public agendas here and in key European countries have been miles apart. The important distinctions, moreover, have less to do with differing "urban" programs and land use controls than with other national policies, the consequences of which are less understood.

Lavish agricultural subsidies in Europe, for example, keep more farmers in business and help dissuade them from selling their land to developers. Thanks to light taxation of gasoline, the price of automotive fuel in the United States is almost a quarter of what it is in Italy. Is it surprising that Italians live closer to their urban centers, where they can more easily walk to work or rely on public transportation? (On a per capita basis, residents of Milan make an average of 350 trips a year on public transportation. People in, say, San Diego make an average of 17.) Gasoline is not the only form of energy that is much cheaper in the United States than in Europe. Electric power and furnace fuels are too. The expense of heating the equivalent of an average detached U.S. suburban home, and of operating the gigantic home appliances (such as refrigerators and freezers) that substitute for neighborhood stores in many American residential communities, would be daunting to most households in large parts of Europe.

Systems of taxation make a profound difference. European tax structures bear down on consumption. Why don't most Dutch people and Danes vacate their tight towns and cities where many commuters prefer to ride bicycles, rather than sport-utility vehicles, to work? The sales tax on a new, medium-sized car in The Netherlands is approximately 9 times higher than in the United States; in Denmark, 37 times higher. The U.S. tax code, by contrast, favors spending over saving (the latter is effectively taxed twice) and then provides inducements to purchase particular goods—most notably houses, the mortgage interest on which is deductible. The effect of such provisions is to lead most American families into the suburbs, where spacious dwellings are available and absorb much of the nation's personal savings pool.

Suburban homeownership has been promoted in the United States by more than tax policy. Federal Housing Administration and Veterans Administration mortgage guarantees are estimated to have financed more than a quarter of all single-family homes built in the postwar period. Meanwhile, in Europe, the housing stocks of many countries were decimated by the war. Governments responded to the emergency by erecting apartment buildings and extending rental subsidies to large segments of the population. America also built a good deal of publicly subsidized rental housing in the postwar years, but chiefly to accommodate the most impoverished city-dwellers. Unlike the relatively mixed income housing complexes scattered around London or Paris, U.S. public housing projects further concentrated the urban poor in the inner cities, turning the likes of South Central Los Angeles or Chicago's South Side into pits of social degradation and violence. The effect was to accelerate the flight of urban middle-class families from the vicinity of these places to safer locations on the metropolitan fringe.

Few forces are more consequential for the shape of cities than are a society's investments in transportation infrastructure. Government at all levels in the United States has committed hundreds of billions to the construction and maintenance of highways, passenger railroads, and transit systems. What counts, however, is not just the magnitude of the commitment, but the *distribution* of the public expenditures among modes of transportation. Where, as in the United States, the share claimed by roads has dwarfed that of alternatives by almost 6 to 1, an unrelenting increase in automobile travel and a steady decline in transit usage, however heavily subsidized, was inevitable.

Dense cities dissipate without relatively intensive use of mass transit. In 1945 transit accounted for approximately 35 percent of urban passenger miles traveled in the United States. By 1994 the figure had dwindled to less than 3 percent—or roughly one-fifth the average in Western Europe. If early on, American transportation planners had followed the British or French budgetary practice of allocating between 40 and 60 percent of their transport outlays to passenger railroads and mass transit systems, instead of 73 percent for highways as in the U.S. case, there is little question that many U.S. cities would be more compressed today.

Dense cities also require a vibrant economy of neighborhood shops and services. (Why live in town if performing life's simplest everyday functions, like picking up fresh groceries for supper, requires driving to distant vendors?) But the local shopkeepers cannot compete with regional megastores proliferating in America's metropolitan shopping centers and strip malls. Multiple restrictions on the penetration and pricing practices of large retailers in various European countries protect small urban businesses. The costs to consumers are high, but the convenience and intimacy of London's "high streets" or of the corner markets in virtually every Parisian *arrondissement* are preserved.

For Richer or for Poorer?

To conclude that a wide range of public policies in Europe has helped curb suburban sprawl there is not to say, of course, that all those policies have enhanced the welfare of the Europeans—and hence, that the United States ought to emulate them. Most households are not better off when farmers are heavily subsidized, or when anticompetitive practices protect micro-businesses at the expense of larger, more efficient firms. Nor would most consumers gain greater satisfaction from housing strategies that assist renter occupancy but not homeownership, or from tax and transportation policies that force more people out of their cars and onto buses, trains, or bicycles. Arguably, the economies of some nations in Western Europe have faltered in recent years amid these sorts of public biases, while the United States has prospered in part because it has successfully resisted them.

Still, if we wonder why the cityscapes of America and Europe typically look so different, we would do well to get beyond clichés (about underfunded

U.S. urban programs, inadequate U.S. land use planning, or "balkanized" U.S. metropolitan governments) and to recognize the full breadth of hard policy choices that make for international differences.

32

Fred Siegel

IS REGIONAL GOVERNMENT THE ANSWER?

Suburban sprawl, the spread of low-density housing over an ever-expanding landscape, has attracted a growing list of enemies. Environmentalists have long decried the effects of sprawl on the ecosystem; aesthetes have long derided what they saw as "the ugliness and banality of suburbia"; and liberals have intermittently insisted that suburban prosperity has been purchased at the price of inner-city decline and poverty. But only recently has sprawl become the next great issue in American public life. That's because suburbanites themselves are now calling for limits to seemingly inexorable and frenetic development.

Slow-growth movements are a response to both the cyclical swings of the economy and the secular trend of dispersal. Each of the great postwar booms have, at their cyclical peak, produced calls for restraint. These sentiments have gained a wider hearing as each new upturn of the economy has produced an ever widening wave of exurban growth. A record 96 months of peacetime economic expansion has produced the strongest slow-growth movement to date. In 1998, antisprawl environmentalists and "not-in-my-backyard" slow-growth suburbanites joined forces across the nation to pass ballot measures restricting exurban growth.

Undoubtedly, the loss of land and the environmental degradation produced by sprawl are serious problems that demand public attention. But sprawl also brings enormous benefits as well as considerable costs. It is, in part, an expression of the new high-tech economy whose campus-like office parks on the periphery of urban areas have driven the economic boom of the 1990s. And it's sprawl that has sustained the record rise in home ownership. Sprawl is not some malignancy to be summarily excised but, rather, part and parcel of prosperity. Dealing with its ill effects requires both an understanding of the new landscape of the American economy and a willingness to make subtle trade-offs. We must learn to curb its worst effects without reducing the wealth and freedom that permit sprawl to develop.

Rising incomes and employment, combined with declining interest rates, have allowed a record number of people, including minority and immigrant families, to purchase homes for the first time. Home ownership among blacks, which is increasingly suburban, has risen at more than three times the white rate; a record 45 percent of African Americans owned their own homes in 1998. Nationally, an unprecedented 67 percent of Americans are homeowners.

Sprawl is part of the price we're paying for something novel in human history—the creation of a mass upper middle class. Net household worth has been increasing at the unparalleled annual rate of 10 percent since 1994, so that while in 1970, only 3.2 percent of households had an annual income of $100,000 (in today's dollars), by 1996, 8.2 percent of American households could boast a six-figure annual income. The new prosperity is reflected in the size of new homes, many of whose owners no doubt decry the arrival of still more "McMansions" and new residents, clogging the roads and schools of the latest subdivisions. In the midst of the 1980's boom, homebuilders didn't have a category for mass-produced houses of more than 3,000 square feet: By 1996, one out of every seven new homes built was larger than 3,000 square feet.

Today's Tenement Trail

Sprawl also reflects upward mobility for the aspiring lower-middle class. Nearly a half-century ago, Samuel Lubell dedicated *The Future of American Politics* to the memory of his mother, "who pioneered on the urban frontier." Lubell described a process parallel to the settling of the West, in which families on "the Old Tenement Trail" were continually on the move in search of a better life. In the cities, they abandoned crowded tenements on New York's Lower East Side for better housing in the South Bronx, and from there, went to the "West Bronx, crossing that Great Social Divide—the Grand Concourse—beyond which rolled true middle-class country where janitors were called superintendents."

Today's "tenement trail" takes aspiring working- and lower-middle class Americans to quite different areas. Kendall, Florida, 20 miles southeast of Miami, is every environmentalist's nightmare image of sprawl, a giant grid carved out of the muck of swamp land that encroaches on the Everglades. Stripmalls and mega-stores abound for mile after mile, as do the area's signature giant auto lots. Yet Kendall also represents a late-twentieth-century version of the Old Tenement Trail. Kendall, notes the *New Republic*'s Charles Lane, is "the Queens of the late twentieth century," a place where immigrants are buying into America. Carved out of the palmetto wilderness, its population exploded from roughly 20,000 in 1970 to 300,000 today. Agricultural in the 1960s, and a hip place for young whites in the 1970s, Kendall grew increasingly Hispanic in the 1980s, as Cubans, Nicaraguans, and others who arrived with very little worked their way up. Today, it's half Hispanic and a remarkable example of integration. In most of Kendall, notes University of Miami geographer Peter Muller, "You can't point to a white or Latino block because the populations are so intermixed."

Virginia Postrel, the editor of *Reason*, argues that the slow-growth movement is animated by left-wing planners' hostility to suburbia. Others mock slow-growthers as elitists, as in the following quip:

Q: What's the difference between an environmentalist and a developer?
A: The environmentalist already has his house in the mountains.

But, in the 1990s, slow-growth sentiment has been taking hold in middle- and working-class suburbs like Kendall, as development turns into overdevelopment and traffic congestion becomes a daily problem.

Regional Government

One oft-proposed answer to sprawl has been larger regional governments that will exercise a monopoly on land-use decisions. Underlying this solution is the theory—no doubt correct—that sprawl is produced when individuals and townships seek to maximize their own advantage without regard for the good of the whole community. Regionalism, however, is stronger in logic than in practice. For example, the people of Kendall, rather than embracing regionalism, are looking to slow down growth by *seceding* from their regional government. Upon examination, we begin to see some of the problems with regional government.

Kendall is part of Metro-Dade, the oldest major regional government, created in 1957. The largest of its 29 municipalities, Miami, the fourth poorest city in the United States, has 350,000 people; the total population of Metro-Dade is 2 million, 1.1 million of whom live in unincorporated areas. In Metro-Dade, antisprawl and antiregional government sentiments merge. Despite county-imposed growth boundaries, residents have complained bitterly of overdevelopment. The county commissioners—many of whom have been convicted of, or charged with, corruption—have been highly receptive to the developers who are among their largest campaign contributors. As one south Florida resident said of the developers, "It's a lot cheaper to be able to buy just one government." The south Florida secessionists want to return zoning to local control where developers' clout is less likely to overwhelm neighborhood interests.

When Jane Jacobs wrote, in *The Death and Life of Great American Cities*, that "the voters sensibly decline to federate into a system where bigness means local helplessness, ruthless oversimplified planning and administrative chaos," she could have been writing about south Florida. What's striking about Metro-Dade is that it has delivered neither efficiency nor equity nor effective planning while squelching local self-determination.

The fight over Metro-Dade echoes the conflicts of an earlier era. Historically, the fight over regional versus local government was an important, if intermittent, issue for many cities from 1910 to 1970. From about 1850 to 1910, according to urban historian Jon Teaford, suburbanites were eager to be absorbed by cities whose wealth enabled them to build the water, sewage, and road systems they couldn't construct on their own. "The central city," he explains, "provided superior service at a lower cost." But, in the 1920s, well before race became a central issue, suburbanites, who had increasingly sorted themselves out by ethnicity and class, began to use special-service districts and innovative financial methods to provide their own infrastructure and turned away from unification. Suburbanites also denounced consolidation as an invitation to big-city, and often Catholic, "boss rule" and as a threat to "self-government."

In the 1960s, as black politicians began to win influence over big-city governments, they also joined the anticonsolidation chorus. At the same time, county government, once a sleepy extension of rural rule, was modernized, and county executives essentially became the mayors of full-service governments administering what were, in effect, dispersed cities. But they were mayors with a difference. Their constituents often wanted a balance between commercial development, which constrained the rise of taxes, and the suburban ideal of family-friendly semirural living. When development seemed too intrusive, suburban voters in the 1980s, and again in the 1990s, have pushed a slow-growth agenda.

The New Regionalism

In the 1990s, regionalism has been revived as an effort to link the problem of sprawl with the problem of inner-city poverty. Assuming that "flight creates blight," regionalists propose to recapture the revenue of those who have fled the cities and force growth back into older areas by creating regional or metropolitan-area governments with control over land use and taxation.

The new regionalism owes a great deal to a group of circuit-riding reformers. Inspired by the arguments of scholars like Anthony Downs, one of the authors of the Kerner Commission report, and sociologist William Julius Wilson of Harvard, as well as the example of Portland, Oregon's metro-wide government, these itinerant preachers have traveled to hundreds of cities to spread the gospel of regional cooperation. The three most prominent new regionalists— columnist Neil Peirce, former Albuquerque mayor David Rusk, and Minnesota state representative Myron Orfield—have developed a series of distinct, but overlapping, arguments for why cities can't help themselves, and why regional solutions are necessary.

Peirce, in his book *Citistates*, plausibly insists that regions are the real units of competition in the global economy, so that there is a metro-wide imperative to revive the central city, lest the entire area be undermined. Less plausibly, Orfield in *Metropolitics* argues that what he calls "the favored quarter" of fast-growing suburbs on the periphery of the metro area have prospered at the expense of both the central city and the inner-ring suburbs. In order both to revive the central city and save the inner suburbs from decline, Orfield proposes that these two areas join forces, redistributing money from the "favored quarter" to the older areas. Rusk argues, in *Baltimore Unbound*, that older cities, unable to annex the fast growing suburbs, are doomed to further decline. He insists that only "flexible cities"—that is, cities capable of expanding geographically and capturing the wealth of the suburbs—can truly deal with inner-city black poverty. Regionalism, writes Rusk, is "the new civil rights movement."

There are differences among them. Orfield and, to a lesser degree, Rusk operate on a zero-sum model in which gain for the suburbs comes directly at the expense of the central city. Peirce is less radical, proposing regional cooperation as the means to a win-win situation for both city and the surrounding region. But they all share a desire to disperse poverty across the region and, more importantly, recentralize economic growth in the already built-up areas. The latter goal is consistent with both the environmental thrust of the antisprawl movement and the push for regional government. In a speech to a Kansas City civic organization, Rusk laid out the central assumption of the new regionalism. "The greater the fragmentation of governments," he asserted, "the greater the fragmentation of society by race and economic class." Fewer governments, argue the new regionalists, will yield a number of benefits, including better opportunities for regional cooperation, more money for cash-strapped central cities, less racial inequality, less sprawl, and greater economic growth. However, all of these propositions are questionable.

Better Policies, Not Fewer Governments

Consider Baltimore and Philadelphia, cities that the regionalists have studied thoroughly. According to the 1998 *Greater Baltimore State of the Region* report, Philadelphia has 877 units of local government (including school boards)—or 17.8 per 100,000 people. Baltimore has only six government units of any consequence in Baltimore City and the five surrounding counties—or 2.8 per 100,000 people. Greater Baltimore has fewer government units than any other major metro area in the United States. As a political analyst told me: "Get six people in a room, and you have the government of 2,200 square miles, because the county execs have very strong powers." We might expect considerable regional cooperation in Baltimore, but not in Philadelphia. Regionalism has made no headway in either city, however. The failure has little to do with the number of governments and a great deal to do with failed policy choices in both cities.

Rusk does not mention the many failings of Baltimore's city government. He refers to the current mayor, Kurt Schmoke, just once and only to say that Baltimore has had "excellent political leadership." In Rusk's view, Baltimore is "programmed to fail" because of factors entirely beyond its control, namely, the inability to annex its successful suburbs. In the ahistorical world of the regionalist (and here, Peirce is a partial exception), people are always pulled from the city by structural forces but never pushed from the city by bad policies.

Baltimore is not as well financed as the District of Columbia, which ruined itself despite a surfeit of money. But Baltimore, a favorite political son of both Annapolis and Washington, has been blessed with abundant financial support. Over the past decade, Schmoke has increased spending on education and health by over a half-billion dollars. He has also added 200 police officers and spent $60 million more for police over the last four years. "His greatest skill," notes the *Baltimore Sun*, "has been his ability to attract more federal and state aid while subsidies diminished elsewhere." But, notwithstanding these expenditures, middle-class families continue to flee the city at the rate of 1,000 per month, helping to produce the sprawl environmentalists decry.

Little in Baltimore works well. The schools have been taken over by the state, while the Housing Authority is mired in perpetual scandal and corruption. Baltimore is one of the few cities where crime hasn't gone down. That's because Schmoke has insisted, contrary to the experiences of New York and other cities, that drug-related crime could not be reduced until drug use was controlled through treatment. The upshot is that New York, with eight times more people than Baltimore, has only twice as many murders. Baltimore also leads the country in sexually transmitted diseases. These diseases have flourished among the city's drug users partly owing to Schmoke's de facto decriminalization of drugs. According to the Centers for Disease Control and Prevention (CDC), Baltimore has a syphilis rate 18 times the national average, 3 or 4 times as high as areas where the STD epidemic is most concentrated.

Flexible Cities

Rusk attributes extraordinary qualities to flexible cities. He says that they are able to both reduce inequality, curb sprawl, and maintain vital downtowns. Rusk was the mayor of Albuquerque, a flexible city that annexed a vast area, even as its downtown essentially died. The reduced inequality he speaks of is largely a statistical artifact. If New York were to annex Scarsdale, East New York's average income would rise without having any effect on the lives of the people who live there. As for sprawl, flexible cities like Phoenix and Houston are hardly models.

A recent article for *Urban Affairs Review*, by Subhrajit Guhathakurta and Michele Wichert, showed that within the elastic city of Phoenix, inner-city residents poorer than their outer-ring neighbors are subsidizing the building of new developments on the fringes of the metropolis. While sprawl is correlated with downtown decline in Albuquerque, in Phoenix it's connected with what *Fortune* described as "the remarkable rebound of downtown Phoenix, which has become a chic after-dark destination as well as a residential hot spot." There seems to be no automatic connection between regionalism and downtown revival.

Orfield's *Metropolitics* provides another version of an over-determined structuralist argument. According to him, the favored quarter is sucking the inner city dry, and, as a result, central-city blight will inevitably engulf the older first-ring suburbs as well. He is right to see strong pressures on the inner-ring suburbs, stemming from an aging housing stock and population as well as an influx of inner-city poor. But it is how the inner-ring suburbs respond to these pressures that will affect their fate.

When Coleman Young was mayor of Detroit, large sections of the city returned to prairie. But the inner-ring suburbs have done fairly well precisely by not imitating Detroit's practice of providing poor services at premium prices. "Much like the new edge suburbs," explains the *Detroit News*, "older suburbs that follow the proven formula of promoting good schools, public safety and well-kept housing attract new investment." Suburban Mayor Michael Guido sees his city's well developed infrastructure as an asset, which has already been bought and paid for. "Now," says Mayor Guido, "it's a matter of maintenance . . . and we offer a sense of history and a sense of community. That's really important to people, to have a sense of belonging to a whole community rather than a subdivision."

Suburb Power

City-suburban relations are not fixed; they are various depending on the policies both follow. Some suburbs compete with the central city for business. In south Florida, Coral Gables more than holds its own with Miami as a site for business headquarters. Southfield, just outside Detroit, and Clayton, just outside St. Louis, blossomed in the wake of the 1960s' urban riots and now compete with their downtowns. Aurora, with a population of more than 160,000 and to the east of Denver, sees itself as a competitor, and it sees regional efforts at growth management as a means by which the downtown Denver elite can ward off competition.

Suburban growth can also help the central city. In the Philadelphia area, economic growth and new work come largely from the Route 202 high-tech corridor in Chester County, west of the city. While the city has lost 57,000 jobs, even in the midst of national economic prosperity, the fast growing Route 202 companies have been an important source of downtown legal and accounting jobs. At the same time, the suburbs are creating jobs for residents that the central city cannot produce, so that 20 percent of city residents commute to the suburbs while 15 percent of people who live in the suburbs commute to Philadelphia.

The "new regionalists" assume that the prosperity of the edge cities is a function of inner-city decline. But, in many cities, it is more nearly the case that suburban booms are part of what's keeping the central-city economy alive. It is the edge cities that have taken up the time-honored urban task of creating new work.

According to *INC* magazine, the 500 fastest growing small companies are all located in suburbs and exurbs. This is because local governments there are very responsive to the needs of start-up companies. These high-tech hotbeds, dubbed "nerdistans" by Joel Kotkin, are composed of networks of companies that are sometimes partners, sometimes competitors. They provide a pool of seasoned talent for start-ups, where engineers and techies who prefer the orderly, outdoor life of suburbia to the crowds and disorder of the city can move from project to project. Henry Nicholas, CEO of Broadcom, a communications-chip and cable-modem maker, explained why he reluctantly moved to Irvine: "It's hard to relocate techies to L.A. It's the congestion, the expensive housing—and there's a certain stigma to it."

Imagine what the United States would be like if the Bay Area had followed the New York model. In 1898, New York created the first regional government when it consolidated all the areas of the New York harbor—Manhattan, Brooklyn, Queens, the Bronx, and Staten Island—into the then-largest city in the world. The consolidation has worked splendidly for Manhattan, which thrives as a capital of high-end financial and legal services. But over time, the Manhattan-centric economy based on high taxes, heavy social spending, and extensive economic regulation destroyed Brooklyn's once vital shipping and manufacturing economy.

In 1912, San Francisco, the Manhattan of Northern California, proposed to create a unified regional government by incorporating Oakland in the East Bay and San Jose in the South. The plan for a Greater San Francisco was modeled on Greater New York and called for the creation of self-governing boroughs within an enlarged city and county of San Francisco. East Bay opposition defeated the San Francisco expansion in the legislature, and later attempts at consolidation in 1917, 1923, and 1928 also failed. But had San Francisco with its traditions of high taxation and heavy regulation succeeded, Silicon Valley might never have become one of the engines of the American economy. Similarly, it's no accident that the Massachusetts Route 128 high-tech corridor is located outside of the boundaries of Boston, even as it enriches the central city.

The Portland Model

The complex and often ironic history of existing regional governments has been obscured by the bright light of hope emanating from Portland. It seems that in every generation one city is said to have perfected the magic elixir for revival. In the 1950s, it was Philadelphia; today, it's Portland. In recent years, hundreds of city officials have traveled to Portland to study its metropolitan government, comprehensive environmental planning, and the urban-growth boundary that has been credited with Portland's revival and success.

While there are important lessons to be learned from Portland, very little of its success to date can be directly attributed to the growth boundary, which was introduced too recently and with boundaries so capacious as not yet to have had much effect. Thirty-five percent of the land within the boundary was vacant when it was imposed in 1979. And, at the same time, fast growing Clark County, just north of Portland but not part of the urban-growth boundary, has provided an escape valve for potential housing pressures. The upshot, notes demographer Wendell Cox, is that even with the growth boundary, Portland still remains a relatively low-density area with fewer people per square mile than San Diego, San Jose, or Sacramento.

Portland has also been run with honesty and efficiency, unlike Metro-Dade. Blessed with great natural resources, Portland—sometimes dubbed "Silicon forest," because chipmakers are drawn to its vast quantities of cheap clean water—has conserved its man-made as well as natural resources. A city with more cast-iron buildings than any place outside of Manhattan, it has been a leader in historic preservation. Time and again, Portland's leadership has made the right choices. It was one of the first cities to reconnect its downtown with the riverfront. Portland never built a circumferential freeway. And, in the 1970s, under the leadership of mayor Neil Goldschmidt, the city vetoed a number of proposed highway projects that would have threatened the downtown.

In 1978, Portland voters, in conjunction with the state government, created the first directly elected metropolitan government with the power to manage growth over three counties. Portland metro government has banned big-box retailers, like Walmart and Price Club, on the grounds that they demand too much space and encourage too much driving. This is certainly an interesting experiment well worth watching, but should other cities emulate Portland's land-management model? It's too soon to say.

Good government is always important. But aside from that, it's hard to draw any general lessons from the Portland experience. The growth boundaries may or may not work, and there's certainly no reason to think that playing with political boundaries will bring good government to Baltimore.

Living with Sprawl

What then is to be done? First, we can accept the consensus that has developed around preserving open space, despite some contradictory effects. The greenbelts around London, Portland, and Baltimore County pushed some development back toward the city and encouraged further sprawl as growth leapfrogged the open space. The push to preserve open space is only likely to grow stronger as continued growth generates both more congestion and more wealth, which can be used to buy up open land.

Secondly, we can create what Peter Salins, writing in *The Public Interest*,[1] described as a "level playing field" between the central cities and the suburbs. This can be done by ending exurban growth subsidies for both transportation as well as new water and sewer lines. These measures might further encourage the revival of interest in old fashioned Main Street living, which is already attracting a new niche of home buyers. State and local governments can also repeal the land-use and zoning regulations that discourage mixed-use development of the sort that produces a clustering of housing around Main Street and unsubsidized low-cost housing in the apartments above the streets' shops.

Because of our strong traditions of local self-government, regionalism has been described as an unnatural act among consenting jurisdictions. But regional cooperation needn't mean the heavy hand of all-encompassing regional government. There are some modest, but promising, experiments already un-

---

[1]"Cities, Suburbs, and the Urban Crisis," *The Public Interest*, No. 113 (Fall 1993).

der way in regional revenue sharing whose effects should be carefully evaluated. Allegheny County, which includes Pittsburgh, has created a Regional Asset District that uses a 1 percent sales tax increase to support cultural institutions and reduce other taxes. The Twin Cities have put money derived from the increase in assessed value of commercial and industrial properties into a pot to aid fiscally weaker municipalities. Kansas and Missouri created a cultural district that levies a small increase in the sales tax across the region. The money is being used to rehabilitate the area's most treasured architectural landmark, Kansas City's Union Station.

Cities and suburbs do have some shared interests, as in the growing practice of reverse commuting which links inner-city residents looking to get off welfare with fast growing suburban areas hampered by a shortage of labor. Regionalism can curb sprawl and integrate and sustain central-city populations if it reforms the misguided policies and politics that have sent the black and white middle class streaming out of cities like Baltimore, Washington, and Philadelphia. Regional co-operation between the sprawling high-tech suburbs and the central cities could modernize cities that are in danger of being left further behind by the digital economy. In that vein, the District of Columbia's Mayor Anthony Williams . . . seized on the importance of connecting his welfare population with the fast growing areas of Fairfax County in Northern Virginia. The aim of focused regional policies, argues former HUD Undersecretary Marc Weiss, should be economic, not political, integration.

Sprawl isn't some malignancy that can be surgically removed. It's been part and parcel of healthy growth, and curbing it involves difficult tradeoffs best worked out locally. Sprawl and the movement against sprawl are now a permanent part of the landscape. The future is summed up in a quip attributed to former Oregon Governor Tom McCall, who was instrumental in creating Portland's growth boundary. "Oregonians," he said, "are against two things, sprawl and density."